HEALTH PSYCHOLOGY

second edition

Howard S. Friedman
University of California, Riverside

Prentice Hall

Upper Saddle River, New Jersey   07458

Library of Congress Cataloging-in-Publication Data
Friedman, Howard S.
    Health psychology / Howard S. Friedman—2nd ed.
        p. cm.
    Includes bibliographical references and indexes.
    ISBN 0-13-895244-2
    1. Clinical health psychology. 2. Medicine and psychology. I. Title.
    R726.7.F75
    616'001'9—dc21

                                                    2001021419

Editorial Director: Laura Pearson
VP, Executive Editor: Stephanie Johnson
Managing Editor (editorial): Sharon Rheinhardt
Sr. Managing Editor: Mary Rottino
Production Liaison: Fran Russello
Project Manager: Karen Berry/Pine Tree Composition
Prepress and Manufacturing Buyer: Tricia Kenny
Art Director: Jayne Conte
Cover Designer: Bruce Kenselaar
Director of Marketing: Beth Gillett Mejia

This book was set in 10/12 Times Roman by Pine Tree Composition, Inc., and was printed
and bound by R.R. Donnelley & Sons Company. The cover was printed by Phoenix Color Corp.

© 2002, 1989 by Pearson Education, Inc.
Upper Saddle River, New Jersey 07458

Printed in the United States of America
10   9   8   7   6

ISBN 0-13-895244-2

Pearson Education LTD., *London*
Pearson Education Australia PTY, Limited, *Sydney*
Pearson Education Singapore, Pte. Ltd
Pearson Education North Asia Ltd., *Hong Kong*
Pearson Education Canada, Ltd., *Toronto*
Pearson Educación de Mexico, S.A. de C.V.
Pearson Education—Japan, *Tokyo*
Pearson Education Malaysia, Pte. Ltd
Pearson Education, Upper Saddle River, New Jersey

For my students, past, present, future.

Brief Contents

Contents

Foreword

Dr. Friedman,

I have really enjoyed your class. I have learned much and from a patient's perspective, I will be better off for it. Your class has stimulated me to think about a lot of issues as I deal with a chronic illness—leukemia. I will be facing the decision of a bone marrow transplant that could bring about a cure, but it is very risky. In studying the procedures, as well as studying iatrogenic illness, I realize I could easily become another statistic.

Although it may not be reflected in my grades, I have truly benefited from this class and will be able to apply many of the principles toward being a better patient.

I hope those who go on to be doctors and medical professionals from this class will remember the psychological aspects of health presented to them.

Respectfully,
[name withheld]

Preface

I have been developing course materials and texts for health psychology as the field itself has taken shape and become an established discipline. In the early 1980s, when I published my first books in health psychology and attended the Arden House conference, I dreamed that in 20 years health psychology would be a major subfield of psychology, bringing important insights for understanding health and illness. And happily, this dream has come true.

Writing the first health psychology textbook in those early days was extremely difficult, because no paradigm or accepted organizing principles existed. Each chapter had to be formed from the mass. Indeed, no formal academic discipline really existed. However, as a core of forward-looking psychologists turned to serious analysis of health, important themes emerged, and it is now clear that we health psychologists have created a remarkable new discipline of which we can be very proud. In this new book, based on my previous work, I have endeavored to capture the maturity of the health psychology discipline while maintaining the excitement of a young and fast-moving field.

Although in one sense this volume involves a natural progression from my previous work, in another sense it is new. In this volume, I have included an ongoing explanation of how health psychology yields an approach that is superior to the traditional medical model of disease. Five distinguishing characteristics mark this book.

First, this book attempts a *conceptual integration* rather than a simple litany of research findings. The biopsychosocial health psychology model is explicitly contrasted and compared to the traditional biomedical model. Theories and concepts provide the basis for an integrated approach to understanding health and illness. Without good concepts, even the best data lose value.

Second, underlying this approach is a belief that health psychology is most importantly a set of intellectually sophisticated ways of thinking about health rather than a narrow "how-to" profession. It is a socio-behavioral science rather than a branch of medicine. To be a successful health psychologist, one has to be able to *think in social science terms*, with understanding of probabilities and uncertainties, influences of culture, interactions of the individual and the social group, and inherent individual differences.

Third, this book views health psychology as the application of psychological theories, concepts, and methods to health: the *psychology* is primary. Thus this book has chapters like "Adaptation to Chronic Illness" and "Quality of Life and the Self-Healing Personality" rather than chapters like "Cancer" or "Heart Disease." Medical issues like cancer are considered not in chapters of their own but rather are integrated throughout as appropriate (coping with chronic illness, personality and health, psychophysiology, stigma).

Fourth, this book employs many examples, illustrations, and applications to society, and it explains the historical roots of many key concepts. Students learn best when fascinated with the material, and attention to literary style does not mean a sacrifice of scientific rigor.

Fifth, this book emphasizes critical thinking, as students learn a specific content while they are learning how to evaluate theory and research. Students will be best able to promote their own health and the health of others when they understand the nature of health and the nature of research.

The text is aimed at the broad middle of the market, rather than at an advanced specialty course.

In May 1983, about 50 researchers interested in the new field of health psychology gathered for four days (and long nights) at the Harriman mansion called Arden House in upstate New York. Under the guidance of conference chair Stephen Weiss, we laid out models for research, education, policy, and training. So primitive was the field that the conference felt it necessary to assert, "Health psychology is a generic field of psychology, with its own body of theory and knowledge, which is differentiated from other fields of psychology" (Conference consensus, 1983).

Not surprising, many of those at the conference, along with their colleagues and students, have gone on to become major forces in the new field—Nancy Adler, Chris Dunkel-Schetter, Karen Matthews, Lee Sechrest, Neil Schneiderman, Jerome Singer, Shelley Taylor, Camille Wortman, and others. The exhilaration engendered by that meeting has served to inspire countless efforts of research collaboration, student training, and professionalization. I wrote this text with the hope that it captures the excitement of those dreams come to fruition.

Howard S. Friedman
University of California, Riverside

Acknowledgments

For this second edition, the advice and input of many colleagues and students made a significant contribution, including Roslyn Mianglee Chaisanguanthum, Kathleen Clark, Alanna Daniels, Elissa Epel, Tiffany Lin, Charlotte N. Castro Markey, Jade Quijano, and Sophia Kes Rath.

About the Author

Howard S. Friedman is Distinguished Professor of Psychology at the University of California, Riverside. He is an elected Fellow of the Division of Health Psychology of the American Psychological Association, from whom he was awarded the career honor for Outstanding Contributions to Health Psychology. He is also an elected Fellow of the Society of Behavioral Medicine, the AAAS, the Society of Personality and Social Psychology, and the American Psychological Society. An honors graduate of Yale University, Friedman received his Ph.D. from Harvard University.

In 1995, Professor Friedman was awarded UCR's Distinguished Teaching Award, and in 2000, he received the Outstanding Teacher Award from the Western Psychological Association (WPA). Best known for his research on personality and health, Friedman has also published work on education and training in health psychology, life-span health and longevity (using the seven-decade archival Terman data), doctor-patient communication (especially nonverbal communication), social support, and health promotion interventions. His research has been supported by the National Institutes of Health, the American Cancer Society, and the American Heart Association.

Some other books authored or edited by Howard Friedman are:

The Self-Healing Personality (Henry Holt, 1991; republished 2000 at [www. iuniverse.com]) (also reprinted in French and German).

Personality: Classic Theories and Modern Research (Boston: Allyn & Bacon, 1999, 2003).

Readings in Personality: Classic Theories and Modern Research (Boston: Allyn & Bacon, 2001).

The Encyclopedia of Mental Health (editor-in-chief) (San Diego: Academic Press, 1998) (3 volumes).

Hostility, Coping, and Health (American Psychological Association, 1992).

Personality and Disease (New York: John Wiley, 1990) (also available in Japanese edition, 1997).

Interpersonal Issues in Health Care (San Diego: Academic Press, 1982).

PART I

Introduction to Basic Concepts and Methods

Chapter 1

THE FIELD OF HEALTH PSYCHOLOGY

In college at UCLA, Jackie Robinson was a four-sport letterman, and he was such an excellent athlete that he chose professional baseball and went on to be named a Most Valuable Player with the Dodgers. When he joined the team, he had trouble with airlines, with hotels, and with other players. Some of his teammates wanted to be traded rather than play with the first African-American player in the major leagues. Fans, opposing players, and opposing managers taunted him. Although he was a tremendous success as a player, Robinson died at age 52 from complications of diabetes.

Did stress help destroy his health? As the case of Jackie Robinson well illustrates, the answers to such questions are complex. On the biological front, Robinson was a star athlete, in excellent physical shape; but diabetes clearly has its roots in genetics and physiology. On the psychological and emotional front, Robinson had tremendous drive and strength of character to be a pioneering hero in such a challenging field; yet anyone would be disheartened and upset in the face of such unfair abuse. On the social front, Robinson was personable, and he established good friendships, but many of his social interactions were troublesome. And on the cultural front, Jackie Robinson faced the habits, biased expectations, and prejudiced laws of a whole society, as he tried to do his interesting job—playing baseball.

Scientific understanding of what it means to be healthy has undergone a dramatic change in recent years, but most people and many health care professionals do not fully understand the new conceptions. Most people believe that they are healthy unless they contract a disease (for example, catch the flu), at which time they are "sick" and should go to a physician to be treated. But there is much, much more to health. Similarly, the health care system is, in some ways, poorly focused to prevent disease and promote health. Huge amounts of effort and money are directed towards treating ill people, and fairly large sums are spent on searching for new treatments, but only relatively tiny efforts are made to keep people healthy in the first place.

Health research and policy in the 20th century proved extremely effective in combating most infectious disease, through vaccinations, antibiotics, and sanitation. Further, surgery corrects many injuries and physical breakdowns. In fact, medicine has been so successful that, in developed nations, curing disease through drug regimens and surgery is no longer the single major challenge to progress in health care, although of course it is still important. Rather, other issues have come to the forefront to challenge health and health care in the 21st century. These challenges concern individual psychological reactions, health-relevant psychosocial relations with others, and health-promoting and health-protecting behaviors (Knowles, 1977; Matarazzo, 1982; USDHHS, 1995, 2000). The scientific study of psychological processes related to health and health care, or **health psychology,** is the topic of this book.

CAUSES OF DEATH

The **major causes of death** in the United States are as follows (U.S. National Center for Health Statistics, 1999):

1. Cardiovascular disease (heart disease and stroke) (about 55%)
2. Cancer (about 24%)

3. Injury (accidents, suicides, and homicides) (about 6%)
4. Lung disease (chronic obstructive pulmonary disease) (about 4%)
5. Pneumonia and influenza (about 3%)

The English statesman Disraeli is said to have proclaimed that there are three kinds of lies: lies, damned lies, and statistics. In other words, statistics can be reconfigured in various ways to make various points. Still, it is useful to draw out several interesting observations from these and related cause-of-death statistics. First, note that once we consider cardiovascular disease and cancer, we have included more than three-quarters of all American deaths. Second, note that acute infectious diseases like pneumonia account only for a small proportion of deaths. This is a dramatic change from the beginning of the 20th century, when infections such as influenza, pneumonia, tuberculosis, enteritis, diphtheria, and typhoid fever dominated the leading threats to health.

Third, note that these deaths are often preceded by many months or years of chronic diseases—many people do not die shortly after they are diagnosed with cancer or heart disease; rather, they may live for years. Finally, note that many of these deaths have a well-documented, significant behavioral component, such as smoking as a contributor to heart disease, and alcoholism as a contributor to automobile accidents.

How strong is this behavioral component? One often-cited study endeavored to identify and quantify the major external (nongenetic) factors that contribute to death in the United States (McGinnis & Foege, 1993). According to these researchers, about half of all deaths were found to have a significant psychological or behavioral component. These major contributors to mortality in the United States in 1990 were:

- tobacco (about 400,000 deaths)
- diet and activity patterns (300,000)
- alcohol (100,000)
- microbial agents (90,000)
- toxic agents (60,000)
- firearms (35,000)
- sexual behavior (30,000)
- motor vehicles (25,000)
- and illicit use of drugs (20,000)

This study, and others, also found that socioeconomic status and access to medical care were important contributors. Note that this study did not try to measure many other psychosocial factors such as stress, which undoubtedly contribute at times to premature mortality. Note also that microbial agents (viruses, bacteria, fungi) seem to be a relatively minor (but still important) contributor to mortality in current-day America.

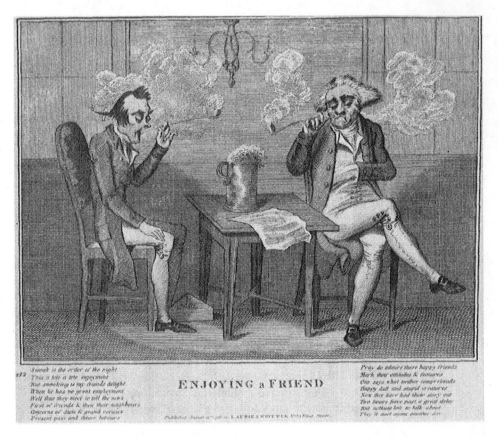

Figure 1–1   The poem on this old inscription states, "Smoak is the order of the night; This a tete a tete enjoyment; But smoking is my friend's delight; When he has no great employment." Unhealthy behaviors, often done with friends, are major contributors to premature mortality and cannot be easily "treated" by traditional medical care. *(Reprinted by permission of Arents Collections, The New York Public Library, Astor, Lenox, and Tilden Foundations.)*

Age and Years of Life Lost

Most Americans die when they are more than 65 years old, and very few live to greater than age 95. So another informative way of looking at death statistics is to examine leading causes of death at a given age. This highlights **years of life lost,** since a 20-year-old who dies of a gunshot loses many more potential years of life than a 75-year-old who has a stroke.

For men ages 15 to 24, the significant and leading causes of death are accidents, homicide, and suicide, with HIV infection (human immunodeficiency virus infection) also of importance if a slightly older age range is considered. For young women, accidents are a significant risk.

Even these statistics can be further refined: The death rate by homicide for young black males is more than nine times greater than that of young white males. General statistics can hide striking relations that emerge if a more refined approach to the data is taken.

During middle age (ages 40 to 59), cancers (especially lung cancer and breast cancer) are the greatest risk. Accidents, suicide, and HIV-infection remain very important, with heart disease of increasing importance. Few young or middle-aged adults now die from the classic infectious diseases that killed such adults throughout most of human history.

Study of death statistics can yield interesting clues to the major threats to the population's health. Indeed, such statistics make it clear that in a utopian, unpolluted world in which everyone ate properly, drove carefully, and behaved peacefully, and in which no one smoked cigarettes or took illegal drugs or acted promiscuously, the rate of premature death would drop dramatically. If we add into this equation the hard-to-measure but still significant health-impairing effects of low socioeconomic status, psychosocial disharmony, and psychological stress, the impact would likely be even greater. Think also of the tremendous economic, social, and productivity gains that would result.

What is missing from this analysis, of course, is any consideration of the individual. It is the individual person who behaves or misbehaves, and individual human bodies that become ill or remain healthy. Health psychology studies the emotional, psychological/psychophysiological, social, behavioral, institutional, and societal/cultural processes that interact with human biology to produce illness or health, premature mortality or longevity.

THE EMOTIONAL CONTEXT

In Salt Lake City, Utah, the heart of a dying 16-year-old was cut out of his body and transplanted into the body of his grandfather. The teenager had been fatally injured in a car-train collision that occurred just at the time that the grandfather had been placed on the hospital's heart-transplant list. Ironically, the grandfather began having severe pain (and needed an immediate transplant) after hearing about his grandson's accident. The grandfather didn't want to accept his grandson's heart, but did consent after the family convinced him that his grandson would have wanted it that way. The heart tissue was an excellent match.

In Baltimore, not long after, surgeons again made medical history when they performed a heart-lung transplant on a man with cystic fibrosis and then transplanted the man's own heart into another person. This man thus became the first living heart donor. The man's own heart was healthy—it was his lungs that were diseased; but the doctors thought he would have a better chance at survival if both the heart and lungs of another were transplanted to him together. Now he had to face the fact that someone else had his heart.

Broken Hearts

Anatomically, the human heart is a hollow, muscular organ that contracts and relaxes to circulate blood throughout the body. It is an efficient pump. Human hearts, however, are inside human beings, people who may have other thoughts and feelings about what a heart is. When a lover speaks of a **broken heart,** the reference is not to a malfunctioning valve or the need for a pacemaker. There is an emotional as well as a biological aspect to the heart. With such emotional meaning invested in hearts, it is apparent that questions about emotional reactions should be considered when a person loses his or her own heart and gains the human heart of another in a heart-transplant operation (Lynch, 1977; Thompson, 1971).

In fact, emotional and related psychological reactions turn out to be an integral part of physical well-being and the process of medical care. Although such processes are

Figure 1-2   Donating and receiving organs for transplantation raise many health psychology issues that are not usually addressed by traditional medical care. *Copyright Howard S. Friedman. Drawing by Robin Jensen.) Reprinted by permission*

often overlooked today, they were a key focus of past medical care. Creative doctors and nurses would talk to their patients, examine them, and, using their intuition, suggest measures that sometimes helped the patients feel better and behave in a more healthy manner. The emotional bond was very important, but little science was involved (Frank, 1977; Hippocrates, modern edition, 1923; Lown, 1996; Shapiro, 1960). With progress in the biological sciences such as physiology and biochemistry, and the discovery of the link between microbes and disease, medicine became much more of a science. Rules were discovered that described the effective treatment for many diseases, but the emotional context was often lost. Health psychology revives attention to these key issues, using modern scientific knowledge of these matters.

Does the emotional distress of a broken heart really interfere with the body's physical function? Can a person die of a broken heart? The scientific answer is yes. Various aspects of psychological stress and emotional upset produce unhealthy and even ultimately fatal bodily reactions (Booth-Kewley & Friedman, 1987; Glass, 1977; Kamarck & Jennings, 1991; Lynch, 1977; Totman, 1979). The problem is that there is no simple relationship—rather, many factors contribute. The various psycho-emotional influences on illness, and the pathways through which they operate, are described in detail later in this book.

THE PSYCHOLOGICAL AND PSYCHOPHYSIOLOGICAL CONTEXT

To my kidney sister: I think of you whenever I go to the bathroom.

This was inscribed on a picture given by a 17-year-old girl named Maria to her 14-year-old "sister," Laura (Schowalter, 1970). These two girls were very interested in each other's health, shared close feelings, and asked to room together whenever they were both hospitalized at the same time. But it was not their close friendship that made these girls consider themselves to be sisters. Rather, it was that each of them had received a kidney transplant from the same cadaver.

Identity—who we think we are—is an important element of coping with the stresses of life. How do you know who you are? Are you your body? How do you know when you are ill?

Although it is hard to know for sure, it appears that a newborn infant cannot understand the difference between pain due to diaper rash and pain caused by a sharp toy poking its foot. With age, the infant learns to move its foot and other body parts in response to environmental stimuli and thus discovers that the body is an important part of its identity (James, 1890; Mead, 1934; Piaget, 1960). A woman with breast cancer, for example, may find that losing a breast significantly affects her sense of self. If someone receives a kidney transplant from someone else, this person may begin to believe that the organ donor is a new part of his or her identity (Cramond, 1967; Fox & Swazey, 1974).

A much more important part of identity comes from interactions with other people. To understand this point, it is helpful to begin by thinking about animals. Does a dog have an identity? Sure, it will answer to "Fido," but does it really have a self-concept?

Psychologist Gordon Gallup studied this question in primates (Gallup, 1977). Gallup gave primates mirrors to play with. Later, he painted an odorless red stripe above their eyebrows. Higher apes like chimps looked into the mirror, saw the stripe, and reached up to their faces to try to pull it off. Thus they recognized themselves in the mirrors and so had at least some sense of self. Lower primates such as monkeys never developed this ability. Importantly, chimps raised in isolation (away from other chimps) never did develop this "sense of self."

Now think about a little girl who tells visiting relatives, "I'm very pretty but I have asthma." This statement is part of her identity, but where did it come from? We might first think that it came from an objective self-examination, but such self-knowledge usually comes from people around the child, especially parents. If Mommy and Daddy continually say, "You're a pretty little girl but sometimes you have trouble breathing because you have asthma," the child will develop a certain self-conception. This point was made early in this century by the philosopher-sociologists George Herbert Mead and Charles Cooley (Cooley, 1922; Mead, 1934). They suggested that identity comes from what people think others think of them. But identity is always changing, especially if people become ill and are cast into the role of a patient.

As we will see, patients encounter many communications and expectations from others. If patients think that others around them think they are "ill" or "weak," they will often come to believe it themselves and act accordingly. Social support turns out to be a key element both of disease prevention and of coping with illness. The field of health psychology examines factors that make patients define themselves as ill, the expectations others have of people who are ill, and the special treatment afforded the ill. (See also Box 1–1).

Box 1-1   Patients' Perceptions and Health

One way in which a patient's perceptions can affect health is through the patient's behavior. A strange but fascinating example comes from the case of a young Florida woman who died from an overdose of water.

Tina's mother died of stomach cancer. Tina soon became convinced that she also had stomach cancer. Doctors told her she did not. But her expectations were more important than the doctors' diagnoses. She did not cooperate with medical treatment.

To cleanse her stomach of cancer, Tina developed a treatment in which she didn't eat, but flooded her body by drinking gallons of water each day. The tremendous amount of fluid intake upset her body's chemical balance. Furthermore, Tina was drinking so much water that her kidneys could not keep up with it. Some of the water drained into her lungs and she drowned. News reports quote the medical examiner as saying, "It's unbelievable, but it happened."

[*Newsweek*, March 14, 1977.]

Psychophysiology

Epinephrine and norepinephrine (hormones related to bodily arousal) are released into the bloodstream in response to stress and, primate studies of pregnancy have shown, may reduce uterine blood flow, resulting in fetal hypoxia (low oxygen in the fetus), hypotension (low blood pressure), and bradycardia (slow heartbeat). In addition, the process of giving birth depends upon the actions of various hormones such as oxytocin, cortisol, and androgens, but these hormones are also involved in our response to stress. Thus, stress can affect the outcome of pregnancy and childbirth (Ivstan, 1986; Lobel, 1998; Myers, 1977; Wadhwa, 1998).

In humans and other mammals, severe stress impairs the number and motility of normal sperm, suppresses ovulation, and decreases sex drive. Stress during pregnancy may also disrupt the brain development of the fetus, possibly by interfering with neurotransmitter regulation, although there are few such studies on humans (Hanson, Spencer & Rodeck, 1995; Wadhwa, 1998). Yet many obstetricians are not especially focused on stresses that women may feel. They are more likely to administer an ultrasound test to view the fetus than they are to administer a psychological assessment test to study the mother. They are trained in the former but not much in the latter. As we will see, there is a separation of issues of psychology from issues of biology: there is a dualism.

There is another significant, but more indirect, route by which maternal problems affect the fetus. An overstressed mother may be more likely to smoke cigarettes, drink alcohol, and eat a poor diet. In other words, psychological factors can be related to health through different mechanisms.

Many pregnant women take classes in which they prepare for childbirth. The focus is on dealing with pain through the use of techniques of breathing, relaxation, and imagination. For many women, these techniques reduce the need for painkilling drugs. In other words, psychological techniques and behaviors can sometimes substitute for or enhance traditional physiological pain control techniques (anesthesia). This book extensively examines the various psychological factors involved in the relationship between physical and mental states, including the value of placebos and the effects of faith and personality on healing.

THE SOCIAL (INTERACTIONAL) CONTEXT

Friend: Did you visit the doctor?
Grandma Ethel: Yes.
Friend: What happened?
Grandma Ethel: The doctor feels better.
Friend: What? I don't understand.
Grandma Ethel: I wrote him out a big check and so now the doctor feels better.

Long-standing concern with the relationships among practitioners and patients and their families is reemerging as a significant issue in health psychology. However, intuition and the doctor's "art of medicine" (sensitivity) are no longer sufficient.

Patient Cooperation (Adherence)

Clearly, a surgeon is not supposed to be motivated purely by financial incentives. Although surgeons are well paid, people take offense at the idea of exchanging life or health for money. In the medical situation, the patient provides many other "social commodities" to the physician besides money. For example, the patient discloses a great deal of personal information to the doctor or nurse, disclosures usually made only to intimates. The patient trusts the practitioner with his or her thoughts, feelings, and body. In return, the practitioner offers a genuine interest in the patient's health (King, 1962). Medical interactions involve very special social exchanges.

In the early part of the 20th century, the anthropologist Marcel Mauss (1967) analyzed the practice of giving gifts in various societies. The gift and the demands for reciprocity and equity that go with it were shown to have important legal, economic, religious, aesthetic, and moral functions to many societies. Patients expect practitioners to return the respect they are given. But the demands and traditions of the medical setting often require that the practitioner assume a "fatherly" or "motherly" type of care. Patients often are asked to give up control of their health and equity in their relationship. Unfortunately, as we will see, while this arrangement may promote a sense of organization in medical settings, it may have many negative effects on the patient's willingness to cooperate with medical treatment. There is now a science of cooperation and a science of health communication.

Communication between Patients and Practitioners

I was born 40 years ago but I'm three years old.

This puzzling statement was made by the recipient of a heart transplant. The patient dates his age not from the date of his natural birth, but rather from the date he received a new heart and was able to resume many normal activities and so "begin life again."

Your distention of the rectum and other symptomatology results from habitual neglect of afferent impulses and accumulation of dry fecal masses.

This statement may be confusing to a layperson. It makes perfect sense to the physician who uttered it, however, as a result of years of medical training and constant exposure to medical journals and medical personnel.

Although such statements are not unknown, most communication between patients and medical personnel involves some shared language and shared expectations. Yet significant misunderstandings are common and widespread. Medical personnel misunderstand patients, and patients misunderstand medical personnel. To make matters worse, both patients and doctors generally think they understand each other when they actually do not. Ineffective communication is a major problem in modern medicine. Many factors may contribute to the problem, ranging from poor habits to an active desire to withhold significant information (McIntosh, 1974). It is clear, however, that significant improvements can be made (Roter & Hall, 1992).

Social Support

The third element of the social-interactional context of health involves social support. Social support entails the information, clarification, assistance, and reassurance that an individual receives from others (Caplan, 1979; Cobb, 1976; Cohen & McKay, 1984; Gottlieb, 1983; Rodriguez & Cohen, 1998). As we will see, social support is clearly associated with better physical and mental health, but the reasons for these relations are complex.

Often, stress comes from (follows) illness. Millions of Americans suffer from a chronic illness—some condition such as kidney disease, arthritis, heart disease, or paralysis—that prevents them from engaging in some major, normal activity. Even if they appear "normal" to the casual observer, many people must live daily with one or more serious problems. They deal with occasional medical crises, control their symptoms, and manage their daily lives while at the same time avoiding social isolation and other problems in dealing with people (Strauss & Glaser, 1975). People with chronic illness can often be completely successful if they have the cooperation of others. As we will see, such issues of coping with chronic illness are an important subfield of health psychology.

The poet John Donne wrote "No man is an island, entire of itself." People are involved with and dependent on many other people. Almost everyone is lonely at one time or another, but people without close intimate relationships, such as people who have lost their spouses, are especially likely to be lonely. Donne's poem continues, "any man's death diminishes me because I am involved in mankind; and therefore never send to know for whom the bell tolls; it tolls for thee." A bereaved person passes through various cycles of recovery (Kastenbaum, 1992). Knowledge of these reactions can help ease that transition. The death of a patient also has effects on health care personnel, although such factors and stresses were mostly ignored until recent years. Now, however, they are seen as an integral aspect of medicine, and they are discussed in this book.

THE BEHAVIORAL CONTEXT

Heart transplants are extremely expensive and very risky. They epitomize a traditional medical approach; that is, wait until something goes wrong, then fix it. Sometimes, as in the use of antibiotics to treat infection, this approach is reasonable and successful. In the case of heart disease, however, it of course seems much more sensible to *prevent* the development of disease. Fortunately, research has established that the likelihood of developing heart disease can be greatly reduced.

The idea that lifestyle—including behaviors like diet and exercise—might have significant effects on serious disease like heart disease began to take hold as evidence emerged from the Framingham Study. Starting in 1948, about 5,000 residents of Framingham, Massachusetts began being followed to see what behaviors might affect (predict) heart disease and stroke. To the surprise of the researchers and other physicians, it gradually emerged that hypertension (high blood pressure) was a significant risk factor. Previously, until the 1970s, medical students were taught that it was normal and healthy for blood pressure to increase with age. And, subsequently, hypertension has been found to be related to lack of exercise for many people.

Smoking, Drinking, Exercise, Prophylaxis

The study of behavioral factors in health and disease is now a central aspect of overall health promotion and health care. We will examine major risk factors, including tobacco use, alcohol, illegal drug abuse, nutrition, and exercise. We will also consider various forms of prophylaxis (protecting against disease), such as using sunscreen and clothing to prevent skin cancer and condoms to prevent sexually transmitted diseases such as chlamydia and AIDS. Contrary to common expectation, lack of education is not the main problem.

Interestingly, it also turns out that it is insufficient to consider behavioral risk factors one at a time. Unhealthy behaviors tend to cluster together and are associated with both social and personal factors. We will consider the idea of a general "disease-prone personality" (Friedman, 2000; Friedman & Booth-Kewley, 1987).

THE INSTITUTIONAL CONTEXT

On December 3, 1967, Dr. Christiaan Barnard of South Africa carried out the first human heart transplant. This operation, a major scientific breakthrough, ushered in a new era of medical technology. However, the timing of the event and the accolades to Dr. Barnard were not purely scientific. It became obvious that the technology for the operation had existed for a long time, because once the first transplant was performed, many others were soon undertaken at various medical centers around the world (Thompson, 1971). Institutional factors influenced whether the operation was seen as "acceptable." Today, a similar situation may exist regarding the cloning of human beings.

Surgeons receive nine or more years of very specialized training after college, more training than is required for almost any other occupation. Most of this training is very demanding, requiring long hours and both extensive knowledge and a high degree of manual skill. In the operating room, the patient's life is in the hands of the surgeon. Surgeons are also among the most highly paid professionals and are accorded a high degree of respect from the general population. It is interesting to note that few surgeons are women (Conley, 1998; Fidell, 1980).

As we will see, becoming a highly trained health professional like a surgeon is not only a technical scientific process; it is also a social and psychological process, with intense socialization that begins on the first day of medical school. For example, the stresses and contradictions of being a medical intern are dramatized with sardonic humor in *The House of God*, a novel by Samuel Shem (1978). Although the public expects physicians to be wise, knowledgeable, dedicated, hardworking, and selfless, the medical intern may see medical training as a challenge to his or her own survival. There are many contradictions between the goals of helping others according to hospital policy and the necessity of maintaining one's own physical and mental health and one's own personal relationships (Caplan, 1979; Cartwright, 1979). In the hospital called the House of God, the interns are advised that when there is a cardiac arrest, the first thing they should do is take their own pulse. Similarly, Shem writes that a key law of the hospital is that "the patient is the one with the disease."

Hospitalization

Prior to surgery, a heart patient will have his or her heartbeat recorded by an electrocardiogram, have blood flow studied with cardiac catheterization, be given various blood and urine tests, have x-rays taken, and so on. The surgery itself may be extremely complex, and postoperative care may require sophisticated monitoring equipment. Yet hospitalization also involves many other changes and procedures that are nonmedical and may at first be overlooked. Patients trade their usual clothes for hospital gowns, are awakened and served food at regular hours, live and sleep in close proximity to strangers, may have their sleep interrupted for testing, and encounter a number of different staff members. In short, the patient's social life is novel, lacking in privacy, and strictly regulated. These psychological factors in hospitalization may in some cases be just as important to consider when treating the patient as the strictly medical procedures (Kastenbaum, 1998; Lorber, 1975; Moos, 1979; Taylor, 1982). Disregard of social and psychological factors in hospitalization has caused many people to dread hospitals, and a poor social environment in a hospital may interfere with the patient's recovery.

Illness and institutional care may also promote loneliness (Revenson, 1986; Moos & Tsu, 1977). Many of our relationships come from our work and our involvement in the community. If one is confined to a hospital, these social relationships are disrupted. Furthermore, relationships with health care personnel are built on the basis of social expectations or roles, not usually on the basis of true intimacy. You are not likely to invite your physician to your home to sip wine and watch TV.

Hospitals did not dominate the American health care system until the middle of the 20th century. To a fascinating extent, the centralization process is now reversing. There are more and more so-called storefront, or walk-in, clinics out in the neighborhoods. Further, more and more procedures are now being performed on an outpatient basis rather than in hospitals. Simultaneously, however, the private physician in independent practice is becoming rarer. More and more people now receive their health care from large groups of health professionals banded together into Health Maintenance Organizations (HMOs). Changes in the health care system have direct implications for the psychology of health and health care.

THE SOCIETAL AND CULTURAL CONTEXT

AIDS, or acquired immunodeficiency syndrome, is a deadly infectious disease that can be spread through sexual relations, and as noted, it has become one of the leading causes of death of young adults. Many other sexually transmitted diseases (STDs), such as gonorrhea and chlamydia, also are occurring in epidemic proportions. Avoidance of tainted blood coupled with abstinence from sexual relations or limiting sex to a single, uninfected partner offers complete protection. Properly used, condoms are highly, though not perfectly, effective. In theory, STDs are nearly completely controllable and should be a minor health problem. The theory does not match reality.

Disease prevention—intervention to prevent a disease for which a person is at risk—now is an important part of health care. Yet disease prevention was (and often still is) left to public health professionals, a small minority of the medical community. Most physicians treat diseases but do not help prevent diseases. They see the cirrhotic liver but not the alcoholic patient. Psychologists too have traditionally not been much involved in disease prevention, but that changed with the rapid emergence of the field of health psychology.

Health psychologists are being employed in health centers, government health agencies, and university medical schools, as well as in private practice (Altman & Cahn, 1987). It is becoming clear that interventions aimed at individuals, one by one, will not be effective in addressing the problems. Disease prevention—from the effects of cigarettes, alcohol, poor nutrition, illegal drugs, guns, STDs, contaminated foods, and many other threats—necessitates a society-wide effort, with multiple levels of intervention.

Society and Self-Image

A more subtle example of the cultural context of health involves self-image. **Self-image** is directly relevant to the idea of a healthy body. Maintaining a healthy and attractive body is partly under an individual's control, but the individual's desires are shaped by so-

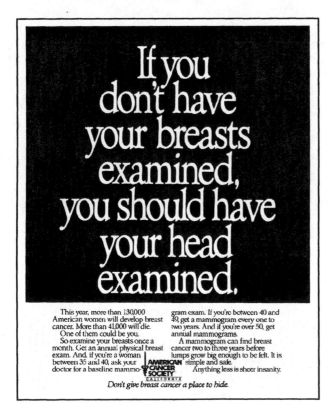

Figure 1-3 Disease prevention should be a key aspect of health care. But should disease prevention be forced upon people? What are the most effective psychological techniques? Why are they effective? *(Reprinted by permission of the American Cancer Society, Inc.)*

ciety. Overeating, under-eating, poor nutrition, suntanning, smoking, and lack of exercise have dramatic effects on both appearance and health. Abuses are often closely tied to problems of self-image, which arise in a cultural context.

For example, consider obesity, a major health problem and a state in which the body's physical structure and the self-identity are closely related (McFarlane, Polivy, & Herman, 1998; Rodin, Silberstein, & Striegel-Moore, 1985). Obese people may tend to think of themselves as "fatties" and "dessert pigs." They often have trouble attracting members of the opposite sex, holding top jobs, as well as other problems in society. Effective treatment usually necessitates an improvement in self-image as well as changing habits: from feeling hopeless, ugly, and fat to achieving a sense of control over one's body (Davidson & Davidson, 1980; Henderson, Hall, & Lipton, 1979; McFarlane, Polivy, & Herman, 1998). Health promotion—the encouragement of healthy individual habits—depends to a large extent on societal influences on the individual. Furthermore, as we will see, it is also the case that socioeconomic status is a key influence on health (Adler, Boyce, Chesney, & Cohen, 1994).

MEDICAL ETHICS

Several years ago, the case of a man with aplastic anemia made headlines. This often-fatal disease of the bone marrow can sometimes be helped by a bone marrow transplant. In the case in question, the only known perfect "match" for a tissue transplant was the patient's cousin, who refused to agree to the relatively safe procedure.

The patient went to court, asking the judge to order the cousin to consent to the procedure. However, the judge ruled that such an operation could not be forced on an individual, even to save another's life. Needless to say, the family relations involving these people became quite strained.

Modern medical procedures raise many questions of **ethics.** Sometimes the ethical challenges grow directly out of a biological issue, such as whether a dangerous but promising new drug should be tried. Often, however, the problems involve a significant element of psychology. Health psychology often helps us understand how and why people interpret information and make decisions. We touch on such ethical issues throughout this book and examine them in more detail towards the end of this book.

Prosecution?

An interesting example of the new ethical issues that arise with changing conceptions of health promotion involves the rights of a fetus. Direct focus on fetal rights arose from a case in San Diego in which a young pregnant woman had the condition of placenta previa, in which the placenta is poorly located and can separate from the uterine wall and cause hemorrhaging before the baby is born. The woman was warned by her doctors to stay off of street drugs, refrain from sexual relations, and seek prompt medical care as needed. But the woman took amphetamines, had sexual relations, and delayed in calling paramedics. The baby was born brain dead. The woman was charged with a crime.

Although the charges were eventually dismissed, the case raises many disturbing questions, and subsequent court cases have produced varying results. Is a mother responsible for the life of her unborn child? Can she be prosecuted for drinking alcohol or smoking cigarettes while pregnant? Should courts be able to order cesarean sections if the doctor thinks it necessary for the health of the fetus, even if the mother objects? Should pregnant women have police at their sides?

More generally, as the detrimental effects of certain behaviors become more apparent, should the state have the right to step in? For example, should smokers be prosecuted for attempted suicide? Should parents who do not properly immunize, educate, or apply seatbelts to their children be prosecuted for homicide if there is a resulting fatality? Such questions may seem farfetched at the moment, but the expectations we have about necessary health behaviors have already changed dramatically during the past 50 years.

In many such cases, the legal issues disappear if there are good relations among patients, their families, and the health care providers. Often, however, the ethical dilemmas remain.

METHODOLOGY

Newspapers and magazines are full of interesting reports linking aspects of psychology to aspects of health. Many of these reports involve useless pseudo-scientific quackery, but some represent major scientific breakthroughs. How can we devour the kernels and discard the chaff?

Two processes can help. First, new findings can be evaluated in terms of the existing knowledge presented in this book. Is the new finding reasonable given everything else we know? Second, new findings should be examined as to the method employed by the research. All methods have some advantages and some drawbacks, but some are clearly superior to others in testing a given hypothesis. Health psychologists emphasize sound methods, especially as addressing the key question of causal links. Throughout this book, issues of sound science and inference are pointed out.

Correlation Versus Causation

One basic methodological concern that has extremely important implications in the field of health psychology is the issue of **correlation versus causation.** In understanding illness, we generally want to know what factors cause the illness; by knowing the causal relationship, we can usually attempt to prevent or treat the illness. The most famous and successful causal relationship in medicine is **germ theory** (Clendening, 1960). When we know that certain bacteria cause certain diseases, we can prevent an illness by avoiding the bacteria, or cure a disease by killing the bacteria.

In many types of illness, the causal relationship is not clear (Elstein & Bordage, 1979). Instead, we only have observed associations or correlations between certain attributes or behaviors and certain illnesses. For example, cigarette smoking is associated with lung cancer, depression with chronic illness, food cravings with pregnancy, incidence of AIDS with homosexuality, anxious behavior patterns with heart disease, alcohol with migraine headaches, hostility with heart attacks, and sexual promiscuity at a young age with cervical cancer. The difficulty arises in determining the cause and the effect of the particular illness. Even though correlation does not necessarily imply causation, people are tempted to infer causation. Some of the following examples illustrate this point through exaggeration:

> People sleep less and less as they get older, but does lack of sleep cause aging?
>
> Most teenage heroin addicts were born in hospitals and nursed by their mothers, but does hospitalization and breast-feeding at birth lead to drug abuse?
>
> People who take two aspirins and drink a glass of orange juice often gain relief from headaches, but does orange juice help cure headaches?
>
> People who are anxious often feel relieved after a stiff drink, but does anxiety result from a lack of alcohol?

These contrived examples reveal the nature of the inference problem, but often the nature of the relationship is much less clear. Some more current research topics are: Does jogging help prevent strokes? Do large doses of vitamins and good friendships prevent the common cold? Do business demands cause heart attacks? Does depression contribute to increased likelihood of cancer? Do women live longer than men because of their hormones or their behaviors? Can the will to live affect the results of surgery? Can biofeedback and acupuncture relieve pain and promote healing?

Such questions are extremely challenging, as we will see as we address them later in this book. But the issue of correlation and causation is found throughout medicine. If a doctor prescribes a new antiviral drug for a patient with a very bad cold and the patient soon gets better, will the doctor conclude that the medication did the trick? Would the patient have recovered to the same extent without the medication?

Randomized Trials

As you probably know, the most straightforward way to arrive at a valid causal inference is to design a true experiment (Campbell & Stanley, 1963). In a true experimental design, people are randomly assigned to either a treatment group or a control group, and then the two groups are compared. For example, say we want to see whether providing gory pictures of lung cancer to smokers will lead them to stop smoking. We should do the following: We take a group of smokers and randomly assign half of them to view the lung cancer pictures, while the control group smokers view pictures of an unrelated topic, like people at the beach. Then we follow up with all the people and see if the smokers who saw the lung cancer pictures are more likely to quit. (The determination of "more likely" is done statistically.) If so, we have a good idea that the intervention caused the decrease in smoking.

Because of random assignment to conditions, an experimental design protects us from the possibility that the treatment group and the control group differed in some unknown way. But even in such an experimental design, there can be problems of inference. First, we do not know if the finding can be generalized to other smokers who have

Box 1-2 Tricky Statistics

When analyzing data in the health field, various statistics must be used to help us understand complex relationships. It is important to examine carefully the meaning of any reported statistics to be sure they mean what they seem to mean. Sometimes findings emerge solely because of the way a study is conducted or the way it is analyzed. In other words, the phenomenon is not real. It is human-made—what is called a *methodological artifact*.

A curious example of an artifact comes from statistical analysis after reclassification. Over time, doctors may change the classification (diagnosis scheme) of a disease and people may be moved from one category to the next, even though their condition has not changed. Consider the following illustrative example of two disease classifications, Group 1 (cancer Type X) and Group 2 (cancer Type Z). The classification of eight patients (here named A, B, C, D, E, F, G and H) was done at Time 1, and then later at Time 2. Over time, the classification of one of the patients, Patient E, changed, even though his disease did *not* change.

Time 1

Group 1	Life Expectancy	Disease Diagnosis	
Patient A	2 years	cancer Type X	
Patient B	2 years	cancer Type X	Average life expectancy = 3 years
Patient C	4 years	cancer Type X	
Patient D	4 years	cancer Type X	
Group 2			
Patient E	4 years	cancer Type Z	
Patient F	6 years	cancer Type Z	Average life expectancy = 6 years
Patient G	6 years	cancer Type Z	
Patient H	8 years	cancer Type Z	

Now the classification scheme is changed, so Patient E is considered to have cancer Type X, but all life expectancies remain the same.

Time 2

Group 1	Life Expectancy	Disease Diagnosis	
Patient A	2 years	cancer Type X	
Patient B	2 years	cancer Type X	Average life
Patient C	4 years	cancer Type X	expectancy =
Patient D	4 years	cancer Type X	3.2 years
Patient E	4 years	cancer Type X	
Group 2			
Patient F	6 years	cancer Type Z	Average life
Patient G	6 years	cancer Type Z	expectancy =
Patient H	8 years	cancer Type Z	6.7 years

In other words, both groups now appear to have increased their average life expectancy, even though nothing has changed except the classification scheme! The patients are not living longer.

Artifacts like this do not mean that statistics are worthless. It means that we have to take special care to understand our findings.

different characteristics from those studied. Second and relatedly, we do not know which moderating factors may be important; for example, our intervention may work very well for older people but poorly for younger people. Third, there could have been problems (biases) in the ways our elegant design was carried out; that is, there could have been experimenter errors. Finally, we only compared lung cancer pictures to beach pictures. We do not really know how other interventions would work, nor which are best.

It is always important to keep in mind what the control group represents—that is, *compared to what*. Although a true experiment has these various limitations, the conclusions drawn are of course vastly superior to those based on case studies or patients' testimonials. In medicine, such true experiments are usually termed **randomized clinical trials.**

Unfortunately, in most health research and health psychology research, we cannot use random assignment and so cannot have a true experiment. Let us consider one of the "simplest" examples: Does smoking cause lung cancer? We cannot randomly assign 10,000 teenagers to smoke two packs a day for thirty years, assign 10,000 other teenagers to never smoke, and then see who gets lung cancer. The impossibility of such a study is behind the statements of tobacco advertisers that a link between smoking and lung cancer has not been "proven." In fact, it took many years and many sorts of studies for clarity to

Figure 1-4 What role is played by societal norms in affecting health? *(Reprinted by permission of the American Cancer Society, Inc.)*

emerge on this issue. So, how can we tell about cigarettes and cancer? We have to rely on quasi-experimental designs.

What sorts of evidence can we muster? First, is there a higher incidence of disease among those engaging in the behavior? Yes, smokers have a much higher rate of lung cancer than nonsmokers. Second, is there temporal priority? Yes, smoking precedes lung cancer. (In other words, smoking is not the result of lung cancer.) Third, is there a dose to response relationship? Yes, heavier smokers have a greater incidence of lung cancer. Fourth, is such a relationship consistent with existing knowledge? Yes, we know that cigarette smoke has substances that damage living cells.

Fifth, is the association consistent in different populations? Yes, smoking is related to lung cancer in men, in women, in different ethnic groups, and in countries around the world. Sixth, are there animal analogs? Yes, other animals who are exposed to high doses of cigarette smoke are more likely to develop cancer. Seventh, will an intervention have an effect? Yes, people who stop smoking have better subsequent health than those who continue smoking. Together, these sorts of evidence almost completely rule out competing explanations for the observed relationship between smoking and lung cancer, and so make us very confident in our casual inference. That is why the surgeon general has called cigarette smoking the chief, single, avoidable cause of death in our society.

Box 1-3   Artifact: Is Alcohol Good for Your Health?

When quasi-experimental designs (rather than true experiments in randomized trials) are employed in health psychology, various serious artifacts can creep into the study, especially artifacts involving sample selection biases or selective attrition. Although quasi-experimental designs cannot be avoided in many cases, extreme care is needed in interpreting results.

A good example of a common artifact comes from study of the relationship between alcohol consumption and health. It is well established that high alcohol consumption—three or more drinks a day—is related to deteriorating health and high mortality rates. Alcohol directly damages the liver (causing cirrhosis) and increases the risk of certain cancers, accidents, and poor health habits. But what about more moderate alcohol consumption? A number of studies have found that light drinkers (one drink a day) are healthier than teetotalers (non-drinkers). Does the presence of small amounts of alcohol somehow help the body stay healthy? Recent evidence does support this conclusion in the case of those prone to atherosclerosis (Criqui, 1996), but consider the type of artifact often encountered:

One interesting long-term study of about 8,000 British men suggested that alcohol does not promote good health (Shaper, Wannamethee, & Walker, 1988). In this study, the researchers did indeed find that non-drinking men were unhealthier over an eight-year period. But why? The data suggested that men who had symptoms of cardiovascular disease quit drinking (because they weren't feeling well or were worried about their health). So, in the older adult male population, non-drinkers may be more likely to be ill to begin with, and so of course end up with worse health outcomes. That is, when one examines only initially healthy men, it may not be the case that the drinkers stay healthier or live longer than non-drinkers; or at least, such artifacts make it difficult to be sure of the size of any effect.

[Alcohol and mortality in British men: Explaining the U-shaped curve. *Lancet, 2,* 1267–1273.]

THE DISCIPLINE OF HEALTH PSYCHOLOGY

Health psychology is one of the youngest major scientific disciplines, barely a quarter-century old. Of course, its roots in the fields of medical sociology, medical anthropology, public health, social-personality and experimental psychology, psychosomatic medicine, physiology, and clinical medical psychology extend back throughout the 20th century. But until the late 1970s, there were no programs of study in health psychology, no professors hired in health psychology, and no professional societies or journals. (There were no textbooks until I coauthored the first one, published in 1982.) Now, that has all changed. Thousands of psychologists identify with the field, thousands of students study the field, and there are several scientific journals specifically focused on health psychology.

Development of Health Psychology

Seven major factors converged to facilitate the emergence of this new field (Ader, 1981; Glass, 1977; Matarazzo, 1982; Mechanic, 1983; Pelletier, 1979; Stone et al., 1987). First of all, medical sociologists, who had studied social structure and power relations in medical settings and the social roles (such as the sick role) surrounding health care, began to raise issues of the individual's psychosocial behavior in health settings. For example, why do some people with back pain seek medical care, whereas other people simply live with it?

Second, medical anthropologists, who had long studied healing practices across cultures, drew increasing attention to subcultural and ethnic influences on health, health behaviors, and well-being. For example, there are strong cultural influences on drinking alcohol, eating meat, and sexual promiscuity. Third, public health scientists began expanding their research interests from a traditional focus on sanitation, vector control (of rodents and insects), and the spread of epidemics to issues of risky health behaviors like cigarette smoking and drug abuse.

Fourth, social-personality psychologists applied attitude and behavior theories to issues like patients' nonadherence to treatment, illness attributions, communication between doctors and patients, and personality and disease—including Type A behavior. That is, traditional psychology theories were now applied to and tested in health settings. Fifth, researchers in psychosomatic medicine expanded their interests from a narrow focus on the psychodynamics of a specific disease to a recognition of the importance of general psychological processes in most diseases.

Sixth, physiologists, psychophysiologists, and behaviorists began studying the behavioral aspects of stress reduction, including such issues as biofeedback and meditation. Seventh and finally, clinical psychologists who worked with medical patients expanded their focus from psychopathology (traditionally the province of psychiatrists in medical settings) to a concern with the normal psychological problems and challenges of (medical) patients and patients' families. For example, they began helping patients and families cope with the challenges of cancer. We will see the influences of these various traditions throughout this book.

Organization of the Field of Health Psychology

In 1978, Health Psychology was formed as an independent division of the American Psychological Association. In 1982, the first issue of the journal *Health Psychology* was published, under the editorship of George Stone. Stone had recently started a graduate program in health psychology at the University of California, San Francisco, which served as a rallying point for many psychologists in California and then throughout the nation. The first issue of the journal *Health Psychology* contained an address from the health psychology division president, Stephen M. Weiss (Weiss, 1982, p. 81). Weiss, hopeful but somewhat nervous about the future of the small field of health psychology, proclaimed, "If there ever was a time of opportunity for Health Psychology, that time is *now*." Weiss needn't have been nervous; his words were prophetic, and the field of health psychology exploded during the following two decades—in research, in teaching, and in structure.

Interestingly, health psychology has remained a broadly based field. Students who master it often go on to careers in academic psychology, clinical health psychology, health promotion, social and governmental issues in health, health economics, occupational safety, work-site consultation, social work, family planning, and public and world health—in short, many of the disciplines that contributed to health psychology in the first place. Knowledge of health psychology should also be a key component of the education of medical professionals. Indeed, many premedical students who took a course in health psychology in the 1980s have since commented that they have used the information and framework throughout their medical and nursing careers.

THE ORGANIZATION OF THIS BOOK

This book is organized into four main sections. In Part I, we introduce the field and explore its bases. Health psychology involves both biology and psychology, and we consider the psychophysiological bases and the sociocultural bases of health and illness.

Part II focuses on the psychological contributors to illness and the psychological treatments of illness. We consider faith-healing, pain, stress, personality and disease, the self-healing personality, adaptation to chronic illness, and issues surrounding dying and death.

In Part III, the focus turns to health promotion and the health care system. We thus consider tobacco, alcohol, illegal drug abuse, nutrition, exercise, prophylaxis, patient cooperation with treatment, communication with practitioners, the health care professional, and health care institutions like hospitals.

Part IV, the final section of this book, takes up broader issues of health psychology and society, such as medical ethics, utilization issues, and goals for the future. Throughout the book there is an emphasis on integrating discussion of the most intriguing and important questions with the best scientific evidence available. Although many questions remain unanswered, we health psychologists do have deeper understandings of many more issues than most people might think.

SUMMARY AND CONCLUSION

Most of medicine, even including such highly technical procedures as surgical organ transplantation, involves significant elements of psychology. Traditionally, disease prevention and interpersonal relations were recognized as an important part of medical practice, but as the practice of medicine became more technical and specialized, these matters were often lost. Fortunately, much of the so-called "art of medicine" can be replaced by the scientific prescriptions offered by health psychology. This book applies the findings of psychology to medicine for the student interested in the field of health care.

As the nature of health problems has changed in developed countries, the nature of required health care must change. Many health issues today involve the promotion of healthy life styles, and the prevention of disease-causing behaviors. In a utopian, unpolluted world in which everyone ate properly, drove carefully, and behaved peacefully, and in which no one smoked cigarettes, took illegal drugs, acted promiscuously, or faced psychosocial disharmony and psychological stress, the rate of premature death would drop dramatically. Further, most people live long-term with chronic disease, and the maintenance of their health and well-being requires attention to their cooperation with treatment and their psychosocial and cultural contexts. All of these topics necessarily involve a substantial dosage of psychology.

Many of the shortcomings of modern technological medical treatment grow out of an outdated model of medical care. Health psychology can suggest a new, more appropriate model of health and health care. The outdated model and its replacement are described in Chapter 2, "The Psychophysiological Basis of Health and Illness," and Chapter 3, "The Social and Cultural Basis of Health and Illness."

Recommended Additional Readings

Kaplan, Robert M. (1993). *The Hippocratic predicament: Affordability, access, and accountability in American medicine.* San Diego: Academic Press.

McKeown, Thomas. (1979). *The role of medicine: Dream, mirage, or nemesis?* Princeton, NJ: Princeton University Press.

McKeown, Thomas. (1988). *The origins of human disease.* Oxford, England, New York: B. Blackwell.

Sagan, Leonard A. (1987). *The health of nations: True causes of sickness and well-being.* New York: Basic Books.

Stone, George C., et al. (Eds.). (1987). *Health psychology: A discipline and a profession.* Chicago: University of Chicago Press.

Stone, George C., Cohen, Frances, & Adler, Nancy E. (Eds.) (1979). *Health psychology: A handbook.* San Francisco: Jossey-Bass.

Key Concepts

health psychology

major causes of death

years of life lost

broken heart

psychophysiology

patient cooperation

disease prevention

self-image

ethics

methodology

correlation versus causation

germ theory

randomized clinical trials

Chapter 2

THE PSYCHOPHYSIOLOGICAL BASIS OF HEALTH AND ILLNESS

In 1896, a medical student named Walter Cannon began using the newly discovered x-ray to study digestion. He noticed that stomach movements seemed to be affected by emotional state (Benison, Barger, & Wolfe, 1987). Rather than viewing this finding as noisy data interfering with his study of the biology of digestion, Cannon's interest was piqued. His observation confirmed our subjective feelings of a "knot in the stomach" or "butterflies in the stomach" when facing a stressful or fear-arousing situation.

In 1932, Dr. Walter B. Cannon, by then a famous professor of medicine at the Harvard Medical School, was able to write a detailed analysis of how bodily alterations occur in conjunction with emotional strife and the experiencing of emotions such as anger or fear (Cannon 1932, 1942). He documented that stress causes an increase in the blood sugar level; a large output of adrenaline (epinephrine); an increase in pulse rate, blood pressure, and respiration rate; and an increase in the amount of blood pumped to the skeletal muscles. Cannon called this the **fight-or-flight response.** *When an animal perceives a threatening situation, its response is an integrated physiological reaction that prepares it either for running away or for fighting.*

Throughout history, people have known that how one thinks, feels, and behaves is somehow related to health. What people did not know was how this connection was constructed. In some societies, the connection was thought to be through evil spirits: When a person was possessed by an evil spirit or was ungodly, he or she became ill and acted strangely. In other societies, humoral (fluid) imbalances or excesses were seen as involved in mental and physical problems. It is only recently that we have achieved some scientific understanding of the links among psychology, physiology, and health, and of how the various complex parts of the body communicate with each other.

We now know that health-relevant internal bodily reactions and external behaviors are inextricably tied to our thoughts and feelings. Our brains are key to both our psychology and our health. The brain is the ultimate health-care complex.

Stress is the state of an organism when reacting to challenging new circumstances. Stress is produced by an unexpected or challenging event, and the stressful event requires the organism to readjust itself (Alexander, 1950; Pelletier, 1977; Selye, 1956). Thoughts, feelings, behaviors, and physiological reactions are all involved. Some of our physiological systems react almost instantaneously, whereas others change slowly over time; and there is always feedback. Remarkably, the ties among our different bodily systems turn out to be much closer than anyone previously imagined.

This chapter describes the internal system of nerves, hormones, metabolism, immunity, and fitness that affects health—the psychophysiological basis of health psychology. We do not analyze physiological systems merely as biological entities, but rather as they relate to psychology. This material thus provides the psychophysiological foundation for exploring more complex matters in health psychology that are taken up in later chapters.

A BRIEF HISTORY OF PSYCHOPHYSIOLOGY

Western notions of health have their roots in ancient Greece. Hippocrates described four bodily *humors* (blood, black bile, yellow bile, and phlegm) as the basis of human nature, and these elements were used by the ancient physician Galen (in Roman times) to refer not only to temperament but to the causes of disease. The predominant humor in a person was thought to produce the dominant temperament, and an excess of a humor led to disease. For example, an excess of black bile was thought to produce a melancholic personality, eventual depression, and associated physical illness. Hence, psychology and health, and mental and physical health, were seen as closely related.

The philosophy of the Middle Ages, however, was heavily concerned with religious and spiritual matters. Speculation about man's soul and his ties to God directed attention away from biology. Man was created in God's image and was different from other living creatures.

Descartes' Dualism

Endeavoring to be analytic and scientific as the Renaissance dawned after the Middle Ages, the 17th-century French philosopher René Descartes proposed that a human being has a mind that exists in the spiritual realm and a body that exists in the realm of physical matter. Therefore, the human body could be scientifically studied. Descartes thus saw the mind and body as separate, although very closely related (Descartes, 1955). This separation helped liberate thinking about health from excessive dependence on religious and spiritual matters.

But this mind-body dualism led subsequent thinkers to maintain a mental/physical (mind vs. body) distinction. When they tried to merge the two, some philosophers argued that the body could think, while others proposed that the body existed in the mind. But no one was easily able to conceive of the mind and the body as one entity (Ryle, 1949). Even in modern medicine, "mental" problems are almost always distinguished from "physical" problems. Because of such religious and philosophical concerns about the unique nature of man and the nature of mind, study of biology lagged far behind progress in physics and chemistry. In fact, it was only after Darwin's theory of evolution was proposed in the mid-19th century that the scientific search for the links between the mind and the body began in earnest.

Eastern traditions have less often stumbled into an artificial mind-body dichotomy, but, on the other hand, they have also been less scientific. For example, in yoga and the Hindu traditions, body positioning, breathing, fasting, and other bodily manipulations were (and still are) done with a spiritual goal in mind. Instead of humors, the focus is on vital energies, which supposedly flow through the body. Some such matters have led to deeper insights but not necessarily scientific understanding. For example, it took Western medicine to explore scientifically the relaxation and physical improvements that come from Eastern meditation and focus, and come to term them the "relaxation response" (Benson, 1975). Despite the Eastern emphasis and insights on close ties between psychological and physical matters, most progress in understanding the scientific basis of health has come from Western medicine.

Homeostasis

The roots of this modern work began in Paris over 100 years ago with the ideas of Claude Bernard, the great 19th-century French physiologist. Bernard emphasized the *mileur interne*—the internal environment—the idea that all living things must maintain a constant or balanced internal environment. Importantly, Bernard noted that the key to staying alive and healthy is *keeping our cells alive and healthy;* and that keeping our cells healthy means maintaining them in an internal environment of a certain temperature, with certain energy (food), with water, with oxygen, with waste disposal, and without toxins or invading, attacking cells. Microbes mattered, but often they did not matter as much as the body's defenses. Maintaining internal equilibrium through adjustments in physiological processes is termed **homeostasis.** Bernard helped make the study of physiology and homeostasis scientific, but he could not overcome the Cartesian dualism between mind and body.

Early in the 20th century, the question of psychology and illness hit a turning point with the theories and observations by Sigmund Freud and the psychoanalysts who followed him. Freud, influenced by Darwin, had studied the evolution of fish before turning to a biological study of psychology. Using hypnosis and related psychodynamic techniques, Freud (1955) was able to cure hysterical paralysis (such as cases in which young women were physically paralyzed by psychological problems) and related conditions. The mind was amenable to scientific, medical study. The function of psychological conflict could be investigated. But what about cancer, heart disease, migraines, and so on? Is psychology involved?

These diseases were taken up in the 1930s, 1940s, and 1950s by the field of psychoanalytic psychosomatic medicine. Does mental disturbance contribute to organic disease (Dunbar, 1943)? Based on clinical observation, the psychoanalyst Alexander (1950) said yes, and suggested that various diseases are caused by specific unconscious emotional conflicts. For example, ulcers were linked to oral conflicts (an unconscious desire to have basic infantile needs satisfied) and asthma to separation anxiety (that is, an unconscious desire to be protected by one's mother). Although these ideas are suggestive to clinicians, little controlled empirical research has been performed to test them; indeed it is impossible to test scientifically some elusive psychoanalytic speculations. Nevertheless, these efforts, combined with Walter Cannon's work, constituted the beginning of modern psychosomatic medicine.

Today, scientists have described a more sophisticated concept of homeostasis, called **allostasis** (Sterling & Eyer, 1988). Allostasis—the ability to achieve stability through change—emphasizes how our body is constantly adjusting to meet the demands of the current situation. For example, at night, our blood pressure drops dramatically, when physical demands are lowest. Before we get out of bed, the anticipation (the mere sense) of knowing we will suddenly stand up, causes an increase in blood pressure. Without that adjustment, we might stand up, feel dizzy, and faint. Allostasis emphasizes that our environment is almost never constant, and thus our body is always having to adapt to a changing environment.

When under chronic stress, however, the physiological systems have to work overtime, and may become strained. Imagine driving a car alternating the brakes and the gas; the car's systems are working extra hard and can do damage to a fine-tuned engine. In humans, the physical damage due to chronic stress, to turning on and off the stress response repeatedly, has been called **allostatic load** (McEwen, 1998). Does allostatic load cause chronic disease? The details of stress and allostasis are considered in Chapter 5, and the relations to disease and healing are considered in Chapters 6 and 7.

Life Stress

As a fertilized human egg begins to grow in the womb and a fetus forms, biological factors account for most of its development and regulation. **Genes** will tell it to take a human form, whether to become a male or female, and so on. There is very little psychology involved. Genes continue to exert a strong influence throughout life, but a person's thoughts, feelings, and behaviors also begin to have pronounced effects on human health and development. In other words, the brain becomes a key element in health.

In the 1930s, researcher-physician Adolf Meyer proposed that stressful life events may be important in the etiology of illness (Meyer, 1948). These events need not be negative, bizarre, or catastrophic to be pathogenic (disease-causing). They must simply be interpreted by the individual as an important **life change,** requiring some degree of coping. Examples are changes such as moving from one city to another, changing jobs, marriage, or a death in the family. Meyer noted the effects of these challenges on patients with respiratory, gastrointestinal, cardiovascular, and skin diseases. However, although Meyer examined the relationship between life change and illness clinically, he never documented his findings with systematic empirical research.

In time, more and more illustrations of the relationship between stress and physical deterioration appeared. The Menningers (1936) noted that very aggressive and ambitious men seemed prone to heart disease. Wolf and Wolff (1947) began studying the relationship between stress and ulcers. And, in general, more diseases were seen as having *psychosomatic* components—that is, as being partly caused by psychological factors, especially stress. Note that we say "partly"; diseases have multiple causes.

Cannon, in 1942, wrote about a phenomenon that he called **voodoo death.** Various examples are known in which a person received some kind of curse (e.g., from a witch doctor), was overcome with fear, and died within a few days. Cannon believed that the continuous stress on the body from severe emotional activation produced this effect. However, Curt Richter questioned this straightforward interpretation. Richter studied a similar phenomenon in rats placed into vats filled with water, who died suddenly even though they were good swimmers; he called this phenomenon *sudden death* (Richter, 1957). Yet autopsies on the rats did not show the kind of physiological stress that Cannon predicted. Rather, the opposite kind of physiological overreaction occurred (see the section on the parasympathetic nervous system, below). These lines of research led to a detailed analysis of the psychophysiology of stress.

We now know that stress involves the nervous system and the endocrine (hormonal) system. These systems prepare the body to meet the demands of the environment but endeavor to maintain an internal equilibrium, or homeostasis. Cannon called this robust internal regulation—this amazing ability to self-correct—the **wisdom of the body.**

Fast-acting, easily changeable bodily responses depend on the nervous system. The nervous system consists of billions of nerve cells (neurons) that comprise the brain, the spinal cord, and the peripheral nerves that communicate with the rest of the body. Some of the nerves provide us with voluntary control of our muscles, but many nerves control organs, such as the stomach, that operate without conscious control. These latter nerves comprise the autonomic nervous system.

AUTONOMIC NERVOUS SYSTEM

The part of the nervous system that manages the internal organs not usually under conscious control (such as the heart and viscera) is called the **autonomic nervous system.** It begins in the brain and travels throughout the body, thus allowing for near-instantaneous communication between the brain and other organs. It has two main parts: the **sympathetic nervous system,** which mobilizes the body, such as by increasing heart rate; and the **parasympathetic nervous system,** which generally restores the body's energies, such as by slowing the heart rate. So when we need to react to an environmental stressor, the sympathetic system may signal the heart to beat faster, the energy system to make glucose available, and the blood flow to be shifted towards the muscles that will be needed to fight or flee. The major effects of the sympathetic and parasympathetic nervous systems are shown in Table 2–1.

If you suddenly encounter a large, threatening predator (whether in a real jungle or in a man-made, crime-ridden jungle), the information is processed by the brain, and the sympathetic nervous system fires. Meanwhile, the parasympathetic (anti-stress) system becomes less active. Net effects: The heart beats faster and with more force, and the blood vessels contract. Blood pressure thus rises rapidly. Although such changes may help you to fight or run away quickly, they may also increase the likelihood of disruptions in heart rhythm, or may damage artery walls (Chesney & Rosenman, 1985). Health risks are the other side of the coin of health advantages (Sapolsky, 1994).

Overactivation of the sympathetic system is not the only risk. When Richter studied the sudden death of his swimming rats, he attributed their deaths to overactivation of the parasympathetic system—the rats eventually gave up and their hearts beat slower and slower and slower. Stress and mobilization can give way to helplessness and exhaustion. When the body falls out of homeostasis, health is impaired.

A **neurotransmitter** is a substance that is released by an excited neuron (nerve cell) and travels across the synapse to excite or inhibit a target cell. At the molecular level, much current study of psychophysiology now focuses on understanding the triggers, the actions, and the consequences of neurotransmitter release. Although health psychologists do not typically work at the molecular or chemical level of analysis, it is important to understand certain key actions of neurotransmitters and hormones so that one can read relevant scientific reports in psychophysiology, and so that one's theories in health psychology are compatible with existing physiological knowledge.

The autonomic nervous system does not work in isolation. Rather, it works in concert with the endocrine system. Together, they help regulate every organ system.

ENDOCRINE SYSTEM

The **endocrine system** is a communicative, or regulatory, bodily system that functions by secreting chemicals called **hormones** into the bloodstream. The hormones travel to target cells, where they attach and thereby activate new functions. For example, the pancreas secretes insulin to help regulate the level of sugar in the blood by stimulating the liver.

Table 2-1   The Sympathetic and Parasympathetic Divisions of the Autonomic Nervous System

Sympathetic (Arousing)	Parasympathetic (Restoring)
Increases heart rate	Slows heart rate
Inhibits digestion	Stimulates digestion
Opens lungs	Constricts lung passages
Dilates pupils (eye)	Constricts pupils
Inhibits salivation (dries mouth)	Promotes salivation
Liberates stored energy	Restores energy
Stimulates adrenal gland to release catecholamines	

Many of the body's organs, such as the heart, stomach, and salivary glands, have dual antagonistic innervation, which means that they are affected by both sympathetic and parasympathetic neurons. For example, when the sympathetic system is activated, it releases norepinephrine on the heart muscle fibers, which causes the heart rate to increase. When the parasympathetic system is activated, acetylcholine is released, which inhibits the activity of the heart muscles.

The thyroid gland (a butterfly-shaped gland in the neck) secretes hormones essential to growth and development.

Two relevant parts of the brain that are especially important for health psychology are the hypothalamus and the pituitary gland. The **hypothalamus** (so called because it is located below the thalamus) is the part of the brain that is central to metabolism and hormonal regulation, overseeing most endocrine (hormonal) activity. It influences bodily functions such as temperature control, the metabolism of fats and sugar, and the sex glands. Importantly, it helps control pituitary gland function.

The **pituitary** gland, the body's master gland, secretes hormones that directly influence other key endocrine organs. It is located at the base of the brain. For example, the pituitary releases gonadotrophins, hormones that stimulate the testes or ovaries (which in turn secrete hormones like estrogen and testosterone). Importantly, when so instructed by the hypothalamus, the pituitary releases adrenocorticotropic hormone (**ACTH**), which stimulates the adrenal cortex. Note that the endocrine system is a relatively slow-acting system, since the hormones must travel through the blood. On the other hand, it is a relatively long-lasting system, since the hormones may linger.

The adrenal glands are located above the kidneys. They have two key parts—the medulla and the cortex. When activated by ACTH from the pituitary, the **adrenal cortex** secretes steroid hormones (not surprisingly called corticosteroids), which have pronounced effects on the health of the body. An important one is **cortisol.** Cortisol acts opposite to insulin in that it increases the concentration of glucose in the blood, thus

providing energy for action. Corticosteroids also fight inflammation and have other effects, some beneficial, some perhaps not. For example, while suppressing inflammation,
antibody production may also be suppressed, thus reducing resistance to infection. (When
administered in drug form, cortisol is called hydrocortisone.)

Interestingly, the sympathetic nervous system also directly affects the hormonal
system. It causes the **adrenal medulla** (the other, core part of the adrenal gland on the
kidney) to secrete two hormones—epinephrine and norepinephrine. These two substances enter the blood, travel throughout the body, and increase general arousal. Thus,
during severe threats, there is both immediate sympathetic nervous system arousal and
slower endocrine arousal.

Epinephrine, also called adrenaline, travels through the blood, enabling the fight-
or-flight response, and accentuates the actions of norepinephrine. It provides the "rush"
one feels when excited. **Norepinephrine,** also called noradrenalin, is a key neurotransmitter. It activates organs through sympathetic nerves. Epinephrine and norepinephrine,
along with another key neurotransmitter called **dopamine,** are together referred to as **catecholamines.** The key elements of the endocrine system are shown in Figure 2–1.

Another chemically related neurotransmitter and hormone is called **serotonin.** (It is
synthesized from the amino acid tryptophan.) Serotonin plays an important role in the
regulation of mood, sleep, pain, and eating. Serotonin is heavily implicated in clinical depression and other mood disorders, as well as in eating disorders (Goldstein, Eisenhofer,
& McCarty, 1998).

Interestingly, research in the 1970s showed that the fight-or-flight response exists
in people responding to psychological stressors as well as physical threats (Frankenhaeuser, 1972, 1977, 1980; Glass, 1977). In one study, healthy young adults were put into
resting positions. Then, while trying to solve arithmetic problems under time limits, they
were harassed and pressured with statements from the researchers, such as: "I did that
better than you did. You're not doing very well." Measurements were taken of their pulse
and respiration rates, blood pressure, and the amount of blood pumped to the skeletal
muscles. Those on whom an emotional stress was placed showed a physiological response. Although the fight-or-flight response may still be necessary in some cases for actual survival, the stresses of society today usually do not require such behavior (physical
fight or flight). There aren't too many saber-toothed tigers in the suburbs, yet the physiological response remains. According to Cannon and others, stressful life events trigger
continuous bodily arousal, and this continuous arousal can cause lasting changes in basic
physiological processes. Such notions form the basis for modern health psychology research on stress and disease.

Part of the hormonal system (the adrenal activation) is illustrated in Figure 2–2. A
brief guide to relevant hormones is seen in Table 2–2.

In short, when we are threatened or challenged, sophisticated internal systems go
into effect and influence almost all parts of our body. There are immediate responses (as
our autonomic nerves fire), and there are long-lasting physiological consequences (as
various hormones are released). As the body's equilibrium is upset, various internal systems are affected. Hormones that affect growth, metabolism, reproduction, and the immune system can all become involved, as can the internal opiates involved in pain

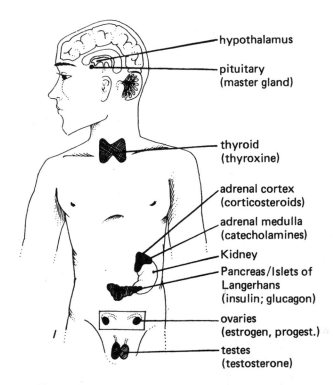

hypothalamus

pituitary
(master gland)

thyroid
(thyroxine)

adrenal cortex
(corticosteroids)

adrenal medulla
(catecholamines)

Kidney

Pancreas/Islets of
Langerhans
(insulin; glucagon)

ovaries
(estrogen, progest.)

testes
(testosterone)

Figure 2-1   Key Elements of the Endocrine System.

control. The long-term psychophysiological consequences relevant to health psychology—such matters as stress and illness, and personality and disease—are considered in detail in Chapters 5, 6, and 7.

The General Adaptation Syndrome

One of the earliest theories that linked stress to illness through endocrine processes was proposed by Hans Selye (1956). Selye argued that any noxious stimulus (emotional or physical) results in a biological response that is characterized by an arousal in the body's system of defenses against the noxious stimulus. In Selye's view, just about any type of threat would produce pretty much the same physiological stress reaction.

Simply stated, Selye's **general adaptation syndrome** consists of three stages: the alarm reaction, a stage of resistance, and a stage of exhaustion. That is, there is a mobilization, there is a fight, and if the challenge continues too long, there is exhaustion, depression, and illness. Selye proposed that there is a specific physiological response developed for defense against noxious stimuli, and that it is possible that many different diseases could result from prolonged adaptive processes using this response. Which disease do we develop? Different organs are affected, depending on the characteristics of the

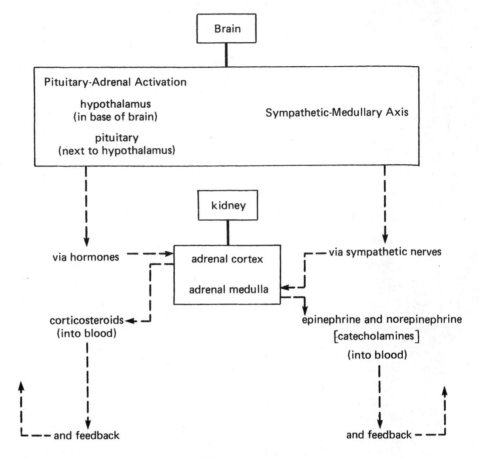

Figure 2-2   Adrenal Activation.

person, and different diseases result. Often the "weakest link" gives out first. The predisposition to disease, often hereditary, is sometimes termed the **diathesis.** It is important to note, however, that in Selye's model, stress does not lead to disease unless the adaptive responses are required for a prolonged period of time; that is, unless the individual must be constantly struggling to adapt.

Although Selye's model did not say exactly how noxious stimuli produce illness, there is an emphasis on the part played by the adrenal-cortical hormones. Selye caused stress in rats by pulling their tails, and after sacrificing them, he examined their adrenal glands and found the adrenal glands to be affected (usually, they were enlarged). He thus hypothesized that as a result of the excessive activation of the adrenal system, bodily resistance to disease is lowered and other biological changes, such as increased blood pressure and damage to tissue, take place. However, Selye was not much concerned with the psychological factors that turn an environmental event into a threat (Levy & Herzog,

Table 2–2   A Brief Guide to Hormones Relevant to Health Psychology

Hormone	Source	Action
Adrenocorticotropic (ACTH)	from pituitary	Stimulates adrenal cortex
Cortisol	from adrenal cortex	Fights inflammation; responds to stress; affects metabolism
Thyroid stimulating hormone	from pituitary	Stimulates thyroid gland
Thyroxine	from thyroid	Promotes growth and metabolism
Epinephrine (adrenaline)	from adrenal medulla	Mimics action of sympathetic NS
Norepinephrine	from adrenal medulla and adrenergic neurons	Constricts blood vessels; mimics SNS; also is a neurotransmitter
Vasopressin	from pituitary	Raises blood pressure
Aldosterone	from adrenal cortex	Regulates sodium and potassium ions
Testosterone	from testes	Promotes male growth and reproduction
Estrogen	from ovaries	Promotes female growth and reproduction
Melatonin	from pineal gland in brain	Has regulatory functions regarding sleep, and others still being studied
Thymosin	from thymus, a small gland behind the breastbone	Supports immune system
Glucagon	from pancreas	Increases blood glucose
Insulin	from pancreas	Affects blood glucose and metabolism; increases fat storage

Note that all of these hormones have complex functions and affect various, interrelated systems. Hormone levels in the blood then feed back to the brain, thus maintaining homeostasis. This table provides only a simple overview of the structure and function of the endocrine system in health and growth, but includes the major hormones usually encountered in health psychology research.

1974; Mason, 1974, 1975). Modern health psychologists, on the contrary, are very concerned with the psychological aspects of stress.

Since Selye's time, his two basic assumptions have been confirmed. First, it is now clear that adreno-cortical hormones are key to the stress response. Second, new discoveries have made it clear that stress does indeed lower bodily resistance, but in more complex ways than initially suspected. Selye thought that in the final exhaustion stage, the adrenal gland runs out of cortisol. Rather than running out of cortisol, it now seems likely that a new allostatic set-point is reached in order to adapt to the new demands; so the adrenal secretes excessively low or high amounts of cortisol. For example, chronic stress can lead to *deficient* exposure to cortisol, such as in post-traumatic stress disorder faced by combat veterans (Yehuda, 1993). Or, it can lead to *excessive* exposure to cortisol, such as often happens to caregivers under chronic stress. In both cases, this altered allostasis can cause trouble. As we shall see, too much cortisol can suppress immunity, predisposing one to infection, whereas too little cortisol reduces any inhibition on immunity, predisposing one to autoimmune disorders (McEwen, 1998). The immune system, described below, is responsive to stress.

PSYCHOLOGY AND THE IMMUNE SYSTEM

As Claude Bernard noted, in some sense, good health means having healthy bodily cells, and one key aspect of maintaining healthy cells is having a suitable defense against foreign invaders like strep bacteria. The skin is the body's first line of defense against microorganisms, keeping them out of our blood and internal organs. Yet even if our skin is unbroken, bacteria and viruses and fungi can invade through other openings, such as the nose, mouth, ears, genitals, and eyes. Thus these areas have mucous membranes or other defenses (such as acid in the stomach) to help trap or kill invaders. Even so, some microorganisms manage to enter the bloodstream.

The **immune system** protects our bodily tissues from invading microbes such as bacteria and from abnormal cells such as cancer cells or those infected by a virus. The functions of the major components of the immune system are summarized in Table 2–3. Such a threat to the body's healthy cells is termed an **antigen,** which involves a recognizable foreign protein on the invader's cell surface. The proteins serve as a warning sign—defense is necessary. Note that the defense of our health is a dynamic process—our bodies are always fighting off such threats, although some of the threats are more severe.

The first line of internal defense involves **phagocytes,** such as macrophages and neutrophils. These cells detect that body cells are being damaged or destroyed, and they go to the site of the infection and attempt to "eat" the antigen. They may also signal for help from lymphocytes.

Lymphocytes are white blood cells that provide **cellular immunity** (T-lymphcytes) and **humoral immunity** (B-lymphocytes). Cellular immunity occurs at the level of the cell, such as when a virus has invaded a cell. Humoral immunity occurs in the blood, involving, for example, the secretion of antibodies to fight invading bacteria. Lymphocytes have developed their specific protective actions through evolution or through prior experience. In addition, infants have some lymphocytes from their mothers.

Natural-killer (NK) cells, the other element of this immune surveillance system, kill their target cells directly, without the production of antibodies. For example, NK cells bind to tumor cells and release lethal chemicals; they thus seem to play a key role in cancer prevention by killing abnormal cells before they multiply.

Although most immune cells originate in the bone marrow, T-cells get their name because they mature in the thymus, a small gland in the upper chest. When T-cells (T-lymphocytes) detect an antigen such as a virus, they attach to the invader and kill it. They may also signal for help from other lymphocytes. T-cells further differentiate into other kinds of lymphocytes. In fact, the complex structure of the immune system is still being unraveled by immunologists.

Table 2-3   Basic Immune System Functions

Component	Funtion
Antigen	Substance that provokes antibody response, usually an invader or foreign substance.
Lymphocyte	White blood cell that attacks invaders; part of the adaptive (learned) immune response.
T-cell	Lymphocyte that learns to recognize invaders and participate in cell-mediated immunity.
B-cell	Lymphocyte that generates antibodies to attack invaders in humoral (fluid)-based immunity.
Helper T-cell	Lymphocyte that helps induce B-cells to divide into antibody-producing cells called plasma cells.
Macrophage	Scavenger cell that eats invaders and helps lymphocytes; part of the phagocyte innate immune system.
Natural killer (NK)	Cell that has a natural affinity for certain infected or tumor cells that does not depend on prior exposure.
Cytokines	Chemical messengers of the immune system (such as interleukin), which coordinate its activation.
Interferons	Proteins that modify immune responses and help uninfected cells resist viruses.

B-lymphocytes, which develop in the bone marrow, release antibodies into the blood stream to attack invaders. They are especially effective against bacteria and against viruses that have not yet entered cells. When B-cells encounter an antigen, they differentiate into two types of cells—one that actively fights the infection, and one that "remembers" the invader, thus termed *B memory cells*. These are the cells that build immunity after you have once contracted an infectious disease.

Because the immune system remembers previous infections (previous invaders), we can teach the immune system to be more effective by using inoculations. That is, by stimulating an immune response (such as by inoculation with a weakened virus), we can prevent contracting the disease in the future.

On the other hand, like any powerful defense system, the immune system can sometimes go awry and attack some of the body's own cells. This produces an **autoimmune disease,** such as lupus erythematosis (a serious disease of the connective tissues). It may be the case that some invading microorganisms have evolved to look similar to normal bodily cells (either in an individual or across generations) in an effort to sneak in and cause an infection. But the immune system may then confuse normal body tissues with foreign substances. Autoimmune diseases, however, are still poorly understood.

The process of fighting a microbe invasion can become quite complex, with some T-lymphocytes helping to regulate humoral immunity. These regulators are called T helper and suppressor cells. There are thousands of kinds of T-cells and B-cells, each responding to a particular antigen. Sometimes, the lymphocytes themselves can lose their self-regulation abilities, thus leading to a disease like some forms of leukemia. It is important to recognize that different studies in health psychology may be examining different aspects of the immune system and so might not generalize to other aspects.

AIDS (acquired immunodeficiency syndrome) is an especially insidious disease because the human immunodeficiency virus (HIV) causes failure of the immune system, and thus subjects the patient to all sorts of other deadly infections and cancers. The virus impairs the helper T-lymphocyte (also called CD4+), a key communicator, and thereby disrupts all usual immune responses (Temoshok, 1998). The advent of AIDS makes it clear just how much we depend on our immune systems on a daily basis; all sorts of infectious agents are constantly challenging our bodies, but a healthy immune system keeps them under control.

The chemical messengers that immune cells communicate through are referred to as **cytokines.** An example of a cytokine is interleukin 1, which helps activate various immune cells. Cytokines are important to health psychology because they are the key chemical control mechanism of the immune response, and so if any process (such as stress) can be shown to interfere with cytokine action, then a likely link to immune suppression has been established. Corticosteroids (like cortisol, elevated in severe psychological depression) can interfere with the normal actions of cytokines.

During the past two decades or so, it has become feasible to measure the production and suppression of these various immune cells through clinical assays. This means that we have been able to begin to assess the mediating mechanisms between psychological stimuli and disease (Ader, 1981; Ader & Cohen, 1998). For example, NK cells are especially important in controlling cancer; they roam the body, looking for abnormal cells. Natural-killer cells have often been used in health psychology studies as a general measure of immune system functioning. They are fairly easy to measure and they seem to vary in predictable ways. The problem with this use of a single measure is that it overlooks the great complexity of immune processes.

Psychoneuroimmunology

Although it has been suspected for a long time that stress can affect the immune system, relatively little attention was paid until fairly recently to the issue of immune-system-mediated disease resulting from human stress. (It was assumed that biology is biology and psychology is psychology, and never the twain shall meet.) A landmark study, published in 1977, looked at the effects of bereavement on immune system function (Bartrop, Lazarus, Luckherst, Kiloh, & Penny, 1977). The investigators examined healthy people whose spouses had died. They found decreased lymphocyte responsiveness at about two months after the bereavement. Although this study did not show whether disease subsequently resulted and did not control for other possible influences on the immune response, this study did spur greatly increased attention to such issues. Because this new field studies how psychological factors affect immunity through the neuroendocrine system, it is termed **psychoneuroimmunology** (sometimes abbreviated **PNI**). This field has the promise of explaining how infection or cancer may be affected by psychological stress. These factors are considered in much more detail in Chapters 5, 6, and 7 of this book.

One of the biggest mistakes that health psychologists can make is to equate some aspects of immune functioning with disease. It is of course true that if your immune system is totally dysfunctional and you are not in a sterile environment, then various diseases will take hold. However, if your immune system is somewhat depressed, this is not equivalent to having cancer. Similarly, you can have a well-functioning immune system and still become very sick. Just as there are people who are overweight, who are out of shape, who drink too much alcohol, and who have a family history of cancer, so too are there variations in immune functioning. There is a difference between being at a higher risk for morbidity and actually being sick.

Immune Phases

Note that the immune response unfolds over time and goes through many phases. For example, if an ill friend sneezes in your face and thus blows virus or bacteria at you, you might be protected by your skin or by your nasal hairs and mucous. Or, phagocytes or NK cells may come to the rescue. Chemo-mechanical reactions also result, such as the familiar symptoms of nasal swelling, discharge, redness, and so on.

If an infection begins taking hold, T-cells and B-cells will be activated and the body begins a coordinated, escalating response. The brain is affected and may trigger changes in eating, sleeping, temperature, and more. Often, after a period of several days to several weeks, the body triumphs and the invader is eliminated. If a researcher studying immunity endeavors to measure levels of various immune cells, the result will depend in part on the phase of the infectious cycle. This time-varying change can greatly complicate the study.

Finally, we can go even further and think about behavior as a component of the immune system. Many animals will go to great lengths to avoid eating rotting, contaminated food, or to stay away from sick and dying members of their own species. In humans, there is certainly, in addition, a conscious effort made to think about behaviors or exposures that have made or are making us ill, or are making those around us ill. To the extent that these efforts protect our healthy cells from threats, they can be considered an element of the immune system. Of course, this conception is stretching the normal views quite far; we usually want to think of such protective efforts in terms of healthy behaviors and public health measures, rather than as immune system function.

FITNESS

Thus far we have seen that psychology is related to physiology (and thereby potentially to health) through our nervous systems and through our endocrine systems and through our immune systems. But there is also a more direct link between behavior and physiology. For the body's cells to function and reproduce, they need nutrients and glucose, they need oxygen, and they need to be clear of wastes and other toxins. Thus, the internal environment depends on good nutrition; a heart, lungs, and circulation that can supply oxygen; and avoidance and elimination of toxins.

Nutrition and Metabolism

Medical students often complain about not learning enough about **nutrition.** They learn what happens when something goes wrong in the body, but there is an underemphasis on how the proper foods help things stay right. This is part of the general overemphasis on pathology in medicine.

Nutrition partly involves getting enough of the right foods that help the body's cells maintain themselves. For example, **free radicals** are molecules that have an imbalance in their electrical charge, which can damage healthy cells; nutrients such as vitamin E function to bind the free radicals and thus protect cells from damage. But proper nutrition also involves not getting too much of the wrong foods, such as saturated fats (animal fats) that can interfere with optimal cholesterol metabolism.

One of the keys to the health of the body's cells is maintaining the proper level of glucose (sugar) in the blood. The body can have too little glucose, or **hypoglycemia,** the light-headed, sick feeling that results when you fast or have too much insulin. Or, it can have too much glucose, or **hyperglycemia,** often a result of diseases like diabetes and Cushing's syndrome. Both can produce hallucination, convulsions, coma, and death.

Glucose is mainly stored in the body as a carbohydrate called *glycogen.* The formation of glycogen from food is termed *glycogenesis.* Conversely, *glycogenolysis* is the breaking down (catabolism) of glycogen back into glucose. This is done through enzymes that are regulated by—guess what—nerves and hormones. In other words, autonomic nerves and hormones, including stress hormones, help establish the proper sugar levels in the blood, and so it is not surprising that stress can upset the usual metabolic homeostasis. However, the details are very complex, varying as a function of a host of other variables. Since the nerves and hormones that are related to stress can also affect metabolism, there are links among psychology, metabolism, and health (Stoney & West, 1997).

Some of the best demonstrated links are among stress, blood sugar control, and body fat storage. When rats are exposed to chronic stress, they develop hyperglycemia and increased amounts of intra-abdominal fat (Rebuffe-Scrive, Walsh, McEwen & Rodin, 1992; Surwit & Williams, 1996). When people with diabetes also develop depression (both conditions being characterized by high cortisol), their glycemic control is worsened (Lustman, Freedland, Griffith, & Clouse, 1998). Conversely, when diabetic people's depression is improved with therapy, their glycemic (blood sugar) control is improved (Lustman, Griffith, Freedland, Kissel & Clouse, 1998).

In addition to the acute effects of alterations in metabolism, there are also many chronic effects. Most obviously, when this aspect of homeostasis fails, there can be conditions of extreme obesity or malnourishment. Further, it has also long been known that stress can affect cholesterol levels in the blood; thus there has been increasing study of this pathway to cardiovascular disease (van Doornen, 1997).

Exercise and Prophylaxis

More than two thousand years ago, ancient Chinese and Greek philosophers and physicians emphasized the importance of exercise to health, but the modern study of the physiology of exercise began in the 18th century, as the French chemist Lavoisier studied oxygen, including the effects of exercise on oxygen intake. It is apparent to any careful observer that people who actively stay in shape are generally healthier, but the many links to psychology, stress, physiology, and health are only now being seriously studied.

In this realm, the term **physical activity** is usually used to refer to use of large muscle groups that results in a significant expenditure of energy, whereas the term **exercise** refers to such activity that is planned and structured. Thus, farm labor is physical activity but calisthenics are exercise. The goal of such planned exercise is usually to achieve **physical fitness,** a hard-to-define term that implies health or the ability to accomplish physical tasks. But why is physical fitness a component of health?

It seems that there are two keys aspects to physical fitness. The first involves the strength to accomplish tasks without excessive strain. That is, if the body is unprepared to tackle an acute task (like shoveling snow) or a chronic difficulty (like working 60-hour weeks), homeostasis will break down, thus endangering health. The second aspect involves **cardiorespiratory fitness,** the ability of the heart (cardio) and the lungs (respiratory system) to supply needed oxygen to the body's cells (Wilmore & Costill, 1999). Well over half of premature mortality in the United States, as well as a large amount of morbidity (disease) is due to malfunctioning hearts or lungs, or to clogged arteries.

Cardiorespiratory fitness is best measured in terms of maximum oxygen uptake. That is, a person runs or cycles as fast as he or she is able, and the composition of expired air is measured. A much easier way to measure cardiorespiratory fitness is simply to assess performance on an aerobic task, such as how long it takes someone to run a mile. As one can see, this leaves much ambiguity. For example, what if one is a good sprinter, or has good endurance? Still, such assessment provides a good rough guide. Before surgery, an anestheiologist may ask the patient, "If you started walking down the block, how long would it be before you became tired and had difficulty continuing?" A patient who looks puzzled and replies that he or she could keep on walking probably has the necessary cardiorespiratory fitness to undergo a surgical operation. In short, much attention in health psychology is now directed toward understanding the development and maintenance of behaviors that keep the body strong enough to accomplish its daily tasks and that keep the heart and lungs functioning in an optimal fashion. Exercise is further considered in Chapter 11.

Toxic Substances

The prevention of or protection from disease is termed **prophylaxis.** Physical activity is thus usually considered an element of prophylaxis. But more commonly, the focus is on prevention of disease through avoidance of toxic substances and infections.

The final aspect of a healthy "internal environment" is thus to keep potentially toxic substances like alcohol away from cells, and to clear away carbon dioxide and other metabolic wastes. Aside from behaviors that keep the toxins away from the body in the first place (such as not smoking), the body has an elaborate filtering system to remove them. The liver and the kidneys are especially important in this respect, and if they fail, the body is poisoned. Some wastes are excreted through perspiration. Waste gases, like carbon dioxide, are brought to the lungs for expulsion. Any actions of nerves or hormones that affect these organs—liver, kidney, lungs, sweat glands—or their blood vessels thus have the potential to affect overall health.

THE TRADITIONAL BIOMEDICAL MODEL

When your automobile is not running right, you bring it into a service center for the attention of a certified mechanic, who will examine your car and do some diagnostic tests. He or she may cut out the old radiator and install a new one, and may follow this with a tune-up. You then pay the bill for parts and service, and go on your way. At some point, too many parts wear out, and you send your car to the wrecking yard.

Does it matter whether the mechanic who fixes your car is in a bad mood, or is hoping to get rich, or thinks your car is an ugly color? We seek only proper repairs at a fair price. In fact, you might talk to the service manager in the waiting area and never even meet the mechanic, who is hidden behind a draped repair stall. The technical skill of the mechanic and the efficiency of the service center are most important.

This mechanical model has striking analogies to the way many physicians and patients view illness. You have a minor basal cell cancer on your hand, you go the dermatologist, the small growth is cut off, and you pay your bill and go back to the beach. You sprain your ankle, you have it x-rayed and taped up, and then you go back to the ball game. You have a strep throat, you go to the doctor and get penicillin, you take the drug for ten days, and you are cured. As you get older, you may need to buy a hearing aid, new teeth, a new hip joint, or a kidney. At some point, too many of your parts wear out, and you die. Comparing physicians to auto mechanics is not meant to be insulting (to either group). In many circumstances, we have truly come to view medical care as a more-or-less mechanical process. After all, do you want a surgeon who has a nice smile or one who knows how to wield a scalpel? Because this view of medical care is so widespread in our society, it is called the **traditional biomedical model of disease.**

The traditional biomedical model of disease (also sometimes called the disease model) developed in 20th-century industrialized societies and reached the height of its prominence in the 1950s and 1960s. It is still the dominant model in the teaching and practice of medicine today. Many factors contributed to its development, and some are worth a brief review here.

One spur to this traditional, or mechanical, view was the development and use of sulfa drugs in the 1930s and of penicillin in the 1940s. Starting in the late 1800s, scientists began to isolate microorganisms as causes of many diseases, and the search for chemicals to kill these microbes began in earnest. For the first time, physicians had a dramatically effective treatment for all sorts of acute problems, ranging from strep throat to infected toes. So-called "internal medicine" rose to prominence, and researchers and practitioners of drug treatment achieved high status. Medical students began receiving

Figure 2-3 The Traditional Biomedical Model (Mechanical Model) of
Disease. *(Copyright Howard S. Friedman. Drawing by Robin Jensen.)*
Reprinted by permission

extensive training in biochemistry, microbiology, and other fields related to the actions of
drugs on human cells. Although little of this detailed basic science information is actually
used in daily practice by most physicians, it creates a certain focus to medical care.

A second factor was the increasing success of surgery. Once aseptic (sterilized)
surgical instruments and operating rooms were used to keep infections out of patients,
and once antibiotics were available to kill those infections that took root anyway, surgeons began helping more patients than they killed. Coupled with increased understanding of anatomy and disease, many wonderful surgical cures were invented.

A third factor promoting this traditional, biomechanical view was the sheer quantity of scientific biomedical information becoming available. No one person could master
all of the medical knowledge known to science, and so specialization developed. Some
physicians became surgeons and some focused on internal medicine; but within these
broad categories, dozens of specialties developed. Specialists included cardiologists, pediatricians, gynecologists, neurosurgeons, ophthalmologists, oncologists, obstetricians,

allergists, urologists, proctologists, neurologists, hematologists, geriatricians, gastroen-terologists, endocrinologists, orthopedists, radiologists, rheumatologists, dermatologists, and otorhinolaryngologists. There is little logical sense to these divisions: Some are focused on organs, some on diseases, some on patient characteristics, and some on the treatment modality. Yet all of them focus on illness as a problem to be repaired, and none of them especially strive for a broad general view of the patient; after all, they are *specialties*. Interestingly, only psychiatrists claimed a direct focus on psychological processes, and no specialty claimed expertise in social, cultural, and structural aspects of health care.

A fourth factor promoting the development of the traditional medical model was the increasing centralization of medical care. Before the 1940s, most patients did not enter hospitals filled with technologically advanced equipment; they were treated at home, they lived at home, and they died at home. Further, before the 1920s, doctors were not organized into strong trade groups like the American Medical Association. Medical training was not formalized and uniform. And, before the 1940s, there was little if any medical insurance and government-provided medical care. Today, however, a patient can walk into a hospital emergency room anywhere in the United States at any time of the day or night and expect to receive standard, competent care by a licensed physician. There are even government-certified diagnostic labels for each disease. This centralization and standardization fit quite well with the evolving traditional medical model.

As anyone who is the recipient of a successful organ transplant or has been cured of a nasty infection can tell you, the traditional biomedical model has achieved many wonderful results during the past 60 years. People expect prompt relief from any illness, and in many cases, they can indeed be cured. Physicians went from the ridicule of past centuries to extremely high status in the America of the 1960s.

New Challenges to Health

However, times have changed. Medical interventions, coupled with improved public health measures, such as immunizations and improved sewage systems (McKeown, 1979), have placed most acute infectious diseases under control. At the beginning of the 20th century, the leading causes of death in America included pneumonia, influenza, tuberculosis, gastroenteritis, diphtheria, and diseases of infancy. Only influenza is still very important. (Smallpox, once a terrible scourge, has been eliminated completely.) As we saw in Chapter 1, today's leading causes of death are heart disease and stroke, cancer, lung disease, and injuries (trauma), which have significant psychophysiological and behavioral aspects to them.

Furthermore, many people now live many years with chronic illnesses like diabetes, arthritis, migraines, emphysema, asthma, and back pain that cannot be cured but can be managed. In other words, as we will see throughout this book, the traditional biomedical model of fixing an acute problem may have outlived its usefulness. It is often inadequate to the challenges of health and health care in today's world, and it does not easily address the psychophysiological and behavioral aspects of health.

It is very important to understand that criticism of the traditional biomedical model is not the same as criticism of physicians or hospitals. In fact, it is often the most learned and eminent physicians who are the most critical of the traditional approach! Rather, traditional health care has outlived its usefulness in some significant ways, in large part because of its own success. But, as we will see, there are also many new matters that have arisen that challenge the old ways of doing things.

EVALUATION

There is now no doubt that psychological disruptions are closely related to the physiological processes that underlie health and illness. We now know that the thoughts, feelings, and actions that we process in our brains can communicate with the rest of our bodies through the endocrine and nervous systems. It makes biological sense to talk about psychology and health. Our hormones and nerves directly affect various physiological processes and so can affect health through various mechanisms.

However, psychophysiological disruption is often neither necessary nor sufficient to produce illness. If you were to be exposed to smallpox and have not been vaccinated, it is very likely that you would become very ill, whether or not you were stressed or depressed. On the other hand, many people seem to go through highly stressful times without becoming ill. In other words, psychophysiological disruption—a failure of homeostasis—is not the same thing as illness.

The psychophysiological study of the bases of health and illness has made great progress in understanding the role of the brain and its related hormonal, nervous, and immune systems. You may have noticed, however, that this chapter has included relatively few psychological concepts, especially social psychological and behavioral concepts. Much research in psychophysiology is still along the lines of a more traditional biomedical model, and it ignores a host of extremely important psychological and social influences on health. This other side—the social and cultural basis of health—is the subject of Chapter 3.

SUMMARY AND CONCLUSION

Throughout history, people have known that how one thinks, feels, and behaves is somehow related to health. Yet only in the last two decades have we achieved some significant scientific understanding of the links among psychology, physiology, and health, and of how the various complex parts of the body communicate with each other.

Descartes' mind-body dualism led subsequent thinkers to maintain a mental/physical (mind vs. body) distinction, a false split that still plagues us. Claude Bernard, the great 19th-century French physiologist emphasized the *mileur interne*—the internal environment—the idea that all living things must maintain a constant or balanced internal environment. Stress is the challenge to this balance, and it involves the nervous system and the endocrine (hormonal) system. These systems prepare the body to meet the demands of the environment, but endeavor to maintain an internal equilibrium, or homeostasis.

Walter Cannon called this robust internal regulation—this amazing ability to self-correct—the wisdom of the body.

The autonomic nervous system has two main parts: the sympathetic nervous system, which mobilizes the body, such as by increasing heart rate; and the parasympathetic system, which generally restores the body's energies, such as by slowing the heart rate. The hypothalamus is the part of the brain that is central to metabolism and hormonal regulation, overseeing most endocrine activity. When so instructed by the hypothalamus, the pituitary releases adrenocorticotropic hormone (ACTH), which stimulates the adrenal cortex.

According to Selye, the general adaptation syndrome consists of three stages: the alarm reaction, a stage of resistance, and a stage of exhaustion. Excessive adrenal activation causes direct damage, such as through hypertension and disruptions in metabolism, and as Selye guessed, bodily resistance to disease is lowered. Chronically challenging situations can lead to damage—allostatic load—and disease.

The first line of internal immune defense involves phagocytes. Beyond that, lymphocytes are white blood cells that provide cellular immunity (T-lymphocytes) and humoral immunity (B-lymphocytes). (Cellular immunity occurs at the level of the cell, such as when a virus has invaded a cell.) The chemical messengers that immune cells communicate through are referred to as cytokines. Cytokines are important to health psychology because they are the key chemical control mechanism of the immune response, and so if any process (such as stress) can be shown to interfere with cytokine action, then a likely link to immune suppression has been established. How psychological factors affect immunity through the neuroendocrine system is termed psychoneuroimmunology.

There is also a more direct link between behavior and physiology. For the body's cells to function and reproduce, they need nutrients and glucose, they need oxygen, and they need to be clear of wastes and other toxins. Thus, the internal environment depends on good nutrition; a heart, lungs, and circulation that can supply oxygen; and avoidance and elimination of toxins.

In many circumstances, we have come to view medical care as a more-or-less mechanical process. Because this view of medical care is so widespread in our society, we call it the traditional biomedical model of disease. This book points out the many significant limitations of this approach, but it is very important to understand that criticism of the traditional biomedical model is not the same as criticism of physicians or hospitals. In fact, it is often the most learned and eminent physicians who are the most critical of the traditional approach. Rather, traditional health care has outlived its usefulness in some significant ways, and health psychology can step in to address many of the new challenges.

Recommended Additional Readings

Cannon, Walter B. (1932, 1939). *The wisdom of the body.* New York: W. W. Norton.
Kemeny, Margaret E. (1994). Stressful events, psychological responses, and progression of HIV infection. In Ronald Glaser, & Janice K. Kiecolt-Glaser (Eds.), *Handbook of human stress and immunity.* San Diego: Academic Press.

Sapolsky, Robert M. (1994). *Why zebras don't get ulcers: A guide to stress, stress related diseases, and coping.* New York: W. H. Freeman.

Selye, Hans, (1975). *The stress of life.* (Rev. ed.). New York: McGraw-Hill.

Thompson, Richard F. (1993). *The brain: A neuroscience primer.* (2nd ed.). New York: W. H. Freeman.

Key Concepts

fight-or-flight response

stress

Descartes' Dualism (Cartesian dualism)

homeostasis

allostasis

allostatic load

genes

life change

voodoo death

wisdom of the body

autonomic nervous system

sympathetic nervous system

parasympathetic nervous system

neurotransmitter

endocrine system

hormones

hypothalamus

pituitary

ACTH

adrenal cortex

cortisol

adrenal medulla

epinephrine

norepinephrine

dopamine

catecholamines

serotonin

general adaptation syndrome

diasthesis

immune system

antigen

phagocytes

lymphocytes

cellular immunity

humoral immunity

natural-killer

autoimmune disease

AIDS

cytokines

psychoneuroimmunology

nutrition

free radicals

hypoglycemia

hyperglycemia

physical activity

exercise

physical fitness

cardiorespiratory fitness

prophylaxis

traditional biomedical model of disease

Chapter 3

THE SOCIAL AND CULTURAL BASIS OF HEALTH AND ILLNESS

In a modern American hospital of the 1950s and 1960s, a particularly severe form of medicalization surrounded childbirth. Expectant mothers were often isolated in labor rooms, and then wheeled into sterile-looking delivery rooms, where they were placed under significant anesthesia and their babies delivered. The mother was then wheeled to a recovery room, while the baby was placed in a nursery. The father was notified so that he could peer at his new child through the glass, pass out cigars, and go home or back to work. All this was "known" by well-intentioned physicians to be in the best interest of the mother and baby.

In rare, life-threatening births, such strict environmental control is necessary. Many premature or ill babies are given heroic, life-saving care. However, with most births, such dehumanized procedures tended to interfere with the natural birth process, increase the anxiety of the mother and the difficulty of the birth, produce a less relaxed (or a drugged) infant, decrease the psychological bond within the family, and cost a small fortune (Herzberger & Potts, 1982). The mother would often spend at least six days in the hospital.

Today, in striking contrast, there is controversy about how little *biomedical care is sometimes offered during childbirth. Women may be discharged from the hospital within hours after childbirth (unless there is objection, now protected by law). The father or another partner may be present in the homey "birthing room," and may assist in cutting the umbilical cord. The baby might be immediately breast-fed and remain with the mother. There is much less anesthesia, sometimes for good reasons, sometimes not. In fact, some women on Medicaid (care for the poor) have sued their doctors, claiming they were denied anesthesia because they could not pay for it. (In 1998, in response, California passed a law prohibiting doctors from denying anesthesia to poor, pregnant women in active labor.) Yet hardworking obstetricians still explain sincerely how they are proceeding in the best interests of the mother and baby.*

We generally think that medical help-seeking, medical care, and hospitalization depend on how sick the patient is and on how the best treatment can be administered. Treatment is assumed to be determined by and focused on curing an organic disease. To a significant degree, this assumption is valid. However, social and cultural influences are also always present. As we will see, these components are not ancillary but are fundamental to understanding health. This chapter explains the social and cultural basis of health and illness. It also goes on to present the biopsychosocial health psychology model.

MEDICAL HELP-SEEKING

A large number of patients who experience an acute myocardial infarction (heart attack) die before receiving any type of medical treatment. The deaths are most often the result of ventricular fibrillation (uncoordinated quivering of the heart chamber). With medical help, this condition is potentially reversible. Furthermore, clot-dissolving drugs such as tissue plasminogen activator (tPA) and streptokinase can actually end the heart attack, preventing further damage. However, many patients get to the hospital too late. Some wait and see if their "indigestion" will go away. Other victims go home to bed to "rest," and they die before receiving any treatment at all. Why?

One might expect that a person who is experiencing the symptoms of a myocardial infarction—chest pain, perspiration, shortness of breath, and dizziness—would seek immediate medical attention. Despite the serious consequences, however, help is often not immediately sought. A typical response is to delay seeking medical advice or treatment beyond the critical period of 1 hour after the onset of acute symptoms. In fact, while about half of coronary patients seeking treatment arrive at the hospital within 4 hours of the onset of symptoms, a quarter take from 4 to 14 hours, and many arrive after more than 14 hours. The median time from onset of symptoms to arrival at the hospital emergency room has been estimated as between 2 and 6 hours (Bleeker, Lamers, Leenders, & Kruyssen, 1995; Dracup, Moser, Eisenberg, & Meischke, 1995; Gentry, 1979; Gentry & Haney, 1975; Jorgensen, Nakayama, Reith, Raaschou, & Olsen, 1996; Petrie & Weinman, 1997; Simon, Feinleib, & Thompson, 1972).

The delay in seeking treatment is not primarily because of transportation problems. Transport takes only about 10 percent of the time. Rather, most of the delay is caused by patient decision time—the interval between the onset of symptoms and the patient's decision that medical help must be sought. The length of this delay before a person seeks medical attention is influenced by several basic factors. Together, these factors help to answer the important question, "What is illness?"

Perceiving Symptoms

The first key factor that influences reactions and delay time involves the psychological process of the patient's perception of illness. The decision to seek help requires perceiving the **symptoms** (the chest pain, perspiration, etc.), understanding their seriousness, and deciding that medical care is necessary. Some coronary patients fail to attribute their initial symptoms to a heart problem. They are not so sensitive to pain, or they attribute their pain to such things as gall bladder problems or a chest cold. Or, they may associate their symptoms with fatigue or depression, and so delay deciding that they are ill (Matthews, Siegel, Kuller, Thompson, & Varat, 1983).

In addition, many patients use denial to deal with the anxiety aroused by the symptoms; they avoid defining their sensations as symptoms of serious illness (Gentry, 1979; Olin & Hackett, 1964). While denial ("I'm really just fine") may have a useful purpose in momentarily reducing the feelings of overwhelming panic in the coronary patient, it may also reduce the patient's chances of survival by preventing the patient from seeking the needed emergency medical care. Finally, some patients feel that something is wrong but they do not recognize the urgency. This is why patients with more knowledge of disease are more likely to seek treatment. But knowledge is only part of the story.

Background, Situation, and Culture

The second factor affecting medical help-seeking involves the background and characteristics of the patient. Reactions to physical symptoms vary as a function of cultural and demographic differences, such as social class, age, sex, and ethnicity. For example, older or female patients may take longer to seek help than younger or male patients. As another classic example, persons of British descent tend to be stoical and therefore reluctant to express the pain of a heart attack (Pilowsky & Spence, 1977; Saunders, 1954; Segall, 1972; Zborowski, 1952, 1969). People follow the personal patterns that govern other areas of their lives.

A third set of very important influences involves the social situation. The social context in which the symptoms first appear affects how long it takes the patient to seek medical treatment (Bleeker et al, 1995; Dracup et al., 1995; Gentry, 1979; Gentry & Haney, 1975; Jorgensen et al., 1996; Moss & Goldstein, 1970; Petrie & Weinman, 1997; Simon et al., 1972; Tjoe & Luria, 1972). Even the day of the week and the time of day when the symptoms begin can affect delay in seeking care. For example, greater delay occurs when the symptoms appear during the day on weekends, whereas patients are more likely to seek help right away if the symptoms occur at work, among coworkers. There is also significantly less delay if patients are in the presence of other persons, particularly spouses, when the symptoms begin. Social rewards influence illness behavior and help us define symptoms, and these effects are described in this chapter.

A final set of influences on medical help-seeking involves the economic and societal structure. People are more likely to seek health care if they can afford to, if the care is readily available, and if the society encourages such behavior. As we will see, a poor, rural farmer may be less likely to seek help than a rich, urban executive.

The earlier the heart attack patient arrives at the hospital, the more likely is recovery. This situation itself justifies a detailed psychological study of the meaning of "illness." Yet

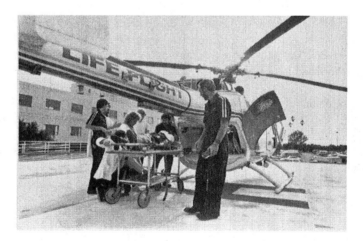

Figure 3–1   Helicopter ambulances can bring patients to an emergency room in a matter of minutes. However, the real problem is usually not one of transportation but rather the patient's delay in seeking treatment. *(Photo courtesy of University of California, San Diego, Medical Center.)*

the same sets of factors also influence the decision to seek medical treatment in cases where life is not immediately threatened. Will a child with a runny nose stay home from school? Will a woman with a breast lump tell her doctor? Will a man with back pain ignore it, complain to his friends, quit his job, or go immediately to a hospital?

WHAT IS ILLNESS?

When an individual feels ill and begins to engage in activities that indicate a problem (such as taking aspirin and going to bed), the individual is engaging in **illness behaviors** (Kasl & Cobb, 1966). People with symptoms and illness behaviors can then adopt a role in society known as the **sick role** (Berkanovic, 1972; Parsons, 1958). A person can enter the sick role if a doctor confirms that the person is ill (or sometimes if the family or influential friends of the individual define this person as ill). It is a societal (not an individual) confirmation or certification.

The Sick Role

An individual enjoys certain advantages as a result of entering the sick role. The ill person is not considered responsible for the illness—it is beyond the patient's control. As a result, the sick individual has a legitimate basis for exemption from normal activities and obligations. That is, the patient does not have to go to work or fulfill other normal expectations. If a mother of five children is hospitalized, she is not labeled a bad mother because she can no longer take care of her children. Illness (the sick role) is also a legitimate basis for seeking assistance from others. *Illness is a social phenomenon.*

It is therefore often useful to distinguish the term *illness* from *disease*. Disease usually refers to an organic problem with the body. A person with organic disease may or may not show illness behaviors and may or may not enter the sick role. On the other hand, a person who shows illness behaviors may or may not have an organic disease.

Certain responsibilities accompany the benefits of the sick role. One of the obligations is that the individual see the role as undesirable—the patient is expected to feel uncomfortable in the role and to try to cooperate with others to get well. The person must also seek help from health care professionals when such care is seen as available and beneficial.

How do we understand and deal with an individual who, after exhibiting various symptoms, is defined as being ill, but then does not profess any desire to get well and does not cooperate with the treatment prescribed by health professionals? Suppose a 40-year-old woman complains of headaches, is defined as ill, and is exempted from her role as a school librarian and as caretaker of her two children. Further suppose, however, that she consistently forgets to take her prescribed drugs, and that she watches television all day. What do we conclude? Is she ill? A loafer? Is she perhaps refusing to cooperate with treatment because of some hidden reasons stemming from her background or social relations?

Becoming Ill

Illness is relative, not absolute. It depends upon interpretation. There is no laboratory test that detects "illness." A number of conditions that make people more likely to interpret their bodily symptoms as illness (and to exhibit illness behaviors) were identified by sociologists David Mechanic and Irving Zola.

Mechanic and colleagues have isolated the following variables (Mechanic, 1959, 1962, 1966, 1978):

- The number of symptoms and their persistence.
- The individual's ability to recognize the symptoms and the amount of medical knowledge available to the person.
- The perceived seriousness of the symptoms.
- The extent of social and physical disability resulting from the symptoms.
- The cultural background of the person and of the defining group in terms of emphasis on stoicism (indifference to pain or pleasure).
- The degree of personal needs to deny the illness.
- The extent of interfering (competing) needs and interpretations.
- The availability of sources of help—including not only the availability of clinic and hospital care, but also the patient's physical distance from it and its cost in money, time, and effort. This factor includes the fear, stigma, and feelings of humiliation associated with treatment, and the patient's relationship with the health care professionals.

Relatedly, the sociologist Irving Zola identified these five triggers affecting the timing of a patient's decision to seek medical care (Zola, 1964):

1. An interpersonal crisis that serves to call attention to the symptoms, causing the patient to dwell on them.
2. Social interference that occurs as the symptoms begin to threaten a valued social activity, such as work.
3. The individual receives sanctioning for seeking care; that is, others encourage the patient to seek care.
4. The patient perceives the symptoms as threatening in nature.
5. The symptoms are seen as similar to previous symptoms, or to those with which the person is familiar because relatives or friends have had them.

These various factors, which seem sensible when described but are often ignored in medical care, will now be discussed in terms of cultural and demographic influences on illness; social perception, attribution, and illness (the psychological processes of social cognition); and the rewards of illness.

CULTURAL AND
DEMOGRAPHIC INFLUENCES

Cultural factors have an enormous influence upon patients' interpretations of symptoms and their responses to these symptoms (Davitz, Sameshima, & Davitz, 1976). An informative example involves comparing Americans of English-speaking, European background to Americans of Spanish-speaking, Mexican backgrounds.

The Example of Mexican-Americans

Euro-Americans tend to prefer medical science and hospitalization to deal with illness, whereas many Mexican-American patients tend to prefer to rely more heavily upon tradition-based medicine and family care as an important aspect of treatment. For example, regarding symptom interpretation, one study found that only 16 percent of Mexican-American teenagers interpreted "hearing voices" as evidence of insanity or hallucination, as compared to 90 percent of the Euro-Americans. The Mexican-American children tended instead to regard hearing voices as evidence of a religious experience, just as biblical prophets heard the divine voice (Clark, 1970; Nall & Speilberg, 1967; Padilla & Ruiz, 1973; Saunders, 1954).

Special problems arise when two cultures clash. The Mexican-American population in the United States is rapidly increasing, and communication difficulties encountered between Euro-American health care professionals and Mexican-American patients are common. They illustrate the profound influence of culture on perception of illness: To many Euro-American physicians, illness means disease—an organic condition brought about by a natural agent, and as such it should be dealt with unemotionally. To many Mexican-American patients, however, illness relates to their life, to their community, and to their family and interpersonal relationships. Furthermore, Mexican-Americans traditionally may tend to be more likely to believe that illness is significant only when there is pain or visible symptoms (Clark, 1970; Kato & Mann, 1996; Kiev, 1968; Lurie & Lawrence, 1972; Quesada, 1976; Vega & Miranda, 1985).

The folk curer, or **curandero,** is a member of the traditional Mexican-American community, makes house calls, and deals with the entire family of the patient. The stark efficiency of the Euro-American physician's office may be unsettling to a Mexican-American patient, who prefers a friendly, calm, courteous physician. Considering the other issues to be discussed in this book concerning the body and mind, we might reasonably conclude that the support of the curandero will lead to a greater chance of effectively treating conditions that have a strong emotional component.

Tradition-oriented Mexican-Americans may also feel that in-depth discussions of their illness must involve their families. The patient may agree to a treatment plan, but the family makes the final decision. Any infringement on the family rights by the health care professional may result in noncooperation on the part of the patient. In short, the basic conception of illness held by a cultural group can have dramatic effects on various aspects of health and health care.

The Example of Jewish and Italian Patients

Other, more subtle, cultural factors are also relevant to health care. In a classic work, Mark Zborowski conducted research in New York City on the reactions of patients from various ethnic groups to pain. He noted that Jewish and Italian patients tended to exaggerate pain experiences, responding in a very emotional manner, while patients of English ("Yankee") or Irish descent were inclined to be more stoical and to deny pain. While the outward expressions of the Jewish and Italian patients were usually similarly emotional, there was a difference in the meaning of pain to the patients in these two ethnic groups. The Jewish patients were concerned with the cause of the pain and its future significance, whereas the Italian patients tended to seek relief from the pain and were more likely to be satisfied when they felt better (Zborowski, 1952, 1969). Zborowski's basic findings have been supported by other research (Kato & Mann, 1996; Mechanic, 1962; Sternbach & Tursky, 1965; Zola, 1963). For example, Italian-Americans and Jewish-Americans are more likely than other groups to report a great number of illness symptoms when questioned in surveys. Cultural and social conditioning bring about differences in illness behavior, with sometimes healthy and sometimes unhealthy consequences.

Most illness behaviors are learned in childhood. For example, Italian and Jewish parents are often extremely protective about their children's health, and crying in response to illness or pain is usually responded to by the parent with sympathy and attention. The children learn to pay attention to painful experiences and distressing symptoms, and also to seek assistance. Familial responses to illness behavior of the child may set a pattern for the child's life.

The patients' illness behaviors, in turn, can affect the attributions that are made about these patients in the health care setting. That is, illness behaviors can influence how the health care professional evaluates the medical condition of the patient. Classic research illustrating this point was conducted at Massachusetts General Hospital (Zola, 1966). The subjects in the study were patients who voluntarily went to the ear, nose, and throat clinics with symptoms for which no medical disease could be found. Zola discovered that patients' modes of cultural expression strongly influenced the way in which they expressed the symptoms, which, in turn, influenced strongly the physicians' decisions about their care. Patients' usual methods of expressing symptoms (primarily culturally based) affected how they were viewed and evaluated by the physician. These examples are not meant to stereotype any ethnic group, but rather to emphasize the importance of culture to illness. Of course, many individuals within a given ethnic group differ from each other and may have more or less identification with their traditional ethnic group.

Age and Sex Roles

Age and sex roles—what is expected of people because of their age and sex—also partially explain illness behavior. Chest pain in a teenager is unlikely to be interpreted as a heart attack by the teenager or by others. Failure to take medications may be seen as rebelliousness in a 20-year-old, but may be excused as forgetfulness in a 7-year-old or a 70-year-old. Differences in expectations also apply to males and females. Traditionally, females have been seen as the "weak sex," and sometimes as frail. In fact, weakness has sometimes been viewed as attractively "feminine." Hence the same symptom—weakness or fainting—may be interpreted very differently, depending on the sex of the patient. Women are also more likely to use health services than men, probably at least in part because it is more socially acceptable for women to disclose information about themselves and to admit weakness (Nathanson, 1975).

A final but striking example of the influence of culture and background on reactions to bodily functions concerns menstruation (Paige, 1973). Since biblical times and throughout history, the same biological process has been given many different and often strange interpretations. Menstruating women have been subjected to many rituals, often involving isolation and even including special menstrual huts. Even the word menstruation itself is often avoided, and euphemisms such as "the curse" are used. Depending on the culture, women will not cook, pray, exercise, have sexual relations, go out in public, and so on, when menstruating. The tremendous variety of reactions illustrates that the "illness" is not solely biological; reactions depend instead on social factors. Even in modern American society, relationships between menstrual distress and social factors have been found to be related to religion (Paige, 1973). For example, Catholics who are very traditional in their views (e.g., believing that women should stay home and care for children) are more likely to experience menstrual distress than are more liberal women. For Jewish women, menstrual distress tends to occur among women especially concerned with social rituals and personal hygiene during menstruation. The way in which people are reared affects their illness behaviors.

Thus, various factors in culture and upbringing may affect whether a person senses certain symptoms, whether the person defines the symptoms as illness, and whether the person (and others) thinks it necessary to seek medical attention for the symptoms.

SOCIAL COGNITION: SOCIAL PERCEPTION, ATTRIBUTION, AND ILLNESS

Consider the following interview with a first-year medical student:

Questioner: How do you know that a person is ill?
Med Student: He says that something hurts, or that he doesn't feel well, or cannot manage to work as before. Of course, once the person comes to the hospital or doctor's office, we look for a specific organic cause of the symptoms.
Questioner: So it is the report of symptoms to the health professional that defines illness?
Med Student: Well, of course, a person can be ill and not seek health care. He or she could simply stay home from work. Then again, the doctor could find something wrong even if the patient feels okay.
Questioner: How do you know how ill a person is?
Med Student: That is a tough one. There are objective indices such as fever and tissue damage. Also with regard to a specific pathogen, we have measures of the extent to which the disease is life threatening. The more life threatening the dis-

ease, the sicker the person is, I guess. However, with most conditions, since they are not life threatening, we often go by how much the condition tends to impair the functioning of the individual. For example, I just met a lady the other day who went back to work five days after a radical mastectomy. She said that it was psychologically healthier for her to do that. Another lady had the same operation and took months to go back to work and to really take on her family responsibilities again. The two women had the same amount of tissue damage and the same cancer prognosis. They had the same surgery. I still don't completely understand the difference between the two.

Questioner: How do you know someone has gotten better?

Med Student: Primarily, he or she acts healthy.

We go through an inference process before we confer upon an individual the label of "ill" or "well." Of the two women who had had mastectomy surgery, the woman who continued to exhibit illness behavior was defined as ill. The woman who went back to work was considered recovered. Both patients' perceptions and observers' perceptions are important.

The process of interpreting a symptom or behavior is one of **attribution** (Jones et al., 1972); that is, we search for a causal explanation for an event. Consider the case of a coworker who calls in sick and does not show up for work on a fine spring day. We are not only concerned about this person's behavior (that is, the fact that the person failed to come to work), but we are also very interested in the reason for the absence. We make attributions of responsibility for behavior, attributions that are influenced by many factors. First, we might recall the *past behavior* of the coworker. If this person always calls in sick when the weather is nice and there is something to do away from work, we may become suspicious of his or her present motives. Or, we might examine this person's *past medical history,* assuming that he or she is justified in staying away from work if we know that this person recently underwent a series of operations. We might also *discuss the matter with others,* such as coworkers, asking them how this person looked yesterday and why they think he or she is absent from work. If we find that our absent coworker is often absent from the job, likes to have a good time, *responds to situational pressures,* does not spend much time visiting doctors, and loves to go to baseball games on nice spring days, we may then conclude that the coworker is not really ill.

Note that the behavior, or action—the fact that this person is not at work—remains the same; only our explanations change. And of course there may be severe consequences for abusing sick leave. Although we constantly make attributions about behavior in our daily lives, attributions about illness are especially important because of the importance of the sick role. An element of interpretation must enter into play before we are willing to speak of illness (Mechanic, 1966; Pennebaker, 1982).

Labeling Arousal

Sometimes the attributions we make are about ourselves (cf. Bem, 1965). As we saw in Chapter 1, aspects of our identity come from other people. We are not born knowing what a headache or a stomachache is. A young boy who looks pale, is holding his stomach, and has just eaten a bowl full of chocolate may be asked by his mother, "Do you have a stomachache?" It is in such ways that we learn to interpret symptoms and behaviors of illness. Understanding the attribution process is important because our decisions are not always rational, but are often biased or distorted.

An interesting insight into how people interpret internal body events is provided by research on the self-labeling of emotion, which was pioneered by the social psychologist Stanley Schachter (Schachter & Singer, 1962). Schachter noticed two interesting phenomena. First, people sometimes feel that their body is physiologically aroused, although they are not sure about the cause of the arousal. For example, something may be affecting their hormonal balance, or they may have received a drug or treatment that (unknown to them) produces sympathetic nervous system arousal. (For example, over-the-counter drugs given to relieve nasal congestion caused by an allergy can cause bodily changes similar to amphetamines, including insomnia, restlessness, tremor, alertness, and feelings of anxiety, tension, and agitation.) Second, Schachter noticed that people sometimes gather information about their own feelings and reactions from other people. For example, in times of fear people seem to gather together and look to each other to decide how to deal with their fear. In fact, experiments have shown that people who have had fear aroused in them are more likely to want to be with other fearful people (Schachter, 1959).

Using these two observations about arousal and social comparisons, Schachter concluded that there is no simple one-to-one relationship between bodily states and our feelings and reactions. Instead, each body sensation must be interpreted before it has meaning. If we are surrounded by people who tell us that our symptoms are typical of a heart attack, we are much more likely to think that we are ill and to seek medical attention. Thus, a man experiencing chest pain in the presence of his worried wife is more likely to seek medical assistance (Gentry, 1979).

Attributions

The attributions we make for our symptoms can in turn affect the symptoms. An interesting case concerns insomnia. While there are many factors that can interfere with a person's sleep, a prominent factor in chronic insomnia often involves a person's anxiety about being insomniac. That is, insomniacs worry that they are insomniacs, and this worry helps keep them awake even more. Hence, an important means of treating sleeplessness involves breaking this vicious circle of insomnia leading to anxiety leading to insomnia. One way is to convince the patient that the insomnia is caused by a common problem such as noise, which can be solved. The anxiety then disappears as the attributions change from "I'm an insomniac" to "I can't sleep because of a problem in the environment." It then may be relatively easy to modify the environment and reduce the insomnia.

For example, in an interesting related study, researchers gave insomniacs a placebo pill but told them the pill would produce the symptoms of insomnia (Storms & Nisbett, 1970). Since the patients now had an external explanation for their insomnia, their anxiety was reduced, and they were indeed able to go to sleep more quickly. By the same token, a patient who cannot fall asleep after taking a sleeping pill may become more anxious about the problem and have even more difficulties. Furthermore, if we have certain expectations about our bodies, then we will selectively monitor our bodies for confirming sensory information (Pennebaker, 1982). Thus, the use of pills must be considered in light of the attributions that the patients will make about them. However, at least one study has failed to replicate these findings, suggesting that small or subtle changes in a person's attributions may have large effects on the outcomes.

An important factor that influences the interpretation of symptoms as illness and produces the desire to seek medical care is the **salience,** or prominence, of the symptoms. The salience of symptoms is dependent on the disruptive effect of the symptoms. For example, if we are at work and feel so weak that we cannot continue working, we may see ourselves as ill; however, if we are at home and do not feel well enough to continue watching the late show on television, we might simply decide that we are tired and go to bed. Social interference is usually the most important component of salience, but other matters can also be very significant. These variables are the visibility of the symptoms, the extent to which they are life threatening, and their frequency of appearance.

One interesting study looked directly at people's attentional focus (Pennebaker, 1982). In this study, males walked on a treadmill while wearing headphones. The men were randomly assigned to hear one of three things over the headphones: their own breathing, distracting street sounds, or nothing. When the walking was finished, the men reported their physical symptoms (racing heart, shortness of breath, etc.) and their fatigue level. It was found that degree of symptom-reporting and fatigue were greatest for the breathing condition and lowest for the distracting sounds condition. In other words, with physiological arousal controlled, symptoms were a function of attention.

A related factor influencing reactions to illness is the availability of relevant information. Can the patient match the symptoms to previous illnesses or to illnesses others have? For example, when there is a flu epidemic, it is easy for both doctors and patients to diagnose the flu. But if a patient has an exotic parasitic infection while there is a flu epidemic, definition of the illness may be much more difficult.

In one experimental study of people's evaluations of the seriousness of a health disorder, 60 college students were told that they were being tested for a (fictitious) enzyme deficiency (Jemmott, Ditto, & Croyle, 1986). After being administered a saliva test, the students were led to believe either that they had an enzyme deficiency or did not (according to experimental condition). They were then led to believe either that the deficiency was rare or that it was very prevalent. The students then completed questionnaires about their conditions, which served as the dependent measures. Results indicated that the people who thought the deficiency was rare rated it as more serious than those who thought it was prevalent; perceptions of prevalence influenced judgments of seriousness. A follow-up study confirmed that students view diseases thought common to be less life-threatening, and also found that students who had a history of a condition rated it as less life-threatening than did their counterparts without such a history (Jemmott, Croyle, & Ditto, 1987).

There are other systematic influences on our attributions (Michela & Wood, 1986; Miller & Diefenbach, 1998). When we infer causes of behavior, we generally give special weight to actions that seem unpopular or that go against our expectations. If a surgical patient refuses postoperative pain medication, cooperates with and compliments the health care personnel, and is able to leave the hospital early, we are more likely to make inferences about this patient than we are about the patient who proceeds in the usual manner (Kelley, 1967).

Other, related attribution principles indicate that the consistency of information affects the inferences we draw. Suppose a friend catches the flu and responds distinctively by going to bed with the illness. If this is something this person has not done during past illnesses, you may conclude that your friend is now very ill. If it is also true that almost everyone else who has this type of flu is very ill and also must stay in bed, you then become very confident that your friend is really quite ill and it is legitimate for your friend to stay home in bed. In other circumstances, for example, if everyone else says this flu is like a minor cold, you might conclude that your friend is not really very ill. It is important to note that the interpretation of a friend's illness behavior does not depend to a great extent on biological symptoms. Our interpretations are instead a function of the patient's behavior in the context of what we know about the patient, the circumstances of the illness, and a comparison with other people. Interpretations occur in the minds of observers; in this sense, illness is socially defined.

There are also individual differences in how people think about threats to their health (Miller & Diefenbach, 1998; Miller, Rodoletz, Shroeder, Mangan, & Sedlacek, 1996). For example, some people with the AIDS virus will be very cognitively vigilant in looking for signs of illness, which may help in early detection of developing problems but may lead to difficulties in coping emotionally with the threats.

Differences in Point of View

A patient's perspective on illness differs from that of health care personnel. For example, consider a patient admitted to a hospital with a nonspecific virus that causes this person to be very weak, feverish, nauseous, and depressed. The patient may be aware of having an aching body, being unable to stand up, feeling dizzy when lifting his or her head up, being unable to eat, and being better off resting than trying to carry on normal conversation with people. However, to health personnel, such as nurses, this patient may appear in a very different light. The virus may produce no obvious physical symptoms except perhaps the fever; there are only behavioral symptoms. Furthermore, the nurses probably had never seen this patient as a well person leading an active life. These differences in information and perspective between the patient and the practitioner may produce an actor-observer difference in attributions (Jones & Nisbett, 1972). The patient, or "actor," will interpret his or her behavior (such as the refusal to joke or eat) as caused by the illness. This interpretation is a situational explanation ("I don't usually behave this way"). However, the nurses, or "observers," may attribute the same behaviors to something characteristic of the patient, such as seeing the patient as uncooperative (sometimes termed a "crock"), especially if the patient is not a sympathetic character. That is, the practitioners will have a tendency to make a dispositional attribution (explanation), blaming the behavior on the personality or fixed characteristics of the patient. As an antidote, the proper type of interviewing is helpful (see Chapter 13). Practitioners might also try to imagine themselves in the patient's position. In fact, many health practitioners have had their eyes opened wide when they became patients!

Patients' judgments of salience do not necessarily coincide with those of the medical professional. Certain symptoms that are disruptive to the patient may be medically trivial and not require attention. Other symptoms, such as initial signs of cancer, might be very serious but have no disruptive effects. Illness behavior usually represents the patient's rational attempt to make sense of the symptoms and to cope with the problem, given the limits of the patient's knowledge, social situation, and culture. But this behavior may not be at all rational from the point of view of the medical professional.

The Social Situation

In addition to the individual attributional processes that affect definitions of and reactions to illness, the presence and actions of other people are important. One reason for individual differences is that somatic (body) complaints are often signs of underlying emotional problems (Balint, 1957; Costa & McCrae, 1987; Mechanic & Volkart, 1960, 1961). The emotional problems might be motivating the expression of physical distress. In fact, emotional distress may be more influential in the patient's decision to express illness and to seek help than is the actual occurrence of any organic condition (Mathis, 1964). Complaining of a physical symptom (however trivial the symptom) is one way for a person who is emotionally distressed to seek reassurance and support.

The ill individual might not recognize the existence of underlying emotional problems. Even if they are recognized, emotional problems are often difficult for a patient to reveal (disclose) in an undisguised form. A socially acceptable source of help—the physician—is consulted instead of a psychologist, clergyman, or social worker (Phillips, 1965). Illness behavior may be part of a coping repertoire—an attempt by the patient to make a challenging situation (e.g., losing a job) more manageable by imposing a familiar explanation on it ("I am upset because I am sick"), especially if this person can deal better with being ill than with losing a job. The sick role gives the individual an acceptable excuse for making claims on others for care and provides a reason for failure. Under conditions of manageable difficulties, people may ignore the same symptoms. Someone who has successfully used the sick role in the past (i.e., has utilized medical services) will use this particular coping strategy more frequently than someone who has not often utilized health care services (Mechanic & Volkart, 1961).

Self-Presentation and Conformity

There are other important ways in which the social situation affects illness definition. In most social situations, people want to present themselves in a favorable light; that is, they want to look good. People often try to present a certain "face" to the world and hide potentially embarrassing information behind the scenes (Goffman, 1963). For example, persons with a stigmatizing condition such as epilepsy or a colostomy may try to present themselves ("pass") as perfectly "normal." This desire may directly affect how they define and react to illness. People who suspect that they have syphilis may try to ignore the symptoms and not immediately seek medical help. Similarly, people who have symptoms of a heart attack may refrain from calling the doctor in the middle of the night in order to avoid bothering health personnel and appearing stupid if it turns out to be a false alarm.

If you think about it, you can probably list certain symptoms and diseases that are socially undesirable, some that seem neutral, and perhaps others that are desirable. Consider the different social meanings of such diseases as lung cancer, flu, breast cancer, tennis elbow, AIDS, hemorrhoids, runner's knee, stroke, indigestion, gonorrhea, muscle strain, cirrhosis of the liver, myopia, sunburn, and leprosy. An important element influencing the reactions to these problems involves their social desirability.

Conformity to group pressure is very relevant to people's reactions to illness and to their health behaviors (Aloise-Young, Hennigan, & Graham, 1996; Asch, 1951). People look to relevant others—that is, to members of their reference groups—to determine what behaviors are appropriate. For example, American teenagers often dress alike and appreciate similar music; lawyers may have similar-looking offices and similar automobiles; and so on. Such conformity pressures also apply to the definition of and reaction to illness. Reporting certain diseases is fashionable, while others are quite deviant.

Mass Psychogenic Illness

A more dramatic but relatively rare instance of the group's influence on definitions of illness involves collective behavior. The term *collective behavior* refers to actions that seem to arise spontaneously, are guided by a general rationale, and spread rapidly from one member to another in a group (Smelser, 1963). Fads are an example. Most interesting is *mass psychogenic illness,* or "assembly line hysteria." A typical case involves the "blue mist" that someone in a midwestern furniture assembly plant thought she saw. One by one, the other female workers began to feel dizzy, lightheaded, and weak, supposedly from the blue mist. Actually, analysis of air samples showed that the air was fine. A similar incident occurred in West Virginia. Workers in a shoe factory began fainting, felt weak, and had headaches and nausea. Government tests found no toxins, which makes it seem likely that the workers were victims of **mass psychogenic illness.**

This phenomenon is well known to social psychologists. In one case in a textile factory in which an imagined biting insect caused nervousness, nausea, and weakness, psychologists found that the spread of the "disease" affected persons who were nervous, who were isolated, and who knew other workers they thought had been bitten. This process is a special form of suggestion in which illness is created purely from the social psychology of the group. Another odd example comes from West Africa, where there are periodic reports of "penis-snatching" episodes, in which victims blame penis shrinkage on handshakes with sorcerers (Sunday Telegraph, 1997). Fear spreads through a crowd (and a penis may indeed shrink as the blood flows out).

It is important to recognize that the individuals involved do indeed feel ill and may even vomit or faint; however, the cause of these symptoms is the belief that one is sick. This suggests that the social situation may strongly affect the collective illness behaviors of a group of people (Gamino, Elkins, & Hackney, 1989; Kerchoff & Back, 1968; Colligan, Pennebaker, & Murphy, 1982; Mechanic, 1962; Zola, 1972).

Thus, the same physical symptoms may be interpreted and reacted to in different ways, depending on the social situation. In fact, illness is especially likely to be subject to the influence of other people since it usually has important implications for a person's

"No Mr. Emerson, you do not have runner's hernia or a naturalist's sunburn. You have gonorrhea."

Figure 3-2 The Social Desirability of Illness. *(Copyright Howard S. Friedman; drawing by Robin Jensen; reprinted by permission.)*

friends and associates. If a man is defined as ill and stays home in bed, there are often important consequences for his wife and children, his employer and coworkers, his bowling partners, and so on. Hence, it is difficult to overestimate the importance of social influence in deciding "What is illness?" (See also Box 3–1.)

THE REWARDS OF THE SICK ROLE

Consider the case of a man who shows up at one hospital, with blood in his urine, saying he is a football player, but then shows up in another town in another hospital saying he is a former fighter-pilot and has been coughing up blood. He seeks out medical care and gets various exotic treatments, but he is not really sick. He is a fake.

Munchausen Syndrome

Baron von Karl Friedrich Hieronymus Munchausen was an 18th-century German soldier and adventurer who told unbelievable tales. In medicine, the **Munchausen Syndrome** refers to patients who tell wild tales, often to gain medical treatment, drugs, or admission to

---

Box 3-1   When Do People Cough?

A traditional medical model would consider a cough as an innate reflex in which air is rapidly discharged from the lungs. Complex muscle and nerve actions are seen as central. However, the psychologist James Pennebaker (1980, 1982) has shown that even coughing is influenced by social factors.

Pennebaker monitored coughing in a number of natural situations, such as in classrooms. He found three important influences on the incidence of coughing. First, people are more likely to cough in large groups than when they are in small groups. Second, people are more likely to cough when they hear others cough and when they are close to someone who is coughing. Finally, people are more likely to cough in boring rather than interesting situations. The precise social psychological mechanisms affecting coughing have not yet been isolated, but it seems likely that the subtle suggestions and expectations of others have a pronounced effect.

---

hospitals (Feldman & Eisendrath, 1996). For example, one case concerned an impressive-sounding man who claimed to be an oceanographic physicist working with Jacques Cousteau. He complained of chest pains and claimed to have sustained many injuries in the Vietnam war that had necessitated extensive surgery. Later investigation showed that this same man had been hospitalized in other medical centers around the country, sometimes as a major in the Strategic Air Command and other times as a counter-intelligence agent. This "patient" seemed to be attracted to medical centers because of the narcotics and other drugs he would receive. This treatment, which rewarded his behavior, evidently continued for many years.

Other patients with this syndrome are reinforced by more *social* rewards from medical settings. They may derive great satisfaction from the attention they receive from medical professionals. That is, they like talking to doctors and nurses. They are also likely to become litigious (bring malpractice suits) in an effort to retaliate against health professionals who try to end their treatment.

Sometimes, a parent may make a child ill, in hopes of receiving sympathy, attention, or access to experts. This is termed **Munchausen Syndrome by Proxy** (Goldfarb, Lawry, Steffen, & Sabella, 1998). For example, the child may present repeatedly with bacterial infections of the blood (after the mother secretly gives injections to her child). In very rare cases of repeated Sudden Infant Death, the mother may even be a serial murderer (Kelleher & Kelleher, 1998).

WELLNESS

Consider the following patient:

> Mrs. Ortiz is medically normal in every way—all of her blood chemistries are in the normal range, she feels okay, and there are no unusual results from a complete physical exam. However, Mrs. Ortiz does not exercise at all, and she has little muscle tone

and stamina. Physical stressors (such as a fall) are potentially devastating, and it would be hard to recover from any surgery. Her diet is adequate but not very well balanced; she loves desserts and is somewhat overweight. She smokes filtered cigarettes but has no signs of lung problems. Is Mrs. Ortiz healthy?

Too often, physicians and scientists describe what is an unhealthy state, or *disease* but fail to appreciate what is a healthy state, or *health*. There is a wide range of fitness among people who are free of disease; people may be more or less healthy. For this reason, some health practitioners have adopted the concept of wellness. **Wellness** describes the state of people who are not only free of disease but are also taking positive action to improve their health.

Wellness Activities

For example, well people may exercise regularly, eat nutritious and well-balanced meals, avoid tobacco, and carefully monitor physical signs such as their blood pressure. In addition, wellness-seekers pay attention to the special, individual needs that are unique to their own bodies, rather than merely following general medical advice. From this perspective, wellness-seekers are actively responsible for matters relating to their health, with a special emphasis on prevention of illness. This view is quite different from the traditional view in which medicine is seen primarily as a curing or repair system needed when medical problems strike.

Wellness can be viewed as an ideal state of self-realization toward which a person strives but never reaches. We have seen that a large part of illness involves the inability to engage in normal kinds of behavior. The wellness-seeker builds stamina and fitness, thus expanding the range of what is to be considered "normal," and may also develop added flexibility in dealing with life.

Because it is a relatively new concept in medicine, wellness has been misunderstood by many traditional medical practitioners and even some of its most vociferous proponents. Unfortunately, wellness is sometimes viewed as a crazy new fad or as some kind of mystical road to truth and self-fulfillment. Actually, the concept is a sensible antidote to the narrow but well-established view that achieving health involves the "fixing" of a diseased body. Many patients who seek "alternative care" are very well-educated (Astin, 1998). As they become more accepted, concepts of wellness may be subsumed under the rightful conception of "health."

THE BIOPSYCHOSOCIAL HEALTH PSYCHOLOGY MODEL

Genital herpes is an infection of the genital area involving a herpes simplex virus. It produces painful blisters and may be accompanied by fever and other signs of infection. It is acquired through sexual contact. After a period of weeks, the blisters usually heal, but the virus remains in the body, and so the symptoms may recur at unpredictable intervals. Some people have monthly attacks but other people have no recurrences at all. Some people are bothered by these attacks, but others simply go on with their lives. Certain treatments are helpful in the control of symptoms, but there is no cure (Gunby, 1983; Stanberry, 1996). Further, note that some people are exposed to the virus but never develop symptoms at all.

Many people with herpes report that it seems most likely to recur when they are overworked or stressed. They may have an attack right before a final exam or right after completing a long project. There is some research evidence that indicates that psychological stress helps bring on a herpes attack, but the bulk of the evidence is inconclusive (Hoon, Hoon, Rand, & Johnson, 1991; VanderPlate & Aral, 1987). As we will see later in this book, it is difficult to define and measure "stress" and even more difficult to assess the effects of stress. Is it even plausible to assume that disease can be affected by psychological factors? In the case of herpes, it appears that the body's immune system may play a complex mediating role between stress and disease (Bierman, 1983; Kemeny, Cohen, Zegans, & Conant, 1989). Further, as with many other diseases, one can help maintain health through proper diet, exercise, and stress management. Sufferers can also benefit from emotional support and clear medical advice.

Although it is not commonly discussed at the dinner table, millions of Americans have herpes. In addition to transmission through sexual contact, herpes also can be transmitted from a pregnant woman to her fetus during childbirth and can be fatal to the baby. It is obviously important to try to prevent the spread of herpes though sexual abstinence during herpes outbreaks (although sometimes the virus is present when symptoms are not), avoiding contact with infectious sores such as by using condoms, or limiting sexual activity overall. But who will be responsible for controlling the spread? Doctors do not usually probe into patients' sexual partners and sexual habits, and they certainly do not make announcements about patients' infections to the community.

Herpes is a disease—a viral infection—but a patient with herpes is much more. There are many issue surrounding the disease that involve health and illness but not "medical" issues. As we have seen, there is much more to illness than contracting an infection.

Health Psychology Model

Picture an approach to health and health care that has these psychosocial, cultural, preventive, and behavioral aspects of health as its main focus. This approach would involve health-promoting psychoemotional relations with others; healthy behaviors (such as the avoidance of cigarette smoking, prophylaxis, and the eating of a balanced and low-fat diet); enthusiastic cooperation with prescribed medical regimens; immunization and well-child care; the social and psychological management of stress; social support for those with chronic illness; the prevention of injury and contagious diseases; and the proper, whole-person care of the aged, the dying, and the bereaved, *as well as* the proper use of traditional drugs and surgery when needed. These matters are the focus of what we call the **health psychology model.**

This broad approach is sometimes termed the **biopsychosocial model** because it assumes that health is influenced by biological factors (such as invading microorganisms and the immune response), psychological factors (such as a person's thoughts, feelings, and behaviors), and social factors (such as the influence of others) (Engel, 1977). However, the word *biopsychosocial* is quite a mouthful, and at the same time is not particularly informative about its emphasis. Many writers have complained that a biopsychosocial approach applied to traditional medical settings quickly degenerates into a traditional biomedical approach. Therefore, in this book we refer to the *health psychology model,* or approach. Health psychologists generally take a true biopsychosocial approach, in which the *psychosocial* as well as the *bio* is given a rigorous, scientific treatment.

Of course, most traditionally trained physicians understand that psychosocial influences affect health. Sometimes physicians therefore refer to the *art of medicine.* By this term, they generally mean those nonmechanical aspects of patient care emphasized by the health psychology model. However, the term *art of medicine* assumes that these matters are just that—an *art.* In other words, they are seen to be intuitive, nonscientific, nontechnical, and informal. Nothing could be further from the truth! The health psychology approach is very scientific, organized, and detailed. *This book is* not *about the "art" of medicine.* It is about the science of the so-called art of medicine, a science that is every bit as complex and technical as internal medicine and surgery. (See Box 3–2.)

The Traditional Biomedical Model of Disease vs. the Health Psychology Model

There are a number of differences between the traditional biomedical model of disease, which emphasizes anatomy, physiology, and pharmaceuticals, in the context of centralized (physician-dominated) medical care, as compared to the health psychology model, which emphasizes behavior, culture, social relations, and self-healing. These are listed in Table 3–1. Most basically, the traditional biomedical model focuses on pathology (the cause of disease), whereas the health psychology model focuses on staying healthy. Further, the traditional biomedical model of disease is built around surgeons in hospitals providing dramatic, life-saving or life-enhancing operations, and around internists and other clinicians in clinics prescribing anti-microbial pharmaceuticals or other focused treatments. The health psychology model, in contrast, is built around improving the health-

---

Box 3–2   Mechanical Model Run Wild

A somewhat humorous example of what happens when the traditional mechanical model of disease is carried to its logical extreme appeared in a brief article in *Bride's Magazine* (February/March, 1987). This magazine caters to women who are planning their weddings.

The article points out that the wedding day is stressful and tiring, and that the new husband may drink alcohol at the wedding. Taken together, such factors can cause temporary impotence, which is extremely embarrassing on the wedding night. A possible solution involves penile injections of the drugs papaverine (a smooth muscle relaxant/vasodilator) and an alpha-blocker (which affects the nerves). The article notes that these injections offer up to three hours of "erectile potential." However, sexual arousal is needed if a climax is desired. Today, there is also Viagra.

Table 3-1   The Traditional Biomedical Model Versus the Biopsychosocial Health Psychology Model of Health

The Traditional Biomedical Model of Disease	The Biopsychosocial Health Psychology Model of Health
Looks for pathology.	Looks for health.
Looks to cure or contain disease.	Looks to maintain, restore, and promote health.
Has large, well-organized groups of professionals (physicians, nurses, clinical psychologists) who earn a living treating disease.	Has scientists concerned with the public health and promoting mental health, including some government agencies like the Center for Disease Control and Prevention.
Individuals pay for medical treatment or health insurance.	Society pays for legal and social changes relevant to health.
Treatment focuses on surgery and pharmaceuticals, with ancillary focused interventions (such as rehabilitation).	Focuses on healthy behaviors, understanding of wellness, good health communication, coping with stressors, and adaptation to disease, rather than focusing on drugs and surgery treatments.
Traditionally dominated by male physicians, with the most technically sophisticated practitioners (such as surgeons) receiving the highest pay.	Focuses on healthy families and healthy communities.
Treatments not controlled by physicians are termed *alternative medicine.*	Individual typically viewed as a consumer, with health professionals as expert advisors.

Note also that the traditional approach claims an emphasis on science, even though many medical treatments have not been rigorously evaluated in controlled studies. On the other hand, the biopsychosocial health psychology model often attracts self-proclaimed healers and other charlatans. The challenge to health psychology is to complement the best of scientific traditional medicine with a rigorous socio-behavioral science perspective.

enhancing features of the individual's thoughts, habits, and behaviors, and the strengths of the community's health-promoting and disease preventing efforts.

Remember two basic points that are sometimes misunderstood. First, no one should underestimate the tremendous value of the clinical treatment given by the internists, surgeons, and clinical psychologists working in the traditional biomedical approach. Important treatments and cures often result from this expertise. Second, it should be remembered that many of the best physicians, psychologists, and public health officials work within the health psychology biopsychosocial approach. (See Box 3–3 on Dr. Oliver Cope.)

Developmental Processes

The issues surrounding the health care of a screaming infant, a robust college student, and an arthritic 80-year-old are quite different. Of course, people of different ages have different physical characteristics. But people of different ages also have different levels

---

Box 3–3   Dr. Oliver Cope

A while back, Harvard Medical School honored Dr. Oliver Cope, a distinguished surgeon. It is interesting to see what was so remarkable about the career of this surgeon (*Focus,* 1983).

One of Dr. Cope's first breakthroughs was his discovery in the early 1940s that many goiters (thyroid problems) could be treated without surgery. His approach was at first bitterly fought by other surgeons, but was eventually adopted.

Soon after, while making major contributions to the treatment of patients who had been severely burned, Dr. Cope came to recognize and publicize the tremendous psychological problems faced by burn patients.

Dr. Cope then began treating victims of breast cancer. It took him quite a while, but he eventually decided that removal of the tumor followed by radiation therapy was vastly superior to the radical mastectomy (total removal of the breast and surrounding tissue) then in vogue. He understood the tremendous importance of women's feelings about their breasts. For a while, he was one of the only surgeons advocating this alternative approach (which is now the norm). He wrote a book to help patients understand their health problems and question their treatments.

Dr. Cope was also especially interested in the psychosomatic origins of disease and the treatment of ulcers. But even this was not enough to keep him busy. He was concerned with the problems of medical education, especially the fact that by the 1960s, medical students were being crammed full of facts but had little time to develop their powers of thinking. This leading surgeon was also concerned that many young doctors are afraid of delving into the personal or emotional difficulties of their patients. Sometimes, it is the very best physicians who reject the traditional biomedical model of disease and embrace the health psychology approach.

---

of understanding, different emotional needs, different relations with families, and different life goals. Would a week spent in a hospital, removal of a breast, development of heart problems, or the need for daily oral medication be the same for a 3-year-old, a 30-year-old, and a 70-year-old? The overall context of a person's life is necessary for a good understanding of health and health care (Tinsley, Holtgrave, Reise, & Erdley, 1995).

It is also the case that the state of our health waxes and wanes over time. When the fuel injector in an automobile fails, it needs to be replaced. But a person is a living *system,* constantly being repaired. Many of the developmental issues relevant to health care are considered at appropriate points in this book.

The health psychology model takes into account the special importance of the patient's family. Of course, physicians have always had to deal with patients' families in cases of death or serious disease. However, the focus in the traditional biomedical model is on the patient; the family is just an extraneous part of the problem. Mechanical-minded physicians have sometimes told health psychologists and social workers, "I'm glad you're here to deal with the family and keep them out of my hair while I try to treat this patient." In contrast, the health psychology model views the family as an integral part of medical care.

The family is a key influence on whether a patient will cooperate with a prescribed regimen. The family is also the unit that sets healthy or unhealthy habits in the areas of eating, exercise, and accident-avoidance. It is also a key factor in reducing or exacerbating stress. Families should not be considered merely an adjunct aspect of health care (Tinsley, 1997).

Why Health Psychology?

It is worth reiterating that people who employ the health psychology model are not trying to disparage traditional medical care. The biomedical side of medicine is extremely important; many times, technological interventions by physicians literally save lives. However, anyone who seriously studies the nature of health and health care will come to the conclusion that the traditional biomedical model of disease is inadequate. Unfortunately, although there are many notable exceptions, the typical physician and the typical health groups, or HMOs, do not fully appreciate the complete range of significant influences on health, and they are not trained or equipped to address them. That is why the health psychology model has the promise of revolutionizing our approach to health care.

SUMMARY AND CONCLUSION

Health psychology starts from a different set of assumptions about health than does the traditional field of medicine. The health psychology approach to health and illness thus provides a different perspective than does the traditional biomedical model. Health psychologists are much more attuned to issues of stress and illness, to help-seeking and illness behaviors, to interpersonal issues such as doctor-patient communication and patient cooperation with treatment, to the institutional and societal context of health, and to health promotion efforts. Since health psychology is a very new and rapidly growing field, this book provides a comprehensive attempt to systematically apply this new health psychology perspective to the vast array of health-related concerns.

Although we generally think that medical help-seeking, medical care, and hospitalization depend on how sick the patient is and on how the best treatment can be administered, the meaning of health and illness does not exist in a vacuum. Attributions, behaviors, family circumstances, and society are key components of an individual's health. When an individual feels ill and begins to engage in activities that indicate a problem, the individual is engaging in illness behaviors, and can be allowed by society to adopt the sick role. There is no laboratory test that detects "illness." It depends upon interpretation.

Cultural factors have an enormous influence upon patients' interpretations of symptoms and their responses to these symptoms. For example, Italian-Americans and Jewish-Americans are more likely than other groups to report a greater number of illness symptoms—a function of upbringing, values, and social rewards. The same symptom can also be interpreted very differently (by both practitioner and patient), depending on the sex of the patient.

The process of interpreting a symptom or behavior is one of attribution and involves a search for a causal explanation for the pain, sensation, or disruption. We are not born knowing what a headache is. As observers, our interpretations are a function of the patient's behavior in the context of what we know about the patient, the circumstances of the illness, and a comparison with other people. The ability of the health care professional to assign the illness label to the patient likewise depends in part upon societal values and the restrictions placed upon health care professionals. The Munchausen syndrome refers to patients who tell wild tales, often to gain medical treatment, drugs, or admission to hospitals. Some patients may derive great satisfaction from the attention they receive from medical professionals.

Too often, physicians and scientists describe what is an unhealthy state, or *disease,* but fail to appreciate what is a healthy state, or *health.* The health psychology model is an approach to health and health care that has psychosocial, cultural, preventive, and behavioral aspects of health as its main focus. It involves health-promoting psychoemotional relations with others; healthy behaviors (such as the avoidance of cigarette smoking, prophylaxis, healthy diet); enthusiastic cooperation with prescribed medical regimens; immunization and well-child care; the social and psychological management of stress; social support for those with chronic illness; the prevention of injury and contagious diseases; and the proper, whole-person care of the aged, the dying, and the bereaved, *as well as* the proper use of traditional drugs and surgery when needed.

It is important to remember that there are thousands of dedicated and well-intentioned physicians who work long hours to combat disease. It is a mistake to blame individual physicians for the shortcomings of health care. They excel, as they have been trained to excel, in situations in which the traditional medical model is applicable. They fail when the traditional approach is inadequate.

In the chapters that follow, the several basic components of health psychology are considered in turn. First, psychological aspects of illness are examined. These chapters discuss the roles played by psychological factors in the development and progression of illness. Second, people's reactions to chronic and terminal illnesses are examined. Third, health promotion issues, including issues of tobacco, alcohol, nutrition, exercise, and prophylaxis, are presented and evaluated. Patient cooperation and communication between practitioner and patient are discussed. Fourth, the societal and institutional influences on health issues are examined, including the health care system, the health professional in this system, and the role of society in promoting health and preventing disease. Finally, goals for the future are discussed. Only when all these influences are taken into account can we have a full appreciation of the role of psychology in health.

Recommended Additional Readings

Engel, George L. (1977). The need for a new medical model: A challenge for biomedicine. *Science, 196* (n4286), 129–136.

Friedman, Howard S., & DiMatteo, M. R. (Eds.) (1982). *Interpersonal issues in health care.* New York: Academic Press.

Mechanic, David. (1986). *From advocacy to allocation: The evolving American health care system.* New York: Free Press.

Pennebaker, James W. (1982). *The psychology of physical symptoms.* New York: Springer-Verlag.

Zborowski, Mark. (1969). *People in pain.* (Foreword by Margaret Mead). San Francisco: Jossey-Bass.

Key Concepts

medical help-seeking

symptoms

illness

illness behaviors

sick role

curandero

age roles

sex roles

attribution

salience

self-presentation

conformity

mass psychogenic illness

Munchausen Syndrome

Munchausen Syndrome by Proxy

wellness

health psychology model

biopsychosocial model

PART II

Psychological Contributors to and Treatments of Illness

Chapter 4

BELIEF, PAIN, AND HEALING

Each year, millions of sick people visit the healing shrine at Lourdes, France. These pilgrims have tremendous faith in the possibility of cure. They pray, and sometimes medical miracles occur. People who were paralyzed walk again; people with tremendous pain are suddenly relieved of it. Although biological impossibilities do not occur at Lourdes (for example, people do not grow new arms or legs), some who are crippled get up from their wheelchairs, and others with serious illnesses recover despite the poor odds given them by their doctors. Why?

Some people make remarkable recoveries from serious, and even life-threatening, diseases or dangerous surgery, but other seemingly similar people succumb—they become more debilitated or die. In many cases, it seems that the only major difference between success and failure is an abstruse quality of the patient known as the will to live.

An interesting case of the will to live involves Norman Cousins, a former editor of the Saturday Review. *Cousins developed a degenerative disease that was progressively paralyzing him. His doctors told him that he had one chance in 500 of recovering. Cousins checked himself out of the hospital and into a hotel room. He devised his own treatment: laughter. He watched old* Candid Camera *films and read humorous stories, and he recovered (Cousins, 1979). Can laughter relieve pain or cure certain diseases? If so, how?*

Jerome Frank, of the Johns Hopkins University Medical School, studied American soldiers who were infected with a parasite during World War II. Hundreds of soldiers surprised their doctors and failed to recover on schedule from this disease, despite adequate medical treatment. Their symptoms continued; they were weak and had cramps and headaches. Purely medical explanations failed, but as Frank discovered, negative expectations seemed to contribute to the soldiers' problems. Confused and hopeless about their recovery, these soldiers were demoralized by seemingly conflicting reports from doctors. They believed they would die, and despite recommended treatment, their symptoms continued (Frank, 1946, 1977).

In the early 1950s, medical researchers reported discovery of a new drug called **Krebiozen,** which was believed to be a cure for cancer. When the news was made public, a panic was created as thousands of cancer patients tried to obtain the drug, which was not generally available. Some patients did obtain it, and in many cases the drug was dramatically effective ("Earthquake in Chicago," 1951). Some patients who were very ill and bedridden with cancer were given Krebiozen and soon were out of bed, their tumors shrinking miraculously. However, when later research showed that Krebiozen was ineffective, patients who had been helped by the drug suddenly had relapses and died of their cancer.

Researchers who have studied pain, as well as doctors, dentists, and nurses, marvel at the differences among people in their ability to tolerate pain. After surgery, for example, some people cry out for more and more pain medication, while others lie quietly or become ambulatory soon after surgery. Likewise, some people insist on taking pain killers after dental work, while others go on with their daily business. Studies of these differences in people suggest a pattern: Psychological factors affect the perception of pain.

This chapter begins to consider the relationship of the mind and the body, including such topics as faith healing, religiosity, expectations, placebos, and pain. We attempt to understand phenomena such as "miracle cures," and in doing so, we apply a psychological framework to achieve a scientific understanding of some of the most fascinating phenomena in medicine.

HOLISTIC HEALTH

In modern medicine, "mental" problems are almost always distinguished from "physical" problems. Most physicians focus on physical problems such as infections, broken bones, and blocked arteries. Matters such as depression, stress, unexplained pain, and the lack of a will to live are usually labeled mental problems and referred to mental health experts. This separation dates from the 17th-century French philosopher René Descartes, who proposed that a human being has a mind that exists in the spiritual realm and a body that exists in the realm of physical matter.

As noted in Chapter 2, this Cartesian dualism led subsequent thinkers to maintain a mind-body distinction. No one was easily able to conceive of the mind and the body as one entity. This is still true for many people today, but this false dualism is actually so inaccurate that it leads to serious errors in the approach to many important illnesses. What is the problem?

First, the mind-body dualism incorrectly assumes that the mind and body operate independently, whereas, in fact, mental and physical factors are almost always closely intertwined. A prime example is pain, which is discussed later in this chapter. Pain can be caused by so-called physical problems, such as an infection or a tumor pressing on a nerve, but pain is also affected by so-called mental difficulties—the conditions of the brain involving perception, emotion, motivation, and action. Pain is intertwined with consciousness (we do not feel pain when we are unconscious) and so is closely tied to psychology.

Furthermore, pain can be controlled through so-called mental means as well as through drugs or surgery, and it is misleading to consider pain (and illness) as either exclusively physical or exclusively mental. Although we can emphasize one aspect or the other, in truth, the mind and the body are parts of one system.

Second, as is described later in this book (see Chapter 12), the patient's cooperation with treatment often depends on proper interpersonal relations. Ignoring a patient's mind—the patient's understanding, feelings, and motivations—while trying to cure his or her body may result in a patient who does not cooperate with the treatment and so does not recover.

Third, many health problems result from a poorly regulated lifestyle—too much smoking, drinking, eating, and too little exercise. A doctor who focuses only on the physical results of such behaviors—cancerous lungs, cirrhotic livers, and diseased hearts—is surely being shortsighted and inefficient. What is it about belief, personality, stress, and culture that leads to such unhealthy behaviors?

Chapters 5 through 7 present a detailed examination of the relationship between psychological factors and illness. First, however, we need a more general analysis of the relationship between the mind and body.

Psychosomatics

In medicine, the mind-body relationship has been explored under the rubric of **psychosomatic medicine.** This is the effect of the mind (psyche) on the body (soma). However, the term psychosomatic medicine has too many meanings to be of much value. Sometimes psychosomatic medicine refers to the use of principles of psychology in understanding and treating illness. (This broad definition applies to most of this book.) At other times, psychosomatic medicine refers to medical problems that are caused by psychological states. This latter definition encompasses three different but important areas.

First, a significant proportion of patient complaints (at least 25 percent) made to physicians are psychological in nature and have no significant physical counterpart (Costa & McCrae, 1985, 1987; Escobar & Gara, 1998; Marsland, Wood, & Mayo, 1976). If the psychological problem is resolved, all symptoms disappear. For example, a patient may complain to a doctor about vague symptoms such as pain, headaches, or weakness for which no physical explanation can be found. These symptoms might result purely from tension, such as an unhappy marriage. The presenting of symptoms that have no known medical explanation and which seem affected by psychological processes is often termed **somatization.**

Second, the term psychosomatic illness sometimes refers to organic disorders that are directly caused by psychological and emotional problems (Deutsch, Jones, Stokuis, Fryberger, & Stunkard, 1964). That is, people with certain psychological difficulties are much more likely to develop specific, definable, and detectable physical problems. For example, a person with excessive worries who does not cope well and constantly experiences tension may develop symptoms, as the autonomic nervous system provokes increased gastrointestinal motility and spasm. In this second type of psychosomatic illness, the physical symptoms have an observable "physical" explanation as well as a relationship to underlying psychological difficulties. However, there is no detectable damage to the organ and so the condition is sometimes termed **functional.** Some of the important factors in this type of problem are considered in more detail in Chapter 6.

Third, psychosomatic medicine sometimes focuses on the body as an environment that may be changed by psychosocial factors. In this emphasis, illness is seen as caused mostly by outside agents invading the body, but the body's defenses are affected by psychological factors. The psychological factors do not cause the disease but rather weaken the body's resistance. For example, it is theoretically possible for all people to contract bacterial pneumonia. But certain psychological difficulties may make some people more susceptible than others (Cohen & Herbert, 1996; Jemmott & Locke, 1984). This use of the term psychosomatic is gaining wider popularity as medical researchers increasingly focus on immunology and as psychological researchers focus on the notion of wellness and disease prevention (Dubos, 1978). These effects are often termed **psychoimmunological.** Although all three of these aspects of psychosomatic medicine are important, we should be specific in defining the phenomenon of interest in any particular analysis.

Somatopsychology

In studying the relationship between the mind and the body, we must consider that disease processes affect psychological reactions. The study of the influence of so-called physical states on so-called mental states is called **somatopsychology.**

Sometimes the body affects the mind through direct action on the nervous and endocrine systems. For example, a tumor on one of the endocrine glands, which causes too little or too much hormone release, can have striking effects on a person's psychological state. Examples include hypothyroidism (an underactive thyroid gland, which results in lethargy) and Addison's disease, involving gradual destruction of the adrenal glands. Other cases include problems in neurotransmitter production or uptake. In the most extreme case, brain damage (whether from external or internal injury) will of course likely affect psychological reactions. Further, many medications have significant psychological effects, although these are often neglected.

Another important, but often-overlooked, way in which the body affects a person's psychological state is through the reactions of others. A disabled or a disfigured person may receive negative reactions from others and may incorporate these reactions into his or her own self-image.

A third source of influence of the bodily state on a person's psychology involves sensory impairments. For example, people who lose vision, or sense of smell, or mobility may learn to approach the world and understand it in different ways from people who are not handicapped in this way.

The temporary impairment caused by hospitalization or serious illness can also affect psychological reactions. For example, bed rest imposed on a normally active person, or the lack of control over the environment that is so much a part of hospitalization, can produce anxiety or depression.

A final area of somatopsychology concerns the body's level of comfort and activity. As we will see, tense muscles, lack of sleep or excessive sleep, pain, sunburn, muscle fatigue, and similar physical ailments can affect a person's psychological state and produce a state far beyond simple discomfort. On the other hand, sexual fulfillment, muscle relaxation, and other such physical influences can also serve to produce a marked improvement in general psychological functioning. In short, just as the mind can affect one's physical state, so too can the body affect one's mental state. Often, both sorts of influences are in effect.

Holistic Health Care

To address the problems of the Cartesian dualism, there is a growing modern movement to bring the mind and body together in what is known as **holistic health.** Simply put, holistic health involves viewing and treating the person as a whole *physical-and-mental* human being, with the mind always affecting the body and vice versa. This is generally the approach taken in this book.

There is a problem with the holistic movement, however. While its basic goals are important and scientifically based, the term and the concept are sometimes used in highly unscientific approaches to health and medical treatment. For example, imagination, megavitamins, or hypnotism may be used as therapies for all sorts of serious maladies without first establishing their therapeutic value for a given illness through controlled experimentation. Even worse, some self-proclaimed "holistic" practitioners may rely on unproven treatments in lieu of a scientifically established medical treatment. Of course, such efforts can be dangerous.

Holistic health care can be scientific. There is an enormous amount of evidence that thoughts, feelings, and behaviors are inextricably tied to the organic processes traditionally studied in medicine. In fact, it is *unscientific* to ignore the so-called mental aspects of general health.

BELIEF AND ITS FUNCTION IN HEALTH

In converted theaters or under tents, thousands of people gather each week, and they may sway with the music, writhe and shout, or close their eyes and hold hands. Many are in pain or have some disability. On the front stage is a charismatic figure urging the followers to believe. These people are at a faith healing gathering.

Faith Healing

There are dozens of prominent "healers" in the United States, many of whom are religious zealots who call on a higher power beyond themselves. Goals and techniques vary; some attempted cures involve the development of a quiet inner peace while others involve dramatic attempts to raise the handicapped from their wheelchairs. Although such healing is shunned by modern medicine as unscientific (and because some faith healers are outright frauds), faith healing often works (Chrisman & Kleinman, 1983; Herrick, 1976; Jaffe, 1980). Belief can materially affect the outcome of treatment. The principles of faith healing are very powerful.

Who are the faith healers? The word "quack" might bring to mind a thin man who curls his black waxed mustache while selling snake oil (a worthless preparation sold as a cure-all). This stereotypical quack is hard to find these days, because laws closely regulate the practice of medicine and the prescription of drugs. But health quackery is rampant in America. Part of the reason is that traditional medicine gives insufficient attention to psychosocial factors. When the scientific establishment disregards issues of faith and belief, the unscientific practitioners provide it. The unscientific healers are an assortment of self-proclaimed nutritionists, self-selected religious healers, gurus, and fitness packagers.

Although drugs are controlled by law, food is not. Many faith healers have led people to fad diets and faddish nutrition therapies. There is little scientific evidence that most of the diets work to promote health and cure disease; in fact, they may do harm. Yet diet books proposing medically unwise diets are often best-sellers in the bookstores. Many Americans gulp enormous quantities of vitamins and other diet supplements. Like snake oil, these supplements are often touted to prevent baldness, stop aging, and increase sex drive. To a large extent, such fads represent a rejection of the health establishment's separation of the mind from the body. People are dissatisfied with physicians who solely focus on fixing bodily malfunctions while mostly ignoring the whole person (including diet) (Cobb, 1954; McKinlay, 1973, 1975). On the other hand, many traditional herbs and exercises are ignored by western scientific medicine, in part because there is no financial incentive for pharmaceutical companies to do expensive testing on substances that cannot be patented. This lack of information further feeds patient mistrust of traditional medical care.

Earlier we mentioned the drug Krebiozen. Extracted from the blood serum of horses, the main evidence for the effectiveness of this drug was the testimonial of cancer patients. Patients given this new miracle drug in the 1950s felt less pain, had improved appetite, and lived longer than expected. The U.S. Food and Drug Administration was dubious about claims for Krebiozen for years, although it was not until the early 1960s that interstate dealings in Krebiozen were banned. The drug was eventually found to be ineffective against cancer, but even after its official ban, some congressmen were calling for Krebiozen to be given another chance (*Newsweek,* 1952; *Time,* 1963).

Interesting observations can be made about Krebiozen. First, evidence for the drug's effectiveness came from individual case studies, not from controlled experiments. Second, the drug was claimed to cure cancer, a fear-provoking and poorly understood disease. Third, there was secrecy associated with the development of the drug, with one scientist proclaiming the need to protect the drug from falling into Communist hands. Fourth, the drug soon acquired an almost mystical or religious significance. And finally, bitter charges of fraud and counterfraud against its developers were involved. These factors are familiar to the medical scene.

A surprisingly similar set of circumstances surrounded the development of another so-called cancer drug, Laetrile. Laetrile is an extract of apricot pits, although there is some doubt about what the chemical structure of "true" Laetrile is. Although it was developed many years ago, Laetrile did not become a public issue in the United States until the 1970s. Since Laetrile has not been shown to be safe and effective, many legal disputes exist over its use. Americans travel to Laetrile clinics and similar clinics in Mexico for cancer treatment (*Newsweek,* 1977; *Time,* 1977). However, patients who ignore conventional, partially effective treatments and instead take unproven cancer drugs or therapies may incur enormous costs for themselves and also for their family, the community, and society as a whole. (See Figure 4–1).

These drugs and these healers, and the belief that people have in them, dramatically illustrate the importance of faith and expectation, which are crucial to all medical treatment. Through a variety of mechanisms, the proper beliefs can promote cures. Fortunately, the healing power of faith can be studied scientifically.

Expectations

Phenomena such as faith healing, the will to live, and the power of fraudulent drugs can be partly understood in terms of people's expectations, most of which arise in interactions with other people (Jones, 1977, 1982). People are social beings and their actions are heavily influenced by the actions of others. Many times, the expectations of others are very subtle.

At the turn of the century, many scientists were interested in the special powers of the horse named Clever Hans (Pfungst, 1965). Hans was a very smart horse and when asked questions, he would tap out the correct answer with his right forefoot. Hans could even perform various mathematical functions. Trickery on the part of his owner was ruled out. Yet

Figure 4-1   One of the most challenging issues in health psychology is
distinguishing innovative new health information about
mind-body ties from quackery and fraud. This Quack
Busters logo is an early logo of the National Council
Against Health Fraud, a nonprofit, voluntary health agency
that focuses on consumer protection in public health
(*http://www.ncahf.org*). (*Reprinted by permission.*) *The National
Council Against Health Fraud, Inc.*

it was some time before a psychologist, Oskar Pfungst, figured out the key to Hans's success. Pfungst determined that the horse could not answer questions correctly if the questioner was not visible to Hans or if the person asking the question did not know the correct answer. Hans, it turns out, was detecting cues from people about when to start tapping the answer with his hoof and when to stop tapping. After systematic investigation, Pfungst found that when observers leaned forward to watch Hans's hoof, he would start tapping. When Hans neared the correct answer, the observers would change their posture; this was the clue to Hans to stop tapping. Hans would respond to a lifted head and even the observers' raising their eyebrows. Hans was not an extremely intelligent horse but he was an extremely astute observer of nonverbal communication (Blanck, 1993).

Hans did not intend to appear to be a very smart horse and behave according to his observers' expectations. Similarly, many patients do not intend to behave according to the expectations of their physicians, family, and friends. Nevertheless, people do pay close attention to the subtle expectations of others.

In the early 1930s, social scientists investigated the productivity of employees at the Western Electric Company's Hawthorne Plant in Chicago (Roethlisberger & Dickson, 1939). These researchers were attempting to identify specific influences on production but stumbled on an important general social-psychological effect. The researchers expected certain changes, such as increased lighting, to raise productivity and other changes to lower productivity. To their surprise, they found that everything they did resulted in greater productivity. The workers were producing more because someone was paying attention to them. Thus the term **Hawthorne effect** refers to the phenomenon by which production rises when special attention is paid to the workers, independently of changes in the working conditions.

The Hawthorne effect has important implications for doctor-patient interactions. Patients often appear at a doctor's office and want a doctor to do something. It is likely that as long as the doctor pays attention to the patient, anything the doctor does will have at least some beneficial effect in many cases. When medical treatments were few and ineffective, doctors counted on their very presence to have a positive effect on the patient. Of course, any treatment must be considered in light of the medical injunction to "First, do no harm."

Wise physicians know that they should use new drugs while they are still effective (Shapiro, 1971). Many new treatments work for a while, that is, as long as they have positive expectations associated with them. However, as failures are reported and as the drugs or treatment procedures become commonplace, their efficacy often fades. Fortunately, positive expectations need not depend on the existence of new treatments. The expectancy effect of belief on physical well-being is usually termed a *placebo*.

Placebos

Throughout the history of medicine up to the 20th century, almost all medical treatments had no specific biological foundation. Yet physicians were able to retain respect, and they sometimes even produced cures. This happened because of the **placebo effect.** Arthur Shapiro defines a placebo as *any therapy that is without specific activity for the condition being treated.* The effects of placebos may be psychological or psychophysiological. Placebos may be "drugs" such as sugar pills, but they can also be surgical procedures, physical manipulations, prescribed diets, exercises, or other regimens (Shapiro, 1960; Shapiro & Shapiro, 1984).

Placebo effects are sometimes dismissed in medical circles because it is incorrectly assumed that they do not have physiological effects. However, placebos have long been shown to produce dramatic beneficial physiological changes, like improvements in skin condition, increased activity, and recovery from fever (Jospe, 1978; Wolf, 1959). On the other hand, a number of studies indicate that placebos can induce symptoms such as weakness, nausea, rashes, and pain. Examples of this phenomenon can be seen in the advertisements for new pharmaceuticals, now commonly seen in magazines. Participants studied with a placebo (in the control group) usually report a wide range of physiological effects!

The psychological state of the individual can either enhance or inhibit the individual's reactions to specific diseases or specific drugs. Human beings are active biological organisms that respond in complex ways to the introduction of foreign agents. Just as the body may be more or less susceptible to various diseases at various times, the body will also react to various therapies and treatments in different ways at different times, depending on the psychological and emotional state of the person (Kirsch, Capafons, Cardena-Buelna, & Amigo, 1999; Leigh & Reiser, 1980).

Throughout the history of medicine, every imaginable substance and treatment has been used in the attempt to cure disease. Drugs ranged from crocodile dung to the spermatic fluid of frogs. Sometimes, the reasoning was that "like cures like." For example, parts of a hairy animal might be given to a patient in an attempt to cure baldness, or muscles of a strong animal be eaten in an attempt to cure muscle disease. Some of these treatments were actually very destructive, such as the well-known treatment of bleeding or leeching. In 1799, an ill George Washington was given a drink to induce vomiting and diarrhea, and was bled of several pints of blood; he died soon after. Nevertheless, because of the placebo effect, treatments were also sometimes helpful.

In a classic review of various work on placebo effects, Henry Beecher found that about one-third of all patients are helped by placebo effects (Beecher, 1959). This is a significant percentage, and it means that any given treatment will help a substantial number of patients. Other estimates place the percentage of patients influenced by placebo effects as high as two-thirds (Roberts, Kewman, Mercier, & Hovell, 1993); it depends on the definitions, situations, and measures. This also means that many successful treatments probably owe some of their success to placebo effects. Thus, even "miraculous" cures such as shrinking cancer tumors are not that unusual, but they cannot be repeated with predictability in well-controlled studies.

The mechanisms underlying placebo effects are not well understood, but two basic processes are probably at work. First, behavioral changes, sometimes very subtle, result from expectations. Patients who expect a cure try harder; for example, they may drink more fluids and sleep and walk more, and these behaviors may lead to improved health. Second, as noted, a person's thoughts and feelings can produce physiological changes through the actions of the nerves and hormones. These matters are considered in more detail in Chapters 6 and 7.

Placebos can also produce severe negative physiological effects, resulting from negative expectations. One example is the American soldiers studied by Frank, which was mentioned earlier. Negative placebo effects include fainting, vomiting, diarrhea, changes in blood flow, and detrimental respiratory effects.

Since placebo effects are probably closely related not only to the patient's expectations but to the doctor's expectations, valid research on all new therapies demands the use of **double-blind** experimental procedures (Rosenthal, 1966). In this procedure, neither the doctor nor the patient knows whether the patient is receiving the new treatment being tested, the old treatment, or a placebo control. For example, a new pain reliever might be compared to aspirin, codeine, or a sugar pill, but neither the medical personnel nor the patients would know which treatment was which. (Only the researcher would know.)

It is sometimes difficult for medical personnel to believe that their expectations, which they try to keep to themselves, can influence a patient's recovery. They may assume that a new treatment either will or will not work, no matter what they do. However, such an approach is a serious mistake, and also very unscientific. Without strict controls in a double-blind procedure, the results of a study of a new treatment are scientifically worthless (see also Box 4–1).

Box 4-1   The Ethics of Placebo Control Groups

To determine their effectiveness, new drugs must be tested against old drugs or inert substances. In this way, any improvement caused by the specific activity of the new drug can be distinguished from any improvement resulting from placebo effects. However, if the new drug is truly effective, some patients would have been deprived of a potentially lifesaving drug during the period of the test. Although this deprivation might at first appear unethical, it is actually extremely ethical in terms of the overall progress of medicine.

The results of a two-year study of stroke prevention showed the importance of careful experimental tests. A new drug, contrary to expectation, was not effective when compared with a placebo and aspirin. However, there was some evidence that the aspirin itself was effective in preventing stroke. If this study had not been conducted, patients might have gone on receiving the new useless drug, while the discovery that aspirin was better would not have been made. In research, any treatment has certain risks and costs, and these must be weighted against the likelihood of any benefit.

Ethics cannot be decided on the basis of the results of a study. New treatments must be compared against old treatments in an experimental design that also assesses placebo effects. Indeed, it is unethical if medical researchers do not conduct methodologically sound research to insure that every new treatment that is used is effective!

For further reading:

S. Bok, The ethics of giving placebos, in R. Hunt and J. Arras (Eds.), *Ethical Issues in Modern Medicine* (Palo Alto, CA: Mayfield, 1977), pp. 278–290.

RELIGIOSITY

Since healthy behaviors and healing bodily reactions are more likely among people who have high motivations and positive beliefs, we might expect that people with a strong, positive religious belief are generally more healthy. Various evidence indicates this tends to be the case, so long as the religious belief does not interfere with or preclude needed medical treatment (Ferraro, 1998; Idler & Kasl, 1997; Koenig, Kvale, & Ferrel, 1988; Jarvis & Northcott, 1987; Krause, 1998; Levin & Schiller 1987; McCullough, Hoyt, Larson, Koenig, & Thoresen, 2000; McFadden & Levin, 1996; Seeman, Kaplan, Knudsen, Cohen, & Guralnik, 1987; Strawbridge, Cohen, Shema, & Kaplan, 1997). The problem in uncovering simple relations, however, is that people are religious or not religious for many different types of reasons.

Religiosity, Social Integration, Nutrition, and Activity

One key way that religiosity—being religious or pious—can promote good health is that religious people tend to have beliefs in protecting and maintaining their God-given bodies. They also associate with other people who share these beliefs. So, they may frown upon smoking, alcohol and drug abuse, promiscuous sex, and gluttony, as well have strong sanctions against suicide and violence.

People who practice one of the major religions also typically attend church services, participate in church activities, and so on. Motivation is thus provided to get out of the house, develop relationships with others, and seek physical and mental stimulation.

In one long-term study, the relation of religiosity to longevity was studied in 547 male and 446 female Californians. Women who viewed themselves as more religious in mid-adulthood (when they were approximately 40 years old) had a lower risk for premature mortality (during the next several decades) than those who were less religiously inclined. These religious women had healthier behaviors, more positive feelings about their futures, and reported being somewhat happier than their less religiously inclined peers. Overall, although religiosity seemed to be part of a generally healthy lifestyle for these women, it was not necessarily a direct cause of it. The relationship between religiosity and mortality was not significant for males in this sample (Clark, Friedman, & Martin, 1999).

Since there are also many secular Americans concerned with their health for scientific reasons, the relationship between religiosity and health is not universal. In fact, it is sometimes the case that people with health problems—obesity, disease, addiction—seek out religion to help them. An overly simple analysis might thus be misleading. It is important to be careful about uncovering the complex causal links (Jarvis & Northcott, 1987; Krause, 1998; Levin & Schiller 1987; McFadden & Levin, 1996; Seeman et al., 1987; Strawbridge et al., 1997).

Religiosity, Faith, and Self-Healing

There may also sometimes be more direct, stress-mediated links between religiosity and health. For example, people who are religious may be less likely to have high blood pressure (hypertension), stress-induced unhealthy habits, insomnia, anxiety, and so on, if their religious practice helps provide a suitable means of coping with life's challenges. As we will see in later chapters, people at peace with themselves are generally healthier. For example, it is generally healthy to be altruistic and helpful to others. Religion also helps many people cope with bereavement. However, not all religious groups actively promote this peace and altruism, and not all religious members adopt them in their own lives.

Prayer often shares many characteristics with meditation and other relaxation states. Repetitive chanting and focused concentration reduces stress for many people. However, some peculiar studies endeavor to see if praying for an ill person will help that patient recover even if the patient and the doctors do not know that prayers are being offered. In other words, such studies are not dealing with the faith, expectations, self-regulation, and psychosomatics that are the subject of this chapter, but rather are trying to prove scientifically the existence of God or a divine healing spirit. Since such studies by definition abandon the natural and search for the supernatural, they are beyond the province of health psychology.

PAIN

When we touch a hot stove or a sharp needle, we feel pain. At a young age, we learn to associate the feeling of pain with the destruction of our body tissue (as through burning or cutting). Since this association is strong, many people assume that pain means that the body is sensing tissue destruction. In other words, people generally think that pain is a natural, fixed reaction to an intrusive stimulus; for example, if we are pricked by a pin, our nerves carry the message to our brain and we feel pain. (In fact, René Descartes described just such a sequence in the 17th century.) This assumed sequence of pain perception is actually inadequate and misleading. There is no necessary and direct link between tissue damage and pain (Melzack, 1973, 1983).

Meaning and Measurement of Pain

Soldiers who are injured on the battlefield often do not feel as much pain as they would if they received an identical injury at home in their kitchens. Athletes frequently report not feeling the pain of injury until they are off the playing field and in the clubhouse. Two patients with the same degree of physical degeneration as the result of a disease may experience very different degrees of pain. Such phenomena are partly the result of psychological influences on pain.

On the other hand, sometimes people feel great pain, but the physician cannot find much if any organic damage or disturbance. The pain is probably really there, but there is no simple, direct biological evidence. This issue is an important one for society because disability benefits and other benefits (such as compensation for "pain and suffering" from an auto accident) are often awarded on the basis of severe pain.

Pain is essentially a subjective experience. There is no "pain meter" we can apply to assess pain. We can ask people to describe their pain (burning pain, stabbing pain, etc.) or rate their pain (mild, excruciating) (Melzack, 1983), and we can observe the behavior of the pain patient (Fordyce, 1976). But ultimately, we can never really know another person's pain. How can it be that pain is so dependent on psychological factors?

Suggestion and Symbolism

In the early 19th century, before anesthetics had been discovered, mesmerism (hypnotism) was used successfully to control pain. For example, it has been reported that the French surgeon Cloquet performed an extensive operation to remove a malignant tumor from a woman's breast. During the surgery, the woman talked quietly to her doctor and showed no signs of pain. Pain-free surgery procedures done under hypnosis (and related techniques) still occur today (Chaves & Barber, 1975; Kessler & Whalen, 1999). Thus, even the pain of surgery can sometimes be significantly decreased with a process based essentially on psychological factors. Pain depends in part upon what we "think" about our pain sensation. In one study of the role of attentional factors in pain, people were instructed to place their hands in a jar of painfully cold water. Those who were told to pay close attention to their hands experienced greater pain than people told to try to detach themselves emotionally from the pain. The worse you expect the pain to be, the worse it is (Pennebaker, 1982).

There is a story about a stage hypnotist who used a swinging watch to hypnotize four suggestible audience members who had been brought on stage. While hypnotizing the last subject, he dropped his watch and exclaimed, "Oh, crap!" According to the story, there was quite a mess to clean up on stage. Could this really happen? Probably not. There are limits on how effective a sudden suggestion can be. Simple, direct suggestion usually does not have a profound effect. However, over time and with sufficient psychosocial and behavioral support, expectations can prove powerful.

According to Sigmund Freud and his followers, pain sometimes may be symbolic of a psychological problem in interpersonal relations. For example, a patient may feel a pain in his or her derriere when in the presence of the boss. These musing have led to the recognition that pain depends on one's psychosocial state. Commonly, people feel headaches in various unpleasant situations (Rapoport & Sheftell, 1996). Furthermore, pain may be associated with emotional disturbances (Leventhal & Everhart, 1979; Sternbach, 1974). For example, people often feel pain more when they are depressed. It is not necessarily true that such people have absolutely no organic disturbance (although it is possible, of course), but rather that various bodily sensations become painful when the psychological environment is right.

Rewards of Pain

Why is pain related to psychological and social factors? One answer points out that the sensation of pain partly serves a function of communication (Szasz, 1957; Zborowski, 1969). Expression generally brings compassion and help from others; the expression of pain may be a request for comfort. The rewards and punishments received from others may affect reactions to pain.

There are many examples of the social benefits of pain. A child who reports a minor sensation of pain and is given ice cream to make him feel better may soon begin to feel the pain more severely and more frequently. Lonely patients who report pain may receive significant attention from various medical practitioners or friends, thus helping to maintain the pain. Since it is very difficult to rule out undiscovered organic influences on pain, a patient who seeks attention for pain relief may be constantly rewarded for feeling pain. This does not mean that pain should be ignored but rather that this element should be considered as part of the overall pain relief treatment plan.

Can these various psychological influences be explained in physiological terms? The gate control theory of pain provides a promising approach to this question.

The Gate Control Theory of Pain

> No amount of knowledge about the physiologic, anatomic, and biochemical substrates of pain perception will suffice to fully explain the common clinical syndrome of low back pain (Loesser, 1980).

This striking statement from a pain researcher reaffirms the key role of psychological factors in pain. Low back pain is a common and important medical problem. In addition to chronic suffering for the individual, it may lead to early retirement and to disability benefits. Hundreds of thousands of Americans each year undergo tests and face surgery or dependency-producing medications for back pain. Yet significant bone or nerve dysfunction is generally not found in these patients. However, in many cases, low back pain will disappear in response to a variety of placebo treatments ranging from hot (or cold) compresses to doctors' orders to remain active (or inactive). Other psychological interventions are also often effective. What is the specific physiological evidence for mind-body ties and application to pain management techniques?

A groundbreaking physiological theory of pain by Ronald Melzack and P. D. Wall, which is called the **gate control theory,** attempts to explain how psychological factors can influence pain perception (Melzack & Wall, 1965; 1982). Melzack became interested in pain when he was studying Scottish terriers that had been raised in isolation. When the terriers first came out of their cages and met people, they ran around excitedly and bumped their heads and were sometimes accidentally stepped on. But they seemed to show no pain. If there were a fixed relationship between noxious stimulation and pain, the dogs' reactions shouldn't have been affected by their earlier experiences (Warga, 1987). Then Melzack met a woman who felt terrible pain in a "leg" that had previously been amputated; this is termed **phantom limb pain** (Sherman, 1997). Even after a limb has been amputated and can no longer send impulses to the brain, the brain may still feel "pain" in that limb. That really got him thinking. A few years later, he teamed up with the physiologist Wall, and an important new theory was born.

Simply put, the gate control theory proposes that there are special nerves that carry intense sensation (such as from extreme heat, like a stovetop) to the spinal column. Receptors that transmit noxious stimuli are termed **nociceptors.** But these signals do not necessarily go directly to the brain because there is a "gate" in the spinal column that can be closed by signals coming down from the brain. Thus, thoughts and feelings can provide gate-closing signals and influence whether the sensation of pain reaches the pain systems of the brain and is perceived as painful. (See Figure 4–2.)

In addition, neurochemical changes may slowly occur in the gate area, making it more or less likely that pain will be perceived as time goes by. This model, in which psychological factors influence the processing of sensation, does seem to be able to account for much of the existing data about pain. Part of the nervous system, including cells of the brain stem and fibers descending from them to the dorsal horn of the spinal cord, can block the incoming (nociceptive) pain signals.

Endogenous Opioids

Certain brain cells contain specialized receptors that respond to opiates like morphine and heroin. These opiates, of course, deaden pain. It turns out that our bodies have their own internal pain control system. The neurons of the central nervous system release various kinds of peptides (chains of amino acids linked by peptide bonds) to affect or to directly communicate with other cells. Some of these peptides act on the opiate receptors and are termed **endogenous opiods** (Terman, Shavit, Lewis, Cannon, & Liebeskind, 1984).

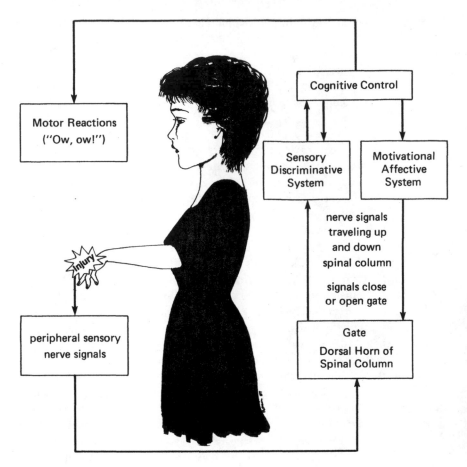

Figure 4–2   This schematic presents a simple overview of the Gate Control Theory of pain. *(Copyright Howard S. Friedman; reprinted by permission.)*

The first such opiods to be discovered were termed *enkephalins* ("in the head"). The two key known enkaphalin neurotransmitters each have five amino acids and are called *met-enkephalin* and *leu-enkephalin.*

Since brain opioids are naturally occurring morphine-like substances found in the body, they have been termed **endorphins**—the word endorphin comes from "endogenous morphine." They seem to be a key part of the body's built-in narcotic system (Ader & Cohen, 1998; Basbaum & Fields, 1984). One important endorphin, beta-endorphin, is produced by the pituitary. Interestingly, endogenous opioids may also stimulate the nerve systems involved in reinforcement (learning), which is part of the reason that opiates are often abused.

Many specialized receptor sites for opiates are concentrated in an area of the brain known as the periaqueductal gray (PAG). When neurons in this area are activated, there is evidently blockage of other neurotransmitter substances down the spinal cord (Basbaum & Fields, 1984; Fields & Liebeskind, 1994). In other words, here is a likely partial mechanism for the gate control theory: Endorphins affect the PAG, which in turn affects other neuron systems in the brain (including raphe neurons in the medulla) that affect neurons descending the spinal column, which then block incoming pain signals. Support for this model also comes from studies that activate the PAG through direct electrical stimulation (thereby producing analgesia) or that destroy the descending spinal neurons (thereby increasing pain).

Because of the mind-body dualism, many people were at first surprised to learn that placebo effects may be able to induce the body to produce endorphins, which help the body control pain (Levine, Gordon, & Fields, 1978; Snyder, 1977). However, it is now better understood that peptides are in some way the physiological counterparts to what we experience as emotions. When we feel or reduce emotions, peptides are involved, and when we feel or alleviate pain, peptides are likewise involved. So although the complete links between psychoemotional states and pain have not yet been completely unraveled, it is likely that we are well on our way to understanding these so-called mind-body links. However, given the body's many redundancies, it is also likely that there are other pain regulation mechanisms.

What implications does the gate control model have for the psychological management of pain? A number of psychological techniques do work in pain control.

PAIN MANAGEMENT

When John Bonica's wife Emma Louise was giving birth to their first child, she almost died from the ether that was given to her as anesthesia. Dr. Bonica set out to find a different way to control the pain of childbirth. One of his innovations involved the epidural analgesia; an *epidural* numbs the lower half of the body by anesthetizing spinal nerves but leaves the patient conscious. Many women now also use breathing, concentration, and relaxation exercises to cope with the pain of labor and delivery. Bonica went on to found one of the first pain control clinics (in the late 1940s) and make many advances in controlling pain. Interestingly to health psychologists, Bonica died of a stroke one month after the death of his wife of 52 years (*NY Times,* 1994).

Pain Prone Personality?

Because pain is ultimately a subjective experience, there has been much speculation about a possible **pain prone personality.** That is, due to their biopsychosocial makeup, some people are hypothesized to be more likely to develop and suffer from pain. Overall, the evidence suggests that although pain is highly associated with personality problems, there is no useful unitary conception of a pain prone personality (Elliott, Jackson, Layfield, & Kendall, 1996; Gatchel, Polatin, & Kinney, 1995; Savidge & Slade, 1997; Simmonds, Kumar, & Lechelt, 1996; Turk & Okifuji, 1998).

Pain patients are more likely to be characterized by hypochondriasis—preoccupation with symptoms of having a serious disease. They are also more likely to be depressed—and in fact many symptoms (such as fatigue) overlap between the two conditions. Pain sufferers are also more likely to have a personality disorder, such as being dependent or passive-aggressive. Some may have factitious (phony) disorders—seeking the rewards of treatment. Finally, pain patients are more likely to suffer from substance abuse.

Note, however, that such associations are to be expected, given our understanding of the complex nature of pain. Biological and psychological states and traits that make one more sensitive to and concerned with bodily sensations are naturally likely to increase feelings of pain. Similarly, people who have bodily injury or disruptions, exacerbated by poor coping, are more likely to try to alleviate their suffering through substance abuse and seeking support from others. It is not difficult to predict who is more likely to suffer pain after an auto accident when comparing a stoic, happily married, well-employed ex-marine to an insecure, overweight, lonely, former victim of child abuse. In other words, it is an incorrect oversimplification to say that chronic pain is "caused" by personality problems; but it is helpful in approaching treatment to understand that pain is often significantly intensified by other biopsychosocial disruptions.

Behavioral Modification

Since the expression of pain is partly a communication to others that has been rewarded by others, the expression and even the feeling of pain can sometimes be eliminated through extinction or punishment. For example, if an employee is rewarded for working even when experiencing tension headaches (but punished by loss of pay for stopping work for every minor ache), the headaches may eventually be minimized or disappear. This is sometimes called "mind over matter," but it is really a form of learning. That is, sometimes pain management can be attained if the patient and those around the patient ignore pain as a symptom when no organic causes can be found over a long period of time. On the other hand, if emotional disturbances seem prominent, direct psychological intervention may be necessary (Gatchel & Turk, 1996).

The discouragement of pain expression (after treatable conditions have been ruled out) is valuable in pain management for another set of reasons. There is evidence that the suppression of pain responses and expressions may directly lessen pain. Examples of this process from common folk wisdom are "whistle while you work" and "let a smile be your umbrella." According to this approach, behavioral changes will produce psychological changes such that a person's body feels good and the person feels happy when working productively and smiling. In psychology, this idea can be traced all the way back to Charles Darwin (1872) and William James (1910). Darwin noted that the expression of an emotion intensifies it, while the repression of an emotion softens it. Expressing rage may increase a person's rage, while keeping it in may reduce the intensity of the experience. William James hypothesized that all emotion develops following bodily changes. According to this theory, the act of crying makes someone feel sad and the act of trembling makes someone feel fearful. Although more complex theories of emotion have since evolved, it is true that inner feelings can sometimes be affected by outer expressions. Thus, if the painful activity is performed with a positive attitude and a smile on one's face, the pain may eventually lessen. This may be especially true of facial expression. Controlling the facial expression of pain (hiding pain) may help to reduce the pain (Lanzetta, Cartwright-Smith, & Kleck, 1976; Blackman, 1980). (Of course, if patients do not express pain, medical personnel do not receive valuable information about the progress of a disease or the course of recovery. The suppression of pain expressions may be a valuable means of controlling pain after the disease, or a lack of any detectable disease, is well diagnosed.)

Modeling is also an influence on pain. Children who see their mother receive an injection without overtly expressing negative emotion, such as crying, are less likely to cry themselves and may feel less pain. Even in burn units in hospitals, where pain is often very intense, a social norm to minimize crying and the expression of pain may help each patient deal with pain (Weisenberg, 1977). At the other extreme, men sometimes experience "labor pain" in sympathy with their pregnant wives, a phenomenon known as the **couvade syndrome** (Richman & Goldthorp, 1978). For example, they may experience nausea and loss of appetite around the time the baby first begins to move in the womb. Much of a person's knowledge about what is painful and when to experience pain comes from observing others.

Cognitive Coping, Distraction, and Guided Imagery

As we have seen in the first part of this chapter, such social influences as suggestion, hypnosis, and placebo effects can affect bodily reactions. This relationship is especially true of pain. If people believe that a certain medical procedure or illness is not painful, they are less likely to feel pain. These processes resemble modeling as a pain control technique in that they depend on expectations transmitted from one person to another. But they are somewhat different in that the process is clearly focused on the individual's thoughts.

Practice in cognitive coping may help to minimize pain. If people know what types of sensations to expect and how to think about these sensations, their pain can be more easily managed. For example, an athlete who is prepared for and experienced in the feelings that occur in the practice of the particular sport is more likely to be able to continue activity without pain than would someone who unexpectedly suffered an identical painful bodily injury. This may partly be explained by a phenomenon known as *pain induced analgesia,* in which animals who know that a painful shock is coming seem better able to tolerate pain, by secreting endorphins (Bolles & Fanselow, 1980; Fanselow & Sigmundi, 1986).

People in chronic pain often are angry or suffer from repressed anger (Fernandez & Turk, 1995). Chronic pain often results from an accident, or injury, or preventable medical condition, and so there is a tendency to try to assert blame. Further, there is often a motivational aspect to pain—a desire to take action to escape from the pain—that is closely associated with anger motivation. The result may be anger at others, anger at oneself, anger at God or nature, or anger at the world. Techniques that help to redirect the anger in a more productive direction may help in coping with pain.

A number of related cognitive variables, such as **distraction,** also affect pain (Johnson, 1973; Kaplan, 1982). For example, thinking pleasant thoughts as compared to concentrating on unpleasant sensations may minimize pain. If a child's minor pain is minimized and the child is sent to school despite it, the stimulation and distraction of other activities may help the pain to disappear. Distraction also can be effective during immunization (Cohen, Blount, Cohen, Schaen, & Zaff, 1999). Similarly, studies in attribution theory in social psychology have demonstrated that the explanations people have for their bodily feelings affect their subsequent reactions to such feelings. It is thus also important to consider the content of somatic attention as well as the direction and degree of distraction (Cioffi, 1991). If one pays attention to one's pain but does so in a mindful way that reduces distress, fear, and anger, then the pain may become more tolerable even though it is still there. (See Figure 4–3.)

Taken together with behavioral techniques, these influences are often termed *cognitive-behavioral* therapies (Turk, Meichenbaum, & Genest, 1983). They involve the social learning techniques of modeling and control of reinforcement, control of emotion and pain expression, the use of intense suggestion and distraction, and the practice of cognitive coping mechanisms.

Conditioning and Biofeedback

The technique of classical conditioning is well known. In this type of learning, the body's autonomic responses become conditioned to a previously neutral stimulus in the environment. For example, when Pavlov paired the ringing of a bell with the presentation of food, his dogs learned to salivate to the bell ringing. The new behavior is known

Figure 4-3   Mesmerism. This eighteenth-century engraving shows people holding their arms or legs under iron bars for "therapy" from "animal magnetism." Mesmer is attending the woman in the left foreground. *(Courtesy of the National Library of Medicine.)*

as a *conditioned response.* Classical conditioning of pain may sometimes occur if a certain activity is always associated with pain. For example, pain may occur whenever a child enters the doctor's office where inoculations or other aversive treatments have been given in the past. In such cases, the worst thing that can be done is to avoid the threatening situation; instead, the situation must be faced and the association with pain unlearned.

The classical conditioning type of learning differs from *operant conditioning,* in which an organism learns those behaviors for which it is rewarded. For example, rats may learn to turn right in a maze if that is where the food is usually presented, or children may learn to brush their teeth if they are often praised by their parents for so doing. Although learning in response to rewards usually involves voluntary behavior, some research indicates that autonomic responses such as heart-rate and intestinal contractions may be subject to operant conditioning. That is, people can gain some control over their "involuntary" responses (Birbaumer & Kimmel, 1979; Labbé, 1998). **Biofeedback** is a self-regulatory technique by which a person may learn to gain some control over autonomic bodily processes and gain increased control over some voluntary processes.

Electrodes on the skin and transducers (like thermistors, which detect temperature, or plethysmographs, which detect blood flow) convert bodily signals to electrical impulses and send them to an output device. In a typical biofeedback scenario, patients hear a tone that changes from unpleasant to pleasant as their physiological response changes. For example, by hearing the tone change as their muscles relax, some patients can evidently learn to relax some muscles not usually controlled in this voluntary way. Visual feedback on a computer screen may also be used. Biofeedback thus holds special promise in treating headaches and in treating neuromuscular problems.

Biofeedback is controversial and much more research is needed to define the boundaries of its effectiveness (Labbé, 1998; White & Tursky, 1982). No doubt biofeedback helps some patients, but that is not scientific evidence. Even when controlled studies are conducted, the biofeedback treatment usually contains some elements of relaxation or suggestion or cognitive stress reduction. Are biofeedback patients receiving a treatment that goes *beyond* the effects of suggestion and relaxation? This aspect of the mind-body link is not yet well understood. At the very least, however, biofeedback can help people to learn muscle relaxation, which may be useful in combating anxiety; anxiety is known to increase pain perceptions.

Acupuncture

Most people are familiar with the phenomenon of referred pain; that is, stimulation to one part of the body is felt somewhere else. For example, the pain of a heart attack may be felt in the left arm or in the jaw. It is also known by most people that stimulation to one part of the body can reduce pain in another part. For example, a hot water bottle applied to the neck may reduce back pain for some people, or a foot massage may relieve a headache. We have also seen that pain is affected by expectations. These phenomena function together in the Chinese-developed technique called **acupuncture** (Bowsher, Mumford, Lipton, & Miles, 1973).

In acupuncture, a patient may undergo surgery while fully conscious (Melzack, 1973). The only analgesic (pain-killing) mechanisms are acupuncture needles inserted at certain critical points in the body and the patient's faith in the effectiveness of the technique. The precise mechanisms underlying successful use of acupuncture are not well understood because pain itself is not well understood. However, consistent with the gate control theory of pain, it seems clear that stimulation of one part of the nervous system can interfere with the sensation of pain produced by stimulation of another part of the nervous system (Takeshige, Oka, Mizuno, & Hisamitsu, 1993).

For example, when Zang-Hee Cho, a California physicist, found that his back pain was relieved by acupuncture, he decided to investigate, using functional MRI (fMRI) imaging. To analyze the effects on brain activity of stimulation by acupuncture needs, Cho first stimulated the eyes of his human subjects by directly using light flashes, and obtained the usual results of activation (increased blood flow) in the occipital lobes of the brain (Cho et al., 1998). The experimenters then studied the vision-related acupoint, located in the foot, which is used by acupuncturists for the treatment of eye disorders. Sure enough, this acupuncture stimulation of the foot likewise resulted in activation of the brain's occipital lobes, as seen by the fMRI. (Stimulation of other—non-acupoint—areas of the foot did not result in this effect.) The precise mediators (links) underlying such effects of nerve stimulation on brain activity are unknown.

This assumption and similar processes also underlie **transcutaneous nerve stimulation,** in which a mild electrical current applied to the skin seems to ease chronic pain in some people. (This is also sometimes called transcutaneous electrical nerve stimulation, or TENS.) Perhaps this stimulation helps release endorphins and close the spinal gate. Perhaps the brain is distracted by the additional stimulation and ignores the pain stimuli (Walsh et al., 1998). However, like biofeedback, acupuncture and transcutaneous nerve stimulation have not yet been proven to be a more reliable or effective treatment than the various cognitive-behavioral influences.

Pain Clinics

Because of the complexity and prevalence of pain, some hospitals have developed pain control clinics. Such clinics create a comprehensive pain management program (Guck, Skultety, Meilman, & Dowd, 1985). They often begin with a detailed assessment of the patient's social situation and psychological state. Training in relaxation, the proper way of thinking about pain, a monitoring of situational influences on pain, and perhaps biofeedback are all used in conjunction with such physiological techniques as drugs, surgery, and transcutaneous nerve stimulation. Some such pain clinics take a truly holistic view of pain, an approach to pain that should be adopted in everyday medical care.

SUMMARY AND CONCLUSION

In sum, there is substantial scientific evidence documenting the influence of psychological and emotional states on so-called physical health. Similarly, there is a link between the condition of a person's body and the resulting mental state. Thus, a mind-body dualism is an inappropriate model. Health involves both the physical and psychological factors at the same time; they are inseparable. This link is most clearly seen in pain perception and control, where instances of the phenomenon of "mind over body" are readily observed.

Yet psychological and emotional factors are relevant, to a greater or lesser extent, in every illness. The "will to live" and related phenomena of placebo effects are a basic element of health care. A placebo is any therapy that is without specific activity for the condition being treated. Sometimes dismissed in medical circles because it is incorrectly assumed that they do not have physiological effects, placebos can produce dramatic beneficial physiological changes. The psychological state of the individual can either enhance or inhibit the individual's reactions to specific diseases or specific drugs.

Interesting observations can be made about phony miracle drugs like Krebiozen and Laetrile. First, evidence for the drug's effectiveness comes from individual case studies, not from controlled experiments. Second, the drug is claimed to cure diseases like cancer—fear-provoking and poorly understood diseases. Third, there is secrecy associated with the development of the drug (with some proclaiming the need to protect the drug from falling into evil hands). Fourth, the drug soon acquires an almost mystical or religious significance. And finally, bitter charges of fraud and counterfraud against its developers emerge. These factors are familiar to the medical scene and are a signal that psychosocial factors are at issue.

The gate control theory partly explains how psychological factors can influence pain perception. There are special nerves that carry intense sensation to the spinal column. But these signals do not necessarily go directly to the brain, because there is a "gate" in the spinal column that can be closed by signals coming down from the brain. Thus, thoughts and feelings can provide gate-closing signals and influence whether the sensation of pain reaches the pain systems of the brain. In addition, neurochemical changes may slowly occur in the gate area, making it more or less likely that pain will be perceived as time goes by. Even within the brain, pain perception is a complex process and is not automatic.

We have seen that belief and faith can be understood in terms of expectations, most of which arise in interactions with other people. People with strong, positive religious beliefs that engender healthy habits and adaptive attributions are generally more healthy, so long as the religious belief does not interfere with or preclude needed medical treatment. Even though all the precise physiological mechanisms through which psychological factors influence disease processes have not yet been identified, faith healing is not necessarily unscientific. It is up to the health care system to study and incorporate the proper social and psychological environments into treatment programs in order to provide the most effective, *scientific* health care.

Recommended Additional Readings

Blanck, Peter David (Ed.). (1993). *Interpersonal expectations: Theory, research, and applications.* New York: Cambridge University Press.
Bonica, John J. (1990). *The management of pain.* (2nd ed.). Philadelphia: Lea & Febiger.

Cousins, Norman. (1990). *Head first: The biology of hope and the healing power of the human spirit.* New York: Penguin Books.

Frank, Jerome D., & Frank, Julia B. (1991). *Persuasion and healing: A comparative study of psychotherapy.* (3rd ed.). Baltimore: Johns Hopkins University Press.

Melzack, Ronald, & Wall, Patrick D. (1983). *The challenge of pain.* (Rev. ed.). New York: Basic Books.

Turk, Dennis C., & Melzack, Ronald (Eds.). (1992). *Handbook of pain assessment.* New York: Guilford Press.

Key Concepts

Krebiozen	gate control theory of pain
psychosomatic medicine	phantom limb pain
somatization	nociceptors
functional condition	endogenous opioids
psychoimmunological	endorphins
somatopsychology	pain prone personality
holistic health	couvade syndrome
faith healing	distraction
Hawthorne effect	conditioning
placebo effect	biofeedback
double-blind	acupuncture
religiosity	transcutaneous nerve stimulation

Chapter 5

STRESS AND ILLNESS

The New York Stock Exchange was one of the first businesses to install a defibrillator, which uses an electric shock to restart a stopped heart. It seems that heart attacks are relatively common in this high-pressure atmosphere, where millions of dollars of stocks are traded every second. A popular assumption is that stress causes illness. It has been said that heart attacks are a way of life on Wall Street.

A while back, the elderly father of the mayor of San Diego passed away. Within 48 hours, his wife of more than 50 years had a stroke, and she too died! Such stories are not uncommon, again implying that something about psychology— one's perceptions and emotions—can show up in a deadly biological event.

In January 1995, an earthquake measuring 7.2 on the Richter scale rocked Kobe, Japan. For the month following the quake, the blood pressures of cardiac patients (who were being measured daily) rose significantly, as did their pulse rates. However, beta-blockers (a type of antihypertensive drug) helped keep down the increase (Saito, Kim, Maekawa, Ikeda, & Yokoyama, 1997).

Although the details may differ, many people are in stressful situations analogous to those above. Can stress play a role in the etiology (causes) of illness? If so, how? Are there steps that can be taken to cope with the stress?

This chapter looks in detail at how life events and our reactions to them can contribute to illness. There are at least two major psychological dimensions that play a part in the precipitation or exacerbation of physical illness. The first involves the person. How does a person deal with the challenges of life? The issue of coping with challenge is considered in detail in this chapter; the related issue of personality and its effects on the likelihood of illness is considered in the next chapter. The second psychological dimension affecting the development of illness involves the environmental challenge itself. The stress stemming from difficult life situations is also examined in detail in this chapter.

In research on the etiology of illness, these two psychological dimensions are typically examined separately. That is, researchers examine either the contribution of a patient's personal characteristics to illness or the role played by a multitude of stressful life situations in the development of illness. These two variables actually operate in concert, however; people respond differently to different life crises. It is important to remember that people's personalities and coping styles—their usual ways of responding to life— tend to "interact with" the situational challenges.

WHAT IS STRESS?

Stress is the state of an organism when reacting to challenging new circumstances. Stress is produced by an unexpected or challenging event in the environment, and the stressful event requires the organism to readjust itself (Alexander, 1950; Dougall & Baum, 1998; Pelletier, 1977; Selye, 1956). Thoughts, feelings, behaviors, and physiological reactions are all involved.

Stressors

The environmental events themselves are usually termed **stressors.** A great variety of environmental conditions (both positive and negative) can produce stress, but different individuals respond to the same conditions in different ways. For example, in response to challenge on the job, some workers experience stress, whereas others can easily tolerate the same event. Even the response of a given person to a stressful event may vary depending upon the physiological and psychological state of the person. For example, consider a student's response to an environmental event such as a term paper. The term paper deadline might be dealt with in a straightforward manner by the individual when feeling well, but may produce severe stress when the student is tired, depressed, lonely, or suffering from a virus.

The degree of stress that a person experiences depends in large part upon the meaning attached to the intruding (challenging) environmental event. The thoughts and actions a person uses to deal with stress comprise the process of **coping** with stress. The resources people have available for coping with the stressful events are considered in this chapter. Again, reaction to environmental challenge varies considerably among individuals and within each individual as well.

Stress affects everyone, not just harried business executives. On the positive side, stress is a necessary part of the psychological growth and change of each individual. An individual experiences stress when attempting a new endeavor like starting college or beginning a new job. Similarly, added stress is usually associated with increasing opportunities and potential resources for the individual. A certain amount of stress can help to keep a person alert and interested in life. Without new challenges, life would become dull, and so would our responses. However, sometimes the amount of readjustment demanded by modern life is so excessive that the person's level of stress is overwhelming (Toffler, 1971).

Although many observations suggest that stress may lead to disease, this does not always occur. Challenge is inherent in life, but many people remain healthy. A number of questions therefore arise concerning the relationship between stress and illness. What happens to the body when it faces a significant challenge? What are the properties that distinguish more stressful life events from less stressful life events? And, perhaps most importantly, why do some people become ill while others do not, given the same stressful life events?

MODELS OF STRESS AND ILLNESS

There are various pathways by which stress is related to illness. To simplify matters, the important elements of various explanatory models can be combined into one overview model. Figure 5–1 illustrates this comprehensive model of stress and illness.

The Illness Behavior (Sick Role) Model

The first important model linking stress and illness is described by the pathway a-b-d-h in Figure 5–1. This model suggests that certain people respond to certain stressful life events by entering the sick role (Mechanic, 1968; Mechanic & Volkart, 1961). For example, someone facing a forced job transfer might respond poorly to the pressure of moving to a new place by avoiding responsibilities—by oversleeping, being lethargic, drinking alcohol, staying away from work, and remaining home, sick in bed. One might complain

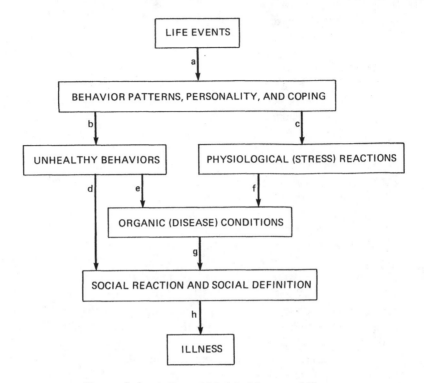

Figure 5-1   A General Model of Stress and Illness.

of headaches and other pains, such as stomach pains. These actions are all illness behaviors. If one exhibits enough illness behaviors, then he or she enters the sick role.

Note that in this model, no organic condition such as heart disease or a brain tumor is involved. Rather what is important is the person's behavior (including what the person says). People sometimes turn to unhealthy habits and exhibit illness behaviors in situations that are extremely stressful—illness is one method of coping with unpleasant challenges (Mechanic, 1968). In our society, it is considerably easier and more socially acceptable for a person to seek medical care from a doctor and to adopt the sick role than it is to seek help for an emotional problem (Phillips, 1963).

The attempt to cope with stress also makes the person more likely to *attend* to physical symptoms. If things are going well in someone's life, attention tends to be focused elsewhere. Most healthy people (those who are functioning normally in day-to-day life) would report at least one or two symptoms of illness if they are asked whether they have any symptoms. Medical students, for example, constantly direct their attention toward bodily functions they are learning about, and as a result, they often report experiencing a cornucopia of symptoms—**medical student syndrome.** The reporting of symptoms is clearly affected by psychological processes (Mechanic, 1972; Pennebaker, 1982; Wolff & Goodell, 1968).

As psychologist James Pennebaker has suggested, symptom perceptions are affected by several factors (Pennebaker, 1982; Pennebaker, Burnan, Schaeffer, & Harper, 1977; Pennebaker & Skelton, 1978). In addition to a person's attention to bodily sensations, symptom reporting is influenced by *interpretive set;* that is, symptoms are affected by what people think about their sensations—what meaning they attach to them. For example, if people think prolonged fatigue is a symptom of illness, they are much more likely to define themselves as "ill" when they experience prolonged fatigue. Others might see fatigue as a normal part of everyday life.

In addition, the interpretation of a bodily sensation as a symptom of illness is affected by the person's mood and chronic emotional state. Negative moods such as depression increase the likelihood of defining symptoms as indicative of illness. In fact, it has been suggested that much symptom-reporting is better regarded as an indication of neuroticism (anxiety, hostility, and depression) than as a sign of organic disease (Costa & McCrae, 1985). People who are depressed and psychologically vulnerable seem more likely to respond to stress by exhibiting illness behaviors that, through social definitions, allow them to enter the sick role (Canter, Imboden, & Cluff, 1966; Cohen, 1979).

In sum, there is one pathway connecting the stress of life events to illness that involves no physiological mechanism. This first model suggests that a person can become ill in response to stressful events without the involvement of an organic condition. Some people simply have a poor psychological response to challenge and turn to illness behaviors. Stressful events can also lead people to pay more attention to fluctuations in their bodily state and to interpret these fluctuations as illness. The sick role may then provide relief from the changes in the environment.

The Stress and Unhealthy Behavior Model

We have seen that the first model linking stress and illness does not involve an organic condition. Although the next two models do involve organic conditions, they differ significantly in the character of the link between stress and physical condition.

The second model is described by the path a-b-e-g-h in Figure 5–1. In this model, the person's psychological responses to stress lead the person to unhealthy behaviors such as cigarette smoking, alcoholism, poor diet, and lack of rest and exercise; these behaviors in turn lead to disease or trauma. There are many unhealthy behaviors that place people at high risk for various medical problems, and many of these behaviors are instigated by stress. A simple example involves traumatic injury: Stress leads to careless or fast driving, which then leads to injury in an automobile accident. Another common example involves stress, drinking, and cirrhosis of the liver. Perhaps the most important such pathway involves lung cancer caused by stress-related cigarette smoking.

Physiological Stress and Illness Model

The third and final important model of the link between stress and illness also involves organic conditions. However, in this model there is a direct link from stress reactions to organic conditions through physiological responses. This path is represented by a-c-f-g-h in Figure 5–1. This third model is provocative and is taken up in the next major sections of this chapter.

Other Models

Of course, it would be possible to draw in other links in Figure 5–1. For example, someone who is defined as ill would be likely to experience different life events from someone not defined as ill. In addition, organic conditions can affect coping mechanisms. For example, the physical weakness resulting from a serious illness like heart disease can induce depression (Brummett et al., 1998). Or, hypoxia (oxygen deprivation) may also lead to depression (Katz, 1982), which might then lead to further problems.

Personality might affect the life events that people encounter and with which they must deal. For example, some people are naturally cautious and therefore remain content to take few risks in their lives. They might be less likely than others to put themselves in situations where they must deal with a new job or a new city in which to live (see Chapter 6). Furthermore, genetic factors undoubtedly play a complex role in health (affecting both personality and specific vulnerabilities to disease), but are not portrayed at all in the model. The web of interlocking relationships that affects health actually constitutes the entire subject matter of this book. The purpose of Figure 5–1 is to focus attention on the stress processes that are examined in this chapter.

LOSS, LIFE CHANGE, AND ILLNESS

Many people become ill after a big change in their life occurs. For example, Richard Nixon became seriously ill with phlebitis soon after he resigned from the presidency, and his wife Pat had a stroke. Or, the detrimental effects may occur years later. For example, children whose parents divorce are at higher risk of premature mortality decades in the future (Schwartz et al., 1995).

When a person becomes seriously ill soon after the death of a loved one, we might say that the person is suffering from a "broken heart," and we may not be surprised to hear of such cases (see Box 5–1). In fact, widows and especially widowers are more likely to die than are those who are not bereaved (Burman & Margolin, 1992; Clayton, 1974; Jacobs & Ostfield, 1977; Rowland, 1977; Stroebe, Stroebe, Gergen, & Gergen, 1982).

There are various causes of such important effects. First, some of the increased risk of death immediately following widowhood is clearly due to unhealthy behaviors: The widowed are more likely to die from violent causes such as accidents and suicide, or from malnutrition. Second, some of the increased risk is due to the physiological effects of acute stress. For example, people who have recently lost their spouse are also more likely to die of heart disease, an effect that seems due to the physiological stress effects of disruptions in heart rhythms and lipid metabolism (Kaprio, Koskenvuo, & Rita, 1987). This leads to ventricular fibrillation, in which the heart loses its rhythmic contractions and so cannot pump blood. The sudden death that results is a major cause of fatality in industrialized societies (Lown, 1979; Verrier, DeSilva, & Lown, 1983).

Box 5-1   The Broken Heart

Social support—the existence of strong, meaningful relationships—are crucial coping mechanisms that weaken the link between stressful life changes and illness. When such ties are shattered, can some people die from a "broken heart"?

Lack of human companionship and love has been thought since antiquity to contribute to death and disease, but the effect of human contact on the health of a person's heart has not been carefully examined until recently. Pioneering work by James Lynch studied the effects of human contact and of loneliness on the heart. He began with a qualitative analysis of "folklore"—of the many instances in human interaction in which the heart is implicated as a significant participant in the drama. For example, people use phrases such as "heartbroken," "heartsick," and "a broken heart." Lynch also observed that human contact had important effects on the hearts of patients in the coronary care and other intensive care units of hospitals. He examined systematically how cardiac rhythms are affected by human contact. In lab studies, he found that human contact with laboratory animals (especially dogs) could have marked effects on the animals' hearts.

Lynch then examined death statistics. Looking at the average annual death rate per population of 100,000 between the ages of 15 and 64, he found that widowed, divorced, and single people have significantly higher death rates than married people. For all age groups (in 1959–1961), the rate of death from coronary heart disease was about twice as high among divorced people as among married people, and about one and one-half times as high among widowed people as among married people. Other research has generally confirmed Lynch's findings, although the causal links are not simple (Tucker, Friedman, Wingard, & Schwartz, 1996).

It is interesting to examine how Lynch reconciles his theory of broken hearts with other explanations of heart disease. He considers, for example, the statistics showing a low incidence of coronary heart disease in Japan as compared to the United States. Experts have attributed this difference to the diet in Japan and have shown that when Japanese move to the United States, their risk of heart disease goes up. The conclusion usually has been that when Japanese men change their diets, they become prone to heart disease. Lynch, however, noted that the family structure in Japan is very strong—there is relatively little divorce. People live in extended families and there is a great deal of companionship. When people come from that environment to the United States, they often experience increased loneliness, and their family ties are weakened. Although current research shows many interrelated factors are involved, the "broken heart" is a legitimate health concern.

For further reading:

J. J. Lynch. (1977). *The broken heart: The medical consequences of loneliness.* New York: Basic Books. See also Chapter 7 of this text.

Giving Up

Third, some people with a "broken heart" seem simply to "give up." The precise biological mechanisms that underlie this phenomenon are still in dispute. Remember that when Curt Richter studied rats who had died a sudden death, he found (on autopsy) that there was, surprisingly, an excess of parasympathetic activity. It seems that initially there was a fear response and the appropriate sympathetic nervous system activity in the rats; however, there was then a tremendous rebound in *para*sympathetic nervous system activity— a fatal excess of relaxation of the heart muscle. Since other rats, who were first given experience in escaping the water, did not die a sudden death, the excessive parasympathetic activity may have occurred when the doomed rats gave up. Thus, both sympathetic and parasympathetic mechanisms may be involved.

Note also that many widowers or others facing loss do recover and go on to live healthy lives. They somehow cope with the challenge. In the next sections of this chapter, we consider in more detail these issues of loss, giving up, life change, and illness. We then consider coping with stress. Related matters are taken up again in Chapters 6 and 7, when we consider issues of personality and health.

MASTERY AND CONTROL OR RELINQUISHING CONTROL

During the Korean War, thousands of American soldiers were captured by the enemy. Many of them, living under severe challenge, became apathetic and listless. These soldiers were more likely to die. The other prisoners called it "give up-itis."

The loss of a significant component of a person's life, particularly a key interpersonal relationship, can bring about severe stress as a person must reorder his or her life (Engel, 1968, 1971). The response of giving up as a result of a severe loss repeatedly has been linked with vulnerability to illness, but what does this mean? George Engel and his colleagues suggested that a giving up response in the face of situations of loss may precede the development of various illnesses in individuals who have *predispositions* to the particular illnesses. While Engel emphasizes the occurrence of loss, he also clearly specifies that the key component of the problem is the ability or inability to cope in the face of a negative environmental event (Engel & Schmale, 1967; Schmale, 1972; Schmale and Engel, 1967). The giving up involves a sense of psychological impotence—a feeling that, at least for a while, the person is totally unable to cope with the changes in the environment. In the extreme, the person loses all interest in life and in other people (see Box 5–2).

Mastery

Many psychologists have argued that people have a basic motivation to gain a sense of mastery over their environments (Kelley, 1967; White, 1959). Most people (especially in the Western world) seem to need to be able to predict and affect what will happen. For example, it is distressing and injurious to health to have responsibility at work but no control (Karasek, Theorell, Schwartz, Pieper, & Alfredsson, 1982); sociologists call such situations of conflicting expectations *role ambiguity* or *role conflict* (House, 1981; Kahn,

---

Box 5-2   Taunts and Death

A sad event can provide a dramatic reminder of the link between stress and illness. The case concerns a seven-year-old African-American girl with sickle cell anemia.

This little girl was bussed to a new elementary school in a white neighborhood of Chicago during controversial efforts at forced integration. She and other black children were met with cries of angry whites to "go back where you belong." The little girl was quite upset by the incident. After some time at the school, she went to the principal's office crying and complaining of chest pains. She died later that day in the hospital, apparently from a sickle cell crisis brought on by stress. As she died, she kept repeating, "Go back where you belong."

Wolfe, Quinn, Snoek, & Rosenthal, 1964). In one large-scale study, it was found that employed males with jobs that were simultaneously low in decision latitude and high in psychological workload had a significantly higher prevalence of myocardial infarction (heart attack) (Karasek et al., 1988). A healthy work environment is one in which a person has a challenging, socially valued job and the resources and support with which to do the job (Antonovsky, 1987).

Similarly, a series of studies of responses to loud noise found that noise that is unpredictable and uncontrollable has much more deleterious effects than noise (of the same loudness) that is predictable or controllable (Glass & Singer, 1972). The deleterious effects of the unpredictable loud noise include physiological reactivity and impaired task performance—that is, both physiological and cognitive problems.

It is worth noting, however, that some theorists have argued that it is not a sense of control per se but rather a sense of coherence that is healthy (Antonovsky, 1987). According to this view, someone (even someone with little power) who felt that some higher power (such as fate or God) were looking out for things would also be at low risk for disease. This matter is taken up again later in this book.

To examine in detail the physiological effects of lack of control, Jay Weiss (1971, 1972) conducted a series of studies on laboratory rats. Rats were placed into one of three groups. The first rat received electric shocks but could (and did) learn to exercise control in response to an audible warning and so avoid the shock. The second rat was "yoked" to the first rat; whatever happened to the first rat also happened to the second rat. In other words, the second rat had no control. The third rat in each group received no shocks. The results showed that the first group of rats who had control developed much less ulceration than their helpless partners. The rats who did not receive any shock showed the fewest problems. As we will see in following chapters, the issue is more complicated in humans.

Methodology.   At this point, it is worthwhile to take a slight detour in order to examine an important methodological issue in this research domain. Research linking psychological factors and illness is often retrospective in nature. That is, the research is conducted by asking the patient (after diagnosis of the illness) to recall and report the pre-illness emotional state or stressful life events. Or, the research is often concurrent in nature—the patient is asked about stressors and moods at the time the illness is being diagnosed. However, the knowledge that someone is ill as well as the actual experience of illness (e.g., the debilitation and pain of a heart attack) can affect the recall or interpretation of the events leading up to the illness. Illness can also affect how people recollect their personality characteristics before the illness (e.g., "I used to be too energetic—running around all the time." or "I was very nervous."). In addition, the doctor's or researcher's expectations can affect what the patient reports. Hence, retrospective reports are often biased.

For example, a study of stress reactions contributing to a heart attack is retrospective if the researcher assesses precoronary life stress after the heart attack. This is done by asking the patient to recall the life events and stresses leading up to the time of the heart attack. Such an approach is likely biased because of the patient's knowledge of having had a heart attack, and also by the patient's physical and emotional state after the attack. Anxiety, hopelessness, helplessness, fear, and agitation resulting from hospitalization and the threat to life can affect the patient's recollections and reporting of the precoronary events. The patient might focus only on the stressful life events or exaggerate their intensity, thereby giving a distorted picture of the relationship between the stress and the subsequent heart attack. Retrospective analyses have inherent biases.

Another example of how this retrospective methodology can lead researchers astray involves research on Down's syndrome (Mongolism). Researchers once believed that Down's syndrome was the result of emotional stress during pregnancy, because when asked about their pregnancy, mothers of Down's syndrome children recalled very stressful events. But after it was discovered that Down's syndrome was actually the result of a chromosomal abnormality, stressful events during pregnancy were no longer the focus of research and were no longer reported (Brown, 1974).

A more valid method is a prospective research study, which involves collecting predictive information before the event to be predicted. For example, we might examine life events and reactions to these events by interviewing a large number of people. After all the data are collected, the researchers simply wait to see which persons develop illness (e.g., who suffers a heart attack). If there is a correlation between stress and whether or not this person eventually has a heart attack, we have a good indication that the connection is not the result of biased reporting.

Much of the data that initially supported the theory of giving up and its relationship to illness has been retrospective in nature, but there has since been much prospective research (Goodkin, Antoni, & Blaney, 1986; Levy, 1985; Schmale & Iker, 1966, 1971; Taylor, Kemeny, Reed, Bower, & Gruenewald, 2000). For example, a study might look at patients who are asymptomatic for cervical disease, but who require a diagnostic biopsy because of suspicious cells in their PAP tests. The researchers interview the patients prior to the biopsy for evidence of loss and feelings of hopelessness. The researchers then make predictions on the basis of the patients' psychological state about which patients will be found to have cancer—predictions based on the hopelessness expressed by patients in the face of loss. These predictions are then confirmed statistically as better than chance occurrences. While all studies are limited by the special characteristics of the patients and other aspects of the particular research design, we still can draw some conclusions from this kind of research, particularly when it is coupled with and supported by other research.

Helplessness and Hopelessness

How can the ideas of lost control and giving up be applied to a more general analysis of human stress? Consider the example of Anna Jones, a 76-year-old widow who lived alone in a tiny New York City apartment. Although it took her all day to perform her chores, she did her own shopping and cleaning. She saw her friends a few times a week, and she entertained herself by cooking, talking on the phone, and watching her favorite television programs. Her only son lived in California.

The low-rent apartment building in which Anna had lived for 20 years since her husband's death was sold one day to developers, who planned to build a group of high-rise condominiums in its place. Anna was sent an eviction notice. Since she lived on meager social security checks, she was overwhelmed at the thought of searching for affordable housing. Even though she was independent with respect to her daily living, Anna was unable to cope with the thought of making a major transition to a new place to live. She needed help. Her son, however, wishing to settle things as soon as possible and also recognizing that his mother's faculties might soon be failing, arranged to place her in a modern nursing home. Despite Anna's protests, her son argued that he knew best. Anna was moved to the nursing home, where all of her meals were cooked and served to her. Her clothes were washed; her room was cleaned every day, and she was allowed to go to the TV room to watch whatever happened to be on television. Within four weeks of her arrival, Anna gave up doing anything, went to bed, and died of heart failure.

Helplessness, according to psychologist Martin Seligman (1975), is a psychological state that often results when a person encounters events that are uncontrollable. Anna, for example, experienced many such events. She could do nothing that would have much impact on her environment. No one needed her in the nursing home, and none of her actions had any consequence. She had nowhere to go. Seligman suggests that people (as well as animals) who are in stressful situations that they cannot control develop **learned helplessness.** They can no longer cope, and therefore they may give up and die. A physiological response develops from a psychological stress. Anna probably would have been better off if she had been placed in an environment similar to her old apartment and had maintained some control over her life (Rodin & Langer, 1977).

Seligman found that people may lose the motivation to control many other events in their lives once they experience significant loss of control in one realm. They also have difficulty in recognizing that any successful responses they have actually are successful in affecting the environment. That is, experience with uncontrollable events can result in learned helplessness. Learned helplessness can lead people to emotional disturbance, serious depression, and even sudden death.

Explanatory Style

Individual differences in how people understand and explain the causes of bad events is termed **explanatory style** (Peterson & Seligman, 1984). The three main dimensions of explanatory style are:

a) internality—"it is all my fault" (versus something external is to blame).

b) stability—"the bad news is going to last forever" (versus more temporary).

c) globality—"the problem is going to ruin everything" (versus it is limited and specific).

Explanatory style is a reformulation of learned helplessness, in terms of cognitive explanations and attributions. Although all three dimensions of explanatory style seem relevant to depression, globality seems predictive of poor health (Peterson & Bossio, 1991). That is, the pessimism of catastrophizing one's failures—saying that some disappointment is a major misfortune—can lead to unhealthy behaviors. For example, one study examined the kinds of explanations people gave for significant disappointments at mid-life, and then followed their longevity and cause of death (Peterson, Seligman, Yurko, Martin, & Friedman, 1998). It was found that catastrophizing men were more likely to die sooner, and they were especially more likely to die injury deaths (of accidents or violence). Such people may be poor at problem-solving when facing life's challenges, and may take unnecessary risks.

Learned Optimism.   Where does an optimistic or pessimistic style come from? Some people have emphasized providing children with unconditional regard and unconditional positive feedback to promote self-esteem. But raising children simply to feel good about themselves often will not prepare them to face challenge and take responsibility. In fact, one long-term study of depression indicated that teaching children life skills is the better way to bolster genuine self-esteem. Further, teaching children to challenge their pessimistic thoughts can help "immunize" them against depression (Seligman, Reivich, Jaycox, & Gillham, 1995).

All in all, losses and even a temporary sense of hopelessness are quite common in most people's lives, and loss can be found in the history of most people. These losses are part of a broader pattern of stressful life changes that everyone must face to a greater or lesser extent. Yet when they become the expected pattern, there are various pathways to illness. As we will see, passive patients may be less likely to follow treatment regimens, less likely to have help from others, and may be predisposed to sickness to start with. There are often associated physiological disturbances. It is ironic that patients who, on the surface, seem "adjusted" and "compliant"—that is, the least rebellious and angry—are often likely to be ill or dead on follow-up.

LIFE CHANGE

All of us have heard of cases in which a person seems in worse health several months after changing jobs, or someone dies soon after retiring or even while on a long-anticipated vacation. In other words, illness follows an important change in a person's life. Working along the lines of Selye's general adaptation model, researchers have investigated the relationship between stressful life events and the onset of illness. This research examines life stress in terms of events that require a significant amount of adaptation in the ongoing pattern of the individual's life (Holmes & Masuda, 1974; Holmes & Rahe, 1967; Rahe, 1974).

The role of stressful life events in the etiology of illness has been studied for many years. More than a half century ago, the physician Adolf Meyer organized medical data as a dynamic biography that contained information not only about a patient's medical history (specific illnesses) but also about the patient's psychosocial history. He began to recognize the importance of life events preceding patients' illnesses. Meyer called this method of organizing data the *Life Chart*. In the late 1940s, other researchers began to use the same method. However, this area of research began in earnest with a study of U.S. Navy personnel patients. This research showed that stressful life events tended to cluster within two years before the onset of disease. This research, conducted in the 1960s and early 1970s, led to the general public's increasing concern with the stresses of life (see also Box 5–3).

Box 5–3 Public Recognition of Stress

The idea that stress is often an important component of illness has made its way into the public consciousness. Stresses that used to be considered the personal problem of the individual are now being used in claims of illness and disability. For example, workers may take a sick day when they become very anxious on the job. A more striking example is claims for disability payments.

According to various news accounts, some public employees are claiming that the stresses of their work are so severe that they are ill and deserve full disability payments. In one case, a county assessor claimed that the nerve-racking pressures of his job incapacitated him. Instead of simply quitting his job, the official saw his problem as an illness and decided to fight for a retirement pension. In another case, a transportation officer claimed that certain problems on his job led to shot nerves and an aggravated case of gout. He too can no longer work and has filed a medical disability claim.

According to the National Council on Compensation Insurance, more than 15,000 occupational-disease claims per year are stress related. Courts are often upholding these claims, especially when there is clear evidence of disability, such as ulcers or mental breakdown. The good news is that public recognition of stress is leading many companies to institute stress-reduction programs in the workplace.

Measuring Life Change

Research on "life events" attempted to demonstrate a connection between the onset of illness and the sheer number of life-change events that required adaptive responses. The effects of these events were assumed to be additive; that is, more events were expected to have a greater effect.

Initially, the researchers counted the number of stressors, but it became clear that some events are more stressful than others. They found a way to measure the general impact of these events by having a large number of people rate various events as to how much readjustment was required. The scale indicating these ratings is called the Social Readjustment Rating Scale (SRRS) (Holmes & Rahe, 1967). For example, death of a spouse is rated 100, the highest point on the scale; divorce and separation are highly stressful, as is a jail term. Interestingly, even positive events appear—marriage is rated 50, a change in recreation is 19, and a vacation is rated 12.

Most investigators working in this field adopted a modified form of this checklist. People might be asked to check off each event that happened to them during the past year. The items represent common situations that arise from family, occupational, personal, or financial aspects of an individual's life. They are events that require an adjustment in the individual's way of life. The checklist is called the Schedule of Recent Experience (SRE).

The early studies by Richard Rahe and colleagues were retrospective. The researchers asked Navy personnel to report life changes and instances of illness during the 10 years before the study. The number of illness episodes that occurred was found to be related to the amount of social readjustment that was required during that period. Scores on the SRRS are referred to as LCUs—that is, life change units. The researchers claimed that subjects who reported fewer than 150 LCUs for a given year reported good health for the following year. However, among those with an annual LCU rate of between 150 and 300, about half reported serious illness in the next year. When the LCUs exceeded 300, as they did for a small portion of subjects in the research, illness followed in more than 70 percent of the cases. Furthermore, the higher the LCU rating, the more episodes of illness that occurred in a given period.

In prospective studies of naval personnel between the ages of 17 and 30, shipboard medical records for an entire six-month cruise were examined. These medical records were compared to a record of life events that had occurred six months prior to shipboard duty, information that was collected before the start of the tour. A statistically significant difference was noted in the amount of illness found during the six months on board ship by individuals who had experienced many life changes versus those who had experienced few life changes before the tour of duty. Personnel who were in the lowest quartile of LCUs had an average of only 1.4 illnesses in six months, whereas personnel in the highest quartile of LCUs had an average of 2.1 illnesses (Rahe, 1972, 1974).

Over the ensuing years, various studies have shown that the number and intensity of life events and the probability of future illness are related. In most of these studies, the data about life events are gathered from very large homogeneous samples, using questionnaires. Information about illness is gathered from medical records. The samples include military personnel, employees of large corporations, and clinic or hospital patients. In both retrospective and prospective investigations, there have been statistically significant relationships noted between a life change and the occurrence of sudden heart attacks, accidents, athletic injuries, leukemia, tuberculosis, diabetes, and many minor medical complaints. High scores on life change have also been associated with psychiatric symptoms and disorders. Finally, some researchers have noted that the number and magnitude of life change events experienced influence the course of recovery in some medical patients (Cohen, Kessler, & Gordon, 1997; Rabkin & Struening, 1976; Rahe & Arthur, 1978). The variety of populations and the large sample sizes are impressive, although closer scrutiny of the methodological and theoretical aspects of the research leads to a host of questions.

Problems in Life Change Research

There are several methodological problems in the life change and illness research (Depue & Monroe, 1986; Kasl, 1983). First, many studies involve retrospective accounts of life changes and retrospective accounts of illness. Since people are asked to report both their life changes and their illnesses, the hypotheses of the study may have been obvious to the subjects, or they make look for stresses to report. Relatedly, illness may make a person more aware of stresses. Furthermore, many times the researchers make little attempt to tell the subjects what types of illnesses to report.

Second, although the results in this area are statistically significant (reliable) because of the large sample sizes, the results are often of small magnitude; that is, actual differences between the high LCU subjects and the low LCU subjects are often quite small. In some studies, characteristics of the occupational environment, personality variables, and demographic variables such as socioeconomic status, age, and sex are better predictors of illness than the life events.

Third, some of the life events in the SRE could be considered indicative of oncoming illness. For example, subjects are asked to report changes in eating or sleeping habits. These changes might be indicative of developing disease. Thus, some life changes may be a result rather than a cause of illness. Similarly, developing disorders might cause behaviors that lead to life changes such as divorce or a new job. Furthermore, sometimes subjective, self-report scales are used to measure both stressors and illness. For example, self-reported heavy increases in highway traffic might be used to predict subsequent headaches; but the initial report may actually be an indirect indication of headaches. People who are already feeling ill may be more likely to report life difficulties. In short, although life stress is associated with illness, its precise degree of importance depends in part on other factors. These criticisms do not by any means invalidate the general approach; they simply indicate that we must be careful in drawing our conclusions.

There are also some more theoretical problems with the original Holmes and Rahe approach. One criticism is that the researchers theorized that all life change, whether it is positive or negative, increases the probability that disease will develop. However, there is evidence that undesirable (negative) events are the events most strongly correlated with reports of illness, especially if they remain unresolved (Liem & Liem, 1976; Rahe, 1987;

Sarason, Johnson, & Siegel, 1978; Thoits, 1994). Although positive changes require adaptation and thus can probably sometimes bring about illness, data do not strongly support this relationship. Furthermore, measures of life change are weighted in the direction of negative changes.

Could no change have negative effects on an individual's health? It could be imagined that the absence of certain changes could have a negative impact on the individual, and might itself require adjustment (Gersten, Langer, Eisenberg, & Orzeck, 1974; Graham, 1974). For example, if a person does not get a job promotion that he or she feels is deserved, or does not have an opportunity to move to a different location, a negative impact on the individual may result from frustration, understimulation, or simple boredom. Understimulation (as well as overstimulation) by the environment can lead to physiological activation, the need for adjustment, and the wearing down of the person's resistance to disease. Finally, note that the life-change approach emphasizes the negative effects of life changes, but it does not deal with the substantial number of people who undergo a major life change without developing illness.

Hassles

If major life events can sometimes affect health, what about minor life events like being stuck in traffic? Intuitively, we feel as if such daily hassles can give us a headache or make us feel stressed. Could the cumulative effect of daily hassles become serious? Analogously, could minor daily uplifts, such as a delicious lunch, reduce stress and improve health?

The research that has been conducted on this topic to date does suggest that **daily hassles** may indeed affect longer-term psychological and physical health (Kanner, Coyne, Schaeffer, & Lazarus, 1981). Such research typically uses a self-report hassles scale, which asks about things like losing possessions, concerns about weight, and home maintenance hassles. In one study of well-educated adults in the San Francisco area, the frequency and intensity of self-reported hassles was significantly correlated with degree of illness (DeLongis, Coyne, Dakof, Folkman, & Lazarus, 1982). In another study of low-income, elderly persons with osteoarthritis, hassles again were related to self-reported physical health over a six-month period (Weinberger, Hines, & Tierney, 1987).

Hassles may be the mechanism through which life event stressors sometimes operate; that is, large disruptions (such as moving to a new city) create lots of daily hassles. However, daily hassles will presumably sometimes affect people's psychological and physiological reactions in ways that are qualitatively different from the effects of major life events. For example, the death of a loved one will produce deep emotions, ongoing thoughts, and physiological disturbances that would not result from the hassle of facing tall grass and a broken lawnmower. The ways in which hassles relate to and differ from major life stresses remain to be researched. Still, hassles are of interest in themselves since there is evidence that minor daily fluctuations in mood are related to immune system competence; that is, some antibody response (IgA) may be lower on days that people have relatively high degrees of negative moods (Stone, Cox, Valdimarsdottie, Jandorf, & Neale, 1987).

There are potential methodological difficulties with the hassles approach, as with life change (Kohn, Lafreniere, & Gurevich, 1991). First of all, self-report artifacts may arise when both hassles and health are measured by asking people how they feel. It is not surprising that people who say they are feeling ill also report that they are being hassled. Second, there may be a confounding with depression, anxiety, and other negative emotional states. People who are depressed and anxious may report that they have interrupted sleep, traffic problems, job worries, and so on. In other words, chronic emotional state rather than real environmental hassles may be being measured.

Chronic Stress

Although occasionally it is sudden, acute stress that brings on a heart attack or stroke, the more common and insidious stress is **chronic stress**—challenge that causes psychophysiological reactions over many months. One well-studied cause of chronic stress is chronic noise. Chronic noise, such as living near a noisy airport, has been shown to affect task performance, disrupt cardiovascular functioning, increase levels of stress hormones, and even contribute to learned helplessness (Cohen, Evans, Krantz, & Stokols, 1980; Evans, Hygge, & Bullinger, 1995).

What is the effect if you happened to live near the nuclear leakage accident at Three Mile Island? Let us say that experts assure you that you have had no significant radiation exposure, but you remain unsure. In fact, you feel a loss of control and frequently experience intrusive memories—thoughts about disaster. In such cases, chronic stress may persist for years (Baum, Cohen, & Hall, 1993). In fact, although only such dramatic national incidents are likely to be studied by scientists, many people encounter similar threats (such as seeing a horrific automobile accident) and may become more vulnerable to stress-influenced disease for many years to come. But reactions will be a function of pre-event personality, type of involvement with the accident or event, and perceptions of and reactions to the accident (Dew, & Bromet, 1993). In other words, here again we see that the body endeavors to establish homeostasis in a complex biopsychosocial way, and so simple predictions of health outcomes are usually not possible.

Severe Stress

In the extreme case, people are subjected to tremendous life stress and then have their social ties taken away. Such a scenario applied to many American veterans of the Vietnam war, who returned home from horrifying experiences to find an uncaring country. Many reacted with ongoing nightmares, survivor guilt, and continued social alienation. The problem was so severe that it has been given a special name, **posttraumatic stress disorder** or PTSD (Keane, Scott, Chavoya, Lamparski, & Fairbank, 1985).

In posttraumatic stress disorder, the trauma victim is disoriented, may have trouble sleeping, may have trouble concentrating, and may have intrusive thoughts, flashbacks, angry outbursts, and other symptoms of ongoing arousal (Jaycox & Foa, 1998). Alcoholism or drug abuse may follow. The psychoneuro-hormonal system is disrupted to such a degree that it cannot seem to right itself. There is a kind of permanent stress. For example, in reaction to a high sense of loss following a major hurricane, some people will face

Figure 5-2   The occasional threat to a cave man or cave woman from real
danger, which was adaptive, has turned into chronic stress for
modern people, as the noises, hassles, and challenges of modern life inundate us. *(Copyright Howard S. Friedman. Drawing by
James Dalby. Reprinted by permission.)*

ongoing intrusive thoughts, sleep disruptions, and effects on the immune system (Ironson
et al., 1997).

One comprehensive study of over a thousand male U.S. army veterans who served
in the 1960s compared those veterans who had significant combat experience in Vietnam
and had been diagnosed with PTSD to those who were not so stressed. Reports of serious
diseases were collected about two decades later. Importantly, the study controlled (statistically) for socioeconomic status, intelligence, volunteer status, age, substance abuse,
smoking, hypochondriasis (complainers), and other variables. The results showed that the
traumatized veterans were more likely to suffer circulatory, digestive, musculoskeletal,
nervous system, respiratory, and infectious diseases during the two decades that followed
(Boscarino, 1997). Since these men were not followed with yearly medical exams as part
of this study, we cannot be sure about the physiological mechanisms that mediate this
stress-to-disease relationship. Nevertheless, other studies of traumatized veterans or traumatized Holocaust survivors have found high catecholamine levels and cortisol alterations symptomatic of long-term disturbance of the hypothalamic-pituitary-adrenal axis
(Boscarino, 1996; Yehuda, 1998).

In sum, a large body of research indicates that adapting to life's challenges (both large and small) can sometimes lead to illness. This research suggests, however, that the relationship between life events and illness is not a simple, direct, or absolute one. How a person copes with the loss or the change may be more important to health than the occurrence of the loss or the change itself.

STRESS PSYCHOPHYSIOLOGY

As we have seen, biomedical researchers have traditionally focused on physiology without much attention to psychology, and psychological researchers have typically done the opposite. Health psychologists aim for an integration, and the psychophysiological basis of health is described in detail in Chapter 2. Fortunately, collaborations among neuroscientists, immunologists, and health psychologists are finally starting to yield even more meaningful and comprehensive explanations of stress psychophysiology.

Allostasis

One influential cross-disciplinary researcher is Bruce McEwen. Recognizing that stress can either help or hurt the body, McEwen (1998) has analyzed how the body adapts to stress by what can be termed **allostasis**—the ability to achieve stability through change.

The process of allostasis uses the autonomic nervous system, the hypothalamic-pituitary-adrenal (HPA) axis, and the cardiovascular, metabolic, and immune systems to respond to stress. When these systems are used *frequently* to help respond to a lot of stress, allostatic load occurs, and the body is damaged.

When in action, allostasis mainly first activates the sympathetic nervous system and HPA axis, which initiates the series of responses that result in the release of the catecholamines and cortisol (see Chapter 2). That is, the hypothalamus stimulates the pituitary gland to release adrenocorticotropic hormone (ACTH), which stimulates the adrenal cortex to release corticosteroids. And the sympathetic nervous system causes the adrenal medulla (the other core part of the gland on the kidney) to secrete epinephrine and norepinephrine. After the challenge is gone, the levels of these hormones gradually return to normal. If there is repeated stress over time, increased exposure to these stress hormones harms many physiological functions.

There are four main causes of allostatic load. One is *frequent stress*, which can come from environments (life change) such as high-pressured jobs in which a person must face new crises every day. *Lack of adaptation* to a repeating stress is the second possible cause. A person who does a lot of public-speaking but does not learn to reduce their anxiety after repeated times may experience this type of allostatic load. This is usually a failure of coping.

Interestingly, the third possible cause is the *inability to turn off* the allostatic response when the stress is gone. An example of this problem occurs if a person's blood pressure does not go back down to normal after a large challenge that initially made the person very anxious. This may be due to biological factors, psychological factors, or a combination.

The fourth cause of allostatic load involves *inadequate responses by some allostatic systems* so that other systems have to increase their activity. For example, if sufficient cortisol is not released in response to stress, inflammatory cytokines will be secreted instead, which will result in an inflammatory response greater than normal. In other words, an impairment in one part of our adaptation can reverberate throughout other critical bodily systems.

Allostatic load has been associated with many negative effects, including effects on the cardiovascular system (Seeman, Singer, Rowe, Horwitz, & McEwen, 1997), the brain (Meaney, Tennenbaum, & Francis, 1994), and the immune system (McEwen et al., 1997). For example, one study showed that increased cortisol secretion in women correlated with a decline in memory (Seeman, McEwen, Singer, Albert, & Rowe, 1997). Although the idea of allostasis is not radically different from some previous notions of stress, it emphasizes the *change*—the constant reestablishment of homeostasis—as the likely source of disease susceptibility. It also emphasizes the close relevance of the cardiovascular, metabolic, and immune systems to understanding stress.

Although the interactions among psychological perception, cognition, physiological reactivity, behavior, metabolism, and immune function are extremely complex and not fully understood (Conrad, Galea, Kuroda, & McEwen, 1996), it is striking how much of the stress and allostasis system involves the same basic bodily adaptation systems. (This is just as Hans Selye hypothesized.) Study after study on stress points to the sympathetic nervous system and the HPA axis. As we gain better understanding of the many functions and triggers of the catecholamines and cortisol, we move ever closer to understanding homeostasis—Cannon's "wisdom of the body."

COPING WITH STRESS

Death of a spouse produces a big change in a person's life. For most people, this loss is devastating. However, some people were not attached to their spouses, live independent lives, and have many same-sex and opposite-sex friends; they soon get on with their lives. Other people are glad to get rid of a demanding spouse, collect insurance money, or try new adventures. They may have a strong faith that everything works out for the best. They face life changes, but happily do so. Similarly, we have seen that negative life events such as divorce have a greater impact on health than positive events such as marriage. Such findings indicate that the *meaning* of a life change to the individual, rather than the change itself, is of significance. The meaning of events is influenced by our interpretations and by personal, social, or biological coping mechanisms.

Analysis of the psychophysiological stress response usually begins with the lower, more primitive areas of the brain, namely the hypothalamus, the pituitary gland, and the relevant parts of the autonomic nervous system. This analysis would be fine and complete if we were talking about certain primitive species. However, people have a more developed brain, with a large cerebral cortex, and are capable of thinking. When exposed to an environmental event, people perceive and *interpret* the event. This interpretation has a profound effect on our physiological responses.

In Figure 5–1, in the links between life events and illness, all pathways included link a, which passes through "behavior patterns, personality, and coping." We now consider in more detail the use of coping mechanisms in the face of life change.

Many people experience traumatic life changes but do not become ill. They may even use the stress for a positive end. For example, an individual may be successful at channeling the physiological arousal that accompanies the experience of stress into positive outcomes such as accomplishment or opportunities to gain new friends. It is interesting to note that the definition of the verb "to cope" in the *American Heritage Dictionary* is "to contend, to strive, especially on even terms or with success." This suggests that coping with stress involves not only contending with stress, but also contending *successfully*.

The thoughts and actions a person uses to deal with stress comprise the process of **coping** with stress. In other words, coping refers to interpretations and behaviors that people use to protect themselves from being harmed by new situations. Coping mediates the impact that stressors have on a person's health (DeLongis & Newth, 1998; Lazarus, 1966; Lazarus & Folkman, 1984). See Box 5–4.

Box 5–4   Ways of Coping

How is a person dealing with the challenges of a specific situation, such as a problem with an annoying friend or colleague? Pioneering work on assessing coping through a self-report questionnaire was conducted by psychologists Richard Lazarus and Susan Folkman (1984). They termed their influential approach the "Ways of Coping."

Although researchers have debated about the optimal number of ways of coping that should be assessed, the following eight ways of coping give a good flavor of this approach:

Confrontive—you might try to get your annoying friend to change his mind.

Distancing—you just go along with your fate.

Self-controlling—you try to keep things to yourself and not further antagonize your annoying colleague.

Seek social support—you talk to other friends in order to help you think about and address the challenge.

Accepting responsibility—you apologize to your friend or do something to make up.

Escape-avoidance—you do things like pigging out, or watching TV, or over-sleeping.

Planful problem-solving—you work even harder to make things right with your friend.

Positive reappraisal—you use the challenge as an inspiration to go out and do some worthwhile things.

At the heart of the concept of coping is the assumption that people are better off if they respond actively to the forces that impinge upon them. In part, this means interpreting or attributing challenges to controllable factors—things we can act on (Amirkhan, 1998). Coping mechanisms can take three forms (Pearlin & Schooler, 1978): psychological resources, social resources, and specific coping behaviors.

Psychological resources are personal characteristics upon which people draw from within themselves to help them deal with threats imposed by the environment. Examples are self-esteem, feelings of mastery and competence, and the feelings of control people have over their lives. On the other hand, self-denigration may lead to giving up and can interfere with successful coping.

Social resources are aspects of people's interpersonal networks. They involve the social support available from family, friends, fellow workers, neighbors, and other associates. Although social support is often equated with emotional support, it may also involve more tangible resources, such as information and cooperation. Finally, while psychological resources represent the thoughts and personal characteristics that people have, and social resources represent the supports that they have, specific coping responses represent the things that people do—their concrete efforts to deal with specific strains of life. These specific coping responses may be influenced by both the psychological resources of the individual and social resources, as well as by biological factors. In the next sections, we consider the empirical research on psychological resources, social supports, and biological aspects of coping.

Emotion-Focused and Problem-Focused

Efforts at coping may serve one of two major functions. **Problem-solving** (or problem-focused) **coping** involves efforts to do something constructive about the stressful situation, such as finding a new job or studying hard for an upcoming exam (Cohen & Lazarus, 1983; Lazarus & Launier, 1978).

Emotion-focused coping involves efforts to deal with the emotional distress, such as by going out jogging, denying the threat, or having a few stiff drinks. Perhaps the most apt comment about emotion-focused coping as "mind over matter" was offered by baseball pitcher and wit Satchel Paige, who reportedly said, "If you don't mind, it doesn't matter." Emotion-focused coping may be useful when dealing with a loss, whereas problem-focused coping may be better for addressing a threat or challenge (Aldwin, 1994).

Both types of coping are very common and frequently occur simultaneously (Folkman & Lazarus, 1980). The success of any effort will of course depend on the individual involved and the nature of the challenge. Ascertaining the types of and successes of coping mechanisms people use is currently an active area of research in health psychology.

Psychological Resources

Generally speaking, an event is not stressful unless the individual appraises (interprets) it as dangerous or challenging (Lazarus, 1966; Tomaka, Blascovich, Kibler, & Ernst, 1997). Thus, psychological coping mechanisms basically involve efforts at controlling meaning. That is, specific interpretations can be made to neutralize the effect of the stressful life event. The individual can learn to think in certain ways in order to make the stressful life event less important or less traumatizing. For example, the person who is experiencing a great deal of stress at work can learn to view work as only one part of life. The degree of stress experienced may be reduced simply because the critical importance of work is minimized. In addition, a person may actually change the perceived meaning of the event, such as viewing a break-up not as a failure but rather as a release from an unpleasant relationship.

Relatedly, the individual can seek to reduce stress by interpreting the event as a positive challenge. Someone who is facing a job transfer, for example, might choose to interpret the transfer as an exciting new opportunity. This person has thus changed the meaning of the situation to allow successful coping. Many "self-help" or "self-insight" groups and classes seek to facilitate coping by changing the person's view of life's challenges.

Because coping is an intervening process that occurs between stressors (like loss of a job) and outcomes (like finding a satisfying new job), it can become quite complicated to conceptualize and measure (Lazarus & Folkman, 1984). Analyses run up against all the difficulties psychologists face in trying to understand what is going on inside someone's head.

A classic example of work involving psychological resources concerns coping mechanisms in facing the stress of surgery. This work was initiated during the 1950s by the psychologist Irving Janis (1958). His research showed that before surgery, some patients were worried about their operation and felt very vulnerable; other patients were somewhat concerned and asked for information about their surgery; whereas still other patients were extremely cheerful and relaxed before their operation and did not want to know anything about it.

Reactions differed after surgery, and these differences were related in systematic ways to the presurgery behaviors. The highly fearful as well as the totally fearless patients experienced poor postoperative reactions, while patients with a moderate amount of anticipatory fear recovered best. These patients rehearsed ways of dealing with the stresses they faced—a phenomenon referred to by Janis as the **work of worrying.** Mental rehearsal of solutions to realistic problems, a moderate level of anticipatory fear, and a preparatory "working through" of difficulties helped the patients deal with the stresses of medical procedures.

Although subsequent research has not always found this sort of curvilinear relationship between fear level and outcome, this process of preparatory worrying has been proven effective by subsequent research in medical settings (Kaplan, 1982). For example, in one study half the subjects were given accurate sensory information about the effects of an upcoming blood pressure test. This prepared group then experienced less distress during the procedure than unprepared control subjects (Johnson, 1973). Similarly, in a study of endoscopy—an uncomfortable procedure in which patients must swallow a tube so that the doctor can see the stomach—patients given preparatory instructions about the sensations that would be encountered showed reduced emotional distress (Johnson & Leventhal, 1974).

However, it has also been found that provision of too much information to patients who don't want to think about what is upcoming can be counterproductive (Shipley, Butt, & Horowitz, 1979). So, adding coping training to the provision of preparatory information about sensation may be the most successful approach (Kaplan, Atkins, & Lenhard, 1982).

Although historically it was usually assumed that coping by distorting one's perceptions of reality was a kind of unhealthy "defense mechanism," more recent research documents that certain misconstruals of challenge sometimes can prove helpful. Unrealistically positive perceptions or interpretations of challenge have been termed **positive illusions** (Taylor, 1989; 1998). Sometimes, when facing a great challenge like having AIDS, unrealistic optimism can be helpful, as the person attempts to proceed with a relatively normal life (Reed, Kemeny, Taylor, Wang, & Visscher, 1994).

On the other hand, this does not mean that it is advisable to blithely ignore stress. A longitudinal study of change in the physical health of family members caring for heart transplant recipients during the first year after transplant showed that individuals who did not feel in control of things that happened to them and who engaged in avoidant coping (e.g., oversleeping) were most likely to show a decline in health and weight loss (Dew et al., 1998).

Social Resources

Although loss of one's child seems to be among the greatest sources of stress, it does not seem to be the case that the death of one's grown-up child affects one's risk of dying, if one is married. A comprehensive study of bereaved parents was conducted in Israel. The parents of all 2,518 soldiers who were killed in the Yom Kippur war in 1973 were followed for 10 years. Parents of accident victims were also studied. The bereaved parents were not more likely to die than non-bereaved Israeli parents (Levav, Friedlander, Kark, & Peritz, 1988), if the parents were married. This study thus suggests that sometimes even very stressful life events do not directly affect health. There must be other factors also contributing. Why is this?

The second major source of coping is social support. When faced with life change and the stress experienced as a result of it, the support of family and friends can be a significant aid to coping, especially if one is satisfied with the support (Cohen & Wills, 1985; Donald, Ware, Brook, & Davies-Avery, 1978; Lynch, 1977; Moss, 1973; Sarason & Sarason, 1984; Rodriguez & Cohen, 1998). In other words, social support will sometimes buffer the relationship between stressors and illness. (See Chapter 8 for a discussion of social support in response to illness.)

Social support comes from the friendly ties an individual has with family, associates, neighbors, and the community. A single person who moves to a new job in a new community may be isolated and have little or no social support, whereas a married person living and working in the town where this person grew up (who still has childhood friends and an extended family) probably has a great deal of support.

Married people are healthier on the average than divorced or widowed people, partly due to the stress of losing one's partner, but also because single people have a more difficult time dealing with environmental stressors (House, Robbins, & Metzner, 1982). The loss of other social ties seems to have a similar effect. A striking example of the importance of the community to one's health is provided by the sociologist Kai Erikson (1976). Erikson studied the effects of a terrible flood in the mountain town of Buffalo Creek, West Virginia. Social ties and the sense of community were destroyed by the flood, and many people became ill. They felt drained, exhausted, and weak, and often these feelings were incapacitating. As Erikson put it, their emotional shelter was stripped away and the community could "no longer enlist its members in a conspiracy to make a perilous world seem safe" (1976, p. 240).

In the 1960s, a pioneering study turned away from the usual sociological focus on demographic characteristics and instead looked at social cohesiveness in Roseto, Pennsylvania. This study concluded that the tight social network in this close-knit Italian-American community may have produced better health (a low mortality rate from heart attacks) (Stout, Morrow, Brandt, & Wolf, 1964). This is sometimes termed the **Roseto effect.** The nearby comparison town of Bangor had the same doctors, hospitals, climate, and traditional risk factors for cardiovascular disease; but it had less of a sense of community and more myocardial infarctions. A follow-up study examined the heart attack rates from the 1960s throught the 1980s, a time in which traditional extended family ties in Roseto were being broken, as Roseto became more Americanized. Sure enough, the mortality rate rose to the level of Bangor's (Engolf, Lasker, Wolf, & Potvin, 1992).

Similar findings were reported among Japanese-Americans living in California (Marmot & Syme, 1976) when they were compared to similar groups who had lost their close community ties. Various community studies have also shown effects of social ties on physical and mental health (Gottlieb, 1983). Most noteworthy, a prospective study done in Alameda County, California followed the community for almost a decade and found that people with fewer community ties were more likely to die (Berkman & Syme, 1979; 1994). Such group findings are very suggestive. But psychologists must always return to look at the individual in order to understand the precise process by which an influence like social support can have its effects.

How does social support work? First of all, social support can sometimes influence an individual's coping by affecting how stressful events are appraised. For example, if you know many other people who have gone through the same challenging experience, you may see the experience as less stressful. In this way, social support functions in concert with psychological resources for coping.

More importantly, social support may help the person deal with the emotional consequences of stress, thus minimizing the risk of illness. Not surprisingly, this is often termed *emotional social support.* One study of unemployed men, for example, found less illness, lower cholesterol levels, and less depression among men with supportive marriages and friendships than among men without this kind of support (Gore, 1978). Disclosure to others who are close, with their resulting reassurance and support, can directly reduce the anxiety of the individual.

Social support may also aid the individual in coping with life stresses in the following manner: Assume that a crisis event is experienced that creates anxiety in the individual. The usual coping mechanisms, such as trying to relax, are ineffective. If the individual has a social support network available, however, the network can encourage a person to take control of the situation, and to take responsibility for action. This responsibility could head off any sense of helplessness that the individual might feel. For example, one study of stress and social support in Chinese-Americans measured social support in terms of feelings about the neighborhood, interactions with friends and neighbors, and involvement in community activities (Lin, Simeone, Ensel, & Kuo, 1979). Illness was defined in terms of such symptoms as restless sleep, depression, overeating, drinking, anxiety, and lack of concentration (all self-reported). The researchers found that the greater the social support, the fewer the symptoms.

Social support can also help the stressed individual develop new coping strategies by providing information about how to deal with the stress, sometimes even when the recipient is unaware of the support (Bolger, Zuckerman & Kessler, 2000). This informational support often goes hand in hand with emotional support, but sometimes it comes alone in the form of written materials about how to deal with the challenge. This information then feeds into one's psychological coping efforts.

Finally, social support may also operate by providing tangible resources. This support is often called *instrumental support*. For example, loss of one's job is presumably less stressful if one's family can provide financial help. On the other hand, tangible support might be harmful if it made the recipient feel inadequate, indebted, or unduly manipulated (Cohen & McKay, 1984; Penninx et al., 1998; Revenson, Schiaffino, Majerovitz, & Gibofsky, 1991). Furthermore, tangible support might not be helpful if the primary problem was emotional distress. It is important to remember that both the individual and the specific environmental challenge must be examined in understanding stress and coping.

Social support is especially important when a person faces a severe challenge, such as the challenge of illness. Social support and its effects on coping with chronic illness are discussed in Chapter 8.

Pets.   Various models of human-pet interaction propose that interacting with pets promotes health in some of the same ways in which human social interaction promotes health. For example, playing with pets may have psychological benefits such as providing the owner with love and companionship, a sense of purpose and responsibility, and feelings of security. This greater psychosocial well-being, in turn, is hypothesized to reduce arousal or promote healthy behavior. Or, the physical stimulation of petting (a dog) may be physiologically relaxing itself (Siegel, 1993; Wilson, 1991; Winkler, Fairnie, Gericevich, & Long, 1989).

People throughout the country were not surprised when 11-year-old Donny Tomei was evidently helped out of his coma by the soft nuzzle of his dog Rusty. Unfortunately for pet lovers, the studies of pets and health are usually very weak methodologically. One of the few long-term, prospective studies of noninstitutionalized people examined 343 males and 300 females as a function of their pet interactions. In survival analyses of documented longevity, playing with pets at around age 67 was not associated with mortality risk during the next dozen years, even among the socially isolated. Further, playing with pets was not associated with other healthy attributes or healthy behaviors such as personality, social ties, education, smoking, and drinking (Tucker, Friedman, Tsai, & Martin, 1995). Although human-pet interactions may be useful for some institutionalized individuals or those recovering from a major stressor such as surgery or the loss of a loved one, human-pet interaction has not been clearly shown to promote health or longevity.

Biological Resources

Coping with stress can sometimes be achieved through direct biological means. Examples of relevant behaviors are running and meditation, as well as related techniques (Jaffe, 1980; Kostrubala, 1976; Pelletier, 1977; Sheehan, 1975). These various behaviors attempt to encourage a different physiological reaction in the individual from the usual fight-or-flight response. Relatedly, feedback techniques provide a chance to control the physiological arousal resulting from anxiety.

Exercise.   In the 1970s, a report by the U.S. Surgeon General first suggested that vigorous physical exercise, including running, can help a person cope effectively with stress (1979). The exact mechanisms by which this relaxation occurs are still not clear, although several processes are probably involved (Sime, 1984). First and most simply, it is probable that going outdoors to run serves to remove the individual from the stimuli that cause stress—such as work pressures at the office or family pressures at home. Second, focusing on one's body, breathing, and visceral sensations with repetitive movements may serve the same purpose as in the relaxation technique (described in the next section). Finally, direct physiological responses are also implicated in stress reduction. For example, the "runner's high"—a feeling of euphoria felt during vigorous exercise—may be caused directly by physiological factors involving the changed metabolism. Exercise is considered in more detail later in this book.

Meditation and the Relaxation Response.   Although there are undoubtedly many types of meditation and many mechanisms (Haruki, Ishii, & Suzuki, 1996), many forms of biological coping can be classified as a relaxation response. An interesting technique that can be used by individuals who face stressful situations, this meditative behavior can cause better feelings and positive physiological effects. The physiological result of such successful meditation, called the **relaxation response,** can reduce blood pressure, respiration rate, and other physiological indicators of stressful arousal (Benson, 1975). People who develop the relaxation response may also be better able to reduce their intake of hard liquor, their abuse of drugs, and their cigarette smoking (cf. Wills, 1986).

The techniques of the relaxation response have been familiar to people in the Far East for many years and have been used in various religions. This method of relaxation is geared to reducing the physiological consequences (sympathetic arousal) of the fight-or-flight response. The technique can be simple and requires only four basic elements: a quiet environment, a mental device, a passive attitude, and a comfortable position. First, the person chooses a quiet room. Second, a mental device must be employed; this device is usually a syllable that is repeated silently or in low gentle tones. Although many different words or sounds have been used in traditional religious and other meditation practices, Herbert Benson suggests the use of the syllable "one" because of its simplicity and neutrality. Third, a passive attitude is necessary. The person should not think about his or her own performance or try to force the relaxation response. Whenever a person becomes distracted—that is, whenever a thought enters the individual's mind—the distraction (the thought) should simply be disregarded. Finally, the meditator should sit in a comfortable position. The purpose is to reduce muscular effort to a minimum.

Benson suggests the following technique: In a quiet environment, sit in a comfortable position and close your eyes. Deeply relax all muscles, beginning with the feet and progressing up to the face. Allow them to remain deeply relaxed. Then, breathe through the nose, concentrating only on breathing. As you breathe out, say the word "one" silently. Then breathe in. As you breathe out again, say "one" to yourself, and breathe in. Whenever a thought enters your mind, disregard it. Continue this practice for 20 minutes. Although there is some question about how meditation differs from daydreaming and how the various types of meditation taught by different yogis, gurus, and therapists differ from each other, there seems to be little doubt that the relaxation response can produce a decrease in sympathetic arousal.

Humor, Music, Massage.   There are many other devices people use to deal with the stresses of a challenging world. Many of these seem to have little to do with the challenge itself but rather reduce anxiety or increase feelings of self-worth. Unfortunately, the success of these techniques in promoting health has not yet been fully and systematically evaluated through controlled research, but many hold promise. For example, body massage is well known to reduce anxiety and may have some salutary effects on immune function (Field, 1998; Ironson et al., 1996; Montague, 1978). This is probably due both to cognitive effects of feeling secure and attached, and physiological effects of pressure-induced stimulation of the parasympathetic nervous system, which calms arousal of the sympathetic nervous system.

The writer Norman Cousins pointed out that humor can be very useful as both a mechanism for neutralizing the stress and as a method of actually changing the meaning of the situation so that it is no longer stressful (Cousins, 1979). Other writers propose sexual activity as a means of reducing tension. Various investigators and artists have suggested music, art, and dance as ways of reducing stress. In fact, there are practicing music therapists, art therapists, and dance therapists. Presumably, these techniques sometimes also act directly on parts of the brain that are incompatible with stress reactions. Again, however, these techniques have not yet been rigorously evaluated by health psychologists, although most Americans would agree that listening to good music with a humorous, attractive lover is a good means of combating stress.

Finally, it should be noted that ingestion of alcohol and other drugs could be considered a direct biological means of coping with stress. In the short term, a stiff drink or a tranquilizer may indeed prove effective. But in the long term, of course, a drug habit usually creates many more problems—physical problems, emotional problems, economic problems—than it solves.

In sum, coping involves many intriguing aspects—some psychological, some social, and some biological. Various techniques seem to work for various people at various times. Many of these coping techniques can be taught, but it is unlikely that universally applicable advice will soon become available.

Diathesis-Stress and Coping

Health psychologists sometimes refer to a **diathesis-stress model. Diathesis** is the predisposition (often hereditary) of the body to a disease or disorder. The predisposition or weakness might come from genetics or upbringing—for example, having sensitive lungs. However, the illness (such as asthma) would not come unless and until it is elicited from the environment, such as engaging in an occupation like mining or farming that challenges the lungs. Generalized stress usually exacerbates such problems.

This model depends on the idea of individual characteristics interacting with the situation. If we now expand individual characteristics to include the various sorts of coping, we have a sophisticated model of stress and illness. We have: a) the background, history, genetics, and other characteristics of the individual; b) the environmental challenge; and c) the psychological, social, and biological resources the person brings to cope with the challenge. As we will see in the next two chapters, this model allows a deep and insightful approach to understanding psychological contributors to illness.

SELF-INDUCED STRESS

Sometimes, stress can occur even though no external conditions seem to account for it. This kind of stress is generated internally. It consists of the demands that people place on themselves, their own fears (which may be irrational), and their tendencies to reproach themselves. Some people have no obvious external problems to account for the stress they experience. The physician or other health care professional, or even a friend, may try to tell the patient simply to stop worrying about benign situations. Such statements as "You worry too much" or "You take things too seriously," however, merely reinforce the person's own perception of him or herself as unstable, inferior, and unable to deal with stress.

Certain people are likely to become ill as a result of such internal stress (Beck, 1976). Health care professionals often call such a patient "neurotic," and it may not be long before patients like this begin to see themselves in those terms as well. But there may be many causes. The motivation behind this constant state of tension may be a fear of not reaching their goals. Because their self-worth and self-image are based wholly on achievement, these people usually exaggerate the importance as well as the difficulty of what must be achieved. They also exaggerate the ultimate consequences of failure. Because they regard each task as a major confrontation with major consequences, they are constantly racing to try to prevent some fantasized disaster.

People whose stressors are internally originated may operate from *faulty cognitions.* Often, these patients can be helped by logically and rationally sorting out the consequences of failure (pointing out their continued value as an individual) and also by helping them assess realistically their probability of achieving their goals. Social support and specific behavioral coping responses may also be helpful. However, psychological counseling and therapy support groups are sometimes necessary.

Sometimes, this internal stress is biologically based. Or it may be psychologically instigated but biologically maintained, as in the case of posttraumatic stress. A person may have a hormonal imbalance or problems with the hormone receptors in the brain. Since normal stress reactions involve hormone release, problems with this biological system can mimic the effects of externally caused stress. Such people may become seriously and chronically depressed. Or they may be abnormally agitated. Although such problems have traditionally been termed "mental illness" (and been treated by psychiatrists), we have seen that it makes more sense to treat these illnesses on the same continuum and with the same broad perspective that we apply to the rest of health psychology.

SUMMARY AND CONCLUSION

People face stress each time they are in a situation that requires adjustment to personal, social, and environmental challenges. There have been numerous changes in our culture in recent years that require a high degree of adaptation and may thus be highly stress-inducing. On a social level, these changes include the changing status of women and minority group members, and the enormous mobility of people. Other stress triggers are economic changes, growing old in a youth-oriented culture, and the removal of constraints preventing marital breakup. In addition, technological advances may require adjustment on the part of the individual to situations he or she has never before encountered.

Our bodies are well-equipped to face new challenges, but often the challenge becomes overwhelming for a given person at a given time. There is little doubt that the resulting stress is closely linked to illness. Often, stress is a cause or contributor to illness, although there are different pathways for the link. This chapter examined in detail the various links.

Among the coping techniques we have considered, it is not yet clear which techniques are most effective. A happy, secure person with a sense of control, adequate social support, and healthy recreational activities will likely do well, but such a state is not always easy to achieve. A combination of techniques can often help a person during a stressful time.

A health care professional can assess each patient's coping repertoire—that is, the usual behaviors in which the patient engages in order to cope with stress. Early recognition of maladaptive coping mechanisms or lack of adequate coping is important so that such behaviors can be changed. Understanding a patient's usual coping repertoire, supporting healthful coping behavior, and extinguishing unhealthy behaviors constitute an important goal for preventive health care.

While it may also help to assist people in avoiding especially stressful life events, this kind of approach is usually unsuccessful. Stressful events may be closely tied to the person's social and economic situation—a person is likely not to be willing to give up family and work responsibilities. In addition, the individual may desire new and exciting things in life. As mentioned earlier, health is not simply the absence of disease. It may, in fact, involve the resiliency to deal with potentially stressful life events. In this context health may involve the flexibility to adapt to life change (see Box 5–5).

Box 5-5   The Autonomous versus Identified Person

Deviation from psychosocial norms—that is, going against the expectations of the cultural group—can be a source of stress for the individual. If someone is willing to go through life fitting in with the behavior expected by members of his or her religious group, community, family, and so on, he or she may never have to experience the stress of thinking about how to behave. However, people differ in the extent to which stability, lack of change, and predictability are important to them. People differ in how much they rely on continuity in social and cultural structure to keep stress at a manageable level for them. These different orientations have different implications for the life course of the individual. For example, patients with autonomous self-regulation are more likely to adhere to medical regimens (Williams, Rodin, Ryan, Grolnick, & Deci, 1998).

The sociologist Gordon E. Moss (1973) has called the individual who accepts psychosocial norms fully and merges his or her identity into that of the community an **identified** person. The **autonomous** person, on the other hand, resists psychosocial norms and tries to achieve a sense of identity outside of and apart from the community. There is of course a range of behaviors that falls between the two extremes. People who are identified attempt to reduce the amount of uncertainty in their lives and to maximize their security by associating themselves closely with organizations and other established social structures. They will accept the beliefs and goals of the group as their own. Autonomous people see uncertainty as an unavoidable aspect of life. They believe that security can be achieved only through complete self-sufficiency. Autonomous people develop their own moral codes in a variety of settings. Their expectations for their own behaviors and achievements are those they have formulated for themselves. They may be considerably more socially and geographically mobile than identified people. Autonomous people train themselves to deal adaptively with changes. They develop inner resources to deal with challenges without having them disrupt their lives or throw them off balance.

As you might guess, identified individuals experience less social change than autonomous individuals. In their insulated structure, identified persons will probably have fewer stress-related health problems. This is true, however, only if the structure remains completely intact. Because this is often not possible, these protected individuals might then begin to experience stress in reaction even to minor disruptions. Autonomous persons will experience more stress than identified persons as a matter of course in their attempts to develop independence and autonomy. They build up a tolerance for stress, however. If the group or social structure to which they belong is destroyed, or if their place in the group is lost (e.g., because of the death of a spouse or loss of community), autonomous persons can better manage the change.

Which orientation is healthier? That of course is not an easy question to answer. It depends on what happens in the social structure of the individual. If it can be guaranteed that the group (community, family, religious or cultural structure) will continue, then the least stress and the best health are likely to be experienced by identified persons. But it is never certain that the social structure will be maintained. Thus, autonomous people often may be better off in the long run, especially in times of rapid social change.

In an ideal world, coordinated health care by physicians, social workers, marriage counselors, psychologists, school administrators, and community agencies can help relieve some of the pressures on stressed individuals and help his or her entire family function better as well. Such preventive efforts may be difficult and costly, but so are the consequences of chronic stress.

Because personality can have such an important effect on stress responses and health, it is worthy of special attention. The relationship between personality and health is considered next.

Recommended Additional Readings

Dunkel-Schetter, Christine, & Bennett, Tracy L. (1990). Differentiating the cognitive and behavioral aspects of social support. In Barbara R. Sarason, Irwin G. Sarason, & Gregory R. Pierce, (Eds.), *Social support: An interactional view.* New York: John Wiley & Sons, p. 267–296.

Glaser, Ronald, & Kiecolt-Glaser, Janice K., (Eds.). (1994). *Handbook of human stress and immunity.* San Diego: Academic Press.

Monat, Alan, & Lazarus, Richard S., (Eds.). (1991). *Stress and coping: An anthology* (3rd ed.). New York: Columbia University Press.

Sapolsky, Robert. (1998). *Why zebras don't get ulcers: An updated guide to stress, stress-related diseases, and coping.* New York: Freeman Press.

Selye, Hans. (1975). *The stress of life.* (Rev. ed.). New York: McGraw-Hill.

Weiner, Herbert. (1992). *Perturbing the organism: The biology of stressful experience.* Chicago: University of Chicago Press.

Key Concepts

stress	posttraumatic stress disorder
stressors	allostasis
coping	problem-solving coping
illness behavior (sick role) model	emotion-focused coping
medical student syndrome	work of worrying
learned helplessness	positive illusions
explanatory style	Roseto effect
life change	relaxation response
daily hassles	diathesis-stress model
chronic stress	diathesis

Chapter 6

PERSONALITY AND DISEASE

About a century ago, a patient came to see Dr. Emil Kraepelin. Kraepelin was the German psychiatrist who helped found and synthesize the modern classification of mental disorders. The patient was a 59-year-old farmer. This man appeared quite dejected, and when questioned, he broke into lamentations about how he was so wretched, apprehensive, and anxious. Why might this man and other such patients go to see a doctor? He suffered from headaches, severe stomachaches, insomnia, and generally felt very sick. Trembling, he reported that he felt so ill that he was even contemplating suicide.

Unfortunately or fortunately, the doctor did not have CT scans available to check out the headaches, nor endoscopes to look into the stomach. As Kraepelin figured out, this man was suffering primarily from a classic case of clinical depression.

Can people be such worriers that they develop ulcers, or be so tense and anxious that they develop migraine headaches? Is there justification for the idea that people with cancer or asthma have a repressed personality? What about the cultural truism that having a "workaholic" personality leads to heart attacks? Although we have seen in Chapter 5 that stress plays an important role in illness, what is the relationship between personality and disease?

There is a long history of speculation about such links. The ancients believed the four bodily "humors" (blood, black bile, yellow bile, and phlegm) formed the basis of personality, and these elements were extended by the ancient physician Galen to refer not only to temperament but to the causes of disease (Allport, 1961). The predominant humor in a person was thought to produce the dominant temperament, and an excess of a humor led to disease. For example, an excess of yellow bile would produce a choleric irascible, bilious personality, eventual chronic hostility, and associated physical illness.

Although no modern physiologist would search a body for "humors," we still speak about the hopeless, depressed "melancholic," the angry, hostile "choleric," the apathetic "phlegmatic," and the optimistic "sanguine." Links among emotion, personality, and health have been written about for two thousand years, suggesting both that there may be some truth to these conceptions and that the ideas are too flexible—they can accommodate any observations. We are not surprised to hear that a depressed, listless associate of ours has developed cancer, but is there any scientific validity to such beliefs?

Early in the 20th century, the question of personality and illness was studied by Sigmund Freud and the psychoanalysts who followed him. Using hypnosis and related psychodynamic techniques, Freud (1955) was able to cure hysterical paralysis (such as cases in which young women were physically paralyzed by psychological problems) and related conditions. But what about cancer, heart disease, migraines, and so on?

Although there is no doubt today that many illnesses have a significant psychological component, the more challenging question is whether chronic mental disturbance contributes to organic disease (Dunbar, 1943). Based on clinical observation, the psychoanalyst Alexander (1950) said yes, and suggested that various diseases are caused by specific unconscious emotional conflicts. For example, he linked ulcers to oral conflicts (an unconscious desire to have basic infantile needs satisfied) and asthma to separation anxiety (that is, an unconscious desire to be protected by one's mother). Although these ideas are suggestive to clinicians, little controlled empirical research has been performed to test them. Indeed it is scientifically impossible to test certain vague psychoanalytic speculations. However, the basic idea that personality sometimes relates to the development of illness began to gain more scientific credibility as research on stress and illness developed in the mid-20th century.

Danger of Blaming the Victim

There are dangers in looking for personality causes of disease. In many primitive societies, diseases were blamed on demons (Murdock, 1980). Demons are psychologically appealing culprits for two reasons. First, they provide an explanation for illnesses that have an unpredictable onset and course, and so seem unexplainable. Second, demons allow for some blaming of the victim, who must have been immoral to allow such possession. For example, frightened observers may have felt more comfortable and less threatened themselves if they could blame a young woman's epileptic seizures on her being a "witch," possessed by the devil.

In recent years, some have argued that "mental disturbance" is the modern replacement for demons. According to this argument, personality explanations for illness merely involve collective rationalization and victim-blaming. There is certainly some truth to this point of view. Tuberculosis was seen as caused by the character of those afflicted until the tubercle bacillus was discovered (Sontag, 1978). Thus, it is important to be very careful in examining the links between personality and disease.

This chapter follows up the preceding chapter by considering the relationship between personality and health. We examine possible links between personality and disease, and review the scientific literature on disease-prone personalities. Cardiovascular reactivity, the immune system, and unhealthy behaviors are examined as possible mediating mechanisms. Finally, we evaluate the implications for health care in our society.

MODELS OF PERSONALITY AND DISEASE

Personality could be related to disease through a variety of very different types of mechanisms, some causal, some not. For example, a finding that angry, "choleric" people are more likely to have heart disease could be due to a number of very different reasons. Each of these mechanisms undoubtedly operates at some times, with some people, or with some diseases. It is important to keep these various mechanisms in mind when evaluating research designed to study the links between personality and health.

Unhealthy Habits and Behaviors

First, personality can lead to disease through unhealthy behaviors. For example, chronic anxiety leads some people to continue smoking, and smoking leads to lung cancer. In this way, anxiety is a causal factor for lung cancer. However, in such cases, of course, curing the anxiety will not necessarily prevent the cancer unless the smoking is also affected.

In general, many personality problems make unhealthy habits more likely. Depressed, impulsive, or neurotic persons are more likely to have eating problems, tobacco habits, alcohol-consumption problems, and so on (Wills, Gibbons, Gerrard, & Brody,

2000). Studies investigating the links between personality and disease should therefore take into account unhealthy behaviors. Unfortunately, many studies do not. There are so many potentially relevant behaviors! As future research becomes more focused, it may be easier to take these influences into account.

Disease-Caused Personality Changes

Some observed links between personality and disease emerge because certain aspects of personality are the *result* of disease processes. For example, some (though not all) patients with serious illnesses such as cancer become fearful or depressed (Dunkel-Schetter & Wortman, 1982). So clinicians may notice that ill people appear psychologically disturbed; for example, oncologists may see what they believe to be a "cancer personality." Even worse, they sometimes may elicit a "cancer personality" through their own expectations. These personality changes result from the disease.

Furthermore, harmful biological processes may induce certain chronic mental disorders. For example, it has been suggested that lack of oxygen (hypoxia) can bring about depression (Katz, 1982). In addition, many diseases, including syphilis, AIDS, and Alzheimer's disease may affect the brain and thus cause personality changes (Friedman, 1994). Since the changes in personality may be noticed by family members well before a physician decides to do expensive medical testing, it may appear (falsely) that personality is predicting or causing the disease.

Finally, many drug therapies for disease cause depression, mood swings, anxiety, lowered sex drive, and other psychological side effects. Unfortunately, as more and more people are placed on long-term medications for chronic conditions like hypertension and high cholesterol, there has not been a corresponding major increase in the amount of research on medication-influenced changes in personality and behavior.

In all these cases, there is a link between personality and disease, but it is caused by the disease or the treatment for the disease.

Direct Influences of Personality

Personality can affect disease directly through physiological mechanisms. For example, if an angry, or "choleric," personality leads to artery damage, which in turn encourages the development of coronary heart disease, then this personality would be a cause of heart disease; changing the personality would then presumably reduce the likelihood of heart disease. This type of model combines Selye's (1976) notion of a general adaptation response to a noxious stimulus with the idea of individual coping mechanisms we considered in Chapter 5. In other words, depending on a person's view of the world, typical pattern of emotional responding, and psychological resources, he or she would be more or less likely to experience certain physiological responses when confronted by environmental challenge. Therefore, personality would play a causal role in disease.

This model is what people generally mean when they refer to a "coronary-prone personality," an "asthma-prone personality," and so on. It is closely related to what investigators have termed **psychosomatic illness or psychophysiological disorders.** This relationship is the main focus of this chapter.

This model does not mean that personality is the only cause of the disease (Weiner, 1977). Most disease processes are probably multi-factorial; they are caused by multiple factors. For example, a genetic predisposition to the disease, invading stressors (such as viruses), age, and other factors may be involved in the etiology of a disease. Thus, according to this model, many people prone to a given disease will not develop it; but on the other hand, relatively few people who are not psychologically prone to the disease will develop it.

Biological Third Variables

Sometimes personality is related to disease through an underlying biological third variable. In other words, some biological predisposition leads to the likelihood of both a certain type of personality and a certain disease. For example, there is evidence that a hyperresponsive (overly active) nervous system is an underlying factor in the development of an anxious personality and is an underlying factor in the development of heart disease. Thus, according to this model, an anxious, reactive personality may be related to heart disease, but the anxiety per se would not necessarily play a *causal* role in the development of heart disease. Rather, chronic anxiety would be a sign of increased likelihood of heart disease but may not lead to its development, depending upon the nature of the mechanisms involved (Kahn, Kornfeld, Frank, Heller, & Hoar, 1980; Krantz & Durel, 1983; McCabe, Schneiderman, Field, & Wellens, 2000).

When challenged, some people react more than others do, with changes in their blood pressure and heart rate. That is, there are individual differences in **psychophysiological reactivity** (also called **cardiovascular reactivity**). It is not yet clear whether this variable is a reliable individual difference that is relevant to both personality and disease risk (Swain & Suls, 1996; Swan, Ward, Jack, & Javitz, 1993).

Various theories have been proposed that relate the nervous system, personality, and health. These theories tend to involve the constructs of emotional expression and extraversion. This work began with the famous Russian physiologist Pavlov (1927), who wrote about strong versus weak nervous systems. The British psychologist Eysenck's (1967) well-known theory of **introversion/extraversion** proposes that introverts and extraverts have basic differences in the sensitivities of their nervous systems that affect their emotional responses and how they react to socialization. Extraverts may also be more likely to seek added stimulation, such as by smoking cigarettes (Eysenck, 1984).

In a related line of work, the psychologist Ross Buck (1984) developed a general model of relationships among nervous system activity, emotional expression, personality, and health. Simply put, a main conclusion of this approach is that inhibition of emotional expression is likely to be a correlate, and may be a cause, of poor health (Richards & Gross, 1999).

Biological third-variable models are not necessarily inconsistent with personality-causing-disease models, if the biological models, allow for feedback to and changes in the nervous system as a function of personality-influenced emotional responding. In other words, although anxiety and some disease proneness may both be physiologically based, it still may be possible to affect internal disease resistance by controlling the anxiety.

Tropisms: Seeking Unhealthy Situations

Another interesting link between personality and disease involves the seeking out of unhealthy situations. Certain kinds of people are pulled towards certain kinds of situations, which then pose a health threat. For example, people who are impulsive and psychologically unstable are more likely to wind up in situations that encourage such things as smoking, drug abuse, and sexual promiscuity. These behaviors then damage health.

In other words, just as photo-tropic plants move towards a source of light, some individuals gravitate towards more health-promoting spaces while other individuals remain subject to darker, health-threatening environments. Understanding the forces that pull some individuals towards unruly drinking clubs, drug abuse, drag-racing competitions, violent gangs, or promiscuous cliques while their peers gravitate towards computer clubs, church groups, track teams, vegetarian restaurants, and studying remains one of the least-studied areas of personality and health. These forces can be termed *tropisms* (Friedman, 2000b).

In such situations, personality leads to disease, but only indirectly. If the unhealthy environments are inaccessible, then the person stays healthy despite his or her personality (Friedman, 2000a,b). For example, if an impulsive, unstable person is raised in a supportive family, with safe schools, in a tight-knit supportive community, with perhaps a supportive religion, then the opportunity for unhealthy behavior greatly diminishes. This is why there can be marked variation in rates of things like alcoholism and drug abuse across time and place.

Measurement Artifacts: Illness Behaviors and Selection Biases

Sometimes, observed relationships between personality and disease are artifactual (not valid). As the health psychology model tells us, illness is partly a socially defined state that involves being diagnosed by a physician and entering the sick role. Social factors and methodological factors may sometimes artifactually produce or inflate a link between personality and disease.

One **artifact** involves measurement. Personality is related to symptom sensation and to symptom reporting. For example, neurotic people are more likely to feel and report pain and other bodily symptoms. Chest pains and choking feelings may lead to a diagnosis of angina or heart disease; but the same symptoms are also closely related to diagnoses of anxiety or depression. The cardiologist might diagnose angina while the psychiatrist was diagnosing anxiety. The resulting personality-to-disease link is not a direct personality influence on organic disease. It is a method artifact. Of course, such problems can be minimized if we can distinguish "chest pain due to anxiety" from "chest pain due to coronary artery narrowing"; but such distinctions are more difficult than they sound.

When should we be on the lookout for such an artifact? If personality is correlated with disease because of artifacts associated with the way that disease is assessed, then we should find such associations stronger when medical diagnosis depends on interviews and self-report measures (as does the assessment of personality). The artifact is more likely when the assessments are similar. Such artifacts are even more likely when the self-report measures themselves are similar.

As an example of this issue, consider the interesting case of coronary heart disease (discussed further later in this chapter). Two kinds of assessment apply: Diagnosis of angina (chest pain) relies heavily on patients' reports, whereas diagnosis of myocardial infarction (heart attack or MI) relies very little on the patients' reports. It has been argued that anxiety predicts better to angina than to MI (Costa & McCrae, 1985)—that is, that the link may be artifactual. However, although such an artifact may sometimes be operating, a comparison of angina and MI outcomes as related to personality found similar associations in the two cases (Friedman & Booth-Kewley, 1987a). The associations between personality and coronary heart disease (CHD) do not always change when MI rather than angina is the end point employed. That is, associations between certain aspects of personality and heart disease are not necessarily due to this type of measurement artifact. Still, this type of artifact is always a threat.

A second type of artifact can also inflate personality-to-disease associations. This artifact involves a **subject (patient) selection bias.** It can arise as a function of the control group used in a study. This artifact can occur if certain people are more likely than others to enter the health care system. For example, let us say that patients at a headache clinic are found to be more depressed than the population as a whole; in other words, there is an association between headaches and depression. This personality-to-disease correlation will be artifactual if there are many people with headaches who are not depressed, do not enter the headache clinic, and so are not included in the study. In other words, if the nondepressed people with headaches had bothered to go to the headache clinic, the clinic population would not be full of depressed patients.

To test for this type of artifact, studies in which the cases and controls are both in or out of the medical care system can be compared to studies in which the cases are in the medical care system but the controls are not. Evidence in the study of personality and disease suggests that the correlations between personality and disease are indeed somewhat smaller when cases and controls are both either in or outside the medical care system (Friedman & Booth-Kewley, 1987a). Since this type of artifact may sometimes be occurring, research designs should take this factor into account.

The Body as a System

Each of the models we have been considering is relatively simple and works in a single direction. In fact, however, the human body is a complex system comprised of many subsystems (Lobel, Dunkel-Schetter, & Scrimshaw, 1992). In many cases, it is likely that a variety of different causal influences and feedback loops will be at work in the relationship between personality and disease. For example, excessive anxiety may lead to smoking, drinking, and insomnia, which will set in motion a series of physiological processes (influenced partly by genetic makeup), which will in turn affect various aspects of health, behavior, and the anxiety itself; and so on. Some of the important links are illustrated in Figure 6–1. It is an oversimplification to say that any single factor is the cause of the disease that results. Nevertheless, personality dimensions having potentially deleterious effects on health should be investigated by health psychologists.

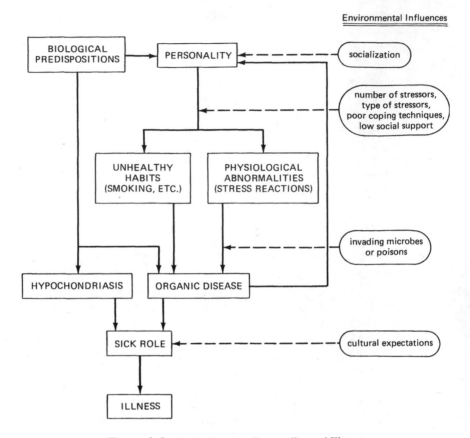

Figure 6-1   Links Between Personality and Illness.

THE CORONARY-PRONE PERSONALITY

The medical community has long suspected a link between emotional behavior and heart disease. It has been known for thousands of years that excitement increases pulse rate and that emotions like fear and love can cause pain in one's breast. As early as the 19th century, the medical educator Sir William Osler proposed a link between high pressure activity and **coronary heart disease** (Leibowitz, 1970). In the 1930s, Karl and William Menninger (1936), brothers who were famous American physicians and psychiatrists, asserted that CHD is related to repressed aggression. However, the dichotomy between body and mind, which many physicians followed, delayed systematic study of the association between emotional behavior and heart disease until the 1950s.

Coronary heart disease refers to impaired blood flow to the arteries that supply the heart muscle, producing symptoms such as angina (chest pain) or a myocardial infarction—heart attack. Atherosclerosis is the buildup of fatty and diseased tissue in the artery wall, sometimes termed *hardening of the arteries*. This process usually occurs over many years. When atherosclerosis occurs in the arteries feeding the brain, a stroke may develop. Remember that cardiovascular disease (CHD and stroke) is by far the greatest cause of premature mortality in western countries.

The incidence of cardiovascular disease in the United States increased dramatically during the first three-quarters of the 20th century, but then began a fairly significant decline. Furthermore, epidemiological studies have isolated vast differences in the incidence of heart disease in different cultures. However, cultures obviously differ on numerous variables (such as diet, exercise, toxins, and living habits) that may affect health. Thus, it is difficult to ascertain which variables are critical. Nevertheless, because such risk factors as diet and exercise are only moderately successful in predicting risk of heart disease, research also has focused on the high pressures and stresses of modern life as causal factors in CHD.

Type A Behavior Pattern

In the 1950s, two cardiologists noticed some interesting relationships between behavior and heart disease (Friedman & Rosenman, 1974). When an upholsterer arrived to repair the chairs in their office waiting room, he asked them what kinds of physicians they were. He wondered why only the front edges of the chairs were worn out. In other words, it seemed that heart patients were especially likely to sit on the edge of their seats! Of course, this incident is only illustrative, not scientific proof, but it does suggest a possible link between persistent agitated behavior and heart disease.

Four decades of research on the possible links between personality and heart disease have studied the **Type A behavior pattern,** or Type A personality (Dembroski, Weiss, Shields, Haynes, & Feinlieb, 1978; Matthews, 1982; Miller, Turner, Tindale, Posavac, & Dugoni, 1991). Type A people are defined as those involved in a constant struggle to do more and more things in less and less time, and they are sometimes quite hostile or aggressive in their efforts to achieve them. Type A people always seems to be under the pressure of time, constantly having a deadline to meet. Extreme Type A individuals live a life characterized by competitiveness, and they are always striving for achievement. They are hasty, impatient, impulsive, hyperalert, and very tense. When under pressure, most people may exhibit some behaviors that are similar to this Type A pattern, but Type A individuals exhibit this behavior very often, for example, turning even the most potentially relaxing situation (recreational sports such as tennis) into a high-pressure event.

On the other hand, people who do not show these characteristics are called **Type B.** They are able to relax, do not worry about time, and are less concerned with accomplishment. Consistent with the traditional medical model, note that Type B was considered a default state, with no independent consideration as to what a healthy personality style might be.

Type A behavior is assessed by means of a structured interview or a questionnaire. In the standardized, **Structured Interview,** the interviewer asks people a number of questions and observes their responses. The manner of the response is often more important than the answers themselves. The speed, volume, and tenseness of the individual's

Figure 6-2 Type A Man. *(Copyright Howard S. Friedman. Drawing by Robin Jensen.)*

words are important, as are gestures, posture, and body movements. Voice analysis is also sometimes used. A hostile executive who was eating rapidly, hurrying others along in conversation, clenching his hands and teeth, and trying to do two things at once would surely be classed as Type A.

A common questionnaire measure of the Type A behavior pattern is called the Jenkins Activity Survey (JAS) (Jenkins, Zyzanski, & Rosenman, 1978). The measure consists of 52 multiple-choice items that inquire into a person's degree of impatience, job involvement, and competitiveness.

Does Type A behavior cause CHD? Many studies of people with CHD have found them to be more Type A than comparison groups who are disease free, and the early evidence was generally consistent with a causal interpretation (Siegel, 1984). In fact, a quantitative summary (using summary statistics) of the published research through 1984 found Type A behavior to be reliably associated with CHD, and the size of relationship was comparable to other CHD risk factors (Booth-Kewley & Friedman, 1987). The structured interview assessment was clearly superior to the JAS questionnaire in predicting CHD. However, the issue of retrospective versus prospective data collection rears its ugly head in the study of the Type A personality. Heart disease might cause people to report more time pressure or to act more competitively; diagnosed Type A coronary patients may be more likely to be selected for study; and there are also other possible confoundings.

Some prospective studies show a Type A effect, however. The Western Collaborative Group Study found that Type A (as opposed to Type B) predicted occurrence of

CHD across a decade. Furthermore, the Type A pattern also predicted subsequent (second and third) heart attacks as well as hardening of the arteries (Rosenman et al., 1970, 1975). This finding was confirmed to some extent by other prospective studies, including the Framingham Heart Study (Haynes, Feinleib, & Kannel, 1980) and the French-Belgium Collaborative Group (1982). Among previously healthy individuals, Type A behavior as assessed through a structured interview sometimes can predict the likelihood of subsequent CHD (Manuck, Kaplan, & Matthews, 1986; Matthews & Haynes, 1986), independent of other risk factors such as smoking and high blood pressure. But this finding has sometimes failed to replicate in large prospective studies (Schwalbe, 1990), and so questions remain unanswered. To address these inconsistencies, the concept of Type A has been further refined.

Hostility, Cynicism, Struggle

Review of past research suggests that the idea that the speed and job-involvement aspects of the Type A pattern are key aspects of coronary proneness may be incorrect (Booth-Kewley & Friedman, 1987; Miller et al., 1991). Instead, research now focuses more on hostility and other chronic negative emotional states (Miller, Smith, Turner, Guijarro, & Hallet, 1996). One program of research in this area is consistent with the idea that hard work can be healthy if it is in the context of a committed and meaningful devotion. In particular, it has been suggested that some individuals who are diagnosed as Type A may not be coronary prone, but rather may be misidentified due to behavioral similarities to individuals who are active, fast moving, dominant, and vigorous (Friedman, Harris, & Hall, 1984). Furthermore, some people labeled as Type B because they are soft-spoken, slow to speak, and passive may actually have repressed hostility and frustrated ambition.

Two independent investigations were conducted to test these hypotheses (Friedman, Hall, & Harris, 1985; Friedman & Booth-Kewley, 1987b). In the first study, men at high risk for CHD were divided into four groups on the basis of whether measures suggested they were healthy expressives, true Type A's, unhealthy unexpressives, or true (relaxed) Type B's. As predicted, the healthy expressives and the true type B's had less peripheral artery disease, less tension, and a less negative nonverbal emotional style than the two other groups. In other words, there may indeed be some healthy Type A's and unhealthy Type B's. Some people who work hard at a fast pace may be healthy; but on the other hand, some people who are slow moving and quiet may be disease prone if their manner is hiding some inner conflict.

The second study examined 100 men, half of whom had had a heart attack (Friedman & Booth-Kewley, 1987b). Again, healthy (expressive) Type A's and true (relaxed) Type B's were distinguishable from unhealthy (true) Type A's and unhealthy Type B's. This study also showed that the Structured Interview seems to take into account the negative emotional states that are relevant to CHD, but that the questionnaire JAS measure misses them. These studies led to more attention to the validity of the Type A/Type B construct. It now appears likely that only certain components of Type A (hostility and competitiveness), and not others (like hurrying and job involvement), are relevant to heart disease (Booth-Kewley & Friedman, 1987; Wiebe & Smith, 1997). Contempt, cynicism, and an alienated bitterness may be toxic (Friedman, Tucker, & Reise, 1995; Rosenberg, Ekman, & Blumenthal, 1998; Smith, McGonigle, & Benjamin, 1998).

Biobehavioral Mechanisms

Causal links between personality and heart disease become more believable as plausible physiological mediating mechanisms, so-called **biobehavioral mechanisms,** are discovered. That is, it makes sense to study psychological causes and interventions if we have some idea of how they translate into biological results. Although the nature of the atherosclerotic process and heart attacks is not completely understood, there are promising directions for investigation (McCabe, Schneiderman, Field, & Wellens, 2000; Krantz, Lundberg, & Frankenhaeuser, 1987; Williams, 1988). Basically, atherosclerosis involves the forming of fatty plaques in the arteries throughout the body, a process that can be affected by stress.

Attention has focused on the sympathetic nervous system and related neuroendocrine activity. Hostile, dominating men are more likely to show increased catecholamine response when subjected to environmental challenge, and higher blood levels of cortisol and testosterone in such situations (Guyll & Contrada, 1998; Pope & Smith, 1991; Williams et al., 1982). How could this lead to heart disease? Catecholamines (such as epinephrine) affect the activity of the heart and arteries, and so excesses may injure the lining (endothelium) of the arteries. This hemodynamic damage to the arteries may be (but is not necessarily) accompanied by chronic high blood pressure.

Catecholamines also affect the metabolism of fats (lipids), and it is these fats that are deposited on the arteries to form atherosclerotic plaque. Furthermore, these effects may be increased by the presence of corticosteroids, such as cortisol. This constellation of bodily changes associated with CHD is sometimes termed the **metabolic syndrome** and involves changes in insulin resistance, glucose tolerance, blood pressure, obesity, and cholesterol and triglycerides (dyslipidemia) (Hurwitz & Schneiderman, 1998). It is associated with the personality traits just discussed (Ravaja, Keltikangas-Jaervinen, & Keskivaara, 1996).

Experimental research on monkeys *(cynomolgus macaques)* also suggests links between atherosclerosis and both competitive behavior and sympatho-adrenal activation (stress). In aggressive males of this monkey species, striving for behavioral dominance combines with social instability induced by the experimenters by switching monkey group membership. In this circumstance, there is especially increased development of atherosclerosis in the presence of a high-fat diet (Kaplan & Manuck, 1998). Interestingly, when the monkeys are given a beta-adrenoreceptor blocker (a drug that blocks the effects of catecholamines), this intervention prevents this exacerbation of atherosclerosis. In short, this is experimental evidence for a direct role of sympathetic nervous system activity in the origin of coronary heart disease. Note, however, that physiology patterns, behavior patterns, and environment all combine to produce the health problem. It is generally *not* the case that a condition like chronic anger is associated with single physiological measures like high blood pressure (Suls, Wan, & Costa, 1995).

Although men die from CHD at younger ages than women, do women have analogous risks? Studies of female *cynomolgus* monkeys offer intriguing hints. Some female monkeys naturally have much lower social status than other female monkeys, and researchers also manipulate their social status by experimentally altering which (captive) monkeys must live together in social groups. Subordinate monkeys face more aggression, they must spend more time in fearful scanning of the social environment (monitoring the more powerful monkeys), and they are less likely to receive affiliative behavior (like being groomed). Importantly, they have more variable heart rates in response to the challenge of a novel environment, and they have greater coronary artery disease. Their ovaries do not work quite right, and these subordinate females also are hypercortisolemic (have high cortisol levels). In fact, their brains seem to adapt to the constant stress, and they are more prone to depression (Shively, 1998; Shively, Watson, Williams, & Adams, 1998).

Cholesterol

More than 1 in 20 adult Americans now take cholesterol-lowering drugs in an attempt to prevent heart disease. Bananas come with stick-on labels saying "cholesterol free!" Cholesterol, technically a type of solid alcohol, has become the most famous organic compound in health-conscious America. Serum cholesterol (cholesterol in the blood) is clearly associated with coronary heart disease: High levels increase the risk of disease. Since some foods, such as eggs, are high in cholesterol, some scientists have urged people to make drastic changes in their diets so as not to eat much cholesterol. However, the human body processes the cholesterol in food and makes its own cholesterol. In fact, many important chemicals, including all the steroid hormones, are derived from cholesterol; we cannot do without it. The level of cholesterol in the blood is affected by hereditary factors, by the amount of fat (especially saturated fat) in the diet, by exercise, and by stress. Avoiding eggs will by itself have little or no effect on serum cholesterol (Glass, 1977a,b; Krantz, Baum, & Singer, 1983; Thompson, 1985). However, controlling one's serum cholesterol level will have a beneficial effect on health.

It is interesting to consider the response of the medical establishment to the discovery of the link between high cholesterol levels and heart disease. What will the traditional medical model of disease predict? Intervene and directly remove the cholesterol from the blood! Sure enough, in recent years, cholesterol-lowering drugs (such as cholestyramine, clofibrate, and gemfibrozil) have been developed and prescribed. One of the better drugs, lovastatin, works directly on the liver, interfering with its production of cholesterol and so causing it to draw cholesterol out of the blood. However, these drugs are expensive and they often produce side effects, although it is now clear that they sometimes save lives. These drugs are supposed to be prescribed only when changes in diet, exercise, and stress management have failed to lower dangerously high levels of cholesterol. However, as we might expect, such drugs are fast becoming routine treatment, with the other key elements of cholesterol control being given little attention. In other words, while no one would quarrel with the use of these effective drugs to save lives, we can and should ask whether any particular drug is being properly used as compared to alternative therapies.

In short, although the precise mechanisms of heart disease are unknown, there is ample reason to suspect that the sympathetic-adrenomedullary system, the pituitary-adrenocortical system, and metabolism of lipids (fats) play a key role. They contribute to processes (physical and biochemical) that damage the artery walls. It could be, however, that these stress effects simply exacerbate another (undiscovered) disease process involving microbes or toxins that is key. Nevertheless, it makes physiological sense to think of a coronary-prone personality (Manuck, Kaplan, & Matthews, 1986; Stoney, Bausserman, Niaura, Marcus, & Flynn, 1999; Williams, 1988). And stress management must be an important part of coronary health care, since psychosocial therapy can reduce mortality rates in a high risk population (Powell & Thoresen, 1988).

THE DISEASE-PRONE PERSONALITY

Coronary-prone behavior is only one important part of a larger picture. To achieve a complete understanding of the relationship between personality and health, it is necessary to consider other aspects of personality and other diseases. To speak sensibly of a particular disease proneness (such as a "coronary-prone personality"), we need to know whether a certain type of personality is related to only one or to many diseases, and similarly we must discover whether a given disease is related to only one or to many aspects of personality. In other words, we must evaluate **construct validity.**

Unfortunately, researchers typically pick a single disease, such as heart disease, and look for its personality correlates. Even worse for purposes of construct validation, a researcher may pick only a single aspect of personality and try to relate it to a single disease. For example, a researcher may try to see whether repression leads to cancer, without seeing if repression also relates to other diseases.

Disease-Prone Traits

In addition to the hostility, cynicism, and chronic struggle postulated and documented to be relevant to coronary heart disease, researchers often focus on aspects of neuroticism, including especially anxiety and depression, and on introversion. Impulsiveness (a lack of conscientiousness) is taken up in the next chapter.

Neuroticism is a broad term for people who are generally more emotionally unstable, nervous, high-strung, and worrying. It is well known that people who are emotionally volatile can turn to unhealthy behaviors such as drinking, smoking, drug abuse, or overeating in an attempt to regulate their anxious states. It is also the case that neurotic people face and experience more stress. For example, in one study of the daily hassles of 42 men, those scoring high in neuroticism reported having more daily problems, reacted more to challenges, and reported being more distressed by ongoing problems than were the men who scored low in neuroticism (Suls, Green, & Hillis, 1998).

Introversion (the opposite of extroversion) is the broad term for people who are shy, submissive, and relatively unsociable and quiet. It is often postulated that introversion is unhealthy, but as we have seen and will see again, the issue is more complex than that.

Box 6-1   Assessing Personality and Assessing Health

"Depressive," "neurotic," "hypochondriacal," "anxious"—in research on personality and health, various psychological diagnoses are employed that seem to have a technical meaning. How are such concepts measured?

Psychologists have developed various criteria for determining whether an assessment is a good one. Most basically, a measure must be *reliable* or repeatable; the measure cannot give a different result every time the same thing is measured. Second, the measure must be *valid;* the measure must measure what it claims to measure and not something else. Assessments vary in how good they are, and insuring proper validity is especially difficult. The best measures have dozens or even hundreds of validation studies, which reveal what different scores mean.

What are some common measures? A well-known personality test is the MMPI, or Minnesota Multiphasic Personality Inventory. Respondents agree or disagree with a wide range of statement, and the items are scored in a standard way to produce a personality profile involving a number of dimensions, such as depression, hysteria, paranoia, and extroversion. For a focus on basic dimensions of normal personality, researchers often turn to the NEO Personality Inventory (NEO-PI). It measures five fundamental personality dimensions derived from factor analysis of how many people are described or rated.

Another commonly used scale is a symptom check list in which the participant is asked to indicate how often he or she experiences symptoms such as headaches, hopelessness, back pains, nervousness, and so on. The symptoms are then combined into primary dimensions, such as depression, anxiety, and somatization (bodily distress). A fourth popular assessment tool is the Millon Behavioral Health Inventory (MBHI). Developed for medical settings, this instrument provides information about the patient's likely style of relating to health care personnel in addition to assessing more general information about personality and disease-relevant states. Patients are asked to agree or disagree with statements such as whether they always have medical problems and whether doctors care only about money. Results include predictions about health-related attitudes and the likelihood of various psychosomatic inclinations. All these measures rely on people's self-reports, and so are subject to error or distortion.

On the illness side, there is a similar necessity for assessment techniques. Although it is usually clear if someone is living or dead, it is not always so clear which medical diagnosis to make or how severe the condition is. These assessments are often termed *health status* and constitute a field of study in themselves. Many determinations of health status must rely heavily on patients' self-reports, just as do psychological diagnoses. There is no medical tool that can measure headaches, chest pain, shortness of breath, frequency of dizziness, or ability to climb stairs.

Insufficient attention to construct validity has led some physicians and health researchers to skepticism about the whole field of personality and disease. An editorial in *The New England Journal of Medicine* asked, "What about heart attacks, peptic ulcers, asthma, rheumatoid arthritis, and inflammatory bowel disease? Are they caused by stress in certain personality types, and will changing the personality change the course of the disease?" (Angell, 1985, p. 1570). The answer given was that it is time to "acknowledge that our belief in disease as a direct reflection of mental state is largely folklore" (p. 1572).

That editorial was clearly an uninformed overstatement that ignored the vast amount and type of research in this area. To try to direct attention to appropriate information and promising areas, a quantitative review focusing on construct validity was done (Friedman & Booth-Kewley, 1987b). This review took several theoretically important and commonly studied aspects of personality—depression, anxiety, anger/hostility, and introversion/extraversion—and reviewed their relationships to five chronic diseases. To aid in simplifying the mass of data, the results were combined by using the quantitative techniques of meta-analysis.

Meta-Analysis

Meta-analysis is a method of quantitative integration of research studies (Glass, McGaw, & Smith, 1981; Light & Pillner, 1984; Rosenthal, 1984). It is a useful tool for combining the results of independent studies so that they may be more easily viewed. Meta-analysis helps us organize and understand the information we already have gathered in a series of studies. Meta-analysis cannot provide missing information when the appropriate controlled studies have not been conducted, but it can reveal interesting patterns. If the relationship between two variables in a study (like anxiety and disease) is expressed in terms of a correlation coefficient (Pearson r), then meta-analysis tells us how to combine the coefficients found in the different studies to get a summary statistic.

Concerning the possibility of a causal link between personality and disease, meta-analysis is useful in addressing three basic questions: First, is the bulk of the evidence encouraging, or should the matter be dropped and our attention turned elsewhere? Second, what is the size of any relationships being uncovered? This information is very important for designing research studies, for evaluating failures to replicate, and for ascertaining the possible economic savings that could be produced by large-scale interventions. Third, meta-analysis draws our attention to discriminant validity—namely the question of whether there are different patterns associated with different diseases or whether there is a more global, or general, "disease-prone" personality.

The five diseases selected for study were asthma, headaches, ulcers, arthritis, and heart disease. The quantitative summary results are presented in Table 6–1. The personality and disease categories are listed in the left column, followed by the combined correlation coefficient (r), the number of independent samples, and the statistical significance level.

Overall, the average magnitude of the relationship between personality problems (depression, anxiety, hostility) and disease was in the range of about .10 to .25, when

Table 6-1   Results of Meta-Analysis of Personality and Disease

Disease and Personality Variable	Combined r	No. of Samples	p
CHD and anxiety	.136	14	<.0000001
CHD and depression	.238	10	<.0000001
CHD and anger/hostility/aggression	.143	24	<.0000001
CHD and anger/hostility	.167	17	<.0000001
CHD and extraversion	.078	14	.0013
Asthma and anxiety	.362	13	<.0000001
Asthma and depression	.167	8	.00003
Asthma and anger/hostility/aggression	.224	10	<.000004
Asthma and anger/hostility	.258	9	<.0000001
Asthma and extraversion	−.132	5	.0297
Ulcer and anxiety	.186	7	<.000001
Ulcer and depression	.079	7	.0022
Ulcer and anger/hostility/aggression	−.031	8	.4623
Ulcer and anger/hostility	−.014	7	.4410
Ulcer and extraversion	−.174	7	.0044
Arthritis and anxiety	.200	9	<.0000001
Arthritis and depression	.156	11	<.0000001
Arthritis and anger/hostility/aggression	.147	3	.0006
Arthritis and anger/hostility	.158	3	.00008
Arthritis and extraversion	−.175	4	.0056
Headache and anxiety	.205	5	.00005
Headache and depression	.187	9	<.0000001
Headache and anger/hostility/aggression	.052	2	.3016
Headache and anger/hostility	−.013	2	.4502
Headache and extraversion	.089	9	.0216

Note: CHD = coronary heart disease; r is the correlation coefficient; p is the probability that the results could have been due to chance. Correlations (r's) above .10 are usually meaningful for public health purposes.

stated in terms of the correlation coefficient r. Although the magnitude of this relationship is small when compared to those found in certain realms of experimental psychology, it is moderate or high when compared to other medical risk factors. For example, in the well-known prospective Framingham and Western Collaborative Group studies of heart disease, the correlations between cholesterol and CHD, and between smoking and

CHD, were all under $r = .15$. (An r equal to zero indicates no association, whereas an r equal to 1.0 means a perfect association.)

The size of these relationships are quite important (Rosenthal & Rubin, 1982). In a population of hundreds of millions of people, true causal factors of this size refer to thousands of lives yearly. For example, a relative risk of two—meaning that those with the risk factor are twice as likely to suffer the disease than those with out it—would typically translate into a correlation coefficient of just about this magnitude. Or stated differently, assuming that there are equal numbers of people with and without the personality predictor (risk factor) in question, then an effect size of $r = .20$ could mean the difference between a 60 percent incidence of the disease (in people with the predictor) versus only a 40 percent incidence (in those without the predictor). In short, the risks associated with the personality factors investigated in this review seem to be of meaningful size and of the same order of magnitudes as more well-established risk factors.

The size of the relationships revealed in the meta-analyses helps explain in part why the links between personality and disease are such elusive phenomena for researchers. In evaluating research results, investigators first look to see if relationships are "statistically significant"; if not, the results may be due to random fluctuations in sampling, and so prove nothing. However, with a correlation of .15, a sample size of 300 is necessary for the effect to be statistically significant at the .01 probability level. Small-sample studies are therefore inappropriate for studying these links. Their statistical power is too low and they may miss relationships that are really there.

As can be seen in Table 6–1, all five personality variable categories were found to have positive and reliable associations with CHD. Higher levels of anxiety, depression, anger, hostility, aggression, and extraversion are associated with a greater likelihood of heart disease. Moreover, the combined effect sizes for anxiety, anger/hostility, anger/hostility/aggression, and depression are of similar magnitude to that observed between Type A behavior and CHD (Booth-Kewley & Friedman, 1987).

Asthma

Bronchial asthma affects about 1 in 20 Americans. It is characterized by obstruction of air exchange in the lungs. Muscle spasms and tissue swelling narrow the bronchial tubes, sometimes for days. Although it is often triggered by allergens, psychological factors have long been implicated in this disease. In traditional reviews, anxiety seems to be the most commonly mentioned psychological cause. The asthmatic personality is supposedly also dependent, aggressive, and neurotic, although the empirical evidence is weak (Weiner, 1977; Creer, 1978). Many asthmatics also suffer from other immunologic disorders (e.g., eczema, allergic rhinitis, and food allergies), making plausible the idea that psychological influences on the immune system play a role in asthma.

In the meta-analysis, the variables of anxiety, depression, anger, hostility, and aggression are positively and reliably associated with the disease, but higher levels of introversion are also associated with asthma. Given the known links between stress and respiration, it does seem likely both that negative or repressed emotions exacerbate (and possibly prolong) an asthmatic attack, and that people with chronic negative emotions, who face a biological predisposition to asthma and an asthma-inducing environment (such as one filled with cockroaches), are more likely to experience an attack (Lehrer, Isenberg, & Hochron, 1993; Pennebaker & Traue, 1993). Of course, losing one's ability to breathe can make anyone anxious, and it is important not to blame the victim. Yet, personality does seem to be one contributing factor.

Headache and Ulcers

Headache is one of the most common medical problems and accounts for tens of millions of medical visits yearly. Muscle contraction headaches (involving the muscles of the head and neck) are almost always attributed to psychological factors. Migraine headache, which involves abnormally dilated blood vessels in the head (and which is often treated by drugs that reduce this dilation), is also often attributed to psychological conflicts. The "migraine personality" is usually thought to involve anger, repressed hostility, and/or emotional tension, but the evidence is mixed (Adams, Feurstein, & Fowler, 1980). There is clearer evidence that migraine (and probably other headache) attacks are often *precipitated* by psychological stress (Bakal, 1977). In the meta-anlysis for headaches, anxiety and depression show positive and reliable associations with illness. This association is confirmed by a wide variety of other research (Breslau & Andreski, 1995; Breslau, Chilcoat, & Andreski, 1996).

Peptic ulcer, a lesion of the stomach or duodenum (part of the small intestine), affects 1 or 2 percent of the general U.S. population, often causing a burning sensation and severe pain. Ulcers seem to be caused by excessive levels of hydrochloric acid and/or problems with the protective lining of the GI tract. Psychoanalytic theorists, including Alexander (1950), posited a link between emotional conflict and various gastrointestinal disorders (perhaps captured in such expressions as "I'm fed up with you" or "You make me want to vomit"). One study of army recruits (Weiner, Thaler, Reiser, & Mirsky, 1957) gave rise to the general perception of a link between personality and ulcers. As mentioned in Chapter 5, it has long been known that gastric lesions (ulcers) in rats (personality unknown) can be brought about by psychological stress (Weiss, 1968, 1971).

The meta-analysis for ulcers found that associations with anger, hostility, and aggression are not significant, but chronic anxiety is clearly associated with ulcers. Subsequent research confirms a role for chronic stress and anxiety in risk for ulcers, but operating through a variety of the pathways discussed earlier in this chapter, including recall bias, distress, and a variety of unhealthy behaviors, as well as pituitary-adrenal axis activation and altered blood flow (Levenstein, 2000; Overmier & Murison, 2000; Soll & Isenberg, 1983).

Arthritis

The pattern of results that emerged for rheumatoid arthritis is similar to the pattern found for asthma, but the correlations are somewhat weaker. Rats susceptible to arthritis are known to have disruptions in their hypothalamic-pituitary-adrenal axis (McCann, Lipton, Sternberg, & Chrousos, 1998), so there is at least some plausible biological basis for these associations.

Emotional disclosure as well as stress appears relevant to the improvement or exacerbation of arthritis symptoms (Kelley, Lumley, & Leisen, 1997; Zautra, Burleson, Matt, Roth, & Burrows, 1994). Concerning extroversion, it is sometimes the case that extroversion is likely to be associated with the ability to obtain social support (Von Dras & Siegler, 1997). Arthritis is currently an active area of research.

Overall, the Friedman and Booth-Kewley (1987) meta-analysis reveals that the degree of consistency across diseases is quite remarkable. If there were a separate "arthritic personality," a "coronary-prone personality," and so on, we would expect clear evidence of independent associations between particular aspects of personality and the particular diseases. Such differences were not generally found. These findings do not rule out the possibility that such illness-specific, disease-prone personalities will eventually be discovered, but such a direction does not seem promising. The consistency of the findings also argues against the idea that specific diseases cause specific personality problems through direct physiological mechanisms (Stanwyck & Anson, 1986).

Depression

Perhaps the most striking and unexpected single relationship to emerge from the meta-analysis is the association between depression and disease (in particular, depression and the four diseases other than ulcers). In the 1980's, there was a great deal of attention directed to the role of anger and hostility in disease (Chesney & Rosenman, 1985), but insufficient attention given to depression. In fact, some prominent researchers reacted indignantly to the idea that something other than hostility was key. This meta-analysis and its follow-ups changed all that. There is now significant evidence for a causal link between depression and disease, including heart disease and stroke (Anda et al., 1993; Jonas & Mussolino, 2000).

Stress and depression are closely linked, though in complex ways. People who face severe stress as children (such as molestation or a troubling parental divorce) are at higher risk for disorders like depression later in life. There are many reasons that this may occur. For example, if these children grow up fearing other people, they may have less social contact and fewer sources of social support. But there is also evidence that an early biological predisposition may be created. For example, one study stressed baby rats when they were young and nursing, but otherwise let them grow up normally. These rats had much higher levels of stress hormones in their blood when they were later subjected to a stressor (mild foot shock) as adults (Ladd, Owens, & Nemeroff, 1996). People with major depression as adults may be reacting so severely to stress because their nervous systems were impaired by their early experiences, such as early sexual abuse. Here again we see that links between personality and disease are often not simple ones.

What about other diseases not included in the meta-analysis? Neurological diseases, such as epilepsy and multiple sclerosis, are usually not seen as "psychosomatic." However, since chronic stress affects the nervous system, perhaps even such conditions are affected by personality and stress. This line of thinking becomes more plausible when we note that sleep deprivation is a well-established trigger of epileptic seizures, emotional shock can trigger spasms of internal organs and vessels, and multiple sclerosis is thought to be at least partly related to immune system function. In fact, it has been argued that life stress and personality do indeed play a role in these neurological disorders (Grant, 1985; Stoudemire, 1995). Although probably not usually a primary cause of such diseases, psychological factors may help precipitate or may exacerbate the disease.

Cancer and Disclosure

Cancer (or the progression of cancer) is another disease that often has been examined in terms of its psychological correlates (Levy, 1985; Spiegel, Sephton, & Stites, 1998). There is special interest in the possible role of hopelessness, isolation, and depression. However, research on cancer has special difficulties. "Cancer" is actually a number of very different diseases—different types of cancer. Furthermore, the stigma of cancer makes its study especially susceptible to issues of "victim-blaming" and other unscientific influences. Cancer was therefore not included in the meta-analysis on personality and disease, but it is definitely worth examination from a psychological perspective.

For example, one study administered psychological questionnaires to 52 women with breast cancer and to a control group, and then followed up their health status after about two years (Jensen, 1987). Various relevant factors, such as the original disease state and physiological aspects, were controlled statistically. The results showed that the spread of cancer was greater among women who had a repressed personality and did not express negative emotion. Similar results were found in another study, a 10-year follow-up of breast cancer patients: Patients originally categorized as helpless, hopeless, and stoic were less likely to have a recurrence-free survival (Pettingale, 1984). Other evidence suggested the repression of anger or other emotions may also be relevant (Greer & Morris, 1975; Cunningham, 1985). In other words, some persons who appear easygoing and calm may be holding back internal conflicts.

In fact, there is a enough evidence along these lines (of the effects of repressed emotions on health) for health psychologist Lydia Temoshok and others to write of a **Type C,** or cancer-prone, personality (Temoshok & Fox, 1984; Temoshok et al., 1985). This Type C personality is sometimes thought to be the opposite of the Type A personality: The Type A person is hostile, tense, and controlling, whereas the Type C person is repressed, apathetic, and hopeless. However, there is no clear evidence proving that the emotional factors that may be relevant to cancer are different from those that predispose a person to other diseases. Stress, poor coping, and negative emotions are relevant to a variety of diseases.

Relatedly, it was proposed that the experience of a traumatic event can have long-range effects on health due to repression of thoughts about the terrible event (Pennebaker, 1985; Pennebaker & Beall, 1986). In one early study, it was found that people who avoided talking about the trauma (such as the death of a parent) were more likely to be ill many years later. In another series of studies (Emmons, 1986; Emmons & King, 1988), personality conflicts are conceptualized in terms of "personal strivings," or what a person is characteristically trying to do. For example, striving to "appear more intelligent than I am" may be in conflict with a striving to "always present myself in an honest light."

These kinds of internal conflicts have been shown to be related to negative feelings and depression, to physical symptoms like headaches and dizziness, and to making more visits to a health care center.

Subsequent research indicates that writing about past traumatic experiences can lead to more positive mental and physical health outcomes (Esterling, L'Abate, Murray & Pennebaker, 1999). Although research from several domains suggests that talking with friends, confiding to a therapist, or praying may improve health, increasing evidence reveals the efficacy of putting ones feelings into words, through writing. Understanding how this works is currently an active area of research in health psychology.

Finally, it is interesting to note that the description of an apathetic, stoic, unemotional, repressed individual fits the ancient Greek description of a "phlegmatic." Today, this condition is sometimes termed **alexithymia**—literally meaning the absence (*a*) of words (*lex*) for emotion (*thymos*) (Sifneos, 1973).

Again, it is important to remember that many factors undoubtedly contribute to these diseases and that there is a great danger of blaming victims for their own terrible diseases. Nevertheless, the area is obviously worthy of continued study. We will now continue this line of thinking by looking at personality influences on the immune system.

PERSONALITY AND THE IMMUNE SYSTEM

To design the "perfect" study of personality and disease, we would first randomly assign people to have a given personality, then intervene with various environments, and then follow them to see which diseases developed. Along the way, we would monitor physiological processes. Obviously, people cannot be randomly assigned to a given personality and environment and then followed. So no single study can ever "prove" a causal link. Hence, important evidence will have to come from physiological research that identifies disease mechanisms and shows how they may be affected by psychological factors.

This task is more difficult than it first appears because most serious chronic diseases are complex and not fully understood. Furthermore, psychological constructs like stress, personality, and coping are not readily operationalized in physiology labs: There are differences between the electric shocks administered to a dog or a pig and the emotional shocks administered to a recently bereaved widow.

The physiological and biochemical systems of the human body (the immune system, the endocrine system, the nervous system) are interrelated and often interdependent. As one system is thrown out of equilibrium, others may be affected, making study of psychophysiology and the immune system very complex. Nevertheless, progress has been made, beginning in the 1980s (Ader & Cohen, 1998; Solomon & Amkraut, 1983; Temoshok, 1990). As noted in the Chapter 2 section on **psychoneuroimmunology,** the immune system does not work independently but rather is closely tied to psychophysiological processes; it is subject to modulation by the brain.

In Chapter 2, we saw that T-lymphocytes, B-lymphocytes, and natural killer (NK) cells protect our body against invading microbes. These same parts of the immune system also look for and fight cancer cells in our bodies. The T-lymphocytes are primarily involved with cell-mediated immunity, such as fighting fungi, cancer, and viruses in the cells. When they are weakened (as they are in AIDS), cancers and certain infections grow rapidly. The B-lymphocytes, involved in humoral immunity, produce and release antibodies (immunoglobulins) that fight invading bacteria. However, since the immune system has many interacting components, there are many ways that it can be impaired; so it is difficult for investigators to know the exact "health" of the immune system at any given time.

As we have seen, stress reactions result in the release of high levels of corticosteroids (from the adrenal cortex). In turn, various animal studies suggest that high levels of corticosteroids interfere with the actions of the immune system cells. In other words, substances like cortisol have **immunosuppressive effects.** Furthermore, there is also evidence to suggest that cancer development is promoted by metabolic disturbance involving the utilization of fatty acids in the blood (Fox & Newberry, 1994; Antoni, 1987). But what are the links to psychological stressors?

Stress, Emotion, and Immunity

An important first study of the physiological consequences of bereavement, published in 1977, compared the endocrine and immune systems responses of healthy people who had unexpectedly lost their spouses to the responses of age-matched controls. They found decreased lymphocyte responsiveness at about two months after the bereavement (Bartrop et al., 1977). A subsequent investigation found that recently bereaved women had significantly lower natural killer cell activity than matched women whose husbands were healthy (Irwin, Daniels, Smith, Bloom, & Weiner, 1987). However, this research also found some hint that becoming depressed, not merely losing one's spouse, is related to the impaired NK activity.

This latter finding is consistent with a large body of evidence that suggests a relationship between depression and impaired immune system functioning (van Dyke & Kaufman, 1983; Locke et al., 1984; Levy, 1985; Miller, Cohen, & Herbert, 1999). Interestingly, most severely depressed patients have markedly increased levels of cortisol. Finally, there is evidence that degree of major life stresses (as measured by the Social Readjustment Rating Scale) is related to NK activity, possibly mediated by depression (Irwin et al., 1987).

In short, there is good reason to believe that negative life events and their associated chronic negative emotional states are closely tied to impaired immune system functioning, although a number of complicating factors, such as physical activity, sleep disturbances, and other behaviors, may also be involved (Cohen & Herbert, 1996). Furthermore, stressors can produce the symptoms of infection, as the immune system communicates to the rest of the body (Maier & Watkins, 2000).

Sometimes anxiety level is related to impairments in some kinds of immune function (but not others), but sometimes anxiety level is related to increased immune function. The apparent contradictions are likely due to the phases of immune response (its cyclic nature), the level of the anxiety for that person (whether stimulating or overwhelming), and other existing conditions and coping mechanisms (Cohen & Herbert 1996; Koh, 1995; Koh & Lee, 1998; Temoshok, 1990; Zorrilla, Redei, & DeRubeis, 1994). This research warns us against any simple interpretations. Stress and personality are influences on immune response, but there are rarely simple and direct links to subsequent disease. Further, the more complex the disease, the more complex will be the links.

Another program of work along these lines was initiated by the health psychologist John Jemmott and the personality psychologist David McClelland (Jemmott, 1987). Working in the area of motivation, they proposed an **inhibited power motivation syndrome.** People with this syndrome have a high need to influence others, but also have a high need to inhibit their own activity. For example, they may be effective but ruthless leaders who get their way but keep their cool. Several studies suggest that people with inhibited power motivation are more susceptible to illness; other studies suggest that such people may show lower immunologic competence—lower NK cell activity—especially when stressed (Jemmott & Locke, 1984; Jemmott, 1987). This work is reminiscent of the studies of repression and cancer, but comes at the question from the viewpoint of motivation. However, it has not been shown *how* and *why* motivation is related to the strength of the immune system, and the further direct link to illness has also not yet been made.

Figure 6-3 The effects of stress are felt before birth and continue throughout life, as stress during pregnancy can increase the likelihood of prematurity or low birth weight. These pregnant teenagers may face interpersonal, behavioral, or financial stress during their pregnancies, which may be ameliorated to some extent by social support. *(Reprinted by permission of the American Cancer Society, Inc.)*

A more current direction of such types of efforts is illustrated by a study of whether emotional expression of traumatic experiences influences immune response (Petrie, Booth, Pennebaker, & Davison, 1995). In this study, 40 medical students were randomly assigned to write either about personal traumatic events or control topics (irrelevant events) during four consecutive daily sessions. The day after completion of the writing, the students were given their first hepatitis B vaccination, with booster injections at 1 and 4 months after the writing. The results showed that participants in the emotional expression group showed significantly higher antibody levels against hepatitis B at the 4- and 6-month follow-up periods (compared with the control group). In other words, something about emotional disclosure (the writing intervention) affects the response of the immune system.

It has also been established that people with a history of non-melanoma skin cancer are at increased risk of cancer mortality from various kinds of cancer (Kahn, Tatham, Patel, Thun, & Heath, 1998). The researchers speculate that excessive exposure to ultraviolet rays from the sun, a known risk for skin cancer, may also play a role in suppressing immune function. But there is no evidence for such speculation, and indeed good levels of sunshine-induced vitamin D are cancer protective. A more likely explanation is that people under chronic stress are more likely to develop not only skin cancer but other cancers as well.

In sum, there is little doubt that psychological stress and coping can sometimes affect immune system function. There is, however, only scattered evidence that planned psychological interventions might promote healthy immunity in humans (Miller & Cohen, 2001). It is important to note that these processes are not necessarily specific to a particular disease. Although some researchers have argued that depression leads to cancer while anger leads to cardiovascular disease, there is no clear evidence that a specific pattern of psychological responses leads to a specific set of physiological reactions that in turn lead to a specific disease.

Elevation of either corticosteroid or catecholamine levels may result in immunosuppression and metabolic abnormalities, and such disturbances are relevant to both cardiovascular and neoplastic (cancerous) diseases (Cohen & Herbert, 1996; Crary et al., 1983; Fox & Newberry, 1984; Goodkin, Antoni, & Blaney, 1986). That is, disturbed psychological states and stress reactions are associated with dramatic changes in metabolism and in immune system functioning, and these alterations in bodily functions are plausibly considered to be relevant to the development and progression of various diseases. The key conceptual point is that there is dysregulation of internal systems: Feedback functions are altered and homeostasis breaks down. Or, as Cannon (1932) knew, stress disrupts the wisdom of the body.

IMPLICATIONS FOR SOCIETY

Chronic diseases such as asthma, arthritis, migraines, ulcers, cancer, and coronary heart disease afflict millions of Americans and cost billions of dollars in medical expenses and missed work. Of course, they also cause untold suffering. To the extent that these diseases are caused or promoted in part by psychological factors, tremendous opportunity exists for improving the health of the population.

The evidence we have reviewed gives clear reason to believe that associations between personality and disease are fact, not folklore. Furthermore, the size of such relationships seems comparable to that of other disease risk factors. Given the potential for tremendous gains, it is worth taking the chance that the strength of the causal links between personality and disease may be overestimated in some cases.

Interventions

What kinds of actions are possible? One good example of a possible action involves an intervention study regarding heart disease. In that study, over 800 victims of a myocardial infarction were randomly assigned to receive or not to receive psychological counseling to reduce Type A characteristics (M. Friedman et al., 1984; Friedman, Thoresen, & Gill, 1986). Over a period of several years, those receiving the counseling had a significantly reduced rate of recurrence of nonfatal MIs. Such studies are not perfect because some patients drop out and because the counseled patients and their counselors know who is getting the special treatment. Still, it is instructive to examine the nature of the psychological intervention used in this study. It consisted of extensive instruction in progressive muscle relaxation, modification of exaggerated emotional reactions, self-management, and establishment of new values and goals. Although such activities were aimed at reducing Type A behavior, it seems likely that such counseling was also effective in dealing with anxiety, hostility, and depression. Although this study yields valuable evidence concerning the role of personality in causing heart attacks, it would have been even better if other aspects of personality were measured and if other diseases were also included.

More generally, perhaps attention should be focused less on changing the Type A style of heart attack victims or the repression of cancer patients and more on the promotion of psychological well-being in the broader population. Although some aspects of personality are probably genetically based, personality forms and is modified by society. Children who grow up with abusive parents, with oppressive teachers, and then take boring or degrading jobs and encounter neighborhood strife are not likely to have the personalities that we regard as healthy. Currently, billions and billions of dollars (more than one-tenth of our gross national product) is spent on medical care for people when they become ill. Perhaps some of this money would be better spent on developing psychosocial conditions that encourage health (Albee, 1982).

In the short term, ameliorative action can be taken by health psychologists. Such action does not require that we know the precise physiological mechanisms, just as we can suggest changes in diet for heart patients without knowing the precise physiological mechanism linking diet and heart disease. Fortunately, there seems to be an obvious direction in which to begin. States of depression, and anger or hostility, seem to be unhealthy for a wide variety of diseases.

Since most previous studies do not examine more than one or two aspects of personality, it is impossible to tell whether each aspect acts independently of, interactively with, or redundantly with the other aspects. For example, there has been speculation about the deleterious physiological effects of chronic anger and the deleterious physiological effects of chronic depression. Are disease-prone people both angry and depressed, or angry but not depressed, or is either of these states sufficient? This is a question that deserves additional attention.

Furthermore, since the average correlations between personality and disease are of modest size, other factors are also relevant. Personality therefore needs to be examined in concert with social factors, genetic factors, and health-risk behaviors such as smoking. Additionally, work is needed on the definitions and assessments of the relevant aspects of personality and the diseases. Finally, physiological and emotional mediating mechanisms between personality and disease should be vigorously investigated. The nature of the mechanisms linking personality and disease will have direct implications for treatment—for example, whether personality affects the development or progression of disease, predicts the development or progression of disease, or does none of these things.

SUMMARY AND CONCLUSION

Personality-based explanations for health and illness, although very old and very plausible, have never been conclusively proven. There are many research traps and many threats to a valid inference, but there is also much evidence supporting a causal link. This chapter has taken a broad and comprehensive view of the issue, rather than focusing solely on specific diseases.

Different studies have used different personality measures, different disease criteria, different populations, and different control groups. These variations make simple interpretation difficult. However, this varied evidence does provide a degree of validity uncommon in psychological research. Furthermore, meta-analysis and a broad perspective direct our attention to the data, to the size of the relationships being uncovered, and to the overall picture. Any single finding (or failure to replicate) becomes less important. A single study might find a relationship that is not real, or can fail to uncover a relationship that is real.

It does not appear that different diseases each have different personality traits linked with them. Constructs such as the ulcer-prone personality, the coronary-prone personality, and so on may have to be revised. However, there may exist a generic "disease-prone personality."

The possible moderating role played by unhealthy behaviors has not been much studied, and the physiological processes linking personality and disease are still being explored. Work on the immune system and studies of metabolic disruption are very promising. Overall, the accumulated evidence is definitely not inconsistent with a causal role for personality. The empirical evidence is consistent across research domains, across diseases, and across a wide variety of methods. The size of the relationships between personality and disease is found to be comparable to that which exists between many well-known risk factors and disease. It is also interesting to note that there is no good evidence that most personality-to-disease links are created by disease-caused personality changes.

In sum, given existing evidence, it may be the case that Selye's general adaptation syndrome is close to the truth. Personality may function like diet: Imbalances can predispose one to all sorts of diseases. Such a conclusion is supported by the considerable evidence emerging from physiological studies. Although the precise physiological pathways appear to be very complex, psychological disturbance seems to produce systemic effects on immune system function and on metabolic processes, rather than effects on particular organs. Although we do not know enough at present to answer certain key questions about causality, we do know enough to begin to direct our efforts to improve the psychosocial health of the population.

Recommended Additional Readings

Friedman, Howard S. (Ed.). (1990). *Personality and disease.* New York: Wiley & Sons.
Friedman, Howard S. (Ed.). (1992). *Hostility, coping, and health.* Washington, DC: American Psychological Association.
Friedman, Howard S. & Schustack, Miriam W. (1999). *Personality: Classic theories and modern research.* Boston: Allyn & Bacon.
Pennebaker, James W. (Ed.). (1995). *Emotion, disclosure and health.* Washington, DC: American Psychological Association.

Key Concepts

disease-caused personality changes	Structured Interview
psychosomatic illness or	biobehavorial mechanisms
psychophysiological disorders	metabolic syndrome
biological third variables	disease-prone personality
psychophysiological reactivity	construct validity
cardiovascular reactivity	meta-analysis
introversion/extraversion	Type C behavior
method artifact	personal strivings
selection bias	alexithymia
coronary heart disease	psychoneuroimmunolgy
Type A behavior	immunosuppressive effects
Type B behavior	inhibited power motivation

Chapter 7

QUALITY OF LIFE
AND THE SELF-HEALING
PERSONALITY

Confirming a great sports comeback, Lance Armstrong won his second Tour de France bicycle competition in the summer of 2000. The 28-year-old Texan was cheered as he rode down the Champs-Elysees in Paris, smiling broadly. At the fin-

ish line, his wife brought him their 9-month-old baby son. "It's a great day for our family," Lance said. On the winner's platform, the band played "The Star Spangled Banner."

Lance had previously won an even greater race, a fight against cancer. He was diagnosed in 1996 with advanced testicular cancer. With less than a 40 percent chance of survival, Lance had a testicle removed, and underwent brain surgery and chemotherapy. (For the cancer story, see It's Not About the Bike: My Journey Back to Life, *by Lance Armstrong and Sally Jenkins, 2000).*

What did Lance Armstrong do after his grueling but triumphant ride through the Alps and Pyrenees? He attended a charity benefit for cancer research.

Is there any relation between the personality that could beat cancer and the personality that could win a 2,250-mile race across swathes of France, Germany, and Switzerland? Did it matter for the race that Armstrong's young son was dressed in a yellow racing jersey that matched his father's?

Thousands of pages are published each year answering the question, "Why did Ms. X become ill, and how can she be treated?" But little is asked about "Why did Ms. Y remain healthy?" Or, "Why did Mr. Z recover so well?" Each week, the prestigious *New England Journal of Medicine* publishes a "Case Record of the Massachusetts General Hospital," detailing the pathology of an unusual or informative patient's case. There is no corresponding "Case Record of a Person Who Remained Well Throughout a Long Life."

What Physicians Don't Say

The physician who does a fine job at implementing currently accepted medical treatments will usually not worry about individual differences among patients. For two 50-year-old women with similar breast tumors and normal physiological stamina, the same treatment will be instituted; if one soon dies of her cancer, the treatment failure is attributed to "probabilities." Few physicians can be concerned, as was psychosomatic researcher Franz Alexander (1950), as to why two patients with similar biological conditions responded so differently to medical treatment.

Many people are exposed to harmful bacteria (and other patho-microorganisms) but do not get sick. This exact situation was documented many years ago in a study by two pediatricians. They followed a number of families for about a year, doing throat cultures for strep bacteria every few weeks. They found that most of the strep infections did not produce any symptoms of illness! The strep bacteria by themselves could not cause illness. When the people were stressed, however, the strep illness was more likely to develop. On the other hand, of course, no one developed the strep illness without exposure to the bacteria (Meyer & Haggerty, 1962).

Many people regularly encounter various environmental and physiological challenges and yet never seem to become ill. Others recover quickly and "miraculously" from serious illness. These observations have led to intriguing studies that seek to determine the personality structures that characterize individuals who remain healthy under challenge, or who recover rapidly from illness. The self-healing personality is the subject of this chapter.

HEALTHY WORK

As we have seen, stress involves challenge, and challenge can be unhealthy. It therefore has often been assumed that the challenge of significant work is unhealthy. We are more likely to hear and say, "Relax, you are working too hard and getting too stressed" than we are to say, "Work harder, you are taking it easy and it is damaging your health!" Yet there is good evidence that challenge and involvement are often important aspects of good health.

The Hardy Executive

Some of the earliest evidence of the beneficial effects of challenge and involvement, especially if controllable, emerged from studies of the workplace. About two decades ago, an extensive analysis of business executives under stress in a large Midwestern firm examined the psychological differences between those who became ill and those who did not. Over a period of eight years, several key factors emerged, seen as constituting **hardiness** (Kobasa, Maddi, & Kahn, 1982; Maddi & Kobasa, 1984).

First, the executives' feeling of control was significant. Those who remained healthier did not feel powerless in the face of external challenges but instead had a sense of power. They believed that challenging situations could be dealt with through their own efforts.

On the other hand, one of the executives studied, "Andy," clearly lacked this sense of control. He appeared polite and eager to please, despite feeling increasing pressures of job responsibilities and job security. He carefully transmitted job orders from his superiors to his subordinates, but exercised little authority himself. He worried that his workload was getting out of control. At home, trouble was developing with his wife and children. Andy had an ulcer and was on a restricted diet. He experienced sleeplessness, appetite loss, and heart palpitations. Although only in his forties, he had a tendency toward high blood pressure. He lacked the strength of personality to cope with his job stress.

The second characteristic of executives who remained healthy was their commitment to something they felt was important and meaningful. Those individuals who felt committed to their work, the community, and their families were less likely to become ill. For example, one executive, "Bill," was seen as especially successful and healthy, even though his wife had been killed in an accident seven years earlier. He had a "twinkle in his eye" and a zest for his work. He enjoyed learning from his work, felt its social importance, and welcomed changes in the company as interesting and worthwhile.

Third, executives who did not become ill viewed life as a challenge rather than as a threat. They responded with excitement and energy. They were searching for novelty while remaining true to the fundamental life goals that they had already established. One of the successful, healthy executives, "Chuck," was involved in difficult customer relations work. As his company began reorganizing, Chuck reported feeling more challenge, but said it made his work that much more interesting and exciting. He was not threatened. Chuck is the kind of executive who views every problem as an opportunity to improve on the status quo.

This insightful research by Suzanne Ouellette Kobasa and Salvatore Maddi did much more than reveal specific characteristics that protected executive health. It also provided a framework for thinking about staying healthy. Subsequent research has further analyzed and described the personal characteristics that help a person remain well.

Healthy Lawyers

Lawyers face many challenges in their work—the duties are, by definition, adversarial, and the pace is fast. Impressions of self-healing have been suggested in two large studies of lawyers.

The first study involved 128 lawyers who were originally examined when they were in law school in the 1950s. At that time, they were administered a psychological test, which since has been refined into subscales, including the **Cook-Medley hostility scale.** Cook-Medley measures aspects of the disease-prone personality; of special interest are subscales that measure cynicism, hostile feelings, and aggressive tendencies. A sample item is "It is safer to trust nobody" (true or false).

By 1985, 13 of the lawyers (10 percent) in this study had died. As might be expected from population statistics, the deaths were due to heart disease, cancer, and diabetes. Was mortality related to personality? The results clearly showed that the higher one's choleric tendencies (being hostile and cynical), the greater the risk of dying over the 30-year period. In fact, the lawyers who scored at around the 75th percentile were about five times as likely to die as those who scored around the 25th percentile (Barefoot, Dodge, Peterson, Dahlstrom, & Williams, 1989). Unfortunately, we do not know much about the social environments and the other behaviors of these lawyers during this time period.

The second study of lawyers looked at 157 lawyers in general practice. First, the numbers of recent stressful challenges in their lives (such as hiring and firing staff members) were measured. Then, the lawyers reported illnesses and symptoms experienced during the past year. Finally, their personalities were assessed. Contrary to pop psychology theories, the happy-go-lucky, lackadaisical lawyers were not especially healthy (Kobasa, 1982).

The healthiest lawyers were those who felt a greater sense of personal power, and who were involved with and vigorously committed to their work. The healthy lawyers actively and positively addressed the challenges they faced. Interestingly, these healthy lawyers did not talk much to others about their work; it seemed as if professional demands and training precluded use of this usual means of maintaining psychological balance. Instead, they drew strength from their professional successes.

In short, given the special challenges of practicing law, certain personal characteristics appear more protective against stress-related physiological imbalances. An aggressive, choleric manner is not healthy, but neither is a relaxed, laid back style. Instead, active, involved lawyers, with a positive motivation to do a good job, seemed most likely to be healthy.

QUALITY OF LIFE

As we have seen repeatedly in this book, conceptions of health and applications to health care have been dominated by the traditional biomedical model of disease. Health economists have also had an influential voice in designing health care. Thus, common outcome measures involve the presence or absence of organic disease, time lost at work, costs of medical care, and longevity. For most physicians, disease, incapacity, and death are the bottom lines.

Ironically, for most people, their feelings or subjective state of health and well-being are most important. Most people are more concerned with being involved and self-fulfilled than they are with whether they will spend three months in the hospital before they die, or whether they will die at age 83 rather than age 80. (Of course, this perspective sometimes changes for someone who is now 79 years old.) So, to address such issues, health psychologists and many public health researchers prefer to talk about **quality adjusted life year (QALY)** (Kaplan, 2000). As its name suggests, QALY simultaneously considers longevity, morbidity, symptoms *and* psychosocial functioning.

In many cases, quality of life is related to medical and physiological assessments of functioning (Kaplan et al., 1997). That is, you are more likely to have a good quality year if you have less biomedical (disease) impairment, but this is not true in all cases. At best, you report optimum functioning without symptoms, and at worst, you are dead. In between, people have periods of symptoms and/or impairments. These can be quantified, taking both quality and quantity into account. For example, you may have asthma attacks that make you anxious and tired and keep you out of work several days each month. Importantly, it has been found that physiological and psychoemotional symptoms cluster together (covary) (Schwartz, Kaplan, Anderson, Holbrook, & Genderson, 1999). As we have argued, separating them is a false dichotomy.

But what about the other side of the coin? That is, to what extent does a good quality (psychosocial) life mean that you will have less biomedical (disease) impairment? Why not focus first on the important biopsychosocial elements of well-being? This is precisely the focus of the new approaches in health psychology on self-healing. It is also consistent with a growing concern with positive aspects of psychology.

Growth Psychology

There are indications, from fundamental research in personality psychology, that the psychological characteristics found in Maddi and Kobasa's work are indeed important in moderating the stress-illness relationship. Many supporting ideas come from basic theories of personality. Growth psychology (Schultz, 1977) and the work of the famous humanistic psychologist Carl Rogers, for example, fit into this framework quite well. Rogers (1961) sees the same characteristics (described in Kobasa's studies) as necessary for the development of a healthy personality and a fully functioning person. The "mentally" healthy personality is able to maintain a healthy physical condition as well.

In fact, the construct of hardiness has not yet been fully discriminated from other related constructs. For example, it has been suggested that lack of hardiness is equivalent to general maladjustment and that the specific components of hardiness have not yet been adequately specified through empirical research (Funk & Houston, 1987; Hull, Van Treuren, & Virnelli, 1987). In other words, although research generally supports the notion that a hardy personality is less prone to illness, it is by no means settled exactly what the hardy personality is. Sometimes, quality of life is best analyzed by examining four aspects: physical, psychological, social, and environmental (Power, Bullinger, & Harper, 1999).

HEALTHY CONTROL

Philip Carret was a well-known investment advisor who, shortly before his death, was managing investment portfolios of $225 million. Carret arrived in his office on 42nd Street in New York City early every morning, nothing remarkable until you realize that Carret was 92 years old. He started money management in the 1920s! A magazine described Carret as follows: "He chuckles often; his personality radiates benevolence. When his stocks go down, Carret remains completely unruffled. Indeed, his friends do not detect any chink in his temperamental armor" (Train, 1989).

In Kobasa's studies of executives and lawyers under stress, she found that those who remained healthier did not feel powerless in the face of external forces, but instead had an **internal locus of control** (Rotter, 1966). Internal locus of control refers to the generalized tendency of people to believe that whatever happens to them is under their own control. Locus of control is also directly relevant to whether a person will engage in healthy behaviors, although it may be difficult for a person to change his or her orientation (Wallston, 1992; Wallston & Wallston 1978).

Mr. Carret had, as any investment advisor has, of course, very little control over his work world. Sometimes, the unexpected and the terrible will occur. Ships can sink and stocks can crash. So how could he have had such a healthy personality at age 92? The answer is that it is not simply control over the world that is important to health. This is where the studies of rats revealed only part of the truth about humans. For people, it is a personal *feeling* of control, a sense that one can do as much as anyone can do, that is key.

A wild sense of optimism is not necessary for a healing personality. Rather, a sense that one can control one's own behaviors is most important. Mr. Carret could gather all the financial information available, and he had complete discretion over which investments to make. In this sense, he was in complete control, even if the investments turned sour. This basic point is one of the most misunderstood in this area. It is a gross oversimplification to assert that more control is better (Amirkhan, 1998).

Choice is therefore important to health. A good example of loss of choice can arise when a worker is involuntarily laid off from work. One interesting classic study compared employed workers to workers who were laid off for long periods due to plant closings and who remained out of work. In terms of psychological states, many of these unemployed men felt a lowered self-esteem and a loss of control. They thought they had nowhere to turn. In terms of emotional reaction patterns, the unemployed men were more depressed, anxious, angry, and irritable. These emotional states are in marked contrast to the investor, Mr. Carret, who "radiated benevolence." In terms of physiological responses, the unemployed workers showed detrimental disturbances in blood pressure, cholesterol levels, blood sugar, and hormone levels. Rates of arthritis and ulcers increased. It was clear that those workers with a high perceived sense of control over their lives remained healthier, both mentally and physically (Cobb & Kasl, 1977).

Outside of prisons, it is hard to imagine a situation with less control than that faced by elderly residents of a nursing home. They have no job, limited choices, and sadly, little social value. Are such residents doomed to deterioration and early death? Often yes, but a series of studies by psychologist Judith Rodin demonstrated that even minor interventions that increase the degree of control felt by nursing home patients can improve their health. Such interventions can be applied to almost all patients (Rodin, 1986).

Competence and Proactive Coping

Why is a sense of control so important? It seems that people have a basic motivation to gain a sense of mastery over their environments. Many years ago, the Harvard psychologist Robert White called it a motivation towards *competence*. Most people need to try to predict what will happen in their world. It is distressing and injurious to health to have responsibility but no sense of control. A healthy work environment is one that provides a challenging, socially valued job and the resources and support with which to do the job. It does not matter that the job is sometimes very difficult.

In a conceptual analysis of the processes through which people anticipate or detect potential stressors and act in advance to prevent them or to mute their impact, health psychologists Lisa Aspinwall and Shelley Taylor (1997) distilled five stages of this process, termed **proactive coping.** First, there is resource accumulation. This involves gathering time, money, friends, and so on, to be ready for a challenge. Second, there is recognition of potential stressors. The person may watch the environment and think about the future.

Third, there is the process of making an initial appraisal. A proactive coper must define the problem or make sense of the challenge. Prior experience or access to a relevant expert is helpful here. A person must also manage his or her emotions and direct them towards the challenge. Fourth, there are preliminary coping efforts. A person must understand the severity and potential consequences of the impending threat, and feel that he or she has the self-efficacy to address the challenge. Fifth, there is elicitation and use of feedback concerning initial efforts. A person using proactive coping will see how things are going and will change strategies as necessary. Note that blind optimism is not likely to be useful.

Control When III

> When I entered the hospital, I felt I was rapidly losing control of my life.

These words can be found in any number of books by cancer patients. For people who are already seriously ill, many of the issues surrounding the healing personality come together in hospitals.

The word *hospital* derives from the same root as the word *hospitality,* but hospitals are not very hospitable places to be. Modern hospitals are organized with two goals in mind. The first is to bring together in one place all the equipment and personnel—diagnostic equipment, life support equipment, treatment equipment, physicians, nurses, technicians—to assist a body that has lost the ability to heal itself. The second goal of a hospital is to make efficient use of a doctor's time.

In hospitals, patients lose control over what and when they eat, what they wear, when they sleep, and whom they can see. They have little say about who can touch them or when they can receive pain control medication. Some of these losses are necessitated by the demands of their disease, but most are not. Although near-miraculous treatments sometimes take place in hospitals, and although the staffs are dedicated and hardworking, hospitals are not very healthy places from a psychological point of view.

Radical changes should be wrought in hospitals, and some reforms are already being made in response to pressures from social scientists. The best example of change concerns labor and delivery. Not that long ago, a woman in labor would be isolated from her husband, confined to bed, and often heavily anesthetized. The newborn baby was removed to a glass-enclosed nursery, away from the parents. Visiting hours for other family members were severely restrictive. All this was thought to be in the best "medical interest" of the mother and baby. It was instead a misjudgment. Today, many women can have their babies in homey hospital "birthing" rooms; their families can be present and they can feel comfortable and "at home." Even though high-tech medical interventions are available for emergencies, the women feel more in control.

Regular hospital rooms and procedures should be similarly altered. In some cases, patients need special treatment or protection that necessitates extraordinary confinement. But in most cases, patients could have more control over what they wear, when and what they eat, who visits, and when they will sleep. Hospital staff needing to enter the room could introduce themselves and explain what they need to do. The result would be healthier patients and happier staff. This is not to minimize the suffering and the life-and-death procedures that go on in hospitals. But a proper psychosocial climate will enhance rather than interfere with the usual medical treatment.

Some patients develop a somewhat odd type of perceived control. They have learned to give up decision-making to their caretakers when ill—at first to their parents and now to their doctors. Some such patients do quite well for a while by insisting, "Whatever you say, doc." Again, the sense of choice is relevant—they have voluntarily given up power to the physician. In general, though, this strategy is less flexible in the long run. For the most severely ill patients, high control over treatment can result in poorer adjustment (Eitel, Hatchett, Friend, Griffin, & Wadhwa, 1995).

In sum, for most people, a sense or feeling that they are in control is healthy. For some people, the feeling that someone else is temporarily taking care of them can also be healthy, especially if they cannot realistically be expected to exert control themselves. In general, the more people feel self-confident, in control of their lives, and engage in proactive coping, the healthier the population will be.

COMMITMENT

When Natan Sharansky was convicted of treason in Moscow and was sentenced to many years at hard labor, his real crime was that he was a Jewish activist who was trying to emigrate to Israel from the (former) Soviet Union. At the end of his trial, whose outcome had been predetermined, Sharansky stood up in court and addressed the following remarks to the observers:

> Five years ago, I submitted my application for exit to Israel. Now I'm further than ever from my dream. It would seem to be cause for regret. But it is absolutely otherwise. I am happy. I am happy that I lived honestly, in peace with my conscience.

Sharansky survived many years in Soviet prison and was eventually permitted to emigrate, in good health. While waiting, he did what he could, with help from his wife Avital, to advance his cause.

Although few westerners face the challenges Sharansky faced, almost everyone is subject to environmental pressures. Yet many hard workers thrive anyway. Exactly opposite to what writers about workaholism and the Type A personality often claim, living life to the fullest seems to provide protection from disease, even though the pace is sometimes hectic. A key element of this healthy style, however, involves a commitment to an ideal greater than oneself.

Not Workaholism

Mohandas K. Gandhi (also called Mahatma, or "Great Soul") was one of the greatest workaholics of all time. He was not sickly, although he spent over 2,300 days in prison and endured numerous self-imposed fasts. On the contrary, he had the personal strength and commitment to be one of the most influential leaders of the 20th century, and perhaps of all time. He pioneered nonviolent political resistance *(satyagrapha)*, instituted numerous social reforms, and won political freedom for India. He was assassinated in his 78th year.

What defined Gandhi's life was a commitment to principle. As he aged, he grew more and more content with his life, but remained humble. He certainly was not blindly optimistic, carefree, or lackadaisical.

Various studies document that alienation is unhealthy. Obligation and dedication are healthy. Some people find this commitment in religion, others in philosophy. Other people seek political reform. Some people simply have a hobby, such as preserving old cars or old trees or old books. What they have in common is a sense of purpose.

Figure 7–1   Although Mohandas K. Gandhi (also called Mahatma or "Great Soul") was one of the greatest workaholics of all time, he was not sickly. His life was defined by a commitment to principle, and he is a good example of Friedman's concept of the *self-healing personality.*

Remember that a key characteristic in Kobasa's study of executives who did not become ill involved their commitment to something they felt was important and meaningful. Those workers who felt committed to their work, social institutions, interpersonal relationships, and families were less likely to become ill. They also had a strong commitment to themselves and were able to recognize distinct values, goals, and priorities. By being committed to other aspects of life, executives who remained healthy were able to see that work was not the only thing that defined them as people.

Japanese society is known for fostering commitment to hard work in general and to one's company in particular. This commitment is healthy up to a point. But it also can be carried to an unhealthy extreme. Many competitive Japanese are now working longer and longer hours, with a consuming passion. The result? Japanese workers are now concerned about *pokkuri byo*—sudden death—and *karoshi*—death from overwork. With little effort spent on anything but work, the workers lose their equilibrium. Emotional reaction patterns change from pride and contentment to distress and fatigue, and general homeostasis begins to break down. Work is harmful when it loses its reason for being.

CHALLENGE

As in most proactive coping, workers who do not become ill view life changes as positive challenges rather than as threats. They respond with excitement and energy. They are cognitively flexible, but they do not engage in irresponsible adventurousness. Rather, they search for novelty while remaining true to their fundamental life goals.

Boredom puts one at higher risk for disease. People who are constructively challenged find it easier to remain healthy. Yet, many health promotion efforts do not appreciate this fact. Middle-aged cholerics are advised to slow down, retire, take it easy, and rest. Starting down this path may lead them to dwindle and subside right into a "rest" home.

The runner, Mary Decker Slaney, who broke four world records, faced many extreme stresses of competition. Yet she stayed healthy and kept competing. When asked why she runs, she answered, "I love it. Running is something I do for myself more than anything else." This is the healthiest view of challenge—something that brings positive emotions and a sense of personal triumph.

Boredom is a warning sign that health problems may be on the way. The German philosopher Arthur Schopenhauer, in his *Essays on Personality,* said that the two foes of human happiness are pain and boredom. Healthy personalities take risks appropriate to their personal strengths and individual situations.

Emotional Training

When an athlete begins training, there is a period of struggle, weakness, and pain. A runner or water skier will have sore legs, a weight lifter will have sore arms, and they will all feel fatigue. Soon, however, their muscles grow, and they will be stronger and more proficient performers.

A similar situation occurs as our bodies fight an infection or other disease. Certain physiological systems weaken, while others go into emergency response mode. As the disease is slowly conquered, however, the systems return to a homeostatic state, often stronger than ever.

Not surprisingly, an analogous sort of training occurs in the self-healing personality. Emotional balance can also become "fit" and "hardy." Individuals who seek out moderate emotional challenge may initially feel weak and discouraged, they may feel fatigued, and they may feel emotional pain. But this pain or struggle in the short run enhances their emotional stability in the long run. Contrary to some simplistic advice to "avoid stress," the experience of moderate challenge can help condition healthy emotional responses.

Physiological research supports this view. Arousal reduction is not necessarily healthy. Rather, a kind of physiological toughness can develop in competitors that serves to buffer the effects of future struggles. This is especially true for playful, challenge-seeking individuals (Dienstbier, 1991; Martin, Kuiper, Olinger, & Dobbin, 1987).

Walter Cannon, who developed the idea of homeostasis, emphasized that the body has developed a margin of safety. By this, Cannon meant that the body is not built with what he termed *niggardly economy,* but rather has allowance for contingencies, that we may count on in times of stress. The lungs, the blood, and the muscles have much greater capacity than is ordinarily needed. The liver, pancreas, stomach, and other digestive and metabolic centers can be seriously damaged and yet still sustain life. And so on. In other words, the body naturally prepares itself for the rare "extra" challenge.

So, we now have some answers as to why only some people drop dead from emotional shock. The model originally proposed by cardiologist Bernard Lown appears applicable. Lown proposed a three-part explanation to account for the variability in sudden cardiac death after encountering stress. First, some electrical instability must already be present in the heart muscle; this is often, but not always, due to partially blocked arteries (atherosclerosis). Such people may also show mental stress-induced ischemia (inadequate blood flow leading to low oxygen state) upon testing. Second, the person must be feeling a pervasive emotional state, such as depression. Third, there must be a triggering event, such as the loss of a job or the death of a loved one, that challenges the person's sense of meaning (Jiang et al., 1996; Lown, 1979).

The 19th-century philosopher and psychologist William James, who anticipated much of our modern scientific understanding of emotional responses, succinctly summed up this idea of emotional training when he advised, "Keep the faculty of effort alive in you by a little gratuitous exercise every day. That is, be systematically ascetic or heroic in little unnecessary points, do every day or two something for no other reason than that you would rather not do it, so that when the hour of dire need draws nigh, it may find you not unnerved and untrained to stand the test" (James, 1890, ch. 4).

HEALTHY SUBTYPES

Self-healing people have an inherent resilience, but they are not identical. They share an emotional equilibrium that comes from doing the right combination of activities appropriate for the individual.

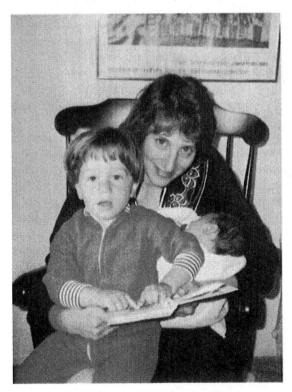

Figure 7–2 Females may have evolved special additional means of responding to challenges and threats. They may focus more on tending to their young and creating associations with others to provide resources and protection, a response termed *tend-and-befriend. (Photo by Howard Friedman.)*

It is useful to think about two major types of self-healing people. The first is the more active, gung-ho type. This includes the busy but confident lawyer and the hard-working, fulfilled executive. These people actively seek out stimulation, are highly extraverted, and tend to be spontaneous and fun-loving.

The second main type of self-healing involves the more calm, relaxed type. In American society, it is a person who is active, alert, involved, and responsive, but calm, philosophical, and bemused. This is serenity. Although these people also enjoy the presence of others, they are more likely to have a few close friends than a wide gang of party-goers.

These two types of healthy people have different optimal levels of stress. For the second, more reserved and content type of person, it is better to have conflicts resolved and stimulation under control. For the first, more excitement-seeking type of healing personality, a higher level of challenge is healthier.

In line with this way of thinking, research suggests that these two types of people have different tendencies toward negative emotions and stress hormones in similar situations. The low-key, goal-oriented individuals show more distress and greater release of stress hormones when challenges remain unresolved. The more spontaneous and arousal-seeking individuals, on the other hand, are especially likely to be distressed by a lack of stimulation and are threatened only when challenges become too much to handle. Thus, here again we see that blanket health recommendations for the whole population can lead to serious problems. The individual must also be considered.

Gender Differences: Tend-and-Befriend

As more attention is being paid to women's health issues, increasing attention has turned to gender differences in staying healthy. Both men and women use the fight-or-flight physiological response to stress (see Chapter 2). In addition to the catecholamine release, an organism under attack will often fight or flee for survival. But, in most mammal species, it is the males who are most concerned with aggression and defense. The females, in contrast, are often especially invested in pregnancy, nursing, and raising the offspring.

Females, therefore, may have evolved special additional means of responding to challenge or threat. They may focus more on tending to their young and creating associations with others to provide resources and protection. This biobehavioral response has been termed **tend-and-befriend** (Taylor et al., 2000). As other research has shown, females are generally more nurturing and affiliative than males, and one might speculate that this is part of the reason that women outlive men.

Although both males and females show similar responses from the sympathetic nervous system and the pituitary-adrenal system when challenged, females also have a strong, biologically-based attachment system. The key hormone here may be **oxytocin,** which has known roles in pregnancy and child-rearing as well as in stress (Panksepp, 1998). Oxytocin, a peptide hormone from the hypothalamus secreted by the pituitary, is secreted, for example, when a nursing mother hears the distress cry of a hungry infant; it facilitates the let-down, milk-flow response. Although not much is yet known, the oxytocin system may provide a key physiological basis for the tend-and-befriend response.

OPTIMISM

A related approach might be summed up as "positive thinking." There is a good deal of evidence suggesting that optimism is sometimes beneficial to health (Scheier & Carver, 1987). Optimism is the general expectation that good things will happen.

In one study, dispositional optimism was assessed on the day before participants had coronary bypass surgery. Results indicated that members of the hospital's staff judged the optimists as showing a faster rate of recovery from the surgery, and the optimists reached certain recovery milestones (such as walking around their rooms) sooner. Optimists seem to cope better, try harder, and take better care of themselves (Aspinwall & Taylor, 1992; Lin & Peterson, 1990; Taylor et al., 1992).

Faster recovery with a positive outlook may also be a result of improved immune system functioning as stress is reduced (Kiecolt-Glaser, Page, Marucha, MacCallum, & Glaser, 1998). However, as with hardiness, it is not yet clear how optimism differs from a variety of related constructs that assess a person's general degree of psychological adjustment.

Optimistic Bias

The other side of the coin of optimism is what can be called **optimistic bias,** or unrealistic optimism or positive illusions (Taylor & Brown, 1994; Weinstein, 1988). This bias involves the faulty belief that negative events are less likely to happen to us than others. For example, we often assume that "people" who do not eat fruits and vegetables are more likely to get cancer, but we may be surprised when the relationship applies to us. Further, if we are too optimistic, we may not take precautions (Peterson, Seligman, Yurko, Martin, & Friedman, 1998; Tennen and Affleck, 1987), or we may not cooperate with medical treatment.

SALUTOGENESIS AND COHERENCE

Going a step further, the medical sociologist Aaron Antonovsky proposed a general theory of **salutogenesis**—a theory of how people stay healthy (Antonovsky, 1979, 1987). He points out that everyone is subject to environmental pressures, but some people thrive anyway. At all times, we are more or less healthy. Rather than asking what causes someone to become ill, Antonovsky asks first what causes a person to remain or become more healthy. Central to successful coping with the challenges of the world is what Antonovsky calls a **sense of coherence**—the person's confidence that the world is understandable, manageable, and meaningful.

According to this approach, the world must not necessarily be controllable, but controlled. That is, someone with a strong sense of divine order (e.g., that he or she is working in concert with God's wishes; Wallston et al., 1999) might be high on the sense of coherence. Thus, Antonovsky's approach is more encompassing than other, similar approaches. The salutogenic orientation leads one to think in terms of those factors that promote health. Although there are daily threats to well-being, it is an achievement to stay healthy. This point may seem obvious when stated this way, but it is actually not the normal way we think about these matters. Instead, we generally assume that the normal or default state is to be healthy, and that it is unusual to be ill. We thus tend to overlook the personality factors that promote a state of health.

Coherence

Viktor Frankl (1962), the existential philosopher and therapist, developed his theories of a healing personality not in a large corporation studying executives, but rather as an inmate in a Nazi concentration camp. Although most inmates died, the quickest to go were those who had their sense of identity and purpose taken away from them. On the other hand, survival was more likely for those who tried living in a meaningful way, even in dire straits.

A person's sense of dignity has more than psychological and ethical importance. It is also an aspect of health. Lack of attention to this crucial factor during medical treatment seems to be what angers cancer patients the most. Much more distressing than the cancer itself is the sense of *being* a "cancer," a "tumor," a "disease." Once a sense of dignity and meaning is gone, the will to live may disappear as well.

Again, the world must not necessarily be controllable, but ordered, in the grand scheme of things. For example, Antonovsky describes the case of a male survivor of the Nazi holocaust, now living in Israel. As a Jewish teenager in Nazi Europe, this individual was quite pessimistic, doubting that he would survive. Yet he had no sense of personal affront or distress—he saw all the Jews in the same sinking ship and carried on with his life as best he could (including resistance efforts). After the war, it seemed natural to him that he would go to Israel and start a new life. This healthy man was hardly an optimist; rather, he had a remarkable ability to take extraordinary challenges in stride.

People with a sense of coherence perceive less stress in their lives and cope better (Flannery & Flannery, 1990). One study examined the relevance of sense of coherence to health-relevant outcomes of older adults facing relocation to new housing. Sense of coherence was measured with Antonovsky's (1987) scale, a self-report measure designed to assess an individual's belief in the manageability, controllability, and meaningfulness of the environment. It was found that those people facing this stress with a low sense of coherence were most likely to have poorer immune function (Lutgendorf, Vitaliano, Tripp-Reimer, Harvey, & Lubaroff, 1999).

This understanding of meaning and dignity, more common among anthropologists and European thinkers than among ethnocentric American scientists, adds an important new twist to our comprehension of health maintenance. For self-healing people, life matters. In their own ways, individuals come to a view of life as ordered and clear, rather than as chaotic and inexplicable. In their own ways, they are intact, thriving protagonists, not isolated, alienated drifters.

THE SELF-HEALING PERSONALITY

An incredible story about Felipe Garza was reported throughout the press. Felipe was a 15-year-old boy, living in California, who fell in love with a 14-year-old named Donna. With echoes of Romeo and Juliet, it soon developed that Donna was dying of degenerative heart disease. Felipe, who seemed in fine health himself, went to his mother and told her that when he died, he wanted Donna to have his heart.

Less than a month later, Felipe suffered a cerebral hemorrhage—a burst blood vessel in his brain—and he died. As he had requested, his heart was transplanted to his girlfriend Donna by surgeons in San Francisco.

Except for some investigation of cases of voodoo death, no one has much studied the idea of a "will to die." It is certainly not apparent how a teenager could will himself a stroke. Puzzling cases like Felipe Garza are useful in stretching our thinking on these issues. It is plausible that we are *underestimating* the powers of self-healing.

Although we hear little about healthy people developing a will to die, the idea of a "will to live" is common both in popular culture and in medical circles. As we saw in Chapter 4, all sorts of examples describe cases of patients who hear some bad news, show some far-off look in their eye, lose the will to live, and quickly succumb; these cases are compared to individuals who "make up their minds" that they will beat their illness.

The will to die involves the disruption of a physiological process to such an extent that it cannot be restored—a passage beyond the point of no return. But the will to live involves growth. It concerns the stimulation of complementary physiological processes that correct the disturbance. It is interesting to note that there is no middle ground—stagnation is unhealthy. Body processes are dynamic and always active. If you are not living, then you are dying.

Most people will accept a description of a sports match in which "willpower" makes the difference. Without any qualms, we accept that intangibles can affect the outcome. The same kinds of intangibles likely can affect health.

For several decades in the mid-20th century, Harry Hoxsey, a former coal miner, sold a "successful" cure for cancer. Hoxsey's clinics spread to seventeen states as patients testified as to the miraculous cures brought on by his potions. Hoxsey's cure for cancer "worked" for some people because it stimulated their bodies' own self-healing systems. The Hoxsey potion was an extraordinary placebo. Unfortunately for Mr. Hoxsey, it did not work on him—he himself succumbed to cancer.

As noted in Chapter 4, placebos do not have to be sugar pills. They can be diets, exercise regimens, consultations with doctors, or any other procedures that might be encountered by patients, even by patients taking the pharmacologically active (real) drug. But these placebo effects are often ignored—they are seen as random variation, or "bias," instead of as an important phenomenon in themselves.

Not everyone is affected by placebos. Some estimates are that about one third of patients are so influenced. Who are these patients? All the evidence is not yet in, but it seems likely that they are the patients who are provided with the means to redress some emotional stability. When people "find their niche" or "hit their stride," the balance and harmonic rhythms of their daily living lead to ongoing positive emotions. It is these positive emotions that are associated with the beneficial physiological changes. The healing emotional style involving a match between the individual and the environment, which maintains a physiological and psychosocial homeostasis, and through which good mental health promotes good physical health, has been termed the **self-healing personality** (Friedman, 1991, 1998).

Will to Live Emotions

In emotional terms, the self-healing personality is most characterized by *enthusiasm*. The word enthusiasm literally means "having a godly spirit within." *Cheerfulness* is another good emotional term. Deriving from the word for "face," cheer at one time referred to facial expression. Cheerful people express good spirits through their faces.

Enthusiastic people are successful in accomplishing tasks and helping other persons. They are alert, responsive, and energetic, although they may also be calm and self-assured. They are curious, secure, and constructive. The emotional aspects of their personality are apparent to the trained observer.

Several good clues indicate emotional balance and an inherent resilience. Such people tend to infect others with their exuberance. They are not ecstatic, but rather are generally responsive and content. They are people who others like to be around. They are not downcast or shifty-eyed. They also smile naturally—the eyes, eyebrows, and mouth are synchronized and unforced. Their gestures are smooth and tend to move away from the body. (That is, they are less likely to pick, scratch, and touch their bodies.) They are

---

Box 7–1   Controlled Study of Chronic Emotional Turmoil and Risk of Infection

Since different people are exposed to different microbes (germs) on a daily basis, how could we ever gain more experimental control to see whether less-stressed, self-healing people are less likely to contract infections? One clever research design has been employed by health psychologist Sheldon Cohen and his colleagues (Cohen et al., 1998). Participants are first screened through medical examinations and laboratory tests to be free of disease. Then these volunteer participants enter a quarantine (a clean room, where they stay). After a day of quarantine, participants are given nasal drops containing a low infectious dose of rhinovirus, which causes the common cold in susceptible people. The quarantine then continues for five days more.

In this way, the experimenters can be sure that the participants had equal exposure to the infectious agent (the cold virus). During this follow-up period, the participants have their nasal secretions sampled for the virus, and they are examined for cold symptons and nasal congestion. The investigators can then compare those participants who developed a cold with those who did not. A host of psychological, social, and biological variables are used as predictors and as statistical controls.

One important finding is that those participants who had *chronic* challenges (stressors) during the past year were at higher risk to catch the experimental cold than were the unstressed participants. During interviews, these stressed participants had reported challenges such as ongoing marital problems or undesired unemployment. Interestingly, using various variables measured in their study, the investigators were unable to provide a further explanation for why those individuals under chronic stress are more susceptible to upper respiratory infectious disease (colds). Nevertheless, such research provides important confirmation that chronic stress based on interpersonal conflicts or work problems can be detrimental to one's health.

unlikely to fidget, and their legs are often uncrossed and open, rather than tight and defensive. They are not apt to make aggressive gestures with their hands.

Emotionally balanced individuals not only walk smoothly, but they also talk
smoothly. They are inclined to show fewer speech disturbances, such as saying "ah," and
their speech is modulated rather than full of sudden loud words. A sanguine person's
voice is less likely to change in tone under stress.

Obviously, there are exceptions to these rules. A single nonverbal gesture does not
tell us much. Still, it is remarkable how much valid information we can gather about a
person's healthy emotional style from just a few episodes of social interaction.

Creativity and Play

It is not a coincidence that performers like Katherine Hepburn, Vladimir Horowitz, and
Pablo Casals, who remained successful late in life, also retain that magical spark and joie
de vivre that audiences find so appealing. The joy, fulfillment, and playfulness of living
are key aspects of the self-healing personality.

As mentioned, the influential psychologist Carl Rogers (1961) was the first to call
scientific attention to personal growth and fulfillment—the joy of being alive. Rogers
saw each person as having an inherent tendency to grow and enhance his or her being—
discovering a true self that may be hidden—in order to produce more positive inner feelings. The fully functioning person lives up to his or her potential and completely
develops and uses any talents.

Rogers was primarily concerned with psychological health, but it turns out that he
described a basic component of general health. This is not so surprising, since the many
patients Rogers saw in therapy were facing major emotional imbalances. Rogerian therapy involves helping patients to clarify their feelings so that they can integrate their
unique life experiences into their self-concept.

The humanistic psychologist Abraham Maslow (1971) spent a good part of his influential career focused on the positive, growth-oriented aspects of human beings.
Maslow recognized that healthy people first need to achieve balance in their basic biological needs, and they then need to obtain affection and self-respect. But he emphasized
what he called **self-actualization**—the realization of personal growth and fulfillment.
People with this growth orientation are spontaneous and creative, are good problem-
solvers, have close relationships to others, and have a playful sense of humor.

As people become more self-actualized, they become more concerned with issues
of beauty, justice, and understanding. They develop a sense of humor that is philosophical rather than hostile. They become more independent and march to the beat of a different drummer. They become more ethical and more concerned with the harmony among
members of the human race. These characteristics of the self-healing personality are not
merely the opposite of such disease-prone characteristics as suspiciousness, bitter cynicism, despair and depression, or repressed conflicts. Rather, they are positive, meaningful
motives, behaviors, and goals in their own right.

Talking to victims of serious illness, it is intriguing to note the ways many of them
have changed their philosophies of life after their brush with death. A reasonable expectation is that recognition of the fragility of life might lead to a callous and hedonistic ram-

page—"I might as well maximize my fun because I won't live forever." In fact, such reactions are rare. For people who make changes (many do not), the direction is almost always towards greater self-fulfillment. "I try to spend more time with my family." "I stop to smell the roses." "I try to see the other guy's side of things."

SOCIAL TIES AND SOCIAL INTEGRATION

One reason that a solely biological approach to health is inadequate is that people are social beings. We are born into families, are raised in communities, and live in societies. All sorts of evidence indicates that major psychological and physiological abnormalities result when a child is raised without sufficient, high-quality human contact.

The basic elements of self-healing personalities develop in childhood. Although this has long been recognized, early psychoanalysts focused on the internal conflicts and frustrations of childhood. The attention was generally on the negative aspects of human nature—what could go wrong. Erik Erikson, on the other hand, turned the Freudian framework on its head. He showed that human struggles could be seen in terms of the positive and successful resolution of tensions, especially in terms of social relations.

Erikson (1950) underscored the idea that although stressed children could come to feel mistrustful, guilty, and inferior, they might instead become trusting, autonomous, and industrious. In adolescence and adulthood, the individual might succumb to identity crises, isolation, stagnation, and despair; but many people triumph over life's challenges and develop self-esteem, intimacy, altruism, and existential satisfaction. Throughout life, the healthy personality continually develops what is best in himself or herself, while also helping others to thrive.

At the risk of oversimplification, healthy psychosocial development in this scheme can be summarized in terms of one basic ongoing process—disclosing one's feelings to loving others (cf. Pennebaker, 1995). For young children, this means expressing joy or despair and having a responsive adult there to understand. For older children, the process is one of trying (or playing) out different roles and having an emerging positive sense of self confirmed by the family. For adults, the self-disclosure is key to developing intimacy and empathy with a spouse and close friends. For the elderly, the sharing of feelings with loving others strengthens the sense of life's meaning and the continuity of the generations. This is one reason why self-absorption can be so unhealthy. Health resides not within an individual, but within a social context.

The Family

When a person develops a serious illness like cancer, it is really the whole family that must fight the cancer; the stress affects everyone. However, usual medical treatment pays little heed to the family's needs. One physician commented to a health psychologist, "I think it's great that there are people like you who can keep the family members out of my hair so that I can get on with treating my patient." He was a good physician but had neither the training nor the inclination to deal with the social context of his patient's illness.

As we have seen, hospitalized patients are routinely cut off from their families and friends. With the restrictions and barriers in place, it is almost like the patient is in prison.

When the patient then returns home and reintegrates into the community, the medical system does not follow along to ease the way and monitor recovery. When physicians stopped making house calls, they thought they were becoming more efficient and effective. In many cases they were. But becoming cut off from the patient's home environment leaves the physician ignorant about how best to treat each patient's individual needs. This is why physicians who do venture out of their protected and regimented office suites are often greeted with such adulation by their patients.

The hospice (see Chapter 9, "Dying, Death, and Grief") is one example of how the family can be brought back into its rightful place in fighting illness. But other changes are also possible. For example, some pediatric hospitals now make it comfortable for a parent to spend the night with an ill child. (This was almost unheard of a generation ago.) Could not similar arrangements be made for spouses or friends of adult patients? As another example, in most treatments, the patient cannot be accompanied by family members. This could be changed; many family members have proven to be valuable medical assistants.

The Community

Men and women living in Alameda County California were asked about their amount of contact with friends, relatives, and community groups. They were followed for nine years (Berkman & Syme, 1979). The extent of social ties was strongly associated with the likelihood of staying alive. A large follow-up study was conducted on data collected in Finland. This study and others confirm the protective effect of social ties, especially for men (Bowling & Grundy, 1998).

There are all sorts of studies indicating that people with closer community ties have better health habits, better mental adjustment, and better physical health (Sugisawa, Liang, & Liu, 1994). In dealing with challenge, people with community ties have better sources of information, more help, and more advice. Most importantly, they have people they can care about and who care about them. It is unhealthy to be lonely.

Ties to health are likely through the stress mechanisms examined in Chapters 5 and 6. For example, one study of healthy young women found that those who perceived their peers as undermining them had higher blood levels of fibrinogen (Davis & Swan, 1999). Fibrinogen is a protein used in the blood clotting process; high levels suggest a possible link to risk of coronary heart disease.

The Society

In Japan, the individual is seen as part of the whole. The individual works for the betterment of his or her family, company, and country. There is a high degree of loyalty, conformity, uniformity, and stability. The individual Japanese is highly integrated into society.

In America, there is relatively more independence. People change spouses, companies, professions, residences, and political loyalties with frequency. The social milieu is more independent, self-reliant, and alienating.

Is one of these societal environments healthier? All other things being equal, the more stable, uniform environment is healthier; it provides identity and meaning for the individual. However, other factors enter the equation. First, societies are not static. As technologies change, economies change, and politics change, the population must adapt. Rigid, structured societies may make these adaptations more difficult for their populations. Second, uniform, structured societies can become stultifying; such boredom and rigidity is unhealthy. Third, even in a uniform, stable society, influences from other cultures become known and create special problems for those to whom they appeal—it is more stressful to be a "rock 'n roller" or an investigative reporter in Japan than in the U.S.

Social and societal disorientation is stressful, but social integration and stability is health-promoting. The paradox is that all societies must and do change. At different times, in different places, and in different ways, the individuals in a society are subjected to special challenges. At these times, attention to steps that facilitate self-healing is especially valuable. A certain amount of change can produce the exhilarating "good" stress; but if emotional equilibrium is totally disrupted, *dis*tress and increased likelihood of illness result.

Some of the best evidence for the importance of social integration to health comes from extensive studies of immigrants. Interestingly, immigrants are not usually at the highest risk of disease. It is their children, the first generation to be born in the new country, who suffer the most. It seems as though the immigrants themselves are usually unwilling to try to adopt all the strange customs of their new country. Rather, they move to a "Little Italy" or a "Chinatown," where cultural support is in place. Their children, however, must often face the greater stresses of leaving family traditions and striking out into a new culture (Moss, 1973; Seeman et al., 1987; Syme, 1987).

LIFETIME PREDICTORS OF LONGEVITY

Although there is little doubt that psychosocial factors play some role in self-healing, there is uncertainty about the nature of the causal pathways. In what ways are aspects of personality related to longevity in general and to heart disease or cancer in particular, across the lifespan? To address this question in a direct manner, we need to follow people for a lifetime. Obviously, this is impossible for any single researcher to do, but such a study has been approximated using a remarkable data archive started by Lewis Terman.

The Human Termites

The psychologist Lewis Terman was one of the leading intelligence researchers of the 20th century. In 1921, Terman began one of the most comprehensive studies in psychology. To investigate his genetic theories of intelligence, Terman recruited bright California schoolchildren—856 boys and 672 girls—intensively studied their psychosocial and intellectual development, and followed them into adulthood. These clever participants nicknamed themselves Terman's Termites. By the 1990s, more than half of Terman's participants had died, and Howard Friedman (your textbook author) and his colleagues have gathered their death certificates and coded their dates and causes of death (Friedman et al., 1995).

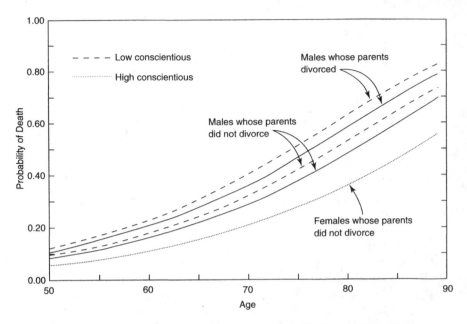

Figure 7-3   **Personality, Stress and Longevity in the Terman Sample.**
These graphs, termed *survival curves*, show that both the personality factor of conscientiousness in childhood, and the social
stress factor of parental divorce, affect the likelihood that one
will die prematurely. Healthy or unhealthy patterns can carry on
to affect health risk many years into the future. *(Copyright Howard
S. Friedman and Joseph Schwartz.)*

When the **Terman Life-Cycle study** began, most of the children were pre-
adolescent (Terman & Oden, 1947). Terman's aim was to secure a reasonably random
sample of bright California children, and so most public schools in the San Francisco and
Los Angeles areas were searched for bright kids, nominated by their teachers and tested
by Terman to have an IQ of at least 135. They have been followed at five to ten year intervals ever since. In this remarkable study, only small percentages (less than 10 percent)
of participants are unaccounted for. Analyses indicate that those lost from study do not
differ systematically from those who remained, so there is not a bias due to dropouts.

The Termites were a bright, well-educated group, integrated into American society,
and they had regular contact with Stanford University. This eliminates certain problems or
confounds common to other psychosocial health studies. For example, the Termites could
understand medical advice and prescription, had adequate nutrition, and had access to medical care. Explanations of poor health involving poverty, ignorance, or discrimination are
generally not applicable to this sample, and so the sample is valuable for focusing on personality. The sample is not, however, representative of the U.S. population as a whole, but
it is a good sample of bright, white children who lived during the 20th century.

Is there evidence that resilient personalities—high in stability, responsibility, socia-
bility, and optimism—are prone to health, whereas aggressive, excitable, impulsive, or neu-

rotic people are prone to disease and mortality? In 1922, when the average Termite was about 11 years old, Terman collected trait ratings about the participants from their parents and teachers. The scales he used are remarkably modern in their appearance and provide a better assessment than the primitive personality tests that were available at the time. It is reasonable to expect that parents and teachers have a good idea of whether an 11-year-old child is a sociable, popular child, is conscientious, is self-confident, and so on. Friedman and his collaborators constructed six personality dimensions from Terman's scales, and used them to predict longevity and cause of death through 1986, using a statistical technique called survival analysis (Friedman et al., 1993; Friedman et al., 1995).

Conscientiousness

Does childhood personality predict premature mortality decades later? The most striking finding is that childhood social dependability, or *conscientiousness,* is predictive of longevity. Children, especially boys, who were rated as prudent, conscientious, truthful, and free from vanity (four separate ratings, which were averaged) live significantly longer throughout the life span. They are about 30 percent less likely to die in any given year. Personality did indeed predict longevity. Conscientiousness assessed in adulthood predicts longevity as well (Friedman et al., 1993; Martin & Friedman, 2000).

This finding that personality predicts survival across the life span raises many fascinating questions concerning causal mechanisms. Why are conscientious, dependable children who live to adulthood more likely to reach old age than their less conscientious peers? Further survival analyses suggest that the protective effect of conscientiousness is not primarily due to a reduction in the risk of injury: Although there is some tendency for the unconscientious to be more likely to die a violent death, conscientiousness is also protective against early death due to cardiovascular disease and cancer. Furthermore, a focus on unhealthy behaviors such as smoking and drinking shows them to be somewhat relevant as explanatory mechanisms, but a significant effect of conscientiousness remains after controlling for drinking, smoking, and other aspects of personality. In other words, a conscientious child grows up being more likely to avoid early death from injury and less likely to engage in unhealthy habits, but also stays healthier and lives longer for other reasons as well. It is a major dimension of staying healthy.

Cheerfulness

Given the findings of other researchers about potential benefits and costs of being optimistic, Friedman and colleagues also examined the Terman children who were cheerful, having a sense of humor and optimism. The interesting finding concerning this childhood cheerfulness was that contrary to expectation, childhood cheerfulness is inversely related to longevity. The cheerful kids grew up to be adults who died somewhat sooner.

It turns out that they grew up to be more likely to smoke, drink, and take risks, although these habits do not fully explain their increased risk of premature mortality. It is likely the case that cheerfulness is helpful when facing a stress such as surgery, but harmful if it leads a person to be careless or carefree throughout his or her life. For example, excessive cheer might lead a person to say, "It doesn't matter if I smoke; it won't affect me." Or, they might not engage in proactive coping.

Stressed Termites

In terms of relevant social factors, this project also looked at those children who faced the divorce of their parents. It is well known that divorce of a person's parents during childhood can have ill effects on his or her future mental health. For example, children of divorce, especially boys, are at greater risk for observable behavior and adjustment problems (Block, Block, & Gjerde, 1986; Hetherington, 1991; Jellinek & Slovik, 1981; Shaw, Emery & Tuer, 1993; Zill, Morrison, & Coiro, 1993). The explanations often concern a lack of social dependability or ego control—that is, impulsivity and nonconformity—although neuroticism or low emotional stability are also often implicated. But there had never before been a lifelong prospective study of family stress predictors of mortality and cause of death, although family stress (particularly parental divorce) has been found to predict unhealthy behaviors such as smoking and drug use in adolescence as well as poor psychological adjustment (Amato & Keith, 1991; Block, Block & Keyes, 1988; Chassin et al., 1984; Conrad, Flay, & Hill, 1992; Hawkins, Catalano, & Miller, 1992). Would these detrimental effects of parental divorce reach across the life span and affect longevity and cause of death?

Friedman and his colleagues looked at the children whose parents either did or did not divorce before the child reached age 21. Children of divorced parents faced a one-third greater mortality risk than people whose parents remained married at least until they reached age 21. Among males, for those whose parents divorced while they were children, the predicted median age of death is 76; for those whose parents remained married, the predicted median age of death is 80. For females, the corresponding predicted ages of death are 82 and 86 (Schwartz et al., 1995).

Is the increased mortality risk of children of divorce due in part to these people's own subsequent divorce? People whose parents divorced were indeed more likely to face divorce themselves. Further, individuals who were divorced or remarried reported that their childhoods were significantly more stressful than did those who got and stayed married. In other words, Terman study participants who experienced a marital breakup were more likely to have seen the divorce of their own parents, and they were more likely to report having experienced a stressful home environment as children (such as "marked friction among family members"). Since parental divorce is associated with a person's own future divorce, and since divorce is predictive of increased mortality risk, it is indeed the case that a person's unstable adult relations "explains" some of the detrimental effect of parental divorce. However, after controlling for (adult) divorce, parental divorce during childhood remains a significant predictor of premature mortality, suggesting that it has some additional adverse consequences in adulthood.

Mental Health

What about personality and mental state in adulthood? In 1950 (when they were about 40 years old), the Termites were asked about tendencies toward nervousness, anxiety, or nervous breakdown. There also had been personal conferences with participants and with family members. Based on this and on previously related information in the files dating back a decade, Terman's team then categorized each participant on a three-point scale of mental difficulty: satisfactory adjustment, some maladjustment, or serious maladjustment. For males, mental difficulty as of 1950 significantly predicted mortality risk through 1991, with unstable males at high risk of premature mortality (Martin et al., 1995).

All in all, undependability, impulsivity, and family instability (parental and personal divorce) are predictive of premature mortality across the life span. On the other hand, there is good confirmation in the physical health arena of the importance of what psychologists have typically called mental stability, or ego strength—dependability, trust, and lack of impulsivity. How large are these effects? These effects are smaller than the influences of gender or smoking on longevity, but comparable to common biological risk factors such as systolic blood pressure and serum cholesterol, and to common behavioral risks such as exercise and diet, as they affect all-cause mortality.

Can people be too conscientious? One obituary reported on the death of a well-known lawyer, while visiting Rochester, Minnesota, the home of the well-known Mayo Clinic. Had this man died of disease despite the best efforts of the Mayo's doctors? No, he died from head injuries sustained in a fall in his hotel room in Rochester, where he had gone for his annual physical exam at the Mayo Clinic.

SUMMARY AND CONCLUSION

If there is a self-healing personality, then there should be all sorts of evidence for it. In the last chapter, we analyzed the evidence for disease-prone personalities. In the present chapter, the emphasis has been not only on avoiding disease-proneness but more particularly on understanding disease resistance. Assorted studies—of health among business executives and lawyers, of the challenges of sports or unemployment, of the physiological effects of challenge, of the goals of successful psychotherapy, of recovery of patients in hospitals, and others—all point to the same conclusion. Each individual can develop a greater or lesser resistance to disease.

Importantly, it is not enough to be optimistic or to "make up one's mind" to be healthy. Rather, a sense of control or choice in life, a commitment to higher goals or principles, an attitude of social integration, an environment of appropriate challenge and excitement, and a sense of creative self-fulfillment together produce the will to thrive and the positive emotions that are at the core of good health. Taken in total, the evidence for a self-healing personality is substantial.

We should not expect to see dramatic effects of self-healing in every research study. Some studies do not examine enough people, some do not continue for a long enough time, and others contain some confounding factor that obscures the true relations. This situation is comparable, however, to that of many other health risks, such as high blood pressure. High blood pressure is a significant risk factor for a number of diseases. But it is difficult to measure reliably, it varies over time, its effects are usually slow to accrue, and in many cases it has no obvious ill effects. Why do so many people and so many physicians worry about blood pressure but ignore emotional balance? The difference is that the traditional health care system expects to find health effects of high blood pressure, but has not known how to think about personality and health.

The essential element of self-healing personalities is an emotional equilibrium. When a degree of emotional equilibrium is maintained, the body's physiological processes can work most efficiently to keep our cells and organs functioning at their best. The challenge is to maintain this emotional equilibrium, a complex process that depends on the individual's resources and the environmental demands. Fortunately, the scientific knowledge about how this can be done is now quite substantial.

The contemporary understanding of the self-healing personality is part of a just-beginning transformation of how society thinks about health. Recent discoveries and insights portend a dramatic reconceptualization of health and health care. The revolution is advancing rapidly in the United States. It is not a fad; the relevant theory and research are solid and comprehensive. Rather, it is a modern scientific realization of principles of emotional balance first suggested more than 2,000 ago.

Recommended Additional Readings

Antonovsky, Aaron. (1979). *Health, stress, and coping.* San Francisco: Jossey-Bass.
Friedman, Howard S. (2000). *Self-healing personality: Why some people achieve health and others succumb to illness.* Available through www.iuniverse.com, 2000.
Friedman, Howard S. (1998). Self-healing personalities. In H. S. Friedman (editor-in-chief), *Encyclopedia of Mental Health.* San Diego: Academic Press. pp. 453–459.
Friedman, Howard S., Tucker, J. S., Schwartz, J. E., Tomlinson-Keasey, C., Martin, L. R., Wingard, D. L., Criqui, M. H. (1995). Psychosocial and behavioral predictors of longevity: The aging and death of the "Termites." *American Psychologist, 50,* 69–78.
Maddi, Salvatore R. & Kobasa, Suzanne C. (1984). *The hardy executive: Health under stress.* Homewood, IL: Dow Jones-Irwin.

Key Concepts

hardiness

Cook-Medley hostility scale

quality adjusted life year (QALY)

internal locus of control

proactive coping (five stages)

hospital policies

Lown's explanation of sudden cardiac death

healthy subtypes

tend-and-befriend

oxytocin

optimistic bias

salutogenesis

sense of coherence

self-healing personality

characteristics of emotionally balanced individuals

self actualization

Lewis Terman and his research

Chapter 8

ADAPTATION TO CHRONIC ILLNESS

When Orville Kelly was diagnosed as having cancer, he reacted as many patients do—with shock, disbelief, and despair. People, however, usually do not die on the day their illness is diagnosed; rather, they face a crisis of adjustment to their new condition. They may need to deal with a period of physical impairment or medical treatments that may last many years.

Cancer is an especially well-known chronic disease, but there are many illnesses that result in long-term challenges. People do learn to cope. Physical impairment itself, however, is only one part of the problem of chronic illness. Social and emotional difficulties are of tremendous importance as well. Unfortunately, traditional medicine has not been well equipped to help patients cope with these problems.

Orville Kelly met the challenge of chronic illness by founding an organization of cancer patients, called Make Today Count (Kelly, 1975). This organization, with branches around the country, encourages mutual support among people with life-threatening illnesses. Kelly lived with his cancer but finally died of lymphocytic lymphoma, seven years after being diagnosed. He died just after winning a fight for veteran's disability benefits; he attributed his illness to exposure to nuclear radiation in the U.S. Army.

Chronic illness refers to conditions that have the following characteristics: The condition involves some disability; it is caused by mostly nonreversible pathological change (the deterioration in the body usually will not reverse itself); and it requires training and motivation on the part of the patient to care for himself or herself. Chronic illness may involve all of the problems of **acute illness,** but it brings special problems as well. The onset of chronic illness can be sudden or gradual, but one characteristic common to all chronic illnesses is that the patient cannot fully return to the pre-illness state of health (Strauss & Glaser, 1975).

About half of the U.S. population has at least one chronic health condition. About 1 in 10 faces some degree of limitation in activity because of their chronic illness. About 2 percent of the total population are unable to carry on major activities such as work, school, and recreation. The average number of chronic conditions per person is about 2.2; multiple chronic illnesses are very common (Belgrave, 1998; Chilman, Nunnally, & Cox, 1988; Costa & VandenBos, 1990; Falvo, 1999; Toombs, Barnard, & Carson, 1995).

Examples of chronic illness are heart conditions, impairments of the back or spine, diabetes, and various forms of cancer. Up to age 44, the most prominent chronic conditions involve paralysis (primarily from accidents) and impairments of the lower extremities and hips. After age 45, the most common chronic illnesses are arthritis, rheumatism, cancer, and cardiovascular conditions. Other common chronic illnesses include Parkinson's disease, AIDS, multiple sclerosis, epilepsy, Alzheimer's, kidney disease, asthma, and emphysema.

Although elderly people are more likely than younger people to have one or more chronic conditions, it is not true that chronic disease is merely a geriatric problem. It has been estimated that in the United States, about 40 percent of those 65 years old or over have one or more chronic conditions that limit a major activity. Of those from age 45 to 64, about one in seven people have at least one chronic condition that limits a major activity.

Chronic illness is becoming an increasingly important health problem. Better emergency treatments allow many patients to now survive the initial critical stages of acute illnesses or trauma (e.g., stroke, accident, or heart attack). Patients live with the effects of these acute illnesses and trauma, and thus face chronic illness from which they will never fully recover. In addition, older persons are likely to develop some form of chronic illness. So, better medical care, coupled with demographic trends that produce an increase in the elderly population, contribute to an increase in chronic illness. The long-term nature of chronic illness often leads to high costs of care. Thus, for a number of economic, social, and psychological reasons, the problems of the chronically ill deserve special study.

When thinking about the problems of someone with cancer or paralysis, most people focus on such difficulties as physical impairment and pain. However, for the chronically ill, one of the most difficult problems (if not the most difficult problem) involves relationships with other people (Burish & Bradley, 1983; Falvo, 1999). In this chapter, we examine the psychosocial and emotional aspects of patients with chronic illness in terms of three issues: (a) the crisis of illness, (b) the process of coping with chronic illness, and (c) the importance of social support. We then examine special cases of chronic illness and the particular problems associated with them.

ADAPTATION TO THE CRISIS OF ILLNESS

The onset of physical illness creates a crisis. Consider James Jones (not his real name), a patient who has recently suffered a severe myocardial infarction. His whole life is disrupted; he was hospitalized for two weeks and out of work for several weeks after that. Not only is his ability to contribute to society now somewhat limited, but Mr. Jones must also deal with a variety of problems and tasks that are related to his coronary attack. He must cope with pain and with some incapacitation, and he must learn to deal with the hospital environment, with special treatment procedures, and with medical personnel.

Initial Crisis

Mr. Jones also faces social and emotional difficulties (Cassem & Hackett, 1973; Michela, 1987). He is unsure whether his life is in serious jeopardy. His relationships with his family and friends are strained; they are worried about him. His family suffers financial hardship. He cannot carry out his usual role in the family as husband and father. It is not clear whether he will be able to go back to his former job, whether he will be able to enjoy normal sexual functioning again, and whether he will be able to participate in all the family recreational activities. These overwhelming problems illustrate the **initial crisis** of chronic physical illness.

Released from the hospital, Mr. Jones retains the identity of "coronary patient." Having suffered a heart attack, his chances of suffering another attack are increased. He must make changes in his usual behaviors and make modifications in his lifestyle. He may have to make changes in his job. In order to prevent a second heart attack, Mr. Jones must follow a special diet, take regular medications, engage in specified exercise, and ease carefully into sexual activities.

The dangers are both physical and socioemotional (Brezinka & Kittel, 1996; Orth-Gomer & Wamala, 2001). For example, some evidence suggests that resuming sexual relations too soon may create additional marital problems, presumably because the sexual activity is surrounded by new fears and pressures (Michela, 1987). In short, Mr. Jones is now suffering from a chronic illness—heart disease. He will probably never be "cured," but his condition can be well managed (Croog & Levine, 1982).

As we have seen, people have certain characteristic ways of behaving, and they use these behaviors to solve minor problems in life. However, when the situation is so new or so major that the habitual coping responses are inadequate, then the situation becomes a crisis. Disorganization, anxiety, fear, and depression may occur, and in the midst of this condition, many matters must be decided. An individual cannot remain in this state of disequilibrium for a long time. Within a few weeks or months after the onset of crisis, the patient needs to reach some resolution; some equilibrium must be restored. The new balance may represent a healthy adaptation for the person, with personal growth, maturity, and self-healing; on the other hand, it is possible that the result may be psychological deterioration and maladaptive responses.

Major Tasks of Adaptation

To provide a comprehensive framework for understanding reactions to illness, researchers Rudolf Moos and Vivien Tsu suggested that the crisis of illness brings with it seven major adaptive tasks (Moos & Tsu, 1977). Some of these problems deal primarily with coping with the physical problems of chronic illness, while others are tied to interpersonal relations.

The first task involves **coping with the discomfort and physical incapacity** of the illness or injury, including pain, weakness, and loss of control. The patient may have never before faced incapacity or chronic pain. The second task involves **dealing with the medical technology.** For example, the patient must adjust to having his or her body invaded for various tests and medical procedures. A third task for the patient involves the **maintenance of adequate communication** with health care professionals. Asking physicians for more attention, requesting help from nurses, and so on, can be difficult for a patient whose psychological resources are already being used up in dealing with the physical illness.

Then there are more general psychological challenges. The fourth category of tasks for the patient experiencing the crisis of illness involves the **preservation of emotional balance.** The patient must try to manage the upsetting feelings aroused by the illness, feelings such as self-blame, anxiety, and thoughts of failure. There may also be a sense of alienation, feelings of inadequacy, and resentment. Relatedly, the fifth task consists of **preserving a satisfactory self-image** and a sense of competence and mastery. Changes in physical functioning and appearance must be incorporated into a new self-image. For example, the patient must find a personally and socially satisfactory balance between accepting help when necessary and taking responsibility and action when possible. Some patients find it difficult to resume being independent after a long period of passivity.

The sixth set of tasks involves **preserving relationships** with the patient's social network—with family and friends. A person who becomes ill may easily become isolated from others and feel alienated both by physical separation and by the new identity as a patient. Seventh, and finally, the patient must engage in a set of tasks that involves

preparing for an uncertain future. Particularly when there is loss of a function as critical as sight or speech, or paralysis of limbs, the loss cannot be denied. It must be acknowledged and mourned, and the patient has to prepare for living with a permanent loss of function. Grief reactions are considered in more detail in Chapter 9.

In brief, new illness is often a significant challenge, with all the features of a major crisis. Eventually, the crisis of the onset of serious illness is overcome, and the long-term problems of the chronically ill take on increasing importance.

The Special Problems of the Chronically III

Even after the first few months of medical crisis have ended, people with chronic illness face many novel social and psychological challenges in their daily lives (Biegel, Sales, & Schulz, 1991; Croog & Levine, 1982; Michela, 1987). The first involves the prevention and the management of a potential medical crisis. The patient's condition, if not kept in

Figure 8-1 The importance of family support for a cancer patient is now well known, but recent research in health psychology documents when and why such support may be helpful (as well as when it may prove harmful). (*Courtesy of the American Cancer Society, Inc.*)

check, may be life threatening. For example, if diabetes is not kept under control with in-sulin, the patient may enter a diabetic coma. The chronically ill patient and the family must be on the lookout for signs that point to an impending medical crisis. A diabetic pa-tient learns to recognize the signs of a depletion or overabundance of insulin. People who have chronic illnesses such as epilepsy usually carry medical identification (such as bracelets or neck chains) so that if they are unconscious, the people around them and medical professionals can immediately identify the problem. Lack of recognition of im-pending crisis and lack of knowledge about what to do to prevent a crisis can put the pa-tient's life in danger.

A second important problem faced by chronically ill patients is the need to manage their treatment regimen. Treatment may seem simple—just following the orders of the physician. However, patients with chronic illness are less likely than patients with acute illnesses to cooperate with and follow medical directions (see Chapter 12). The problem is usually not that patients are willfully noncompliant or even medically ignorant. Rather, in the management of chronic illness, patients must continually juggle the various de-mands made on them in every aspect of life. The treatment regimen is simply one of many demands that are made on the individual.

Initially, patients may be overwhelmed by the realization that the treatment regi-men is a lifelong undertaking. This is particularly true for patients who are learning to give themselves insulin injections for diabetes, or for patients who are learning to un-dergo hemodialysis. Even the use of a bronchial inhalator, which clears breathing pas-sages for patients with obstructive pulmonary disease, can be profoundly disturbing because the patients recognize that use of the inhalators is something upon which their lives may depend. Furthermore, if a treatment regimen interferes sufficiently with a per-son's job or other activities, the patient is less likely to follow it. And if the treatment is socially isolating (i.e., makes it hard for the person to interact with others), the patient must decide whether to follow the regimen and experience some loss of human contact, or to follow the regimen only partially or not at all.

A third major ongoing challenge faced by patients with chronic illness is that of controlling their symptoms and hiding them from casual friends and acquaintances. Most people do not want to spend their days explaining their medical conditions to bored lis-teners. For example, victims of lung diseases and heart diseases (two extremely common sorts of chronic problems) may function very well in some situations and so be unde-tectable, but may be limited in their activities.

Control over others' perceptions may be difficult if the patient lacks social skills. Patients usually do not know what to say to other people about such things as their lim-ited energy level or their inability to go to certain places. For example, a woman who suf-fers severe asthma may have difficulty telling her friends that she cannot visit them unless they dust their houses. Close friends and family may accept these requests and re-design their environment for the patient, but the management of more peripheral friend-ships may be extremely difficult for the patient.

Another example, provided by Strauss and Glaser (1975), involves a woman suffer-ing from multiple sclerosis, who carefully arranged her one-room apartment so that every object she could conceivably require during the day was within arm's reach for her. Other people saw this arrangement as incredibly cluttered, and they encouraged her to tidy up her apartment. Friends were made uncomfortable by the clutter because they did not understand its purpose. Not surprisingly, loss of bodily function, with its related problems in social control, seems to be a main source of distress for victims of multiple sclerosis (Devins & Seland, 1987).

Management of social relationships can also be extremely difficult without knowledge of the prognosis. For example, knowing whether you likely have four months or four years to live is obviously important in making plans. Knowing at what point severe disability is likely to develop can be also important for the patient. That is, estimating what the future will bring is a major problem of patients with chronic illnesses. Furthermore, since no one really knows with certainty what the course of any disease will be, the patient and individuals in the patient's close social environment may be at odds in their predictions. For example, a person with cancer might be considered **"socially dead"** long before actual biological death. While the patient may expect a remission in the disease (a time during which the disease is arrested or appears cured), others in the social environment may assume the patient's life is coming to a close.

Insecurity about the trajectory of the disease can be particularly distressing for the individual whose symptoms are not obvious to others. For example, a high-level executive who is extremely important to a corporation may decide to retire very early because of a heart condition. Without a clear statement from medical professionals about how long this executive can expect to live, and the chances for various levels of impairment, the executive is likely to be seen (in the absence of symptoms) as someone who simply does not want to face responsibilities in the corporation.

In short, social isolation is a major problem that chronically ill patients experience. Social relationships are often disrupted and jeopardized because of the patient's decreased energy, limitations in mobility, communication impairment, or time required for symptom control. In addition, patients, in an effort to hide their disease or certain symptoms, may avoid certain friends and associates.

Thus, people with chronic illness face both a number of short-term (crisis) challenges and many long-term social and emotional difficulties. We now turn to an examination of the ways in which patients cope with chronic illness. We then examine the special importance of social support.

COPING WITH CHRONIC ILLNESS

In Chapter 5, **coping** was defined as contending with environmental challenges—using thoughts and actions to master, tolerate, or minimize demands of the environment (Cohen & Lazarus, 1979; Haan, 1977). The methods that people use in an attempt to cope are never in themselves necessarily adaptive or maladaptive. They must be evaluated in the light of the situation in which each occurs. Any given coping technique for chronic illness can be adaptive in one situation and extremely maladaptive in another (Moos & Tsu, 1977).

The first type of coping technique involves denying or minimizing the seriousness of the medical crisis. Sometimes, this technique of denial is referred to as a *defense mech-*

anism, because it is a self-protective response to stress. People may, in fact, delude themselves into believing that what has actually happened to them really has not occurred. This allows them to protect their self-image. For example, a male patient who has suffered a heart attack might deny this fact to himself, and he might believe that he is in the hospital primarily because of a gall bladder problem. So as long as the patient follows all of the requirements of the treatment regimen and takes care of himself as he should, such temporary denial may be prudent. It may be adaptive for this patient not to think too much about the implications of his massive heart attack; too much anxiety may interfere with his initial recovery. However, denial becomes a maladaptive coping mechanism when the patient refuses to follow the treatment regimen necessary for a cardiac patient. Some degree of denial accompanies many illnesses, but whether or not it is adaptive depends on circumstances.

A second coping technique involves seeking information. If a person is feeling helpless, gathering information about the particular illness may help to restore a sense of control. However, if the patient insists on extensive information in every step of the treatment, and becomes upset if health care professionals cannot provide or will not provide the medical chart, results of laboratory tests, and all physicians' opinions, the information-gathering coping technique becomes maladaptive.

Requests for reassurance form a third type of coping technique. Comfort from others can be a big help. But excessive requests for reassurance and emotional support from the concerned family, friends, and medical staff can of course be maladaptive for the patient. They cannot provide constant assurance and support. On the other hand, suppressing the need for reassurance can also be maladaptive. Patients who keep their feelings bottled up inside them or who withdraw from social interaction and cut themselves off from others also encounter problems. A moderate degree of expression of feelings can serve to relieve tension and help patients open themselves to comfort from others. (We examine this point in more detail when we consider the issue of social support.)

A fourth set of coping techniques involves setting concrete, limited goals. If a patient has something to look forward to and something to work for, a sense of meaning can be restored. This coping technique can help the patient to break an overwhelming number of problems into small and potentially manageable parts.

Fifth, there is rehearsing alternative future outcomes. Through mental preparation (anticipation and rehearsal) of the various alternatives, a patient can learn to deal with eventualities that may arise in the illness. For example, if a breast cancer patient has an unknown prognosis, she may prepare ahead of time for the possibility of additional chemotherapy or radiation treatments. The patient's ability to deal with the additional treatment may depend on her rehearsal beforehand of the feelings and the behaviors that are likely to accompany the experience.

A related technique has been heavily employed in coping with cancer. It is called **visualization.** Patients are taught to relax and form a mental picture of the cancer and their body's response to the cancer. Some physicians hope that this process will help mobilize the body's own natural defenses against cancer, but the process also seems valuable solely in a psychological sense. Patients have the opportunity to rehearse the future of their illness and they may achieve a sense of personal control over some of the emotions that are troubling them. In this way, the visualization process seems to help some patients cope more effectively with their illness (Simonton, Matthews-Simonton, & Creighton, 1978). Definitive studies of the role of visual imagery have not yet been done, because the existing programs combine imagery with relaxation, social support, self-disclosure, and similar coping techniques, thus making it impossible to determine the effects of each component of the treatment (cf. Baum, 1990; McKinney, Antoni, Kumar, Tims, & McCabe, 1997). However, many patients and physicians report it to be very helpful.

A final common coping mechanism involves the patient's **search for meaning** in the illness. This coping technique involves understanding the experience by looking at it with a long-term perspective (with or without a religious orientation). It involves making the crisis work for the good of the patient instead of to the patient's detriment. For example, a woman who has experienced a radical mastectomy may gain from the experience a greater closeness to her family and a new ability to share feelings and understandings. In fact, many victims of chronic illness report a closer family life than they had previously (Taylor, 1989).

Which People Cope Best?

Different people respond differently to chronic illness. Why? What factors influence their reactions to the illness and their ability to cope? Certain individual factors have been found to influence this coping (Cohen & Lazarus, 1983; Felton, Revenson, & Hinrichsen, 1984; Folkman & Lazarus, 1980; Moos, 1977; Pakenham, 1999; Pearlin & Schooler, 1978).

First of all, an individual who has a high level of intelligence and cognitive development may be better able to seek and use information, thus avoiding a sense of powerlessness. This might be true primarily because an individual with high intellectual development and education is more confident in asking for information. Information-seeking coping strategies (a type of problem-focused coping) may work when one's illness or condition can be controlled or affected in some significant way.

The general ego strength and self-esteem of the individual may also have a significant impact on ability to adapt to the crisis of illness. Illness is often a threat to one's self-esteem, and so someone who starts out emotionally strong may be better able to cope. On the other hand, people who are insecure or feel inadequate and who are psychologically vulnerable tend to have difficulty coping with illness. For example, adolescents may have particular difficulty coping with illness because of their limited experience in coping in general, and because they are at a point in their lives when they are struggling to gain emotional independence from their parents. Again, the greater maturity of an individual and the more extensive experience this individual has in successfully coping with crises, the easier it is to deal with the crises of illness (Biegel, Sales, & Schulz, 1991; Cohen, 1979; Greenfield, Roessler, & Crosley, 1959; Kahana & Bibring, 1964).

Characteristics of the illness, such as the type and location of symptoms, tend to influence the degree of successful coping with the illness. For example, if the symptoms are disfiguring or disabling, the individual will generally have more trouble coping with them than if the symptoms are not at all obvious. Relatedly, patients are often overwhelmed when their illness causes damage to their reproductive organs or to their faces; there is a great deal of psychological significance attached to certain regions of the body. Amputation of a breast that cures breast cancer, for example, may have a greater psychological impact on an individual than a very serious chronic condition that is life-endangering (e.g., severe hypertension). Unfortunately, surgeries for breast cancer, testicular cancer, prostate cancer, cervical cancer, uterine cancer, and facial skin cancer are quite common.

One study examined how self-rated physical and emotional intimacy of women with their heterosexual partner, during an illness episode of lupus (a chronic systemic disease), was related to their feelings and relationship satisfaction (Druley, Stephens, & Coyne, 1997). Women who engaged in more intimate behavior with their partner tended to report greater relationship satisfaction. Women who frequently avoided, or who were often the initiators of, physical intimacy had greater negative reactions, however, thus illustrating the dilemmas people face as they try to walk the fine line between giving in to their illness or acting as if nothing were the matter.

Normalization

The chief goal of the chronically ill person is not simply to remain alive as long as possible, under any circumstances, but rather to attempt to live for as long as possible as normally as possible (Goffman, 1963; Strauss & Glaser, 1975) (see Box 8–1). How "normal" a chronically ill person's life can be, however, depends on the social arrange-

---

Box 8–1   Adaptation to AIDS

Many of the worst problems in coping with chronic illness come together regarding AIDS patients. Issues of quality of life clearly come to the forefront.

People with AIDS may face chronic weakness. There may be degeneration. They face high financial costs of long-term care. Although not contagious through casual contact, the disease is caused by a virus, and so some social contacts can be difficult. AIDS patients often face a stigma because the disease is mostly sexually transmitted and was first concentrated among homosexuals and drug addicts. The stigma often remains, even though the illness can be transmitted through contact with infected blood and is increasingly transmitted heterosexually.

AIDS victims may delay in seeking treatment, denying the illness. AIDS often results in a changed appearance, with all the attendant problems of identity and social relations. There may be dementia. There is a long incubation period, creating various problems of uncertainty and unknowing transmission. Because of its modes of transmission, AIDS tends to strike the young, causing special resentments and despair among patients, families, and friends. Finally, the course of AIDS may be affected by stress. In short, just about every factor that can increase the challenge of chronic illness exists with AIDS. For all of these reasons, psychological research on AIDS patients has become one of the most important research topics in health psychology, from its beginnings in the 1980s right up through the present (Coates, Temoshok, & Mandel, 1984; Temoshok, 1998).

ments that the individual can make, how intrusive the symptoms are, the necessary regimens for treatment, and the knowledge and reactions of other people. For example, patients weakened by chronic obstructive pulmonary disease must make it clear to bystanders that they are tired, and not drunk. The process of **normalization** is the attempt by the ill person to establish and maintain as normal an existence as possible.

Some symptoms are immediately obvious, and therefore the sick person cannot choose whether or not to reveal them. Distorted limbs, a disfigured face, a limp, slurred speech, and disagreeable smells are intrusive and obvious. Unfortunately, sometimes these obvious symptoms are interpreted by others as overwhelmingly pervasive—that is, people may view the chronically ill person as incapable of engaging in any kind of constructive behaviors, even though that is not true. This phenomenon is termed **identity spread** (Strauss & Glaser, 1975). Others tend to overgeneralize; an insidious stereotype is at work. For example, people may speak to a blind or physically impaired person in a loud voice, assuming that they cannot hear.

When the symptoms of sick people are invisible or the fact of the disease is not known to other people, the patients have the option of what sociologist Irving Goffman has called **passing** (Goffman, 1963). That is, these people can engage in normal interactions with others because the others do not know that they are not "normal." Examples are a patient who has had a colostomy and a patient who has had a radical mastectomy. The public is not aware of the patient's disfigurement unless, of course, the patient chooses to reveal it.

This passing, however, can cause a great deal of anxiety. Under some conditions, the person may have to reveal the illness condition or disfigurement. This is true, for example, if a woman who has had a radical mastectomy becomes very close to a man that she is dating. At some point, as sexual intimacy develops, the man will discover the fact. The anxiety that builds up as their intimacy level increases obviously can be very distressing. Another problem, in addition to this anxiety, is that the patient who is "passing" is being accepted by others for something that this person is not. The patient cannot disclose feelings about the deformity without acknowledging its existence. Thus, the person is, in a sense, trapped in a deception. The patient is not sure whether acceptance will continue when the problem is revealed. In the case of certain members of ethnic minority groups, chronic stress to conform to the demands of the majority culture can have an analogous negative effect on health (Contrada et al., 2000).

Goffman discusses passing in his interesting book *Stigma*. He notes that people, like stage actors, try to manage their identities and present themselves to others in a certain light. In this "presentation of self," people's actions may not correspond to their "true" selves. This acting has implications for the patient's sense of identity. As we saw in Chapter 1, a person's identity develops to some extent from other people. If, however, others have an incorrect impression of what someone is really like, false self-impressions may begin to form. The conflict between self-impression and the impression given to others may be detrimental to the patients' well-being. For example, if patients give the impression to others that they are physically fine and in turn come to be treated as such, they may overestimate their abilities; in addition, others may then be reluctant to give the extra encouragement and support required in times of medical crisis.

In light of the many problems of passing, why do many patients do so? Why not just be totally honest? One reason is that there is a stigma associated with many illnesses, which produces harmful reactions. An example is the stigma of cancer. **Stigma** refers to some characteristic or attribute of a person that is deeply discrediting and takes priority over all other characteristics that the person has (Goffman, 1963). It is important to recognize that stigma is actually a property of interpersonal relations (rather than physical condition), because people define what conditions are stigmatizing. Cancer has a greater stigma than heart disease, even though heart disease is a more prevalent killer (Wortman & Dunkel-Schetter, 1979). Tuberculosis once had a greater stigma associated with it than it does today, and AIDS now has a tremendous stigma.

What conditions are considered stigmatizing can be changed with proper public education. Some of the many stigmatizing effects associated with breast cancer, for example, were alleviated when several very prominent women announced publicly that they had had mastectomies. The notion of stigma is important because expectations of society are inextricably entwined with how people cope with chronic illness. It is also the case that presenting oneself in a positive manner, as coping well with one's illness, can actually lead to better adjustment to one's illness (Leake, Friend, & Wadhwa, 1999).

SOCIAL SUPPORT AND REHABILITATION

Many of the greatest difficulties faced by chronically ill persons result not from their physical disability but from their relationships with others. It is not surprising, then, that successful coping may depend as much or even more on socioemotional resources received from others than on the individual's personal strength. As is noted in Chapter 5, the information, clarification, assistance, and reassurance that an individual receives from others is called social support (Caplan, 1979; Cobb, 1976; Cohen & McKay, 1984; Cohen, Underwood, & Gottlieb, 2000). This social support can function in several ways in chronic illness.

Social Functions

In their daily lives, people are members of various groups that provide the social resources necessary for living. For example, people receive information about the demands of their career from their coworkers; they receive assistance from their neighbors and associates; they discuss their feelings with friends and family members; and they form a sense of identity from their ethnic, religious, family, or professional ties.

The groups that help people maintain a sense of identity are called **reference groups.** Reference groups help people evaluate their thoughts, feelings, and abilities, and influence what people believe they should or should not do. If a person moves away from these groups (geographically, to a new job in a new state, for example), psychological and emotional pressures on the person may result. These pressures will be relieved when new group ties are developed. The chronically ill person is in a position similar to, but even more difficult than, someone who has moved to a new job. The ill person desperately needs social support but may have trouble becoming "reestablished." For example, a heart patient may no longer be able to play vigorous sports with his or her friends, but may not yet have developed a network of individuals with whom to spend leisure time. A new identity has not yet been established.

Consider now the **informational function** of social support. Ill persons need much new information about their medical condition—its physical effects, prognosis, the side effects of drugs given for the condition, financial demands, government services, transportation, nursing care, and many other matters. The range of questions may be enormous: Who sells and repairs wheelchairs? Is insulin easily available when traveling overseas? Is it safe (and legal) to drive a car? Which company makes a good prosthesis? Unfortunately, most pre-illness friends and acquaintances of patients are not likely to know the answers to many of these questions, and therefore chronically ill people need to establish firm ties with new sources of information.

Another one of the great pressures facing a person who has been newly diagnosed as having a condition like epilepsy or cancer is uncertainty (Dunkel-Schetter & Wortman, 1982). There is uncertainty about how and by whom to be treated, about what friends and acquaintances will think (and who should be informed), and about what the future will bring. Social psychologists have established that in such times of uncertainty, people usually turn to others—to their reference group—for clarification. When they are afraid and uncertain, people generally seek out others in a similar situation to share feelings and compare reactions. However, patients may have great difficulty contacting other people who are relevant. Unafflicted friends may be inappropriate as people with whom the patients can compare themselves because they are too "distant" (in terms of acquaintance with the disease) or the problem may be too embarrassing. Family members may not be knowledgeable about the patient's particular condition. Medical personnel may be too busy or may be seen as able only to treat physical, not social or emotional, problems. Hence, patients may be unable to clarify their feelings and unable to reduce their uncertainty. This may interfere with the patient's recovery.

Uncertainty may also increase the patient's need for reassurance. In facing daily problems, people turn to others for the positive feedback, warmth, and caring that helps them deal with life's difficulties. However, patients may have a greater need for such comfort at the same time that their families are in need of extra support. Nurses and social workers can fill this need to some extent, but they cannot fully replace the supportive role of friends and family.

In sum, although the needs of the chronically ill for social support can be great, the various problems we have considered so far that face the chronically ill may combine to make such support difficult to obtain. In fact, it appears that patients who need the most social support are likely to get the least (Caplan, 1979). Furthermore, patients with insufficient support may not cooperate fully with their treatment, and this uncooperativeness may in turn reduce the little support that they had been receiving. Fortunately, increasing attention has been paid to the problem of social support. Three areas look promising.

The most likely source of beneficial support is the peer group; many patients can be put in touch with other patients with similar conditions (Kulik & Mahler, 1987). For example, the organization called Reach to Recovery offers mastectomy patients the opportunity to talk with a volunteer, herself a former patient. This organization provides information, a chance to discuss feelings, and the encouragement of seeing a "recovered" patient. There may be an unexpected benefit as well—a benefit for the volunteer. Terese Lasser, the founder of Reach to Recovery, asserts that in reaching out to help others, she helped herself (Lasser, 1974).

Organizations for a wide range of chronic illnesses now exist, and in part, they have emerged as a result of the increasing assertiveness of patients. Whereas traditionally, physicians had complete control over the information patients received, the increasing "consumer" demands of patients have helped bring about the formation of support groups. While these groups may initially form to share information, they may in fact often function effectively in promoting the sharing of feelings. At any given time, about 1 in 20 Americans may be involved with some sort of self-help social support group (Jacobs & Goodman, 1989) See Table 8–1 for some examples of support groups.

Since many of these groups have not been carefully evaluated, it is prudent to be cautious in looking at them. Groups that interfere with necessary medical treatment or that

Table 8–1   Social Support Organizations

Alcoholics Anonymous
P.O. Box 459
Grand Central Station
New York, NY 10164-0371
212-870-3400
www.aa.org/

Alzheimer's Association
919 North Michigan Avenue
Suite 1000
Chicago, IL 60611-1676
800-272-3900
www.alz.org

American Burn Association
National Headquarters Office
625 N. Michigan Avenue, Suite 1530
Chicago, IL 60611
www.ameriburn.org

American Cancer Society
National Home Office
1599 Clifton Road Northeast
Atlanta, GA 30329
800-ACS-2345
www.cancer.org

American Diabetes Association
1660 Duke Street
Alexandria, VA 22314
800-DIABETES
www.diabetes.org

American Lung Association
1740 Broadway
New York, NY 10019
800-LUNG-USA
www.lungusa.org

Arthritis Foundation
1330 West Peachtree Street
Atlanta, GA 30309
800-283-7800
www.arthritis.org

Autism Society of America
7910 Woodmont Ave, Suite 650
Bethesda, MD 20814-3015
800-3-AUTISM Ext. 150
www.autism-society.org

Candlelighters (Childhood Cancer)
www.candlelighters.ca

Compassionate Friends, Inc. (Grief support after death of a child)
P.O. Box 3696
Oak Brook, IL 60522-3696
630-990-0010
www.compassionatefriends.org

Cystic Fibrosis Foundation
6931 Arlington Road
Bethesda, MD 20814
800-FIGHT-CF
www.cff.org

Epilepsy Foundation of America
4351 Garden City Drive
Landover, MD 20785
800-EFA-1000
www.efa.org

National Down Syndrome Society
666 Broadway, 8th Floor
New York, NY 10012-2317
800-221-4602
www.ndss.org

National Stroke Association
96 Inverness Drive East, Suite 1
Englewood, CO 80112-5112
800-STROKES
www.stroke.org

**Parents Without Partners
(Single parents)**
401 N. Michigan Ave
Chicago IL 60611
312-644-6610
www.parentswithoutpartners.org

Phoenix Society (Burn Survivors)
33 Main Street
Suite 403
Nashua, NH 03060
800-888-2876
www.phoenix-society.org/

Spina Bifida Association
4590 MacArthur Boulevard, NW
Suite 250
Washington, DC 20007-4226
800-621-3141
www.sbaa.org

United Ostomy Association, Inc.
19772 MacArthur Blvd.
Suite 200
Irvine, CA 92612-2405
800-826-0826
www.uoa.org

United Cerebral Palsy Associations
1660 L Street, NW
Washington, DC 20036-5602
800-USA-5-UCP
www.ucpa.org

Note: Reading the Web sites of these organizations can provide good insights into the role of social support in coping with chronic illness.

---

are led by unqualified people might produce detrimental rather than beneficial effects (L. H. Levy, 1984; Lieberman, 1979). In addition, although people may report being pleased with peer support or self-help groups, a number of as-yet unknown factors may affect whether their psychological adjustment has really improved as a result of their participation (Hinrichsen, Revenson, & Shinn, 1985). Support may help even though the recipient may be unaware of receiving it (Bolger, Zuckerman, & Kessler, 2000).

A second developing area of social support involves the use of psychologists and social workers in medical settings. Although traditionally, psychologists have been called upon to deal mostly with "mental" problems, recognition of the importance of psychology to all aspects of illness is leading to the inclusion of social scientists on medical "teams." The social scientist pays special attention to the social and emotional needs of the patient and can facilitate positive interactions with family and friends. Furthermore, such a "health facilitator" can also improve relationships among physicians, nurses, and patients, thereby increasing the social support available from medical personnel.

A final source of increased social support is the primary care physician. With the increasing addition of social science to medical school curricula, and with the establishment of training programs in community medicine and family practice medicine, physicians are becoming more sensitive to the importance of social support and better able to provide relevant information, treatment, and referral.

Negative Effects of Social Support

When will social support have negative effects? Many studies confirm that sometimes it may not work as intended (Bolger, Foster, Vinokur, & Ng, 1996; Burg & Seeman, 1994; Dunkel-Schetter & Wortman, 1982; Revenson, Wollman, & Felton, 1983; Revenson, Schiaffino, Majerovitz, & Gibofsky, 1991; Wortman & Dunkel-Schetter, 1987). For example, a patient receiving help from others may feel that he or she is receiving help that cannot be reciprocated. Or, a patient may try to present a favorable image to others in order to try to reestablish social relations, but then may fear being "found out"; as we have noted, this state of hiding aspects of one's illness can be very distressing. These issues are very important to those who have found out that they are HIV-positive (Derlega, Winstead, & Folk-Barron, 2000).

Relatedly, contact with others may not be helpful if the others feel that they are being pressured to interact with the patient or if they try to deny the illness by telling the patient that "you will be perfectly all right." Analogously, people who are highly cynical may not benefit from peer support (Lepore, 1995). Further, families sometimes may model unhealthy behaviors like smoking, or may reward unproductive illness behaviors. Physiological or illness events may be maintained in ongoing cycles of social interaction in a dysfunctional family (Minuchin, Lee, & Simon, 1996).

Finally, social support may be of the wrong type for a person's needs. A breast cancer patient in desperate need of emotional reassurance that she can remain sexually attractive may not be helped by detailed informational support about artificial breasts. In one study of group support for women with breast cancer, peer discussion groups were helpful for women who did not get enough support from their partners or from their physicians. But peer discussion groups were found to be harmful for women who had high levels of support (Helgeson, Cohen, Schulz, & Yasko, 2000). Such problems of social networks become especially challenging as people age (Rook & Schuster, 1996).

What about the pressures on the caregivers that comes from the patients' needs for social support? This is an increasing problem as more family members face AIDS, Alzheimer's, and other serious chronic conditions. There is no doubt that there can be long-term physiological consequences of being under such constant pressure (Esterling, Kiecolt-Glaser, Bodnar, & Glaser, 1994). There are no simple answers to the stress on the caregivers. It depends on many variables including the disease, the setting, the needed care, and the interaction between patient and family member (Vitaliano, Schulz, Kiecolt-Glaser, & Grant, 1997). It also seems to be the case that caregivers are much more likely to be affected by the challenges if they themselves already have a developing condition like cardiovascular disease (Vitaliano et al., 1998). This is of course consistent with diathesis-stress models of illness and with notions of self-healing as a function of the match between the person and the psychosocial environment (Friedman, 1991).

What Can the Health Care Professional Do?

> *Urologist:* You have testicular cancer. You will have an orchiectomy, sometimes called orchidectomy, or surgical excision tomorrow, followed by radiation. Your chances of recovery are excellent—the five-year survival rate is over 85 percent, even if it has spread. Do you have any questions?

There are good ways and there are bad ways for the physician to prepare and assist a patient to deal with illness. Throughout the discussion of the process of adjustment to chronic illness, we have focused on the importance of the patients' adjustment to their environment, their management of relationships with friends and family, and their capacity to deal with symptoms. The emphasis has been on the patients' ultimate responsibility for the management of their social and psychological condition. Remembering that it is the patient's decision and ultimate responsibility to carry out the treatment, the health care professional can still provide much support in an effort to help patients accomplish their goals.

The urologist quoted above is not doing a very good job of preparing his patient for cancer treatment. What could be said and done to help the many victims of testicular cancer recover (as most do) to lead normal, happy lives (Cassileth & Steinfeld, 1987)? First, a fixed office appointment should be designated in advance for discussion of diagnosis and treatment. Second, the spouse or a close friend should be present. Third, the diagnosis and treatment should be revealed simultaneously, so that the focus is on the treatment rather than on the cancer itself. Finally, the physician should use simple language, answer questions, encourage discussion, and find out how the news relates to other aspects of the patient's life.

After the treatment plan is formed, what can be done? First of all, it should be recognized that an acute care unit of a hospital may be inappropriate for a chronically ill patient, unless the patient is temporarily in an acute care crisis. The best place for a chronic illness to be managed, and for patients to work at normalizing their lives, is usually at home. Thus, part of the support from the health care professional should involve aiding patients to care for chronic illness symptoms at home with the support of family members and friends. The health care professional should assess the physical setting of the home in which the patient will be living, either through examination of the setting or by interviewing the patient and the family members about it.

To aid in communication and understanding, the health care professional must have information about the patient generally, the patient's reactions to the illness, and about the social support system. Although patients often disclose information to health care professionals, sometimes a concerted effort has to be made in order to obtain detailed information. Often, however, physicians claim that they cannot spend time collecting psychosocial information through lengthy interviews with patients. Strauss and Glaser suggest that the health care professional should engage in **action dialog**, or action interviews, with patients. This technique involves gaining information from patients (and giving information to patients) while doing something to them. For example, when changing dressings on a wound, the physician might talk with the patient and explore the social, psychological, and physical resources available to the patient in a program of rehabilitation. Information about the social and physical settings and also the patient's psychological resources can be gained from interviews with family members and friends.

Because of the inability to cure chronic disease, the work of people who care for and give comfort to the chronically ill may not be valued as highly as the work of those who provide acute care. Care of the chronically ill is usually somewhat routine, and it is regarded as not as exciting as acute care for trauma. On the other hand, the care of the chronically ill can be especially challenging because of the many social and psychological factors involved. The management of patients and their immediate families demands the skill of professionals well versed in both the social and technical aspects of medicine.

SPECIAL CASES OF CHRONIC ILLNESS

Crisis, coping, and social support are issues that are found in all forms of chronic illness. However, each chronic condition also has various unique problems that must be addressed, and as an illustration, we consider three special cases of chronic illness. The first involves a specific age group—children. The second concerns a specific illness—cancer. And the third case involves a type of traumatic injury—burns. Examination of these three cases provides a further understanding of the importance of psychology to chronic illness.

Long-Term Illness in Children

The prevalence of chronic conditions in childhood is surprisingly high (Karoly, 1988; Mattsson, 1972; Quittner et al., 1998). Considering serious chronic illness of primarily physical origin, American and British surveys find that up to 10 percent of all children are afflicted with chronic illness. The most common physical conditions are heart problems, cerebral palsy, asthma, orthopedic problems, and diabetes mellitus, as well as AIDS in some communities. Other serious long-term illnesses in children include hemophilia, muscular dystrophy, rheumatic fever, chronic renal disease, leukemia, and permanent handicaps resulting from physical injuries.

Children with long-term physical disorders tend to be subjected to many stressful situations, but may not have the emotional resources to deal with these stresses. First, children may not have sufficient cognitive development to understand illness. For example, while pain is emotionally stressful to adults, adults are usually able to understand its cause. Children, on the other hand, tend to be extremely confused about the origin of pain and discomfort. They may feel that they are ill as a punishment for disobedience to parents, or perhaps because their parents were not protective enough. If the condition results from hereditary factors, the child may express anger and resentment toward the parents (Mattsson, 1972).

A second source of enormous emotional stress for the child is the health care system itself. Hospital stays involve separation from family, school, and friends. Fears of abandonment may arise. This separation is also often accompanied by frightening situations, orchestrated by the physician, not by the parent. The health care system also removes much control and chances for self-care from patients. This can be especially troubling to children or young adolescents who are just beginning to develop independence in caring for themselves. They may experience anger and humiliation because they are being pulled back to a helpless dependency state. Some children may respond to this helplessness by regressing to even more childish or babylike behavior; they may lose some of the achievements that they have attained in motor functioning and social functioning (Mattsson, 1972).

Finally, surgical invasion of the body may be very difficult for children to deal with because of their fears of bodily mutilation. These fantasies tend to be especially difficult for younger children. Most sick children also find restriction and immobilization particularly stressful emotionally; they are accustomed to freedom of movement in order to express dissatisfaction and to explore the environment. Prolonged restraint of a child may cause anxiety, a buildup of tension, and eventual temper tantrums. On the other hand, the child might respond with withdrawal into an apathetic, depressed condition.

One study had children role-play what they would do and what they would suggest a friend should do when facing a medical procedure (Peterson, Crowson, Saldana, & Holdridge, 1999). For themselves, the children were more likely to choose a negative, reactive strategy like crying. But for their friends, they suggested a more proactive strategy, like thinking about fun things. This finding suggests that children often know how to cope (cognitively) but are still unable to cope. Therefore, they would probably benefit from motivational and emotional training.

A third source of emotional stress for the child involves family members (Brown, 1999). While parents may become more loving and indulgent, siblings may become extremely resentful of the sick child. Or parents themselves may at times reject the ill child, criticizing the child for causing inconvenience. These changes in family attitudes can be extremely confusing to the child who is ill. A good example is childhood diabetes (Benoliel, 1975).

Childhood diabetes is a chronic metabolic disorder that is treatable but usually not curable (Goldston, Kovacs, Obrosky, & Iyengar, 1995; Johnson, Tomer, Cunningham, & Henretta, 1990). The child's life may depend upon receiving daily injections of the hormone insulin; however, this is not the only responsibility of the person caring for the child. Along with the proper scheduling of these injections, dietary restrictions and activity monitoring are needed. The insulin and the body's glucose (sugar) must be balanced within the child or the child can experience a severe medical crisis. Without a regular pattern of food intake and insulin injection, the child could experience symptoms as simple as confusion and irritability or as complex and dangerous as convulsions and loss of consciousness.

The parents of the child implement the treatment regimen but are also responsible for the socialization of the child—that is, teaching the child the rules of conduct and the norms of caring for himself or herself. Balancing the usual routine care of a child in the morning (getting the child ready for school) with the extra demands of the illness (urine tests and insulin injections) can be complex. A major problem faced by parents is rearranging their social activities, including the activities of the other children in the family (Benoliel, 1975). Much of the scheduling of the family's activities revolves around the needs of the chronically ill diabetic child. For example, in order not to tempt the diabetic child, parents may refrain from keeping sweets in the kitchen, thus depriving the other children of sweets.

Children with a serious respiratory disease such as asthma often express fears of suffocation, drowning, or dying while they are asleep. However, asthma can be controlled, and children can be taught to help manage their condition (Mesters, Meertens, Crebolder, & Parcel, 1993). For example, they can be taught to spit out mucus and explain to their friends that such actions are necessary to help them breathe (Evans, Clark, Feldman, & Wasilewski, 1990). In contrast, children with chronic heart disease often find it difficult to understand the nature of their illness, the reasons why their activity is restricted, and why extensive medical procedures and perhaps surgery may be required; they may experience minimal symptoms. At the same time, these children may be very frightened when references are made to the importance of the individual's heart to life itself (Vernon, Foley, Sipowicz, & Schulman, 1965). On the other hand, some children with deformities withdraw almost totally and become very shy and lonely.

Children with chronic renal disease experience special stresses if they are treated with hemodialysis or kidney transplantation. Children may feel overwhelmingly dependent upon a machine and find it difficult to seek independence from their families. Parents may attempt to exert a great deal of control over children who have received a kidney transplant in an effort to prevent rejection of the kidney. If rejection does occur, the child may blame himself or herself for destroying the kidney that was given as a special gift, often by a family member (Abram, 1970; Adler, 1972; Reichsman & Levy, 1972).

Children with leukemia may become very depressed, upset, and uncooperative. They may refuse to confide in their parents and avoid suggested treatment. Such problems generally result in part from miscommunication. The parents, trying to be strong and supportive, may act in a friendly, lighthearted manner toward the child, attempting to minimize the seriousness of the illness. However, a hospitalized child is very adept at detecting such attempted deception; it is obvious to the child that something is very wrong. Thus, the child may interpret the parent's positive act as evidence that they do not really care about the child's illness and the possibility of death. The child thus feels abandoned and becomes alternately depressed and rebellious. The problem can often be resolved if the adults recognize the difficulty and are honest with their child about their true feelings and concerns (Brown, 1999; Cantor, 1978). Therefore, in all chronic illnesses, the psychological problems experienced by children may be quite complex, and not at all immediately evident.

Many children cope quite well with the stresses of long-term chronic illness. In the proper circumstances, with supportive, understanding adults, children can be very adaptable. Many studies of long-term childhood disorders report surprisingly good psychosocial adaptation of children, usually when the children are provided with emotional support and understanding. In fact, most children experiencing long-term disability accept their physical limitations; often, they have never known anything else!

Although we have been focusing on children, there are also other age differences in reaction to chronic illness. People have different needs, different expectations, and different social ties and networks at different stages of the life span. For example, one study of middle-aged and older adults with chronic illness found evidence that older people react to illness with less anger and less emotion than do the middle-aged, perhaps because they have a greater expectation of illness in old age (Felton & Revenson, 1987). A true understanding of adaptation to illness must be based on a broad view of the personal and environmental forces affecting the ill person.

Cancer

It was not by chance that we began this chapter by mentioning cancer. Cancer is an important area of chronic illness (Cassileth, 1979; Falvo, 1999). Millions of Americans have a history of cancer, many of whom had it diagnosed years ago. It is estimated that over 55 million Americans who are now living will have cancer; it will strike two out of three families. A century ago, few cancer patients lived very long. Today, however, many are alive years after treatment. Some of these people are completely cured, some will face a recurrence, and some have a continuing problem or disability: They must cope with the problems of chronic illness.

A classic survey of the social psychological needs of about 1,000 cancer patients and their families was sponsored by the California Division of the American Cancer Society (ACS, 1979). Experienced social workers conducted in-depth interviews with adults who had been living with cancer of varying forms (except skin cancer) for about two or three years. About two-thirds of the sample was female, but otherwise the people were quite representative of the population. A number of important findings emerged.

When is the worst time for a cancer patient? The periods that were reported as being most stressful for both patients and their families were immediately following diagnosis and during hospitalization. Interestingly, a significant proportion of patients reported that *release* from the hospital was the most stressful time! The stress of diagnosis results from uncertainty, whereas the stresses of hospitalization and release from the hospital are in large part due to changed interpersonal relationships. Although people often imagine that pain and weakness are the major problems encountered in cancer, actually the social disruptions are most troublesome for most patients.

One of the significant problems faced by cancer patients is the changes in their physical appearance. Why is appearance so important? First, the physical attractiveness can somewhat affect the reactions of the doctor (Lasagna, 1970). More importantly, however, the patient's appearance affects relations with others. For example, chemotherapy often produces hair loss, and while hair loss in itself is not a terribly severe problem, it can have dramatic effects on family and friends because of its effects on appearance. Hence, it has long been suggested that patients should keep themselves as attractive as possible, including the use of wigs (Donavan & Pierce, 1976). Perceived support from family members has been found to be related to positive emotional adjustment to breast cancer (Lichtman, Wood, & Taylor, 1982).

In the beginning of this chapter we saw that, after his diagnosis of cancer, Orville Kelly had nowhere to turn for social support. A similar finding emerged from this California survey. On the whole, supportive services were said to be missing, inadequate, or unknown. Most people were aware of no social services to which they could turn. While only about one-quarter of the patients felt that they could turn to religious leaders, writings about cancer, or other cancer patients for help, the vast majority of patients who knew these services were available utilized them. In other words, it was found that there was a tremendous need that could be met but mostly was not being met. Consequently, patients turned mostly to their families for help.

An insightful study by health psychologist Christine Dunkel-Schetter (1984) looked directly at social support among patients with breast cancer or intestinal cancer. The patients were mostly middle-aged women in the Chicago area; they were interviewed about a year after their initial diagnoses. What did these respondents report to be helpful? Most mentioned emotional support, especially love and concern by family members, as opposed to other kinds of social support. Interestingly, informational support provided by health professionals was also seen as very helpful, especially when accompanied by emotional support; but information provided by family and friends was seen as unhelpful. Attempts by relatives to provide information, advice, and examples of other patients' recoveries ("so-and-so had her breast removed and is doing fine") were resented. Furthermore, social support was not so helpful when patients had a poor prognosis. In fact, as noted above, such social support can have negative consequences (Revenson, Wolfman, & Felton, 1983). In short, social support for cancer patients can often be extremely important, but the meaning and context of the support must be carefully evaluated (Bolger, Zuckerman, & Kessler, 2000; Wortman & Dunkel-Schetter, 1987).

Many people hold stereotyped views of cancer, in which they see cancer as tied to chronic pain, prolonged weakness, dirtiness, fear, and obsession with death, even though such characteristics are by no means universal. It is also true that cancer patients are often blamed for their illness, much the way people were once seen as "causing" their tuberculosis (Sontag, 1978). Although we have seen that psychological reactions can affect health, there is little justification for asserting that most cancer patients had a decisive role in producing their disease. Rather, the psychological process called "blaming the victim" is at work (Ryan, 1971). Many people desire to believe in a "just world" in which people get what they deserve (Lerner, 1970). Seeing a young, active, "innocent" person who is ravaged by cancer is quite difficult for many people to deal with, and therefore they come to believe that the cancer patient somehow deserved to be stricken; the victim is blamed. This process is part of people's general attempt to make sense out of their world, and it appears with other diseases as well; however, the fear and uncertainty of cancer make it a special target. Such reactions understandably interfere with the cancer patient's ability to cope.

In the California survey, many patients saw their communications with their physicians as inadequate. Their ability to deal with the stresses of cancer was reported to be hindered by lack of sufficient explanation from medical personnel. Problem areas ranged from diagnosis and treatment to rehabilitation to socioemotional matters. We emphasize the importance of proper communication throughout this book. In this case, however, its critical significance is highlighted by the spontaneously volunteered comments of cancer patients on these matters. In addition to providing much-needed information, medical personnel can warn patients about the psychological reactions of others that they are likely to encounter and suggest ways in which they can try to deal with these reactions. As the health psychology model emphasizes, cancer is not only a biological disease; it too has many significant psychosocial aspects.

The California survey also found that cancer had a considerable financial impact on people (ACS, 1979). About one sixth of the sample foresaw a problem with their future financial security. Many patients had to make significant adjustments in their pre-illness lifestyle because of monetary problems. Although financial matters are often seen as an economic problem rather than a medical or psychological problem, financial resources are actually directly relevant to the patient's health. With sufficient money, patients and their families are able to maintain their usual lifestyle and concentrate their efforts on dealing with the illness. Adequate insurance makes a big difference. What was noteworthy in the California survey was that the low-income working people (who most needed insurance) were least likely to have adequate coverage. (This finding is still not unusual, years later.) This means that in many cases the children of the cancer patient had to forego college and the family's house had to be mortgaged or sold. The social and emotional needs of many patients can never be completely addressed so long as the financial burden to families continues to be crippling (ACS, 1979).

Thus, there are various problems of chronic illness to be faced by the cancer patient, but again, the problems are often mostly psychological and social, not simply medical. Whereas the special problems faced by children with chronic illness resulted mostly from their state of dependency and limited understanding, the problems of cancer flow mostly from the stigma of cancer and its attendant fear, uncertainty, and lack of social support. Additional problems result from changes in the body. This latter problem is discussed next.

The Burned Patient

Hundreds of thousands of Americans suffer each year from burns. In the past, most patients died from mutilating burns, but with new medical procedures, many lives are now saved. Recovery is not simple, however. Being burned is a traumatic experience—it is extremely painful and results in deformity and debilitation. There is also an enormous chance of infection. Furthermore, victims of burns continue to be reminded of the trauma they have experienced; throughout their lives they have scars to remind them of the experience (Artz, Moncrief, & Pruitt, 1979).

There are enormous psychological problems that accompany severe burns (Tarrier, 1995; Wisely, Masur, & Morgan, 1983). It was found in one study that about half the victims of the major Coconut Grove nightclub fire still experienced severe emotional problems almost a year after the fire (A. Adler, 1943). Two years after the initial trauma, many of the patients were functioning interpersonally at about the same level that they had been functioning before the injury. But for many, the trauma continued. The enormous negative emotional impact of burns may last for years.

What special kinds of problems are faced by patients who are severely burned? A major identity crisis usually arises directly from the individual's altered appearance. The patient's body image (sense of self) must be redefined to take into account the scarring, deformity, and weakness resulting from the burns. Equally importantly, strained interactions with other people alter the patient's social identity, and so the patient faces feelings of isolation and estrangement.

Although many friends attempt to respond positively to the burn patient, sometimes people respond to the physical deformity with expressions of revulsion and disgust. These reactions can be devastating to the self-concept of the patient. While immediate resumption of a familiar role within the family could help prevent an identity crisis, this usually does not occur because of the prolonged hospitalization that is required after being burned. When finally discharged from the hospital, the patient may have trouble fitting back into the usual family role.

Consider the problems of a young woman who is severely burned. As with mastectomy, women who lose their physical attractiveness because of severe burns tend to assume that they have also lost their sexual desirability. In spite of assurances from their husbands or boyfriends, these women may be overwhelmed by the feeling that they are no longer attractive. Their response is to withdraw. For their part, family members often treat the patient differently from how this person was treated before the accident, partly because of the expectations of the sick role and partly because the burn victim acts differently. Of course, burned patients often experience physical handicaps and limitations as well. They may have to wear bandages for a long time, and their skin, which is scarred or recently grafted, may be painful.

Patients who succeed in resolving their identity crises do so primarily by using certain patterns of adaptive responses. Through support and acceptance from people who are close to and love them, patients may begin to believe that what really matters is their "inner selves." They confront their bodies and the scarred, deformed outer self comes to be seen as unimportant. This denial of the obtrusiveness of the self presented to the world is adaptive in terms of the acceptance of their injury and their ability to continue on with life.

Since the self is partly socially defined, however, problems arise. The patients may unrealistically minimize the obtrusiveness of their appearance. They may consistently underestimate their unattractiveness, and therefore have trouble relating to others. Patients finally adjust if they come to a more realistic self-image (recognizing that they may repulse or scare others who do not know them) accompanied by some kind of rationalization about what has happened to them. A number of patients with severe burns come to the conclusion that what happened to them has made them better people. Severely burned patients eventually describe themselves as drawing closer to their spouses and to their families. They tend to experience a new awareness of life and of their role within their families and their relationships to other people. In other words, they recognize their physical problems but see the good that has come of it.

On the other hand, some of the ways in which patients deal with their disabilities and deformities are quite maladaptive. Some patients withdraw from others and experience a great deal of anxiety about interpersonal relationships. Their extreme shyness and self-consciousness may follow in part from their pre-injury personality, although there is no conclusive evidence on this point. This detrimental coping mechanism prevents patients from recognizing that they are accepted by other people, particularly family members and friends. Withdrawal from social contacts and close social relationships prevents these patients from reestablishing their identity.

As with other chronic conditions, there is significant pressure on the family of the burned patient. Many patients experience confusion and disorientation as a result of a temporary acute brain syndrome (delirium) that often accompanies burn trauma. Relatives may find the patient verbally abusive and of course are distressed by this extremely strange behavior.

In addition, while the initial response of the family is relief that the patient will live, the family soon begins to feel the stresses of the difficulties involved in the patient's hospitalization. They must constantly provide emotional support, but there is usually little support provided for them. The burn patient tends to focus only upon himself or herself, returning little in the way of support to the distressed relative. Finally, the family members must adjust to the altered appearance of the patient. There is pressure on the family members to monitor constantly their reactions to the patient.

About one-third of burn victims are children, who face unique challenges (Artz, Moncrief, & Pruitt, 1979; Wisely, Masur, & Morgan, 1983). During the initial stages of hospitalization, most children almost surely are unable to cope rationally with the severe pain, the delirium, and the many medical and surgical procedures. Thus, subsequent efforts to cope often start out from a very difficult point. As the child starts to recover, there may be severe cognitive and emotional difficulties. Cognitively, the child cannot understand the terrible ordeal and may tend to blame himself for the burning (and the "punishment" received in the hospital). Emotionally, there are so many interruptions of normal social relations that severe emotional disturbances and behavior problems may result. Such issues present great challenges to future work in pediatric health psychology.

Many of the issues relevant to burn patients also apply to victims of automobile accidents, assaults, suicide attempts, falls, and other injuries. Since such incidents constitute the major threat to the health of people from childhood to age 40, the relevant psychological issues are likely to be an increasing focus of attention in health psychology in the years ahead.

Although facing a chronic illness can be challenging, successful adaptation is not rare. In fact, most people who develop a chronic condition can face the initial crisis, learn to cope, and go on to lead meaningful and mostly healthy lives. Many people are motivated by their illness to become closer to their friends and family, more focused in their work, and more appreciative of the daily pleasures of their lives. Encouraged by their friends and by health professionals, and developing new psychological strengths, they learn to make every day count.

SUMMARY AND CONCLUSION

A major area for the application of psychological principles to health and medicine involves adaptation to chronic illness. Improved technological treatments for medical emergencies coupled with an increasingly elderly population have made chronic illness a significant health issue. Millions of Americans suffer from heart disease, cancer, paralysis, chronic lung disease, diabetes, AIDS, and other conditions that create a long-lasting, significant physical impairment. For the most part, however, the physical impairments are not the greatest source of difficulty for the chronically ill. Rather, chronically ill patients often face their greatest challenges in psychosocial matters—the crisis of illness, coping with illness, and the need for social support.

Once the crisis of the onset of serious illness is overcome, and the long-term problems of the chronically ill take on increasing importance, people with chronic illness face many novel social and psychological challenges in their daily lives. Lack of recognition of subsequent medical crisis and lack of knowledge about what to do to prevent it can put the patient's life in danger. It is often difficult to convince a patient that the treatment regimen for chronic illness is really helping, because the alternative is hidden. For the patient, the side effects must be outweighed either by relief of the symptoms or by a sufficient fear of the disease itself.

For the chronically ill, one of the most difficult problems (if not the most difficult problem) involves relationships with other people. A major ongoing challenge is that of controlling symptoms and hiding them from casual friends and acquaintances. It is difficult to be totally honest because stigmas associated with many illnesses can produce harmful reactions from others.

Many problems of social support for patients may possibly be resolved through various social groups and coping techniques. Any given coping technique for chronic illness can be adaptive in one situation and extremely maladaptive in another. Characteristics of the illness, such as the type and location of symptoms, tend to influence the degree of successful coping with the illness. The health care professional can help patients by setting regular appointments (including the patient's spouse or friend) to discuss the ongoing treatment. Children with long-term physical disorders tend to be subjected to many stressful situations but may not have the emotional resources to deal with these stresses.

In all chronic illnesses, the psychological problems experienced may be quite variable, and not at all immediately evident. Discovering the new ways in which they must relate to their social worlds is perhaps the greatest challenge facing the chronically ill.

Recommended Additional Readings And Resources

Moos, Rudolf H. (Ed.). (1986). *Coping with life crises: An integrated approach.* New York: Plenum Press.

Revenson, Tracey A., Schiaffino, Kathleen M., Majerovitz, Deborah S., & Gibofsky, Allan. (1991). Social support as a double-edged sword: The relation of positive and problematic support to depression among rheumatoid arthritis patients. *Social Science & Medicine, v33* (n7) 807–813.

Pennebaker, J. W. (1997). *Opening up.* New York: Guilford.

Taylor, Shelley E. (1989). *Positive illusions: Creative self-deception and the healthy mind.* New York: Basic Books.

Zarit, Steven H., Pearlin, Leonard I., & Schaie, K. Warner. (Eds.). (1993). *Caregiving systems: Informal and formal helpers.* Hillsdale, NJ: L. Erlbaum Associates.

Reach to Recovery (800-227-2345): http://www2.cancer.org/bcn/reach.html

University of Pennsylvania OncoLink Support Groups: http://www.oncolink.upenn.edu/psychosocial/support/

American Heart Association: http://www.americanheart.org/

National Cancer Institute: http://www.nci.nih.gov/

The Phoenix Society for Burn Survivors: http://www.phoenix-society.org/

Spina Bifida Association of America I: http://www.sbaa.org/

Key Concepts

chronic illness

acute illness

initial crisis

seven major tasks of adaptation
  coping with the discomfort and physical incapacity
  dealing with the medical technology
  maintenance of adequate communication
  preservation of emotional balance
  preserving a satisfactory self-image
  preserving relationships
  preparing for an uncertain future

social death

coping

visualization

search for meaning

normalization

identity spread

passing

stigma

social support

reference groups

informational function

action dialog

Chapter 9

DYING, DEATH, AND GRIEF

Something has gone wrong with health care when many dying people fear uncommunicative physicians, loneliness, terminal pain, or dehumanizing artificial life support much more than they fear death itself. Hamlet proclaimed, "To die, to sleep; to sleep: perchance to dream: ay, there's the rub." Today, although many share Hamlet's fear of after-death experiences—what dreams may come, they truly dread being abandoned or belittled or facing terrible suffering while still alive.

For many years of the post–World War II 20th century, many Americans main-
tained a kind of death taboo. Most young adults could look forward to a long life.
Dying was thought to be a kind of curse of the hospitalized elderly and a few unfortu-
nate younger victims; it was not much discussed and not much thought about. Most
young people (except war veterans) had never seen a dead body. However, this inno-
cence is disappearing. The existence of AIDS in epidemic proportions means that so-
ciety has often had to confront dying and death. Further, many young people face
scenes of homicides, suicides, accidents, and drug overdose deaths.

More than any other topic in health psychology, death is intensely personal,
and it calls for some personal reflection. In your personal encounters with death,
who died? Was it a grandparent, parent, sibling, coworker, or fellow soldier?
What aspect of your own inevitable death is the most distasteful to you? Is it that
you could no longer work, or could not finish something you have started? Do you
fear the pain of dying? What does death mean? Is it an end, or a beginning? Is it
a kind of endless sleep with rest and peace, a joining of your spirit with a cosmic
consciousness? Is there nothing after death?

What kind of death would you prefer? A death that is sudden, or one that gives
you time to prepare for it? In the prime of life, or in very old age? If you were told that
you had a terminal disease and a limited time to live (say, six months), how would you
spend the time until you died? Would you make no change in your lifestyle? Contem-
plation of such questions helps us to approach the topic of dying and death.

Consider the following example of a young woman who is dying. Sarah is a 32-year-old housewife who has been married for 10 years. She has two young children. Sarah and her husband work hard to pay for the family's expenses, yet they have a close relationship. They have purchased a home where the school system is good and the children can play safely. Sarah has had a breast biopsy, and the discovery of a malignancy led to radical mastectomy. Cancer has spread to the lymph nodes, and Sarah's chances of long-term survival are fairly low.

The psychological management of death and bereavement is a key issue for society and an important aspect of the role of the health care professional (Kastenbaum, 1992; Stephenson, 1985). How much should the patient and the family be told about the condition of a patient with poor odds of survival? Should hope of a cure always be offered? How can the patient and the family best prepare for death? What reactions can be expected? How can the health care professional deal with these reactions? In this chapter we consider these and related issues.

Thanatology, the study of death, is a relatively new field, but much progress has been made (Kastenbaum, 1992; Koocher, 1986). This chapter first considers the perspective of dying patients—their feelings about their impending death and their attempts to cope with the crisis. Hospice is examined. We then probe the impact of impending death and death itself on the family, and the family's processes of grieving. Next, caregivers' reactions are analyzed. Finally, we consider the special issues of children and death, and suicide.

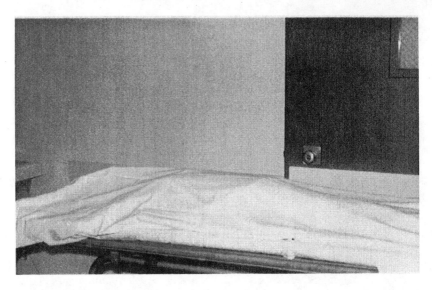

Figure 9-1   Death is a socioemotional experience as well as a biological event, but Americans tend to try to hide away various signs of dying and death. *(Photo by Howard S. Friedman.)*

REACTIONS TO IMPENDING DEATH

For many years, health care professionals would often tell the families of terminal patients, but not the patients themselves, that they were dying. As recently as the 1950s, most physicians, nurses, and other health professionals routinely denied to their dying patients that they were dying. This approach is still taken in some countries, such as Japan, where cancer patients are often not told that they have cancer. (However, in Japan, the issue is now one of active debate.)

Although information might have been given to relatives so that arrangements could be made, many health care professionals saw their involvement with the patient as extending simply to technical medical care. Following the traditional biomedical model, many providers believed that their primary job was to keep the patient alive as long as possible. Although everyone dies, death often was seen as a medical failure.

Of course, we have seen that there are apparently sometimes good reasons for this stance, in terms of patients' expectations. For example, a hematologist's letter to the medical journal *The Lancet* describes the case of a man in his mid-50s with leukemia ("Killed by a Word," 1994). The disease was not severe, and the patient was doing fine for three years, until he happened to look over his physician's shoulder and see the word "leukemia" on his medical chart. He was dead within three weeks. Does this mean that physicians should be more deceptive, or that they should do a better job of explaining the diagnoses?

Legally, death generally means **brain death,** which occurs when there is no longer any activity whatsoever in the brain. (The heart may still be beating, especially if the person is on a respirator.) However, in practice, brain death sometimes means sufficient, extensive brain damage such that the patient could never come out of a coma—could never think or act again. This vagueness opens a number of controversies; for example, a religious argument might be made against harvesting organs for transplant from a comatose patient on a respirator with such massive brain damage.

Just as death is not purely a biological event, dying is a **psychosocial** event in addition to a biological process. That is, the process of dying affects the patient's thoughts, feelings, and relationships (Garfield, 1979). Even if not told directly, a patient often knows that he or she is dying. But the dying may not be readily acknowledged by others (Becker, 1973). The family may deny the information or may refuse to deal with the emotional issues that impending death creates. Dying is partly a social phenomenon because it affects the way in which people react (Kübler-Ross, 1969).

Keeping information about death from patients is often counterproductive. Even 30 years ago, over 80 percent of patients interviewed said they would want to know about their terminal illness (Erickson & Hyerstay, 1979; Feifel, 1965). In other follow-up studies, up to 98 percent of patients undergoing diagnostic tests at a cancer detection center indicated that they would want to be told the truth, even if they had cancer. Yet during the 1950s and 1960s, about 70 to 90 percent of the physicians interviewed said they did not tell patients that they were soon going to die (Erickson & Hyerstay, 1979). Thus, the patient was enmeshed in an atmosphere of deception. Controlling verbal and nonverbal behaviors was virtually impossible, however, and family members were especially poor at carrying out the deception. This produced only conflicts. As Woody Allen (1976) put it, he wasn't afraid to die; he just didn't want to be there when it happened.

Patients thus often faced what is called a **double-bind situation** (Erickson & Hyerstay, 1979; Dunkel-Schetter & Wortman, 1982). Conflicting messages such as "you're going to be okay" combined with very sad or depressed facial expressions of family members confused and alienated the patient, who was already feeling very poorly. The patient would ask himself or herself, "Why are the family members visiting for such a short time? Why do I feel like my condition is getting worse? Why won't the doctor look at me and talk to me?" As the inconsistencies recurred, the patient became more apprehensive and suspicious. Eventually, if the patient asked, "Am I going to die?", the family members would defer to the nurse, the nurse to the physician, and perhaps only after immense emotional pain would the patient receive the answer that by then the patient already knew.

The communication of information (e.g., "The prognosis is poor beyond six months") now occurs with great frequency. However, there are still many psychological factors at work to render the patient lonely and alienated. While once there was a conspiracy of silence with respect to medical information, today there may be a conspiracy of silence with respect to feelings (Weisman & Worden, 1975).

People who find out about their impending death face a crisis with which they have had no prior experience. Everything in a person's life is threatened. Often, the patient experiences psychological shock accompanied by denial—a feeling that this cannot be happening to him or her—and anger. Finally, when death seems inevitable, the patient may experience some grief, a letting go of people and places, and eventual acceptance of the inevitable. Elisabeth Kübler-Ross proposed distinct stages in the reaction of the person who is dying (Kübler-Ross, 1969).

Stages of Dying

In her influential, best-selling book, *On Death and Dying*, Kübler-Ross proposed that dying patients go through five stages. Based upon her interviews with approximately 200 patients in a Chicago area hospital, she suggested that the stages are normal ways of responding to the prospect of death.

Patients may begin with the stage of **denial** in which they are not able to face the information. For example, a patient may insist that the prognosis is a mistake, and this patient may seek new tests or even new doctors. According to Kübler-Ross, denial does not last very long, but patients differ in the amount of time they take in this initial stage.

Kübler-Ross claims that in the second stage, the patient becomes **angry** and asks the question, "Why me?" The patient vents anger and resentment at both family and health care personnel. Concerns of equity may become important as the patient sees other "less deserving" people enjoying good health. The patient may want to assert that he or she is not dead yet and should not be ignored. Anger may also be an attempt by the patient to regain control over his or her life. This concern reflects societal belief that life should be fair.

In the third stage, many patients begin to **bargain.** The patient may try to make a deal with fate for more time or less pain. The patient may offer more compliant behavior in exchange for these benefits. The dying person may try to strike a bargain with God, often because of feelings of guilt. The person tries to exchange good deeds for more life. These efforts reflect our society's view that death is some sort of punishment.

Many dying patients face a number of losses. They may lose their job, financial resources, independence, and even parts of their bodies. There is also the specter of future losses. According to Kübler-Ross, when bargaining does not work, these losses lead many patients into the fourth stage: **depression.** The patient goes through a type of self-grieving. If the patient lives long enough, the fifth and final stage may be reached: **acceptance.**

People at the final stage contemplate death with a quiet acceptance. It is not necessarily a form of giving up, but it is not a happy stage either. Kübler-Ross says, "It is almost void of feelings." For example, one may come to an acceptance of the ways in which one's family will go on. At this stage, the dying person often wants to be cut off from the problems of the outside world; they are no longer relevant to him or her. The patient may severely limit the number of visitors permitted. Sitting together with the family in silence is common. Extraordinary life-prolonging measures are not desired.

Scientific evaluation.   There has been no scientific demonstration of progression through such stages (Wortman & Silver, 1989). Rather, the scheme turns out to be a convenient way of looking at different patient reactions, but there is no convincing evidence that there are only five basic orientations among dying people or that people move from one stage to the next in succession. The stages were developed on the basis of psychiatric interviews, and they represent subjective analyses by Kübler-Ross and her colleagues. In this scheme, there tends to be an enormous concentration on the process of dying, but patients' previous usual coping mechanisms are largely ignored.

Other research on crises, including dying, has found that patients respond to the crisis much the same way they have responded to crises in the past (Kastenbaum & Aisenberg, 1972). If a patient usually responds to a crisis with denial, this patient is very likely to use denial when facing death. If the usual response is anger, that response will probably appear. Some patients move directly to the acceptance stage. Other patients remain depressed throughout the entire time, from first learning about their impending death to the end of life. Others remain optimistic. Knowledge of the patient as a person can be important in both predicting and understanding the patient's reaction to the news of impending death.

Although Kübler-Ross's model of the stages of dying lacks independent confirmation, her work has been important in improving study of and sensitivity to the needs of dying patients. Yet some practical problems have arisen from Kübler-Ross's stage theory. Patients' behavior may be forced into a mold of expectations, although patients differ greatly in their reactions to dying. Patients also react differently to secondary sufferings, such as the loss of self-esteem, fears of separation from those close to them, and the anxieties that come with feelings of hopelessness. A patient's response to dying depends upon his or her age, past experience, personality, and lifestyle, as well as on the specific disease, treatment, and the expectation of time remaining (Kastenbaum, 1992, 1998).

Dying of AIDS

Perhaps not since the Black Plague killed half the population of Europe have thoughts about death been so changed by a single epidemic disease—AIDS. As its name suggests, acquired immunodeficiency syndrome is a collection of symptoms involving the suppression of the normal immune responses. As noted in Chapter 2, it is caused by a virus, the so-called human immunodeficiency virus, or HIV, and is spread by sexual contact or contact with an infected person's blood.

Although many more people die of cardiovascular disease and cancer, AIDS is the leading cause of death among young American males, especially homosexuals and African-Americans. Since the disease is primarily sexually transmitted, young people are especially likely to be its victims. The fear of AIDS and early death is so great in some circles that cases are reported of people who do not have the virus but are entering the sick role and developing some of the symptoms of the disease.

AIDS patients often face a long period of serious illness. Further, in our society, it is otherwise not common for young people to die. Thus, AIDS raises special issues about dying.

The recent use of combination anti-retroviral therapy, which suppresses the virus and prolongs survival, often has turned AIDS into a chronic disease, but a life-threatening one with many impairments. The uncertainty can be quite stressful, as it is difficult to make long-term plans (Kelly, Otto-Salaj, Sikkema, Pinkerton, & Bloom, 1998). Further, the necessity of taking many drugs with side effects makes patient adherence a very challenging issue (Stewart & Gregory, 1996; Ostrow, 1997) (see also Chapter 12). Many AIDS sufferers are marginalized by society, or otherwise isolated. For example, they may be in a gay community where their friends are ill or have died, and where they have been cut off from the community of their childhoods. Or, they may be in prison. Or, they may be a straight person in a middle class community, ostracized for their disease.

People infected with HIV may have to make difficult choices about treatment, and they must cope with the emotional roller coaster of facing new potential cures that turn out to be false hopes. All of this is commonly compounded by a premature confrontation of death, since AIDS is primarily (but not exclusively) a disease of the young.

Coping with Dying

Through church records, peasant life in the 14th century in the small French town of Montaillou has been reconstructed, revealing that an important aspect of life for them concerned death (Ladurie, 1978). Death at a young age was very common, and saving the soul was very important. Yet it was also of great importance to die surrounded by household and family members—not to die alone. Although today, saving the soul is generally less important for many people, dying patients are often still most afraid of being left alone. Included here is the fear of being left in pain without any control over it. These are the key issues in coping with dying.

It is important that patients have some hope (there is always a chance for a longer life), and that they understand "we will be with you" (we will not abandon you). A more positive outlook may facilitate coping and may help in the fight against the disease. For example, in a study of dying AIDS patients, those with a "realistic acceptance"—who accept the objectively pessimistic news about what is happening and simply try to prepare for the worst—are more likely to die sooner (Reed, Kemeny, Taylor, Wang, & Visscher, 1994). However, permission to express feelings and permission to die should be granted in open and honest confrontation with the terminal patient, especially since patients often recognize their poor health status (Kaplan, Ries, Prewitt, & Eakin, 1994). This can be done by the patient's family or by health professionals. In other words, those caring for patients with a potentially fatal illness have to walk the fine line between giving in to unhelpful pessimism and denying frank discussion.

Without open, honest communication, the dying patient is likely to be the most lonely person in the world (Kübler-Ross, 1969). Without social contact, it becomes very hard for a dying patient to validate his or her feelings and even to maintain a sense of identity. In short, it is important to remember that all people need regular social contact, and this need is generally especially urgent in the dying.

One significant means of preventing loneliness and controlling pain is the hospice, a special institutional approach for caring for the dying.

THE HOSPICE

"Cold, uncommunicative physicians are family members' biggest criticism of end-of-life care, a new study concludes." This statement could have been taken from a report written 40 years ago, 30 years ago, or 20 years ago. Unfortunately, it was based on a study done just a few years ago (Hanson, Danis, & Garrett, 1997). Family members are satisfied with medical decisions about life-sustaining treatment, but their primary concerns involve psychosocial failures of communication and failures of pain control.

Such reports are especially frustrating for physicians, who work long hours under difficult conditions to care for the seriously ill. Yet the problem is not primarily one of individual physician behavior, but rather, it is a structural problem. The traditional health care system is not structured to deal with what are essentially psychosocial issues. Doctor-patient discussions that focus on specific treatment decisions do not satisfy the real needs of dying patients and their families.

All of the problems of institutionalization—where people are dehumanized for purposes of standardization and efficiency—may come together to plague the terminally ill in an acute care hospital. The dying may be too weak or come to care too little to attempt to assert any personal control. They may have their various physiological needs met on a rigid schedule by constantly changing members of the medical team. They may be somewhat isolated from friends and family. The terminally ill may be studied by medical residents learning their profession. Simple requests (such as to have pets or favorite foods) may be denied because of hospital rules. In its extreme, such treatment may be so "efficient" that there are extremely negative consequences for the patient. Some of these problems arise from the fact that the patient is dying, but many of the difficulties arise from the hospital environment itself.

The **hospice** attempts to improve the care of the terminally ill. A hospice is a program designed for the care of the terminally ill, which focuses on the psychosocial and comfort needs of the dying person *and* the family.

Traditionally, a hospice has been a place of rest for travelers, the elderly, or the sick. Hospices took on their modern meaning from St. Christopher's, a London hospice founded by Cicely Saunders (Stoddard, 1978). The hospice movement spread to the United States through the National Hospice Organization. Although both the words *hospital* and *hospice* are related to the word *hospitality,* it is the hospice that endeavors to improve the psychosocial care and the quality of life of terminally ill patients.

More specifically, what is hospice? First, it is an approach that accepts death as a natural part of life. Second, it is community-centered, patient- and family-focused, and emphasizes care that minimizes pain, including the psychological aspects of pain. Although a hospice may be a separate building or a wing of a hospital, the majority of hospice patients are cared for in their own home or in the home of loved one. In accord with emphasis on the family, the whole family is counseled, and there is bereavement care even after the death of the patient. There also may be respite assistance, so that family members can take breaks in their care of the dying.

Many private insurance plans cover hospice care, and hospice services are part of the covered benefits of Medicare and Medicaid in most states. Everyone benefits, since hospice care, with less high-tech equipment and with help from family members and other volunteers, is generally less expensive than hospital care.

The Hospice Difference

There are four basic areas in which the hospice differs from the traditional medical approach of the hospital. First, the focus of the hospice is on the person, thus counteracting the dehumanization of hospitals. Through a variety of means, patients are made to feel like people. Patients are introduced as people rather than as medical cases, and acquaintanceships are built among patients and the staff. Hospital gowns are not used. Attention is paid to the patient's thoughts and feelings, and a general emphasis is placed on the patient's overall well-being (Cassileth & Donovan, 1983; McNulty & Holderby, 1983). This is sometimes termed **low tech, high touch.**

Second, the hospice encourages rather than discourages family interaction. Spouses are recognized and welcomed into the health care system, and children are permitted to visit (or stay in the home). Family members are taught to help care for the patient. The family may even get to know other patients. Furthermore, psychosocial support services are offered to the family. Deaths that are associated with a stigmatized condition—such as AIDS—can be especially hard on the survivors.

Third, more attention is paid to the proper control of pain in hospices than in traditional acute care hospitals. Whereas hospitals are likely to view pain mechanistically, in hospices the significant psychosocial aspects of pain are recognized. Instead of administering pain medication on a strict and rigid schedule according to doctors' orders, in the hospice pain medication is administered when the patient needs it. In addition, the patient is assured that pain medication will be available when it is needed; elimination of the fear of pain helps to reduce the pain.

With the focus on the quality of the patient's life, the type of pain medication used in hospices is very important. Hospice personnel endeavor to allow the patient to function normally to the greatest possible extent while pain is controlled. As noted, this hopeful emphasis in itself helps control pain. But hospices have also helped pioneer new pain control preparations. For example, St. Christopher's developed Brompton's mixture for controlling pain in terminal cancer patients. (In England, this consisted of heroin, cocaine, alcohol, chloroform, and sugar. Now, new analgesics are often used.) The precise mixture is not as important as the emphasis on pain control medication that preserves the psychosocial functioning of the patient. Although in principle, there could be excellent pain control administered in hospitals, in practice hospitals are generally less willing to focus intensively on pain relief and patient comfort.

Fourth, hospices are more likely than acute care hospitals to rely on allied health professionals (Larson, 1993). Hospitals give an extraordinary range of duties and responsibilities to physicians. Hospices are more willing to rely on social workers, pharmacists, clergy, and psychologists. The full range of patient and family needs is therefore more likely to be addressed. At the same time, hospices may attempt to address the emotional needs of the providers.

Evaluation of Hospice

One national study of over 1,700 patients evaluated the effectiveness of hospice care as compared to traditional care (Greer & Mor, 1986; Greer et al., 1986). A number of interesting differences were found. Hospice patients were less likely to be subjected to diagnostic testing or to receive therapies such as chemotherapy, radiation, and transfusions; they were less "bothered" during their final months, but they did as well and lived as long. They were more likely to die at home, and their families were satisfied with that. Finally, pain control appeared better in hospices.

The hospice movement fits in well with some promising trends in American health care. Most obviously, it encourages increased sensitivity to dying and death. It is also compatible with increased emphasis on home care. Hospice staff have ties to the family and form a small community; it is easier for seriously ill patients to remain at home and return to the institution only when absolutely medically necessary. Finally, the hospice movement fits in with the trends toward health maintenance organizations and other group practices in which teams of health professionals cooperate to produce efficient health care. Acceptance by insurance companies is a good sign that the health care system itself is changing.

Although hospice care has been established primarily for the terminally ill, its emphases provide promising alternatives to certain types of existing hospital care. Although hospitals as they are now may be excellent places for accident or heart attack victims for a short period in the initial phase of the medical problem, many aspects of hospitalization can, upon careful scrutiny, be much improved. In response to the hospice movements, traditional hospitals have begun to change some of their practices.

Homecare

To enter hospice care, it must be reasonably clear that the patient is within six months of death. However, many patients are clearly on a deteriorating path but are not clearly terminal—they may suffer from Alzheimer's disease, obstructive lung disease, severe heart disease, neuromuscular disease, and so on. Or, they may be terminally ill but may not have access to hospice care. Such people often have what has come to be termed **homecare.** Simply put, homecare is health care for the chronically or terminally ill supplied in the home of the patient or a family member. With the increasing elderly population, the increased number of chronically ill AIDS patients, and the government's desire to save money by limiting hospital costs, homecare has become one of the fastest-growing industries in the United States.

Homecare brings with it a host of challenges, including severe stress on the other family members or caretakers, difficulties in providing advanced medical treatments, financial drains, and many practical difficulties of equipment, supplies, trained visiting nurses, and more. Although there is large scientific literature on this topic, it is mostly about economics, medical care, elder abuse, and utilization. Because of the many relevant psychological issues, this area promises to become an important one for health psychology (Caine et al., 1992; McCorkle, Robinson, Nuamah, & Lev, 1998; Pearlin, Aneshensel, & LeBlanc, 1997).

BEREAVEMENT AND GRIEVING

In the introduction to this chapter, we discussed Sarah, who is dying of breast cancer. Sarah's impending death will significantly affect her family and friends. Her husband is left to face what is perhaps the greatest crisis of his life. As we noted in Chapter 5 on life stress, the death of a spouse is probably the greatest source of stress that an individual encounters. The problems that Sarah's husband will face involve not only his own loneliness, but also the need to bring up young children; he may also have financial burdens. The social network he has developed with Sarah will be partially dissolved, and he will lose his role as a husband and assume that of a widower. He will need to comfort his children and parents-in-law. He may grieve deeply. Before Sarah's death, her husband must begin to deal with making these adjustments at a time when he is still taking care of and hoping to communicate with Sarah.

The children may be profoundly affected by their mother's impending death. She will be ill much of the time, often too tired to play with them. There will be medical crises, requiring trips to the hospital. Mother and father will often express grief. Few plans will be made for the future, and then one day she will no longer be with them. The older children at least will try to understand what it means that Mom is dead.

Sarah's parents and friends are likely to face their own fears and inadequacies in their attempts to communicate. While they want to understand and to share their feelings, they may not know what to say. Because they may be afraid to dwell on a morbid topic like death, they may avoid the subject altogether. In their visits, few people are likely to talk about their own feelings. They may become distressed if Sarah becomes jealous of their good health. They may be unable to deal with her anger, pain, and discomfort. Very often, family members and friends stop touching dying patients, both in a physical and in a symbolic sense.

This withdrawal may be a symptom of **anticipatory grief,** an important phenomenon in understanding reactions to the dying (Chochinov & Breitbart, 2000; Clayton, Desmarais, & Winokur, 1968; Futterman, Hoffman, & Sabshin, 1972; Moriarty, 1967; Parkes, 1972; Parkes & Weiss, 1983; Rando, 2000). Anticipatory grief involves beginning the grieving process before the loss occurs. Sarah's husband may prepare himself for various aspects of widowerhood during the period before her death. Anticipatory grief involves a consideration of the feelings that will occur in the bereavement; it may sometimes help a person to regain a normal level of functioning in a shorter period of time.

The death of someone close puts a person in a condition of bereavement. **Grief** is the psychological response to **bereavement.** It involves how the survivor feels and the effects on thinking, eating, sleeping, and other general aspects of daily life. When someone is grief-stricken, this person is experiencing a serious interruption in the total patterning of his or her life (Chochinov & Breitbart, 2000; Clayton et al., 1968; Rando, 2000; Shephard, 1975).

Components of Grief

There are five common **components of grief,** which include many of the elements of depression and anxiety (Boerner & Wortman, 1998; Gorer, 1965/1977). First is **somatic** (bodily) **weakness**—a grieving individual may be exhausted, or sometimes restless. Usually, there is a marked decrease in appetite. A second component of grief is a **preoccupation** with the image of the deceased. Bereaved persons often report that they find themselves daydreaming of their interactions with the deceased person. They may "hear" the deceased person talk, may see people who look like him or her, and may have recurring dreams about the person. They may be confused and report feeling "hollow" and having a sense of unreality.

A third common component of grief is **guilt.** Bereaved persons may think carefully over the period of time before the death in an effort to understand their contribution to the death. If, for example, the friend or relative died in an accident, the bereaved person may think over and over about what his or her contribution to the accident might have been. Or they might say, "I should have taken him to the doctor sooner." Fourth, bereaved people may act with **hostility** toward others. They may express a sense of anger at others who are not bereaved, and they may withdraw from other people or become very formal and stiff in their manner of social interaction.

Figure 9-2 Vieillard pleurant ("Old Man Grieving") (1882) by Vincent Van Gogh.

Fifth and finally, the daily activities of bereaved people usually show many **changes.** They are restless and lack the capacity to initiate and maintain organized patterns of activity. They may be surprised to find how much of their customary activity was done in meaningful relationship to the deceased and how this behavior has lost its significance (Glick, Weiss, & Parkes, 1974; Parkes & Weiss, 1983; Caine, 1974, 1978; Pincus, 1974). In terms of cognitive changes, bereavement can be understood in terms of three **phases: avoidance,** in which the bereaved struggles to understand what has happened; **confrontation,** in which one comes to grips with the new reality; and **accommodation,** in which the lost person becomes a memory, and new ways of dealing with the world are created (Rando, 1993; Worden, 1991).

For some people, the duration of the grief reaction depends upon the success with which a person does what is called **grief work** (Lindemann, 1944). Grief work involves the rechanneling of intense feelings of attachment. One of the obstacles to grief work is the fact that many people try to avoid the intense emotional distress that can be connected with the grief experience. The length of the grief reaction also depends on the centrality of the deceased individual to the bereaved person, the nature of the relationship, and the degree of dependency of the bereaved person. Interestingly, it has been found that with respect to marital relationships, the more ambivalent the bereaved person's feelings were toward the person who died, the more difficult is the grieving response. There are then contradictory feelings to reconcile. Ambivalence coupled with dependency may make it difficult for the bereaved to work through their grief.

On the other hand, not all people experience grief after loss (Wortman & Silver, 1989; 1992; Lepore, Silver, Wortman, & Wayment, 1996). Some people do not experience much distress and do not try to "work through" their grief. In fact, they may be troubled if they are somehow pressured to grieve deeply. Others, who try to "work through" their grief but are socially constrained from doing so may end up even worse off. In other words, the implications of grieving for future adjustment depend on characteristics of the individual and characteristics of the social situation and society. There should not be a general prescription forced on everyone alike (Boerner & Wortman, 1998).

Nevertheless, if the individuals who are bereaved emphasize positive ideals, they can sometimes expend their energies in grieving by channeling them with enormous productivity into worthwhile pursuits. Bereavement is primarily a loss, which can sometimes be faced by restoring meaning to one's life (Harvey & Miller, 1998). For example, when Candy Lightner was told "We've lost Cari," she responded, "It's okay, we'll find her." "You don't understand; a man came along in his car and killed her." However, Candy Lightner did find Cari in a metaphorical sense. Cari had been struck and killed by a drunk driver who had previously been convicted three times for drunk driving. Drunken drivers were rarely punished. In response, Lightner went out and founded MADD—Mothers Against Drunk Drivers. This organization has had phenomenal success in changing laws and increasing public awareness to keep drunken people from driving. Many other youngsters have thus been spared Cari's fate.

As with most psychological reactions, bereavement is heavily influenced by one's culture (Stroebe & Stroebe, 1987; Stroebe, Stroebe, & Hansson, 1993; Stroebe, Stroebe, Schut, & van den Bout, 1998). In modern western culture, the emphasis is on "working through" the loss, and on getting back to a "normal" life. American parents who have lost a child and leave the child's room untouched as a sort of shrine to the departed are seen as unhealthy, weird, or even mentally ill. Yet Japanese who construct a shrine to the departed are in the mainstream of their culture. Similarly, other cultures or other times in history would encourage the grieving persons to try to keep in touch with the departed through prayer or seances or a belief in reincarnation. Here again, such cultural beliefs are too often seen as psychologically unhealthy by modern western societies.

Effects on the Spouse

One of the deepest forms of bereavement is the effect on an individual of the death of a spouse. There are many similarities, however, between the bereavement process when a spouse dies and bereavement in general. Thus, many of the issues reported here can be generalized to other settings.

A pioneering study of grief among spouses was conducted at Harvard University and reported in a book called *The First Year of Bereavement* (Glick, Weiss, & Parkes, 1974). The researchers attempted to understand the usual or expected pattern of grieving, and they looked for processes that would prevent the person from recovering. The primary method of collecting data in the study involved informal open-ended interviews that concentrated on experiences.

People who suddenly found themselves widows or widowers felt overwhelmed. They felt shock and anguish, and it seemed to them that there were no limits to the suffering. They usually felt numb and feared that they would never be able again to move or act or think. The findings also showed that men and women responded somewhat differently to the bereavement. Women's reactions were more intense than men's, and they often emphasized a feeling of abandonment. The men, on the other hand, felt a feeling of dismemberment. The marriage had sustained the men's capacity to work, and they tended to become disorganized in their existing work patterns. The newly widowed women felt more in control once they were able to realize that they could go to work and take care of themselves. These sex differences reflect the differences in meaning of the marriage itself to the men and women in the study.

After the first shock of the death had been experienced, there were feelings of bewilderment and despair. The individuals experienced periods of weeping, although widowers in the study more often reported feeling "choked up," partly because they were unable to express their feelings with tears. Physical symptoms appeared and sometimes lingered for weeks or months. Symptoms included poor appetite, headaches, dizziness, sleep disturbances, and various pains. Since this is often a time of maximal disruption of homeostasis, the risk of sudden death rises (see Chapter 5). For example, after Alan Shepard, the first American to fly in space, died of leukemia in 1998, his wife Louise died of a heart attack on a plane flight just a month later.

Controlling the expressions of sorrow is often very difficult, particularly for women. It was found in the Harvard study, however, that while some women who could not control their emotions were afraid that they were headed for a "nervous breakdown," most of them assumed a stance of responsibility and competence, and began to trust in their own abilities. Men and women differed in their ability to express emotion, and this factor had an impact on recovery and their ability to come to grips with the death. Whereas the direct expression of emotion by the widows may have seemed at times to be overwhelming, they may have ultimately been somewhat better off than the men who coped ineffectively. Men were more likely to blame themselves for factors contributing to the death of their wives. The men would say, "I wasn't sensitive enough to her" or "I should have made things easier." The guilt reaction was resolved, however, when friends who knew both the husband and wife helped the husband gain some rational control.

Mourning.   A key aspect of the bereavement process is the **leave-taking ceremony,** which usually takes the form of a funeral. The ceremony establishes the fact that the individual has died, making it an emotional reality both for the bereaved survivors and for others. Social validation of the change—agreement of people in the social network of the bereaved—is a necessary transition (Lindemann, 1944).

Mourning is the public or ritual display of grief. Like births and marriages, deaths are social events. Community involvement aids the evolution of social relationships and helps maintain the psychological health of the bereaved. Funerals, cemetery visits, memorials, the wearing of special clothing, and changed social activities are all rituals that may help both mourners and the community to adapt gradually to a death.

Some widowed individuals engage in what Robert Kastenbaum calls an **obsessional review.** The bereaved person reviews over and over again the details of the death, and although this activity may seem worthless, Glick and colleagues suggest that the review serves a vital function in helping the widowed persons integrate the emotional and cognitive aspects of the loss. Mulling over the loss may be painful, but this integrative process can be an important component of the work of grieving. The individual must slowly detach his or her intense feelings from the deceased person, which takes time. On the other hand, a grieving individual could selectively process new information (such as by attending to information about disease, violence, and death), which might lengthen the recovery period or bring on depression.

Glick's Harvard study found that many of the widows felt deeply immersed in memories of their husbands, and they found these memories comforting. At first, they idealized the dead spouse, but as they recovered, they would begin to see the spouse realistically, with both positive and negative attributes. Often, however, the bereaved individual would express a fear of "going crazy" because of having extremely vivid visual and tactile memories of the spouse. These memories were often described by the bereaved individuals as similar to hallucinations.

Social recovery includes becoming involved again in activities, making new friends, reestablishing relationships with old friends, and going back to work. Emotional adjustment involves being able to cope effectively with thoughts of the deceased person, only infrequently having nightmares about the person, and no longer expressing or even feeling extreme sorrow. Women tend to recover more quickly emotionally, whereas men appear to recover more quickly socially. A man may appear to be socially recovered from his wife's death—going back to work, making new friends, and perhaps even dating or remarrying. However, he may not have completely coped emotionally with the death. A woman, on the other hand, may actually "feel better" about the death but still refrain from social activities, which are important to her recovery.

In the United States, mourning has traditionally been a relatively private affair. Faced with the guilt, anger, and disorientation of grief work, widows and widowers may feel lost in modern society, especially when there are few ties to an extended family. Throughout this book, we have seen the importance of social support for a variety of conditions; such support groups also now exist to help people cope with death. Groups exist for widows and widowers, for suicide survivors and their families, and for those of various religions. Especially helpful are groups for parents who have lost a child. The topic of children and death is considered later in this chapter.

The Amish Way of Death

To examine the importance of family systems to dying and death, the Amish way of death was studied by Kathleen Bryer (Bryer, 1979). The Amish are a distinct cultural and religious group who live primarily in Pennsylvania. To preserve their way of life, the Amish have kept strong family ties and avoided the American cultural mainstream. (Many use a horse and buggy instead of an automobile.) Since they are a close-knit and separate society, the Amish behavior concerning death provides a good example of the importance of social and psychological factors.

The Amish, like most societies before the 20th century, emphasize the importance of death. The act of preparing funeral clothing (before death) is a type of anticipatory grief. After a death, neighbors notify the community. The body is embalmed and brought home, where it is dressed in white. Women are placed in the same white cape that they

Figure 9-3   Each society has its own death rituals. *(Photo by Kelly Powell)*

wore at baptism and marriage. The body is placed in the center of the house, where it is viewed by relatives, neighbors, and friends. The coffin is then viewed again at the cemetery.

Many Amish die at home, where caring for the terminally ill is viewed in a positive light. Many of the ill are in the stage of quiet acceptance before their death, and seeing this acceptance helps the family cope with their grief. When a tragic death occurs, other Amish families who have had a similar experience may travel to the bereaved to provide comfort and support. Strong social support is maintained for at least a year after the death; this length of time for continuing support is crucial, since grief may last for a year or two. This support may take the form of visits, letters, and handmade gifts. Quilting projects and similar gatherings are a special source of support for widows. Proper concern with death is used to enhance the quality of life.

The Amish way of death is, unfortunately, very different from the custom dominant in America today. For most Americans, death occurs in an institution replete with restrictions and away from the extended family. Death is often hidden and is certainly not a central aspect of life.

Some aspects of concern with a "proper" death in our culture may even represent a further attempt to deny death. That is, death is seen as an event that can be managed by hospices and therapists; the stark, challenging fact of death itself can be managed. Instead of hiding death, we may now, to some extent, be smothering death with "therapeutic" intervention. Along these lines, Kastenbaum has called attention to the phenomenon of **"healthy dying"** (Kastenbaum, 1982). This paradoxical term refers to the quest for a glorious death in which all psychological and social needs are met. A fine line exists between humanized care of the dying (recognizing the fact of death) and unrealistic expectations of death as a very positive experience.

The advent of AIDS may be encouraging a movement towards treating death in more traditional ways, more like the Amish do. AIDS victims and their friends and families often prepare themselves for the impending death, and social support groups for survivors are available. The death taboo in our culture may be breaking down. However, even many health psychology books and articles still have little mention of dying and death.

THE CAREGIVER'S REACTION TO DYING PATIENTS

Individuals who work intensively with dying patients must come to grips with the feelings that are stirred in them by their day-to-day contact with death. Without successfully facing these emotions, the health care professional may experience the phenomenon of **burnout,** an emotional exhaustion in which concern for patients as people disappears (depersonalization) (Leiter & Maslach, 1998). Without a firm acceptance and understanding of their own feelings about death, practitioners may become overwhelmed by the distress that they experience and may develop an unhealthy insensitivity to dying patients (Feifel, 1959, 1965).

Health care professionals face several stressors when dealing with dying patients. First is an identification with dying patients; that is, the caregiver will tend to recognize his or her own limits and mortality. Second, the process of the disengagement from or "letting go" of the patient can be troubling for the health care professional, as disengagement tends to be accompanied by a sense of loss, and also a sense of failure. Third, health care professionals, who are dealing with an emotional and confused patient and family, may themselves experience confusion, grief, anger, loneliness, inadequacy, and guilt. These feelings might be experienced with such intensity that they can lead the health care professional to withdraw from the care of dying patients (Fishoff and O'Brien, 1976; Kastenbaum, 1992; Wiener, 1970).

Coping by Health Professionals

Some health care professionals attempt to deal with anxiety by intellectualizing the situation and by detaching themselves from a recognition of the patient as a person. This defensiveness allows the health care professional to avoid identification with the patient. For example, the health care professional might perceive the patient's needs as requiring a mechanistic kind of ritualized care. The patient becomes an interesting medical "case." Such treatment is often detrimental, both to the patient and ultimately to the professional.

Since some health care professionals see the death of a patient as a loss of their own control, they may attempt to gain mastery of the situation by engaging in perfectionist technical care. They may find it difficult to acknowledge that there are many situations in medicine in which there is little or nothing that can be done to save the patient and prevent death. Also, health care professionals may react to dying patients with strong emotion, but these feelings are not acceptable in health care settings, such as the intensive care or coronary care units of a hospital. In the structure of caregiving, there is little acceptance of expression of emotion in response to dying patients or of discussion of the caregiver's personal philosophies regarding dying. Furthermore, the action-oriented milieu in which care is provided for dying patients in an acute care hospital prevents the expression of grief among health care professionals, who also experience bereavement when a patient to whom they have grown close dies (Kastenbaum & Aisenberg, 1972). Thus, it is not only the pressures of facing death, but also the need to resolve emotional responses after the death of a patient, that are important for health care professionals. Health care professionals can face loneliness and isolation. When the death occurs, the caregiver, who may have had a long-term relationship with the patient, must return to work immediately and be involved in establishing similar relationships with yet more dying patients. The caregiver is, for the most part, denied the opportunity to grieve.

Changes in some institutions in recent years have helped eliminate some of these problems. In many acute care hospitals, physicians, nurses, aides, and technicians working in high-stress settings cannot function effectively within the old system. Therefore, a number of hospitals have developed support groups for health professionals working with seriously ill or terminally ill patients (Samarel, 1991). In addition, classes on death and dying are increasingly popular for both medical personnel and laypersons. In hospitals, these support groups, seminar discussions, and experiential group meetings are often led by psychologists or social workers on the hospital staff. These groups allow health care professionals to legitimize and recognize each other's feelings. They work together to find meaning in their care of patients, and they help each other find ways of dealing with the stresses and emotional reactions they encounter.

Perhaps most importantly, the training of health care professionals should help them see that the prolongation of life is not the only goal of medicine. As we have repeatedly noted, the meaning of the job of the health care professional is far broader than providing care for the patient solely on a biological dimension. In many cases, the caregiver can enter into a mutually supportive relationship with the family and the dying patient. That is, the health care provider may not only give emotional support to the family but may also derive support from them.

CHILDREN AND DEATH

The death of a child is a special tragedy. It goes against many, many of our society's expectations. Parents expect to see their children grow up, create a family of their own, and fulfill their potential. It seems so unfair that an innocent child would be taken. In one interview survey, many bereaved parents first wanted to follow their children into death, but later resigned themselves to a passive life without happiness (Knapp, 1987). Yet tens of thousands of children in our society do die each year, mostly from accidents, suicides, and cancer. Thousands more infants die each year from congenital defects and from Sudden Infant Death Syndrome (SIDS), an ailment in which babies are found dead in their cribs.

There are two psychological issues that are important in understanding children and death. One involves an understanding of parental and other adult reactions to the child who is dying; it involves the feelings of these persons and their ability to come to grips with the child's impending death. The second issue concerns the child's own view of death. It is useful to understand to what extent children can conceive of death, and how they think of it in different ways at different ages.

Reactions to the Child Who Is Dying

There are two primary demands on the health care professional who is dealing with a dying child. The first is to help the child respond both physically and emotionally as positively as possible to the ups and downs that may accompany a life-threatening illness. The second, but equally important, task of the health care professional is to keep the family together and functioning during this period, which is one of the greatest crises a family can face.

When a child is dying, it may be very difficult for parents to focus on the present instead of the future. Adults tend to see childhood as a preparatory period, rather than as a time in a person's life that is worthwhile in and of itself. Hence, the first step in helping the family involves teaching parents that although the child will not have an adult future, the child is alive in the present. There can be a significant concern for the quality of the life the child has left (Kastenbaum, 1992).

A dying child places a tremendous stress on a family—on parents and on the other children in the family as well (Fishoff & O'Brien, 1976; Kennell & Klaus, 1976). This stress takes its toll; the family is often also a victim. A significant percentage of such marriages (of the parents) either become troubled or fail during or soon after the care of a dying child.

The stress is accentuated partly because, in an effort to construct a more or less normal life for the whole family during the illness of the sick child, parents shelter the child who is ill. The parents withdraw from other people. In their desire to avoid explanations to other people and endurance of their pity, parents may withdraw from close friends and other members of their family. Thus, parents of dying children become isolated at just the time when they require the most support. Some members of couples become more alienated from each other at this time. They sometimes cannot understand one another's reactions to the child, and each thinks the other is indifferent or unrealistic in dealing with the problem (Futterman et al., 1972; Goldman, 1994).

In addition to support from others, most parents of dying children need information. For example, parents should know about the side effects of chemotherapy so that if a child begins to exhibit behaviors that are worrisome, the parents will know that these reactions are to be expected (Lewis and Armstrong, 1977). Second, parents need information to allay their guilt and fears that they are responsible in some way for the child's illness (Futterman et al., 1972). In the case of cancer, for example, public advertising stresses the importance of early detection. If a child's leukemia is diagnosed late and the child has little chance of recovery, the parent may feel a great deal of guilt.

Parents of dying children are increasingly addressing their needs for information and support through special support groups. Support groups provide information to the parent, teach the parent to recognize signals of an impending medical crisis, and show ways in which to deal with the illness, all of which gives parents a sense of control. Parents of dying children also share information with each other about their emotional, reactions; there is some evidence that parents who are able to share their grief over the impending death of a child may stand up better to the burdens of the serious illness than those who are isolated from other people. However, as we have seen with social support and chronic illness, the support groups are not needed by everyone, and some parents may deal with the child's fatal illness better by talking with one person, such as a psychologist or other health care professional. After the death, many parents carry some grief throughout their lives. Some are helped with psychotherapy, and many bounce back in order to care for their other children.

The Child's Conception of Death

In a society like ours, in which we strive to put death out of sight and out of mind, children's reactions to death are slighted, and children are often left to deal alone with their feelings about death. Adults often assume that children cannot understand the meaning of death and that children do not experience grief during bereavement. But according to various research and clinical findings, children do have very definite ideas about death—ideas that change at different developmental stages in their lives (Anthony, 1972; Barnard, Moreland, & Nagy, 1999; Kastenbaum, 1992; Nagy, 1948; Rochlin, 1967).

They think about their own death, and they may react with great (although not always overtly expressed) feeling to the death of someone close to them.

It is easy to misinterpret behavior that children may exhibit concerning death. Robert Kastenbaum (Kastenbaum, 1977) and Maria Nagy (Nagy, 1948) (a psychologist, who in the late 1940s studied Hungarian children) identified three phases in a child's awareness of personal mortality and the mortality of others close to the child. The first stage lasts until about age 5. The child at this age does not recognize death as final, but sees being dead as somewhat like being less alive. The young child regards death as a kind of sleep that takes place in an uninteresting place called a grave. Death disturbs the young child, but only because the child sees it as something that separates people from each other and because life in a grave seems uncomfortable and dull.

Between the ages of 5 and 9, the child develops a second kind of awareness of death. The child sees death as something or someone that strikes people down. Although the child understands that death is final, the child has an important ego-protective feature, believing that death can be avoided. By being clever (e.g., never getting hit by a car), he or she can avoid death.

Finally, around age 9 or 10, the child enters the third stage of recognition of death. The child begins to recognize death not only as final, but also as something that is inevitable. Thus, it is not until nearly age 9 that children can fully understand the concept of death. This is not to say, however, that a child at the age of 6 does not have visions of a friend, sibling, or parent as dead. And this is not to say that the child does not know the person is missing. Even though the child does not fully understand what death means, the child can be profoundly affected by the absence of a person who was close.

A child's conception of death is limited by basic processes of cognitive development. As the Swiss psychologist Jean Piaget has noted, most children under age 7 cannot easily take the perspective of another person. They are egocentric in that they are able to view the world only from their own point of view. They cannot easily imagine the reactions of others to an impending death and cannot imagine themselves in the place of someone who is dying. Furthermore, it is not until about age 11 that children enter Piaget's stage of formal operations and can begin to think about the meaning of death in the abstract (Piaget, 1960).

Children can understand something of what it means if they find out they are dying. The child with a terminal illness may experience significant fear and anxiety about eventually being left alone (e.g., in a grave). This anticipated separation from others, as well as actual disengagement, can be highly distressing. Of course, the approach that involves concentrating on living can succeed only if the parents themselves are successful in concentrating on the present, and they do not withdraw or treat the child in a distressing, ambivalent, or discrepant way (Davies, 1999; Kastenbaum, 1998; Rothenberg, 1967; Wiener, 1970).

Children often know more about their situation than adults believe. The child's fears may bring about questioning, which if avoided could increase anxiety significantly. Because of an erroneous but still lingering perception that children do not feel as much pain as adults, or that they are more susceptible to addiction from painkillers, pain is too often not fully controlled in dying children. Furthermore, children are often insufficiently considered as participants in determining their own care.

The Bereaved Child

What happens when death separates children from someone who is important to them? If a parent or grandparent dies, the surviving spouse or children of the grandparent may be temporarily unable to care for the child. If a sibling has died, the parents may be so immersed in their own grief that they may have little energy for dealing with or even recognizing the impact of the death on the brothers and sisters of the child who has died. Thus, a child who experiences bereavement is likely to face two sources of stress. First, the child may be deprived of the usual support expected from the parents because the parents are too busy dealing with the death themselves. A child is likely not to eat as well or get as much rest as before, thus placing the child at greater risk for accidents and mishaps. Second, the child must deal with his or her own grief. Children do grieve. Adults in this situation often fail to interpret the child's **grief response** accurately (Furman, 1974; Koocher, 1986).

The child's emotional response (the grief response) depends on a number of factors. It may be particularly distressing for the child to lose someone to death very soon after recognizing that death is final. The child has not had a chance to come to grips with this realization, and it may be profoundly threatening. The quality of the child's personal and family situation before the bereavement is relevant as well. If the child is immersed in a close-knit family and has a strong sense of love and security, the child is probably less likely to be threatened by the death of someone close. However, if a child's life is filled with anxiety and insecurity, the child's entire world can be shaken by the death of someone very close. Thus, an understanding of each child's individual situation is important in trying to understand the child's bereavement reaction.

Bereaved children do not always express distress in ways that are obviously related to the loss. Instead, the child might experience serious difficulties in school, show behavioral problems, attack people with sudden anger, and express fears of the dark or of being alone. The child may feel guilty, believing he or she contributed to the death.

Children may express their memories of a person that they have lost by acting out specific activities that were associated with the dead person, although these acts can be distressing to an adult. For example, a child who has lost a sibling might engage in the very activities that were always shared with the sibling, giving a constant reminder to the parents of the painful absence. Even as young as 2 or 3 years old, a child may express longing and sadness over the absence of a parent through actions such as playing with toys that were usually used with the parent who has died, or walking in places where the parent usually took the child (Brown, 1961; Davies, 1999; Kastenbaum, 1977; Krupnick, 1984).

At other times, children withdraw and become aloof or seemingly uncaring. This reaction may lead adults to conclude that the child has forgotten the significant death and that the child does not need to talk about it or to resolve the feelings. Research on childhood bereavement suggests that partially because of a misunderstanding on the part of adults, and partially because it may simply be easier for the adult to choose not to deal with the child's reactions, many children bear an enormous amount of pain completely alone with no one to share their grief. Nevertheless, most children recover from the loss, and there is good evidence that bereaved children face significantly fewer future difficulties than do children who face emotional abuse, parental divorce, and physical abuse (Crook, 1980; Tennant, 1988; Tucker et al., 1997).

SUICIDE

One day, the mother of Dr. David Eddy decided to stop eating and drinking. She had lived a long life, but her health had begun to decline rapidly—colon surgery, gallbladder surgery, incontinence, pneumonia. She ate some birthday cake on her 85th birthday and then stopped food and fluid intake. She died a few days later (Eddy, 1994). Before her death, she reportedly commented, "Tell others how well this worked."

Because Dr. Eddy was a prominent physician, who wrote about these events in the *Journal of the American Medical Association*, this death received a lot attention. But similar events occur daily. Difficult questions arise. Is this death like other suicides? Although it is legal because people have the right to refuse food and medical care, is it moral? Would it have been equally acceptable (to those who find it acceptable) at age 75? Age 35? Should doctors be able to prescribe painkillers to such an individual? Dr. Eddy reported that it was a happy death because it did not come after years of decline and loneliness.

Suicide is not only a concern among the aged infirm, as many people believe. For people between the ages of 15 and 24, suicide is one of the top three causes of death in the United States (and it is the second leading cause of death among college students). Most of these young people shoot themselves. Although the overall suicide rate has been steady for the past 80 years (except for a sharp rise during the Great Depression), the suicide rate among young people has risen dramatically in recent decades (Centers for Disease Control, 1986). There is an epidemic of suicide, especially among young males.

In the epidemiological study of suicide, the information comes primarily from death certificates. The information is very reliable in the sense that few people who are said to have died from suicide may have really died from some other cause. However, there may well be many people who committed suicide but whose death certificates give another cause of death. Our society frowns upon suicide on moral grounds. So, when there is some doubt about whether a death is or is not a suicide, there is pressure to list a different cause. For example, if a depressed young person crashes a car over a cliff, the cause of death is unlikely to be listed as a suicide unless a suicide note is found. For this reason, the actual suicide rate in the population is probably even higher than statistics indicate.

As we have seen, epidemiology does not necessarily tell us much about psychology. Since we have only group statistics, we do not know why any given person may have committed suicide. However, such statistics give us some clues about psychological influences. For example, in recent years, females have replaced poisoning with firearms as the most common means of suicide. The increasing use of firearms is especially apparent in young people. So, we might speculate that the increasing "liberation" of women

Box 9-1 Pulling the Respirator Plug? Yanking the Feeding Tube? Karen Ann Quinlan and Nancy Beth Cruzan

The ethical problems in treating those who are almost dead and the legal questions of the definition of death reached national attention in the case of Karen Ann Quinlan, age 21. In 1975, Karen went into a deep coma. She was placed on a respirator and administered other treatments, including special foods and antibiotics. Karen never recovered from her coma. Her neurologists claimed she had extensive brain damage and had no hope of recovery.

After a good deal of soul searching, Karen's parents decided that she should be allowed to die rather than be kept alive by extraordinary means. But the doctors refused to disconnect Karen from the respirator, mostly because of the legal implications. It was, of course, very costly and very disruptive to keep Karen in special medical treatment even though she showed absolutely no signs of conscious life. Her parents sued for the right to pull the plug on her respirator. After a year, during which Karen never regained consciousness and dropped to 71 pounds, the New Jersey Supreme Court ruled that her parents could turn off the respirator and let her die with grace and dignity. The court's ruling set a legal precedent, establishing a right to privacy for persons who are nearly dead biologically that allows them or their guardians to refuse extraordinary treatment that is deemed hopeless.

Several months later, the respirator was turned off. Ironically, Karen continued to breathe on her own. She was given food and antibiotics through a tube that ran from her nose into her stomach. She continued in this state, unconscious and curled up in a fetal position. She did not die until nine years later, of pneumonia. During that decade, expectations about extraordinary intervention changed to the point that people began thinking about whether even food and antibiotics can be withheld from comatose patients who have little or no hope of recovery.

In the 1980s, the key case of interest was that of Nancy Beth Cruzan, a young woman who in 1983 went into an irreversible coma after a car accident. Could her feeding tube be removed, as her parents wanted? After many years of hearings and court cases, judges ruled that the feeding tube could be removed if her parents could establish that Nancy had clearly stated that she would have wanted it to be that way. Friends and relatives testified in court, in a heartbreaking drama. Finally, in December 1990, a judge ordered the feeding tube removed, and Nancy died 12 days later.

With increasing technology available for prolonging life in terminally ill patients, the ethics of withholding extraordinary treatment has become an important issue in health care. Some aspects of the problem can be addressed through more modern definitions of biological death. However, the answers to many of the questions will depend on society's evolving conception of the social meaning of dying and death.

Box 9-2 Is Your Body Your Own?

A controversial issue of increasing importance in health care involves the extent to which a person retains control over what is done to his or her body. Some of these cases involve extraordinary life-preserving equipment. But many cases concern questions of medical judgment and the quality of life. In one case, a 72-year-old woman with gangrenous feet refused to have an amputation. The gangrene was almost surely fatal, but with the operation, she would have a 50 percent chance to live; the doctors went to court to have her declared incompetent to make this decision. In another case, parents of a child with leukemia refused to allow chemotherapy since they believed that they could better treat the disease through diet and other means. In still other cases, members of certain religious groups refuse promising treatment because it is against their religion to receive blood transfusions, take certain medication, or engage in certain other modern medical treatments.

Should such patients be forced to be treated? Should such parents of ill children be prosecuted as criminals? Are medical personnel who respect a patient's wishes guilty of malpractice or other crimes, including homicide? Questions like these often end up in the courts. In many cases, however, they are not legal questions but ethical questions instead. It is up to patients, medical personnel, theologians, as well as lawyers, to decide such issues. Each individual must participate in the decision and share in the responsibility.

For further reading:

R. Hunt & J. Arras (Eds.). (1977). *Ethical Issues in Modern Medicine.* Palo Alto, CA: Mayfield Co.

may have had the consequence of leading them toward men's method of choice for killing themselves. For example, young women might now have greater access and attraction to guns, or a more macho attitude about guns and shooting. The accuracy and meaning of such interpretations cannot be determined until psychological studies of changing aspects of suicide are conducted.

Nearly all health care professionals encounter the threat of suicide at some point in their careers. However, although psychological research on suicide provides us with answers to some of the questions that are relevant to health promotion and the effective care of patients (Jacobs, 1998; Kastenbaum & Aisenberg, 1972), suicide does not fall within the traditional medical model. So, physicians and nurses may find themselves ill-prepared to address the issue. Health care professionals, who are primarily oriented to saving lives, are likely to find themselves experiencing very negative reactions to individuals who threaten or attempt suicide—unfortunate because such people need help, not anger and hostility.

If a person does commit suicide, the family and friends are likely to need help dealing with the death. Suicide leaves many victims. Bereavement, as we have seen, is difficult enough in itself, but the process of grieving for someone who has died by taking his

---

Box 9–3   Living Wills

A usual will tells how you would like your affairs handled after you die. A living will describes how you want your medical care handled while you are still alive but no longer able to manage your affairs.

In 1977, California became the first state to legally recognize the person's right to issue a written directive concerning "extraordinary" life-sustaining procedures during a terminal illness. Currently, most states have enacted a relevant law. (Groups active in these efforts include the Society for the Right to Die, the Concern for Dying, and the Hemlock Society.) The living will usually becomes effective when you are comatose and expected to die.

Typically, you sign the will (in front of witnesses) when (or before) you are diagnosed as having a terminal illness. It instructs the doctors to withhold extraordinary life-prolonging interventions, such as respirators. Sometimes, the living will is legally binding on the physician. More typically, it provides direction and legal protection for the physician.

Living wills should be distinguished from **euthanasia,** the putting to death of a person suffering from a painful, terminal illness (also called *mercy killing*). Euthanasia is illegal in all states except Oregon, where assisted suicide is legal in special cases of terminal illness. (Note, however, that euthanasia is lawful when applied to pets.)

One difficulty of living wills is that it is hard to predict with absolute certainty how long one will live with a terminal illness, whether a spontaneous remission is possible, or how painful the end will be. Furthermore, an upset, depressed patient may not be in the best position to decide future issues of life and death (Sourkes, 1982).

Living wills are a legal solution to a problem that is primarily interpersonal and ethical. If patients had trust and confidence in their doctors, and if doctors did not fear being sued or prosecuted, many of these issues could be worked out on a case-by-case basis in discussions among the patient, the family, the doctors, and perhaps the relevant clergy.

---

or her own life can be especially hard on family and friends because of their guilt. They wish they had understood, heard the warning signals, and provided support for this person. The study of suicide, **suicidology,** has become a regular scientific discipline.

Myths About Suicide

Although it is often believed that someone who talks about suicide will not attempt it, research suggests that about three out of every four people who eventually committed suicide had given some kind of hint ahead of time to others. An individual's threat of suicide often is a cry for help (Farberow & Shneidman, 1965; Jacobs, 1998). It is also a misconception that suicide is specific to any particular group of people. People in all income and social status brackets commit suicide, and not only depressed people commit suicide. Although people with a psychiatric diagnosis of depression or other mood disorder do have a higher suicide rate than those with no known psychiatric disorder, suicide is not a risk only with depressed people. For example, a drug abuser may not even seem particularly unhappy before attempting suicide (Jacobs, 1998; Kastenbaum, 1992).

Another myth about suicide is that people are "out of their minds" when deciding to kill themselves. While some suicides are related to mental disorders, others have no relationship to psychosis at all. Not surprisingly, therefore, it is also not true that only a psychiatrist or mental health professional can prevent a suicide. There is much evidence that human resources of a community, including people without any professional training, can help to prevent suicides simply by providing emotional support. In particular, when someone who has attempted suicide recovers, this person is in danger. After the first attempted suicide, the individual has received a lot of attention from family members, friends, and health care professionals. After recovery (and discharge from the hospital), however, the person may again feel lonely and detached from others, and may attempt suicide again.

Preventing Suicide

There is consistent evidence that a history of physical or sexual abuse is one risk factor for suicide (Wagner, 1997). There is also some evidence that poor family relations are a risk factor, but this is usually not measured in prospective studies, so we cannot be sure if it is the suicidal symptoms and threats that are causing the poor family relations or vice versa (or perhaps both pathways are relevant). Alcoholism and access to lethal methods are other predictors (Maris, 1998). If guns and poisons are unavailable, the suicide risk goes down, even though there are many ways to kill oneself.

An individual who verbalizes a threat of suicide may be trying to get attention, and it is important to be sure that the individual who has threatened suicide is not dared to carry it out. Sometimes goading is done on a very subtle level. If an individual's troubled state of mind is belittled, this person will respond with a heightened need to do something desperate to have others recognize the seriousness of the threat. Many people end up being successful at suicide when their intention was actually only to get attention by providing an obvious threat.

Telling a troubled person that suicide is wrong is likely to be responded to negatively. An individual may not only be unconvinced not to attempt suicide, but may realize that another's value system is very different from his or her own, and therefore may come to value the act positively. The person's motives may be meant only as a gesture, signifying "I will show them, I'll make them wish they had appreciated me." For example, one study found that passersby on a city street who were standing in front of a funeral home (being reminded of their mortality) evidently had an increased need to feel an appreciated member of a supportive group (Pyszczynski et al., 1996). Fortunately, resources are increasingly available in most communities from schools, religious groups, community crisis intervention telephones, and mental health centers. Talking to someone with suicidal feelings does not put the thought of suicide back into his head.

As in depression, deviations in the usual modulation of the neurotransmitter serotonin in the brain have been implicated in suicidal behavior (Spoont, 1992). In particular, a biological marker of risk is a low level of the serotonin metabolite CSF 5-HIAA. So, serotonin uptake modulators like Prozac have often proven effective in addressing the biological aspects of suicidal inclinations, although paradoxical (opposite) effects can occur.

Occasionally, there seem to be clusters of suicides, such as when a number of students at a high school attempt suicide during a short period of time. In such cases, it is likely that these people share a vulnerability to problems, a lack of social support, and some environmental stress (Joiner, 1999).

Justifiable Suicide?

Is suicide ever justified? Many people fear suffering or old age more than they fear death. This fact was dramatically demonstrated in the 1970s when a British organization produced a manual on how to kill oneself. For example, it described the lethal combinations of common drugs. Many thousands of people tried to join this organization and obtain the book (*A Guide to Self-Deliverance*). Since both the United States and Great Britain have laws against aiding and abetting suicide, a host of legal and ethical issues arise concerning such matters. Do people have the right to such medical information? Or is it better, for example, to risk having people live with extensive brain damage that can result from a botched suicide attempt? As people gain more control over their health care, such questions will join the traditional questions (e.g., Is suicide always wrong?) in the public's interest.

The severe limits of the traditional medical model and the traditional health care system were once again brought to the fore when a similar movement repeated itself in the 1990s. A book entitled *Final Exit: The Practicalities of Self-Deliverance and Assisted Suicide for the Dying* became a best-seller. It was written by Derek Humphry of the Hemlock Society, a right-to-die organization. Newspapers were full of quotes from angry patients saying, "I don't want doctors and hospital bureaucrats to dictate my destiny. I want dignity and humanity in how I die."

Many of these issues were brought to a head beginning in 1990 when a physician, Jack Kevorkian, designed a suicide machine. He brought the machine to a woman who had recently been diagnosed with Alzheimer's disease. She voluntarily pushed a button on Dr. Kevorkian's machine and was killed by a lethal injection; she did not want to face the slow deterioration of Alzheimer's. Dr. Kevorkian was indicted for murder, but a judge dismissed the charges. (He was subsequently imprisoned for further actions.) Many legal issues still swirl around this and subsequent controversial cases.

Also problematic is the so-called passive suicide by the chronically ill. Hemodialysis patients may ignore their diet and refuse dialysis, diabetes patients may refuse insulin, and cancer patients may turn down chemotherapy. There are two ways in which such cases differ from other unhealthy behaviors, like smoking and the refusal to treat an acute illness like an infection: First, the natural process is already one of serious deterioration, and second, there may be severe problems, such as extreme discomfort, associated with the treatment. However, just as active suicide is influenced by psychosocial forces, so too is passive suicide.

While younger persons may attempt suicide as a means of manipulating others, a cry for help, or as a reaction to an overwhelming but temporary crisis, older persons attempt suicide in a determined effort to bring their life to a close. Older persons use more violent and obviously effective methods to kill themselves than do younger persons. They shoot, hang, or drown themselves, or they jump from high places. Firearms represent the major means of elderly suicide. Older people commit suicide for a variety of reasons, but most have to do with loss. Losses may be economic or social (loss of income or job status), physical (loss of health and vigor), emotional (loss of spouse), or psychological (loss of self-esteem and confidence to cope with distressing or challenging events or loss of enthusiasm and resilience).

EVALUATION

Not long ago, the prestigious Institute of Medicine issued a critical report about care of the terminally ill, noting that dying patients often suffer needlessly, that opioids are underprescribed, that physicians are poorly educated about such matters, and that more commitment to and discussion about the dying patient is needed (Field & Cassel, 1997). They suggest better medical education, reform of drug prescription laws, more hospice care, more community involvement, and increased "commitment" on the part of health professionals. Although such actions may be somewhat helpful, they can never fully rectify the root problem, which is that dying is not a disease and so cannot be fully addressed by a traditional biomedical approach and traditional medical institutions. Thus, such recommendations are not fully implemented.

It is not fair to expect physicians to be experts in psychology, social work, religion, and law; and it is not reasonable to expect high-tech hospitals oriented around surgery and chemotherapy to act like counseling centers, pain clinics, and spiritual organizations. Even the best-designed inventions along these lines—trying to "improve hospitals"—repeatedly fail (SUPPORT Principal Investigators, 1995). Even hospice care sometimes can be co-opted into a traditional medical approach (Kastenbaum, 1998). A better solution is to adopt the health psychology model, in which treating disease is understood to be only one part of health, and in which physicians are seen to be only one part of the health care team. As society changes its overall understanding of health, the day may come when dying people no longer fear uncommunicative physicians, loneliness, terminal pain, and dehumanizing artificial life support.

SUMMARY AND CONCLUSION

Death is the greatest crisis of life. In our society, the fact that each of us must die someday is met with profound denial by many people. As a result, dying patients, who exemplify human mortality, are often rejected by the living, and their needs are ignored. The dying frequently become angry, depressed, afraid, and, most of all, lonely. This societal orientation may be changing somewhat as more and more young people are dying from AIDS and other threats to the young. Dying can be made easier for the patient and for family, friends, and health professionals if the emotions surrounding dying are brought out into the open and dealt with knowledgeably. For the survivors, bereavement, though never pleasant, can be an experience of emotional growth.

A hospice is an institution, either community-based or home-based, that specializes in caring for the terminally ill. Unlike a hospital, whose primary goal is to prevent death, a hospice helps to ease the pain of the dying by offering pain control and psychological and community support to both the patient and the family. Patients within hospice care live as long as hospitalized patients. With such emphases as family interaction, increased sensitivity to the process of dying, greater attentiveness to pain control, and the availability of homecare, the hospice is a growing movement, as the health psychology model replaces the traditional medical model of disease.

Grief is a psychological response to bereavement, which follows the death of a loved one. It is often comprised of five common elements, which the bereaved may or may not experience. Many factors influence how an individual will deal with death, including culture, the degree of dependency on the deceased, and the nature of relationships. The death of a spouse is one of the deepest forms of bereavement, as most view marriage as a sacred and particularly close relationship. However, the widowed express and control their grief in differing manners. While some may become so grief-stricken that normal daily activity becomes cumbersome, others find "working through" the ordeal as therapeutic. Support of family and friends is more likely to ease the pain of loss; such support is often apparent in traditional societies such as the Amish of Pennsylvania.

Often overlooked is how health professionals cope with death. Although some may deal with the death of patients every day and may shrug them off as mere medical cases, caregivers may develop close relationships with patients and their families. Health institutions may offer useful support groups for physicians, nurses, aides, and technicians in dealing with the stresses of caring for the dying. However, the training of health care professionals should help them see that the prolongation of life is not the only goal of medicine.

Dying and bereaved children require particular attention because of their limited understanding of the meaning of death. It is also important, however, not to be ignorant of what understanding a child may have. Children often know more about death than adults believe, which can increase stress and anxiety significantly in a given situation. Children also deal with death in different ways than do adults. Depending on the child's recognition of death and the quality of the personal and family situations, death may be a more traumatic or less threatening concept.

Adults who have lost a child often alter their lives in profound ways. Many couples will isolate themselves from society after the death of a child, just when they need support the most. Others alienate themselves from their spouses, not understanding one another's reactions. The parents of dying and bereaved children, as well as the children themselves, often need special support.

Suicide is a relatively common cause of death in our society, especially among young people. Suicide threats are best addressed openly and not belittled. Many myths about suicide cause great misinterpretations, such as to the mental state of a person desiring to take his or her own life. Those who are suicidal are not necessarily "out of their minds," but are more often than not crying out for attention and help. Special cases of suicide involve the elderly infirm and the chronically or terminally ill. These cases raise moral and ethical issues that go to the heart of how we think of ourselves as human beings. Much work remains to be done concerning death, dying, and grief, and health psychology holds the potential to develop many important solutions.

Recommended Additional Readings

Field, Marilyn J. & Cassel, Christine K. (Eds.). (1997). *Approaching death: Improving care at the end of life.* Committee on Care at the End of Life, Division of Health Care Services, Institute of Medicine. Washington, DC: National Academy Press.

Kastenbaum, Robert J. (1998). *Death, society, and human experience* (6th ed.). Boston: Allyn and Bacon.

Kübler-Ross, Elisabeth. (1997). *On death and dying* (1st Scribner Classics ed.). New York: Scribner Classics.

Maris, Ronald W. (Ed.). (1992). *Assessment and prediction of suicide.* New York: Guilford Press.

Nolen-Hoeksema, Susan & Larson, Judith. (1998). *Coping with loss.* Mahwah, NJ: Erlbaum Associates, Inc.

Nuland, Sherwin B. (1994). *How we die: Reflections on life's final chapter.* New York: A. A. Knopf: Distributed by Random House.

Parkes, Colin Murray. (1996). *Bereavement: Studies of grief in adult life* (3rd ed.). London, New York: Routledge.

Stroebe, Margaret S., Stroebe, Wolfgang, & Hansson, Robert O. (Eds.). (1993). *Handbook of bereavement: Theory, research, and intervention.* New York: Cambridge University Press.

National Sudden Infant Death Syndrome Resource Center: http://www.circsol.com/sids/

American Association of Suicidology: http://www.suicidology.org/

The Compassionate Friends: http://www.compassionatefriends.org/

Survivors of Suicide: http://www.suicidology.org/survivorsofsuicide.htm

Parents Without Partners: http://www.parentswithoutpartners.org/

Key Concepts

thanatology

brain death

psychosocial death

double-bind situation

Kübler-Ross' stages of death
  denial
  anger
  bargaining
  depression
  acceptance

hospice

low tech, high touch

homecare

anticipatory grief

grief

bereavement

components of grief
  somatic weakness
  preoccupation
  guilt

hostility
  change in activity
phases of bereavement
  avoidance
  confrontation
  accommodation
grief work
leave-taking ceremony
mourning

obsessional review
healthy dying
burnout
grief response
suicide
living will
euthanasia
suicidology

PART III

Health Promotion, Disease Prevention, and the Health Care System

Chapter 10

TOBACCO, ALCOHOL, AND ILLEGAL DRUG ABUSE

In a Florida courtroom in July 2000, a record $145 billion award was handed down against five tobacco companies. This award made state officials across the country nervous, because they were counting on money from a previous national settlement with tobacco companies to pay for health programs in their states; the states could not collect if the new jury award bankrupted the tobacco companies. Many of the ju-

rors found the tobacco lawyers very insulting, especially in such instances as when they attempted to explain away one plaintiff's throat cancer by saying it was caused by wood dust the clockmaker had inhaled at work, not by cigarettes.

Tobacco makers misled the public about the effects of tobacco since the 1950s, when industry research secretly concluded that smoking causes cancer. According to top industry critics, by the early 1960s, some tobacco industry insiders knew that nicotine was addictive, but cigarettes continually were promoted as nonharmful and a matter of personal choice (Glantz, Slage, Bero, Hanaver, & Barnes, 1996). Although sale of tobacco to minors is illegal, and although all schoolchildren are educated about the grave dangers of smoking, almost all tobacco use and addiction begins before age 21. If no one used tobacco before age 21, the bulk of the tobacco problem (addiction and disease) would quickly disappear.

Issues of how to promote health, prevent disease, and best structure our health care system are key aspects of the field of health psychology. Beyond questions of stress and coping, personality and disease, and adaptation to illness are the broader matters of models and social systems that best enable people to stay healthy or recover quickly. Although there have been countless studies of interventions to help people avoid drugs, stop smoking, lose weight, stay fit, follow treatment regimens, use condoms, and eat right, many studies do not start with a full understanding of basic principles of social, biosocial, personality, and behavioral psychology, and so they repeat and repeat the same sorts of studies, to little effect.

In this section of this book, we examine health promotion, disease prevention, and the health care system. As we will see, it is a complex matter to understand people's healthy and unhealthy behaviors. Indeed, it is often a fascinating human drama involving money, influence, power, beliefs, drives, politics, addiction, culture, and identity.

This chapter focuses on tobacco, alcohol, and illegal drug abuse. The next chapter takes up nutrition, exercise, and various forms of prophylaxis.

MODELS OF HEALTH PROMOTION AND DISEASE PREVENTION

Health psychologists use two different kinds of perspectives in thinking about preventing unhealthy habits and promoting healthy behaviors. One path is to focus directly on specific habits, such as the aspects of tobacco addiction and on quitting smoking. This is a pathogen-based approach.

The other path is to focus on more basic models of human motivation and behavior, such as how people learn about, think about, and are driven (both socially and biologically) to various healthy or unhealthy behaviors. This latter approach ultimately makes more sense, since it can deal with the whole person rather than proceeding one unhealthy habit at a time. Unfortunately, understanding all major influences on healthy behavior is a monumental task and cannot be summarized in one chapter. We will, however, review the major relevant theoretical perspectives on human behavior, so that the assumptions underlying more specific, disease-focused health interventions can be more easily recognized and evaluated.

Biological

Biological approaches to health promotion focus on the genetic, hormonal, and nervous-system bases for motivation and behavior. For example, there is evidence that some people have a greater biological proneness to become alcoholics; but of course this tendency can only be realized in environments that allow or encourage alcohol consumption. As we have seen, it is also the case that some people have a nervous-system basis for their impulsivity, and this may manifest itself in risky behaviors like fast driving or parachute jumping.

When a biological basis for unhealthy behavior is viewed as dominant, the problem is often seen as one of "disease." For example, individuals may be seen to have the disease of drug addiction or alcoholism. These approaches view a person as mostly controlled by the "bio" in biopsychosocial influences.

Learning

Learning models postulate that healthy or unhealthy habits and behaviors are primarily learned. This assumption also implies that they can be unlearned. Learning approaches sometimes try to change people's attitudes and beliefs, with the expectation that behavior change will then follow.

Learning approaches generally involve three components. First, there is **conditioning,** such as the classical conditioning made famous by Pavlov and his dogs, who he conditioned to salivate in response to a tone. For example, most people are comforted, relaxed, and pleased by associations with close friends. If these responses usually occur at parties where drugs and alcohol are in abundance, people may come to associate drugs and alcohol with the relaxed state, regardless of the physiological effects of the drugs.

Conversely, unconditioning or extinction approaches can be used for treatment. For example, if a person has one of the many symptoms often associated with tension and anxiety, such as headaches or stomachaches, he or she may be treated through a conditioning therapy like systematic desensitization: By gradually pairing relaxation training with the tension-provoking stimuli, the person learns to reduce the anxiety. The symptoms may then diminish.

Second, there are many learning approaches that focus on **reinforcement,** sometimes termed *operant conditioning.* When a behavior, like heavy drinking, is rewarded by consequences, like approval by friends and by sexual relations, the reinforced behavior is more likely to occur in the future. On the other side, if a dieter receives some nice new clothing for each week that a diet is successful, the new, healthier diet is reinforced and more likely to be maintained.

The third basic component of learning approaches involves **modeling,** sometimes termed *vicarious learning.* In this process, a person might learn unhealthy behaviors by watching a favored parent or a favorite movie star drink, smoke, take risks, and so on. Many of our health-relevant behaviors are learned by observing those around us. On the other hand, someone trying to lose weight might associate with a well-organized group of weight watchers, who model proper behavior.

Educational

A very weak form of learning approaches are educational models. These naïve approaches assume that if people learn that a behavior is unhealthy, then they will not do it. Thus, schools often preach ("educate") about the dangers of cigarettes, drugs, and unsafe sex.

Education and knowledge are the first steps in a healthy lifestyle. But education itself is not enough for many people. Consider, for example, the label that is placed on cigarettes warning that smoking is dangerous to your health and can cause cancer and birth defects. This information alone led some people to avoid cigarettes. Almost no one thinks that smoking is healthy, yet millions smoke and thousands take up the habit each month. Education is often touted as the answer to a wide variety of health problems, but as we see throughout this book, it is rarely effective by itself.

Cognitive Learning: Health Belief Model

Most popular in health psychology these days are cognitive learning models of healthy behavior. These models take into account that people think about their worlds and are more likely to engage in healthier behaviors if they believe that the behavior will make a difference in their lives and also have the sense that they are able to succeed in changing their behavior. Thus, notions of self-monitoring, self-reinforcement, and self-efficacy (see next section) are common in health promotion programs.

These psychological characteristics are not personality traits per se, but rather relate more to the way people think, what they believe, and how they learn about healthy behavior. Such factors are part of the **Health Belief Model** (Becker, 1974; Becker et al., 1979; Janz & Becker, 1984; Rosenstock, 1974). The Health Belief Model proposes that people's health actions are a function of whether they perceive a personal threat to their health and whether they think the health action will reduce the threat. For example, it has been found that patients who do not cooperate with their medical treatment believe themselves to be less susceptible to and less threatened by their illness (or possible future illness). To these patients, the physician's assessment of the danger of their illnesses does not matter very much. Rather, to them it is their own perception of the severity of the illness that is important, even if this estimation is not correct.

People who engage in unhealthy behaviors and do not cooperate with their medical regimens tend to be generally less concerned about their health, in an interesting way. Their unhealthy behavior and noncooperation often does not involve lack of education, but rather depends on a host of cognitive influences—that is, patients' thoughts and beliefs about themselves, their habits, and their disease (Ajzen & Fishbein, 1980; Eraker, Kirscht, & Becker, 1984). It also matters whether one's behavior is ripe for change. That is, different people are at different stages of readiness to change, depending upon other things going on in their lives.

Box 10–1   Basic Models of Health Promotion

Model	Brief Description
Biological	Focuses on the genetic, hormonal, and nervous-system bases for motivation and behavior. Usually sees at-risk individual as having a disease.
Learning	Postulates healthy and unhealthy habits are learned through conditioning, reinforcement, and modeling. They therefore can also be unlearned. Sometimes tries to change people's attitudes and beliefs, with the expectation that behavior change will follow.
Educational	A common form of learning model that assumes that if people are taught that a behavior is unhealthy, then they will not do it. Unfortunately, education is often not enough to promote health.
Cognitive Learning	This approach considers that people think about their worlds and are more likely to engage in healthier behaviors if they believe that the behavior will make a difference in their lives and also have the sense that they are able to succeed. Health Belief Model focuses on the relationship between perceived threat and whether health actions are thought to reduce that threat to one's health.
Ego/Identity	Postulates individuals will take care of their health according to how they think about themselves, especially in terms of the concepts of self-efficacy and self-image. May also employ fear appeals.
Societal/Cultural	The focus is on cultural bases of health behavior and attempts to facilitate wide-ranging changes in societal norms.
Socio-Economic/Political	The focus is on the economic and legal pressures on people's health-relevant behavior. For example, cigarettes may be taxed and restricted.
Existential	These models believe that people freely choose styles of living, for a noble or meaningful purpose. Do not try to coerce healthy behavior.
Personality Trait	Disease can be caused or influenced by individual personality traits and emotional reaction patterns. See Chapters 6 and 7.
Interactional, multimodal	Intergrates two or more systems of health promotion. Very valuable in public health campaigns. May reward and model healthy behaviors, provide education and social support, intervene physiologically in difficult cases, and employ ads, laws, and societal pressure.

Ego and Identity

Ego and identity models of healthy behavior postulate that how you think about yourself is key to understanding whether you will take care of yourself. These models are cognitive in the sense that they involve thinking, but they are identity models because self-image and self-esteem are central.

A key concept here is that of **self-efficacy,** which is a person's belief that he or she is in control of relevant actions. People who have high self-efficacy have stronger beliefs in their capabilities to successfully perfom given behaviors. For example, obese people with low self-efficacy cannot take charge of when, what, and how much they eat. People with the most unhealthy habits are often aimless, alienated, or depressed.

Models that focus on self-esteem also fall under this ego and identity category because they assume that people who feel good about themselves and view themselves as good people will want to take care of themselves. These approaches to health promotion therefore consider the influences on a person's identity, such as whether the person came from an abusive childhood, lives in a stable relationship, and has self-worth from a satisfying career. The focus may be on improving early childhood social environments.

Fear appeals are a particular type of ego approach because they postulate that a threat to one's well-being will motivate change. For example, smokers or sunbathers might be shown color pictures of gross, ugly cancer tumors. Fear appeals that are too threatening, however, are often ignored or tuned out by their targets.

Societal and Cultural

As we have seen throughout this book, health practices vary dramatically from culture to culture and even among subcultures. Sociocultural approaches to health promotion focus on these cultural bases of health behavior. For example, people in Italy eat lots of olive oil and tomatoes, people in Japan eat lots of soy and fish, and people in America eat lots of hamburgers and french fries. This is not because people with soy-eating genes or fish-eating personalities live in Japan, but rather because of the norms of the society and culture. Sociocultural approaches attempt to capitalize on these bases, encouraging those culture-based behaviors that are healthy.

More broadly, sociocultural approaches attempt to facilitate wide-ranging changes in societal norms. For example, few people ever went jogging or running before the 1960s. In only a generation or so, American society rapidly developed jogging trails, marathons, running clothes, running shoes, and much more. The Nike company did not even exist in 1960.

Socioeconomic and Political

Socioeconomic and sociopolitical models of health promotion focus on the economic and the legal pressures on people's health-relevant behavior. For example, alcohol usage is legal but marijuana usage is illegal, and there is a much higher usage of alcohol than marijuana. There are many critics of this sort of approach, which outlaws or restricts unhealthy behavior. For example, critics point out that there is wide usage of marijuana anyway, but since it is illegal, there is therefore now no monitoring of the quality of marijuana consumed (such as for adulteration); furthermore, the huge marijuana trade is dangerous and untaxed.

Poor people tend to eat inexpensive foods, some of which are healthy (like beans and vegetables) and some of which are unhealthy (like Twinkies and lard). The government does not subsidize or require the sale of broccoli or asparagus, and it is usually impossible to find these healthy vegetables in fast-food restaurants. However, the government does subsidize many products such as dairy products (and for many years, tobacco), for a variety of socioeconomic and sociopolitical reasons. Almost all major industries have lobbyists in Washington, D.C.

Socioeconomic and sociopolitical models of health promotion range from economic incentives on consumers to society-wide economic control and advertising. It is well-established that consumption of unhealthy products like cigarettes and liquor goes down as taxes on these substances go up (at least to some extent). It is also well-established that large companies that sell tobacco, alcohol, gambling, medical devices, and prescription drugs all advertise heavily and also often make large contributions to politicians and officeholders. In some cases, these large economic and political interests are allied, as large corporations seek favorable public policy.

Existential

Although many scientists do not like to admit it, some people drink, smoke, or take illegal drugs as part of a desire for mind expansion or spiritual improvement. Such use has long been part of human history. Aztecs and other early Americans used peyote, a small psychedelic cactus. Other people use ritual wine. All sorts of other rituals affect health. Many religions employ fasting. Some religious people refuse prescribed medications or vaccinations.

Existential approaches to healthy and unhealthy behaviors generally assume that people freely choose styles of living, often for a noble or meaningful purpose. These approaches are diametrically opposed to health promotions that attempt to coerce cooperative behavior. The self-fulfillment may prove very healthy. For example, people may choose the relaxation of yoga or turn to vigorous exercise to seek the runner's high. Of course, when a nature-seeking motorcyclist who refuses to wear a helmet needs a surgical operation to repair a brain injury, controversy arises over whether the tax-supported health care system should pay for it.

Because much of behavioral science assumes that most of people's behavior is determined (by genes, learning, and social pressures), existential models are the least studied. In reality, issues of choice and responsibility are relevant to understanding all models of health promotion.

Personality Trait

The personality trait approach to understanding disease and healthy behavior was discussed in detail in Chapter 6, "Personality and Disease," and in Chapter 7, "Quality of Life and the Self-Healing Personality." Personality trait models often overlap other approaches because, as we have seen, personality is affected by biological, psychological, and social influences. Personality is closely tied to health behavior across the life span.

Interactional, Multimodal

Interactional, **multimodal approaches** attempt to integrate two or more systems of health promotion. Although commonly used in clinical health psychology in attempts to treat unhealthy patients, multimodal approaches are also often valuable in public health campaigns.

A multimodal approach may reward the individual for healthy behaviors, model appropriate behaviors, provide social support groups, provide education, send mass media advertisements, provide necessary physiological interventions, and use laws or economic incentives to support healthy behavior. For example, drug abuse might be addressed with cognitive-behavioral counseling, the social support of a 12-step group (based on Alcoholics Anonymous), physiological interventions to reduce cravings, education, and laws restricting access and providing punishment.

A successful multimodal approach will include not only the early diagnosis and treatment of disease but also the promotion of healthy lifestyles. Although prevention efforts that rely on diagnosis have produced limited benefits, primary prevention efforts focusing on lifestyle may have substantial benefits (Kaplan, 2000). Yet most preventive health resources in society are currently focused on this diagnosis-dependent secondary prevention, rather than on primary prevention. Society is willing to try to change the diet of someone with heart disease, but relatively less willing to promote good nutrition overall throughout the population.

It is important to think about these basic models of health promotion when considering any particular problem or intervention. If we understand the assumptions and orientations that are the foundations for our approaches, then we are more likely to design valid and comprehensive health research.

There are thousands of studies that test health promotion using one or more of these basic models. Unfortunately, they often do not fully explore the assumptions underlying their interventions and conclusions. A well-versed health psychologist should be able to evaluate the relevant theories and assumptions and notice the limits thereby imposed. There are no simple solutions to many health promotion problems. But by taking this broad view, a health psychologist can observe parallels across different types of health problems and select the most appropriate solutions.

We will now consider several of the key behavioral factors in disease prevention, namely those involving tobacco, alcohol, and illegal drug abuse.

TOBACCO

In 1492, Columbus encountered tobacco in the New World, and not long after, tobacco use began to spread through European culture. By the mid-20th century, this deadly habit (sometimes called "slow-motion suicide") had conquered the world. Tobacco is by far the single greatest cause of preventable death in developed countries.

Cigarette Smoking

Cigarette smokers are about twice as likely to die from heart disease as are nonsmokers. (And because heart disease is the major killer in the nation, the health implications are phenomenal.) Cigarette smoking causes more cancer than any other single element; smokers are much more likely than nonsmokers to develop lung cancer, cancer of the mouth, and cancer of the urinary bladder. Cigarette smoking is also associated with many other diseases, especially various lung diseases. Smoking is a major health problem, associated with as many as one in every four American deaths (U.S. Public Health Service, 1997; Warner, 1986).

Traditional medical approaches have been relatively ineffective in dealing with this health problem. For example, medical and surgical interventions for lung cancer are mostly ineffective. Yet in theory, smoking-related deaths are 100 percent preventable. There was little lung cancer 100 years ago. People begin smoking because of the influence of other people in their culture. Smoking is thus a major issue in the field of psychology and health.

Millions of Americans smoke, and millions more are exposed to the smoke of others, so-called **involuntary smoking.** Involuntary, or *passive,* smoking also increases the risk of disease and death (Environmental Protection Agency, 1990; Garland, Barrett-Connor, Suaret, Criqui, & Wingard, 1985). Even the unborn fetus is affected by smoke.

In 1964, the first Surgeon General's report on smoking and health was published. This widely publicized report documented the causal relationship between smoking and lung cancer. This was the beginning of organized, modern efforts to combat smoking. Since 1964, the percentage of American males who smoke has significantly decreased. Many males, especially educated white males, began to stop smoking in response to the very real threat of an early death.

However, the 1960s also marked the beginning of women's liberation from traditional sex roles. Although it was previously thought deviant, unfeminine, and even sinful for women to smoke, liberated women no longer faced such social pressures. More began to smoke even as others quit. So the percentage of female smokers has not changed as much during the past 25 years. Recently, women "caught up" to men ("came a long way, baby," as the cigarette ads put it), as lung cancer became the leading cause of cancer death in women.

Smoking tobacco is the most common form of tobacco intake and leads to the most serious problems, because smoke also contains carbon monoxide and carcinogens in addition to those found in the tobacco itself. Nevertheless, smokeless tobacco—snuff or chewing tobacco—is also a serious health problem, analogous to cigarettes, with many deadly consequences (Tomar & Giovino, 1998). The tobacco-chewing baseball player, as well as the pipe-smoking philosopher, may face an intriguing array of cancers of the mouth, tongue, throat, and vocal chords. Sigmund Freud, a great cigar smoker, commented that sometimes a cigar is just a cigar, but he slipped towards death with cancer of the mouth and jaw.

Why People Smoke

Adolescents are especially susceptible to the social pressure of their peers, and it is during adolescence that most people begin to smoke. About 4,000 American adolescents begin smoking cigarettes each day. Almost no one who has not smoked by age 21 takes up smoking as an adult, but teenagers who experiment heavily with friends who smoke are especially likely to gradually get hooked (Choi, Pierce, Gilpin, Farkas, & Berry, 1997). Once a person becomes a regular smoker (a process which may take two years), it is very difficult to quit.

Nicotine is physically addicting. The nicotine in smoke rapidly enters the bloodstream and travels to the brain. The brain then signals for the release of catecholamines, thus producing the smoker's "lift" or "fix." Withdrawal from this physical addiction can produce headache, nausea, constipation, irritability, fatigue, and other unpleasant states. Smoking may also be an especially rewarding behavior because of nicotine's effects on stimulating dopamine release in the brain (Bloom & Kupfer, 1995). Nicotine gum is thus sometimes helpful in easing the transition to being a nonsmoker.

However, smoking addiction involves a complex biopsychosocial process. Smoking becomes intimately related to our regulation of our emotions (Leventhal & Cleary, 1980). That is, people may use cigarettes to relax, to control social anxiety, to provide regular routines of behavior, and even to have something to do with their hands. For example, a smoker who regularly lights up with his friends after a meal has developed an habitual *social* reaction, an habitual *behavioral* reaction, and an habitual *physiological* reaction that interacts with the postprandial (after eating) digestive process. Upon quitting, the ex-smoker might find difficulties with after-dinner social interaction, awkwardness in controlling bodily movements and positions, and unusual bodily feelings as the digesting meal has its effects in the absence of nicotine. It is not surprising that it is so difficult to quit.

Pressures to Start Smoking

Smoking should be a major focus of pediatric medicine and primary care medicine (see Figure 10–1). Yet, although physician-delivered interventions are somewhat effective (Ockene, 1987), many physicians and dentists do not even discuss smoking with their patients and so do not urge them to avoid or quit smoking (even though very few physicians themselves smoke). Following the traditional medical model, many health care practitioners wait until a disease develops before addressing the problem (Marlatt & Gordon, 1985).

Even so, why do teenagers begin smoking even though they know the health risks? Very simply, it is because certain important aspects of our culture glamorize smoking. The tobacco industry spends hundreds of millions of dollars each year promoting cigarettes. For example, thousands of young men became hooked trying to be like the rugged, masculine cowboy, the original Marlboro Man. Ironically, the Marlboro Man died of lung cancer, and his widow sued cigarette maker Phillip Morris.

Advertisements for cigarettes promise sex appeal and financial success. Many popular magazines would go bankrupt if they refused to accept cigarette ads. The various pressures exerted by the tobacco industry have created an uproar in the public health community (Glantz et al., 1996; Iglehart, 1984; P. Taylor, 1984). Societal glamour (from cigarette advertising) attracts some teenagers, and then the peer pressure influences many more teenagers.

Figure 10-1   Modeling is one of the strongest influences on smoking initiation. Modeling, together with conditioning and reinforcement, comprise *learning approaches* to the development of health behaviors. *(Reprinted by permission of the American Cancer Society, Inc.)*

In the late 1960s, the Federal Communications Commission ruled that cigarette advertising was subject to the Fairness Doctrine; opposing viewpoints (i.e., antismoking ads) were required on radio and TV. Per capita consumption of cigarettes fell dramatically, until finally smoking ads were removed from the airwaves (Warner, 1986). But smoke still fills the air. There is no requirement that magazines give equal time to antismoking ads.

There are other forms of important cigarette promotion. Events like the Virginia Slims Tennis Tournament pushed cigarettes to sports fans, although it is doubtful that many cigarette smokers would have enough wind to become tennis champions. The Kool Jazz Festival hoped that many fans would follow jazz greats into chain-smoking, although many, such as Duke Ellington, died from lung cancer (Warner, 1986). Free cigarettes were often given out at events that young people and working-class people were likely to attend, although political pressure has stopped many of these practices.

Figure 10–2   *Cognitive approaches,* which emphasize notions of self-monitoring and self-reinforcement, and *ego approaches,* which emphasize self-efficacy, assume that people who have optimistic thoughts about health and who feel good about themselves (as good or attractive people) will want to take care of themselves. *(Reprinted with permission.* Country Fresh Air, *1981,* © *Copyright American Heart Association.)*

There are other important reasons for adolescent smoking besides cigarette advertising and promotion. Most teenagers are not concerned about future health or death; they see a long life ahead of them. In addition, adolescents are trying to show their independence and show they are adults. Since parents clearly see smoking as adult behavior and as undesirable for their children, smoking becomes a perfect way for adolescents to appear to be independent and adult-like.

Smoking also needs to be considered in the context of the tobacco industry, one of the wealthiest and most politically active businesses in the country. Tobacco industry-sponsored research, significant political donations to politicians, and tobacco-financed attorneys and lobbyists have played a significant role for many decades in hiding the severe health hazards of tobacco and preventing its regulation (Glantz et al., 1996; Koop, 1989; Warner, 1986). Certain tobacco industry executives worked to delay public knowledge of the health dangers of smoking, to formulate products that would hook their consumers, and to aggressively market tobacco to many of the most vulnerable members of society.

Figure 10–3   Societal and political influences, such as forbidding smoking in indoor public places, have proved to be very effective means of health promotion, even though they do not directly target the individual. Often, societal changes will change norms, which will change attitudes. *(Reprinted by permission of the American Cancer Society, Inc.)*

Preventing Smoking

What can be done to prevent smoking? As we have seen, education has had some effect. Some people make rational decisions to avoid or to quit smoking, but many people do not or cannot. As social psychologists well know, most people are more conforming than they are rational. So, most important are social expectations. Most people will avoid cigarettes if their peers believe it to be an unhealthful and undesirable addiction.

An important first step in creating these expectations is to make it clear that non-smokers are in the majority and have taken an active decision to protect their health. Non-smoking areas in restaurants and smoking bans on public transportation and in public buildings are an important step. Smoking bans communicate the general societal message that smoking is a threat to public health that will not be tolerated. Community activism on such matters is being facilitated by nonprofit public interest groups like ASH (Action on Smoking and Health). Not that long ago, people would not dare to ask smokers to extinguish their cigarettes; now, many smokers are too embarrassed or fearful to light up outside the privacy of their own homes. It is now sometimes joked that smoking is hazardous to your health because of the danger of assault from nonsmokers.

Raising cigarette taxes also discourages smoking (Biener, Aseltine, Cohen, & Anderka, 1998). So does making cigarettes hard to obtain, such as by banning vending machines. All in all, education and modeling, supported by laws and regulations, has begun to change social expectations. It is this peer pressure that will have the greatest effect on smoking.

Adolescents may need additional special protection (Petraitis, Flay, & Miller, 1995). For example, one project attempted to deter smoking among seventh-grade students, a time when adolescents are at high risk (R.I. Evans et al., 1978, 1981). Role models of children resisting social pressures to begin smoking were found to be effective. In addition, the immediate physiological consequences of smoking were stressed, rather than the threat of lung cancer 40 years hence.

Relatedly, the Waterloo Smoking Prevention Project intervened with adolescents in Canada (Flay et al., 1985). In a school-based program, students taught each other about the dangers of smoking, made commitments not to smoke, and practiced responses to peer pressure. The project included control-group schools and careful assessment techniques. The results were very encouraging. Just as teenagers can learn that it's "cool" to smoke, they can learn that it is cool not to smoke, but to have healthy, attractive bodies instead. And they can learn the social skills with which to act on their beliefs. Smoking prevention programs work, but we are not yet sure exactly why or under what conditions (Flay et al., 1985; 1995).

Smoking Cessation

What about quitting smoking? While there are currently many efforts to help people quit smoking, evaluations generally show mixed results (Dijkstra, DeVries, Roijackers, & Van Breukelen, 1998; Leventhal & Cleary, 1980; Hunt & Matarazzo, 1982; Shiffman et al., 1996). There is a high rate of relapse (recidivism). Certainly, information about the ill effects of smoking and appropriate advice from medical practitioners will help. Encouragement from valued others is useful; divorced or separated people (lacking such social support) are less likely to quit (Kabat & Wynder, 1987). Removal of cigarettes and ashtrays from the house and changing relevant habits (such as not lingering after dinner with a cup of coffee) may also be helpful.

Because of the biological effects of nicotine, quitters can gain weight, feel anxious or tired, and become constipated. Thus for many quitters, nicotine gum provides a helpful bridge between being a smoker and an ex-smoker (Doherty, Militello, Kinnunen, & Garvey, 1996). Regular exercise, a low-fat diet, lots of water, and high fiber foods are also often of real benefit. Physiological aids may be especially useful for those individuals who have a genetic predisposition to enjoy smoking, possibly due to the make-up of the dopamine transmission system in their brains (Lerman et al., 1999; Sabol et al., 1999).

More recent research on smoking cessation focuses on special populations and on readiness to change behavior (King, Borrelli, Black, Pinto, & Marcus, 1997; Morera et al., 1998; Orleans, Boyd, Bingler, & Sutton, 1998). That is, subcultures (such as whites vs. blacks, men vs. women, young adults vs. older adults) have different influences on their behaviors, so different techniques may be more effective. These interventions consider the specific pressures on individuals in their daily lives. For example, having a supportive friend (who also quits) can prove quite helpful.

Some people simply announce they have had enough and are able to quit spontaneously (Schachter, 1982). Various behavior management techniques are sometimes helpful. For example, association of smoking with unpleasant sensations (such as by forcing people to "oversmoke" by puffing heavily) helps a smoker to quit. This type of conditioning is termed **aversion therapy.** Others substitute gum chewing or the eating of sunflower seeds for their smoking habit. Still others reward themselves for not smoking, such as by going to a gourmet restaurant they can now afford and eating food they can now taste.

However, the primary emphasis must be placed on *prevention* of smoking. Just as people learn to avoid accidents and eat nonpoisonous foods, so can people learn to avoid cigarette smoking.

Understanding Risk

As a final point, it is worth asking whether most people really understand the risks from smoking. The public is often provided with **relative risk** statistics that compare mortality rates for smokers (the persons with the risk factor) to rates for nonsmokers (persons without the risk factor). Or, people may hear statistics about **attributable risk,** which is incidence of the disease in exposed persons that is due to the exposure (i.e., the excess disease associated with the risk factor). For example, about 90 percent of lung cancer deaths are attributable to smoking.

However, such statistics say nothing about the actual probability that a person will die from the disease. So, for example, although a man may believe that smoking increases his chances of lung cancer, he may place the risk as comparable to that of pesticide traces in food or artificial sweeteners in soft drinks. He may think that he faces comparable risks daily—in driving a car or taking a plane flight. In fact, however, a 35-year-old male heavy smoker has about an 18 percent chance of dying of smoking-caused lung cancer before age 85, about a 36 percent chance of dying from some smoking-related disease by age 85, but only about a 1 percent chance of dying in a car crash and a very tiny chance of dying in a plane crash by age 85 (Mattson, Pollack, & Cullen, 1987).

In short, there are various ways of looking at health-risk statistics, which may have different implications for a person's understanding of the health issues. Many people believe that smoking is simply one risk among many (like obesity or not having smoke detectors), but in fact it is far and away the most significant preventable threat to one's health (Warner, 1986). When actor Michael J. Fox heard of the death of choreographer Bob Fosse (a heavy smoker), he enrolled in a quit smoking program, saying, "Granted he was 60, but I want to live a hell of a lot longer than that."

Overall, studies suggest the following approach to preventing smoking and encouraging cessation:

First, society should limit access to tobacco to young people through laws and taxes that make tobacco expensive and that make it difficult for children to obtain (restricting vending machines, sales to minors, and so on). Further, tobacco advertising should be limited to print informational appeals (consistent with free speech rights and a desire for the free flow of information), controlling sexy, emotional appeals. Restriction of smoking in all public places further discourages use.

Second, cultural institutions like churches, schools, government bodies, and entertainment producers should make it clear that smoking destroys human life and so is not a desirable activity, just as these institutions discourage violence.

Third, role models appropriate to the various groups in society should show the example of a healthy, well-developed body. Relatedly, social and peer groups can exert tremendous positive influences. Also, people living in stable families in stable communities are less likely to take up dangerous habits.

Fourth, on the more individual level, a sense of control and efficacy in one's life, coupled with goals for the future, significantly reduce intent to use tobacco and other dangerous substances.

Have all the efforts against smoking had an effect? Yes, indeed. The Centers for Disease Control reported that just about one in four or five adult Americans smokes cigarettes. (Well over half of American males smoked in the 1960s.) However, the U.S. Surgeon General's goal of a smoke-free society by the year 2000 turned out to be not within reach.

ALCOHOL

Several million Americans are physically addicted **alcoholics;** they neglect other responsibilities, need large quantities of alcohol, and experience withdrawal when they stop drinking. Several million more are **problem drinkers**—they get drunk several times a month and face significant negative consequences (such as with drunken driving or problems with their spouses) but can stop if they want to stop (Bennett & Miller, 1998). For these people, biology plays less of a role, and psychosocial factors play more of a part in their drinking.

Alcohol threatens health directly through such diseases as cirrhosis and indirectly through accidents such as auto crashes. Overall, most alcohol use begins with social pressure, but as with other drugs and cigarettes, a physiological addiction can also develop. Although the physiological reactions are different than those to smoking, the relevant health psychology models are very similar.

Most alcoholics are not skid-row bums. An alcoholic can be (and usually is) a business executive, a member of Congress, a schoolteacher, a teenage soccer player, a physician, and so on. Hundreds of thousands of lives are ruined each year as alcohol drinkers destroy their own livers and brains, abuse their families, and kill or maim others on the highways. The children of an alcoholic mother may suffer from fetal alcohol syndrome, involving a wide range of birth defects, including possible brain damage (Abel, 1998). Alcohol plays a significant role in many falls, drownings, homicides, and suicides, and it is involved in many crimes.

Alcoholism has such devastating effects on families that special social support organizations exist for spouses of alcoholics (Al-Anon) and their teenage children (Alateen). Even when they grow up, children of alcoholics (COAs) often face psychological and social difficulties (Woititz, 1983).

Disease or Behavior Pattern?

In many cases, there is a biological influence on susceptibility to alcoholism. Children of alcoholics have high rates of alcoholism. Alcoholics seem to metabolize alcohol differently, have different physical reactions to it, and may be more readily addicted. Alcoholics also are likely to have psychological problems and may have physiologically based problems in emotional regulation (Miller & Heather, 1998; NIH, 1996). Alcohol affects the levels of neurotransmitters in the brain, including dopamine, serotonin, and glutamate (Lowman, Hunt, Litten, & Drummond, 2000).

So, some researchers view alcoholism as a disease. The main benefit of this view is that the alcoholic is seen as someone with a serious problem who needs a lot of help from others; there is less blame and self-blame involved. It may become easier to break a cycle of lower and lower self-esteem.

On the other hand, viewing alcoholism as a disease raises many of the problems of an overgeneralized medical model. Although children of alcoholics have a higher rate of alcoholism than children of non-alcoholics, most children of alcoholics do not become alcoholics themselves; their overall social environment is important. Different cultural and ethnic groups have markedly different alcoholism rates. For example, there are low rates of alcoholism among Mormons, Jews, and Chinese Americans. Social expectations, such as sex roles, affect alcohol use (with men more likely to be abusers). Stressful life events can promote alcohol use. And even laws and taxes affect alcohol use. For example, when excise taxes on alcohol go up, drinking goes down. When alcoholism is viewed as a disease, many of these important influences may tend to be overlooked (Vaillant, 1983; Tuchfeld & Marcus, 1984; Marlatt & Gordon, 1985).

Treatment and Relapse

As with similar problems, the best way of dealing with alcoholism is prevention. However, our society mostly ignores prevention, and so treatment is necessary (Marlatt & Gordon, 1985). Some of the most successful treatment programs for alcoholism are the groups called Alcoholics Anonymous (AA). (There are also other "Anonymous" groups for other addictions.) Alcoholics Anonymous is a group that involves the use of other alcoholics to provide social definition, social support, and social influence to keep an alcoholic sober. Alcoholics must announce their addiction, swear off alcohol, and work to help other alcoholics stay away from the dangerous liquid. In brief, AA incorporates the social factors that we have seen are most successful in influencing behavior.

Young people usually do not start drinking unless they are influenced by their peers to do so, and ultimately it is the peer group that can help end problem drinking. It is more difficult to stop drinking, however, if one has learned to use alcohol as a coping mechanism in times of stress. Individuals raised by attentive, warm, and nurturing parents may be more likely to turn to supportive and helpful others (McIntyre & Dusek, 1995).

As with smoking, aversion therapy is sometimes used with alcoholics. In this case, a medication like disulfiram (Antabuse) is used—it causes vomiting when alcohol is then drunk. This can condition the body to avoid alcohol. Other behavior therapies focus on the environmental cues that trigger drinking, and simply avoiding situations where alcohol is readily available.

Can recovering alcoholics ever take a drink or is that the beginning of a relapse? Alcoholics Anonymous groups preach total abstinence from alcohol. In theory, some people can learn to control their drinking, but in practice, the many forces—biological and psychosocial—that led to an alcohol problem in the first place make "drinking in moderation" a risky goal for someone who has experienced alcohol problems.

With both smoking and drinking, individuals may relapse, despite the best intentions. Overall, the research suggests that disease prevention training should include strategies for recovery from relapse when it occurs (Marlatt & VandenBos, 1997). For example, the individual should well understand that taking a smoke or a drink is not necessarily the "beginning of the end," and a social support network could immediately be called upon to help prevent further escalation.

Preventing Alcohol Abuse

Our society deserves much of the blame for the problems of alcohol. Many party hosts push alcohol on their guests. The amiable drunk is a fond character in our comedies. The view of drinking as "macho" each year leads college students to kill or injure themselves during fraternity initiation rituals. The glamorization of alcohol among young people has made alcohol a key factor in many "date rapes," in which many young people wake up to the sober facts of pregnancy and criminal prosecution.

Even small amounts of alcohol can impair judgment and relax inhibitions, making more likely driving accidents, risky sexual behavior, sports accidents, and more. Yet about a third of the population mixes alcohol with sports, parties, and recreation. This is especially a problem with male adolescents and young adults. Alcoholism decreases with age, in part because problem drinkers tend to die young.

Are there any benefits of alcohol consumption? There is consistent evidence that a small amount of alcohol—about one drink a day—is protective against cardiovascular disease. This seems to be due to beneficial effects on high density lipoprotein levels (HDL cholesterol) (Criqui, 1996). However, detrimental physiological effects appear with greater consumption, and given the great potential for problems and abuse, alcohol intake is not recommended by public health officials.

Many well-adjusted adults relax with an occasional beer or cocktail with no ill effects, and so it is also important not to exaggerate the potential risks of alcohol. It is not the case that "everything enjoyable is bad for you." Rather, health psychology can help design policies that influence and warn against the more dangerous combinations and risks.

The health psychologist Meg Gerrard and her colleagues make the case that, contrary to popular expectation, there is a complex relationship among personality, self-esteem, and risky behaviors such as teenage drinking (Gerrard, Gibbons, Reis-Bergan, & Russell, 2000). Overall, well-adjusted adolescents with high self-esteem are usually less prone to unhealthy behavior like alcohol abuse. However, individuals with high self-esteem who engage in risky behaviors may utilize a variety of self-serving cognitive strategies that protect them from having to acknowledge their vulnerability to the negative results that may follow. Although people with high esteem value their well-being, and so are motivated to take care of themselves, they may also be more stubborn about listening to the advice of others. This is especially a problem when the society views drinking as cool.

In short, alcohol is not a benign joy but is a mind-altering drug, with significant health-damaging potential. Although many people certainly can enjoy an occasional drink without any problems, many other people live to regret their "one drink too many" or even enter a nightmare of addiction. The study of alcohol and the prevention of alcohol abuse will likely become an increasingly important topic in health psychology.

ILLEGAL DRUG ABUSE

Society is filled with contradictory messages about drugs. On the one hand, people are urged to take various pills to feel better, control pain, aid in sleeping and relaxing, stay alert, and so on. At the same time, there is a stigma attached to relying on drugs, and the dangers of drug addiction are well known. This contradiction was well illustrated at the national level by the case of Dr. Peter Bourne, an advisor on drug abuse to the President. Bourne was well known for his opposition to the abuse of common drugs like sleeping pills; but when asked for help by a distressed colleague, Bourne wrote a prescription for Quaaludes (a powerful sedative). To protect his colleague from embarrassment, Bourne wrote the prescription in a phony name, thus violating the drug laws. When the story became public, Bourne was forced to resign from his position.

For drugs like cocaine and heroin, the proportion of the population that has used them is low, but the proportion of users who have drug problems or become addicted is high. As with alcohol and cigarettes, a combination of factors puts one at higher risk for illegal drug abuse—an impulsive personality with problems of self-regulation, a family that is unstable or abusing, a peer group that contains drug abusers, and a subculture where drugs are readily available and commonly used (Baer, Marlatt, & McMahon, 1993; Rouse, 1998; Wills, 1998). Abusers of illegal drugs are also likely to use alcohol and tobacco.

As with cigarettes, users of illegal drugs generally begin their pattern in adolescence. It would be highly unusual for a 40-year-old schoolteacher to suddenly start using heroin. Although one in seven American adults are heavy drinkers, only about one in a hundred abuse cocaine or heroin. Since this rate varies dramatically across families and subcultures, it is often unclear where the problem arises. Treatment programs that focus on one substance (e.g., alcohol) as an individual problem will generally be ineffective, since abusers typically use multiple substances and are caught in a biopsychosocial pattern of continuing abuse (Bukstein, 1995; Gorsuch & Butler, 1976).

In general, there are four main influences on whether or not someone is likely to use illegal drugs like amphetamines, heroin, or cocaine. First, parents seem to have a significant influence on whether their children will become drug abusers, in two ways. On the one hand, the warmth of the parent-child interaction and the cohesion of the family unit are often related to a child's sense of identity and self-esteem; this is in turn related to whether the child will turn to drugs. Parents also influence their children through modeling. If parents use, encourage the use of, or abuse drugs, their children are likely to follow suit.

Second, the use of drugs is clearly related to the influence of peers, and this factor also operates in two ways. Both the lack of involvement in healthy groups in which drugs are not used and direct involvement in drug-abusing peer groups will lead to an increased likelihood of drug abuse. Campaigns to "Just Say No" to drugs endeavor to operate through this mechanism. If they provide children with a relevant reference group of other children who are refusing to use drugs, then they can help prevent some drug abuse.

Third, general social adjustment is related to the potential for drug abuse. People who are heavily involved in normal social activities and have close relationships with others are less likely to become drug abusers.

Finally, initial experiences with drugs may affect subsequent drug use and abuse. If the initial experiences are unpleasant, dangerous, or troublesome, there is less likelihood of subsequent abuse.

Cocaine is a psychostimulant that is an especially widespread and dangerous drug. There is evidence that cocaine prevents the reabsorption of the neurotransmitter dopamine by binding to the dopamine uptake transporter and hence inhibiting dopamine reuptake (Bloom & Kupfer, 1995; Volkow, Fowler, & Warp, 1999). When dopamine concentrations rise due to cocaine, emotional highs are initially created; but the brain is disrupted as dopamine levels later crash. It is likely that some people have natural defects or disease-caused weaknesses in their dopamine systems, and such people may be especially susceptible to cocaine addiction. Even in initially healthy people, chronic cocaine use tends to produce symptoms of paranoia. Users may become hypersensitive—to light, to noise, and to other people. They may worry, become obsessed with details, and feel they are being persecuted. Cocaine addicts may also become nervous and depressed, as dopamine levels regress. See Box 10–2 for a neurological-homeostasis view of addiction.

Cocaine can permanently affect infants exposed in the womb, and the fact that dramatic changes occur in personality and social relations in abusers makes drug abuse a prime topic for health psychology. Interestingly, it has long been noticed that people with Parkinson's disease seem to be stoic; since Parkinson's disease involves a defect in the dopamine system, it may be the case that this defect is related to this aspect of personality as well as to cocaine abuse. Unfortunately, this whole field of neurotransmitter abnormality and health psychology is still in its infancy (Alessandri, Sullivan, Bendersky, & Lewis, 1995; Menza & Liberatore, 1998; Wills, 1998).

Box 10-2   A Neurological Homeostasis Model of Drug Addiction

A person, often an impulsive or anxious person under peer pressure (such as an insecure teenager at a party), ingests an opiate or euphoric like heroin or cocaine.

↓

The drug travels to the brain, where it affects the pathways that normally make us feel pleasure in response to rewarding experiences. It thus creates "artifical" or purely biological pleasure. Neurotransmitters, especially dopamine, are affected.

↓

In the case of drugs like cocaine, normal dopamine re-uptake is hindered, keeping dopamine levels high, and pleasure intense. In the case of drugs like heroin, more dopamine is released.

↓

Over time, the brain senses that homeostasis has been disrupted and too much neurostimulation is occurring. The body responds by decreasing the amounts of neurotransmitters available or decreasing their effects (such as by decreasing the numbers of dopamine receptors).

↓

The person becomes tense, unhappy, or driven, as normally pleasant activities are no longer sufficient to produce a sense of pleasure or well-being. Reinforcement turns from being provided by the social environment to being provided by the drug.

↓

The person seeks higher or more frequent drug doses to compensate. The brain further adapts. The social environment, in turn, becomes increasingly unrewarding. The person is addicted (hooked).

For further information:

National Institute on Drug Abuse. (2000). *Principles of drug addiction treatment: A research-based guide.* Rockville, MD: National Institutes of Health Publication, no. 00-4180.
Or see: (www.nida.nih.gov)

Prevention and Treatment

Due to the great societal toll of drug abuse, all sorts of intervention problems have been designed and tested (Goldberg et al., 1996; Schinke, Cole, Diaz, & Botvin, 1997; Warner, Kessler, Hughes, Anthony, & Nelson, 1995; Wills, 1998). These are often community-

Figure 10–4   This informational poster appeals to people's desires to strive
for a meaningful life, full of noble accomplishments. It thus is
based on the *existential approach* to health promotion, rather
than trying to coerce, scare, threaten, or reward people toward
healthy behavior. For some people, philosophical or religious
appeals succeed where others have failed. *(Reprinted by permission of the American Lung Association.)*

based and fairly effective, at least in the short term. These programs could be even more effective if they were more general and comprehensive (Jessor, Van Den Bos, Vander-ryn, Costa, & Turbin, 1995). Specifically, drug abuse in a community tends to be low when the following conditions are satisfied:

1. Individuals with high-risk personalities receive special attention; these are people who are impulsive, frequently unhappy or angry, have academic problems in school, seek high levels of stimulation, and generally have poor self-control.

2. Family relations are good; loving families in which adolescents have someone they can trust are at lower risk for substance abuse.

3. There is supportive religion or other inspiring social support; people who feel a larger purpose in life are less likely to abuse.

4. People understand the harm that comes from drug abuse, especially if this information comes from respected others.

5. The subculture clearly disapproves of illegal drugs and makes them difficult and expensive to obtain.

6. Parents with abuse problems of their own receive intensive treatment.

7. There is sufficient supervision of adolescents—by parents, schools, and community officers—so that troublesome peer groups cannot exert their influence.

Of course, satisfying these conditions is not easy. People often do not worry about substance abuse until it becomes a serious problem. Note also that although these conditions seem to be sensible ways of preventing and minimizing substance abuse, they are often not fully adopted even when a community decides to attack the problem. For example, the community may turn to police action and other punitive measures, which address only one or two of the seven conditions. Or, communities may emphasize education, but education is only one part of the overall solution.

Harm Reduction

What do we do about the core of people who cannot be easily prevented from engaging in unhealthy behaviors? Should we attempt to reduce the extent of their unhealthy behavior and the harm that it does to them and others? For example, should we give methadone (a synthetic narcotic) to heroin addicts so that they will not obtain adulterated heroin on the streets nor steal to support their habits?

Efforts directed at reducing the damage rather than at preventing the behavior are collectively known as **harm reduction.** Some important examples are the following: giving out condoms in high schools to prevent sexually transmitted diseases and unwanted teenage pregnancy; providing filtered or low tar cigarettes; needle exchanges (giving out clean needles) for intravenous drug users to prevent the spread of infections like HIV; and putting in airbags for unsafe (or alcoholic) drivers (MacCoun, 1998).

Such programs are often opposed by some politicians due to the belief that such harm reduction efforts will legitimate and thus encourage the unhealthy behavior. However, research generally suggests that programs such as needle exchanges do not lead to much if any increase in drug abuse. In fact, by bringing the unhealthy behavior into the public health system, there may be better opportunities for providing information and treatment (Lurie & Reingold, 1993). However, it is still unknown whether such recognition of unhealthy behaviors will be seen as permissiveness and will lead to an increase of unhealthy behaviors in the long run.

SUMMARY AND CONCLUSION

This chapter well illustrates that issues of health promotion and disease prevention go way beyond basic psychological processes. Much larger psychosocial issues, socioeconomic issues, and sociopolitical issues come to the fore, as health behavior is affected not only by individual factors but also by family factors and cultural factors. As the eminent scientist and physician, former Surgeon General C. Everett Koop, put it, "I frequently spoke of the sleazy behavior of the tobacco industry in its attempts to discredit legitimate science as part of its overall effort to create controversy and doubt. Well-funded tobacco interests attacked (and continue to attack) not only the surgeon general, but also the Environmental Protection Agency, the Food and Drug Administration, the Occupational Safety and Health Administration, and individual scientists who are working to end the scourge of tobacco" (Glantz et al., 1996, p. xiv).

Issues of how to promote health, prevent disease, and best structure our health care system are key aspects of the field of health psychology. Health psychologists endeavor to go beyond a pathogen-based approach to focus on more basic models for health promotion and disease prevention.

The biological approaches to health promotion focus on the genetic, hormonal, and nervous-system bases for motivation and behavior. Drugs and behaviors that change physiology are the focus.

Learning models postulate that healthy or unhealthy habits and behaviors are primarily learned and, therefore, can be unlearned. Conditioning, reinforcement, and modeling are three basic components of the learning approach. A very weak form of learning approaches is educational models. Though education and knowledge are the first step in a healthy lifestyle, education itself is not enough for many people.

Cognitive learning models of healthy behavior take into account that people think about their worlds and are more likely to engage in healthier behaviors if they believe that the behavior will make a difference in their lives and also have the sense that they are able to succeed. These include the theory of reasoned action and the Health Belief Model.

Ego and identity models of healthy behavior focus on self-image and self-esteem. Sociocultural approaches emphasize the cultural bases of health behavior, even attempting to facilitate wide-ranging changes in societal norms. Socioeconomic and sociopolitical models of health promotion focus on the economic and the legal pressures on people's health-relevant behavior, ranging from economic incentives on consumers to society-wide economic control and advertising. Existential approaches to healthy and unhealthy behaviors generally assume that people freely choose styles of living, often for a noble or meaningful purpose.

Use of nicotine, alcohol, and illegal drugs, with their significant negative consequences, is a complex biopsychosocial issue. Most people start using such substances due to a variety of peer pressures or appealing advertising that make these substances desirable and available. Both biological and psychosocial factors in turn contribute to the person's dependency on that substance. There is a high rate of relapse for those trying to quit, and the variety of treatment programs available vary in their success, depending on design and implementation. A better understanding of the risks involved in the use of these substances may help prevent their abuse by some people, but overall, there needs to be a much greater focus on well-designed prevention.

Recommended Additional Reading

Glantz, Stanton A., Slage, John, Bero, Lisa, Hanauer, Peter, & Barnes, Deborah. (1996). *The Cigarette Papers.* Berkeley: University of California Press.

Marlatt, G. Alan. (Ed.). (1998) *Harm reduction: Pragmatic strategies for managing high-risk behaviors.* New York: Guilford.

Marlatt, G. Alan, & VandenBos, Gary R. (Eds.). (1997). *Addictive behaviors: Readings on etiology, prevention, and treatment.* Washington, DC: American Psychological Association.

Alcoholics Anonymous: http://www.aa.org/

National Institute on Alcohol Abuse and Alcoholism (NIAAA): http://www.niaaa.nih.gov/

The National Institute on Drug Abuse: http://www.nida.nih.gov/

Key Concepts

models of health promotion and disease prevention

conditioning

reinforcement

modeling

reasoned action

Health Belief Model

self-efficacy

fear appeals

socioeconomic and sociopolitical models

multimodal approaches

involuntary smoking

aversion therapy

smoking prevention

relative risk

attributable risk

alcoholics

problem drinkers

behavior pattern

harm reduction

Chapter 11

NUTRITION, EXERCISE, AND PROPHYLAXIS

When Jack LaLanne started his pioneering fitness show in the early days of television in 1956, his message was scorned by the medical establishment. LaLanne touted vitamin supplements, and mineral supplements, and whole grains and fresh fruit (and he guzzled carrot juice); but the medical establishment warned of vitamin overdoses and touted whole milk (and doctors ate white bread).

    Jack urged vigorous physical fitness training and weight lifting; he started his own health club in 1936 and invented weight-lifting equipment. But most coaches and doctors warned of becoming "muscle-bound" and overdeveloped. Certainly, women should not do such exercise—they would become "mannish." Even jogging was quite unusual until the 1970s.

None of this rejection stopped Jack or some of his viewers and fans. Slowly but surely, others began opening gyms for the average person, developing weight training, switching away from an animal-based diet, inventing running shoes, making exercise videos, studying vitamins, and more. Progressive physicians joined those questioning traditional approaches. Yet it is still difficult to find a government program that will pay for a fitness center or a weight machine instead of a hospital or a surgery; or a physician who can speak knowledgeably about vitamins, herbs, and supplements; or a public health program on highway safety. There is movement in LaLanne's direction, but it is very, very slow.

When last heard from, at age 84, Jack LaLanne was still traveling around the country, doing push-ups, drinking vegetable juice, gobbling lots of vitamins, and urging his elderly audiences to get out and muscle build. He was also wondering out loud if they would wake up and feed their dogs a cup of coffee, a piece of cheese on toast, and a doughnut for breakfast. Most of Jack's more traditional contemporaries (and doctors) are either in a nursing home or dead.

The rate of gain in adult Americans' life expectancy has slowed dramatically. In the past, most Americans could expect to live longer lives than their parents, but that may no longer be true to any significant degree. We may be reaching the limits of how long the human body can last. However, the evidence suggests that much old-age morbidity and most deaths in the United States are still "premature"—that is, they are due to conditions other than the natural aging processes of the body.

In the late 1970s, the U.S. Surgeon General issued a report on health promotion, called *Healthy People* (U.S. Public Health Service, 1979). The remarkable conclusion of this report was that further improvements in the health of Americans were most likely to result from efforts to prevent disease and promote health. In other words, the most important future advances would come *not* from sophisticated medical technology, new drugs, nor specialized doctors. Rather, the improvements would occur *before* the individual even entered the medical care system!

Traditional medical approaches still dominate health care, but there is movement toward more health promotion, often led by health psychologists. The topic of health promotion also encompasses concerns from the fields of public health, health education, primary care medicine, medical sociology, and clinical psychology. To remain healthy, people need to do much more than avoid harmful and toxic substances like cigarette smoke. They need to eat the right foods, engage in the right amount of exercise, live in physically safe environments, and take prophylactic measures as appropriate. (These measures are of course in addition to the many matters of stress-management discussed earlier in this book.) People also need to cooperate with treatment (discussed in the next chapter of this book.) All of these actions involve human behavior.

This chapter focuses on key psychological aspects of healthy orientations and environments, especially nutrition, exercise, and prophylaxis. We endeavor to present the general philosophy and principles of health promotion that emerge from health psychology research.

NUTRITION AND EATING

Healthy Diet

The *Joy of Cooking* cookbook is in the kitchen of many serious chefs. Before presenting the thousands of recipes, one edition of the book opens with a story about a physician. In this story, the "old-fashioned" doctor, upon entering the home of the afflicted, goes straight to the kitchen to thank the cook for giving him a new patient. Then the doctor goes up to see the patient. Moral: There is no doubt that poor diet plays a key role in illness.

Diseases caused by a **deficient diet** (such as pellagra, caused by a vitamin B deficiency) are now quite rare in the United States, although a disturbing number of pregnant women and infants in inner-city ghettos suffer from inadequate nutrition. However, there is increasing evidence that **dietary imbalances** may have important links to many acute and chronic illnesses (USDA, 1995). That is, people often eat too much of certain foods and too little of other foods.

Health care has paid relatively little attention to the types of foods eaten. Since the development of germ theory in the 19th century, the perceived importance of the human host to health and illness has been low. That is, disease is usually conceived to be the result of the invasion of the body by an external microorganism rather than a failure or breakdown of the body's defenses. As the importance of the body's own "environment" has been increasingly recognized, nutrition has emerged as a key aspect of maintaining the healthy body (Dubos, 1968; Harper, 1984; Hegsted, 1984).

There is controversy about which diets are best because unambiguous data are hard to find: It is impossible to isolate two groups of people who are the same on all other attributes except that one group eats a lot of lobster and the other group doesn't. Forced to rely on indirect, quasi-experimental evidence, reputable scientists disagree. However, there is increasing consensus that people should:

- Eat a variety of foods;
- Eat five or more servings of fruits and vegetables each day; and
- Choose most of what is to be eaten from plant sources, including lots of whole grains (American Heart Association, 2000).

In other words, the "good" foods are whole-grain breads and cereals, fruits, vegetables, and nuts, with some protein from fish and low-fat meat. The "bad" foods (when eaten in excess) are those high in saturated fats (fatty meat and skin, butter, foods fried in animal shortening, many dairy products, many processed baked goods) and high-sugar foods like soda pop, lacking in vitamins and minerals. Monounsaturated oil like olive oil and polyunsaturated canola oil have not been shown to be unhealthy.

This healthy diet is remarkably simple! All it advises is to choose one's food primarily from among foods like oranges, apples, grapefruits, melons, berries, pears, apricots, avocados, bananas, grapes, dates, nectarines, peaches, plums, strawberries, raisins, watermelon, pineapple, corn, potatoes, asparagus, beans, tomatoes, beets, yams, carrots, onions, cabbage, spinach, green salads, broccoli, squash, Cornflakes, oatmeal, granola, rice, walnuts, breads such as wheat bread, rye bread, and whole-grain, and pastas such as spaghetti and ravioli. Pizzas made with whole-grain crusts and topped with tomato sauce, olive oil, spices, mushrooms, olives, asparagus, peppers, and lots of other vegetables are not "junk food" (unless loaded with saturated oil and fatty cheese) but are probably one of the healthiest meals you can eat.

If this were a nutrition book rather than a health psychology book, we could go into the physiologic reasons for these recommendations. For example, saturated fats (like those found in ice cream) can raise levels of low-density lipoproteins (LDL cholesterol), which is the so-called bad cholesterol that helps clog arteries. Antioxidants like the carotinoids found in carrots and squash and the vitamin C found in citrus fruits can travel through the body and help destroy **free radicals,** which are ionized (chemically active) molecules that damage healthy body cells. Cruciferous vegetables like cabbage (the main ingredient of cole slaw) are high in isothiocyanates, which help destroy toxic chemicals that have been ingested or formed in the body (Saltman, Gurin, & Mothner, 1993). Many plants, including tea and green vegetables, are high in flavonoids, which help remove toxins. Cereals and the B vitamins control homocysteine levels and other potentially harmful substances.

The problem with this kind of approach is that it leads to ever-longer and more complicated lists: Eat this, don't eat that. Further, the science of nutrition is complex, and most of the details are still unknown. Health psychology should be focused instead on the problems of how and why people come to eat healthy and unhealthy amounts of the basic healthy and unhealthy foods.

Promoting Healthy Eating

Interestingly, there is evidence that regularly eating breakfast is associated with good health (Berkman & Breslow, 1983; Kaplan, Seeman, Cohen, Knudsen, & Guralnik, 1987). However, we do not know for sure whether the breakfast itself makes the difference or whether people who eat breakfast are more likely to engage in various other health-promoting behaviors. Such conundrums again illustrate that health promotion must be broadly considered, and that endless lists of instructions are not the answer.

Yet despite the importance of diet to health, it is difficult to induce people to change their eating habits. First, although eating is a biological necessity and some taste preferences are biologically determined, eating is mostly a social and cultural phenomenon (Friedman & Brownell, 1998; Rozin, 1984; Wadden & Brownell, 1984). Meals, especially dinners, are often social occasions in which friends or family gather together. The kinds of foods eaten depend in part upon the desires of others. (It is hard to eat fish at a pizza party). Similarly, eating is often tied to holidays like Thanksgiving and to various celebrations and parties. In America, what is a birthday without a birthday cake?

Second, eating certain kinds of foods involves habits from childhood; foods are often part of a family's tradition (Birch & Fisher, 1996). People may learn that a breakfast is incomplete without buttered toast or that a dinner is incomplete without meat and potatoes. Or a family may take pride in its Sunday morning omelets. Relatedly, eating habits are part of a general cultural influence. Only certain foods are available in local markets, certain foods are heavily promoted through advertising, and certain foods are proscribed because of religious or other moral grounds. For example, in American culture, well-marbled red meat is a highly prized food, but insects are not. Restaurants further restrict people's options, often frying foods in saturated fats. And cultures maintain their distinctive food choices for hundreds of years.

Because of their strong ties to social factors, eating habits are most effectively changed through a general shift in social norms rather than through an individual's efforts. For example, it is easier to help an individual cut down on fat consumption if there is a general social belief that too much fat is a bad idea for reasons of health or economics or appearance than it is to rely on logical argument. Clear guidelines from public health and related social agencies, and influences in economic policy will, in the long run, have a more significant impact on eating habits than simple education (Kumanyika et al., 2000).

Still, public health promotions are sometimes helpful. For example, one ambitious mass media campaign attempted to alter the diet of a whole community in order to improve cardiovascular health (Maccoby, Farquhar, Wood, & Alexander, 1977). Termed the Stanford Three-Community Study, this project measured the diet and the blood cholesterol and fat of people in three California communities. Then, two of the communities were exposed for two years to television and radio programs and ads, newspaper columns, and posters and billboards promoting heart health. People in the communities were followed and reassessed. The project found that the mass media campaigns were somewhat effective in changing diets and reducing the blood fat and cholesterol levels. This study had the methodological strength of a control group (actually a control community) that did not see the media campaigns and did not show the improvement.

The importance of this work was to show that carefully planned mass media campaigns, which cost relatively little per capita, can work. These efforts were followed up in a five-city study, the Stanford Five-City Multifactor Risk Reduction Project (Farquhar et al., 1984; Rimal, 2000; Schooler, Chaffee, Flora, & Roser, 1998; Winkleby, Flora, & Kraemer, 1994). As predicted by models of health behavior, diets improve if people feel they are at risk, think that they can do something to change their risk, and receive a message appropriately targeted to them.

For some people facing particular disease risks, individual influence is helpful. An obvious though relatively minor role can be played by the individual health provider in patient education. For example, patients can be warned about foods containing high fat contents (contributing to heart disease and cancer) but very little protein or fiber. However, few medical providers include extensive questions about daily diet in medical examinations, although almost all would admit the importance of diet to health. The general expectations of the medical environment do not yet give sufficient attention to diet.

Although there is still a long way to go in improving diet education and diet advice, it is important to emphasize again that limits exist on how effective such individual educational techniques can be. A good example is obesity.

Obesity

It is unhealthy to be extremely overweight or extremely underweight. Obesity is measured in terms of **body mass index** (BMI). BMI is weight divided by height squared. This is weight in kilograms divided by the square of your height in meters; or your weight in pounds multiplied by 704.5 and then divided by the square of your height in inches. BMIs greater than about 26 are unhealthy. Very low body masses are also predictive of increased risk.

More than one-third of middle-aged women and one-fifth of middle-aged men are obese. Although precise causal pathways have not yet been proven, obesity is related to diabetes, gall bladder disease, high blood pressure, and various other health-threatening conditions. In addition, obesity can affect a person's self-concept and physical attractiveness.

A "cure" for obesity in many cases involves a proper, restricted diet and adequate exercise. Although many people have a genetic tendency toward being heavy, excessive weight usually results simply from eating more calories than are burned up through activity. Yet obesity remains one of the most stubborn health problems. Diet books are regularly on the best-seller lists. Obesity is intimately tied to psychological issues (Friedman & Brownell, 1998; Wadden & Brownell, 1984).

One of the largest studies of the relations of obesity and mortality risk studied over one million Americans between 1982 and 1996 (Calle, Thun, Petrelli, Rodriguez, & Heath, 1999). This study confirmed that obesity is a significant risk factor, especially for death from cardiovascular disease. This risk held even for initially healthy people who did not smoke.

What can be done? The Stanford Five-City Multifactor Risk Reduction project confirmed classic psychological studies indicating that feelings of personal control and responsibility are very important in successful control of obesity (Mahoney & Mahoney, 1976; Rodin & Janis, 1979). There are often many opportunities for people to eat throughout the day or the night. People who are aware of when and how much they are eating and who have a sense of control over this behavior are more likely to be successful in controlling overeating. Of course, gaining such a sense of control is not easy.

Diet Control

In the short term, the specific weight-loss diet is unimportant. Crazy diets range from eating all you want of a nonfattening substance (such as grapefruit) that will soon make you nauseated, to ordering any foods you want as long as you don't eat much of any of them.

All these diets help people lose weight (as they focus attention on eating), but the weight is soon regained. Permanent weight loss requires a change in habits and in self-image.

Consider the self-image aspects. Part of the problem people have in gaining control over their overeating and other unhealthy behaviors involves explanations or attributions for behavior. People who blame their obesity on their genes or metabolism, their cooking partners, or their personalities are likely to experience difficulties in controlling their weight. Placing the blame on the environment or on heredity makes it next to impossible for someone to gain the sense of control that often is necessary to control overeating.

For highly motivated people who must change their diet for health reasons, certain specific techniques may be helpful (Friedman & Brownell, 1998; Kanfer, 1980; Karoly, 1980; Wadden & Brownell, 1984). First, it is useful if they keep a written record of both the type and quantity of all food eaten each day, as well as of their daily weight. This process is termed **self-monitoring.** These objective records promote awareness of the need for change and help prevent rationalization of poor eating habits.

Second, diet can be modified by controlling the external or environmental cues. This is termed **stimulus control.** To eliminate unnecessary snacks and overeating, for example, meals could be confined to the dining room at mealtimes; dieters can be instructed to take the proper portion of food on their plate all at once and then eat and chew the food slowly. Similarly, shopping can be controlled by using shopping lists or being accompanied by others, and unwanted foods can be kept out of the house.

Third, diet modification on the individual level can be encouraged through the use of **diet rewards.** For example, people could buy new clothes as they lose weight, or they could buy gifts with the money saved from spending less on food. Finally, as with other situations in which stress may arise, eating may be controlled through participation in **social support,** such as having a dieting "buddy" or joining Weight Watchers or Overeaters Anonymous. Commercial weight-loss programs that include an ongoing follow-up work for some people, especially if the program is a good match for the participant. Simply telling people which foods are healthy is rarely effective if other forces are working against the change.

In some cases, physiological disturbances are the root cause of overeating. There is some evidence that the body has a **set point,** which is the body's sense of its own ideal weight (Gosselin & Cabanac, 1996; Stallone & Stunkard, 1991). Getting older, becoming pregnant, eating a very high-fat diet, and perhaps various other influences might raise the set point, making the body feel that it is starving if it is below that point, and thus motivating eating. This might be adaptive if one is pregnant and needs to eat more, but it is often likely a problem.

Unfortunately, most obese people face a lifelong struggle to control their weight. It is difficult to control one's behavior by oneself. It is much easier if the social environment is conducive to healthful eating habits. It is also easier if people develop good exercise and eating habits when they are children. Most people are naturally attracted to fatty and sweet foods because of evolved preferences for high-caloric nutrition, but experience, culture, and availability also play a significant role in food preferences (Schiffman, Graham, Sattely-Miller, & Warwick, 1998).

Stress and Overeating

There is a joke about the healthy diet that helps one deal with the mounting stress of the day:

BREAKFAST

½ grapefruit

1 bran muffin, dry

8 oz skim milk

LUNCH

Slice whole wheat toast

4 oz lean broiled chicken breast

1 cup steamed spinach

1 cup green tea

MID-AFTERNOON SNACK

Package of M&Ms

2 pints of chocolate ice cream

DINNER

2 loaves garlic bread with cheese

Large meat lasagna

6-pack Bud beer with potato chips

Twinkies and apple pie with vanilla ice cream

It is well known that stress can lead to overeating. But nonobese, nondieters who are under stress actually may eat less. Rather, strong emotional or motivational states, including distress, can cause normally "restrained eaters" (dieters) to overeat (Polivy & Herman, 1999). The psychophysiological basis for this is still being studied.

Overeating or binge eating may distract you from the distress you are facing. Or, overeating may help the person hide the true source of distress or dysphoria. ("I am miserable because I can't stop eating and I look terrible. It has nothing to do with my break-up.")

It also may be the case that cognitive load can also disinhibit eating by restrained eaters (Ward & Mann, 2000). People who are trying to lose weight may be less able to monitor the dietary consequences of their eating when they have too much on their minds. This is yet another way that excessive stress is a threat to health.

Developmental Concerns

Special factors affect diet and weight control in children (Epstein & Wing, 1987). Obese children are likely to grow into obese adults and become prone to a variety of diseases. Obese children may be at risk for cardiovascular disease, for disturbed family relations, and for social problems with their peers. Children who develop good habits are likely to carry them into adulthood. Yet children themselves have relatively little understanding of and control over their eating and exercise habits.

When given complete freedom, young children often choose food solely on the basis of taste. However, it is also true that children can become aware of and act on the healthfulness of different foods (Michela & Contento, 1986). They will follow good examples set by adults. For many children, the environment can be structured by the parents to promote balanced nutrition. For example, children can eat only in one place (rather than munching all day long), be taught that healthy snack foods (like cheese or carrots) are a "treat," and be reinforced for choosing healthy, nonfattening foods. In the appropriate social environment, it is likely that many healthy foods will be perceived as extremely tasty. Finally, children who are gaining excessive weight can be placed into environments that encourage a lot of exercise.

It is also the case that children have a different conception of health than do adults (Altman & Revenson, 1985). Few are actively concerned about their health (unless they are ill). Younger children may view illness simply in terms of the presence of specific symptoms like a runny nose, whereas older children begin to think in more adultlike terms of a general feeling state and the possibility of a recurrence of symptoms. Before designing interventions to promote healthful eating in children, it is important to know how the children will understand and react to different kinds of information. When worries about weight become intertwined with issues of self-esteem and family power, dangerous eating disorders can develop.

Anorexia and Bulimia

Imagine a young woman who eats one Cheerio for breakfast each day. People who suffer from extreme malnutrition and loss of weight caused by insufficient food intake are diagnosed as having **anorexia nervosa.** Such people are generally young women with no known medical disease or other psychiatric disorder, although they often are depressed and have disturbed family relations. Anorexics have a distorted attitude toward food and weight. The Grammy Award–winning pop singer Karen Carpenter was one such victim. She died at age 32 from an irregular heartbeat brought on by a diet-induced chemical imbalance.

Many anorexic patients report a desire for an extremely thin appearance that they perceive to be attractive. They have a distorted body image. Although it is well documented, anorexia nervosa is still a controversial medical syndrome, probably because psychological factors are heavily implicated. In most cases, there is no simple "germ" or "disease" that can be isolated, and therefore the traditional medical model may have a difficult time addressing the problem. Yet it is unquestionably a serious illness. Estimates of mortality rates range from 2 percent to 25 percent (Mussell & Mitchell, 1998).

Although the phenomenon has received public attention in recent years, anorexics were first recognized more than a century ago (Lasegue, 1873; Schwartz, 1986). Sometimes people starved themselves for political reasons—so-called hunger strikes. For example, American women suffragists went on hunger strikes at the beginning of the 20th century (and some were force-fed). Although political protest is different from psychiatric disturbances, it is interesting to note two points about hunger strikes: First, the loss of weight is being used as a means of asserting control or power. Second, *thinness* is being associated with virtue; the suffragists didn't threaten to eat themselves to death. Similar issues are often relevant to anorexia in teenage girls: They may be trying to assert control over their parents and they are trying to achieve a virtuous self-image.

There are clear sex differences surrounding the meaning and uses of food. Women are much more likely to suffer eating disorders, and women diet more frequently than men (Mussell & Mitchell, 1998; Rodin, Silberstein, & Streigel-Moore, 1985). These differences are socially based. For example, in one study, male and female students were presented with diaries of the food allegedly eaten in two recent meals by other young people (Chaiken & Pliner, 1987). Actually, the description in the diary was controlled by the experimenter. Some of the diaries described small meals and some described large meals. The students were asked for their impressions of the eaters. The results showed that the female target who ate smaller meals was seen as more feminine, less masculine, and probably better-looking than the females who supposedly ate larger meals. If the eater was a male, ratings were not influenced by the size of the meal.

Regardless of the origins of anorexia, it is clear that family interactions are, or become, an important part of the illness. Most anorexic patients are teenagers who live with their parents, and, of course, a severe weight loss produces worry and strained relations within the family. Family reactions often lower the patient's self-esteem and sense of control, which may be very low to begin with. For patients who enjoy the attention given them by their new illness, family worries may serve as a reward for maintaining the poor eating behaviors. Family therapy, which addresses the patient's needs for independence and self-identity, is thus sometimes helpful (Minuchin, Rosman, & Baker, 1978; Rattie, Humphrey, & Lyons, 1996).

Bulimia nervosa is a related disorder involving binge eating followed by purging. For example, a college student worried about her weight may eat several bags of donuts and a couple of chocolate cakes in one sitting, and then swallow a box of laxatives to get rid of the food. Other bulimics induce vomiting. Although bulimics may have personal psychological problems, part of the difficulty arises from societal mixed messages about food and eating.

Ninety percent of bulimics are women. For many, the bulimia may develop as follows. First, the teenage girl receives societal messages about the importance of being thin to be attractive. Girls who are predisposed to be heavier thus develop a low self-esteem and go on a weight-loss diet. This diet disrupts their eating habits and their physiological mechanisms, perhaps even slowing down metabolism. If the girl is rewarded for losing weight, that behavior is further encouraged; if her family protests, her self-esteem falls. As her diet becomes more and more restrictive, certain food cravings arise. When these cravings become strong enough, she will go on an eating binge, but then follow it with purging. Self-esteem then falls even further (Striegel-Moore, Silberstein, & Rodin, 1986).

In short, severe weight loss and other accompanying symptoms (such as amenorrhea in women) have a significant impact on self-concept and family relations. A vicious circle often develops, in which physical problems, family concern and worry, low self-concept, excessive concern with food, and strained interactions with health providers all become related as causes and effects of each other. It is important to understand the complex nature of the various psychosocial factors in this health problem before appropriate treatments can be instituted. Currently, psychotherapy and group therapy, combined with drug treatments (usually anti-depressants), are often most effective in treating eating disorders.

Relapse

As with preventing smoking and drinking, the promotion of healthy eating, diet, and exercise needs to take into account the potential for relapse. Despite the best strategies, people can and do relapse. Therefore, maintenance of a healthy lifestyle across the life span needs to include strategies for recovery from relapse (Marlatt and VandenBos, 1997). With eating, this might involve increasing one's self-monitoring through daily food logs and weekly discussions with a counselor or other knowledgeable friend or colleague.

Dental Health

Most people do not like to think about dental disease or dentists, but dental caries and periodontal disease account for a hefty portion of medical care costs, not to mention pain. Most dental problems can be prevented or reduced through changes in behavior (Kegeles & Lund, 1984; Melamed & Fogel, 2000).

Almost all Americans brush their teeth, but most do not floss. About half of all community water supplies are now fluoridated, and so the incidence of dental caries has decreased markedly. But further improvements in dental health will likely depend on more and better flossing, keeping sugar off the teeth, and regular visits to the dentist.

Various school educational programs to promote dental health have been developed and tested over the years. Most have only limited success. Dental care is mostly a habit. If children learn the proper techniques, are rewarded for proper dental care, and incorporate it into their self-image, then the habit will be maintained. Otherwise, the proper behaviors will likely taper off over time.

Aside from bad habits, one old but still significant threat to dental health is fear of dentists. This fear is obviously a psychological factor, and so psychologists have long been involved in addressing this problem. The challenge is a significant one because it revolves around pain and avoidance. Patients who are fearful and anxious feel more pain when treated. They also delay seeking treatment (until their conditions worsen) and so encounter more extensive and painful procedures. Thus, their worst fears may come true. Furthermore, it is well known that avoidance of a fear increases the fear and may lead to a phobia. In short, vicious cycles arise in which patients feel more and more pain and develop greater and greater fears.

Successful treatment thus involves the use of the techniques to fight pain and anxiety described earlier in this book. Relaxation training, biofeedback, preparatory cognitive instructions, systematic desensitization, modeling, distraction, guided imagery, hypnosis, and related techniques can all be found in the dentist's office.

EXERCISE AND PHYSICAL ACTIVITY

In the summer of 1984, James Fixx had a heart attack and died while jogging through a small town in Vermont. Fixx was the author of the 1977 book *The Complete Book of Running*, a work that probably did more than any other to get Americans out jogging to improve their health. Before then, there were few joggers (and no industries of running shoes, running clothes, etc.). The irony of his death at age 52 while running brought questions about the real benefits of exercise into the public eye.

Many people, including many athletes, die while exercising. Sometimes this death is due to failure of a cardiovascular system that was temporarily weakened by some medical condition like a virus. At other times, vigorous exercise brings on an attack that was likely to occur in the near future anyway. In other cases, such as when a middle-aged businessman shovels snow, a person overtaxes a system that is generally not challenged.

It is important to recognize the various health hazards of exercise in order to achieve a balanced understanding of the topic and to avoid a mindless adoption of the propaganda of some exercise cults. Heavy exercise is a stressful challenge to the body (Blumenthal & McCubbin, 1987). On the other hand, there is good reason why "getting proper exercise" is usually included in lists of health tips for the public.

Exercise and Physiological Fitness

Aerobic exercise (exercise like jogging, swimming, and bicycling that elevates the heart rate to about 140 beats per minute) has beneficial physiological effects. In a well-conditioned person, the heart beats more slowly and efficiently, there is better oxygen usage, the cholesterol level may be reduced, and there may be faster adaptation to stress (Blumenthal, Shocken, Needels, & Hindle, 1982; Sebregts, Falger, & Baer, 2000). Exercise also strengthens muscles and burns calories; it helps us maintain proper weight.

Hints of the effects of behaviors like diet and exercise on serious diseases like heart disease first began emerging from the Framingham Study. Starting in 1948, about 5,000 residents of the small town of Framingham, Massachusetts (about a fifth of the population) began being studied and followed to see what factors might be relevant to heart disease and stroke. The study is still going on. Much to the surprise of the researchers and other physicians, it gradually emerged that high blood cholesterol levels and hypertension (high blood pressure) were significant risk factors. (In fact, until the 1970s, medical students were taught that it was normal and healthy for blood pressure to increase with age.) And hypertension seemed related to inactivity and lack of exercise.

In 1984, a longitudinal study of thousands of middle-aged men (who had first been studied as students at Harvard College) provided the first clear evidence for the health benefits of exercise (Paffenberger, Hyde, Wing, & Steinmetz, 1984). Men who engaged in regular exercise lived longer than those who did not. This effect held even if hypertension, body weight, and cigarette smoking were taken into account (i.e., controlled statistically). This study also found a large detrimental effect of cigarette smoking, and interestingly, suggested that heavy exercise (expending more than 3,500 kcal per week) might also negatively affect health. Moderate, regular exercise throughout one's life seems best.

It is also likely that the benefits of regular exercise continue through old age (Kaplan, Seeman, Cohen, Knudsen, & Guralnik, 1987; U.S. Department of Health and Human Services, 1996). For example, one study examined whether walking is associated with a reduced risk of coronary heart disease in a sample of elderly men, who were participants in the Honolulu Heart Program. Distance walked was measured over a 2- to 4-year follow-up period. Among these elderly men, the risk of coronary heart disease was reduced with increases in distance walked (Hakim et al., 1999).

Most Americans who make a New Year's resolution to exercise regularly discontinue their program within six months (Dishman, 1982). As with other issues of patients' cooperation, people are much more likely to stick to regular exercise programs if they can be readily incorporated into daily life. People are relatively unlikely to come home from work, eat dinner, and then miss their favorite TV shows to drive through a rainstorm to get to a gym. However, if there are exercise facilities at the workplace and a regular time to use them, long-term activity (especially by men) is much more likely to occur (Sallis, 1986). Thus, many progressive businesses began developing such facilities in order to promote the health of their employees. For example, Johnson & Johnson, the large health care products company, started a program that includes exercise group leaders and on-site exercise, shower, and locker facilities (Nathan, 1984). In addition, tips about how to manage their own behavior, such as by keeping an exercise record and forming new good habits to replace old bad habits, may also prove successful in helping people maintain regular exercise (Belisle, Roskies, & Levesque, 1987).

People who are in good shape live longer. Although this finding seems obvious, there are two significant puzzles that have only been partly addressed by research. First, what does it mean to be in good shape? For example, can one exercise too much? Second, why is fitness related to health and longevity? Is there a causal relation or a spurious (noncausal) association?

Too Much Exercise

Throughout this book, we have seen that health generally involves a homeostasis, in which the bodily systems can deal with challenges that arise, and in which the individual is in harmony with the environment. This conception of health, coupled with the many reported sudden deaths during vigorous exercise, suggests that there may be such a thing as too much exercise.

In fact, if we carefully examine some of the research studies, we see that at very high levels of exercise, there is an increase of morbidity and mortality risk—the risk curve tips up. For example, in the longitudinal Paffenberger studies, too much exercise raised mortality risk. As we saw in Chapter 2 on the psychophysiological basis of health, the term **physical activity** usually refers to use of large muscle groups that results in a significant expenditure of energy, whereas the term **exercise** refers to such activity that is planned and structured. Thus, farm labor is physical activity but calisthenics are exercise. We are unlikely to engage in too much physical activity if it is a part of our daily lives; but we might very well over-exercise. For most Americans, the terms are interchangeable in their implications, since most jobs these days do not involve constant physical activity. It is most important to remember that the exercise is not the goal in itself. The goal of exercise is usually to achieve **physical fitness,** a term that implies health and the ability to accomplish the physical tasks and face the stressors that arise.

　　Another important prospective study examined the relations between physical activity and all-cause mortality, and incidence of major coronary-heart-disease events in about 6,000 older men in 24 British towns (Wannamethee, Shaper, & Walker, 1998). Comparing sendentary men to progressively more active men, physical activity improved both cardiovascular mortality risk and non-cardiovascular mortality risk. However, the men who engaged in the most vigorous activity were at greater risk than those who engaged in moderate activity. Although this finding has appeared before, it is generally overlooked or minimized in research summaries.

Figure 11-1　　For both weight control and physical activity, it is helpful to develop regular schedules and to keep objective written records. Programs designed to improve physical fitness that specify frequency (how often), intensity (how hard), and time (how long) provide the best conditioning to stay *F.I.T. (Reprinted with permission. The F.I.T. Formula for Exercise, 1987, © Copyright American Heart Association.)*

Exercise and Mental Health

Regular exercise seems to reduce anxiety and increase self-esteem in some people, although the mechanisms underlying such an effect are not fully known (Dishman, 1998; Folkins & Sime, 1981). It even helps the mental state (as well as the physical state) of people with serious conditions like chronic obstructive pulmonary disease (Emery, Schein, Hauck, & MacIntyre, 1998). Sedentary people are more likely to be depressed, but exercise has so many correlates that it is difficult to draw clear inferences.

Although it has been hypothesized that exercise improves mood through direct physiological mechanisms, such as the release of endorphins or effects on the production of norepinephrine, this has not been proven (Dishman, 1998; Hughes, 1984). Opiate antagonists have not blocked the mood elevation often reported after exercise. More complex effects on neuroendocrine function have also been mixed.

However, exercise usually removes people from stressful work or family situations and may involve pleasant social contact. So, sedentary people may face more stress and weaker social ties. Or, exercise may improve mood by providing a simple, rhythmic, focused activity, similar to meditation. Distraction (from stressors) is another possible mechanism mediating between exercise and mental health (Morgan, 1997).

Finally, if exercise produces improvements in appearance, mood may improve due to compliments from others. Or, one's body may look better and be able to accomplish more things. Self-esteem is generally associated with better mental health. Yet about half the adult population in most developed nations spend most of their lives sitting—sitting in cars and busses, sitting in front of televisions, sitting at desks, and sitting at meals.

Promoting Exercise

As we have seen with other health promotion efforts, social expectations and the social environment, rather than individual influences, are most effective (Pate et al., 2000). Thirty years ago, almost no Americans jogged, and there were no jogging suits, no jogging shoes, and few marathons. It is unlikely that millions then simultaneously made the individual conclusion that they would like to be joggers. Rather, a complex sociological evolution occurred.

The reasons for the low levels of physical fitness and the low levels of regular physical activity in developed countries have been studied in various ways by the health psychologist James Sallis and his colleagues. One important study used a diverse national sample of young Americans in grades four through twelve (Sallis, Prochaska, Taylor, Hill, & Geraci, 1999). It was found that three factors had strong and consistent associations with levels of physical activity among the children. These were: using time in the afternoon for sports and other physical activity; reporting enjoyment of physical education; and having family support for physical activity. In other words, when the social environment favors physical activity and when the available activities are those that appeal to youth, high levels of physical activity are likely. Although these findings may not sound particularly surprising when stated in this way, they confirm the superiority of the broad health psychology model as compared to an informational or educational approach.

Box 11-1   Sunbathing and Skin Cancer

Opportunities for disease prevention are all around us, although they often go unnoticed. For example, one very common cancer-causing behavior has been ignored until the past decade by health psychologists and public health officials. This behavior is excessive exposure to the sun's rays.

It is well established that sun exposure plays a significant causal role in basal cell carcinoma, squamous cell carcinoma, and melanoma (the so-called black cancer). Although the first two types of skin cancer are easily cured when detected early, they may cause blemishes or deformities; further, since they affect hundreds of thousands of Americans, they engender a major health care cost. Melanoma is often fatal, and its incidence is rapidly increasing.

Many of these cases of cancer can be prevented through the use of protective clothing and sunscreens, or simply by staying out of the sun. Yet suntanning has progressed to the point that some people enter "tanning contests," and others place themselves into tanning booths that function sort of like a giant toaster.

One foundational study examined psychological and social behaviors in excessive suntanning (Keesling & Friedman, 1987). A number of California residents were interviewed in detail while on the beach. Some of them had dark tans, but other beachgoers had protected their skin and were very light-skinned. What differentiated the tanners from the nontanners?

Sunbathers had an image of themselves as active, healthy, and attractive, although they were *not* likely to engage in health-promoting behaviors that are unrelated to physical appearance (like wearing a seat belt). Second, sunbathers have friends who are sunbathers, who reinforce this behavior. Third, suntanners seem to be risk-takers. That is, they tend to have the kind of personality that is willing to be adventuresome without worrying about possible harm. In short, suntanners are not seeking health but are looking for an appearance and social identity that indicates a relaxed but adventurous approach to life. A health promotion model that takes a number of different variables like self-image, social influence, and personality into account can begin to provide a good level of understanding of a complex health-damaging behavior. Such an approach is necessary before effective health-promoting interventions can be designed.

Nevertheless, in recent years there have been a number of intervention trials to improve nutrition and physical fitness. For example, the Child and Adolescent Trial for Cardiovascular Health (CATCH) was a very large school-based field trial. The CATCH intervention programs were implemented in 56 schools (in four states) that were typical of schools throughout the country (Perry et al., 1997). The program produced positive changes in the school food service and physical education programs, leading to likely improvements in students' fitness.

Such programs demonstrate that intensive efforts in schools *can* improve fitness, and that they are more feasible than intervention at the individual level (with a focus on changing each individual). However, such improvements and emphases must become a societal norm, rather than a limited, expensive federal effort, before a great impact will result.

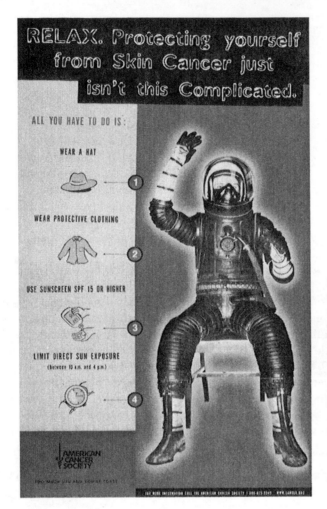

Figure 11-2 Sun exposure and resultant skin cancer have reached epidemic proportions in many areas of the world. Simple educational campaigns (to wear a hat and use sunscreen) have some impact, but a more sophisticated approach to skin cancer prevention relies on an understanding of the interrelated factors affecting sun exposure, including clothing fashions, peer activities, people's views about appearance (self-image), personality, and other sociobehavioral influences. *(Reprinted by permission of the American Cancer Society, Inc.)*

Imagine now a situation in which everyone in the family gets vigorous exercise every day, eats almost no meat, has no tobacco and little alcohol, has no risk of traffic fatality, low risk of suicide, and spends a lot of time together in family pursuits. Is this nirvana? Consider that this is the situation of most serfs during the Middle Ages, toiling on farms. Average life expectancy was less than 40!

This example reminds us of the complexity of health—that homeostasis has many aspects. Even today, a subsistence farm family, living and working hard (physically) in the rural South, generally would not have a high life expectancy compared to a wealthy family living on Manhattan's upper east side. It is a flawed argument to try to enumerate a few isolated behaviors—such as exercise—that by themselves will be the royal road to health.

INJURY

The extent of death and injury from physical trauma is phenomenal. Remember (from Chapter 1) that injury deaths come third in their toll (after cardiovascular disease and cancer), and they rise to first when years of life lost are considered. In the United States, about 40,000 people are killed each year in automobile accidents alone, and about half a million are injured. The paraplegic wards of hospitals are filled with paralyzed young people who went for a motorcycle ride. Three hundred thousand people suffer injuries that cause brain damage. For young people, injuries, especially those sustained in auto accidents, are by far the greatest threat to their health (Dershewitz, 1984; Goldbaum, Remington, Powell, Hogelin, & Gentry, 1986; National Center for Injury Prevention and Control, 2000).

Automobile Accidents

When the loss in person-years is computed, the amount is astounding, and it puts auto accidents as the leading threat to the health of the population. However, the traditional medical model can do little to address this problem. In recent years, many hospitals have been designated as "trauma centers" and can offer advanced treatments for accident victims. But usually very little can be done by the time the teenager's mangled body is pried loose from the crumpled remains of the car.

Two effective solutions exist to the problem of highway fatalities. The first involves keeping impaired drivers off the roads. (About half of all auto accidents involve drunk or drugged drivers.) The second is slower speeds when conditions warrant and the use of safety devices such as seat belts and child restraint seats. Both these solutions are psychological in nature: Human behavior must be influenced.

One way to reduce the number of drunken and drugged drivers is to reduce the general use of drugs, an issue we discussed earlier in this book. A second way of keeping impaired drivers off the road involves using increased law enforcement, such as highway patrols, sobriety checkpoints, controlled liquor sales, and strict driver's license regulation. These measures have all been tried in recent years and have had some positive effects. However, the most powerful influence would be a societal expectation that impaired driving is totally unacceptable behavior. Currently, many people who would never serve heroin to their party guests feel free to provide unlimited liquor and then turn their guests loose on the roads.

A child traveling unrestrained in a car has about a 14 times greater chance of being killed than does a child strapped into a safety seat. Adults, too, face much better odds of surviving a crash if wearing a seat belt. In addition, using seat belts costs nothing but could save over $10 billion a year in medical costs (Goldbaum, Remington, Powell, Hogelin, & Gentry, 1986).

Public educational campaigns were often tried to increase seat belt usage. Yet usage typically remained relatively low after such campaigns. What did seem to work? A more complex process. First, the state enacts a mandatory seat belt usage law. Second, the mass media public education campaigns are used to reach that small percentage of the population (perhaps 10 to 20 percent) that will respond directly to the educational message. Third, one-to-one educational campaigns are instituted in pediatricians' offices, community groups, and schools. This *combination* of influences helps people remember the message and at the same time creates a public expectation or norm for seat belt and child restraint usage. For example, a family leaving church after hearing the minister remind them to buckle up, who see a town police officer drive by, and who enter a car that contains reminder stickers that the children brought home from school and child restraint seats that their pediatrician sold to them are very likely to buckle up.

In states where this approach has been tried, seat belt usage has climbed from about 10 to 20 percent to well over 60 percent. However, since all these changes are occurring at once and are confounded with other changes in society, it is next to impossible to know for sure the precise mechanisms producing the improvement.

Other Accidents

Some serious accidental injuries come from unexpected sources. For example, scald burns caused by hot tap water result in thousands of hospitalizations each year. This problem cannot be cured through drugs or surgery, but it can in theory be perfectly controlled through behavior modification. The problem could be eliminated if people would simply measure their water temperature and turn down the thermostats on their hot water heaters (to about 120° F)! Unfortunately, as with all issues involving human behavior, this is easier said than done (Katcher, 1987). Although thousands of millions (that is, billions) of dollars are spent each year on research on heart disease and cancer, almost no money is spent on such issues as preventing tap water burns.

Job-related injuries also take a big toll. There are tens of thousands of traumatic occupational fatalities in the United States, most of them potentially preventable (Bailer, Stayner, Stout, Reed, & Gilbert, 1998; CDC, 1987). Many more workers are injured. Miners and construction workers are at high risk, but even workers in wholesale and retail commerce are at risk, especially more elderly workers. Many cases involve the failure of workers, supervisors, or planners to follow established safety standards. In other words, much of the problem is one of safe behavior.

Other important sources of injury and death in the United States involve fires, poisonings, drownings, and falls. Many of these threats have been partially addressed in recent years through the use of technologies such as smoke detectors, childproof container caps, and better architectural design. However, technology alone can never make a safe world. Most injuries are not really due to "accidents;" they could have been prevented.

Finally, people can be injured by pollutants and toxic substances in the water, air, and food supply. Health psychologists undoubtedly have some role to play both in the prevention of government policies and human errors that cause the environmental pollution and in the encouragement of individual reactions that minimize the pollutants' effects. Professional training in such areas as environmental toxicology is often available in schools of public health (Matthews & Siegel, 1987). However, health psychologists have thus far conducted little research in these areas.

Weapons and Aggression

No discussion of injury and safe environments is complete without some mention of aggression and weapons. In particular, two classes of weapons pose a significant threat to the health of Americans: guns and weapons of mass destruction.

As noted, aside from injuries, homicide and suicide are the greatest threat to the health of young Americans. Although people can and do kill other people and themselves without guns or fancy weapons, the ubiquitous presence of guns seems to lead to higher homicide and suicide rates, at least in cross-national comparisons. In addition, homicide rates appear to rise after a nation has been at war, possibly because the government has made the use of lethal weapons seem socially acceptable (Archer & Gartner, 1976).

Most violent crimes are committed by young men. The typical offender is not a suburban housewife on her way home from a shopping trip, but rather is a young, urban male, often on drugs or alcohol. Thus, it is usually illegal guns (or stolen guns) that are involved in crime, despite the large number of gun-owning Americans (Stolzenberg & D'Alessio, 2000). Political posturing about "gun control" often misses the key issues, which generally involve the widespread availability of cheap handguns to those people most likely to abuse them. The issue of gun possession and use is a complex one with wide-ranging implications, but it should not be ignored by those interested in health psychology.

One prospective study of handgun carrying among adolescents followed a sample of 2,200 high school students in 9th grade and again in 12th grade (Simon, Richardson, Dent, Chou, & Flay, 1998). Interestingly, several psychosocial measures, including risk-taking preference, depression, stress, temper, and drug use assessed in 9th grade were predictive of handgun carrying in 12th grade for both male and female students. Here again, both psychological and social instability raised the risk.

War

Another major weapons threat is from nuclear bombs and other weapons of mass destruction. In some ways, war and terrorism can be viewed as the greatest health threats of all. An all-out nuclear exchange or a mass attack with biological toxins could probably destroy life on earth. Recognizing this threat, groups of physicians, psychologists, and other health workers have organized, analyzing and acting to find ways to reduce international tensions and promote disarmament (Deutsch, 1983; Wagner, 1985; Fiske, 1987; Frank, 1987). With the collapse of the Soviet Union and the rise of so-called "rogue states," the dangers from terrorism have come to the fore.

Even when there is not direct physical injury from war or terrorism, the stress of attack can have damaging long-term health effects, especially on those who have faced other stressors in their lives, are socially isolated, or are children (Hobfoll et al., 1991). The claim has been made that the prevention of war should be a key aspect of public health (Levy & Sidel, 1997). Issues of war and peace are usually left to politicians, statesmen, and generals, while public health officials and health psychologists concern themselves with matters like cigarette smoking and exercise. Yet environment destruction, diversion of resources, injury, and posttraumatic stress are certainly issues that cross into the health psychologist's domain.

HUMAN SEXUALITY

Fifty years ago, most health practitioners were woefully ignorant about human sexuality. First, training about sexuality was absent from most medical education programs. Second, most medical students, busy with long hours of studying and pressured to uphold high moral standards, were likely to be less sexually experienced (in a personal sense) than many other people their age. Not only were they ignorant, but many health students and practitioners held erroneous beliefs—for example, that masturbation leads to insanity.

Figure 11-3 Sometimes embarrassment over issues of sexuality, or excretion, or other private matters interfere with educating people about disease prevention, or prevent people from seeking treatment, or discourage societal efforts at attacking serious health problems. (*Reprinted by permission of the American Cancer Society, Inc.*)

Most people have some kind of sexual problems at some time in their lives. Often, they are related to psychosocial issues, but they are also commonly caused by disease states. In our society, most of these people turn to physicians for assistance. Yet many physicians have traditionally not only been ignorant about sexuality, but have also been uneasy talking about the subject and unwilling to bring it up as a part of a routine medical history. Even with the advent of AIDS and its close ties to sexual practices, many physicians still do not take a full sexual history from their patients (Lewis, Freeman, & Corey, 1987). Extensive classic research by Harold Lief showed that health personnel often have a long way to go before they become proficient in promoting healthy human sexuality (Lief & Karlen, 1976).

Today, many American medical students, during their first year of medical school, are exposed to sexual materials or films including scenes of masturbation, intercourse, homosexuality, and oral-genital sex. This may be followed by a lecture or two. Nevertheless, because of ties to issues of morality, religion, family structure, and tradition, matters of human sexuality have been difficult to view in an unbiased scientific manner. However, research by Alfred Kinsey, William Masters and Virginia Johnson, and others laid the basis for significant progress in scientific understanding (Diamond & Karlen, 1980; Hunt, 1974; Kinsey, Pomeroy, & Martin, 1948; Kinsey, Pomeroy, Martin, & Gebhard, 1953; LoPiccolo & LoPiccolo, 1978; Masters & Johnson, 1966).

Overall, it has been found that there are various means of sexual arousal and none is superior to the others in a biological sense. Masturbation, oral-genital contact, stimulation through mechanical means, sexual intercourse, and other activities may all lead to the same sexual arousal and to orgasm. The different activities may have different meanings or implications for different people, but the biological response is the same.

Second, research has shown that sexual response is heavily influenced by learning and by technique. There is a tremendous range of sexual activity. People can learn to become aroused or to lose their desire by various activities and may choose various objects as sexual goals. It is impossible to say that these activities are more or less healthy in a biological sense; of course, some activities have implications for other issues, such as the rights of others.

STDs and AIDS

On the larger, societal level, the lack of information and openness about sexuality can lead, and has led, to various dangerous problems, ranging from teenage pregnancy, illegitimate births, and high abortion rates, to the many problems of sexually transmitted diseases (STDs), including AIDS. Although many people have religious and moral beliefs about restrictions on sexual behaviors, these beliefs sometimes get mixed up with issues of societal understanding and knowledge about sexuality in the service of human health.

Sexual knowledge is different from sexual activity. In fact, it can easily be argued that religious or moral restraint is most meaningful when the individual understands what decisions he or she is making, and why.

Ignorance and fear about human sexuality and sexually transmitted diseases has led to epidemics of gonorrhea (a bacterial infection of the genital tract and urethra), chlamydia (a bacterial parasite that can cause sterility in women if it infects the fallopian tubes), syphilis, and genital herpes (a common viral disease with painful lesions and no cure). Most cases of AIDS are also sexually transmitted, as the human immunodeficiency virus (HIV) spreads through open mucous membranes during sexual contact.

The tremendous human, social, and economic costs of the AIDS epidemic have led to a number of research efforts in health psychology to try to reduce the spread of HIV. One representative, well-done study evaluated programs to encourage abstinence or safer sex (condom use) among a population at high risk of contracting HIV (Jemmott, Jemmott, & Fong, 1998). The study focused on inner-city African American adolescents (who were about 12 years old on average). The abstinence intervention stressed delaying sexual intercourse until one was older, or reducing its frequency. The safer-sex intervention stressed the importance of condom use. There was also a control condition. Interestingly, the participants who received the abstinence intervention were somewhat less likely to report having intercourse at a 3-month follow-up (compared to the control group), but this effect did not hold at the 6-month or 12-month follow-ups. Similar findings emerged regarding condom usage with participants in the safer-sex intervention condition. It also turned out that it did not matter whether the intervention was done with adult facilitators as compared with peer (adolescent) cofacilitators.

This study and others in this field well illustrate certain key health promotion points of this chapter and the preceding chapter. Individual intervention efforts, if done in a focused and knowledgeable way, can have an effect on part of the population, but they will also miss (fail at) a significant portion of the population. Further, the effects will fade over time. This is not surprising if we think about the behavior of a 14-year-old with a hot new boyfriend or girlfriend, who has received sex education when 12 years old. On the other hand, in a society of stable families, with good knowledge and discussion of sexuality, and tight-knit communities with strong social norms for good mental and physical health, it is much easier to minimize the likelihood of epidemics of sexually transmitted diseases.

IMMUNIZATIONS AND VECTOR CONTROL

Johnnie has the whooping cough
Jennie has the measles
That's the way the money goes
Pop goes the weasel.

Many readers are not familiar with this verse of the well-known "Pop Goes the Weasel" nursery rhyme. Due to inoculation, cases of whooping cough (pertussis) are now about as common as weasels in most communities. Smallpox has been totally eliminated and very few cases of rubella and polio are reported, although there have been occasional resurgences (e.g., cases of pertussis) when immunization programs are not thorough.

It is also no longer true that "that's the way the money goes." Spending on infectious diseases has declined dramatically in relative terms, and mass inoculation saves $10 or $20 for every dollar spent (Chang, 1981).

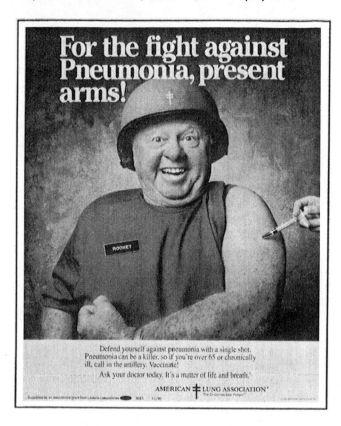

Figure 11-4 Due to inoculation, many previously-devastating infectious diseases have been nearly or totally eliminated. Such societal-level health promotion efforts may remain effective only as long as multiple segments of society (governments, schools, health clinics, etc.) cooperate and vast numbers of people are immunized. *(Reprinted by permission of the American Lung Association.)*

Why are these disease prevention programs so successful? There seem to be two reasons. First, there is almost total societal cooperation, with schools and pediatricians insisting on vaccination (paid for by public funds, if necessary). Second, only one quick event (the inoculation) is involved; occasional boosters may be helpful, but there is little need for extensive lifetime follow-up. In other words, these programs are a good example of a wonderfully effective societal measure that involves very little individual decision making.

Sanitation and Vector Control

Americans also do not suffer from typhoid fever, cholera, or the Black Plague. They have not been immunized against these deadly diseases. Rather, the sanitation system prevents them by controlling the possibility of polluted drinking water and flea-ridden rats in every home. A **vector** is an organism (such as a mosquito) that transmits a pathogen (such as the malaria microbe). If our streets and water supplies were filled with garbage and sewage, these diseases would quickly return.

People live longer and healthier lives because of (1) control of diseases like plague, typhus, and malaria, which are vector-borne (i.e., carried by rats, mice, ticks, lice, and mosquitoes); (2) control of diseases like cholera, dysentery, and typhoid, which are water- and food-borne; and (3) minimizing of respiratory diseases (like tuberculosis) that are spread through the air under crowded living conditions (McKeown, 1979). Here again, the individual's motivation or decision making has very little influence on his or her health. The threats can be almost completely controlled by direct government action. But the various governments—federal, state, and local—need to be coordinated and prepared to tackle such issues.

SUMMARY AND CONCLUSION

As Thomas McKeown (1979) points out, death rates in Western countries were declining long before the introduction of the "miraculous" drugs and surgeries of the mid-20th century. Longevity increases and health improves when a society can prevent disease and promote health. The internal environment of the human body can be strengthened to resist disease, and the external environment can be altered to minimize the risk of infection.

Researchers who look for simple explanations and simple interventions for successful health promotion efforts are often disappointed. The process of affecting the ongoing health behavior of human beings is complex (Henderson & Enelow, 1976). Nevertheless, a sensible outline of the influence process has emerged. People's health behaviors are heavily influenced by the social environment in which they live. If children grow up in an atmosphere where few people smoke and use drugs (and such behaviors are frowned upon), but most people exercise, eat right, and use seat belts, they will be very likely to follow the majority's expectations and good examples. The majority's expectations are in turn influenced by information and logical arguments, by laws, by economic costs, and by their own past experiences and habits.

For people who need to manage specific behaviors, such as their eating or exercise habits, certain behavioral management techniques have proven useful. Rewarding oneself regularly for following a diet or avoiding cigarettes, keeping a written log of food or exercise, talking to an abstaining or dieting "buddy," substituting new habits for harmful old habits, associating harmful behaviors with noxious or unpleasant reactions, making a public commitment to new behaviors, learning verbal skills to respond to temptation, and joining social support groups like the "Anonymous" groups are all helpful. However, the elimination of a long-time habit or addiction is always difficult; it is much better to prevent the problem in the first place.

Furthermore, as we have seen earlier in this book, self-esteem and self-concept play a key role in health. Problems with eating, drinking, drug usage, and so on all seem to be associated with low self-esteem and a deviant self-concept. And solutions, including exercise, positive social expectations, learning good habits, and social support, all seem to be related to a stable, positive self-image. We have not talked about "mental health" per se in this chapter, but it does appear that a population with good psychological adjustment will be more likely to have good health-promotion efforts.

Most people have some kind of sexual problem at some time in their lives. Yet many physicians traditionally have not only been somewhat ignorant about sexuality, but have also been uneasy talking about the subject. Today, even with additional training, matters of human sexuality have been difficult to view in an unbiased scientific manner because of ties to issues of morality, religion, family structure, and tradition. On the larger, societal level, the lack of information and openness about sexuality can lead to various dangerous risks to human health.

Some health promotion and disease prevention issues lie outside the direct control of any one individual. Vaccination, pollution control, avoidance of war, availability of healthful foods at a reasonable price, fluoridation of water, provision of exercise and recreation areas, and many other issues depend upon societal decisions and actions. For these matters, a strong government role in public health is essential, one that can prevent disease from developing and spreading rather than one that merely treats disease that has already spread. Thus, health psychologists must also address these larger societal issues in their work.

Suggested Additional Readings and Resources

Capaldi, Elizabeth D. (Ed.). (1996). *Why we eat what we eat: The psychology of eating.* Washington, D.C.: American Psychological Association.

Sallis, James F. & Owen, N. (1999). *Physical activity and behavioral medicine.* Thousand Oaks, CA: Sage.

Thompson, J. Kevin & Smolak, Linda (Eds.). (2001). *Body image, eating disorders, and obesity in youth: Assessment, prevention, and treatment.* Washington, D.C.: American Psychological Association.

American Heart Association dietary recommendations: http://www.americanheart. org/Health/Diet_and_Nutrition/AHA_Dietary_Recommendations/eatplan. html

National Cancer Institute dietary guidelines: http://rex.nci.nih.gov/NCI_Pub_ Interface/ActionGd_Web/guidelns.html

Key Concepts

deficient diet	anorexia nervosa
dietary imbalances	bulimia nervosa
free radicals	physical activity
body mass index	exercise
self-monitoring	physical fitness
stimulus control	prophylaxis
diet rewards	immunization
social support	vector
set point	

Chapter 12

PATIENT COOPERATION (ADHERENCE)

Patient "A" (Alice) is a 22-year old woman with leukemia. Her prognosis is pretty good if she cooperates with treatment. She was instructed to take maintenance medications, and she takes most of them and always keeps her clinic appointments. But she stopped taking corticosteroids because they make her look fat.

*   Patient "B" (Bob) is a 47-year-old truck driver with angina and high blood pressure. His doctor prescribed antihypertensive medication, a diuretic (water pill), and a salt-free diet. He was also told to "take it easy," to stop smoking, and to lose weight. Bob stopped taking the blood pressure medicine when, to his dismay, it*

seemed to cause him to be impotent. He sometimes forgets to take the diuretic. Because he is on the road so often in his job, the salt-free diet is almost impossible for him to follow. He eliminated desserts from his diet and was able to lose a few pounds. Driving his truck at all hours of the night, however, tempts him to smoke and to drink a great deal of coffee. He cannot take it easy because he is determined to save the money required to send his children to college.

Patients face many obstacles in their search for medical advice. They have to make advance appointments and obtain transportation to their clinic or physician. They must fill out forms, disclose personal information, wait long periods of time, and explain their conditions to the health care professionals. They must then submit to a physical examination and diagnostic tests. Some of these tests may be painful or carry some risk. Finally, the patient is usually required to pay directly or indirectly (through insurance) for the service. After all this, many patients fail to follow their doctors' instructions!

Patient noncompliance with medical regimens thus seems at first glance to be clearly irrational behavior. It is certainly a costly waste of medical expertise and the re-

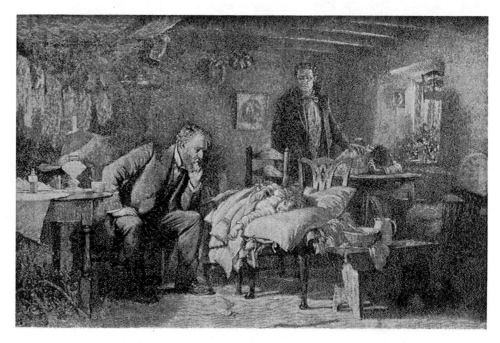

Figure 12-1   The so-called art of medicine should now be more properly considered the science of adherence and practitioner-patient relations. *(Courtesy of Historical pictures service, Chicago.)*

sources of health care. The noncompliance of patients with medical regimens is also dangerous to patients—they may remain uncured or develop serious complications from their conditions (Muehrer, 2000). In spite of these dangers, lack of cooperation is widespread. About one-third of all patients do not cooperate with the medical recommendations given to them for short-term treatments, and half or more do not cooperate with long-term treatments (Becker & Maiman, 1980; DiMatteo & DiNicola, 1982; Kaplan & Simon, 1990; Sackett & Snow, 1979). How can we explain this behavior? How can we prevent it?

A key problem with this issue is reflected in the terminology traditionally employed. The matter is usually referred to as **patient compliance** with medical treatment. Such terms tend to reflect and perpetuate the image of patients as unable to make their own health care decisions. This conception creates expectations that providers of health care are all-knowing and all-powerful, and can decide what is best for the patient. If recommendations are not followed, it is the fault of the patient. As we shall see, however, noncompliance often results from particular aspects of the practitioner-patient relationship and the way in which health care is delivered. Having the patient and health care practitioner work together as a team often is a key element of effective patient care. Therefore, a preferable term is **patient cooperation.** Throughout this chapter, the emphasis is on the "give and take" that is characteristic of all successful social relationships. We also sometimes use the more neutral term **patient adherence.**

This chapter examines the extent of the problem of noncooperation, the forms that it takes, the ways in which it is measured, and its causes. It also explores the more general issue of doctor-patient relations.

THE PROBLEM OF NONCOOPERATION

The failure of a patient to follow precisely the recommendations of the physician or other health care professional is termed **lack of cooperation with treatment** or **noncooperation with treatment.** (In the case of a young child, of course, noncooperation involves the failure of the parent or guardian of the child to carry out specific recommendations for the care of the child.) Noncooperation is often taken to mean the failure of the patient to carry out the recommendations as the health care professional *intended* they be carried out (Haynes, 1980). This is an important point because it brings up a key question: Did the patient understand the regimen when it was described? In many cases, it is unrealistic to assume that the patient understood what to do.

Noncooperation can occur in many ways and take many forms. For example, a patient may fail to keep an appointment for follow-up care. Or, when sent to a specialist-consultant, the patient may fail to follow through with the visit. In such cases, the patient has not followed the recommendation of the physician (or other health care professional) to invest time, energy, and money into another health care encounter.

Patients' lack of cooperation can occur in relation to primary prevention. **Primary prevention** involves measures designed to prevent illness from developing, such as measures to maintain proper weight and programs to prevent adolescents from beginning to smoke cigarettes. Noncooperation can also occur regarding so-called **secondary prevention,** namely, regarding measures taken once a problem begins to develop—such as with interventions designed to lower blood pressure to prevent stroke. Finally, patients may also not cooperate with therapeutic measures that are designed to alleviate symptoms or fight disease.

Patients can fail to cooperate with treatment by deviating from their physician's exact prescriptions for medication. They may vary the size of the dose of medication that is taken, the number of doses taken, and the number of days over which the therapy is continued. A patient with a urinary tract infection may be instructed to take an antibiotic four times a day for 10 days. The patient might take a pill only once or twice a day, for example, or take two pills at once after skipping a number of pills scheduled, or fail to evenly space the four pills taken over the day. The patient might discontinue taking antibiotic pills after four days, when the symptoms have subsided; this is a common but dangerous practice. The patient's health is endangered by failing to follow the instruction to take the medication for 10 days, since the infection can recur in a severe form if it is not totally eradicated.

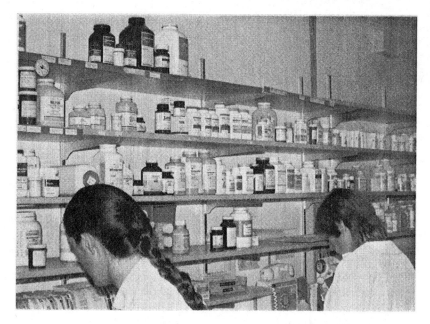

Figure 12-2   An important type of non-adherence involves patients who fail to cooperate with treatment by deviating from their physicians' prescriptions for medication. They may vary the dose of medication that is taken, the number of doses taken, or the number of days (the amount of time) the therapy is continued. The problem is not merely one of education but rather involves various psychosocial, situational, and cultural influences. *(Photo by Howard S. Friedman.)*

In short, any significant deviations from the recommended treatment are examples of noncooperation. This analysis points out that what is termed **noncompliance** or lack of cooperation on the part of the patient could easily involve lack of understanding or lack of ability rather than willful disregard of the regimen. If a patient is supposed to carry out recommendations for appropriate dosage, temporal spacing, and duration of medication ingestion, the patient often needs to understand fully what is to be done, why it is to be done, and how to do it (Haynes, Taylor, & Sackett, 1979).

Noncooperation with treatment frequently involves a patient's unwillingness to make major changes in lifestyle for the sake of health. Recommendations to change diet, to engage in exercise, or to avoid smoking require changes in the living patterns of patients, and most such preventive health behaviors are difficult because they require immediate behavior change in the face of only possible future dangers (Sackett, 1979). Furthermore, the recommended treatment may not be thought helpful by the patient, and sometimes in fact may not be helpful.

Measuring Noncooperation

How do we know that one-third or more of all patients fail to cooperate with their medical regimens? As in all of health psychology, it is important to understand the nature and sources of our information in order to gain a better understanding of what it means.

Estimates of the degree of noncooperation depend in part upon the specific measure that is used (Gordis, 1979; Muehrer, 2000; Stone, 1979). The estimate is positively related to the objectivity of the measure. That is, the more patients' or health care professionals' own subjective reports are relied upon, the higher the estimate of cooperation; the more objective the measure, the lower the rate of cooperation. Consider this finding in more detail: An example of a very subjective measure of patient cooperation is the opinion of the health care professional (the physician or nurse) regarding whether or not the patient has followed orders. The impressions of the health care professional concerning patient cooperation tend to be inaccurate; health care professionals are often not very good at recognizing noncooperation (Charney, 1972; Kasl, 1975; Shumaker, Schron, Ockene, & McBee, 1998).

Patients' own reports of their behavior—whether or not they have taken their medication for example—are also often inaccurate. Because they do not want to disappoint or even be scolded by the health professional, because they are reluctant to admit that they have not followed the advice of the expert whom they have sought out, or because the issue is not important enough to remember, patients overestimate the extent to which they have cooperated with treatment.

More objective measures of cooperation with treatment include the checking of medical records to determine the patient's faithfulness in returning for visits or in seeking consultation visits. Some researchers have tried to examine pharmacy records to determine whether patients have had their prescriptions filled, but we can never be certain that a patient who has filled the prescription will take the medication as prescribed. Most noncooperation with medication treatment consists not in the patient's failure to fill the prescription, but rather in the patient's taking too little medication or taking it at the wrong times (Sackett & Snow, 1979). This is now a special problem with HIV-infected patients, who must take an assortment of antiviral drugs (protease inhibitors) on a fixed schedule (Kelly et al., 1998).

Sometimes, researchers or practitioners have used **pill counts** to determine the extent of patient cooperation with medication regimens. If the patient brings the pill bottle to the health care setting, and the nurse counts the remaining medication, the practitioner may be able to determine whether the correct amount of medication was taken. Of course, it is still impossible to know for sure whether the medication was taken or whether the proper schedule was followed

Perhaps the most objective measure of patient cooperation with medication regimens is the direct measure of the medication in the patient's body by means of a tracer or the medication's metabolic by-product. For example, if a patient is taking penicillin, it is possible to test for urinary excretion of the antibiotic. Patient reliability in reporting is often measured against this objective criterion. Patients state that they have taken their medication much more often (close to 40 percent more often) than their objective tests corroborate (Gordis, Markowitz, & Lilienfeld, 1969; Stone, 1979).

Pill counts and direct-assay measures are not so important if the relationship between the health professional and patient is a partnership. If the patient feels comfortable admitting difficulties in cooperation to the health professional, and if those difficulties are accepted with understanding, the reports of patients may be the least expensive as well as most useful and accurate of all measures of cooperation (Shumaker et al., 1998).

CONSEQUENCES OF NONCOOPERATION

If patients do not follow the recommended courses of action, one result is clearly a waste of valuable health resources. Such a loss may be irrelevant to the condition of the patient, however. Of greater immediate consequence are the health problems that patients encounter when they are derelict in carrying out the terms of their medical treatment.

The Treatment Regimen

The consequences of noncooperation vary with the nature of the condition or regimen. Most obviously, recurrence of symptoms or inability to stop the progress of disease may result if medication is not taken regularly, or if it is terminated too soon. This problem is common and especially troubling in cases like hypertension (high blood pressure), where the patient usually doesn't feel ill but the consequences (such as stroke or heart disease) are serious. Relatedly, there are about 5,000 deaths in America from invasive cervical cancer each year, which are preventable with early detection and treatment. Yet many women do not follow recommendations to get a Pap smear, and even more surprisingly, many with an abnormal test result do not return for follow-up treatment.

Noncooperation can lead the health care professional to prescribe an overdose of a drug believed to be having no effect at a lower dosage. For example, suppose the patient has been given 2 milligrams (mg) of an antihistamine for allergy symptoms, and the patient reports no improvement. The physician might raise the dosage to 4 mg, using the patient's lack of response to 2 mg as a gauge of the patient's tolerance. Because the patient has not taken any of the 2-mg tablets of the drug, the patient's sensitivity is still high and 4 mg may be too much. In another case, a physician might prescribe two drugs that must be taken in conjunction with each other in order to be safe and effective. If the patient takes only one of these medications, a detrimental reaction might occur.

Diagnoses are often made on the basis of the responses of the patient's symptoms to a particular medication. If the patient has not actually taken the medication that was prescribed, whereas meanwhile the physician believes that the medication is not working, a misdiagnosis might occur.

Relatedly, when new drugs or treatments are tested, researchers should obtain estimates of the compliance of the patients in the study. Although a new drug may appear to work much better than an old drug in eradicating an illness, its efficacy might be brought about solely because patients take the new drug and do not take the old drug. On the other hand, when a new drug or treatment is being tested for its clinical efficacy (effectiveness), a small fall-off in the number of fully cooperating patients will seriously interfere with the likelihood of valid study results. Sometimes, studies of new drugs actually assess the level of the drug circulating in the blood, but this is very expensive and not always feasible.

There is a final consequence of noncooperation that is often overlooked. As we have seen, the manner in which care is delivered—the positive expectations that are communicated to the patient—may at least in part be responsible for the patient's getting well (Leedham, Meyerowitz, Muirhead, & Frist, 1995). So, if lack of cooperation disrupts the doctor-patient relationship, there could be various other serious consequences, including further lack of adherence.

REASONS FOR LACK OF COOPERATION

The issue of noncooperation is not part of the traditional medical model of disease, and so it is poorly understood by many practitioners.

Practitioner Misconceptions

Many physicians believe that noncooperation occurs mostly in the clinic setting, but that in their own private practices, their patients cooperate with treatment. This is not true. Noncooperation can occur in any setting in which recommendations are offered (Haynes, 1979; Sackett & Snow, 1979).

A second misconception is that noncooperation is limited to patients who are uneducated or of low social class. However, there are few sociodemographic variables that are consistently related to noncompliance.

Another misconception of some health care professionals regards the extent of the noncooperation problem. Physicians and other health care professionals tend to underestimate the rates of noncooperation in their practices (Charney, 1972). In addition, health providers are not very accurate in identifying which patients are not cooperating with treatment (Metry & Meyer, 1999). This lack of knowledge and understanding is one of the key obstacles to reducing the incidence of noncooperation.

Finally, there is a great deal of misunderstanding concerning the reasons for nonco-operation. The reasons are worth considering in detail. First we will examine personality and situational influences on rates of cooperation, and then look at the influence of the illness. Finally, we will consider the practitioner-patient relationship as it affects cooperation with treatment.

Psychological Attributes of the Patient

Some health care professionals believe that lack of patient cooperation with treatment can be attributed to the **"uncooperative personalities"** of their patients, but few personality characteristics are clearly related to compliance among patients (Haynes, Taylor, & Sackett, 1979). By personality characteristics, we mean traits that are measurable and stable. Labeling patients who do not comply as uncooperative personalities, without further explanation, is uninformative.

It has been suggested that patients who do not comply are more dependent or more irrational people, and while attracted to the authority of the physicians, seek their independence by rebelling against it (Christensen, Moran, & Wiebe, 1999; Gillum & Barsky, 1974). In this conception, noncooperation stems from the resistance of the patient prompted by unconscious fears and conflicts. This hypothesis is interesting in that it reveals the possible complexity of the processes motivating noncooperative behavior. Occasionally noncooperation may be due to some personality disorder (see Box 12–1 for a discussion of the extremes of patient personality), but such cases are the exception rather than the rule.

Finally, the anxiety level of patients can influence the extent to which they can remember and act on what their physicians have told them (Ley & Spelman, 1967). Intermediate levels of anxiety are best. When patients have very low anxiety, they may not remember what they have been told. If their level of anxiety is too high, patients are so afraid of what is happening to them that they cannot process information, and hence do not follow their recommended treatments.

Environmental, Social, and Cultural Factors

So-called **health literacy** is a significant problem. In one study of 2,659 poor patients, 42 percent were unable to understand directions for taking medication on an "empty stomach." A quarter of the patients were unable to understand information regarding their next appointment (Williams et al., 1995). Communication issues are further discussed in Chapter 13, "Communication Between Patients and Practitioners."

Each patient has limited time, money, and energy. Health care is only one concern. Very often, patients who have limited resources cannot comply with their prescribed medical regimens (Gillum & Barsky, 1974). In a study of mothers of pediatric patients who did not keep their clinic appointments, for example, it was found that the three most common explanations were lack of money, lack of transportation, and other pressing problems at home (such as other children to take care of). Other studies have shown that mothers with fewer opportunities for help in the home were less compliant with regimens designed for the care of their children. In general, if people have a great many factors in

Box 12-1   The Hateful Patient

Certain patients arouse strong negative emotions in physicians. The psychiatrist James Groves labels these patients "hateful." These patients create problems for their physicians, but can be dealt with by a well-trained practitioner. Groves claims that there are four basic types of problem patients, necessitating special attention to the nature of the doctor-patient relationship.

The first type of troublesome patient is called the dependent clinger. These patients need repeated attention, reassurance, explanation, and affection. Their dependency will eventually exhaust the doctor. Such patients must be dealt with by a firmly enforced schedule of follow-up appointments.

A second group of problem patients consists of entitled demanders. These patients also ask for excessive service, but they do not flatter or cooperate with the physician. Rather, they threaten and control the physician's behavior. For example, they may withhold payment, threaten malpractice suits, and appeal to the physician's guilt. Such patients may actually be terrified by their illness. Hence, the physician should reassure the patient of his or her rights, help the patient deal with his or her fear, and endeavor to rechannel the patient's energies into coping with the illness rather than the doctor.

Grove's third category of problem patients involves manipulative help rejecters. They are commonly known as "crocks." These patients believe that no treatment will help them. When some symptoms are cured, others often develop. These patients may undergo a series of operations. They fear losing their medical care. It is unlikely that the pessimism of these patients can be quickly eliminated.

The fourth type of problem patient is called the self-destructive denier. Self-destructive deniers are very dependent and frequently suicidal in some sense. For example, an alcoholic patient may keep drinking even when told it will soon kill him. Physicians may become very upset or even angry at such patients. They may be tempted to abandon such patients. However, all the physician alone can usually do is provide normal service and try to help the patient find the reason behind the self-destructive behavior. However, a broader, societal-based prevention and health promotion approach to health care can address such issues.

When patients can evoke hateful feelings in doctors, problems in diagnosis and treatment are not far behind. It does no good to blame or dislike patients. Instead, physicians should try to understand the patient's needs and maintain a friendly orientation and positive expectations. Most patients will cooperate with treatment if the doctor-patient relationship is good and the regimen is feasible. However, even when the practitioner-patient relationship is a good one, a small number of patients will continue to be a problem.

(From J. Groves, Taking care of the hateful patient, *New England Journal of Medicine,* 1978, 298, 883–887.)

their lives competing for few resources, they may find it difficult to channel resources into their own (or a child's) care (Alpert, 1964; Dahl, 1977; MacDonald, Hagberg, & Grossman, 1963).

Adopting a medical regimen usually involves changing habits and developing new patterns of behavior, which often requires the encouragement, reinforcement, and assistance of family and other intimates (Caplan, Robinson, French, Caldwell, & Shinn, 1976). In other words, behavior change requires social support. Thus, as one might guess, when patients are faced with disharmony in their families, family instability, or social isolation, they are less likely to cooperate with their medical regimens (Baekeland & Lundwall, 1975; Porter, 1969). Social support, considered elsewhere in this book, is again relevant here, as it relates to cooperation with treatment.

Social support.   Studies of the drug treatment of hypertensive patients indicate that if patients are perfectly adherent to their drug regimens and consistently restrict their salt intake by maintaining a low-sodium diet, they can produce an impressive drop in their blood pressure and considerably reduce the chances of stroke and heart attack. Adhering to hypertension regimens is difficult for patients, however. They usually have no symptoms and they feel fine. Why deny themselves salted foods and remember to take their medication every day? In fact, taking the medication can sometimes precipitate negative side effects. There may be muscle weakness or even impotence (though the physician will usually change the drug if impotence does occur). Certainly, the avoidance of salty foods is difficult when there is only a less-than-certain probability that one will develop some trouble in the future. The treatment of hypertension represents a situation in which the person is "at risk" and must deny present gratification to produce a possible future well-being.

Understandably, perfect cooperation with regimens for hypertension is rare. Only about half the people in the United States receiving treatment for hypertension are under effective control. But family support can make cooperation considerably easier. This was a finding of some pioneering research on patient education and social support done at the University of Michigan (Caplan et al., 1976).

These researchers defined social support for adherence as encouragement from family and friends. Encouragement from loved ones can help the patient to carry out the regimen, and can increase his or her feelings of self-competence and motivation. One factor that made a large difference in adherence was support to the hypertensive from his or her spouse. Support from the spouse was associated with low levels of depression, with higher motivation to adhere, and with greater knowledge of the regimen.

A special patient education program was then set up in which some patients received information in lectures while others were assigned to social support groups with their spouses. Patients in the social support experimental groups were involved in sharing their thoughts and feelings with other hypertensive patients and their spouses at the periodic meetings. They also shared problems that they encountered, such as learning to cook good-tasting, low-sodium foods. These patients were more likely to achieve and maintain a clinically controlled level of blood pressure than were those who were not in the social support experimental group.

Culture.   Cultural factors also affect cooperation with treatment. In Chapter 3, the influences of culture on reactions to illness, to medical care, and on health behaviors are described. However, cultural factors are also related to cooperation. Cultural and religious factors influence cooperation by placing restrictions on the person's actions (Kato & Mann, 1996; Nall & Speilberg, 1967; Snow, 1974). Few patients are willing to cooperate with behavior that goes against what is prescribed by their cultural group. If they do, they will face social rejection.

Relatedly, the symbolic meaning that patients attach to various behaviors are affected by ethnic, cultural, and religious values. For example, to individuals from cultures that value the importance of food (where food is equated with love and attention), restrictions on food intake are very difficult. These restrictions will necessarily be bound up with emotional meaning (Bloom, 1963; King, 1962; Penn, Kar, Kramer, Skinner, & Zambrana, 1995).

Furthermore, cultural factors are important in influencing the attitude of patients toward responsibility for their health. Some cultures are more fatalistic than others. The individual's belief in self-efficacy versus the random influence of fate is likely to be influenced by his or her cultural upbringing. This belief in turn will affect the person's willingness to assume responsibility for care. The influence of the family is also a function of culture and ethnicity. Few patients will cooperate with a regimen if that regimen goes against family requirements, responsibilities, and values.

The Influence of the Characteristics of the Treatment

A patient's ability and willingness to cooperate with medical treatment depends to some extent on the nature of the illness and on the nature of the treatment. When a patient has an acute illness with painful symptoms that are directly alleviated by a short-term dose of medication, the probability of compliance is high. Even when the symptoms are alleviated, but the medication must be continued for a few more days (such as in the case of a urinary tract infection for which the patient must take medication for 10 days, although the symptoms disappear after 4 days), cooperation is likely to occur if the patient understands what is expected of him or her and the reasons for continuing the medication for 10 days are explained (Haynes, 1980).

However, in the case of chronic illness requiring treatment of long duration, patient cooperation is comparatively poor (Sackett & Snow, 1979). For example, in a study of diabetic patients, large errors were found in insulin dosage among patients who had the disease for 1 to 5 years. Moreover, when patients had the disease for more than 20 years, the dosage errors occurred in about 80 percent of the cases. Taking a medication that may be troublesome, time-consuming, or associated with side effects (and without any immediate discernable positive consequences) is difficult for patients.

The more complicated the treatment regimen, the less likely it is that the patient will follow the regimen precisely as prescribed. Among patients with diabetes or congestive heart failure, errors in medication were found to increase as the complexity of the treatment increased. For example, the error rate (or noncooperation) was only 15 percent when one drug was prescribed and 25 percent when two drugs were prescribed, but it exceeded 35 percent when three drugs were prescribed (Hulka, Cassel, Kupper, & Burdette, 1976).

Relatedly, the greater the interference with patient's usual habits, the more difficult it is for a patient to cooperate with treatment. Taking oral medication one, two, or even three times a day is a relatively minor change in habit for a person. However, if the patient must totally restructure his or her usual routine (e.g., lose weight, stop smoking, and exercise), the likelihood of total adherence to the entire routine is low. Interestingly, some studies have shown that patients adopt only a portion of their therapeutic regimen if it is particularly difficult. They pick and choose the parts of the regimen that are least difficult for them (Gillum & Barsky, 1974).

Another aspect of treatment that may influence what the patient does involves the effects of the treatment. Sometimes, the treatment is inappropriate for a certain patient. For example, the patient may develop an unusual side effect. At other times, the treatment is generally accepted medical practice but is actually harmful for many patients. For example, x-ray treatments for skin problems created more problems than they cured. There are many, many other examples. Illness caused by physicians is called **iatrogenic illness;** it is discussed in Box 12–2. It is worth remembering that sometimes, noncooperation turns out to be in the patient's best interest.

In sum, treatment influences on patient cooperation are easy to understand when examined; but they are not obvious. In practice, they are often ignored by health practitioners. Interestingly, while they are important, these factors are not the most important influences on cooperation.

The Doctor-Patient Relationship

The factor that has consistently been found to be very strongly related to patient cooperation with medical regimens is the quality of the relationship between the health care professional and the patient (Stone, 1979). There are two different aspects of the practitioner-patient relationship. One is the degree and quality of the communication of information between the patient and the health care professional. The second aspect of the relationship is the rapport between them, which is also referred to as the socioemotional component of care.

There is a strong relationship between the quality of communication between the practitioner and patient and the patient's degree of adherence to the therapeutic regimen. The vocabulary, ways of thinking, and expectations of health care professionals are often very different from those of their patients (Ley & Spelman, 1967). Numerous studies have documented extensive communication problems between health professionals and their patients. In one study, over 60 percent of the patients misunderstood the oral instructions given by their physicians for taking medication (Boyd, Covington, Stanaszek, & Coussons, 1974). Another study found that more than 50 percent of the patients made at least one error when they were asked to describe their physician's recommendations for their treatment only a week after their visit to the clinic (Svarstad, 1976). Writing instructions down for patients sometimes helps, but these written instructions must be clear and unambiguous in order to be useful. (See also Chapter 13.)

Box 12-2   Iatrogenic Illness

Should a patient always cooperate with a doctor's advice? Is adherence necessarily in the best interest of the patient?

Countless examples of iatrogenic illness suggest that the answer may be NO. Iatrogenic illness is illness that is caused specifically by medical intervention. It can be the result of problems occurring in surgery (e.g., perforation of the bowel with resultant peritonitis during abdominal surgery). Or it can be the direct result of the side effects of drugs or the dangerous interaction of two drugs administered by the physician. Iatrogenic illness also commonly involves infections contracted during hospitalization.

This problem is complex. Can the occurrence in a patient of an improbable but still possible side effect of a drug be considered an iatrogenic illness? Probably, since the side effect would not have occurred without administration of the drug. But this does not mean that the physician was incompetent or negligent, or that the patient should have refused to take the drug in the first place. But what if the physician has not told the patient that the side effect might occur? Is the illness as well as the resulting anxiety of the patient then the fault of the physician? On the other hand, what about the patient's anxiety that results from knowledge of what might happen if a certain drug is administered?

The issue is complicated still further by the fact that the medical management of a patient might never be questioned because the patient remains unaware of the role of the physician's treatment in the exacerbation of this medical problem. It is easy to hide iatrogenic illness, disguising it as the normal course of the patient's problem.

It has been reliably estimated that at least 44,000 Americans die each year as a result of medical errors. The number may even be as high as 100,000 annual deaths (Kohn, Corrigan, & Donaldson, 2000).

Thus, some have argued that patient noncompliance may sometimes, in fact, be adaptive. Sometimes, patients do not cooperate because the treatment can be worse than the disease.

For further reading:

Ivan Illich, (1976). *Medical nemesis: The expropriation of health.* New York: Random House.
Institute of Medicine (L.T. Kohn, J.M. Corrigan, & M.S. Donaldson, Eds.). (2000). *To err is human: Building a safer health system.* Washington, DC: National Academy Press.

The importance of clear and open communication between the health care professional and the patient has been discovered again and again in research. In one classic series of studies conducted in Children's Hospital in Los Angeles by Barbara Korsch and her colleagues (Francis, Korsch, & Morris, 1969; Korsch, Gozzi, & Francis, 1968), researchers tape recorded conversations between pediatricians and the mothers of their patients. Analysis of these tape recordings revealed that physicians whose patients were noncomplying were often vague in communicating with the mothers. They tended to use medical jargon often (e.g., "We have to watch the Coombs titre") and did not take time to answer questions thoroughly or to determine whether each mother understood what was wrong with her child and exactly how to carry out the prescribed treatment.

An explanation that only involves giving information from the health professional to the patient is not sufficient to be effective. There often needs to be a give and take of information between the health care professional and patient so that the health professional can obtain continual feedback from the patient about what he or she understands and what needs to be made clearer (Stiles, Putnam, Wolf, & James, 1979). In fact, social psychologists have consistently found in research on human interaction that **reciprocity** (give and take) is necessary in order to maintain a relationship and to continue it in a mutually satisfying manner (Blau, 1968). Reciprocity in self-disclosure requires disclosure by the health care professional as well as the patient. Self-disclosure is important to the development of a respectful and caring health professional-patient relationship. Such communication is discussed in detail in the next chapter.

The second critical interactional element in cooperation is doctor-patient rapport. The studies at Children's Hospital in Los Angeles found that acceptance, appreciation, and respect were requisite for mothers of pediatric patients to follow recommended courses of care for their children (Korsch, Gozzi, & Francis, 1968; Korsch & Negrete, 1972). However, it is also likely that patient satisfaction with care is more likely to result in cooperation with directly relevant aspects, such as keeping follow-up appointments, than it is to result in cooperation with less relevant activities such as taking medication (Richardson et al., 1987).

Why does good rapport help? A conceptual analysis of cooperation concludes that good rapport is a necessary factor in the development of so-called **referent power** (Rodin & Janis, 1979). Because of the nature of the physician-patient relationship, only a few sources of social power are available to the physician or other health professional (French & Raven, 1959). The physician or health care professional actually has no way to guarantee control of the behavior of the patient. Reward power (the ability to withdraw rewards for noncompliance) is limited because the physician controls few of the patient's needs, except perhaps for caring and esteem. **Expert power** is part of the professional-patient relationship, because the health care professional is seen as an expert in matters of health and illness. Patients follow advice partly because they know the health care professional has more knowledge and expertise than they do. But for the most part, the greatest influence that the health care professional can have on the patient's health behavior is by using referent power, the process of forming a social unit with the patient. Through mutual caring and respect, patients come to trust the health care professional and to model themselves after the health care professional as someone who values healthy, responsible behavior.

Unfortunately, when faced with noncooperation, many physicians usually take the following steps: First, they explain the regimen to the patient, and then they try rational arguments to persuade patients. After that, physicians and other health care team members may resort to threat tactics. Finally, they withdraw from the case. The resulting arousal of fear in the patient might bring about the patient's denial of the problem altogether, or else bring about behavior that is the opposite of that desired.

In short, the doctor-patient relationship is critically important to patient cooperation with treatment. However, this relationship also has other related, important implications that are worthy of special attention.

THE CARE OF THE PATIENT

In 1926, Dr. Francis Peabody gave an address at Harvard Medical School on the care of the patient (Peabody, 1927). Peabody emphasized the importance of personalized, intimate care; he warned of the dehumanizing and isolating experiences of hospitalization and specialty care; and he recognized that physicians can often do no more than provide psychological support to their patients. Today, this essay is often read by first-year medical students and cited by eminent physicians. Ironically and unfortunately, it is disregarded in much of the modern structure and practice of medicine.

From the earliest times in the history of medicine, physicians such as Hippocrates (the fourth-century B.C. Greek physician, called the "Father of Medicine") recognized how important it is for health care professionals to deliver care to their patients with understanding and sensitivity (Hippocrates, 1923). Hippocrates wrote about the interpersonal transaction between health professional and patient, stating that while the health care professional should not allow the patient's sentiments to lead him or her to deliver care that is inappropriate, the health care professional should practice a science of effective human relations. The health professional should learn to modify the negative sentiments and fears of patients with hope and positive behavior. Hippocrates also spoke of the importance of the health care professional's manner in dealing with patients. He suggested that "the patient, though conscious that his condition is perilous, may recover his health simply through his contentment with the goodness of the physician."

In the early 20th century, the prominent medical educator Frederick Shattuck wrote that a serious problem in health care would occur if the gap between the science of medicine and its actual practice were to grow (Shattuck, 1907). Shattuck suggested that the gap could be bridged by the art of medicine. Shattuck wrote of the importance of sensitivity and genuine concern for patients' feelings when taking a history; much can be learned about patients from the way in which they tell their stories. Another prominent educator, Sir William Osler, in 1899 recommended that a health care professional listen to the patient, for the patient may actually reveal the diagnosis (Osler, 1904). Peabody, Shattuck, and Osler all noted the importance of remembering that disease is one phenomenon, whereas the diseased person is another. The early physicians were, in sum, suggesting a certain sensitivity on the part of the health care professionals in dealing with patients.

Physicians often see the art of medicine as "common sense." However, these behaviors are far from simple. There are many pressures from within the structure of the health care delivery system to treat patients as objects and to attend to the disease and not the patient.

The art of medicine does not belong in a nebulous, ill-defined realm. In order to practice successfully the art of medicine, the health care professional needs to understand verbal and nonverbal communication and the sociocultural context of behavior. The health care professional also needs specific information regarding the problems in social relationships that are faced by patients with problems like cancer. All of this information is necessary for effectively dealing with patients by developing a "science of the art of medicine." That is why so much of this book deals with the psychological, interpersonal, cultural, and societal influences on health and health care, based on scientific studies.

Complete, effective care of a patient is not an accident (Bloom, 1963). It has to be planned by knowledgeable practitioners with support from larger societal factors. One means of teaching doctors more about effective care is described in Box 12–3. The education of the health care professional is described in more detail later in this book.

In short, the overall care of the patient should be an essential element of health care. However, in addition to its dramatic impact on patient cooperation with treatment, the so-called art of medicine has effects on two main areas: patient satisfaction with care and the outcome of treatment (Roter, 2000).

A key outcome of health care involves the patient's satisfaction with the medical care received. When rapport is missing, patients tend to switch health plans, or turn from the medical profession to nonmedical healers, or bring malpractice suits against physicians and hospitals. The health psychology approach to health care allows us to consider the success of the health care industry as judged by its consumers, especially the quality of the doctor-patient relationship (Caplan & Sussman, 1966; Roter & Hall, 1992; Skipper & Leonard, 1965).

Doctor-Shopping

Each time a patient changes doctors, it is an expensive and time-consuming event. The new primary care physician must repeat a medical history, conduct a physical examination and systems review, and also perform the necessary diagnostic tests. Many times, patients end the physician-patient relationship simply because they are displeased with the interpersonal behavior of the physician (Ben-Sira, 1976, 1980; Bloom, 1963; DiMatteo & DiNicola, 1982; Kasteler, Kane, Olsen, & Thetford, 1976).

Few patients terminate the relationship with their physician because they believe the physician is incompetent technically. Rather, it is because of the way in which health

---

Box 12–3   Patients Teach Doctors

An interesting innovation that may improve doctor-patient relationships involves the use of patients as instructors. Physicians-in-training usually do not receive any direct feedback from their patients as to how well they are conducting themselves. Patients are often expected to remain silent unless asked a direct question. However, certain patients with chronic illnesses are in an excellent position to evaluate how well a young doctor is doing both technically and interpersonally, and they may be able to help him or her improve.

The patient-instructor may be someone suffering from multiple sclerosis, emphysema, a heart murmur, or other chronic condition. After medical students have received some basic medical training, such patients are made available to them. The patients are encouraged to respond to and instruct the students. Such patients are also willing and able to tell medical students such things as that their hands are too cold, they forgot to wash their hands, or that certain mannerisms are anxiety provoking. In this way, medical students can quickly learn through experience to correct various difficulties.

professionals have behaved toward the patients. In fact, most patients probably cannot effectively judge the technical competence of their physicians or other health care practitioners. Patients instead tend to base their trust in the physician on the socioemotional aspects of care—the components of the art of medicine that we discussed earlier.

For example, in one classic study, patients changed primary care physicians almost exclusively because of what they called inadequate interpersonal treatment and attention. When questioned further, they revealed that their dissatisfaction was with the socioemotional dimension of care; patients were most likely to terminate the physician-patient relationship if their physician was too busy to talk with them or appeared to be uninterested in their welfare (Gray & Cartwright, 1953). In another study, it was found that doctor-shopping was significantly increased if patients disliked the doctor as a person, were dissatisfied with the amount of time spent in health delivery, or if they felt the physician was not interested in them as people (Kasteler, Kane, Olsen, & Thetford, 1976). The patients' perceptions about their physicians' degree of intellectual capability and seriousness, as well as their specific technical performance, were less important.

Rejecting the Medical Establishment

Another distressing result of patients' dissatisfaction with their medical care leads patients to inflict serious harm on themselves. If their health care professionals do not provide the important socioemotional aspects of care, seriously ill patients can easily feel abandoned by their physicians. Then, they are likely to reject the medical establishment and seek nonmedical cures.

In a pioneering study, Beatrix Cobb examined the reasons why some cancer patients reject the medical establishment and seek nonmedical cures (usually religious healers or worthlesss drugs) (Cobb, 1954). From Cobb's many interviews, she learned that these patients felt they received little understanding and reassurance from their physicians and other health personnel and were not sure that all that could possibly be done would be done for them. The patients felt that because their illness was very serious and had a low cure rate, their health professionals treated them as terminal cases. Therefore the patients turned to nonmedical healers. This process still occurs today.

Unfortunately, dissatisfied patients who have turned to quacks in foreign countries or to faith healers in this country are usually not even considered in analyses of patient noncooperation. These patients have left the formal health care system and so in some ways have vanished from view. Of course, the social and economic consequences of these actions are still with us.

Malpractice Litigation

Malpractice insurance rates have skyrocketed, and the entire health care system is alarmed at the extensive patient retaliation against physicians, hospitals, and even nurses and other health professionals. Nearly all patients tend to recognize and acknowledge that there is a risk attached to any medical procedure and that medicine is not foolproof. After a failed treatment, this sort of objective analysis does not always occur, however. Often, patients' emotionality and anger result from a breakdown in the health care professional-patient relationship.

In the ideal situation, the health care professional explains the medical procedures to the patient. All of the attendant risks are described, the expected results considered, and a trust is built up between the physician and the patient. A joint decision is then made, and if the treatment does not go as expected, the patient is informed and takes part in the additional decision-making.

In this ideal case, the patient can rely on the health care professional for continued support and for respect, care, and concern for him or her as a person. The patient is an active, rather than a passive, participant. Under these conditions, patients deal relatively well with problems that arise in their health care—even with physicians' errors.

Regularly, though rarely, cases occur in which a sponge is left in the patient during surgery; or a serious, correctable condition is missed in reading an x-ray. Surprisingly, the health care professional is not always sued. If communication with the patient had been open and honest, a solution to the problem can often be found without calling in a third party (i.e., a lawyer). Such is not the case, however, when the health care professional-patient relationship has gone awry. Psychologists and lawyers have written about the overwhelming influence of the health care professionals' behavior toward patients as an influence on the patients' decision to sue if the results are not completely satisfactory (Blum, 1960; Gordon & Edwards, 1995; Lander, 1978; Vaccarino, 1977; Wyatt, 1991).

It is important to note that this does not mean that "malpractice"—the actual practice of medicine with negligence, in which the health professional makes serious errors—does not exist. There are many cases, however, in which health professionals have practiced standard acceptable medical techniques. Yet, because of some unfortunate circumstance, the results were less satisfactory than expected. The patient then brings a lawsuit against the physician. Under which conditions do patients decide to attempt to file a malpractice suit, regardless of the actual degree of malpractice? Often, the nature of the health care professional-patient relationship determines the patient's behavior. A lawsuit is especially likely when the physician ignores the patient's complaints and sends the usual bill.

Ironically, the threat of lawsuits makes physicians more likely to order extensive diagnostic testing (in order to protect themselves). This testing in turn makes the practice of medicine more technical and more mechanical, thereby likely increasing rather than decreasing the incidence of lawsuits.

Outcome of Treatment

Many years ago, researchers from Massachusetts General Hospital in Boston demonstrated the importance of good anesthetist-patient communication in the outcome of treatment (Egbert, Battit, Turndorf, & Beecher, 1963; Egbert, Battit, Welch, & Bartlett, 1964). In this study, almost 100 surgical patients were randomly divided into two groups, an experimental group and a control group. The experimental group patients were told about the postoperative pain they would experience and how to relax in order to reduce the pain. The anesthetist gave these patients both information and a pep talk about how to deal with the impending surgery. The other patients, from the control group, were not told about their postoperative pain, and they received the usual preoperative preparation.

While the experimental and control groups did not differ on the first postoperative day, after that time the group of patients given the special anesthetist visit and information required significantly less pain medication than the patients from the control group. Furthermore, their surgeons decided that some of these patients were well enough to be discharged from the hospital earlier than the control group patients. The surgeons were "blind" to the condition in the experiment in which the patient had participated; that is, they were unaware of which kind of preoperative preparation the patient had received. The patients in the experimental group were discharged an average of 2.7 days earlier than the other group of patients.

The results of this study demonstrate that a proper relationship between the health care professional and patient can influence the outcome of a purely technical procedure such as surgery. Similar research by the same authors has shown that visits by an informative, caring anesthetist relaxed patients and made them as calm and drowsy before surgery as did phenobarbital. Patients who are drowsy and calm before surgery require less anesthesia during the surgery—a distinct positive therapeutic effort contributing to the patient's more immediate postoperative recovery as well as his or her chances of surviving surgery.

As noted earlier in this book, the interpersonal behavior of health care professionals toward their patients can also influence the patients' observable physiological condition. In one study, it was found that a significantly large number of cardiac patients who had been stable and recovering from their heart attacks in the hospital suddenly died of a second heart attack during or very shortly after ward rounds. Ward rounds are generally very stressful for patients, often because physicians behave in a formal, aloof manner and frequently discuss the patient's illness (with others) in front of him or her (Jarvinen, 1955). Other researchers partially explained the sudden deaths by showing that human contact can have a major effect on the cardiac rhythm and the electrical impulses of the hearts of cardiac patients (Lynch, Thomas, Mills, Malinow, & Katcher, 1974). (See also Chapter 5.) Interestingly, a visit to the physician can provoke an increase in blood pressure. This is termed **white coat hypertension** because the higher pressure results from the patient's anxiety about the high-status physician in a white coat (Dubbert, 1995).

In sum, proper interpersonal care of the patient can affect the outcome of treatment as well as patient satisfaction and its attendant effects on doctor-shopping, rejecting the medical establishment, and malpractice litigation. These effects are beyond those on patient cooperation already noted. It is curious that doctor-patient relations have not assumed a central place in the structure of modern medicine.

DOCTOR-PATIENT RELATIONS

In all cultures, certain individuals are designated caretakers of the sick. In traditional Mexican culture, for example, the curandero treats patients with religious symbols and herbal remedies. In American Indian cultures, medicine men have traditionally treated illness with a variety of techniques, including dancing, herbs, shaking rattles, and beating drums. American evangelical religious leaders may include singing, prayer, and other religious rites in their approach to healing. These diverse individuals play the role of healer (King, 1962).

In mainstream American society, on the other hand, the healing roles are filled by physicians, nurses, psychologists, pharmacists, and social workers. These healers possess many attributes that are not logically required by their work. For example, American physicians have a great deal of prestige and power. Americans do not value their leaders, their workers, or their craftsmen as much as they value their physicians. In exchange for this prestige, most Americans expect their health providers to be wise and professional, caring and sensitive, and generally deserving of respect (Bloom, 1963; King, 1962; Parsons, 1951).

Public perceptions about practitioner quality and dedication have become more negative in recent years. People think doctors are too concerned with making money and don't care as much as they used to. Practitioners, on the other hand, feel patients have unrealistic expectations, are too likely to sue for malpractice, and are too accepting of having insurance companies manage medical practice. We will thus conclude this chapter with a more general and formal analysis of doctor-patient relations.

The Roles of Doctors and Patients

Respect and power are accorded physicians for three major reasons. First, the job of a health professional requires a high degree of technical competence. Physicians, nurses, dentists, and so on are extensively trained: Their formal education may continue for up to ten years beyond college. They differ from other skilled individuals, however, in that they have access to a particular body of knowledge that is difficult or impossible for a person who is not a health professional to acquire. A person with a severe sore throat and earache finds it nearly impossible to make an accurate diagnosis and obtain treatment without help from a health expert.

Even if the knowledge and resources of health professionals were generally available, health professionals probably would still be held in awe. Automobile mechanics, for example, have a distinct body of knowledge that is not generally available to most untrained individuals. So do the computer programmers in a bank who diagnose and repair problems in monthly bank statements. But the car mechanic and the computer programmer are dealing with problems that have limited impact on the individual who must deal with them. People can forget for a while that their car does not work or that their bank statement does not match the checkbook total. But it is difficult to forget a very painful sore throat when continually trying to swallow. Problems with body functions are problems central to the person; they are not easily ignored and are usually accompanied by strong emotion (Moos, 1977). The health care professionals who can solve these problems find themselves endowed with great respect and awe; they often deal with issues of life and death.

Second, the power and respect accorded health professionals is hinted at by the following questions: Should physicians devote a great deal of their time to financial invest-

---

Box 12–4   Ways to Minimize the Risk of Suits

In recent years, various task forces, including one by the American Academy of Family Physicians, have issued recommendations about the best ways for practitioners to minimize the likelihood of medical malpractice suits. Interestingly, they note that many malpractice suits come from patients improperly informed about the procedures to be carried out or the risks involved. In other cases, suits are brought because once the patient develops a complication, the physician appears to be less than honest and acts in a secretive manner, suggesting to the patient that the doctor really is at fault.

Therefore, capable practitioners should:

- Refer or consult with other medical experts as soon as needed.
- Participate in continuing medical education to keep skills updated.
- Give patients an adequate explanation of risks and possible complications and frankly discuss the fees involved before initiating treatment.
- Involve the patient in treatment and diagnostic decisions and document this involvement.
- Give all patients having major surgery or serious diseases the opportunity of a second opinion and document it in the record. (With any medical high-risk or unusual procedure, insist on a second opinion.)
- Investigate all incidents to make sure that the patient is helped in a concerned and sympathetic manner.
- If complications develop, be completely honest.
- If a patient is upset, meet with the patient as soon as possible and discuss the apparent concerns. Try to settle differences reasonably.

---

ments? Should physicians be involved in elaborate real estate sales deals or in owning convalescent homes? Should nurses demand higher wages and go on strike, leaving hospitalized patients unattended? Many professionals invest their money, and many union members strike. Should health professionals be any different?

These questions illustrate the point that the health professional is expected to show a high degree of commitment to serving people. It is expected that nurses, paramedics, and physicians chose the health profession primarily because of their desire to serve others. Money, status, power, and even intellectual challenge are expected to be secondary considerations. Whether this assumption is realistic or not, the primary goal of health professionals is expected to be caring for people, and not financial gain. Health professionals are respected partly because they are presumably less concerned with their own financial gain than are other workers in society. For this reason, "transgressions" by health care professionals receive very negative responses from society.

Third, respect given to health professionals derives in part because they are viewed as nonjudgmental and emotionally neutral. Health professionals learn a great deal of intimate information about patients. For example, a physician might ask a patient if he or she has had regular bowel movements or ask about the most intimate details of sexual functioning. Patients in fact often disclose their thoughts and feelings more readily to physicians and nurses than to their closest friends or spouses. Therefore, the physician or nurse is put into a position that requires objectivity. It would not be appropriate for a nurse or doctor to be judgmental toward a patient—for example, by giving a lecture on religious morality. The health professional's role involves simply learning as much as he or she can about the patient, avoiding negative judgments about the patient as a person, and helping the patient to engage in healthful behaviors.

Sociologists and psychologists who theorized about the relationship between health care professionals and patients originally proposed that emotional neutrality and objectivity also meant cold detachment (Parsons, 1951). It was assumed that because health professionals deal all day long with such traumatic events as patients dying, they must remain emotionally detached from their patients. The assumption was that they needed to treat the disease and ignore the person with the illness. But research on physician-patient relationships, shows that detachment is really not possible for physicians and other health care professionals (Fox, 1959). They become acutely aware of the patient as a person and are strongly affected by the human side of medicine.

Thus, patients' expectations about their doctors' behavior are very specific, and these expectations need to be fulfilled in order for doctors to command their patients' respect. In exchange for prestige and power, all health professionals are expected to develop a significant degree of technical expertise, be totally oriented toward serving people (often at cost to themselves, such as overwhelming fatigue), and in a nonjudgmental manner be caring and concerned with the feelings of patients (Cartwright, 1979). This is a tall order for anyone to fulfill.

There are also demands made on patients. When people become ill, they occupy "the **sick role**" (Parsons, 1958, 1975). The sick role involves expectations people share about the rights and obligations of the person who is ill. As noted in Chapter 3, the sick individual is relieved of normal social responsibilities such as going to work and taking care of others. In return for this right, the sick person is expected to seek competent medical help and to profess a desire to get well. Just as the doctor has a clearly defined role, the individual who is ill has an obligation to seek the advice of a medical expert and to follow that advice (Mechanic, 1968; Parsons, 1975).

MODELS OF THE PRACTITIONER-PATIENT RELATIONSHIP

A classic and still useful framework for summarizing practitioner-patient relations describes three basic models (Szasz & Hollender, 1956). This framework allows us to examine the appropriate role of the health care expert in encouraging patient cooperation.

First, there is the **activity-passivity model.** In this relationship, the health professional does something to the patient but the patient is passive. An obvious example of this model occurs when the patient is unconscious during an emergency or while undergoing surgery. Something is done to the patient and the patient has no control or responsibility. On occasion, this model is legitimately applied to a conscious patient, for example, when the patient is too sick or old to be a participant in the care. Sometimes also, the patient is too fearful or confused to take an active role. Of course, if the physician or other health care professional ministers to most patients as if the patient were not a living, thinking human being, this activity-passivity model may lead to the various problems discussed earlier.

The second model is very common in medical practice. It is the **guidance-cooperation model,** and it typifies the relationship that exists when the illness is not very serious. The patient is aware of what is happening and is capable of following instructions. The practitioner tells the patient what to do and the patient is expected to cooperate. In this model, the health practitioner (expert) decides what is best for the patient and makes the recommendation. The patient is expected to follow the recommendation.

In this guidance-cooperation relationship, health professionals try to be supportive, but the practitioner assumes responsibility for deciding the right treatment. The patient is simply expected to follow the rules. However, the physician cannot be with the patient to deal with problems that arise, and also cannot determine whether the patient is cooperating. As we have seen, cooperation is problematic in this situation because the patient is following someone else's recommendations about how to behave in many areas of challenge.

The third model of the practitioner-patient relationship is **mutual participation.** Szasz and Hollender stated that in modern medicine, this model is still rare; however, things have been changing in recent years. This model is based upon the belief that the physician and the patient are pursuing common goals of eliminating illness and preserving the patient's health. The practitioner and patient have equal power in the relationship; they need each other (i.e., are mutually interdependent), and their behaviors must be mutually satisfying in order for the relationship to continue.

In the mutual participation model, the patient's dignity and respect are maintained. In this model, there is a true sharing of responsibility. While it avoids a false sense that patients and the physician are equal in knowledge or in education, this model provides the opportunity for patients to maintain freedom of control over their lives and the decisions that are made concerning their bodies. The patient's input is included in medical decisions before they are made. This model suggests an open and responsible partnership.

The Health Transactions Model

A detailed analysis of this successful mutual relationship was offered by the health psychologist George Stone; it is called the health transactions model (Stone, 1979). It is based around solving problems with patients—the idea that cooperation with medical regimens is the positive result of a successful transaction between the health care provider and the patient. There are three stages: (1) the statement of the problem by the patient and the exploration of symptoms by the physician; (2) the development of the diagnosis and the decisions regarding treatment; and (3) the implementation of treatment.

In the first stage of the health care transaction, the patient brings a problem to the physician. For example, the patient describes a set of symptoms and notes when they occur, explaining something about their personal meaning. The expert should question the patient extensively about the symptoms and history. While the patient probably describes the problem in common behavioral terms, the medical expert usually redefines the problem in purely medical terms (Stiles, Putnam, Wolf, & James, 1979). An example of this kind of transaction is the patient who describes feeling faint and dizzy and having difficulty breathing while walking outside. The physician will probably define the problem in terms such as "shortness of breath upon exertion." It is possible, of course, that the patient is having heart trouble, but it is also possible that the patient is having an anxiety reaction. Although questions will usually center on the physical aspects of the case, it could be equally important in the care of the patient to know about the patient's lifestyle, beliefs, family or other support systems, coping mechanisms, and general emotional health. Combinations of physical and emotional data are needed in order to be able to make an accurate diagnosis.

During the second stage of the health care transaction, the health professional makes a decision about the diagnosis and recommends the treatment. The health care professional has a great deal of knowledge about the intricate details of various treatments—for example, how much each costs, what the side effects and restrictions are, and what the duration of the treatments will be. But a rational selection among these possible treatments demands some knowledge of the values assigned by the patient to the various complicating factors and outcomes. For example, suppose one treatment requires the patient to remain sedentary for a few weeks. A physician may decide upon this remedy, placing a low value on mobility. Suppose, however, that the patient is an athlete; the prescription of a restriction in movement is likely to be very distressing for the patient's social, psychological, and physical health. A better treatment may be available for this patient.

The health transactions model, like the mutual participation model, maintains that although traditionally health care professionals have made the sole decisions about treatment, such unilateral decision-making is inappropriate. The health care professional can never completely know or anticipate the values of the patient, the meaning of various outcomes, or the problems the patient would face in trying to cooperate with the therapeutic regimen. Rational selection of a course of treatment requires that the patient take (and the health professional give) some responsibility when the treatment course is being selected. The health care professional must be willing to take advice from the patient.

The third and final stage of the health care transaction is implementing the treatment. Traditionally, total responsibility has been placed on the patient for carrying out the treatment. If full responsibility for carrying out the treatment—say, taking medication for high blood pressure and trying to lose weight—is borne by the patient, both parties to the health care encounter may be reluctant to admit the patient's inability to carry out the treatment regimen. The health care professional is likely to avoid the fact that he or she has not explained the treatment adequately or convinced the patient to follow it. The patient may be reluctant to admit an embarrassing inability to carry out the regimen. The health care professional probes halfheartedly for noncooperation, and the patient hides it as much as possible. Everyone plays a social game, and the patient fails to benefit from treatment.

If, on the other hand, the entire health care transaction is considered the shared responsibility of the health professional and the patient, no fault is assigned when difficulties arise. Difficulties are expected to occur, and noncooperation is addressed by the provider and by the patient, who work together to alleviate the problem. They design or redesign a treatment program that the patient can follow successfully—a program that fits the patient's social, psychological, economic, and cultural situation.

In summary, the health transactions model recommends that in the initial stage of the health care interaction, the health professional explore the situation of every client, examining their beliefs about their illness and symptoms, and their willingness to receive and carry out recommendations. In the second stage, the health care professional should examine the patient's values and engage in open communication with the patient about them. The health care professional should explore the patient's expectations about treatment. Finally, in the stage in which the patient is charged with carrying out the regimen, the health professional should share in the responsibility by remaining an integral part of the treatment. The practitioner should check the patient's progress and discuss the regimen and its modification. The health care professional should listen to the patient, provide an accepting atmosphere in which the patient can admit mistakes and ask for help, and explain the many aspects of the treatment regimen, its purpose, expected outcomes, side effects, and expected duration.

It is important to remember that not all patients will benefit from treatment with the health transactions model. A different approach may be necessary with those patients who need to be or prefer to be more fully cared for by the health professional.

SUMMARY AND CONCLUSION

Despite the time and expense patients put forth in obtaining medical advice, a large number of them fail to follow it. Although many health professionals believe that patients' failures to cooperate are the result of uncooperative personalities, extensive research on this topic has shown that patient cooperation is dependent upon a number of social and psychological factors—many of which can be changed or addressed by the health professional's intervention. In order to cooperate with their treatment regimens, patients must believe they are susceptible to serious disease, they must trust in the efficacy of the treatment, and they must believe its benefits outweigh its costs. They must have clear, open communication with the health professionals, who provide understandable explanations to them and prescribe regimens compatible with the patients' social and cultural norms. Cooperation may also be enhanced by support and help from the patient's family and network of close friends.

Research strongly supports the notions of earlier physicians such as Hippocrates, Shattuck, and Osler, who wrote of the importance of the interpersonal quality of the physician-patient relationship. There is a growing awareness that a *scientific,* rational approach to the teaching and practice of the so-called art of medicine is indeed possible. Research on patient satisfaction strongly suggests that physicians and other health care professionals can learn to develop relationships that discourage doctor-shopping and malpractice suits while encouraging favorable outcomes of treatment. Health practitioners must learn to communicate concern as well as learn to listen to and educate their patients. Details of this communication process are described in Chapter 13.

Recommended Additional Readings

Brody, Howard. (1992). *The healer's power.* New Haven: Yale University Press.

Illich, Ivan. (1976). *Medical nemesis: The expropriation of health.* New York: Random House.

Leigh, Hoyle, & Reiser, Morton F. (1990*). The patient: Biological, psychological, and social dimensions of medical practice.* New York: Plenum Medical Book Co.

Lown, Bernard. (1996). *The lost art of healing.* Boston: Houghton Mifflin.

Myers, Lynn B., & Midence, Kenny (Eds.). (1998). *Adherence to treatment in medical conditions.* Amsterdam, Netherlands: Harwood Academic Publishers.

Shorter, Edward. (1985). *Bedside manners: The troubled history of doctors and patients.* New York: Simon & Schuster.

Shumaker, Sally A., Schron, Eleanor B. Ockene, Judith K., & McBee, W. L. (Eds.). (1998). *The handbook of health behavior change* (2nd ed.). New York: Springer Publishing Co.

Key Concepts

patient compliance

patient cooperation/adherance

lack of cooperation/noncooperation with treatment

primary prevention

secondary prevention

noncompliance

pill counts

uncooperative personality

health literacy

social support

iatrogenic illness

reciprocity

referent power

expert power

reward power

doctor-shopping

malpractice

white coat hypertension

sick role

activity-passivity model

guidance-cooperation model

mutual participation

Chapter 13

COMMUNICATION BETWEEN PATIENTS AND PRACTITIONERS

One evening in March, Mr. A. Arguilez went to see his doctor at his neighborhood health maintenance organization. When the doctor walked in to the examining room, Mr. Arguilez pulled a gun, shot his doctor in the groin, and fled. There was a real problem in this doctor-patient relationship.

As newspaper and television reporters investigated the story, the reasons for this bizarre episode became clear. The 62-year-old patient had prostate cancer. (This is a slow-growing cancer of the prostate gland, which surrounds the urethra of males at the base of the bladder.) According to the patient, his doctor had pressured him to have prostate surgery, promising he would "be like a young man"; but the surgery left him sexually impotent ("Videotape tells why," 1994). After lawyers refused to help him, the frustrated patient decided to take matters into his own hands. "I intend to blow his penis and testicles off of him," the patient reportedly said on a videotape he made before the incident. This was truly a doctor-patient relationship gone wrong, a monumental failure to communicate.

Although this incident is unusual, the psychosocial problems that it captures are quite common. In the urologist's mind, it was intolerable to have a cancer growing untreated in one's body, even if surgery risked sexual performance. He thought the patient understood this. But to the patient, losing the ability to have sexual relations took away his manhood and made him an "android." Of course, there is no justification to excuse or condone such violence, but many patients can sympathize with feelings of frustration that arise in interactions with their health practitioners.

Consider the following example of misunderstood communication.

> With a slight frown at the fact that he was running behind schedule, Dr. Welton said, "Well, Mrs. Gooden, the results of your tests are back. It looks like what we are dealing with here is a simple case of hypertension. There seems to be no kidney involvement at this stage, and your blood chemistries look pretty good."
>
> Looking at the chart, not at Mrs. Gooden, Dr. Welton continued, "Since the hypertension is most likely being exacerbated by your obesity and by excessive stress, I'd like you to follow this diet, which is designed both for weight loss and for decreased sodium in order to reduce fluid retention. In addition, I want you to relax and take these pills three times a day—hydrochlorthiazide, or water pills, for diuresis. You should talk to my receptionist and make an appointment to come in again in three weeks." He glanced at his watch. "Do you have any questions?"
>
> "No thanks, doctor," Mrs. Gooden smiled graciously. "See you in a few weeks."
>
> Later, in the Gooden home, Mr. Gooden asked, "What did the doctor say today?"
>
> Mrs. Gooden replied, "He said I may have a chemical problem in my blood and that is what makes me a little overweight and nervous. He wants me to go back and see him in a while, and then after I see him again, I should start taking some pills if I want to lose weight. I think he's worried about my health. I wonder if there's something he's scared to tell me."

The gross misunderstanding of the physician's explanations and instructions by this patient, Mrs. Gooden, may seem a little farfetched. You may be thinking that such confused communication between the physician and the patient is unlikely to happen. Yet if we look at the research studies that have addressed this question of physician-patient communication, we find that such misunderstanding is actually common.

THE PROBLEM OF PRACTITIONER-PATIENT COMMUNICATION

Faulty communication between health care professionals and patients, and resulting errors in diagnosis and treatment, is disturbingly common. In one disheartening study, for example, researchers tape recorded 25 physician-patient interactions in which the physicians conveyed important information to the hospitalized patients (Golden & Johnston, 1970). These communications were about such matters as the need for surgery or the results of important diagnostic tests. The patients were questioned immediately after the physician left, and asked to describe what they had discussed with the physician. Ten of the 25 patients showed definite distortions of what they had been told. Analyses of the tape recordings showed most distortions to result from inadequate explanation by the physician. Furthermore, in all cases except one, the physician left the room before checking to see whether the patient had understood what was said.

Such problems have long been apparent. For example, a classic study interviewed patients after a visit to an outpatient clinic and a comparison was made between what the patient reported was said and what the practitioner had actually said, according to a verbatim record (Ley & Spelman, 1965). Only 63 percent of the medical statements made by physicians were recalled accurately by patients. Furthermore, 56 percent of the instructions were reported erroneously (although this was true of "only" 27 percent of statements about diagnoses).

Examples of communication failures are commonly reported in the clinical literature, since they are frustrating to physicians and dangerous to patients. For example, one 46-year-old man was given a nitroglycerin transdermal patch to help control his high blood pressure (Letter, 1988). But surprisingly, it was not working. The medication package insert is clear, and it is obvious to anyone familiar with the practice of medicine that the patch is to be attached to the skin, where the medication is slowly and continuously absorbed. However, this man was eating his patches.

What is the source of such significant problems in physician-patient communication? A series of clever studies at a children's hospital tape recorded 800 patient visits to a pediatric walk-in clinic and then conducted follow-up interviews with the mothers of the children (Francis, Korsch, & Morris, 1969; Freemon, Negrete, Davis, & Korsch, 1971). The primary problems involved the physician's failure to take account of the patient's concerns and expectations from the medical visit, and the lack of a clear-cut explanation concerning diagnosis, the cause of the illness, and treatment. In the 800 visits, 19 percent of the mothers reported that they had not been told by the physician what was wrong with their child, and 26 percent said that they had not mentioned their greatest concern to the physician because either they did not have a chance or because they were not encouraged by the physician to do so. There was also significant misunderstanding by patients of what the physicians had communicated to them. While the length of the session that the mother and child had with the physician had no relationship to patient satisfaction or to subsequent cooperation with treatment, characteristics of the communication strongly influenced these results. This is a general finding—some physicians are much better communicators than others, and it is not simply a function of time constraints.

The communication problems had little to do with language barriers. The most severe as well as the most common complaint of the dissatisfied mothers was that the physicians did not show enough interest to relieve their worries about the children and acknowledge their concern. What specifically can be done?

Expectations

One way to think about health communication is to distinguish two functions of the health care professional: the provision of **instrumental care** and the provision of **socio-emotional care** (Bloom, 1963). The former involves the purely technical aspects of the treatment of the patient (e.g., surgery or the administration of a specific drug for a specific condition). The latter involves the emotional and interpersonal dimension of care—the communication of caring to the patient and the understanding of the patient's feelings and problems (Ben-Sira, 1980). This is sometimes assumed to be a distinction between the art of medicine and the science of medicine, but, in reality, there is also a science of interpersonal care and an art of technical care.

Because of the influence of the traditional biomedical model, many physicians focus on the instrumental aspects and have little scientific training on the interpersonal side. Interpersonal expertise involves two basic skills. First, the practitioner must have the proper orientation to and understanding of the role of the health practitioner in health care. This matter was discussed in Chapter 12. Second, the practitioner must be *skilled* in interviewing and in effective communication. Consider the following examples.

Patient:
I don't understand why doctors can't tell their patients what to expect, or explain things in terms the patient can understand. Why do I feel frustrated and confused when I leave my doctor's office? He talks to me in gobbledygook. Then, if I don't get everything exactly right—like if my blood pressure doesn't go down enough to satisfy him—he seems to be annoyed or treats me like a child. I think he likes to keep me in the dark so I can't do without him.

Physician:
What do my patients want from me anyway? I tell them what I think their symptomatology means and I tell them what the results of the diagnostic examinations were. I explain to them carefully what they should do to effect a treatment regimen. I tell them all the implications of each of the treatment regimens. Still, so many of them come back having not complied with treatment or remembering only a small proportion of the things I told them. I guess I assume too much about what patients are capable of comprehending. They probably should not be given very much information. Everybody likes to criticize physicians.

Such common incorrect expectations and incorrect assumptions on the part of both patients and physicians about what the other expects and understands underlie various obstructions in the flow of communication between the health care consumer and provider. Many could be resolved if patients and health care teams talked together about what each can expect and what each can provide.

Another, related way of thinking about these problems is to focus directly on the two components of a successful interaction: issues of medical jargon and issues of nonverbal communication.

WORDS AND MEDICAL JARGON

In one early study of medical jargon (Samora, Saunders, & Larson, 1961), patients defined various medical terms as follows:

1. **Abdomen:** sides; buttocks; heart; bladder; area below the waist.
2. **Appendectomy:** a cut rectum; taking off an arm or leg; something to do with the bowels.
3. **Intern:** same as an orderly; boys that help in the hospital; drugstore man; a man nurse; a doctor with no degree.
4. **Pulse:** a bad hurt or sickness; a nerve; temperature.
5. **Respiratory:** in the arms or legs; venereal; tiredness; a sickness in which you sweat and have hot and cold flashes.

In this study, randomly selected common medical words, which physicians and health care professionals had reported they would readily use with their patients, were repeated to 125 hospitalized patients and scored immediately by an interviewer according to whether or not the patients understood what the word meant. No respondent gave an adequate definition for all of the words, and no single word was known or understood by all respondents. While there was some relationship between education and knowledge of medical terms, there was no overwhelming tendency for patients of higher educational levels to know many of the words. A possible consequence? One poor man was almost catheterized because he answered no when asked if he had "voided." Remember that these medical terms were terms that physicians and other health care professionals had indicated they would readily use in discussing a medical case with a patient.

Because medical jargon is very familiar to the practitioner, the practitioner may believe that the patient understands what has been said when in fact this is not so. For example, many patients do not understand "hypertension," and think that they have an issue with nervous tension. Those on a low-sodium diet may be surprised when they cannot eat salt. Those on a low-sugar diet may be surprised about limits on fruit. Some common examples of current medical jargon are listed in Table 13-1.

Medspeak

In the totalitarian world of George Orwell's novel *1984,* there was a new language called Newspeak (Orwell, 1949). The purpose of Newspeak was to make it difficult or even impossible to think "unacceptable" thoughts. For example, words like *honor, justice,* and *morality* did not exist any longer, and words having to do with freedom were combined into the word *crimethink.*

The idea that our thought is influenced and controlled by our language comes from the psychologist and philosopher Benjamin Lee Whorf (Whorf, 1956). It is called **linguistic relativity.** For example, in English there is only one word for frozen water vapor— snow. But in Eskimo there are three words, describing different types of snow. Although we can all recognize snow and distinguish wet snow from dry snow, the Eskimo may more eas-

Table 13-1   Common Medical Jargon Often Misunderstood by Laypersons

Jargon	True Meaning
negative test result	results are normal (good news)
idiopathic	doctor doesn't know reason
contraindicated	don't do it
lesion	any sore or damage whatsoever
parenteral	not given by mouth
functional	nothing wrong with the structure, or of psychological origin
analgesic	painkiller
hematoma	bruise (swelling filled with blood)
pruritis	itching
subclinical	not yet identifiable
eryth- (erythroderma)	red (red skin)
thrombosis	blood clot (in a vessel)
tissue	cells
trauma	injury
physician	M.D. (to distinguish from other doctors such as osteopaths, dentists, biologists, psychologists, optometrists, chiropractors, and anatomists)

ily recognize and remember the type of snow that fell last winter and may be more sophisticated in thinking about snow. Words facilitate thought, and sometimes our thoughts and memories are interrupted because we cannot think of the right word.

Medical situations are full of special words, with analogous effects. First, health practitioners who have facility with medical terms can think faster about medical topics than the patients with whom they are talking. In a discussion, the practitioner may have gone on to a new topic while the patient is still trying to remember precisely what *vascular* means. Second, practitioners may be better able to remember past discussions and problems than patients because of their greater knowledge of medical language. The patient may have forgotten the explanation received at the last visit because all the terms were new to the patient.

Third, medical jargon may lead practitioners to think about certain medical problems in very different ways from how their patients think about them. For example, *coronary thrombosis* may recall the image of a blocked artery to a nurse, while the term *heart attack* may lead the patient to imagine a deadly substance attacking the heart. Consequently, the patient may not understand the treatment. Finally, medical jargon may create obvious problems of miscommunication, as in the following examples:

Doctor: Have you had a history of cardiac arrest in your family?
Patient: No, we never had any trouble with the police.
Doctor: Do you have varicose veins?
Patient: Well, I have veins, but I don't know if they're close or not.

Surveys of randomly selected patients in the waiting rooms of clinics and private medical practices reveal that a large percentage of the patients feel their doctors do not understand their problems, and that doctors and nurses use words that are too difficult for them to understand. Patients often say that they would like doctors to simplify their language (Barnlund, 1976; Becker & Maiman, 1980; Mazullo, Lasagna, & Griner, 1974). But not too simple. An anesthesiologist in the operating room who tells his patient that he is about to put her to sleep may be communicating the wrong message if she is thinking about the time the vet said the same words about her dog.

Physicians and other health care professionals also use many abbreviations when talking to each other. For example,

- **DOA** means the patient was dead on arrival;
- **zero delta** means that there is no change in the patient's condition;
- **oids** are steroids—that is, corticosteroids.

Physicians use this kind of jargon in talking to each other about patients' conditions. What is distressing for professional-patient communication is that health care professionals sometimes use this language when speaking to each other about the patient in front of the patient, and also sometimes when speaking to the patient.

Of course, medical jargon can be beneficial to practitioners in communicating with each other concisely and precisely. Everyone understands the necessity for scientific precision, but there may also be a more insidious use of medical jargon. It has been suggested by at least several observers of medical communications that health care professionals do indeed intentionally talk a secret gobbledygook. Nicholas Christy, in the *New England Journal of Medicine,* defined a language called **Medspeak** that health care professionals (particularly physicians) use supposedly to facilitate the sharing of information (Christy, 1979). But Medspeak often clouds scientific communication between the health care professionals themselves. An example of Medspeak is to use *symptomatology* synonymously with *symptoms.*

Why is Medspeak used? First, some have suggested that health professionals use their expectations that patients cannot understand medical issues as excuses for avoiding the time and trouble required to communicate with patients (McKinlay, 1975; Pratt, Seligmann, & Reader, 1957). Second, limited communication with patients serves to protect the nurse or physician from encountering emotional reactions from patients (Thompson, 1971). Third, Medspeak may prevent a patient from discovering neglect or error, and fourth, it may even save health care professionals from having to face their own emotional reactions.

Finally, it has been suggested that the control and withholding of information in the health care professional-patient relationship—the careful control of what is said to the patient about the patient's condition and how much is explained—represent an attempt by the health professional to exert a measure of power over the patient (Davis, 1960; Marquis, 1970; Waitzkin & Stoeckle, 1972; Waitzkin & Waterman, 1974; Lorber, 1975). Although most physicians are highly motivated to help their patients, the health care system, like any bureaucracy or guild, also functions to protect its members. Obviously, most of these (power-oriented) reasons for the use of jargon benefit only the practitioner and only in the short run. In the long run, however, excessive jargon will destroy the interpersonal aspects of health care, with detrimental consequences for the patient's health. As a result, the entire medical care system will suffer. The best physicians and nurses typically are the best communicators (see also Box 13–1).

The use of jargon may be so natural in certain medical settings that practitioners are not aware of the problems it creates. In one study of 50 physicians, some of the terms used without explanation were *electrolytes, creatinine, dysrhythmic,* and *stool guiac* (Roter & Hall, 1992). However, the use of jargon is so rarely necessary in communicating with patients that a good rule for practitioners is to always endeavor to explain any medical condition to a patient without using a single technical term! Medical names for conditions, drugs, and so on, can be provided later as needed in treatment.

On the other side of the coin, some patients do know medical jargon, and most can understand clear medical explanations (Segall & Roberts, 1980). In one interesting classic study, clinic patients were questioned about the etiology, symptoms, and treatment of 10 common diseases (Pratt, Seligmann, & Reader, 1957). The questions were then given to physicians to see how well they thought their patients would answer. It was found that 81 percent of the physicians underestimated their patients' capabilities of understanding conceptual explanations. Patients actually had a surprisingly good understanding of medical problems when discussed in ordinary language. Today, with many patients reading about and discussing their problems on the Internet, they may have many intelligent questions.

In the medical encounter, patients can be helped to ask more questions. In one study, half the clinic patients received a 10-minute session with a health educator prior to meeting the physician (Roter, 1984). A list of pertinent questions was developed and given to each patient. These patients did indeed ask more questions of their doctors (than did patients in a control group), but even these patients did not ask all the questions they would have liked to ask.

Detailed analyses of transcripts of doctor-patient interactions reveal that when doctors talk, they are mostly giving information to patients (such as blood pressure readings). About a quarter of their informational talk, however, involves advice-giving (counseling), such as about the need to effect certain changes by taking certain medications. These patient-focused communications also turn out to be signs of a proficient clinician and are appreciated by patients (Roter & Hall, 1992).

Physicians also spend a lot of the encounter asking questions. Unfortunately, these are mostly closed-ended questions that do not elicit sufficient information. There is also some positive talk (encouragement, empathy) and some partnership building, such as seeking the patient's ideas. There is very little confrontation (antagonism) or social conversation (chitchat), which is a good thing, since these are not useful or productive.

Box 13-1   Ethical Issues in Deceiving Patients

The law of the courtroom insists that witnesses not only tell the truth but also that they tell "the whole truth and nothing but the truth." This demand protects against the case in which a statement is true but misleading. For example, if a doctor tells a leukemic youngster that he has a serious chronic disease but does not mention cancer, the doctor has told the truth but not the whole truth. Many people believe that adults are entitled to hear "the whole truth" from their doctors.

The medical setting is quite different from the legal setting, however, and there are various significant factors that complicate the issue of deception in medicine. The most troubling factors concern placebos. Psychological factors can have a tremendous influence on health. Patients who expect to get better will often do much better than patients without hope. Indeed, the creation of positive expectations is a critical aspect of medical care. Thus, if a patient believes that cancer is always painful and fatal, and the doctor consequently tells the patient that he or she has cancer, the communication itself may have a detrimental effect on the patient's health. Further complicating the matter is the fact that the doctor often is not sure of the patient's prognosis. Giving a patient unnecessarily bad news may thus be seen as a serious mistake in treatment. The patient's right to know the diagnosis must be somehow balanced against the ambiguity in the diagnosis and the implications of knowing.

Another problem in telling the whole truth is the fact that medical knowledge can be very technical. Most people can understand the question "Were you in the victim's house on the night of the murder?" But many people cannot fully understand the meaning and implications of certain diseases. Thus, it is almost impossible to communicate "the whole truth" to them.

Patient anger at physicians who did not tell them the whole truth is usually the result of the reasons why the doctor did not tell the truth. Patients may understandably be upset if they were deceived because the doctor did not take the time to talk to them, the doctor was protecting his or her own reputation, or the doctor did not want to face the emotional reaction of the patient. In such cases, the doctor is simply another dishonest person.

The issue of the ethics of deceiving patients does not have to be decided in the abstract. If the doctor and patient are communicating well for the most part and if the doctor-patient relationship is generally positive (according to the criteria described in this book), deception is usually not a problem. Such patients in some situations want to and need to know more of the truth than other patients in other situations, and this matter can usually be dealt with directly in a healthy doctor-patient relationship.

Specific techniques for obtaining accurate information from patients are considered later in this chapter in the section, "Interviewing in the Health Care Context." First, however, we examine the subtle emotional communication that occurs between health practitioners and patients.

NONVERBAL COMMUNICATION BETWEEN PATIENTS AND PRACTITIONERS

Since ancient times, healers have relied upon careful observation of patients as an aid in diagnosing illness, and have developed bedside manners to promote recovery. Medical lore offers numerous suggestions for proper comforting of patients and for correct demeanor. In other words, experienced practitioners rely heavily on the subtle, unspoken messages of practitioner-patient interaction.

However, although scientific procedures have replaced art in much of medical practice, subtle interpersonal communication has not generally been developed scientifically. Such vague notions as intuition, empathy, sensitivity, caring, and similar suggestive but imprecise terms are often used in discussions of face-to-face patient care. But there is much relevant science about the meaning of these notions in terms of nonverbal communication (Buller & Street, 1992; Engel, 1977; DePaulo & Friedman, 1998; Friedman, 1979, 1982).

Nonverbal communication involves facial expressions, voice tones, gestures, touches, and related cues that complement and illustrate aspects of the spoken word. They often express feelings that are not subject to direct conscious analysis by the practitioner or the patient. For example, a patient's grimace or shudder as well as a nurse's comforting touch or facial expression of sadness are messages that may be even more important than the words that are spoken (Daubenmire, 1976; Knapp & Hall, 1997). One experimental study of the presentation of mammogram results showed that if the oncologist looked worried, the patients recalled less information and become much more anxious (Shapiro, Boggs, Melamed, & Graham-Pole, 1992).

Many factors make it likely that patients will be especially watchful of providers' nonverbal cues. First, illness generally provokes anxiety and emotional uncertainty. The patient must deal with such matters as the possibility of death, reactions to drugs, the presence of imposing equipment, new environments, and being separated from loved ones. In such circumstances, patients are likely to have a strong need for what psychologists call **social comparison.** That is, they want to reduce their emotional uncertainty and tend to look to those around them—often medical personnel—for subtle clues to help them understand what they are feeling and how they should respond (Ellsworth, Friedman, Perlick, & Hoyt, 1978; Lederer, 1952).

Second, patients are likely to be searching for factual information about their disease and its prognosis. Some of this information is provided by the verbal diagnosis, but we have already seen the many problems connected with verbal communication in the health care setting. Practitioners may not fully communicate the whole truth for a variety of legitimate and not-so-legitimate reasons, and patients know this fact. Since it is commonly believed that cues about deception are expressed through nonverbal channels, such cues may be given special attention by patients (Knapp, Hart, & Dennis, 1974). For example, patients may look for false smiles or a hurried manner.

Third, patients are especially likely to watch for nonverbal cues because of their position of weakness. Research indicates that inferiors may closely examine the nonverbal cues of their superiors; people with less power need to assess the mood of their superiors and ascertain which of their actions are creating a positive versus a negative effect (Exline, 1972; Henley, 1977). Patients are often at the mercy of the practitioners and want to please them. Furthermore, they may be hesitant to question a busy, high-status professional in detail and prefer to rely on messages left "unsaid" for clues about their medical condition. Finally, certain medical matters interfere with normal verbal communication and therefore require that more attention be paid to nonverbal communication. For example, orders to remain still, being attached to a respirator, and even holding a thermometer in the mouth all limit the patient's ability to question the practitioner and thus increase the importance of nonverbal communication.

In addition to patient sensitivity to nonverbal communication, it is also true that patients tend to be especially nonverbally expressive. That is, important information about the patient's condition is emitted solely through nonverbal channels. First, patients are likely to experience emotions such as fear, sadness, surprise, and anger. Emotions are often clearly revealed nonverbally, particularly through facial expressions (Ekman, Friesen, & Ellsworth, 1972). Practitioners can become experienced at recognizing these emotions. Second, patients are unlikely to have had much experience in hiding or controlling emotions in medical settings, and their usual social graces may disappear. For example, people may know how to control anger when provoked in a department store, but fear of hospitalization or pain caused by a doctor's probing may be directly revealed. Thus, the attentive practitioner can detect valuable information. Third, some patients may prefer to communicate their feelings about certain difficult matters—their attitude toward death, embarrassing disabilities, a desire for additional services, and so on—through channels that are not too explicit, that is, through nonverbal communication. For example, a proud man may ask for pain medication with his eyes, but refuse to ask with words. Finally, various medical conditions may disrupt verbal communication and thus leave the patient with no choice but to communicate nonverbally. For example, weakness may make conversation too difficult for the patient but still allow the possibility of nonverbal messages such as a glance or gesture. The likely meanings of specific nonverbal cues are described next.

The Face and Facial Expression

Hippocrates urged the physician to study the patient's face first. A face with "the nose sharp, the eyes sunken, the temples fallen in, the ears cold and drawn in and their lobes distorted, the skin of the face hard, stretched and dry, and the color of the face pale or dusky" usually portends death (Hippocrates, 1950). In addition to its general sense organs, the face has many muscles and nerves. In modern times, facial features have proved useful in diagnosing genetic disorders (Goodman & Gorlin, 1970). Beyond fixed features, however, facial expressions of emotion provide valuable and detailed information.

Facial expression is an important element in the communication of pain. For example, facial expression has been used to assess the amount of distress of women in labor (Leventhal & Sharp, 1965). In fact, the concept of pain itself has a communicative component in that its expression generally brings help from others; the expression of pain is, in part, a request for comfort (Szasz, 1957). Facial expression of pain may thus be expected to vary somewhat as a function of the nature of interpersonal relationships. If the expression of pain brings rewards other than pain relief (such as sympathy or insurance payments), the patient may show increasingly more pain. If the expression of chronic pain is ignored or punished, on the other hand, it may decrease, although at the cost of avoiding the possibility of relief through treatment.

The practitioner's expectations and the patient's emotions are often clearly and forcefully communicated through facial expression. The human face is fantastically expressive and people can easily and quickly recognize distinct emotional states from facial expression (Vine, 1970; Ekman & Friesen, 1975). The six basic and easily recognized facial expressions are happiness, anger, sadness, surprise, disgust, and fear. Such expressions can effectively communicate a nurse's disgust at a wound or deformity, a physician's anger at a patient's failure to follow treatment regimens, or a technician's fear of a patient's deterioration. On the other hand, facial expressions can, with practice, be effectively controlled by most people (Ekman & Friesen, 1969, 1975). With proper training and motivation, practitioners' expressions might just as effectively communicate a nurse's sympathy and understanding or a physician's positive outlook and expectations. This psychological power of facial expression was not lost on tribal medicine men who wore elaborate masks indicating proper spiritual orientation during healing. In fact, in Ceylon different masks were worn for each disease (Liggett, 1974). Patients, paying special attention to nonverbal cues and especially influenced by the emotional nature of the social interaction, can be strongly influenced by the provider's facial expression (Ben-Sira, 1980).

Touch

Touch is one of the oldest and most widespread forms of traditional medical treatment. For hundreds of years during the Middle Ages, Europeans sought relief from the disease of scrofula (tuberculosis of the lymph gland) with the **King's touch** or the **royal touch** (Bloch, 1973). English and French kings treated thousands of people who came to them to receive divine healing. Despite a very low "cure" rate, the practice persisted, and many people obtained temporary relief after being touched by the king. The power of this technique illustrates the tremendous symbolic value of touch in healing. Not surprisingly, the healing power of this royal touch tended to wane with the disappearing divinity of kings. However, some of this power may have been transferred to physicians.

Patients may feel much better after a routine physical exam but may complain if the doctor "never even touched" them. An interesting example is provided by the brain surgeon I. S. Cooper (1981). Cooper tells a story told to him by a famous surgeon at the Mayo clinic. This distinguished surgeon saw a patient with a brain tumor and planned to operate the next day. But the patient went home and asked for another doctor. Why? The patient was upset that the doctor had never touched his head. From that time forward, the surgeon always made sure to feel all around his patients' heads. In many situations, touch has retained its symbolic value as a kind of blessing involving the transfer of special powers.

Figure 13-1   The Royal Touch: Charles II of England touching a sufferer from scrofula, a tuberculous degenerative disease of the lymph system. The special touch of the king is now often represented in the special touch of the doctor or other healer. *(Courtesy of Historical pictures service, Chicago.)*

The symbolic value of medical touching can be easily seen in folk medicine. Faith healers have long used the technique of **"laying on of the hands,"** and this "therapy" is still quite popular in American society. Since its efficacy is supposedly derived from the transfer of a healing spirit, just as the king transferred the divine spirit, this technique is of course viewed as quackery by modern medicine. However, imbued with a special symbolic value, the practitioner's touch may indeed promote healing. In modern American society, the concept of touching as basic to the process of healing has been enthusiastically adopted by the "human potential movement," people interested in self-actualization. Many popular encounter groups praise the healing value of touching.

One study investigated the effects of being touched by female nurses during presurgical instruction (Whitcher & Fisher, 1979). In the hospital, some patients were touched on the arm by female nurses while receiving information about upcoming surgery, whereas other patients were not touched. Patients who had been touched reacted more positively on a variety of measures than patients who had not been touched, but this beneficial effect was confined to female patients. This study provides evidence that touch is important to medicine, but reactions may depend on other aspects of the doctor-patient situation (Roter & Hall, 1992). In short, touching has a significant psychological effect on many patients. Since positive expectations may result, even brief touches can be beneficial (Riscalla, 1975).

Medical practitioners palpate, poke, and otherwise touch their patients for purposes of diagnosis. Furthermore, routine diagnostic procedures such as temperature taking, blood pressure assessment, and throat and stethoscopic examination all involve touching the patient. Often, as in examinations of the breasts, vagina, prostate, and groin, the touch is in intimate areas not usually invaded by relative strangers. This kind of touching often produces emotional and interpersonal reactions from patients.

There is little doubt that being touched is sometimes comforting and also sometimes emotionally arousing. Some medical touching may even be sexually arousing. However, a certain type of touch at a certain part of the body cannot be shown to have a general, predictable effect. First, there are tremendous individual differences in responses to being touched. Second, many differences arise from the fact that touch has social meaning. Two prominent interpersonal meanings of touch concern intimacy and power.

In normal social interaction, the part of the body touched is generally clearly related to the intimacy of the relationship (Jourard, 1966). Violation of such norms in the medical setting may produce confusion. Nurses report incidents in which patients begin disclosing very personal information or become flirtatious during or after a backrub, a bath, or other usually "intimate" forms of touching, even though such behavior violates the role constraints of being a patient (Johnson, 1965). There are often technical reasons for providers to touch patients, but providers are also people, and thus some patients may react to the social meaning of the touch.

Touching also communicates power (DePaulo & Friedman, 1998). If one man is touching another in a doctor's office, which man is the doctor? Practitioners touch patients routinely, but there is usually very little occasion for the patient to touch the practitioner. The practitioner is of higher status. Of course, most of this one-sided touching is for instrumental means in the technical side of medical care. Doctors do not touch patients for the purpose of asserting their power, although the implication of power differences remains. Thus, on a social psychological level, touching can have an important effect on the overall relationship between the patient and practitioner.

Therapeutic touching. Touching for therapeutic purposes is not standardized and has been left as a relatively unresearched medical "art." Yet there is increasing evidence that not all benefits of touching come from social expectations.

Classic studies of monkeys raised with wire and cloth surrogate mothers showed the importance of touch to healthy social development. Harry Harlow found that infant monkeys were very attracted to the contact comfort of a terrycloth surrogate "mother" (Harlow & Zimmermann, 1959). This terrycloth mother aided the adjustment of the mon-

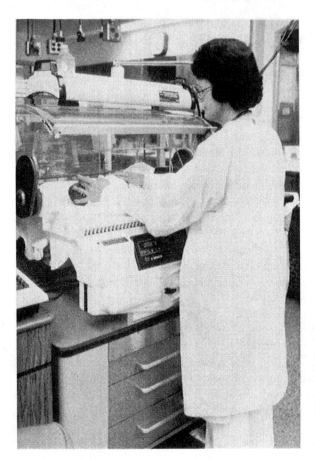

Figure 13-2 The comfort of contact is physiologically based. In newborn intensive care units, nurses, parents or volunteers now endeavor to insure that premature infants receive sufficient tactile stimulation. *(Photo courtesy of the University of California, San Diego, Medical Center.)*

keys and was even preferred to a wire surrogate mother who had a nipple and provided food.

This comfort of contact is physiologically based. For example, lack of touch retards development and has been implicated in skin disease (Montague, 1978). A series of studies by Tiffany Field and her colleagues on infant development indicate that premature or ill infants are more likely to thrive when they are touched (Field, 1998). At the least, humans are physiologically primed for the comfort of touch.

Patting, gentle massaging, backscratching, and other touches are tension reducing, combatting autonomic arousal. Nursing instructors acknowledge that "in nursing, touch may be the most important of all nonverbal behaviors" (Blondis & Jackson, 1977, p. 6). An ill, anxious patient who is surrounded by cold equipment may be especially reassured by a warm touch. A similar conclusion was reached by the anthropologist Ashley Montague, who wrote that "in every branch of the practice of medicine, touching should be considered an indispensable part of the doctor's art. . . . Touch always enhances the doctor's therapeutic abilities" (Montague, 1978, p. 223).

Gaze and Tone of Voice

People generally are aware of and respond when they are being stared at (Ellsworth, 1975; Ellsworth, Friedman, Perlick, & Hoyt, 1978). Gaze is an influential nonverbal cue. Eye behavior is similar to touching in that its total meaning may depend upon other factors in the situation. A stare may be comforting if it intensifies a pleasant situation or opens communication in an uncertain situation; on the other hand, a stare may be arousing or threatening if it is excessive or if the context is negative. For example, glances from a sympathetic nurse or an unhurried doctor may encourage a patient to cope with a difficult time or help a patient bring up a sensitive subject.

The practitioner's avoidance of looking a patient in the eye may be part of the process of dehumanization, common in medical settings, in which the patient is seen as (and comes to feel like) a body rather than a person. A doctor who looks only at medical records while avoiding the gaze of the patient will have difficulty establishing rapport with a patient. On the other hand, excessive staring at a patient, with no apparent cause or in a troubling situation, is likely to have a negative effect, perhaps making the patient feel like a freak or a bad person. Presumably, health providers will generally not stare at a patient's physical deformity, but constant eye contact to avoid doing so is also likely to be recognized by a patient. For example, interaction with a handicapped person (including eye contact) may be less variable, that is, more rigid and unchanging (Kleck, 1968).

As with facial expressions, the specific emotional and motivational states of patients and practitioners may be revealed through their tone of voice (DePaulo & Friedman, 1998). The tone of voice refers to sounds, primarily pitch variations, that accompany the spoken word. Emotions like fear, anger, sadness, interest, and joy and motivational states like pain are readily transmitted through vocal cues. Another message expressed through tone of voice concerns the nature of the interpersonal relationship.

A good example of the influence of voice tone concerns baby talk. Baby talk is the special high-pitched tone parents use when talking to toddlers and infants (Snow & Ferguson, 1977). However, baby talk may also occur between caretakers and patients. In one study, baby talk was found to be a significant aspect of the speech directed towards the institutionalized elderly (Caporael, 1981; Culbertson & Caporael, 1983). Although this speech sounds positive, it also suggests that the recipient is dependent, subordinate, and passive. For example, an elderly patient may be asked (in high-pitched voice), "Can I butter your muffin for you, dearie?" A passive, dependent orientation may thus be encouraged.

Tone of voice also seems important to the transmission of expectancies; it is probably an aspect of placebo effects (Duncan & Rosenthal, 1968). For example, one study found a relationship between the amount of "anger" judged to be present in a doctor's voice and his success in referring alcoholic patients for treatment (Milmoe, Rosenthal, Blane, Chafetz, & Wolf, 1967). Another study has shown a relationship between a physician's ability to express emotions through voice tone (and face and voice) and the way the physician is evaluated by his or her patients; physicians with better voice control were better liked (Friedman, DiMatteo, & Taranta, 1980). Thus, providers' voice tones are likely to affect the expectations and emotional reactions of their patients.

Smells and Distances

Communication through odors is sometimes important in the medical field. Some drugs, illnesses, and treatments may produce unpleasant odors in the patient. On the other hand, medical practitioners may also be associated with particular odors. The use of anesthesia, alcohol, and other chemicals may give practitioners and their surroundings certain smells. Furthermore, the lingering odors of other patients may transmit an olfactory message to the patient.

Social psychological research on "person perception" has shown that negative personal attributes are often associated with malodor. A bad person may be labeled a "stinker" or "stinkpot." In fact, perceiving the outgroup as smelly is a prime characteristic of prejudice (Allport, 1954; Largey & Watson, 1972). The diseased person suffering from malodor is likely to be reacted to with negative feelings. Even some health care providers may unknowingly come to regard foul-smelling patients as less good or moral, especially if the patient has at least some control over the odor. Such reactions of distaste may then be transmitted to patients through facial expressions.

The particular and uncommon smells of practitioners' medical settings may affect the health care process through associations. For unknown reasons, odors often have tremendous power to evoke memories of forgotten times and places (Allport, 1954; Meerloo, 1964; Schab & Crowder, 1995). People often associate certain smells with particular events in their past. Hence, a doctor's office or a hospital may evoke vivid memories of the previous negative experiences of an ill relative or a childhood trauma. These memories may create, even unconsciously, significant negative expectations in the patient.

Bad odors, disfigurement, fear of contagion, and other factors may all affect the distance that health practitioners keep between themselves and patients. Extra distance can have a significant psychological impact on patients since there are firm expectations about the distances that should be used in normal social interaction.

The anthropologist Edward Hall distinguished four **spatial zones** (Hall, 1966): intimate distance; personal distance (a small, protective personal sphere); social distance (for usual social interaction); and public distance. The intimate distance is of course the distance at which very intimate interactions usually occur. We have already seen that closeness and touching by practitioners (that is, their occupying of an intimate distance) may produce psychological reactions in patients that are out of place. Analogous problems can occur at other distances. For example, if a doctor on rounds in a hospital with a group of medical students stands back across the room and addresses the patients so that everyone can hear (public distance), the patient may become upset if intimate matters are being discussed. Intimate matters are supposed to be discussed at the intimate distance; the public distance results in a lack of privacy, a loud voice, more emphatic gesturing, and other incongruent cues that may produce psychological distress. Similarly, interpersonal problems can result if practitioners and visitors stand too far away from patients, maybe because of fear or poor habits, or if they stand too close, perhaps out of curiosity or a desire to comfort the patient. If the type of social interaction does not match the usual distance at which such interactions occur, the patient may be distressed by such deviations, perhaps without even realizing why.

Cue Discrepancy

One of the most important aspects of effective communication involves not what is said nor how it is said but rather the degree of consistency between verbal and nonverbal cues (DePaulo & Friedman, 1998). People with medical problems and other stigmas are very vigilant in watching for clues as to how they will "really" be treated (Goffman, 1963). Even the slightest inconsistency is likely to be noticed. A positive verbal communication, for example, "You're looking better today," accompanied by a negative nonverbal cue like a scowl is likely to be perceived as very insincere even if the negative facial expression results from the fact that the practitioner has just realized that he or she is running behind schedule (Argyle, 1975; Friedman, 1979). If the practitioner is angry, sarcasm and nastiness may be perceived. On the other hand, a relatively submissive, negative verbal message, such as "I hope you won't mind if I tell you that you need additional tests," will probably be perceived as sincere and sympathetic despite its negative verbal content if it is accompanied by a sad face (Friedman, 1979). This sentence may be seen as patronizing by some patients, however, if it is accompanied by a happy face.

One study examined the verbal and voice tone communications between patients and physicians in an outpatient clinic (Hall, Roter, & Rand, 1981). Verbal cues were assessed by asking raters to judge written transcripts of conversations; nonverbal tone was rated using content-filtered audiotapes (in which the words were made unintelligible). Patients' self-reported contentment was a function of an interesting combination. When physicians uttered words that were less anxious, patients were more content; but when the physicians' voice tones sounded more anxious, patients were again more content. This cue combination evidently produced a serious, controlled-sounding but explicitly (verbally) positive atmosphere that these patients liked. In sum, the degree and type of verbal-nonverbal cue consistency creates the "innuendo" that can either be very distressing or very comforting to an ill person. The development of proper demeanor requires some time.

A related matter concerns the intimacy of the relationship. It seems likely that complex nonverbal communication increases in efficiency and becomes more specialized as a relationship between two people develops. For example, spouses are probably better at quickly communicating and detecting distress or encouragement from each other than are strangers. However, illness brings practitioners and patients into an intimate relationship (especially from the patient's perspective) in which communication channels have not been fully developed. The relationship is intimate but its development has been forced. Hence, confusions and omissions may result as patients emit special cues that practitioners miss or misunderstand.

Deception

It is sometimes very important for the health practitioner to know that a patient is hiding some discomfort or is not telling the whole truth. Patients may try to deceive practitioners for a variety of reasons, including a desire to appear healthy to please the practitioner, a wish not to "bother" the practitioner, anxiety or fear about new symptoms, embarrassment about certain intimate matters, and so on. Fortunately, clues as to possible deception can often be detected through attention to certain aspects of nonverbal communication.

A major category of nonverbal communication involves body positions and gestures. Posture, hand movements, how a person is leaning, self-touching, foot tapping, and so on, fall in this category. Slumping posture seems related to feelings of depression (Suzuki, 1996). These behaviors generally receive little conscious attention from people. However, leaning forward indicates an interest in the interaction.

Many people believe that you can tell if someone is lying by carefully watching the face. However, there is theoretical and empirical reason to think that cues of deception are often emitted through body behavior rather than through facial expression (DePaulo & Friedman, 1998). For example, skillful nurses recognize a patient's squirming, gesturing, pacing, and similar body signs of general restlessness (Blondis & Jackson, 1977). They should also watch for these cues of anxiety when questioning a patient. The basic idea underlying this phenomenon is that through feedback from others and detailed internal feedback, many people learn to control their facial expressions, but they do not normally monitor their body postures and movements. Thus, it seems that many people express, or "leak," their true feelings through body rather than facial cues.

If body cues are important subtle indicators of distress, therapeutic success should be related to the skill of the practitioner in reading body nonverbal cues. In one research project, six studies of psychotherapy measured the nonverbal sensitivity of counselors with a test called the **Profile of Nonverbal Sensitivity (PONS)** (Rosenthal, Hall, DiMatteo, Rogers, & Archer, 1979). The PONS test is a film test that provides a quantitative index of an individual's accuracy at decoding (understanding) facial, body, and voice tone cues of emotion. (See Figure 13–3, NVC-PONS.) In these studies, the counselors were also rated by their supervisors on clinical effectiveness. The studies found that counselors who were sensitive to body communication were more likely to be seen as clinically effective. Two additional studies were done in medical settings. These studies again measured physicians' nonverbal sensitivity with the PONS test. However, they also

Figure 13-3   Nonverbal communication (from the PONS test). Tests can isolate ability to detect information from facial expressions alone or body movements alone, often important in understanding emotional state. *(Reprinted by permission of the Johns Hopkins University Press.)*

Box 13-2   Interpersonal Process Recall

Back in 1962, visitors to Michigan State University were videotaped as they lectured to students and other faculty. Videotaping of lecturers was relatively rare at this time, since the technology had just been developed. Many of the visiting lecturers asked to view their videotape recording right after the lecture. Norman Kagan, clinician and psychological researcher, was surprised to find that the videotape stimulated the visitors' detailed recall of the feelings they had during the lecture. Many recalled points in the lecture during which they were panic-stricken, having forgotten passages in their prepared address, although the videotape showed only slight hesitation in their behavior. The visitors often commented on their own behavior, as they saw themselves as others saw them.

Kagan's observations led to the development of a multifaceted project aimed at understanding and influencing human interaction based on videotape replay as a stimulator of recall of feelings. The project and subsequently developed human relations training program were called Interpersonal Process Recall (IPR). It has been used in the training of psychiatric and family practice residents, medical students, nurses, social workers, psychologists, and psychotherapists.

Participants in the IPR program watch films of actual therapeutic interactions. They are asked to label the affective states (or feelings) of the interactants. Students receive feedback based on the actual affective states labeled by the persons in the films. Another aspect of the training consists of the videotape recording of the student's interview of a trained actor or actress (or patient who has a prepared repertoire) portraying a particular character type or problem. The interaction is observed by other students. The interaction centers around psychosocial problems of the simulated patient. The interaction is later discussed by the videotaped student along with the faculty facilitator and the other students in the small group.

Research on health professionals' training has pointed to techniques like IPR as a successful way to teach interviewing skills to health professionals, both improving their ability to gain psychosocial information from patients and increasing their empathy. It also helps to identify health professionals whose natural interaction skills are so deficient that they need remedial work to improve their relations with their patients. Similar techniques have been adopted at various medical schools around the country.

For further reading:

Kagan, N. (1973). Can technology help us toward reliability in influencing human interaction? *Education Technology, 13,* 44–51.

Werner, A. M., & Schneider, J. M. (1974). Teaching medical students interactional skills: A research-based course in the doctor-patient relationship. *New England Journal of Medicine, 290,* 1232–1237.

Box 13-3   DEE-nar: What's in a Name?

DEE-nar is the pronunciation of the acronym DNAR, which stands for Do Not Attempt Resuscitation. This notation is written in the hospital medical charts of some terminally ill patients. It tells the medical staff to not intervene (let the patient die) if the heart stops beating or breathing ceases.

Traditionally, this instruction has been written as DNR—Do Not Resuscitate. However, some medical ethicists believe that DNR incorrectly implies that the patient could usually be resuscitated, but that the physician is coldly letting the patient die. By inserting the word "attempt," some believe that perceptions of the situation could be improved (D. C. Hadorn, 1989, DNAR, NEJM, 320, 673.). Do you think this minor shift in terminology has any impact on the situation, and if so, does it change things for the better or for the worse?

---

obtained actual patients' ratings of the interpersonal effectiveness of their physicians. It was found that physicians who were most sensitive to body nonverbal communication received the highest ratings of patient satisfaction with treatment (DiMatteo, Friedman, & Taranta, 1979; DiMatteo, Taranta, Friedman, & Prince, 1980). Furthermore, additional work suggests that physician sensitivity to vocal cues (which are also hard to control) is related to patient cooperation—more sensitive physicians experienced fewer unrescheduled appointment cancellations (DiMatteo, Hays, & Prince, 1986).

It is impossible to assign a particular, immutable meaning to each body movement or voice cue. However, any changes in normal behavior are probably important as cues to deception, including such things as clenched fists, hand, foot, or body shaking, tapping, drumming, smoking, and tightly closed arms or legs.

In sum, nonverbal communication is especially important in medical settings. Fortunately, it is no longer necessary for medical practitioners to rely solely on concepts like intuition and empathy in dealing with subtle, interpersonal aspects of health care. We can become more specific about what we mean by the "tone," "atmosphere," or "rapport" of practitioner-patient interactions.

Keeping in mind issues of medical jargon and issues of nonverbal communication, we can now further analyze the medical interview.

INTERVIEWING IN THE HEALTH CARE CONTEXT

As a professor and researcher at the Institute for Sex Research at Indiana University at Bloomington, Dr. Alfred C. Kinsey was one of the most widely known scientists of the 20th century. Kinsey devoted most of his life to the study of human sexual behavior (of adults and children) by taking over 18,000 sexual histories of individuals from every walk of life. Overall, these people had engaged in an enormous range of sexual behaviors. Kinsey's research was groundbreaking, and his analyses of sexual behavior were astoundingly complete. Kinsey interviewed various people in the country, ranging from prostitutes and Bowery bums to powerful members of the community and members of the clergy. It is fascinating that this work was conducted primarily during the 1940s and 1950s, times when the subject of sexuality was taboo (Pomeroy, 1972).

In these interviews, Kinsey was able to elicit an extraordinary amount of detailed, sensitive information about respondents' most private behaviors. Kinsey was able to elicit, even from his most inhibited subjects, detailed accounts of their masturbation habits, of their premarital and extramarital sexual behavior, and of their sexual behavior with animals. People revealed much to Kinsey and his colleagues that they had never before told anyone.

The personal interview is a major tool of health care professionals for gathering information about the patient's medical history. It is also useful in discovering a comprehensive picture of the present problems the patient is experiencing. The widespread use of this technique is based, however, on the incorrect assumption that the interview is a straightforward, simple way to collect health information. It is a mistake to assume that, as usually conducted, the interview yields valid information. Actually, interviewing persons about medical facts is not in any way similar to retrieving information from a computer bank or from written files. Aspects of human memory, understanding of the questions, motivation to answer the questions, and especially the quality of the practitioner-patient relationship are crucial aspects of the process of interviewing and strongly affect the kind of information retrieved.

One important series of studies involved thousands of individuals responding to questions about their present and past health; the responses were then compared with the information in their written medical records (Cannell, Oksenberg, & Converse, 1977). Overall, this research found serious problems with the medical interview. For example, the studies showed a very high level of underreporting of illness incidents. Between 12 and 17 percent of recorded hospital episodes were not reported by people in their health interviews, and 23 to 26 percent of recent physician visits were not reported. Furthermore, it was found that at least 50 percent of the medical conditions that appeared in the medical records were not reported by the respondents in the interviews. Reliance on interviewing can thus be quite hazardous. Fortunately, the research also indicated that problems such as underreporting can be remedied.

Interestingly, inaccuracies in interview results are not strongly related to characteristics of the respondents (patients). Rather, the characteristics of the interview itself were more important. Of course, people differ in the extent to which they provide accurate information about their condition, but the respondents' social characteristics and even level of medical sophistication are not so important as factors in the interview situation itself. How can accurate answers be obtained? What makes an interview bad or good? The following factors are especially relevant.

Interviewer Bias

Kinsey never asked whether a subject had ever engaged in a particular sexual activity, such as sex with an animal. Instead, he asked when was the first time that the respondent engaged in the activity. For example: "When did you first have sexual intercourse with an animal?" Kinsey thus communicated the acceptability of the activity. The burden was then on the respondent to disavow the behavior; the response, "I never did that," could be taken as probably true. In an analogous situation, a doctor might ask, "How many times have you had venereal disease?" rather than "You never had VD, did you?" Such questioning is important, for example, to alert the doctor to the possibility that the patient has been exposed to the AIDS virus.

The phenomenon in which a respondent's answer is influenced by the interviewer is known as **interviewer bias**.

Careful phrasing of the question (such as asking "when" instead of "whether") is one way of making various answers socially acceptable and thus minimizing bias. The reporting of an event is more likely to be distorted in a socially desirable direction.

People tend to underreport embarrassing conditions such as disorders of the reproductive system and diseases of the nervous system. Reporting is higher and more accurate for such diseases as gall bladder problems. This underreporting of threatening events can be partly reduced by creating an atmosphere in which the individual is not made to feel unusual because of having the diseases or condition. Relatedly, avoidance of medical jargon lessens the chance that a patient will fabricate a response so as not to have to admit a lack of understanding of the question. Incidentally, it turns out (according to Kinsey's long-time associate, Wardell Pomeroy) that of all the issues considered in the interview, the most embarrassing question, particularly for women, turned out to be "How much do you weigh?" (Pomeroy, 1972). Matters that seem routine to the practitioner may be very embarrassing to the patient unless proper expectations are created.

Bias can sometimes be minimized by suggesting a wide range of possible answers to the patient. Kinsey would sometimes encounter a respondent who found it hard to estimate the frequency with which he or she had engaged in a particular sexual practice. Kinsey was on guard against respondents who were highly suggestible. Thus, a range of possible frequencies, such as once a week, four times a week, more than twenty times a week, or once a year, were suggested. In this way, Kinsey did not communicate to the respondent an idea of what would be considered an appropriate answer.

Sometimes interviewer bias is the result of characteristics of the interviewer (Gordon, 1980). For example, it has been shown that white people are less willing to make prejudiced comments about blacks to black interviewers, and non-Jews are less willing to make negative comments about Jews to Jewish interviewers. Therefore, we might expect male patients to be less willing to discuss marital problems with female doctors than with male doctors. Or medical problems related to poverty might go unmentioned to an obviously wealthy physician. Such matters can be difficult to deal with, since a health provider obviously cannot change his or her sex or status. However, the provider can do certain things to insure an open, supportive atmosphere in which personal characteristics of the provider become less salient.

Positive Regard

Cannell found in his interview research that the interpersonal dynamics of the interaction between the interviewer and the respondent strongly influence the accuracy of reporting. The behavior of many health interviewers was observed by the researchers and subjected to intense scrutiny. An important set of interviewer errors emerged. One of the most striking findings of the research was that the interviewer delivered positive feedback ("yes," "um hum," nods, etc.) for both good and poor respondent behavior. Unfortunately, adequate responses received proportionately fewer positive feedback responses than did less desirable answers. In fact, the worst possible response on the part of the patient, that is, a refusal to answer the question, received the most positive feedback. When the patients were uncooperative, the interviewers acted warmly, thus rewarding and encouraging patients for being uncooperative.

Feedback, if properly used, is an effective means of influencing the behavior of respondents in desired directions. Laboratory studies in social and learning psychology have shown that an experimenter can reinforce specified classes of respondent verbal behavior. For example, some studies have shown that nodding used as a reinforcement can increase respondents' production of plural nouns. Expressed attitudes toward various topics have also been shown to be reinforceable—that is, the listener can subtly reward a speaker for expressing some attitudes and not reward him or her for others, thereby increasing the expression of the first attitudes.

The number of health events reported is greater in an interview with proper reinforcement (Marquis, 1970). Out of 429 interviews, the interview that produced the most information was one in which for every report of morbidity (health symptom, condition, illness, or residual impairment), the interviewer used a programmed reinforcing statement. These statements were used in a natural tone with the interviewer looking directly at the respondent. They included such statements as:

"Yes, that is the kind of information we need."
"This is all valuable information."
"Yes, we need to know about things like that."
"I see, you had [repeat what respondent said]."

The interviewer also smiled, leaned forward, and used appropriate hand gestures.

In the control condition, the interviewer did not look at the respondent, lean forward, smile, or use hand gestures. In effect, the interviewer eliminated what some practitioners would consider superfluous activity, and the interview was conducted in a very businesslike manner, as are most medical interviews. This interview was very poor and ineffective.

The first step toward an effective practitioner-patient relationship involves encouraging the patient to disclose his or her troubles and feelings while offering unconditional **positive regard** (Rodin & Janis, 1982). The provider should not reward a close-mouthed, nondisclosing patient. But once the patient is talking about his or her condition, the provider should give positive responses no matter what the nature of the medical problem. An effective practitioner is generally nonjudgmental.

Precision of Questioning

The questions chosen by Kinsey were always simple as well as single-barreled; that is, only one concept was dealt with in each question. For example, if a respondent was asked about becoming aroused after seeing nude pictures, the effect of male and female pictures were asked about separately. If questioned about male and female pictures, most males would say, "Yes, I am aroused by female pictures." Unfortunately, in this way, arousal from seeing male nudes would not have to be admitted to answer the question fully. Many heterosexual physicians do not find out that their patients have had homosexual experiences; misdiagnoses may result.

Health professionals often ask for, and as a result receive, little information of any value from their patients. If a physician were to ask a double-barreled question like, "Do you sleep better now and does your back hurt less?" a "yes" response would be confusing. The health professional does not know whether the sleep, the back, or both, are better. If the meaning of the patient's response is not obvious immediately, the question is not good (Gordon, 1980).

The careful sequencing of questions can be important. In Kinsey's research, impersonal, nonthreatening questions were asked first, with the interviewer working slowly to the more sensitive topics. Common questions about the subject's childhood (where he or she lived, etc.) were asked. Religion and early sex education followed. Then questions about current sexual practices were asked. What was considered sensitive for the individual depended upon the meaning of that particular issue for the person. The questions became quite detailed (e.g., fantasies during masturbation). Any leads into rare or unusual sexual activity were followed up by the researchers with additional questions that were reserved for these situations. Throughout the interview, Kinsey was careful to use the patient's own language in describing a particular sexual practice. Progressing from less personal to more personal questions is necessary because of patients' natural aversions to the invasion of their privacy.

In eliciting relevant information from patients, it is also useful to begin with general questions and gradually become more specific, although never becoming too limiting. The process of starting the interview with the most broad questions and then moving to more specific detailed questions is called **narrowing.** This method is particularly useful for eliciting spontaneous patient attitudes. A patient will tend to lead the interview toward the specific issue that he or she is interested in and that is relevant to his or her life. Nevertheless, it is also important to help the patient to continue talking freely. Thus, questions should be worded in such a way as to elicit complex answers in many cases—particularly when the health care professional wishes to explore a number of related issues. While the **closed-ended** question can be answered very quickly, the **open-ended** question gives the patient a chance to elaborate and to provide valuable information.

Example
Closed-ended: Was the pain sharp or dull?
Open-ended: Tell me about the pain—what was it like?

When combined with interviewer bias, the wording of a closed-ended question can lead a patient to a particular response that might in fact be inaccurate. For example, questions like "You've been taking your medication, haven't you?" or "You aren't having any more pain, are you?" lead the patient directly to a response that is drastically limited by the expectations of the health professional. Making matters even worse, there is some evidence that closed questioning is more likely to be directed at patients who are young, less educated, lower status, and nonwhite (Stiles, Putnam, & Jacob, 1982). In other words, patients already facing relatively more problems in caring for their health may be the most likely to encounter poor communication.

If deception is suspected, it is important to pay close attention to the patient's responses and behaviors, especially to nonverbal cues. To minimize deception in Kinsey's research, simple questions were asked in rapid succession in an attempt to insure that patients would answer spontaneously without too much time to think and to fabricate responses. Kinsey also maintained eye contact with his subjects. If he thought that the respondent was not telling the truth, he would pay close attention to the nonverbal clues given by the respondent, and he would repeat the question. If the suspicion still remained, Kinsey would confront the interviewee, asking "Now, will you please give the story to me straight?"

In Kinsey's research, guarding against respondents' covering up information was done by cross-checking histories of husband and wife, where possible. Furthermore, a number of retakes were done two to four years after the first interview. Health practitioners should similarly be on the lookout for information that confirms or disconfirms information gathered in the initial interview. Conversations with relatives, the results of medical tests and exams, and the overall cohesiveness of a medical condition or story are valuable checks on interview information.

Finally, it should be noted that many cognitive factors can affect interview responses (Cannell, Oksenberg, & Converse, 1977). As one might guess, as the time between an event and its recall (the interview) increases, there is increased underreporting of the event. What is surprising is the rapidity with which the failure to report information increases with time. In one study of visits to physicians, for example, the failure to report the visit increased from 15 percent one week after the visit to 30 percent two weeks after the visit.

Consider **salience.** Events that are more important to the individual are more completely and accurately remembered than events of less importance. Note, however, that this is subjective importance. An event may be very useful to know about for the doctor, but the patient will not report it unless it had an important impact on the patient's life. While there is no single way directly to improve the patient's cognitive functioning in an interview, proper use of the techniques described above will tend to have a beneficial effect.

SUMMARY AND CONCLUSION

Communication between practitioners and patients, both verbal and nonverbal, is a key element in effective medical care. Sensitivity to nonverbal communication and good interviewing skills are essential to proper diagnoses. Avoidance of jargon, coupled with an understanding of the patient's frame of reference, is crucial to the transfer of information necessary in treatment. Perhaps most importantly, the process of communication is the central component in the creation of the rapport and positive expectations that are so important to health care. Psychology provides knowledge of specific verbal and nonverbal skills that can be learned and practiced by health professionals as part of their medical training.

A physician's sensitivity to nonverbal communication provides valuable insight to information that a patient may not be willing to verbally impart, and utilizing both these verbal and nonverbal cues in practice with good interviewing skills will enable proper and accurate diagnoses and treatment—which is not to underestimate the importance of the patient's ability to read nonverbal cues from their caregivers. The physician's facial expressions, gestures, and the manner in speaking have a significant effect upon the willingness of a patient to give and understand information and on his or her confidence of treatment. Excessive use of Medspeak may not only serve as a scapegoat for practitioners' avoidance of providing vital socioemotional care, but can also confuse patients into misunderstanding their illness and care. By conducting a medical interview, the health practitioner is compiling valuable information from which diagnoses and treatment will be derived. Therefore, it is vital that the interview be conducted in a manner in which this information is as accurate and thorough as possible.

Recommended Additional Readings

DePaulo, Bella M. & Friedman, Howard S. (1998). Nonverbal communication. In D. Gilbert, S. Fiske, & G. Lindzey (Eds.). *Handbook of Social Psychology* (4th ed., Vol. II, pp. 3–40). Boston: McGraw Hill.

Hoyle, Leigh, & Reiser, Morton F. (1992). *The patient: Biological, psychological, and social dimensions of medical practice.* (3rd ed.). New York: Plenum Medical Book Co.

Roter, Debra, & Hall, Judith A. (1992). *Doctors talking with patients/patients talking with doctors: Improving communication in medical visits.* Westport, CT: Auburn House.

Key Concepts

instrumental care

socioemotional care

linguistic relativity

Medspeak

nonverbal communication
    body language, positions, gestures
    facial expression
    touch

social comparison

King's touch or royal touch

"laying on of the hands"

therapeutic touching

gaze

tone of voice

smells

distance: Edward Hall's spatial zones
    intimate distance
    personal distance
    social distance
    public distance

cue discrepancy

deception

immediacy

Profile of Nonverbal Sensitivity (PONS)

interviewer bias

positive regard

narrowing

closed-ended and open-ended questions

salienc

Chapter 14

HEALTH CARE PROFESSIONALS AND HOSPITALS

Doctors are often imagined to be attractive and wise men who are able to solve a tremendous variety of health problems. In other words, many people hold a stereotypical image of the health care professional. The doctor's role may be thought to resemble that of Dr. Albert Schweitzer, the Nobel Peace Prize winner who spent many years ministering to poor people in Africa. Nurses may be imagined to resemble Florence Nightingale, the 19th-century English reformer who improved the training of nurses and the care of patients. In actuality, however, the role of health care professionals is held by a variety of kinds of people, is rarely glamorous, and is stressful and difficult. The Albert Schweitzers with a consuming dedication to help humanity are quite rare. Health professionals themselves are various types of people with various problems of their own.

Physicians, nurses, nurse practitioners, medical social workers, and others on the traditional medical team usually experience intrinsic rewards in helping people, in doing socially useful work, in being exposed to a wide range of human experience, and in facing problems that are intellectually challenging. Hospitals generally function to facilitate treatment and healing. However, health care professionals pay a price in terms of emotional distress, and hospitals can be jungles of pressures in training and in practice. In addition to the triumphs, there is a tremendous psychological drain in taking responsibility for other people's lives and encountering disease and death. Health psychologists are now entering these arenas.

Earlier in this book, we have discussed how health practitioners and the health care system can best promote health and treat patients, but in this chapter we turn the tables and examine health care professionals themselves, as well as the hospitals. We consider characteristics of medical training and of practice, and special problems that health care professionals experience, including physician impairment. We suggest possible solutions for dealing with these problems, both on an individual and on an aggregate level, and examine what structural changes in the medical care system might help to minimize these stresses. Relatedly, the stress of decision-making under uncertainty—which health professionals experience every day—is analyzed.

There are two important reasons why an entire chapter is devoted to understanding the position of the practicing health care professional. First, individuals in the health care professions who are reading about the psychological aspects of medicine will recognize that the psychological aspects of their own lives affect their work. Second, students of psychology need to understand the experiences of medical professionals in order to work more effectively with them. A social scientist who works in the health care field cannot work in a vacuum; communication between the psychologist and the medical professional can be effective only if they understand each other (Stone et al., 1987).

The stresses of health care begin with medical education, and that is where we begin our discussion.

MEDICAL TRAINING

Medical School

Medical students enter training with high expectations; they have reached the pinnacle of their student careers after having prepared for years for this experience. Often, reality does not coincide with these expectations, however, and the resulting problems may be serious.

A popular stereotype of the beginning medical student is someone who is highly idealistic and deeply concerned with the physical, emotional, and social problems that people face. For decades, entering medical students have expressed a hope to be interpersonally sensitive and to "help people" (Radest, 2000; Rogoff, 1957), but actually, by the time the student has begun the first year of medical school, the potential physician has been through many anxiety-provoking experiences that have begun to erode this idealism (Becker, Geer, Hughes, & Strauss, 1961; Wear & Bickel, 2000).

Premedical education is highly competitive, although the competition has eased slightly in recent years. The distress brought about by the competitive pressures of premedical education is often compounded by the fact that some medical school admission criteria are of questionable validity. While the medical profession espouses the belief that a physician should be people oriented and exhibit a sensitive interpersonal approach to patients, almost all of the formal criteria used by most medical schools for admission are academic criteria, such as MCAT (Medical College Admission Test of the Association of American Medical Colleges) scores and grades in science courses. The admission interview is important in some schools, but initial screening is usually on the basis of scientific promise. The applicant to medical school can insure being included in the first wave of the admission procedure by becoming heavily technically oriented. A different admission model—under which all students are evaluated *first* on social and interpersonal grounds and then screened for scientific competence—is quite rare.

Medical school applicants learn that there is a division between their own expectations, or image of the physician's role, and the realities of admission. However, the successful applicant to medical school often expects that constant attention to technical issues, such as organic chemistry, is a phenomenon of premedical days and that, once in medical school, an orientation toward people can be resumed. Unfortunately, idealization of the professional role is often once more frustrated in the medical student. During the first two years of medical school, the major goal of most medical school faculty is to teach as much technical information to the medical students as possible. This goal has an unspoken corollary—that the medical students recognize their ignorance.

Few students receive mostly A's in medical school, although nearly all have received A's as long as they can remember. This overwhelming onslaught of material presented by the faculty humbles many medical students and encourages caution. This approach is considered important in making a physician. However, it demands enormous adjustment on the part of the medical student. This process continues for the first two years of medical school (the preclinical years) in which the academic work is concentrated. After a full year of learning a tremendous amount of basic material about a normal human body, and another year of learning all of the possible diseases a patient can experience, the medical students is then thrust into the world of serious patient care.

During the third and fourth years of medical school, the typical medical student serves as a clinical clerk, although many students now have some community exposure to patients right from their first year. The students work on the wards with interns and residents, attempting to make diagnoses and helping to plan and administer treatments. Feelings of inconsistency are often intensified as the medical students, learning a new role, come to grips with the fact that their self-image as a medical student does not always coincide with reality. In the classic research in this area, the realms in which inconsistency is experienced are called the **zone of discontinuity** (Becker & Geer, 1958; Becker, Geer, Hughes, & Strauss, 1961).

The first conflict, or discontinuity, for the medical student arises right away. The student has to resolve the problem that there is more material to be learned than is humanly possible in the time given. First-year medical students often complain that there is more material to be memorized in a particular time period than can even be read. Furthermore, medical students become anxious thinking about taking care of patients later and realizing that they might be missing a critical piece of information, something that was taught but they failed to grasp and memorize. And as they begin to recognize their own limitations, students have to understand that medical knowledge itself is limited. There is a disagreement among even the most prominent physicians as to how to treat patients; and medicine does not have all the answers. Students find that their faculty members do not always know what to do about a medical problem, and, in addition, many diseases are incurable (Fox, 1959).

Second, medical students often become frustrated when they recognize that they may be becoming cold and callous toward their patients in dealing with the patients' emotional problems. Students focus on a central goal of finishing the necessary laboratory tests and completing the charts. They may begin to cut corners and save minutes in order to be able to sleep during nights on which they are on call. They may recognize that they are developing unhealthy attitudes toward patients and their feelings, but when the demands of clinical work are high, idealism is threatened. This loss of idealism, with the resultant change in expectations, can be a significant source of anxiety for medical students.

Another psychological strain for medical or nursing students is their initial contact with human suffering and death. When a medical student first faces a patient who is severely ill or badly hurt, the anxiety can be overwhelming. Conflict arises within the student, since the only stance the student can take with the patient is that of calm assurance. This calm assurance is expected by patients and also by colleagues; regardless of how much anxiety a student is experiencing, confidence must be projected. As responsibility increases for the student, there is less time to pay attention to internal fears and emotions. However, the need to play the part of the assured professional with competence and confidence eventually helps the student to feel in control (Lief & Fox, 1963).

Finally, student physicians often experience identity crises, which is understandable since the medical student has a dual identity. Among peers and in the eyes of the faculty, the medical student is a "student." But to patients, the medical student is a "doctor." While working with patients, the medical student begins to feel like a doctor, but then the student receives constant reminders from faculty and fellow students that a medical student is not a physician. This dual identity, or **role conflict,** is a common source of stress to medical students.

The stringent medical curriculum often strains the personal lives of medical students (Cartwright, 1979; Distlehorst, Dunnington, & Folse, 2000; Shem, 1978). To survive academically, some students have to become compulsive about their work, leaving little time for recreation, friends, and family. Without ties to the "outside world," students lose perspective on what they are doing and miss the emotional support that friends and family can provide.

In sum, the medical student's self-image is systematically broken down by faculty members, who then proceed to build it up again in the mold of the profession. Many faculty members place the major emphasis on technical accomplishments, research activity, and on becoming a scientist. Many students feel abused in the hierarchical system of medical training, and the treatment they receive from others can translate into their own overall feeling of disrespect for patients. Thus, aspects of the medical school experience may sometimes foster cynicism and a lack of recognition of patients' emotional and social needs (Becker & Geer, 1958; Bok, 1984; Christie & Merton, 1958; Distlehorst, Dunnington, & Folse, 2000; Gough & Hall, 1977; Rosenberg, 1979; Wear & Bickel, 2000).

Improving Medical Education

Student culture involves communication and shared understanding among students in a medical school class. Through informal means, students provide information and support for each other—particularly in assessing and validating the demands of the faculty. In facing the tension experienced during medical education, many students are able to turn to their group members for help (Becker, Geer, Hughes, & Strauss, 1961). This natural response can be used to improve the environment. At some medical schools, discussion groups for medical students are organized by counseling services (sometimes headed by psychological "facilitators"), and they often receive heavy use.

A second mechanism by which medical students cope with the stress of medical school is through their identification with the faculty. Students learn the role of the health professional by watching physicians and sharing a sense of colleagueship with them. As they gain clinical experience, follow in their teachers' footsteps, and are given responsibility for patients, students are rewarded by the fact that they are trusted by others to be competent enough to handle important situations. A new identity is developed through comparison and interaction with established professionals. When the faculty members are well adjusted and lead balanced lives, they set a good example for their students.

A third influence on student coping involves the structure of medical training. The traditional biomedical disease model, which has, up until recent years, been part of the socialization process for the medical student, is now slowly being replaced by elements of the biopsychosocial or health psychology model of medicine. Slowly, medical school training is beginning to incorporate into the study of medicine an understanding of how the social forces, lifestyle preferences, and maladaptive behaviors of patients affect their health. Such ideas can affect the structure of training as well. However, most medical school curricula have a long way to go to reach such an end (Bok, 1984).

A good choice of specialty involves the appropriate utilization of an individual's talents and abilities. For example, a physician who wants close and reciprocal relationships with patients will do well to choose a specialty such as internal medicine, psychiatry, or family practice, all of which entail continual and intense contact with patients. On the other hand, individuals who need some distance from patients do best to choose surgery, radiology, or other consulting subspecialties. A particularly stressful situation will occur if, for example, a physician who is prone to isolation and withdrawal from people chooses a specialty that demands intimacy. Sometimes, medical schools admit students of certain backgrounds and interests in the hope that they will become certain types of physicians. For example, it is hoped that some students will eventually practice in medically underserved rural areas. An evaluation of such a program found that specially recruited rural-based students were indeed much more likely to return to practice family medicine in a rural, underserved area (Rabinowitz, 1988).

In the 1980s, Harvard Medical School began experimenting with a new approach to medical education termed **New Pathway.** The New Pathway program emphasized behaviors and attitudes related to so-called "humanistic medicine," including many of the health psychology issues covered in this book (Taylor & Moore, 1994). The program included problem-based learning tutorials focused around patients (in a broad context), with coordinated lectures and clinical experiences. Since Harvard is a leading medical school, this program was watched closely, and it influenced other medical schools.

An evaluation of the long-term effects of this innovative curriculum was done by conducting telephone interviews of 100 graduates 10 years later (50 who had studied the new curriculum and 50 who had studied the traditional curriculum in a randomized trial) (Peters, Greenberger-Rosovsky, Crowder, Block, & Moore, 2000) Overall, the New Pathway students and the traditional students did not differ that much. It did turn out, however, that 40 percent of the New Pathway students but only 18 percent of the traditional students went on to practice primary care or psychiatry, probably because the New Pathway students had significantly more exposure to these medical fields and mentors. Although the two groups of physicians were mostly similar in their orientations, the New Pathways students were more likely than were traditional students to believe that faculty from the first two years continue to influence their thinking many years later. In short, the basic medical model still prevailed, even though the altered training did dramatically increase interest in and awareness of the broader psychosocial nature of health.

A final suggestion for improvement involves a long-term apprenticeship program for medical training.

An Alternative: Long-Term Apprenticeship

Medical education is run by physicians who have been through its socialization forces and find it hard to think of other models of training. What can be done to break this vicious cycle in which generation after generation of physicians suffer through training that all admit has many flaws? One possibility is a change to a long-term apprenticeship model (Friedman, 1987b).

Changes to medical training are often resisted on the basis of two structural arguments. The first is that there is a tremendous amount of information and skill that must be mastered by a physician. So, it is argued, there must be years and years of intensive learning and practice, 16 hours a day or more, with little time for other activities. This argument is seen to be a very weak one when it is recognized that medical knowledge changes rapidly; the knowledge learned in 1970, or even 1980, is virtually useless today. Yet physicians practice successfully for a lifetime. They engage in *continuing* education rather than relying on their early training.

The second argument for the current medical education system is primarily economic. It is argued on the one hand that medical education is so expensive that it must be very intensive, and on the other hand, that if the medical students and residents did not put in long hours working in hospitals, the costs of hospitalization would be too high. The problem with this argument is that medical students work so hard in school for so many years and amass so much educational debt that they are forced to charge huge fees when they finally do set up a medical practice. In other words, the society pays the economic costs anyway, but does so in a different way.

The competing needs of medical education can be addressed by a **long-term apprenticeship model** (Friedman, 1987b). In this model, medical education never ends, but the workload at any given time in a physician's life is much more reasonable. First, premedical students obtain a liberal arts college education, which teaches them to think, prepares them for a lifetime of learning, and exposes them to the ethical values needed for dealing with other people's lives. Such well-rounded students would be given preference for medical school admissions.

Second, the student enters a new medical training system and progresses through different stages that may last a lifetime! Classroom education is mixed with clinical experience appropriate to the student's knowledge and skills. From the very beginning, students have ties to "real" patients and access to medical school faculty. As the student masters more material, he or she does more direct patient care and also begins to teach and monitor other students. Most physicians would then remain in this system, becoming more and more expert, for most if not all of their careers.

Because the student works for many years providing services, no high education costs are incurred. In fact, medical students can be paid a salary! Of course, they will not earn a fortune in their later years. Similarly, because the training is a lifelong process, the students will have time for other activities. There are more than enough physicians to service the basic medical needs of the American population, especially when other health care providers are brought onto the team.

This model of lifetime training and teaching requires a certain degree of group practice and centralization (with each group having physicians with different levels of expertise), but most physicians are now practicing in groups anyway. In most cities, the group practices would have ties to a medical school, but they could function relatively autonomously, as they now do. The structure could be more socialistic, with a national system, or more capitalistic, with various groups competing for patients. The model might not work for an isolated rural physician, but such practices are rapidly disappearing in any case.

In addition to providing more stable lives for physicians (physically and economically), this approach has many other benefits. Students truly dedicated to a lifetime of helping others would be more likely to apply to medical school. Economically disadvantaged students would be encouraged to consider a medical career, whereas students seeking only money would avoid it. Women could enter medicine without having to worry about waiting until age 35 or 36 to have children, since the early years of training would be more flexible. More physicians would be able to be involved in teaching. Continuing education would be stronger and more natural, since it would be an integral part of the training, rather than an "add-on." Because of ties to other physicians, the stress of medical practice would be reduced.

In sum, a new model of medical education can be instituted by more closely matching the training with the realities of modern practice. Physicians would give up high incomes late in their careers in return for more time and money earlier in their careers. Ongoing ties with other physicians and with medical schools would be necessary. And the selection and training of physicians would be more in line with the exigencies of the health psychology model.

STRESS AND ITS EFFECTS ON PRACTICING HEALTH CARE PROFESSIONALS

A revealing folk tale about doctors describes the case of a cancer patient who had been treated by a famous surgeon, but died and went to heaven. While waiting in line to enter the pearly gates, the patient was surprised to see a doctor walk to the front of the line and enter. The patient wondered to one of the angels whether he was imagining things or whether doctors get special treatment in heaven. The angel answered, "That's no doctor. That's God playing doctor."

This story hints at the many contradictions surrounding the doctor's role, contradictions that can be extremely stressful. In one large cross-cultural study of professional men, it was found that American physicians have a higher incidence of heart disease than other professionals (King, 1970). Recurrent emergency calls for physicians can bring about special stresses. The most important factor, of course, is the emotional response of the health care professionals to the events in their lives; but many are lacking the time and skills to cope with the demands of their profession in an adaptive way.

Many studies have examined health professional stress. This research suffers from methodological problems, however, because distressing symptoms tend to be underreported and covered up by health care professionals. When asked whether they experience various symptoms, many health care professionals who in fact do suffer these impairments simply deny that they do. It is also true that colleagues often overprotect the stressed health professionals instead of referring them to rehabilitative treatment. Yet classic symptoms of occupational stress are highly prevalent among physicians and dentists.

Suicide is the most drastic response to stress, and perhaps one-quarter of the deaths among physicians under the age of 40 are suicides. (This figure probably involves underreporting.) Suicide also has been found to be more prevalent in dentistry and pharmacy and among medical students than in the general population (Aasland, Ekeberg, & Schweder, 2001; Council Report, 1987; Everson & Fraumeni, 1975; Rose & Rosow, 1973; Simon, 1986). Owing to their access to drugs and their knowledge of anatomy and physiology, they may be more likely to succeed at suicide. However, in many physician suicides, the distressed persons simply shoot themselves. Interestingly, nurses, social workers, teachers, and clergy are not at special risk.

Workers in medical environments are also more likely to contract infectious diseases such as hepatitis and tuberculosis. In addition, there are specialty occupational

*"And all my friends told me it would be wonderful to
be married to a godlike surgeon."*

Figure 14-1   The traditional doctor's role engenders many contradictions.

(Copyright Howard S. Friedman. Drawing by Robin Jensen.) Reprinted by permission

hazards—health care professionals involved in anesthesiology sometimes develop lymphomas and leukemias from the gases used in anesthetizing patients, whereas those who work closely with x-rays may suffer the effects of exposure to radiation. These physical occupational hazards can play some role in stress-related problems.

Impaired Health Professionals

Drug abuse among physicians is a major problem. Of all the physicians who are now licensed, perhaps five percent of them may be drug abusers. Among health professionals, it is estimated that the incidence of drug abuse is many times higher than in the general population (Hughes et al., 1999). Alcoholism is also a serious problem.

Health care professionals, particularly physicians, often strongly resist recognition of the fact that they (or any of their peers) are impaired. A **cloak of silence** is the usual reaction to the problem. Impaired physicians and other health care professionals deny that their problems are real and avoid assistance. It is usually only after alcoholism or drug abuse has severely interfered with a physician's practice and personal life that the problem comes to the attention of someone who can help. Recognizing the problem, the American Medical Association and the various state associations have set up Impaired Physicians Committees and programs (Shore, 1987; Talbott, Gallegos, Wilson, & Porter, 1987).

There are a few positions in society in which direct and immediate danger to other people can result from the inability of the individual to function effectively; one of these roles is that of airline pilots. Federal Aviation Administration regulations prohibit pilots from drinking or taking drugs before a flight; careful precautions are taken to assure that pilots comply with these rules. But no immediate, direct regulations or controlling mechanisms exist for the medical profession. Medical professionals are relatively autonomous in their work. There is abundant evidence of the harm that has come to patients as a result of the inability of health care professionals to function effectively because of the influence of drugs and alcohol. A classic example is that of the Marcus twins—two New York gynecologists who were addicted to barbiturates and died of the addiction. However, this addiction was concealed from public view throughout the time they were practicing in a large New York hospital.

It is difficult to identify a physician as an alcoholic or drug abuser and take steps to rehabilitate this physician. Part of the problem lies in the unwillingness of physicians and other health care professionals to interfere with the freedom of physicians to treat patients in their own way. It may also be difficult for an observer to understand the source of the impaired physician's strange behavior. Accusations are unlikely to be made. Therefore, colleagues attempt to normalize the behavior of the physician until something drastic happens—such as a patient recognizing that the physician is unable to deal with the task at hand, or severe consequences befalling a patient. Colleagues then fulfill their moral and legal responsibilities and remove the doctor from practice. In short, impaired physicians present outstanding difficulties. Physician addicts often ultimately commit suicide, and many physician patients leave the hospital against medical advice.

In sum, common causes of physician impairment are the physical and emotional demands of the profession; the enormous amount of time required for training and practice; the easy availability of drugs; and excessive professional autonomy. However, research suggests another key factor: The presence or absence of such problems as drug addiction and suicide tends to be correlated primarily with (poor) life adjustment prior to medical school (Vaillant, Sobowale, & McArthur, 1972). In this longitudinal study of physicians, George Vaillant and colleagues found that emotional adjustment before medical school, even as early as childhood, was highly correlated with adjustment to the pressures of the physician's role. Individuals who go into the medical field unprepared emotionally because of their backgrounds and early adjustment have a great deal of difficulty adjusting to the pressures and strains of a medical career.

Treatment

Increasingly, there have been attempts to identify and treat impaired physicians and those in danger of suicide. An information telephone number and a help hotline are available within various state medical association headquarters to allow physicians to report suspicious behavior by their colleagues or else to ask for help themselves. Family members also can call the telephone numbers to request help for an impaired physician. This arrangement insures the confidentiality of the report and allows trained professionals to contact the physician whose behavior is in question. Care can then be offered on a completely confidential basis to the physicians and also to members of their families.

Formal programs for alcoholism and drug detoxification have been developed by these medical societies, and referral to psychiatrists and psychologists who have expertise in working with the special problems of physicians can be arranged. Sometimes, of course, disciplinary action against the physician must take place. The purpose is usually not punishment, but rather the rehabilitation of the physician. However, all in all, physicians have not applied the rigor and intensity of efforts to this problem that they have shown with regard to many other issues.

In residency or in medical school, programs can be designed to promote adjustment and the sharing of problems among physicians-in-training. Instead of an atmosphere of competition, physicians-in-training could develop a sense of personal responsibility for their own and their colleagues' well-being. Support groups, even including spouses or significant others, could do much to strengthen the feeling among the physicians-in-training that they are not fighting an uphill battle alone.

Second, residents, interns, and medical students can be encouraged to utilize existing mental health facilities for support as a **preventive** measure instead of only to resolve a crisis. Part of the physicians' training in behavioral science and psychosocial issues in medical care should include understanding psychosocial issues in their own life. Third, each residency and medical school program can identify faculty members who are visible and available to help with problems at their early stages. Finally, physicians-in-training should be given a chance to participate in making decisions about the structure of their educational programs.

A final great source of stress on physicians is the necessity of making many decisions, some of which involve life and death. The process of decision-making and its results are a key aspect of the life of the health professional. It is a topic worthy of separate consideration.

DECISION-MAKING IN HEALTH CARE

Uncertainty

An unusually sensitive and perceptive physician practicing in a rural area of Minnesota told the following story (Hilfiker, 1984). Having delivered the healthy baby of his patient (named Barb) two years earlier, he was pleased when she happily appeared in his office saying she thought she was again pregnant. She had all the signs of pregnancy, but her urine pregnancy test was negative. He told her to return for another urine test. Two weeks later, the urine test was again negative. The nearest ultrasound scanning equipment was 110 miles away, and such an exam would be very expensive. Barb's family did not have much money. They waited.

Four weeks later, Barb still felt pregnant, had no menstrual period, and no signs of a spontaneous abortion. But her urine test remained definitely negative. The doctor broke the bad news that probably she had been pregnant but the baby had died, leaving dead tissue in her uterus. A few weeks later, with the urine test still negative, the doctor performed a dilation and curettage (D & C) to clean out the tissue. To his horror, he found that the body parts he was removing were not dead tissue but were alive. The urine tests had been wrong and he was aborting a live fetus.

As the case was reviewed with colleagues over the next several months, it became clear that this doctor had made a number of poor decisions, such as not ordering the ultrasound test. In this case, the consequences of a poor decision were particularly terrible (including further complications from the operation for Barb), but many daily decisions made by physicians can have important implications.

In September 1951, Renee Fox began a study of the reactions of physicians and patients to medical uncertainty (Fox, 1959). The research took place in a 15-bed metabolic research ward in a university teaching hospital. Fox, a medical sociologist, was conducting a participant observation study of physicians and patients in a setting in which medical experimentation on the patients was part of everyday life on the ward. Most of the patients were ill with diseases that were not well understood and could not be effectively controlled by medical science in the 1950s. These patients had agreed to act as research subjects for a team of 11 physicians because it was their only hope for prolonging their lives. The physicians had a dual role: One was to care for their patients and try to keep them alive as long as possible; the other was to conduct clinical research on them.

The physicians were attempting to assess the activity of newly synthesized steroids as clinical agents in the treatment of metabolic and endocrine, cardiovascular, renal, and other diseases. Hence, the procedures were radical and were attempted only on patients who were acutely, seriously, and often terminally ill. The physicians were all relatively young and in early phases of their professional careers; many of them had completed internships and were serving as residents or fellows. They were seriously interested in careers in academic medicine and were trying to strike a balance between caring for patients, teaching, and research.

Fox's sociological research is reported in the book *Experiment Perilous* (Fox, 1959). The physicians who were part of the metabolic research group were confronted with major problems of uncertainty in caring for their patients. This uncertainty sometimes resulted from their own incomplete mastery of the medical knowledge that was available, their limited skills, and their inability to synthesize completely all the relevant material. Their uncertainty, however, also derived from limitations in medical knowledge at the time. There was also stress resulting from the physicians' inability to distinguish between their own personal inadequacies and the limitations of medical sciences.

In her research, Fox found that the physicians reacted with a considerable degree of emotion to problems of uncertainty and to problems concerning the ethics of human experimentation. But these physicians came to terms with the pressures of the uncertainty. To begin with, they found deep personal and professional gratification in being associated with each other. The atmosphere of working together helped them to counterbalance some of the strains to which they were exposed. Their unit provided social support and a chance to exchange both opinions and feelings about common problems that were associated with the research. They also were able to share responsibility for what happened to the patients—something that made the awesome responsibility for patients easier to handle. A number of group meetings took place in which the physicians could express their mutual problems and talk about how they felt about them. The physicians "sounded off" a good deal to one another about the strains that they experienced in the uncertainty and unpredictability of their professional situation. They listened sympathetically and gave active encouragement and support to each other.

Another way in which the physicians dealt with the stresses of their experimentation on human beings involved humor. A highly patterned and intricate form of humor served as a protective device. The physicians' humor and jokes focused on the major problems they faced as a unit. They joked about the problems of uncertainty with which they were confronted:

> *Dr. D:* Mr. Goss is still alive.
> *Dr. S:* Is he putting out urine?
> *Dr. D:* No.
> *Dr. S:* Is he having hemodialysis?
> *Dr. D:* No.
> *Dr. S:* Then how is he alive? (Laughter) (Fox, 1959, p. 78.)

They also joked about the trial-and-error nature of their scientific pursuits:

> *Dr. G:* Are you sure Mr. Stark's adrenals are out?
> *Dr. H:* They must be. His carcinoma got better. (Fox, 1959, p. 78.)

Others joked about the moral ambiguities and conflicts that conducting research on patients involved:

> *Dr. G:* Mr. Powers' test will be over on Wednesday. What are the plans for his management after that?
> *Dr. S:* Why, I supposed we'll finally get around to treating him (Fox, 1959, p. 78.)

The humor of the physicians in the metabolic groups was cathartic, as it enabled them to express and dissipate the tension they felt over the problems they faced. To some extent, their humor was deviant. By laughing at events that were extremely serious, the physicians were able to express their refusal to accept the poor prognoses of their patients as inevitable. They were able to make light of their own feelings and to achieve a more detached attitude toward the pressures of their work. In sum, by freeing them from some of their tensions, humor helped the physicians strengthen their resolve to deal with the problems.

Another way in which these physicians were able to deal with the stresses of uncertainty involved becoming close to the patients. The physicians provided special privileges for their patients, such as a television set, books, and games. They tried to select nurses who would give special attention and consideration to the patients. Patients were given privileges such as permission to move about freely in the ward and visit other patients in the hospital when they were well enough to do so. A close association with the patients after they went home was maintained by the physicians through follow-up visits. The patients were also given a considerable amount of information about their disorders, and the procedures that were done to them were explained in detail. The patients were considered working members of the research group. The physicians expressed indebtedness and gratitude to their patients for the role that they played in facilitating research. The enthusiasm that the physicians generated by developing these cooperative relationships with their patients helped them to overcome the stresses of research (Robinson, 1977).

Reaching Rational Decisions

Although health care professionals perform their duties under conditions of uncertainty, the factors that affect decision-making are not only matters of evidence. Social and psychological issues also influence how medical decisions are made and what form they take (Chapman & Sonnenberg, 2000). When a physician hears a patient's complaint, the physician conducts an examination and makes a decision about what is wrong. This diagnosis is based on answers to questions asked of the patient and on tests that are performed. Even at this stage, a physician has to weigh the risks and costs inherent in a particular diagnostic procedure against the risks of following a treatment plan without the information that would result from performing the diagnostic procedure. In prescribing treatment, the physician also knows that the treatment for one illness may aggravate another illness. These diagnosis and treatment decisions are subject to systematic biases (Chapman & Elstein, 2000; Elstein & Bordage, 1979).

Physicians and other health care professionals usually develop judgment from two sources. First, during training, they observe assessments made by people more experienced in their field. Second, they learn directly through trial and error—they make a diagnosis, prescribe a treatment, and observe the results. It is important to recognize, however, that there is a great deal of disagreement among experts in medicine regarding particular treatments. For example, physicians often do not agree about the use of certain drugs for particular illnesses, and physicians make different value judgments on the question of risk. If a particular procedure has a mortality rate of 2 or 3 percent, some physicians would advise against the procedure because the risk is too high. Other physicians may believe that the patient would encounter an acceptable risk by having the procedure.

Physicians, too, differ among themselves in their approaches to various treatments. This is partly because each works from a different data base. Some physicians are more experienced than others with relevant cases. For example, although a research study may have suggested that a certain treatment has a mortality rate of 50 percent, physicians tend to rely on their own experience with the treatment. Few physicians will jump to any conclusions if the treatment works one or two times; but if among six patients, a high-risk treatment helps five, with one dying (i.e., there is a mortality rate of one out of six), the physician may begin to believe that the mortality rate is much lower than 50 percent. The doctor's data represent only the short run, however.

Psychologists D. Kahneman and A. Tversky have studied such errors in estimating odds (Kahneman, & Tversky, 1972, 1973). They reported that people tend to develop confidence in a treatment that works four out of five times. This result is not significantly different from a 50-50 chance. But this problem of the **belief in small numbers** may lead the physician to place undue confidence in a small amount of data. People believe that their samples, even if very small, are representative of the population from which they are drawn. That is, they extrapolate the findings from a small set to an entire population and judge the probabilities of success accordingly. Faulty inferences result.

It also has been found in work by Tversky and Kahneman that people judge the probability of an event by the **salience** of previous instances of that event—that is, how easily instances of that event come to mind (Tversky & Kahneman, 1974). Thus, physicians may conclude that a treatment is better than it actually is (i.e., has a greater probability of working than it actually has) if they can easily remember patients who succeeded after having had the treatment.

Emotions also affect decision-making. Physicians often have difficulty in deciding whether to give patients bad news; for example, telling a patient that the patient is dying is one of the most difficult tasks many physicians must face. Apparently, there are two reasons for this hesitation. First, people prefer to avoid the unpleasant feelings that occur in sad situations (Tesser & Rosen, 1975). Second, the physician who bears bad news is sometimes held responsible for the bad news; that is, the physician is unfairly blamed for the patient's condition (Haan, 1979). Such influences on decision-making are emotional rather than rational approaches to patient management, however.

The values of the health provider also influence decision-making (Chapman & Sonnenberg, 2000). A victim of his or her own drunken driving or a destitute old person is more likely to be classified as "dead on arrival" by emergency room personnel than would a child upon whom resuscitation would still be attempted (Roth, 1972). Similarly, decisions may be subtly affected by the costs of treatment and whether the patient's case is useful for research or teaching purposes (Waitzkin & Waterman, 1974). To reduce such biases, health professionals might acknowledge their relevant values as explicitly as possible and then analyze them outside the pressures of a specific decision.

Can advertising also have an effect? It is often imagined that physicians base their decisions on an informed reading of the scientific literature. In fact, many social influences and distortions operate. Physicians are regularly contacted by the sales representatives of the pharmaceutical industry, and physicians may receive subsidized meals at conferences, travel, sponsored teaching, and other perks. In return, the influences affect prescribing and professional behavior (Wazana, 2000). One study of physicians looked at the perceptions of two heavily advertised drugs whose effects had been shown by scientific study to be no different from nonprescription alternatives (Avorn, Chen, & Hartley, 1982). (For example, one of the drugs, Darvon, was heavily advertised, expensive, and addictive, but is no more effective than aspirin.) When surveyed, a majority of physicians claimed that they were not influenced by advertisements and drug company detail men. However, their prescribing patterns revealed that they were indeed being influenced. It is no wonder that the medical journals are filled with expensive pharmaceutical ads for expensive pharmaceuticals.

In most cases of medical malpractice, it is not the case that the physician did something wrong, but rather that he or she *thought* something wrong. In other words, poor decision-making rather than botched surgery is the cause of most lawsuits (Payne, Harrison, & Harel, 1986).

WOMEN IN MEDICINE

You may have heard an old but very interesting riddle, which goes like this:

> A man and his son went out fishing on a Sunday afternoon. Driving home, they were in a car accident with a drunk driver and the man was killed instantly. His son was rushed to the hospital, needing surgery.
>
> When the boy arrived at the hospital, the attending surgeon looked at him and exclaimed, "I can't operate. He's my son!"
>
> How can this be?

Even today, many people do not know the answer to this riddle, or else take quite a while to solve it.*

Our expectations about the roles of women in medicine are deeply ingrained. **Gender roles** (also called sex roles) are shared expectations we hold about the appropriate behavior of men and women; they are stereotypes applied to sex. For example, in America, men have traditionally been expected to be aggressive, strong, athletic, dirty, and insensitive, whereas women have traditionally been expected to be emotional, dainty, talkative, sensitive, and neat. Gender roles are important in all areas of social relations, but they are especially important in medicine. Inferior roles for women date back thousands of years to biblical proclamations about the superiority of men and the uncleanliness of women. The ancient Greeks also viewed women as biologically and emotionally inferior. Church laws and Greek philosophy continued to exert a strong influence on the development of the roles of women in medicine until recently.

Gender roles have affected the possibilities for women as health professionals (and the treatment women received as patients). As scientific medicine developed in 20th-century America, women were, on the whole, limited to positions as nurses; even the role of midwife was denied to them!

Women as Physicians

In 1965, only 6 percent of beginning medical students were women. By 1975, three years after the passage of an amendment to the federal Health Manpower Act and of a law that prohibited educational discrimination according to sex, about 20 percent of the nation's incoming medical students were women. Today, the percentage has leveled off at about 40 to 45 percent.

In the early 1970s, most of the female physicians followed very similar career paths. About 22 percent of the pediatricians, about 20 percent of the public health physi-

---

*The answer of course is that the surgeon is the boy's mother.

"No, Mr. Smith, I am not your nurse or your dietician. I am the surgeon who will be performing your emergency hernia repair."

Figure 14–2   *(Copyright Howard S. Friedman. Drawing by Robin Jensen.)*

cians, and about 25 percent of the child psychiatrists in the United States were women. Altogether, about 65 percent of the female physicians worked in pediatrics, public health, child psychiatry, or internal medicine. Perhaps surprisingly, only 3 percent of the obstetrician-gynecologists in the United States were women, but the percentage has been growing since. However, the absence of women from the OB-GYN specialty is more understandable when we remember obstetrics and gynecology often involve surgery.

There are relatively few women in surgery. Why? One female surgeon described typical experiences in her training. When in medical school, male surgeons urged her to go into pediatrics, dermatology, or primary care—anything but surgery. When she nevertheless applied for an internship in surgery, she faced the following interviewers. The first asked her if she were going to have children and quit, as did a previous female intern. The second interviewer thought it might be fun to train an oddity like a female surgeon. The third agreed to train her but (eventually) wound up treating her like a little girl.

During the internship, one of the chief surgeons was shocked to have a woman on his service and tried to make her fail. Another instructing surgeon "clearly preferred his women in bed," but turned out to be helpful. In addition, this female surgical intern had to work much harder than her male counterparts and be careful never to challenge male power (Name withheld to protect the guilty, 1986). (See also Box 14–1.)

Until recently, female physicians were likely to have parents with high education, and professional fathers. They tended to marry physicians or other professionals, but often they made less money than their physician-husbands. It was also true that a large percentage of them did not marry, and those who did had few if any children. Women physicians who married encountered a tremendous workload, often handling cooking, shopping, childcare, and money management in their houses (Cartwright, 1987).

Box 14–1   Doctors Are People Too

In 1991, the *Harvard Medical School Health Letter* polled over 600 members of the Harvard Medical School faculty, asking them about their own personal health practices. The results were quite revealing.

- 39 percent report that they need to lose ten pounds or more.
- Half did not get regular aerobic exercise.
- Most do not have an annual physical exam.
- Fewer than a third of the faculty have an annual flu shot and most have not been immunized for hepatitis B (despite the fact that both are recommended for health professionals).
- More than a third do not maintain a high fiber intake, but most try to avoid eggs and red meat.
- Most regularly eat cakes, cookies, pies, or ice cream.
- Almost half do not regularly examine their breasts (females) or testes (males).
- Only 11 percent practice a specific stress-reduction technique.
- A large minority avoid aluminum products, based on the very weak evidence of a possible link to Alzheimer's disease.

During the decade between surveys (1982–1991), use of seat belts rose significantly to practically all physicians surveyed. The number smokers dwindled from 8 percent to 3 percent. Many other behaviors changed only slightly, in expected directions.

It is worth noting that physicians are influenced by a whole host of psychosocial factors, just like everyone else; their high level of medical expertise is not overwhelmingly important. These physicians are also heavily caught up in social trends (especially medical trends), sometimes to their benefit (as in the current avoidance of cigarettes—35 percent are former smokers) but sometimes irrationally (as in their excessive avoidance of aluminum products and red meat).

A significant number of professional women in medicine report that they experience a conflict between their work and home life (Cartwright, 1979; Schermerhorn, Colliver, Verhulst, & Schmidt, 1986). In addition, women were (and still are) vastly underrepresented in seats of power in medical education.

It is sometimes argued that women make less effective use of their medical training than do men because they are in practice for a shorter period throughout their lives, but there is little evidence to support this claim. The relationship between the professional and personal behavior of female physicians has been changing, and these changes may have a significant impact on the future of medical practice. Women currently entering medicine are more likely to choose an array of specialties, and they are working longer hours than in the past. Both women and men are more attracted to family practice, internal medicine, and internal medicine subspecialties (Babbott, Baldwin, Killian, & Weaver, 1989; Weisman, Levine, & Steinwachs, 1980).

How is medicine different with women in the profession? Some clues come from studies done by psychologist Lillian Cartwright (Cartwright, 1978, 1987). It has been found that women often are more sensitive than men to values concerned with interpersonal issues in health care. Probably because of this orientation, female physicians are more likely to be aware of the patient's psychosocial environment. With encouragement to hold on to what are considered traditionally "feminine" values, female physicians can have a positive impact on the psychological aspects of medical practice. They may also improve the treatment received by female patients. However, the jury is still out on these matters.

Women as Patients

Hysteria, or "wandering womb," an emotional "craziness," has long been expected of women. For example, views of women's health have been heavily influenced by the writings of Sigmund Freud, who believed that "anatomy is destiny" and that a woman's anatomy often led her to a troubled destiny. These and other sex stereotypes historically have led to various detrimental effects in the treatment of female patients (Gallant, Keita, & Royak-Schaler, 1997).

Several generations ago, some women were forced to have their clitoris removed as a "cure" for sexual enjoyment, and this still happens in some African countries. Hysterectomies as treatment for psychiatric disorders were especially common early in the 20th century. As such cultural expectations persisted in one form or another, unnecessary hysterectomies continued into contemporary times. As a more recent example of likely sex bias, it has been shown that physicians see menopausal symptoms as more pathological than menopausal women themselves do; and physicians may tend to blame psychological factors, seeing menopausal symptoms as at least partly "in her head" (Cowan, Warren, & Young, 1985).

Health care is sometimes unhealthy for women (Fidell, 1980; Gumbiner, 1981; Revenson, & McFarlane 1998). Some physicians expect women to be more troublesome as patients than men and expect to find more symptoms with psychological links. For example, women are more likely than are men to receive prescriptions for mood-modifying drugs such as tranquilizers (Cooperstock, 1971; Fidell, 1980; Graham & Vidal-Zeballos, 1998). To some extent, these sex differences may be physiologically based; but there is little doubt that the expectations of society and of physicians play a major role in treatment.

Part of the difference may lie in the greater tendency of women to report symptoms. Females are generally expected to monitor their family's health, while males are expected to ignore "minor" pain; or perhaps women are more attuned to the feelings of their bodies than are men. Various studies find women are more likely than men to use health services (Bertakis, Azari, Helms, Callahan, & Robbins, 2000; Mechanic, 1982). Only a health practitioner, either male or female, who is alert to the long history of differential treatment of men and women can attempt to avoid errors in medical diagnosis that result from unjustified expectations in what might be called the **medical milieu.**

Some people become needlessly defensive when topics like sex discrimination in health care arise. Two important points should be kept in mind. First, gender role expectations, like other roles, are generally very subtle and often unintentional. For example, the fact that "hysterical" women were excluded from many professions or had unnecessary surgery for many years does not mean that men, or anyone else, conspired against women or indeed that anyone recognized what was happening. Sex roles then were just "the way things were." Second, it is important to note that there is a methodological limitation in designing studies to examine the effects of sex role expectations. To use an extreme example, if it is asserted that pregnant women are not given enough pain relief during labor, we cannot test the possibility of sex discrimination by examining the pain relief given to pregnant men. Nevertheless, problems can slowly be uncovered, and careful examination of indirect evidence must be undertaken.

Not too long ago, childbirth in American hospitals had all the trappings of major surgery for a horrible disease. Acting in the "best interests" of the mother and child, physicians banished fathers to isolated pacing during the birth, anesthetized the mother (and thereby the fetus), removed healthy newborns to a glass-enclosed nursery, discouraged breastfeeding, and forbade the newborn's siblings from visiting. Although in the 19th century, husbands could help their wives and monitor the doctor during delivery (Suitor, 1981), changes in the health care system sacrificed such activities to "progress." These developments, more psychosocial than medical in nature, turned out to cause many problems and have mostly been reversed in recent years, in large part due to efforts to change the rigid patriarchal system of health care.

Women's Health Initiative

Because of past relative inattention to women's health issues, the U.S. National Institutes of Health has undertaken the Women's Health Initiative. Begun in 1991, the Women's Health Initiative (WHI; *http://www.nhlbi.nih.gov/whi/index.html*) addresses the most common causes of death, disability, and impaired quality of life in postmenopausal women: cardiovascular disease, cancer, and osteoporosis. The WHI, a 15-year multimillion dollar endeavor, is one of the largest U.S. prevention studies of its kind, with over 150,000 women participating. Its three major components are:

- a randomized, controlled clinical trial of promising but unproven approaches to prevention;
- an observational study to identify predictors of disease;
- a study of community approaches to developing healthful behaviors.

Nursing

In the United States, most of the health care workers are women. We have seen that women do not dominate the positions of medical administration or physician. Rather, over 90 percent of nurses are women.

Nursing is, of course, a very old and honored profession, and for a long time, it was one of the few professions open to women. During the Dark Ages, nurses were considered "the healers" because they used social and emotional remedies more readily than did physicians, and the invasive therapies used by physicians often did more harm than good to the patient.

Nurses have enormous responsibilities in their care of patients. They take on complete care of the patient when the physician is not available. This is particularly true in emergency situations in hospitals, such as cardiac arrests. In fact, nurses are usually responsible for making the important decision about whether or not a particular situation is actually an emergency. Nurses are also often primarily responsible for reducing fear and emotional upset in patients, and they may be directly involved in maintaining a patient's will to live.

A significant source of stress for nurses is the gap that exists between their training and their professional lives (Barron-McBride, 1976; Llewelyn & Fielding, 1987). For nurses, **role training incongruities** arise (Davies, 1995; Kramer, 1974) in which there is a reality shock when it becomes apparent that there is a disparity between professional values and norms learned in school (such as the need to spend time talking with patients) and the bureaucratic norms set in hospitals (such as time limitations). Attitudes and work habits developed in nursing school may not be held in high esteem in the workplace. Nurses often feel that interference from physicians and administrators leaves them unable to do the job that they were hired to do. Nursing shortages then result.

In the Middle Ages, nurses often used herbal remedies and poultices (cloth bags of warmed meal). For their efforts, they were sometimes burned at the stake as witches, privy to the devil's secrets of healing. Life for the female nurse is considerably better now, although she still faces stereotyping and low expectations for performance. One commonly held belief is that nurses are just preparing to be doctors' wives.

Male nurses have their own special share of problems. They face all the usual problems of a male working in a typically "female" profession. But because nurses must provide intimate care for patients, male nurses are sometimes viewed as perverts who seek to molest patients. Thus, in some ways, male nurses face the worst of all worlds. Yet the number of male nurses is slowly increasing.

Nursing has its own academic programs, professors, scholarly journals, and professional organizations. Certain aspects of nursing require very high degrees of technical skill. Yet nurses' primary responsibilities still involve monitoring health, preventing problems, and dealing with many socioemotional aspects of care. It is worth asking the question of why nursing is a relatively low-status profession.

Finally, another health care professional worth noting is the physician's assistant. The physician's assistant is a trained health worker, neither a physician nor a nurse, who is qualified to provide supervised primary health care services to patients. The physician's assistant differs from the nurse practitioner in that nurse practitioners have advanced training and may work independently from physicians, whereas physicians' assistants work directly with physicians. Perhaps the best-known system of using the physician's assistant is in Russia, where the **feldsher** provides a large volume of the medical care to individuals in rural populations. In the United States, it sometimes appears that physicians are hoping that the assistants will take over those matters of medicine involving the psychological, social, and emotional aspects of treatment.

HOSPITALS

A century ago, hospitalization was dreaded. Hospitals were seen as unpleasant and costly places, and most importantly, as places where people went to die. With the advent of medical "miracles," however, hospitals cure millions of seriously ill people each year.

Figure 14-3   The hospital environment in a fifteenth-century French hospital. What has changed today and what is the same? *(Photo Giraudon.)*

Yet hospitals still suffer a negative reputation; the problem is not merely their association with disease.

The words *hospital* and *hospitality* come from the same Latin root. The Latin word for hospitality refers to the way in which guests should be received. Yet hospitals are often not very hospitable, and patients are rarely treated as guests. Of course, there are some medical benefits that accrue from this discrepancy, but there are also negative effects.

Hospitals have their roots in centers set up in the Middle Ages in western Europe by religious groups. They cared for the ill, but also provided shelter for the poor and for travelers (Anderson & Gevitz, 1983). Since little effective medical treatment was available, hospitals sometimes spread more disease than they cured. In America, the idea of separating the ill from the poor was urged by Benjamin Franklin, and the Pennsylvania Hospital was founded in 1751. Today, there are more than 5,000 hospitals in the United States (American Hospital Association, 2001). People no longer go to hospitals only when they are seriously ill. The performance of most surgery, many laboratory tests, and procedures requiring expensive medical equipment necessitates hospital admission. In addition, when a patient needs to be observed for a while, the hospital is where this patient should be, often for the convenience of the health care professionals.

Total Institutions

Hospitals are **total institutions** (Goffman, 1961), which means that they manage every aspect of the patient's life. The hospital is one of the few places where people forfeit almost all control over their life. (Other examples of total institutions are prisons and mental hospitals.) Patients relinquish their clothes for hospital gowns; they are rarely addressed in familiar terms, are highly restricted in where they can go, encounter a fixed schedule of eating and sleeping, and have little privacy. Patients are usually unable to make even the smallest effort to help in their own treatment. Patients must operate according to the schedule of the hospital and follow its rules, with little chance for individuality. Patients may begin to lose their identity in hospitals.

Control

> I am forced to admit that doctors really are bad patients. But better bad than dead. Being a doctor may lower your risks in that most hazardous of places—the American hospital.
>
> Dr. Benjamin Felsom, a distinguished medical school professor, writing about his experiences with coronary artery bypass graft (Mandell & Spiro, 1987, p. 27).

One reason hospitals and nursing homes are generally regarded as unpleasant places to be as patients involves lack of control. People generally wish to maintain some individuality, to have some control over their environment and their schedules, and to gain information about what is happening to them. However, inmates of hospitals and other health institutions quickly learn that this is not the way they are expected to behave. Instead, there is an obligation to be a cooperative patient. Most patients learn that they should not try to play a "consumer" role. They should be quiet, submissive, obedient, and not distinguish themselves as individuals (Lorber, 1975).

The social and health psychologist Shelley Taylor has analyzed the hospital patient role in terms of control. Most patients assume the expected role; that is, they behave in ways that make them "good" patients. However, a significant number of patients are considered "bad" patients; bad patients play the consumer role, insisting on their rights, including the right to know everything that is happening to them. Consumer patients (who may be seen as bad from the perspective of certain health care professionals) insist on their own autonomy and the right to help take care of themselves. These patients may become angry, particularly if freedoms are withdrawn from them for the convenience of the staff. They also resent the hospital bureaucracy (Lorber, 1975; Taylor, 1982). The patient's angry reaction to the seemingly arbitrary withdrawal of freedom is a common psychological reaction, termed **reactance** (Brehm, 1966).

Patients may rebel by failing to take their medications. This petty mutiny may actually function as a form of self-sabotage. Unfortunately, patients in an angry state are also experiencing a physiological arousal that may be detrimental to their recovery. Staff attempts to mollify irascible patients with condescending comfort may increase this anxiety. On the other hand, staff members may ignore angry patients and avoid listening to their complaints; in so doing, they may overlook a complaint that has medical significance.

While it is probably true that most so-called bad or angry patients receive negative reactions from staff members, are treated poorly interpersonally, and may be punished in some ways, they may often be in better physical and emotional shape than good, compliant patients, and may actually get better faster. As we have seen, their fighting for control may be a psychologically healthy response.

Very submissive "good" patients, on the other hand, often have given up control. Because they have received very little information, these patients may remain in a condition of anxiety. These individuals are exposed to aversive stimulation over which they have no control. Most of the time, submissive patients are highly regarded by the staff because they do not complain and are not demanding. Their passivity, however, puts them in a position where they are unlikely to do much that will improve their health. These patients not only do not ask for information, but also, they do not divulge it; they have learned to be quiet.

In short, hospitals should allow patients to maintain as much personal control as is feasible. Neither an angry, rebellious state nor a passive, helpless state is likely to be healthy. In recent years, some hospitals have become more willing to consider this important aspect of patient care.

Helplessness is partly a function of the situation. But it is also true that people differ in their basic beliefs about how much control they can exert over their environment. **Locus of control** refers to an individual's belief about what determines what happens to him or her (Rotter, 1954, 1966). People with an internal locus of control believe that their fate is in their own hands; those with an external locus of control believe that they have no power to determine their fate and that it is up to chance or luck. This personality trait represents a continuum on which a person can be described as more or less internal, or more or less external. People with a predominantly internal orientation are likely to seek constructive solutions to frustrating problems instead of giving up on them.

In a study of hospital patient behavior, it was found that internal patients knew more about their condition, were more inquisitive with doctors and nurses about their illness, and indicated less satisfaction with the amount of information they received than did external patients. Internal patients attempted to gain a greater degree of control over their health by gaining information (Seeman & Evans, 1962). Similarly, in a number of interesting research programs, locus of control has been utilized to predict health behaviors (Walston, 1992; Walston et al., 1999; Wallston & Wallston, 1978).

Unfortunately, the hospital environment may overwhelm even a healthy personality. Ironically, patients with an internal locus of control may be especially upset by the sense of helplessness created by the typical hospital environment. Further, it is especially difficult for patients who must institute and carry out self-care after being discharged from the hospital to overcome the lack of control induced by the hospital. Patients may have trouble assuming the tasks necessary to take care of themselves.

Thus, the degree and nature of control exercised by hospitals and the various resulting reactions by patients can have both short-term and long-range impacts on health. Strict, arbitrary, unexplained hospital rules may harm the very patients they are trying to help.

Dehumanization

The hospital patient is sometimes treated like an inanimate object by most of the staff. Things are "done to" the patient. The patient may have a great deal of trouble acquiring any dignity or respect. Questions from the patient may be put off onto others. Many different people enter the patient's room throughout the day, few of them even bothering to identify themselves. Patients are often referred to by their symptoms, disease, or conditions. Thus, a patient may become "the gallbladder case" or "the kidney in room 200." Medical staff making rounds may talk about the patient in highly technical terms in front of the patient. For whatever reasons that the staff may have, patients are usually told little about what is happening to them (Cartwright, 1964; Coser, 1962; Lorber, 1975). This phenomenon is called **dehumanization.** Dehumanization is the process of treating a person as less than a whole human being (Bernard, Ottenberg, & Redl, 1971; Goffman, 1961).

Dehumanization is often associated with instances of mass violence in that it helps ease psychological restrictions on murder (Sanford & Comstock, 1971). Unfortunately, sometimes an insidious epithet is "patient." How can this be? Interestingly, dehumanization produces an emotional detachment that may sometimes be useful in medicine. For example, it may be beneficial for surgeons not to be emotionally involved with their patients during an operation.

Although it is sometimes helpful, dehumanization produces a decreased awareness of the human attributes of the patient and a loss of humanity in dealing with the patient. The health care professional may stop perceiving the patient as also having feelings, thoughts, and impulses, and instead deal with the patient only on an intellectual level (Skipper, Tagliacozzo, & Mauksch, 1964; Wilson, 1963). Dehumanization in medical settings puts the patient in a position where he or she is responded to with objective, analytical responses, but the responses are lacking in emotion or in empathy. Health care

"Oh, you must be the kidney in Room 200."

Figure 14-4   Dehumanization of patients.
(Copyright Howard S. Friedman. Drawing by Robin Jensen.) Reprinted by permission

professionals may engage in dehumanization partly to protect themselves emotionally from having to deal with pain and illness.

Obedience and Authority

Hospitals and similar institutions have very clearly defined authority hierarchies; that is, there is a well-defined power structure that ranges from the directors at the top to the orderlies at the bottom. There is a clear expectation that each member of the institution will obey a perceived legitimate authority; obedience helps the institution run smoothly. However, like other aspects of an institution, obedience can also produce deadly side effects.

A traditional status ranking in hospitals is that nurses are subordinate to physicians. This status difference has been further supported by sex roles, since most physicians have been men while most nurses have been women. The implications of the status difference are well illustrated by a dramatic study by C. K. Hofling and associates (Hofling, Brotzman, Graves, & Pierce, 1966). In this study, doctors telephoned nurses in a hospital and instructed them to administer a dose of medicine to a patient on the ward. (Prescription by telephone was against hospital policy.) The drug was a "new" drug, unknown to the nurses, but the prescribed dose was an overdose according to directions on the label. Out of 22 nurses who received these telephone orders, 21 of them attempted to administer this potentially fatal overdose to the patient. To protect the patients, the experiment was set up so that the drug was actually harmless and the nurses were intercepted before they could administer it. This study dramatically demonstrated the extent to which nurses would obey authority. Interestingly, many of the nurses reported that they had encountered similar (real) incidents in the past.

A follow-up study helped isolate the factors that produced compliance on the part of the nurses (Rank & Jacobson, 1977). First, the nurses were unfamiliar with both the drug and the doctor; they had little previous information on which to evaluate the order. Second, the nurses were instructed not to discuss the order with other medical personnel. In fact, the Hofling study was done with nurses on the evening shift, when staffing was minimal. If in doubt, the nurses would usually consult with other nurses or endeavor to recontact the doctor. Still, in a replication study in which an overdose of valium was prescribed while other options were available, some nurses obeyed the order completely and few directly challenged the order. Another, more recent follow-up study surveyed nurses about times (in the past) that they had carried out or refused to carry out a physician's order that they felt might be harmful to the patient (Krackow & Blass, 1995). Here again, a significant number of nurses admitted that they had sometimes carried out such an order by a physician, who was perceived as an expert and legitimate power in this situation.

The point of such studies is not how many nurses will obey dangerous orders. The point of the study is also not weaknesses in the nurses' personalities or training. Rather, such studies demonstrate the tremendous power of a legitimate authority in an institution. Such instances of well-intentioned but dangerous obedience to authority are found in many social situations.

The classic studies demonstrating the tremendous power of the social situation to elicit obedient behavior were done by the social psychologist Stanley Milgram (Milgram, 1974). Milgram created a laboratory study supposedly on the effects of punishment on learning. When someone arrived to participate in this study, he or she was assigned to the role of "teacher" and was supposed to teach another person a list of paired words. The learner was hooked up to electrodes, and the teacher was instructed to administer an electric shock to the learner as punishment whenever the learner made an error. As the study progressed, the "teacher" (the experimental subject) was instructed by the experimenter to administer a continually higher dosage of shock to the learner. The shocks became quite painful and eventually very dangerous. The learner, who was in another room and connected to the teacher by an intercom, called out and demanded that the study be stopped. However, the experimenter insisted to the teacher (the person being studied) that the experiment continue. On orders of the experimenter, more than 50 percent of the "teachers" kept administering electric shocks even at a level marked extremely dangerous. Fortunately, unknown to the teacher, the learner was a confederate of the experimenter and was not actually receiving the electric shocks. Just as the teachers in the Milgram study did not desire to do any harm but felt they had no other choice, many nurses and medical assistants feel they have no choice but to obey the orders of a doctor.

Some safeguards can be instituted to help each individual recognize his or her own personal responsibility for actions, but the problem cannot be completely eliminated so long as an authority hierarchy is in place. Such power structures are an integral part of most hospitals, and therefore all medical personnel should be alert to the dangers that may result. We cannot rely on a health professional's "common sense" to avoid the dangerous consequences of erroneous medical orders.

Nosocomial Infection

Should patients remind doctors and nurses to wash their hands? Of the more than 30 million Americans who will be admitted to hospitals this year, about 1 million will develop **nosocomial infections**—infections that are acquired in the hospital. Thousands will die because of entering a hospital. Of course, for most patients the benefits to be gained from hospitalization far outweigh the risks; but nevertheless, the problem is still serious, although mostly avoidable (Mayhall, 1999; Raven & Haley, 1980).

Since the discovery of germs, most nosocomial infections have been controllable in theory. Sterilization of equipment, disinfection of the environment, and isolation of certain patients all help control the transmission of bacteria. Also important is the simple act of handwashing. Yet the biological problem of killing bacteria has become the psychosocial problem of controlling the attitudes and behavior of hospital personnel.

How can weakened patients, often with open wounds, be protected from those trying to help them? Will doctors wash their hands? (See Box 14–2.) A number of social-psychological issues come together to address this question. First, simple precautions like handwashing may lose their importance if the emphasis of the overall hospital environment is on the technological wonders of medicine and miracle drugs. Second, authority hierarchies may preclude a nurse or patient from questioning a doctor about simple infection-preventing measures. Relatedly, patients in a hospital may wish to avoid "insulting" a health care practitioner by implying a lack of cleanliness, even though their lives are at stake. Such matters of embarrassment and manners are psychosocial phenomena. In some hospitals, expectations make it perfectly permissible, perhaps even desirable, for everyone to work together to prevent nosocomial infection. Just as errors in technical treatment are pointed out, so too are lapses in cleanliness. If the people around the health professional are very conscious of nosocomial infection, it is likely that he or she will be also, and will adopt the values and procedures of the surrounding people.

We have singled out nosocomial infection for attention because the danger of disease and death from improper behavior of medical personnel is so obvious here. However, in a total institution like a hospital, the general expectations and standards for behavior are extremely important in many areas. Expectations about patients' chances for recovery, their sensitive treatment, the role of family, and the dignity of the dying are all social psychological factors that are a key part of any hospital.

Children in Hospitals

A child of age four was contacted through an intercom by a nurse from the nurses' station. After a number of calls with no response, an answer was finally received in a tiny, very frightened voice. The child asked, "What do you want, wall?" The child did not un-

---

Box 14-2   Doctors Fail to Wash Hands

Patients in intensive-care units may contract new diseases because practitioners fail to wash their hands. Although nosocomial infections (infections contracted in hospitals) are a common problem, intensive-care patients are especially susceptible because of the frequent use of catheters, wires, tubes, and other "invasive" procedures. The infections can be fatal.

Handwashing is the single most important procedure in preventing hospital infections, yet this simple behavior is often overlooked. This issue reappears in the news every few years but never changes. For example, one interesting study observed handwashing in a university-affiliated hospital under the guise of observing "traffic patterns" (Albert & Condie, 1981). The researchers recorded whether doctors, nurses, and other hospital personnel washed after direct contact with either patients or support equipment. They then followed up these observations with identical observations at a private hospital.

This study found that, on the average, hospital personnel washed their hands after contact with patients less than half the time. This was the case even though urine bags were manipulated, intravenous dressings were changed, and respiratory equipment was adjusted. In other words, basic infection control techniques were often ignored.

Physicians were the worst offenders, washing their hands less than a third of the time. Respiratory therapists ranked best in the study, washing their hands 76 percent of the time at the university hospital and 48 percent at the private hospital. Nurses were intermediate, washing their hands less than half of the time after patient contact. Although these health care practitioners would be appalled to see the wrong drug administered to an intensive-care patient, they would probably not even notice the transfer of a lethal infection through inadequate handwashing.

---

derstand that the nurse's voice was coming through the intercom (Haller, Talbert, & Dombro, 1967).

There is a growing awareness of the traumatic effects of hospitalization on children, particularly children in their preschool years. Studies have indicated that much of the trauma results from separation anxiety—the anxiety experienced by the child in being separated from parents. Coupled with this separation anxiety is an intense fear of bodily mutilation. Even though physicians and nurses involved in the hospital care of sick children recognize that it is often extremely difficult to care for children who are hospitalized, there is often insufficient attention to the child's psychological needs. This situation is slowly changing, however.

The major problem occurs with children from the ages of three to five who are hospitalized for the first time since birth. Hospitalization is a threat to most young children, primarily because they feel betrayed and deserted by their parents. These children are usually too young to understand assurances that they will soon be able to go home. Children may also become quite anxious at the sight of hospital equipment. Toddlers may react to hospitalization with **developmental regression**—that is, regressing to earlier behaviors. These behaviors include nighttime fears and screaming, clinging to and being dependent on their parents, intensified thumb sucking, and loss of bowel and bladder control. Many doctors now advocate that parents remain in the hospital with the child who is under the age of five. In addition, attempts are made to avoid voluntary hospitalization and elective surgery on young children.

Sometimes, hospitalization is necessary and other measures must be taken to reduce the serious emotional problems that can result. Whereas not long ago children were taken into the operating room unaware of what was going to happen to them, it is now believed that giving the child some control may be the best approach (as it is with adults). While it was once believed that it was better not to excite fearful expectations in the child, research suggests that avoidance of the issues proves too traumatic and produces too many long-lasting effects. Providing information to the child can be done in the context of storytelling or play acting. The child can be given a demonstration of the frightening equipment.

Second, the child should be encouraged to express emotion, and there must be a relationship of trust established with the hospital staff. It is not uncommon for a child to feel that he or she is being sent to the hospital as a punishment for being naughty. Furthermore, children should be forewarned about pain that will accompany medical procedures. Telling children "It won't hurt" and then inflicting pain in various procedures that actually do hurt destroys the trust that the child has in the health care professional.

Finally, it is important for the staff to promote autonomy and independence in children. As much as possible, aspects of the child's environment should be child-sized. Between the ages of one and five, children develop skills of eating, washing, dressing, and controlling their bowel and bladder functions. In the hospital setting, it is very easy for the child to be fed, washed, dressed, and changed and to be required to assume no responsibility. But just as an adult may become helpless, so can the child. Regressive behavior could easily make the child lose a sense of responsibility and self-esteem. If the child is given psychological preparation, some control, and is supported in the ability to respond emotionally, hospitalization can become a meaningful learning experience for the child instead of a time of trauma.

SUMMARY AND CONCLUSION

Psychological issues are relevant not only to the care of patients, but also to the training and care of health professionals. Medical education is stressful and contains an overemphasis on biomedical matters. Internship and residency have been compared to a kind of civilized torture. Yet medical training is a large institution, resistant to reform.

Health professionals encounter special challenges in medical training and throughout their careers. They suffer high rates of suicide and drug and alcohol addiction. For the good of both the professional and the patient, stressful challenges must be appropriately managed. Various suggestions for small-scale and large-scale reforms have been suggested.

A key challenge for health practitioners concerns the uncertainty of decision-making. Various biases can distort rational decisions, and the uncertainty itself can be a large source of distress for the professional.

Women in medicine face special difficulties. These problems arise from the gender role expectations of society, but they are compounded by the enormous demands of medical training and practice. These kinds of interpersonal difficulties are often not squarely faced by the hierarchical and conservative medical care system and so are slow in being resolved.

Hospitals suffer a negative reputation, being seen as unpleasant and costly places where people often went to die. Patients are stripped of their individuality and sense of control, and are treated like objects, sometimes for reasons of medical necessity but sometimes merely out of tradition or a misguided sense of efficiency. This can lead to a loss of identity, a sense of helplessness, and dehumanization.

Hospitals and similar total institutions have very clearly defined authority hierarchies, which can be disastrous, because research demonstrates that we cannot rely on a health professional's "common sense" to avoid the dangerous consequences of erroneous medical orders. Behavior is as important as medical technology, as can be seen by the fact that a large number of people will develop infections (including fatal infections) that are acquired in the hospital; many infections still result from lack of the professionals' following simple handwashing procedures.

There is a growing awareness of the traumatic effects of hospitalization on children, which has resulted in important changes in pediatric wards. Traditionally, children felt betrayed, deserted, and punished, with an intense fear of body mutilation. It is now more clearly recognized that the staff can make special efforts to promote autonomy and independence in hospitalized children as well as in adults.

Recommended Additional Readings

Conley, Frances K. (1998). *Walking out on the boys.* New York: Farrar, Straus and Giroux.

Gallant, S., Keita, G.P., & Royak-Schaler, R. (Eds.). (1997). *Health care for women: Psychological, social, and behavioral influences.* Washington, DC: American Psychological Association.

Ludmerer, Kenneth M. (1999). *Time to heal: American medical education from the turn of the century to the era of managed care.* New York: Oxford University Press.

Moyers, Bill. (1993). *Healing and the Mind.* New York: Doubleday.

Association of American Medical Colleges: *http://www.aamc.org/start.htm*

American Medical Women's Association: *http://www.amwa-doc.org/*

American Cancer Society: *http://www.cancer.org/*

American Hospital Association: *http://www.aha.org/*

Women's Health Initiative: *http://www.nhlbi.nih.gov/whi/*

Key Concepts

zone of discontinuity	hysteria
role conflict	medical milieu
student culture	role training incongruities
New Pathway	feldsher
long-term apprenticeship model	total institutions
cloak of silence	reactance
preventive action	locus of control
belief in small numbers	dehumanization
salience	nosocomial infections
gender roles	developmental regression

PART IV

Society, Utilization, and the Future

Chapter 15

MEDICAL ETHICS AND UTILIZATION ISSUES

Artificial insemination, in which a doctor injects donated semen near the woman's cervix, is now a routine medical procedure to address infertility. A newer and much more expensive procedure, fast becoming routine, is in vitro *("under glass") fertilization. In this procedure, an egg is removed from a woman's ovaries and then fertilized in a test tube. The embryo is then implanted in the uterus. Although in vitro fertilization helps couples in which the woman simply has a blocked fallopian tube, these procedures are also wonderfully useful to couples who have problems with the woman's eggs, problem's with the motility or potency of a man's sperm, or problems with the woman's uterus. Using a donor's egg or sperm, or a surrogate uterus, many childless couples are able to have children.*

*Mary Beth Whitehead, a New Jersey homemaker, agreed to be artificially inseminated with William Stern's sperm and bear him and his wife Elizabeth a child. However, when the little girl known as **Baby M** was born, Mrs. Whitehead changed her mind and wanted to keep the baby. Subsequent court battles raged not only about legal agreements, but also about the suitability of each family to care for the child.*

In modern medicine, many interrelated ethical, legal, economic, and psychological problems may arise. Most relevant to fertilization and conception is the issue of paternity and maternity. Does the child belong to the donor of the egg, the donor of the sperm, the owner of the uterus, or the holder of a legal contract? The well-known case of Baby M has become a classic, but many others follow each year.

A society's approach to such issues—whether artificial insemination, surrogate parenting, and in vitro fertilization are allowed, and how they are regulated and paid for—are a part of the society's health care system. The system involves much more than doctors, patients, hospitals, and medical procedures. It reflects how we think about ourselves, our rights and responsibilities, and our world view. It also reflects our economic priorities. That is, judgments are made, implicitly or explicitly, about how our resources are best spent. Ethical matters, utilization issues, and goals for the future are the subject of this chapter.

SOCIO-MEDICAL ETHICS

The unraveling of the human genome—the genetic blueprint—has opened a host of new ethical questions in health care. There is no technical or biomedical answer to issues that arise. Rather, they are best considered in the broader health psychology model, as well as in the broader context of societal values.

From Minneapolis comes the story of 6-year-old Molly Nash, who suffers from Fanconi anemia, a rare genetic disease. Her parents, Jack and Lisa Nash, conceived a son, Adam, through in vitro fertilization (in a test tube). They had the fertilized eggs checked to find an embryo who was free of Fanconi anemia and a transplant match for Molly. After Adam was born, doctors infused stem cells from Adam's umbilical cord blood into his ill sister.

The medical technique has a fancy term: **pre-implantation genetic diagnosis.** In actuality, it means that the parents are selecting some of the traits of a future child. In this case, there seems to be a very good reason, namely to save the life of 6-year-old Molly. But what about parents who have other reasons? For example, we think it is fine for parents to send their children to a private school to improve their grades or to a tennis camp to improve their game. But what about selecting intellectual or athletic traits using new genetic techniques?

Cassandra Genes

In the classical mythology, Cassandra was a prophet who made true prophecies which were not believed. It was a terrible curse to know the future but be unable to do anything about it. A similar situation has been created by advances in modern biology and genetics. For certain diseases, it is now possible to examine genes and discover that a person will someday develop a dreaded disease for which there is no cure. Thus, these genes can be termed **cassandra genes** (Friedman, 1987a).

An example of this situation concerns Huntington's disease, a progressive degenerative disease of the nervous system. This disease is controlled by a dominant gene passed on by the parent. If you have the gene, you will develop the disease, usually in middle life (30s and 40s). Children in Huntington's families used to have to grow up not knowing what would happen to them. Now they can find out, but should they? If you are a 19-year-old college student, would you like to know that you will develop a terrible disease at age 35?

A related situation involves genetic markers that indicate increased risk for certain diseases; for example, such markers exist for colon cancer and for manic-depressive disorder. More and more such markers are being discovered monthly. Should your insurance company know that you are at risk? Can they charge you higher insurance premiums? Should your potential employer know this information during a job interview? Should you and your doctor know this information so that you could plan possible interventions? Should you tell your lover or spouse? Should people with known genetic defects be discouraged from having families?

End of Life Directives

Millions of Americans have completed advance directives such as living wills, hoping that their wishes about medical treatment near the end of life will be followed. It is assumed that these directives improve the understanding by relatives of patients' treatment wishes regarding end of life interventions. Do they help? In one interesting study, 401 outpatients, who were age 65 or older, and their self-designated decision makers (either spouses or adult children) were studied (Ditto et al., 2001).

The participants were randomly assigned to one of five experimental conditions. In the control condition, the family members predicted the patients' preferences for various life-sustaining medical treatments in a number of different medical scenarios (without the benefit of any patient-completed advance directive). Accuracy in this condition was compared to that in four intervention conditions in which the family members made predictions after reviewing either a scenario-based or a value-based directive completed by the patient, and after discussing or not discussing the contents of the directive with the patient.

Surprisingly, the results showed that none of the interventions produced significant improvements in the accuracy of the family's judgment in any illness scenario or for any medical treatment studied. Not only that, but the family members were not very accurate overall in predicting the patients' preferences. In other words, the simple assumption that people can make such judgments accurately or can learn what to do from a living will is called into question. As we have seen throughout this book, the so-called art of medicine is a misnomer. Rather, the understanding of human behavior, including judgment and decision-making, is a socio-behavioral *science*. Health psychology is a difficult field, but it is a scientific one.

As with the right to die issues of Dr. Kevorkian that we discussed in Chapter 9, we again see that health is a complex concept, and maintaining health is different from repairing an automobile. As controversies rage about issues ranging from harvesting sperm from the recently deceased to issues of cloning humans or parts of humans for organ transplants, the health psychology biopsychosocial approach endeavors to consider the full range of our understanding of health.

HEALTH CARE AND THE POOR

In the United States, complete access to good health care is not the right of every individual; the socioeconomic status (SES) of the patient affects the kind of care received and the quality of the supportive environment. Although maintenance of health and success of treatment depend upon such factors as healthy surroundings, personal care, early recognition of symptoms, accurate diagnosis, and application of appropriate treatment, failures at various steps occur all the time for patients of low economic status. These failures are at least partly responsible for the higher mortality rates of the low-income population.

In a classic 1954 study, sociologist Earl Koos conducted a door-to-door household survey to examine the manner in which people from different social classes interpreted the seriousness of various medical symptoms (Koos, 1954). He gave the respondents descriptions of various symptoms (some as nebulous as lower back pain, others as serious as vomiting blood) and asked them whether they would seek help from the medical system (go to a doctor) if they had these symptoms. He found large differences in the willingness of respondents to seek medical help as a function of their socioeconomic status (defined by their economic status and their level of education).

Koos reported that less than one-fifth of the lower-class patients in his sample thought chronic fatigue or persistent backache was worth mentioning to a doctor. Loss of appetite would be ignored by about 80 percent of the lower-class, fainting spells by 67 percent, and continued coughing by 77 percent. Overall, Koos concluded that upper-class persons were more likely than lower-class persons to view themselves as ill when they had particular symptoms, and they were more likely than lower-class persons to say that specific symptoms would lead them to seek the advice of a physician.

Such differences among people in various socioeconomic groups may have little to do with their interest in keeping themselves healthy. Instead, the reasons for the differences in interpretations of symptoms as serious or not serious stem in large part from the willingness of the various individuals to spend family or personal resources for health care. A worker whose monthly earnings barely cover the expenses required for basic necessities is unlikely to readily define a symptom as needing medical attention or warranting a day off from work with the resultant loss of a day's pay. A decision about the seriousness of the symptom is made in the context of the resources of the individual or the entire family.

In addition, among poor patients, good medical care is not always accessible. One of the major problems facing patients from lower socioeconomic classes is that state health (e.g., MediCal, Medicaid) payments to physicians are lower than payments made to physicians by private insurance companies for the same services. Therefore, many physicians refuse to take patients whose only source of insurance is state or federal assistance programs. The physicians or clinics in a given area who do take Medicaid patients are usually quite busy. If the accessibility of care if low, patients tend to avoid seeking care (Segall, 1976).

Another one of the failures of medical treatment for the poor involves the health care professional-patient relationship. Persons of low socioeconomic status in this country often do not have a personal physician, and consequently, they enter the medical care system through the emergency room of the hospital. Persons who enter the medical care system in this way are usually more seriously ill than patients who enter the system via their private physician. They are also more susceptible to various problems of noncooperation and rapport that are described in Chapters 12 and 13.

Patients of low SES are more likely than those of higher SES to delay treatment. First, they have less information about disease than do patients of higher SES and higher education. They are not exposed to health information as much as higher-income groups are, and they are less likely to have a long-term relationship with a physician. In recent years, this has been a special problem facing efforts to fight the spread of AIDS.

Further, in Koos' interviews, survey respondents answered questions about their health in ways such as, "I plan to get this hernia fixed, but it really does not bother me that much right now. My car is a wreck and I need the money to get a new one. There really are other things more important to me right now." Another respondent remarked on the difficulty of taking time out to acknowledge illness: "Sometimes I feel so bad I could curl up and die, but I have to go on because the children need me to take care of them, and besides, I have to go to work and cannot spend the money on doctors" (Koos, 1954). Many of the same problems exist today, half a century later.

Public Hospitals

Patients of low SES may also delay treatment because of public hospitals, where they may undergo procedures done in part for the education of physicians in medical training. Patients of high SES are less likely to be "practiced on" in private hospitals. Therefore, poor people sometimes consider even a top-notch medical center a "butcher shop" (Norman, 1969). Even though the technical care may often be excellent, patients' fears are confirmed if they find the physicians-in-training are interested in their diseases, not in them as a person. For example, in a classic study of patients in a large urban teaching hospital, Raymond Duff and August Hollingshead documented the distressing treatment of patients of low SES by health care professionals in the hospital (Duff & Hollingshead, 1968). This treatment was compared with the treatment of more well-to-do patients. The researchers found that in this elite academic medical center, attached to a famous medical school, patients became acutely aware of their social status in the hospital by the way in which they were treated. Poor patients received much more impersonal treatment.

In addition, poor patients tended to be grossly uninformed about the details of what was happening to them, mostly because the health care professionals viewed them as un-educated and incapable of understanding what was happening to them. Finally, because of differences in social class and education, none of the health care professionals could easily identify with poor patients. The physicians and other health professionals preferred to communicate with patients of their own social class.

In recent years, studies have confirmed the existence of these classic factors affecting health, health care, and the poor. The factors of background, psychological inference, and social and societal situation, all of which affect the definitions and reactions of everyone to illness, have a special influence on poor people (Minuchin, Montalvo, Guerney, Rosman, & Schumer, 1967; Aday, 2001). Together, these factors may seriously increase the time that elapses before a poor person seeks treatment, the access available, and the types of disease prevention and treatments received. Therefore, poor Americans remain at higher risk of premature mortality and of more serious disease states.

Social Class and Illness: The SES Gradient

Interestingly, there are also additional striking but often-puzzling relations between social class and health. As we have just seen, it is easy to understand why poor, lower-class people have worse health. But it turns out that, no matter what level, the higher one's social and financial resources, the greater is one's likelihood of good health.

There is a fascinating phenomenon in public health, called the **SES gradient.** The higher a person's socioeconomic status is, the lower is that person's risk of getting sick and of dying prematurely. This relation has been found in various times and places (Adler, Boyce, Chesney, & Cohen, 1994; Auerbach & Krimgold, 2001). It holds at all ages and at all income levels. For example, old women who are very wealthy live longer than old women who are merely affluent.

There are many sorts of explanations for this gradient, but none of them by itself is fully adequate. For example, less educated people might be less able to request and pro-duce enough money for state-of-the-art, expensive medicines. They might also engage in more unhealthy behaviors like smoking. Or, people who are sickly might drift down to lower socioeconomic status as they lose their jobs or miss promotions.

As noted, poorer people often might have poorer nutrition and less access to the best medical care. Wealthier people may be able to live in healthier environments, such as by avoiding polluted neighborhoods. All of these possibilities would account for a relationship between socioeconomic status and health. Each of these mechanisms surely operates in some cases, but the overall phenomenon is still not well understood. In fact, it is likely that various sorts of explanations are applicable to different people. The topic is one of increasing research.

It is also the case that health care resources are not distributed in any rational man-ner. Massachusetts, New York, and Maryland have the most physicians per capita, well over 300 doctors per 100,000 people. In Idaho, Mississippi, and Wyoming, you will not find many physicians—perhaps less than 150 per 100,000. Are people in Mississippi really so much less in need of medical care? Are doctors in Boston half as productive, or are their patients twice as sick? Surely not.

There are so many physicians in Massachusetts, New York, and Maryland because there historically have been major medical centers and medical schools in and near these areas, and because doctors can support and help each other in these areas, and because these areas have the wealthy, well-educated populations that will pay for these doctors. Further, many well-educated physicians prefer to live in urban areas.

The same comparisons exist on a county-by-county basis. Poor, rural counties generally have relatively little care (regardless of population), but rich, urban counties have very high per capita rates of medical personnel. Such societal influences on health are often missed when one focuses only on individual risks and behaviors.

HEALTH CARE UTILIZATION

The issues we have been considering concerning the biopsychosocial nature of illness will of course have direct implications for the use of medical services. Health psychologists study the psychological and social influences on individual decisions, but such matters assume societal importance when considered in the aggregate. The economists, sociologists, and public health officials who study and regulate this usage of medical care are working in the field called **health care utilization.**

Health services and medical procedures are utilized to a different degree by different people, at different times, and in different settings. It has long been known that at any given time, most people have some condition that is bothering them, but most of them will not consult a physician; and if they do, they may not receive treatment (White, Williams, & Greenberg, 1961; White & Henderson, 1976). The doctors, the patients, and the society are all key determinants of health care utilization.

Cesarean Section

Thus far, we have been concentrating on those factors that affect the patient's decision to enter the sick role and seek medical care. However, many of the same influences also affect the physician's decisions and activities. To illustrate this point in detail, we will consider the case of cesarean sections.

A **cesarean section** (or C-section) is the delivery of a baby by cutting through the mother's abdominal and uterine walls. (The name comes from the Roman general Caesar, who is said to have been born this way.) Sometimes, this surgical procedure is necessary to save the life or preserve the health of the infant or the mother. However, there are risks of surgery (including death), high costs of the surgery, and aftereffects on the mother's health, so of course this procedure should be performed only when absolutely necessary.

There has been a dramatic rise in the C-section rate in the United States over the past several decades. For example, in 1965, only 4.5 births in 100 were cesarean, but the rate had risen to 22.7 in 100 by 1985 (Placek, 1986). This sharp increase raises questions about the use of this procedure (Taffel, Placek, & Liss, 1987).

There are several sorts of possible explanations for this marked increase. The first sort involves medical necessity and medical advances. For example, progress in medical technology has allowed the obstetrician to monitor the condition of the fetus during labor and delivery. In some cases, the surgical procedure (C-section) can now save a fetus experiencing severe distress, whereas in the past the distress may have gone undetected. Similarly, viewing techniques can allow the doctor to see whether the size or position of the fetus will make vaginal delivery difficult or impossible. In such cases (which, by the way, closely follow the medical/mechanical model of disease), the skilled obstetrician can save the life of the mother and the baby.

It is important to evaluate, however, whether the intervention has been shown scientifically to reduce morbidity or mortality. Doctors might believe that a particular fetal monitor report of fetal distress means a C-section is indicated, even though there may be no controlled studies showing that intervention produces a better outcome overall. For example, one of the main reasons cesareans are now performed is because the woman previously had a cesarean. Many doctors fear that a subsequent vaginal delivery will rupture the old cesarean scar, thus killing the mother or baby. In fact, this fatal complication almost never occurs. In short, the second sort of reason for the increase in the C-section rate involves doctors' beliefs and expectations—the **tenor of the times.** Since the mother is much more likely to die during a cesarean than during a normal vaginal delivery, these influences on the procedure rate are obviously very dangerous.

A third set of possible reasons for the rise in the C-section rate involves personal and economic influences on the physicians. Obstetricians are at high risk for being sued for malpractice, so they may be unwilling to take any chances—they may operate at the first sign of fetal distress or difficult labor (called *dystocia*). It is also the case that doctors and hospitals generally make more money from a C-section than from a vaginal delivery. Although most physicians are dedicated to providing the best care for their patients, there may be subtle pressures to maintain a certain level of income for the medical industry. And the woman in labor is in no position to contest a recommended procedure that her doctor says is needed for her baby.

Similarly, in cases where there is some doubt as to whether a C-section is indicated, some physicians may be moved by the challenge of providing the most "advanced" medical care. Some support for this sort of explanation is provided by a study of obstetricians that showed that some of the wide variation in C-section rates is a function of the individual physician, even when the nature of the patient population and the medical risks are taken into account (Goyert, Bottoms, Treadwell, & Nehra, 1989).

A final sort of possible explanation for the rise in the rate of C-sections involves various demographic and statistical artifacts. For example, because older women are now having children, there may be more complications and so more need for surgical interventions. Similarly, if childbearing women are now in poorer health or if the fetuses are now less viable (possibly due to new diseases), then a rising C-section rate may naturally be expected.

We have chosen the case of cesarean sections to illustrate the value of examining the utilization rates of medical procedures. The information provided by looking at such rates does not answer the question of why the procedure is being performed, but it does lead us to ask important questions. Many of these questions lie outside the traditional medical model, since they involve social, psychological, and structural influences; but they can be readily addressed by the health psychology model. These questions can and should be examined by well-designed scientific research.

Are too many cesarean sections being performed? All of the issues we have just raised have not yet been fully addressed by research. However, many studies over the years suggest that more repeat C-sections are being done than are medically justified (NIH, 1982; Taffel et al., 1987). When the economic and social costs of this surgery are added in, the procedure emerges as one deserving of further examination by our society. It may be the case that C-sections are the modern-day equivalent of tonsillectomies and adenoidectomies, whose rates have plunged dramatically during the past 30 years.

Unnecessary C-sections can be made less likely through constant attention to the broad issues raised by the health psychology model (Gregory, Hackmeyer, Gold, Johnson, & Platt, 1999). Interestingly, in the last few years, the number of C-sections has again begun to rise, after falling due to increased scrutiny. The attention of a decade ago has waned, and old habits have set in. As long as the traditional medical model is in place, there will always be pressure to perform the most high-tech procedures.

Allocation of Research Resources

Even within medical research, there is controversy about resource allocation. For example, if you divide National Institutes of Health (NIH) research spending per disease by the number of Americans dying of each disease each year, you find more than 20 times as much research money being spent per AIDS death as per heart disease death (as of the late 1990s). Similarly, figured by number of patients, NIH allocates much more money per HIV/AIDS patient than per heart disease patient, breast cancer patient, or prostate cancer patient. Some congressmen and others have therefore argued that research dollars should be more fairly (proportionately) allocated (Istook, 1997).

These numbers change dramatically if we consider years of life lost as the measure. The average age at death from AIDS is much younger than the average age at death from heart disease. This also means that more productive years of life are lost to AIDS than to diseases of the elderly. In fact, if the measure of disease burden is **disability-adjusted life years (DALY),** disease does correlate with NIH spending, since DALY measures take into account age (years lost) and morbidity (sickness), as well as mortality measures like longevity and number of deaths (Gross, Anderson, & Powe, 1999).

But do we want to value one life as worth more than another? Is saving a young life better than saving an old one?

The Last Six Months

Much of the outlay for health care in the United States occurs during the last six months of life. For example, these final months account for about 30 percent of Medicare expenditures (in the government health insurance program for those over age 65). Yet there are also striking differences in Medicare spending as a function of geographic region (Skinner & Wennberg, 1998). For example, spending in Miami is much higher than in Minneapolis, even taking into account age, illness, and local medical prices. However, high spending areas do not have reduced mortality rates.

Such findings are further evidence of the failings of the traditional biomedical model—more care does not necessarily mean better health. Economists, who usually conduct such studies, point out that health care expenditures are correlated with the number of doctors and hospitals per capita and the existence of a chance for profit. That is, the more doctors and the more health businesses, the more expensive and intensive is the care, with no necessary improvement on health.

Health psychologists should also be involved in such analyses. With a deep knowledge of the bases of health and illness, the result might be better health care at lower cost. At the least, if a broad definition of health and quality of life were considered, more efficient resource use could be discussed.

THE FUTURE OF HEALTH PSYCHOLOGY

At certain times in history, scientific, social, and economic forces converge to produce dramatic, rapid change in the ways things are done. Such a dramatic convergence is now affecting health and health care.

First, the population is becoming older and is more likely to be suffering from chronic as compared to acute diseases. Fewer people suffer untreatable acute illnesses, but more people are living for many years in an impaired or debilitated state.

Second, progress in terms of simple and effective miracle drugs is slowing. Dozens of miracle drugs that can be used to treat a wide variety of diseases were produced in the 50 years between 1930 and 1980. But the easy work has been done and the challenges of the

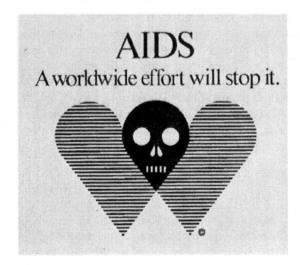

Figure 15-1 Many health threats of the 21st century are likely to resemble AIDS, in that simple cures are difficult to fashion, disease prevention is very important, and living with chronic conditions (including stress management) is common. *(Reprinted by permission of the World Health Organization.)*

new genetic research are great. Analogously, simple medical procedures and surgeries have been perfected. However, these surgical approaches and drugs are often ineffective or inefficient in combating problems caused by so-called "lifestyle" factors. As we have seen, many of today's health problems result from smoking, drinking, drugs, emotional disturbance, pollution, stress, accidents, overeating, inactivity, and so on.

Third, there has been rapid economic change. Health care costs have risen dramatically to the point that society seems unable or unwilling to afford more expense. The crises of "managed care" have resulted.

Some of these issues go well beyond the scope of health psychology. However, what is the potential of health psychology to help resolve these challenging issues?

The Changing and Aging Population

As noted at the beginning of this book, the major causes of death in the United States are cardiovascular disease, cancer, and injuries (trauma, homicide, and suicide). This is in marked contrast to the state of affairs at the end of the 19th century, when people most feared infant mortality (death during the first year of life) and infectious diseases like tuberculosis, bronchitis, pneumonia, smallpox, whooping cough, scarlet fever, and diphtheria. Today, the only infectious diseases that are a major threat are a few serious viral diseases such as influenza and AIDS, and even those may yield to effective treatments. Genetic diseases are also a current problem, but good progress is being made toward understanding them.

The major causes of premature death are not primarily infectious and they are not inevitable results of aging. The most striking aspect of these threats to health is that they are all heavily influenced by **lifestyle factors.** No one knows for sure what would happen if lifestyle threats were eliminated. But imagine a country with no smoking, moderate alcohol use, clear air, clean water, healthy food, safe transportation, moderate exercise, few weapons, stable families, good stress management, and complete cooperation with medical treatment. The results would be astounding. It is likely that the vast majority of children in such a country would live well into their 80s and 90s. Ironically, in such a healthy country, we would need *fewer,* not more, physicians and hospitals.

Cardiovascular disease and cancer often take many years to develop. For example, heart attacks are almost unknown before age 35. Coupled with the fact that the population is aging in demographic terms, this means that there are greater numbers of elderly people, with chronic conditions. In other words, the typical patient is now much more likely to be a 59-year-old man with heart disease or a 65-year-old woman with lung cancer than a 10-year-old boy with smallpox or whooping cough. This phenomenon will be further compounded by the fact that millions of children born in the years following World War II—the post-war Baby Boomers—have begun reaching retirement age.

In short, the major challenges to health and health care involve lifestyle-induced chronic conditions in an increasingly elderly population, with fast-increasing costs. Is the society responding properly to these challenges?

Medicare, national health insurance for the elderly, was created in 1965. It has proved remarkably successful in providing services for the aged, including the millions of retired

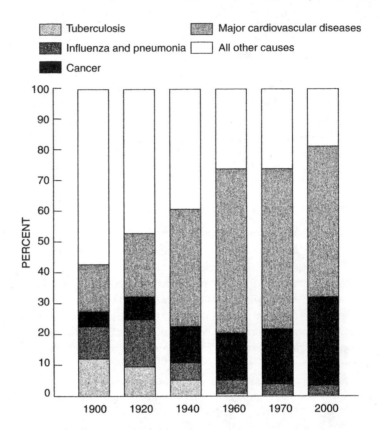

Figure 15-2 Deaths for selected causes as a percent of all deaths (United States). Note that deaths due primarily to infectious causes have decreased markedly, but deaths involving lifestyle factors have dramatically increased. Also, note that the major causes of death are now often preceded by a long period of chronic illness. The "other causes," in decreasing magnitude, include lung disease, injuries, diabetes, HIV, suicide, and liver disease. *(National Center for Health Statistics.)*

people who had little money. However, it does relatively little to prevent disease or facilitate coping. Furthermore, Medicare was created at a time when the numbers of elderly were relatively small. So, the government has decreased payments (in relative terms), and in response, some physicians have been less interested in treating Medicare patients. Therefore, the government has moved to require treatment. This cycle is moving in the wrong direction. It pits patients, physicians, and government against each other as adversaries.

Medicare is a good example of the problems that will be facing our entire health care system. New conceptions of health and health care are needed. As should by now be clear from this book, when long-term chronic conditions, lifestyle factors, and health promotion are involved, health psychology has much to offer.

Healthy People 2010

Healthy People 2010 is an American national health promotion and disease prevention initiative that brings together government agencies, nonprofit organizations, businesses, communities, and individuals to improve the health of all Americans, eliminate disparities in health, and improve years and quality of healthy life (USDHHS, 2000).

The objectives for the year 2010 are based on two main goals:

- Increase quality and years of healthy life.
- Eliminate health disparities.

These goals include four broad categories of objectives:

- Promote healthy behaviors.
- Promote healthy and safe communities.
- Improve systems for personal and public health.
- Prevent and reduce diseases and disorders.

As you can see, this initiative embraces many of the principles and goals of health psychology. It endeavors to head off the problems of an aging society that lives unhealthy lives and cannot be "cured" by physicians.

The Limits of Medicine

There is a story about a physician who summoned her patient into her office with a very grave manner.

> "I hate to be the one to break it to you, Mike," she said, "but I'm afraid you have a limited time to live."
>
> "Oh!" cried Mike, as he sat down. When the information had sunk in, he said, "Do you have any suggestions as to how I could make the most of my remaining time?"
>
> "You haven't ever married, have you?" asked the doctor.
>
> "No," said Mike.
>
> "May I make a suggestion?" asked his doctor. "Marry a lawyer. The time will seem longer."

Only in the last 60 years could most patients enter a hospital with the possibility of effective treatment by knowledgeable doctors (Starr, 1982). Before that time, hospitals were often simply places to suffer and die. The dramatic success of modern medicine has concentrated tremendous power and resources in university medical centers. Perhaps more importantly, it has led to the general expectation that if you are sick, there is surely some smart doctor out there who can cure you. This expectation has distorted our approach to health and often hidden the limits of medicine.

One good example involves our approach to cancer. Fear of developing cancer is one of the greatest fears of Americans; it is repeatedly cited in public opinion polls. To fight cancer, Americans spend billions of dollars each year, a tremendous amount of money when compared to other scientific and health-related expenditures. Is it worth it? In other words, has significant progress been made (U.S. General Accounting Office, 1987)?

The answer is complicated by a number of factors. Most basically, cancer is actually a number of different diseases. Cancer can originate in different types of cells (carcinomas, sarcomas, lymphomas, leukemias, myelomas), at different sites (colon, breast, lung, etc.), and in different forms. Secondly, it can be difficult to define what we mean by survival rate. Who are cancer patients being compared to and where is the information coming from? Finally, there can be various problems in measurement. For example, criteria for diagnoses can change over time, or diseases can become more readily detectable.

Putting these various factors together, we could artifactually increase the cancer survival rate in several ways. We could include patients with a higher survival rate (better prognosis type of tumor) in our new categorization scheme. We could be detecting the cancer earlier, though not curing it any better: If we found the tumor a year earlier, the patient would appear to live a year longer. Or, we could be sampling people with a better prognosis. In other words, patients would not actually be living longer, but the statistics would appear to show longer survival.

Box 15-1   Turning Antagonism into Cooperation

Student A: The class was good, but because I was not a premedical student (I am in sociology), I felt left out. I was appalled many times by the insensitivity of students who are hoping to become doctors, and I deeply and fervently hope that I never go to one of them in the future when I need help with a medical problem.

Student B: The portrayal of all physicians as cold, impersonal, technically skilled, but otherwise ignorant people is inaccurate and overgeneralized. The emphasis should be on teaching attitudes that make a good doctor, as in a medical class that I am currently taking. This approach is more effective, since medicine is not constantly being attacked from a one-sided viewpoint.

These student comments illustrate a dilemma facing anyone endeavoring to teach and apply psychological principles to health and health care. On the one hand, students well-versed in the social sciences are appalled at the problems with the traditional medical model of disease, and they are outraged at the perceived insensitivity of some medical students and professionals. Premedical and medical students, on the other hand, are sometimes indignant at what they see as personal attacks on their good intentions and integrity.

In a sense, both sides are right. The health care system is insensitive to key psychological issues, while most individual health care providers are dedicated, humane professionals. This book has pointed out the many ways in which the health psychology model is superior to the traditional medical model. This book has also assumed, but not stressed, that many biomedical services provided by highly-educated physicians are extremely valuable contributions to individuals and society. Thus, both sides are necessarily left with some dissatisfactions. The challenge is to truly integrate the two perspectives.

Doing so is not easy. It necessitates changes in society's thinking about medical education, medical practice, health promotion, and the structure of health care.

Despite the interpretive difficulties, many important conclusions can be drawn. Most obviously, we have not found a general cure for cancer. Some day, a cure may appear for the various cancers. In the meantime, millions of people will have suffered extensively and died prematurely, billions of dollars will have been spent on research, and further billions and billions will have been spent in providing medical care and lost in missed wages. There are still severe limits on medicine.

On the other hand, consider the fact that 100 years ago, few people died of lung cancer, whereas now more than 100,000 die annually in the United States. With the elimination of cigarette smoking and the development of safe environments in chemical plants, lung cancer would almost disappear again. Similar arguments could be made concerning other diseases, such as AIDS. With no unprotected sex or drug abuse, AIDS could be controlled. There are few limits on the potential of health promotion, especially as compared to the limits on medical treatment.

People continue smoking cigarettes, living in stressful and polluted environments, engaging in dangerous activities, and so on, and so on; they then demand a cure for their diseases. Medicine responds with more and more sophisticated, expensive, and dangerous treatments. Expectations keep rising. Iatrogenic (physician-caused) illnesses and side effects also rise. Such problems brought the field of medicine severe criticism and encouraged the rise of health psychology (Illich, 1976; Millman, 1976), and a more optimistic and balanced view.

The Changing Health Care System

As we have seen in earlier chapters, physicians are, for the most part, ill-equipped to deal with the challenges of modern health care. Premedical students are pressured to major in science in college, are crammed full of biomedical facts in medical school, and severely overworked in medical residencies. Of course, no patient wants to be treated by an ignorant physician, but no one wants physicians to be stressed-out individuals either. There is ample evidence that medical education must be changed, and some progress has been made (Bok, 1984).

Sometimes, medical educators try an easy fix to this challenge. A course on Medical Ethics or Behavioral Science may be added to the curriculum. Unfortunately, a broader perspective that includes health psychology can only be learned when it becomes a full partner in the whole educational process. There are currently several thousand psychologists on the faculties of medical schools, but serious problems remain in integrating them into the mainstream of practice (Clayson & Mensh, 1987). Some student physicians do learn this broader perspective by watching distinguished physicians who have somehow come to understand these issues on their own. However, the education should not be haphazard but, rather, should be integrated into the basic educational process.

Consider one simple example: Will families be allowed to witness emergency room treatment to help ease the stress of both family and patient (Meyers, et al., 2000)? Will such taboos about family involvement fall, just as fathers are no longer banished from delivery rooms?

Even when broadly trained, physicians cannot do it all. Health care has become so complex that a single individual can no longer fill all its needs. Health care teams are

Figure 15–3 A challenge of health psychology is to integrate the traditional and the biopsychosocial approaches to health. This necessitates changes in society's thinking about medical practice, health promotion, and the structure of health care. *(Copyright Howard S. Friedman, drawing by Robin Jensen.) Reprinted by permission*

being and should continue to be developed. More basically, as we have seen, the traditional medical model must be replaced with a broader understanding of health.

THE PROMISE OF HEALTH PSYCHOLOGY

In reading about health psychology, you may have sensed some of the excitement that currently characterizes this field. The promise of health psychology may be summarized in two domains. First, there is hope that concern with health promotion, disease prevention, and patient cooperation will provide a higher quality of life at lower cost. Second, there is hope that better interpersonal relations will improve the health and the health care of the chronically ill, the stressed, the dying, and their families, as well as positively affect the lives of health care professionals themselves.

Quality of Life and Cost Effectiveness

Many people become upset and indignant when a life is lost that could have been saved; they don't care about the costs. Some people refuse to put a dollar value on a human life and human health. Yet, when we refuse to face this issue directly and rationally, we make the decision anyway, but we do so indirectly and irrationally. For example, government or health insurance may refuse to put a cap on the amount it will pay for cancer treatment for any one person. The argument goes, "You can't just let her die due to lack of money for more surgery." But the government may then cut benefits for prenatal care or health education or school lunch programs, saying they cannot be afforded; health may be damaged or life lost.

Or, people may donate large sums of money to help a poor child with leukemia but will rise up in protest if expensive air pollution controls are installed and gasoline prices rise sharply. In other words, many people irrationally refuse to consider monetary costs when a victim is near death, but will then oppose spending comparatively small amounts of money to prevent morbidity and mortality.

In a rational analysis, the monetary costs of health must be considered directly and not hidden. Should we buy a new heart-lung machine and a resonance imager for the hospital, or would that money be better spent straightening the road where car crashes are killing people? Should we provide expensive cholesterol-lowering drugs to the threatened elderly, or should we hire a new physical education teacher for the elementary school kids? These questions, while rational, are not likely to be asked in this form. Although the assessment of health and quality of life may be difficult (Kaplan & Criqui, 1985), such questions must be addressed.

There are two main avenues through which health psychology may be cost effective. The first is through the prevention of unnecessary use of medical services. It has been estimated repeatedly that perhaps half of all visits to a physician are for nonmedical conditions (Mechanic, 1982). That is, the problem does not fit the traditional medical model and may not need expensive treatment by a physician. The patient may be feeling anxious, or wanting to stop smoking, or needing permission to be sexually active or to stop having more children.

For example, one early study examined the effects of psychotherapy within Kaiser-Permanente, a large HMO (Cummings & Follette, 1976). It found that psychological services reduced the use of medical care. Other studies support the view that when psychological services are provided, use of medical services may decrease (Chiles, Lambert & Hatch, 1999; Jones & Vischi, 1979; Mumford, Schlesinger, Glass, Patrick, & Cuerdon, 1984; Sobel, 1995), although the issue is far from settled.

The second, and probably more significant, way in which health psychology may save money is more complex. This way is of course through encouraging the kinds of behaviors that lead to reduced stress, greater patient cooperation, and significant health promotion efforts. Research in this area began, as health psychology began, only several decades ago.

One interesting analysis examined the scientific literature on the effects of psychological intervention on recovery from surgery and heart attacks (Mumford, Schlesinger, & Glass, 1982). For example, the psychological intervention might be a group discussion led by a trained nurse for patients having surgery the next day. This review found that, on average, a brief psychological intervention resulted in patients being discharged two days earlier from the hospital (than were control patients). Such a saving is of course much more than the cost of the intervention. Importantly, note that this monetary analysis does not even include the benefits to the patients' emotional adjustment.

A more recent study did a randomized, controlled intervention on about 1,000 patients with heart disease, lung disease, stroke, or arthritis (Lorig et al., 1999). Half the patients were taught a self-management program for chronic disease. At the end of six

Box 15-2   The Economic Marketplace

Dear Wendy:

I wish to extend my personal THANKS to you for the cooperation you have given me during your dental treatment. The porcelain crowns that I placed in your mouth represent some of the finest dentistry that can be produced. We will be looking forward to seeing you again. We hope that you will need only a pat on the back at that time. Meanwhile, we hope you enjoyed your dental experience enough to tell your friends and family about us. We're not looking for patients, we're looking for the super people of the world. And you are certainly one of those people.

    Have a super fun year. See you soon!!!

Sincerely yours,
R. Henderson, DDS

P.S. Keep smiling!!

This dentist probably didn't mind the $2,000 payment he received. Nevertheless, not that long ago, such a letter from a health care provider was unheard of. Now, it would not be surprising to see such a letter or a TV advertisement extolling one's artificial pacemaker. Economic forces are having a great impact on health care.

Countries that have developed systems of socialized medicine (in which everyone has access to health care services provided by the government) have strictly regulated the numbers of physicians and the access to health care. In this way, costs have been controlled. In the United States, a different approach has been taken. The government has subsidized the education of physicians, and then allowed people to obtain the best health care that money can buy. But people are less and less likely to pay directly for their health care. Most Americans rely either on health insurance (so-called third party payment) or on prepaid plans.

During the past half century, huge hospital complexes have been built, with specialists to staff them and advanced equipment to fill them. In the short term, this tremendous shift of national resources to health care has benefited the pocketbooks of physicians. Many physicians earn over $150,000 per year, and incomes of $250,000 to $500,000 are not unheard of.

In recent years, however, people have reached the limits of what they are able and willing to pay for private health insurance, and government has reached the limits of what it will pay for the uninsured. To participate in the reimbursement system, many physicians have given up much of their autonomy and rely in one way or another on government or institutional subsidies for hospitals, health insurance, and care for the indigent. As the limits of increase in technology are being approached, both in terms of society's wealth and cost-effectiveness, the incomes of physicians are inevitably being squeezed. It remains to be seen whether some of their autonomy will be regained

In many settings, health care services, including doctors' services, are now owned by for-profit private corporations. Not surprisingly, these corporations are in business to make money. They may hire those physicians who make the most money. One physician, writing in the *New England Journal of Medicine,* described how he was fired for not ordering enough tests and bringing in enough money. When his company's regional medical director visited, this director (himself a physician) pointed at the x-ray machine and exhorted the staff, "I want to hear that baby humming!" [R.S. Bock, 1988, *NEJM, 319,* 785–787.] On the other hand, physicians in HMOs may be pressed not to order tests. Since health psychology emphasizes social and cultural factors, communication and cooperation, and health promotion, it provides a perspective that may head off many problems before they become serious. Many of these problems are issues of how to utilize resources.

months, those in the intervention group had spent less time in the hospital than those in the control group, and they reported more exercise, better symptom management, and better self-reported health. This study continues a long tradition in health psychology, but one that it is finally being given new impetus.

On the other hand, it is important not to overstate the potential contributions of health psychology. The health psychologist Robert M. Kaplan (1984, 2000) has pointed out that many simple behavioral changes will by themselves likely have a relatively minor impact on health. However, taken together, many simple steps may prove significant, and there is no doubt that some health behaviors, such as smoking and drunken driving, do have a dramatic impact on health.

Further, it is not easy to change human behavior. So, the benefits of such interventions in terms of quality and length of life should always be weighed against their psychological, social, and economic costs.

Better Human Relations

The second major promise of health psychology lies in the domain of human relations and human dignity. As this book has repeatedly emphasized, when the human characteristics of patients are overlooked and medicine becomes overly technical or mechanical, the results can be devastating. Part of the issue involves dignity, ethics, and compassion. But it is a big mistake to view the health psychology model solely as "humanistic." Rather, the health psychology model is also *scientific.* When psychological and sociocultural factors are given the proper attention, the healing process performs at its best.

SUMMARY AND CONCLUSION

In sum, times of turmoil can be used to produce change for the better. Notions of health and health care are currently in a state of flux and are undergoing significant reevaluation. Health psychology promises to make a positive contribution to this process.

In modern health care, interrelated ethical, legal, economic, and psychological problems continually arise. For example, many Americans have completed advance end-of-life directives, hoping that their wishes will be followed, but family members still are not very accurate in understanding the preferences. On the biological front, advances in genetics sometimes bring with them a curse of knowing the future but being unable to do enough about it.

Complete access to good health care is not yet the right of every individual. Poor patients are less likely to seek and obtain care, may be less able to follow treatment regimens, may receive much more impersonal treatment, and may be uninformed about the details of what is happening to them. Doctors, patients, and *society* are all key determinants of health care utilization. As long as the traditional medical model is in place, there will be pressure to perform the most high-tech procedures, but more care and more expensive care does not necessarily mean better health.

The health psychology model constantly reminds us that patients are people, not machines. People exist in a social and cultural context, people make decisions about their daily health behaviors, people experience emotions and stress that affect their health, and people require a certain amount of respect and dignity. When these matters are recognized, addressed, and studied scientifically, the health care system and the people in the society benefit. When these matters are ignored, even unintentionally ignored, we all pay the price.

Suggested Additional Readings

Dworkin, Gerald, Frey, R. G., & Bok, Sissela. (1998). *Euthanasia and physician-assisted suicide.* Cambridge, England: Cambridge University Press.

Kaplan, Robert M. (1993). *The Hippocratic predicament: Affordability, access, and accountability in American medicine.* San Diego: Academic Press.

Rose, G. A. (1992). *The strategy of preventive medicine.* Oxford, England: Oxford University Press.

Key Concepts

Baby M	cesarean section
socio-medical ethics	tenor of the times
pre-implantation genetic diagnosis	disability-adjusted life years (DALY)
cassandra genes	lifestyle factors
SES gradient	Healthy People 2010
health care utilization	

GLOSSARY

acceptance   a postulated stage of dying during which a patient is "void of feelings" and contemplates death with a quiet acceptance.

accommodation   a phase of bereavement during which the lost person becomes a memory and new ways of dealing with the world are created.

action dialog   action interviews with patients that involve gaining information from patients (and giving information to patients) during the examination.

active patient orientation   the idea suggested by various social scientists to return responsibility for healing into the hands of patients.

activity-passivity model   a practitioner-patient relationship in which the health professional does something to the patient but the patient is passive, so he or she has no control or responsibility and the practitioner has absolute control and responsibility; model most often applied to a patient during an emergency.

acquired immunodeficiency syndrome (AIDS)   an infectious disease that can be spread through sexual relations or blood contact; a disease that develops from attaining the human immunodeficiency virus (HIV), which impairs the helper T-lymphocytes (also called CD4+).

acupuncture   a Chinese technique designed to minimize or eliminate pain by inserting needles at certain critical points in the body.

acute illness   injury or sickness that arises within a short period of time, during which an individual requires emergency medical treatment and attention (i.e., stroke, accident, or heart attack).

adherence   the act of a patient's following medical treatment prescribed by a physician; a term that may reflect and perpetuate the image of patients as unable to make their own health care decisions.

adrenal cortex   a component of the adrenal glands, located above the kidneys in the human body; tissue in the body that secretes corticosteroids, hormones that have pronounced effects on the health of the body.

adrenal medulla   a component of the adrenal glands, located above the kidneys in the human body; tissue which secretes epinephrine and norepinephrine into the blood.

age roles   what is expected of people because of their age, which may also contain a partial explanation for illness behaviors.

alcoholic   an individual who is physically addicted to alcohol, who neglects other responsibilities, needs large quantities of alcohol, and experiences withdrawal when he or she stops drinking.

alexithymia   an absence of words for emotions; a condition in which individuals are apathetic, stoic, unemotional, or repressed.

allostasis   the ability to achieve internal stability through change.

Alzheimer's disease   a chronic organic brain disorder that produces poor memory, an inability of the individual to orient in time and place, and a general marked decline in intellectual functioning.

anger stage   a stage of dying during which a patient vents resentment at both family and health care personnel.

anorexia nervosa   an eating disorder in which people suffer from malnutrition and loss of weight caused by insufficient food intake.

anticipatory grief   a psychological response whereby family members and friends stop touching dying patients, both in a physical and in a symbolic sense, that can leave the patient feeling extremely lonely.

antigen   a threat to the body's healthy cells, which involves a recognizable foreign protein on the invader's cell surface.

artifact   a human-made phenomenon in which findings emerge out of a study solely because of the way a study is conducted or the way it is analyzed.

art of medicine   nonmechanical aspects of patient care emphasized by the health psychology model in a scientific manner.

attributable risk   incidence of a disease in exposed persons that is due to the exposure.

attribution   the process of interpreting a symptom or behavior through a search for a causal explanation.

autoimmune disease   a disease in which the immune system can sometimes go awry and attack some of the body's own cells.

autonomic nervous system   part of the nervous system that controls an organism's internal organs; part of the nervous system that contains the sympathetic nervous system and the parasympathetic system.

aversion therapy   association of a behavior with unpleasant sensations to rid oneself of the behavior.

Baby M   a baby who resulted from artificial insemination and was put up for adoption; but when Baby M was born, the biological mother changed her mind and wanted to keep the newborn.

baby talk   the special high-pitched tone parents use when talking to toddlers and infants; talk that is a significant aspect of the speech directed toward the institutionalized elderly; a positive-sounding speech that also suggests that the recipient is dependent, subordinate, and passive, showing how tone of voice can reveal emotional and motivational states of the speaker.

bargaining stage a postulated stage of dying during which a patient may try to make a deal with fate for more time or less pain.

belief in small numbers a person or physician extrapolates the findings from a small sample to an entire population and then judges the probabilities of success accordingly; may lead a physician to place undue confidence in a small amount of data.

bereavement a loss; can sometimes be faced by restoring meaning to one's life that occurs in three phases: avoidance, confrontation, and accommodation.

biobehavioral mechanisms plausible physiological mediating mechanisms between behavior and disease.

biofeedback a self-regulatory technique by which a person can learn to control some autonomic bodily processes and gain increased control over some voluntary processes.

biological third variable a biological predisposition that leads to the likelihood of both a certain type of personality and a certain disease.

biopsychosocial health psychology model a broad approach to health and health care that assumes that health is influenced by biological, psychological, and social factors.

body language, positions, gestures a major category of nonverbal communication that incorporates any movement or placement of the body that communicates a specific message (i.e., posture, hand movements, how a person is leaning, self-touching, foot tapping).

body mass index (BMI) a measure of obesity which equals weight in kilograms divided by the square of height in meters, or weight in pounds multiplied by 704.5 and then divided by the square of height in inches; a BMI greater than 26 is considered unhealthy.

brain death a state in which there is no longer any activity in the brain.

broken heart psychological stress and emotional upset resulting from a conflict of interest usually occurring between two individuals in a romantic relationship.

bulimia nervosa an eating disorder in which binge eating is followed by purging.

burnout an emotional exhaustion in which concern for patients as people disappears; a phenomenon that health care professionals may experience if they do not successfully face the emotions of working intensively with very ill or dying patients and which can come about from a lack of a firm acceptance and understanding of their own feelings.

Cartesian dualism an idea proposed by the 17th-century French philosopher René Descartes that a human being has a mind that exists in the spiritual realm and a body that exists in the realm of physical matter; a belief in the separation of the mind and body; a common idea in modern medicine where "mental" problems are almost always distinguished from "physical" problems.

cassandra genes genes that can be examined to discover if a person will someday develop a dread disease for which there is no cure, such as Huntington's disease.

catecholamines a group of key neurotransmitters, including epinephrine, norepinephrine, and dopamine.

cesarean section (C-section)   delivery of a baby by cutting through the mother's abdominal and uterine walls; a surgical procedure that is sometimes necessary to save the life or preserve the health of the infant or the mother; a surgery that has had a dramatic rise in rate in the United States, which raises the question about the use of this procedure.

change in activity   a component of grief when the daily activities of bereaved people usually show many changes; when bereaved people are restless and lack the capacity to initiate and maintain organized patterns of activity.

chronic illness   a condition that involves some disability, is caused by nonreversible pathological change, and requires training and motivation on the part of the patient to care for himself or herself.

chronic stress   a continuing stress, common and insidious, that causes psychophysiological reactions over many months.

cloak of silence   a reaction in which health care professionals, particularly physicians, strongly resist recognition of the fact that they or their peers are impaired, so they avoid assistance.

closed-ended and open-ended questions   a closed-ended question provides the respondent with a choice of answers and can be answered very quickly, whereas an open-ended question forces the respondents to come up with their own answers and gives the respondents a chance to elaborate and to provide valuable information.

cognitive coping mechanisms   techniques that focus systematically on the individual's thoughts and thought patterns; techniques that may help minimize stress or pain by helping people know what types of sensations to expect and how to think about the sensations so that their stress or pain can be more easily managed.

compliance   the act of a patient's following instructions to medical treatment; a term that tends to reflect and perpetuate the image of patients as unable to make their own health care decisions.

components of grief   reactions to bereavement that occur in stages; five common components of grief, which include many of the elements of depression and anxiety: somatic weakness, preoccupation, guilt, hostility, and change in activity.

conditioning   a type of learning in which the body's autonomic responses become programmed to a previously neutral stimulus in the environment.

conformity   a reaction to group pressure that involves looking at behaviors of members of an individual's reference group to determine what behaviors are appropriate.

confrontation   a phase of bereavement during which one comes to grips with the new reality.

Cook-Medley hostility scale   a self-report scale that measures aspects of the disease-prone personality, including cynicism, hostile feelings, and aggressive tendencies.

coping   the thoughts and actions a person uses to deal with stress.

coping with the discomfort and physical incapacity   the first major task that researchers Rudolf Moos and Vivien Tsu suggested that the crisis of illness brings with it; the act of dealing with the illness or injury while experiencing pain, weakness, and loss of control.

coronary-prone personality   hostile, cynical, struggling personality; a type of personality that is believed to bring about coronary heart disease.

correlation   degree of association between two variables, such as attributes or behaviors and illnesses

Couvade syndrome   a phenomenon where men experience "labor pain" in sympathy with their pregnant wives, showing that the mind can affect the body.

cue discrepancy   the degree of inconsistency between verbal and nonverbal cues.

curandero   a folk-curer; a member of the traditional Mexican-American community who makes house calls and deals with the entire family of the patient.

dealing with the medical technology   the second major task that researchers Rudolf Moos and Vivien Tsu suggested that the crisis of illness brings with it; the act of the patient adjusting to having his or her body invaded for various tests and medical procedures.

deception   a situation in which an individual may be hiding something, or may not be telling the whole truth, which may be detected through analysis of nonverbal cues, specifically that of body behavior.

deficient diet   inadequate nutrition and a poor diet that does not satisfy daily requirements for vitamins, minerals, and other nutrients.

dehumanization   the process of treating a person as less than a whole human being.

denial   a beginning stage in responding to the prospect of death, where the patient is not able to face the information.

depression stage   a postulated stage of dying during which a patient goes through a type of self-grieving; a psychological state of hopelessness, lost concentration, and lethargy.

developmental regression   regressing to earlier behaviors, such as nighttime fears and screaming, clinging to and being dependent on parents, thumb sucking, and loss of bowel and bladder control.

diathesis   the predisposition of the body to a disease or disorder.

diathesis-stress model   a sophisticated model of stress and illness that depends on the idea of individual characteristics interacting with a situation or stressor.

dietary imbalance   the result of eating too much of certain foods and too little of other foods.

disability-adjusted life years (DALY)   a measure of disease burden that takes into account age and morbidity, as well as mortality measures like longevity.

disease   organic problem with the body, where the individual may or may not show illness behavior and may or may not enter the sick role.

disease prevention   intervention to prevent a disease for which a person is at risk.

disease-prone personality   a personality that may consist of a variety of unhealthy attitudes and behaviors that make an individual more prone to disease.

distance/Edward Hall's spatial zones   the four spatial zones distinguished by anthropologist Edward Hall in 1966; the four zones are intimate distance, personal distance, social distance, and public distance.

distraction   a method that may be used to make pain more tolerable even though it is still present; any event that prevents an individual from focusing attention.

doctor-shopping   the phenomenon of patients' changing doctors repeatedly.

double-blind   a type of experimental procedure in which neither the doctor nor the patient knows whether the patient is receiving the new treatment being tested, the old treatment, or a placebo control; a type of experimental procedure meant to eliminate the effect of the patient's and the doctor's expectations on results of the research.

double-bind situation   what patients often face when conflicting messages of optimism and pessimism are expressed to them, leaving them in a state of confusion and alienation.

dualism   the belief of the separation of issues of the mind from issues of the body.

emotion-focused coping   a type of coping with stress that involves efforts to deal with the emotional distress, such as by going out jogging, denying the threat, or having a few stiff drinks.

emotional social support   social support that helps a person deal with the emotional consequences of stress, thus minimizing the risk of illness.

endocrine system   a communicative or regulatory bodily system that functions by secreting chemicals called hormones into the bloodstream.

endogenous opioids   peptides released from the neurons of the central nervous system that affect or directly communicate with other cells and that specifically act on opiate receptors.

endorphins   a substance produced by the body that helps the body control pain; can be induced by placebo effects.

epidemiology   the study of the distribution of morbidity and mortality throughout the population.

ethics   the study of the nature of morals and moral choices, which often takes into consideration the dynamic between costs and benefits.

euthanasia   the putting to death of a person suffering from a painful, terminal illness, also known as "mercy killing."

exercise   physical activity that is planned and structured.

expert power   the ability of a health care professional to be seen as an expert in matters of health and illness as part of the professional-patient relationship.

explanatory style   individual differences in how people understand and explain the causes of bad events.

facial expression   a major category of nonverbal communication that incorporates any function of the sense organs, muscles, or nerves of the face to communicate a specific message.

faith healing   an attempt to alleviate pain or disability by having the person "believe" he or she will feel better; a practice shunned by modern medicine as unscientific, although it often works.

fear appeals   a particular type of ego approach to behavior change, which postulates that a threat to one's well-being will motivate change.

feldsher   a physician's assistant in Russia, who provides a large volume of the medical care to individuals in rural populations.

fight-or-flight response   discovered by Walter Cannon, a response to stress which causes an increase in the organism's blood sugar level; a large output of adrenaline; an increase in pulse rate, blood pressure, and respiration rate; and an increase in the amount of blood pumped to the skeletal muscles; an animal's integrated physiological reaction that prepares it either for running away or fighting when it perceives a threatening situation.

free radicals   ionized (chemically active) molecules that damage healthy body cells.

Gate Control Theory of pain   a theory that proposes that there are special nerves that carry intense sensation to the spinal column but these signals do not necessarily go directly to the brain because there is a "gate" in the spinal column that can be closed by signals coming from the brain; a belief that thoughts and feelings can provide gate-closing signals and influence whether the sensation of pain reaches the brain and is perceived as painful.

gaze   an influential nonverbal cue that incorporates any eye behavior that communicates a specific message, that is, staring, degree of eye contact, glances, and so on.

gender roles   shared expectations we hold about the appropriate behavior of men and women; stereotypes applied to sex.

gene   unit of information in the form of nucleic acids that codes for biological characteristics unique to an individual.

General Adaptation Syndrome   a theory proposed by Selye that argues that any noxious stimulus (emotional or physical) results in a biological response that is characterized by an arousal of the body's system of defenses against the provocative stimulus in three stages: the alarm reaction, a stage of resistance, and a stage of exhaustion.

germ theory   the most famous and successful causal relationship in medicine that involves the knowledge that certain bacteria cause certain diseases.

grief   the psychological response to bereavement (the loss of someone close), involving somatic (bodily) weakness, exhaustion, a feeling of hollowness, thoughts about the deceased, guilt over the death, and possible hostility, withdrawal, or restlessness.

grief work   the rechanneling of intense feelings of attachment to a deceased person by doing things such as avoiding the intense emotional distress that is connected with the grief experience or transforming the grief process into a meaningful and productive pursuit.

groupthink   group decision-making, which can sometimes replace independent critical thinking; a phenomenon that can occur in the medical setting where health care professionals go along with a group of peers, suppressing their own personal doubts, and have a shared illusion of unanimity; the collective thinking of a group associated with unquestioned belief in its own morality, collective use of the defense of rationalization, stereotyped views of outsiders, and pressure on dissenters.

guidance-cooperation model   medical model in which the practitioner tells the patients what he or she thinks is the best for the patient and the patient is expected to cooperate because both believe the "doctor knows best."

hardiness   a characteristic of a person who lives life to the fullest, feels competent, and has a productive orientation; the belief a person has that he or she can control or influence events, is able to become deeply involved in and is committed to activities in his or her life, and views change as an exciting challenge to his or her further development as a person; personality trait that tends to be associated with healthy individuals.

harm reduction   efforts directed at reducing the damage rather than at preventing the unhealthy behavior.

hassles   minor stressful events that may affect longer-term psychological and physical health.

Hawthorne effect   phenomenon by which production rises when special attention is paid to the workers, independently of changes in the working conditions; a situation in the medical field where a doctor has some beneficial effect on a patient only because the patient appeared at the doctor's office.

health belief model   a model that proposes that people's health actions are a function of whether they perceive a personal threat to their health and whether they think the health action will reduce the threat.

health care utilization   the usage of medical care; studied and regulated by economists, sociologists, and public health officials.

health literacy   the ability to understand subject matter surrounding one's health problem and to accurately follow directions given by a health practitioner.

health maintenance organization (HMO)   health care organization (set up between providers and health insurers) to provide comprehensive medical services to patients at fixed and presumably lower costs.

health psychology   the study of psychological processes related to health and health care.

health psychology model   an approach to health and health care that has issues of healthy interpersonal relations and healthy behavior as its main focus, as well as properly using the traditional model of medicine; model of medicine assuming that health is influenced by biological factors, psychological factors, and social factors; biopsychosocial model.

health transactions model   a model that maintains that although traditional health care professionals have made the sole decision about treatment, such unilateral decision making is inappropriate, since the professional can never completely know or anticipate the values of the patient, the meaning of various outcomes, or the problems the patient would face in trying to cooperate with the therapeutic regimen.

healthy dying   the quest for a glorious death in which all psychological and social needs are met.

Healthy People 2010   an American national health promotion and disease prevention initiative that brings together government agencies, nonprofit organizations, businesses, communities, and individuals to improve the health of all Americans, eliminate disparities in health, and improve years and quality of healthy life; program has two main goals for the year 2010: increase quality and years of healthy life and eliminate health disparities; a program that incorporates four broad categories of objectives: the promotion of healthy behaviors, the promotion of healthy and safe communities, the improvement of personal and public health, and the prevention and reduction in diseases and disorders.

Hippocrates   Greek physician of fourth century B.C., called the Father of Medicine, who recognized how important it is for health care professionals to deliver care to their patients with understanding and sensitivity.

holistic health   a growing modern movement to bring the mind and body together in medical treatment; treatment of a person as a whole "physical-and-mental" human being, with the mind always affecting the body and vice versa.

homecare   health care for the chronically or terminally ill supplied in the home of the patient or a family member.

homeostasis   the process of maintaining internal equilibrium through adjustments in physiological processes.

hormone   a chemical secreted by the endocrine system that travels to target cells, where it attaches and thereby activates new functions.

hospice   an institution that provides special care for the terminally ill.

human immunodeficiency virus (HIV)   a virus that causes the acquired immunodeficiency syndrome (AIDS); spread through the exchange of bodily fluids, such as in sexual relations, blood transfusions, and sharing drug needles.

humors   fluids that the ancient Greeks believed were in the body and determined health and personality, explaining mind-to-body links.

hysteria   "wandering womb"; an emotional disturbance.

iatrogenic illness   illness caused by physicians.

identity spread   a situation in which obvious symptoms are interpreted by others as overwhelmingly pervasive and people begin to view the chronically ill person as incapable of engaging in any kind of constructive behavior, even though that may not be the case.

illness   a social phenomenon that may or may not involve an organic disease and is a legitimate basis for seeking assistance from others.

illness behaviors   actions that indicate an individual feels ill and is engaging in activities that indicate a problem, but may or may not have an organic disease.

immediacy   the mutual stimulation of an interaction.

immune system   a system of the body that protects bodily tissues from invading microbes, such as bacteria, and from abnormal cells, such as cancer cells or those infected by a virus.

immunization   the process of becoming immune to a disease; commonly takes the form of an injection designed to create an artificial immunity in the body, which the body cannot create for itself, prior to being exposed to the pathogen.

immunosuppressive effects   the result of substances that interfere with the action of immune system cells when present in high levels.

informational function   a channel through which patients learn valuable information pertaining to their illness, including its physical effects, prognosis, the side effects of drugs given for the condition, financial demands, government services, transportation, nursing care, and many other matters; a function of social support.

inhibited power motivation syndrome   a syndrome in which people have a high need to influence others but also have a high need to inhibit their own activity; a characteristic that may be associated with people who have lower immunological competence.

initial crisis   a preliminary stage during chronic physical illness in which the individual afflicted with the illness faces social and emotional difficulties.

instrumental care   one of the two functions of the health care professional that involves the purely technical aspects of the treatment of the patient, such as surgery or the administration of a specific drug for a specific condition.

internal locus of control   the generalized tendency of a person to believe that whatever happens is under his or her own control.

internship (and residency)   the training a student physician receives in the first three to five years of post-medical school training.

interviewer bias   phenomenon in which a respondent's answer is influenced by the interviewer.

intimate distance   one of Edward Hall's four spatial zones, where very intimate interactions usually occur.

involuntary smoking   the inhaling of smoke that occurs as a result of being exposed to the smoking of others.

King's touch/royal touch   a technique used by English and French kings to provide divine healing by direct physical contact alone.

Kübler-Ross' stages of death   the five stages dying patients undergo according to Kübler-Ross in her book *On Death and Dying:* denial, anger, bargaining, depression, and acceptance.

lack of cooperation/noncooperation with treatment   failure of a patient to follow precisely the recommendations of the physician or other health care professional.

laying on of the hands   a technique used by faith healers to heal the ill by direct physical contact alone.

learned helplessness   a situation in which an individual can no longer cope and may give up (and even die), which results from learned lack of control in stressful situations.

leave-taking ceremony   an important aspect of the bereavement process, which usually takes the form of a funeral or ceremony to establish the fact that the individual has died, making it an emotional reality both for the bereaved person and for others.

Lewis Terman and his research   psychologist Lewis Terman was one of the leading intelligence researchers who, in 1921, began one of the most comprehensive studies in psychology in his investigation of genetic theories of intelligence; the Terman Life-Cycle study intensively researched psychosocial and intellectual development of bright California schoolchildren (nicknamed Terman's Termites) until their adulthood.

life change   any event in an individual's life that requires some degree of coping and can be related to illness and physical deterioration.

lifestyle factors   factors that involve an individual's way of life, for example (under ideal conditions), no smoking, moderate alcohol use, clear air, clean water, healthy food, safe transportation, moderate exercise, few weapons, stable families, good stress management, and complete cooperation with medical treatment.

linguistic relativity   the idea that thought is influenced and controlled by language, an idea from the psychologist and philosopher Benjamin Lee Whorf; an issue of medical jargon that makes the communication between physicians and patients more difficult.

living will   a description of how an individual wants his or her medical care handled when he or she is still alive but no longer able to manage his or her affairs.

locus of control   an individual's belief about what determines what happens to him or her.

loneliness   the negative psychological feeling of being alone, which can be caused by having no close intimate relationships or by the death of a loved one.

long-term apprenticeship model   a model in which medical education never ends, but the workload at any given time in a physician's life is much more reasonable; a new model of medical education proposed by Howard Friedman that can be instituted by more closely matching the training with the realities of modern practice.

Lown's explanation of sudden cardiac death   a three-part explanation to account for the variability in sudden cardiac death after encountering stress; an explanation for sudden cardiac death that includes electrical instability already being present in the cardiac muscle, feelings of a pervasive emotional state, and a triggering event.

low tech, high touch   a technique used by hospice as opposed to using a traditional medical approach.

lymphocytes   white blood cells that provide cellular immunity and humoral immunity; a part of the immune system that has been known to be affected by stress.

maintenance of adequate communication   the third major task that researchers Rudolf Moos and Vivien Tsu suggested that the crisis of illness brings with it; the act of asking physicians for more attention and requesting help from nurses, which can be difficult for a patient whose psychological resources are already being used up in dealing with the physical illness.

malpractice   the practice of medicine with negligence in which the health professional makes serious errors.

mass psychogenic illness   a psychological-based illness that seems to arise spontaneously but is guided by a general rationale and spread rapidly from one member to another in a group; also known as assembly line hysteria; suggests that the social situation may strongly affect the collective illness behaviors of a group of people.

medical ethics   the study of the nature of morals and moral choices pertaining to the medical field, often brought up by modern medical procedures.

medical jargon   vocabulary familiar to the practitioner but often not to the patient, which may result in the practitioner believing that the patient understands what has been said when in fact it is not so; one of the main barriers to effective communication between physicians and patients.

medical milieu   an area of uncertainty in health care that leads physicians to make errors in medical diagnoses, which result from unjustified expectations.

Medspeak   a language that supposedly is used to facilitate the sharing of information; a language that often clouds scientific communication between health care professionals themselves and especially between health care professionals and patients.

meta-analysis   a method of quantitative integration of research studies useful for combining the results of independent studies so that they may be more easily viewed.

metabolic syndrome   a constellation of bodily changes associated with coronary heart disease that involves changes in insulin resistance, glucose tolerance, blood pressure, obesity, cholesterol, and triglycerides.

modeling   a situation in which a person might learn unhealthy behaviors by watching a favored parent or a favorite movie star drink, smoke, take risks, and so on; vicarious learning.

models of health promotion and disease prevention   ten models split into two kinds of perspectives in thinking about preventing unhealthy habits and promoting healthy behaviors that include the specific pathogen-based approach and the more general and basic model of human motivation and behavior; the categories of health promotion and disease prevention that include a biological model, learning model, educational model, cognitive learning/health belief model, ego/identity model, societal/cultural model, socioeconomic/political model, existential model, personality trait model, and interactional multimodal model.

monism   the belief of the close, integral ties between the mind and the body.

mourning   the public or ritual display of grief.

Munchausen Syndrome   a condition in which patients tell wild tales to gain admission to hospitals, possibly to gain drugs or social rewards.

Munchausen Syndrome by Proxy   a condition in which a second party, usually a parent, may make a child ill in hopes of receiving sympathy, attention, or access to experts.

multimodal approaches   models that attempt to integrate two or more systems of health promotion.

mutual participation   medical model in which the practitioner and patient have equal power in the relationship and their behaviors are mutually satisfying to keep the relationship continuing, maintaining the patient's dignity and respect; a belief that has been rare in modern medicine but has recently become more prominent.

narrowing   the process of starting the interview with the most broad questions and then moving to more specific, detailed questions.

New Pathway   a program started at Harvard Medical School in the 1980s that emphasized behaviors and attitudes related to so-called humanistic medicine, including many health psychology issues.

noncompliance   lack of cooperation on the part of the patient.

noncooperation   failure of the patient to carry out the recommendations as the health care professional intended they be carried out.

nonverbal communication   communication involving facial expressions, voice tones, gestures, touches, and related cues that complement and illustrate aspects of the spoken word; a cue that patients are likely to be watchful of because they want to reduce their emotional uncertainty and so tend to look to those around them for subtle clues to help them understand what they are feeling and how they should respond, to search for factual information about their disease and its prognosis.

normalization   the attempt by a chronically ill person to establish and maintain as normal an existence as possible.

nosocomial infections   infections that are acquired in the hospital.

nutrition   the process of getting enough of the right foods that help the body's cells maintain themselves and not getting too much of the wrong foods, such as saturated fats, that can interfere with optimal cholesterol metabolism.

obsessional review   an activity in which the bereaved person reviews over and over again the details of the death to help integrate the emotional and cognitive aspects of the loss.

optimistic bias   unrealistic optimism or positive illusions that involve the faulty belief that negative events are less likely to happen to us than to others.

oxytocin   an important peptide hormone from the hypothalamus secreted by the pituitary, secreted, for example, when a nursing mother hears the distress cry of a hungry infant; it facilitates the let-down, milk-flow response.

pain-prone personality   an individual hypothesized to be more likely to develop and suffer from pain due to biopsychosocial makeup.

parasympathetic nervous system   part of the autonomic nervous system that generally restores the body's energies, such as by slowing the heart rate.

passing   the engagement of chronically ill people in normal interactions with others because the others do not know that they are not "normal."

patient compliance   a situation in which a patient follows the recommendations of a health care practitioner.

patient cooperation   the dynamic associated with a patient's adhering to a health practitioner's medical advice and treatment; when the patient and health care practitioner work together as a team to better the situation of the patient.

personal distance   one of Edward Hall's four spatial zones that incorporates a small, protective personal sphere around each individual; for the most part, this is a boundary that others should not cross.

phases of bereavement   cognitive changes that occur during a major loss in an individual's life; three phases that include avoidance, confrontation, and accommodation.

physical fitness   a hard-to-define term that implies health or the ability to accomplish physical tasks; health and the ability to accomplish physical tasks and face the stressors that arise.

physical activity   the use of large muscle groups that results in a significant expenditure of energy.

pill counts   an objective measure researchers and practitioners use to determine the extent of patient cooperation with medication regimens.

pituitary   the body's master gland, which is located at the base of the brain, that secretes hormones that directly influence other key endocrine organs.

placebo effect   the effect of any therapy that is without specific activity for the condition being treated, which may bring about results because of the belief that the therapy is supposed to be working.

positive illusions   unrealistically positive perceptions or interpretations of challenge that may help an individual face a great challenge.

positive regard   a technique designed to uncover troubles or the feelings of patients by reinforcing any report of this information with positive behavior on behalf of the interviewer.

posttraumatic stress disorder   a type of reaction to stress commonly found in people who are subjected to tremendous life stress and have their social ties taken away; a problem of many American veterans of the Vietnam war, who returned home from horrifying experiences to find an uncaring country; many react with ongoing nightmares, survivor guilt, and social alienation.

pre-implantation genetic diagnosis   a medical technique that enables parents to select some of the traits of their future child.

preoccupation   a component of grief during which an individual occupies himself or herself with the image of the deceased.

preparing for an uncertain future   the seventh major task that researchers Rudolf Moos and Vivien Tsu suggested that the crisis of illness brings with it; the act of preparing for living with a permanent loss of function.

preservation of emotional balance   the fourth major task that researchers Rudolf Moos and Vivien Tsu suggested that the crisis of illness brings with it; the act of trying to manage the upsetting feelings aroused by the illness, feelings such as self-blame, anxiety, and thoughts of failure; the process behind dealing with a sense of alienation, feelings of inadequacy, and resentment.

preserving a satisfactory self-image   the fifth major task that researchers Rudolf Moos and Vivien Tsu suggested that the crisis of illness brings with it; the act of incorporating changes in physical functioning and appearance into a new self-image.

preserving relationships   the sixth major task that researchers Rudolf Moos and Vivien Tsu suggested that the crisis of illness brings with it; the act of maintaining the patient's social network of family and friends to avoid isolation from others and feelings of alienation associated with physical separation and having a new identity as a patient.

primary prevention   measures designed to prevent illness from developing, such as to reduce patients' excessive weight or programs to prevent adolescents from beginning to smoke cigarettes.

proactive coping (5 stages)   a conceptual analysis of the processes through which people anticipate or detect potential stressors and act in advance to prevent them or to mute their impact, developed by Lisa Aspinwall and Shelley Taylor; processes of coping that include resource accumulation, recognition of potential stressors, making an initial appraisal, preliminary coping efforts, and elicitation and use of feedback concerning initial efforts.

problem drinking   getting drunk several times a month and facing significant negative consequences.

problem-solving coping   a way of coping with stress that involves efforts to do something constructive about the stressful situation, such as finding a new job or studying hard for an upcoming exam.

Profile of Nonverbal Sensitivity (PONS)   film test that provides a quantitative index of an individual's accuracy at decoding facial, body, and voice tone cues of emotion; found that physicians who were most sensitive to body nonverbal communication received the highest degree of patients' satisfaction with treatment and that physicians' sensitivity to local cues is related to patients' cooperation.

prophylaxis   a prevention of disease that may include physical activity, but more commonly, the avoidance of toxic substances and infections.

psychoneuroimmunology (PNI)   the study of how psychological factors affect immunity through the neuroendocrine system; a new field of study that has become more popular since a landmark study in 1977 showed that healthy people whose spouses had died experienced a decrease in lymphocyte responsiveness at about two months after bereavement.

psychosomatic illness (psychophysiological disorder)   an illness that results from a person's view of the world, typical pattern of emotional responding, and impaired psychological resources; an illness where personality plays a causal role.

psychosomatic medicine   the area of medicine in which the mind-body relationship has been explored; an area of medicine that can refer to the use of the principles of psychology in understanding and treating illness or to medical problems that are caused by psychological states.

public distance   one of Edward Hall's four spatial zones, affecting psychological comfort.

quack   one who pretends to have medical expertise and bases treatment on unscientific findings.

quality adjusted life year (QALY)   a measure of the quality of life during a year, involving morbidity, symptoms, *and* psychosocial functioning considerations.

randomized clinical trials   true experiments in medicine in which people are randomly assigned to an experimental group or control group and then compared to each other.

reactance   a common psychological reaction where a patient angrily reacts to the seemingly arbitrary withdrawal of freedom.

reasoned action   action that results from people thinking about their worlds and being more likely to engage in healthier behaviors if they believe that the behavior will make a difference in their lives.

reference groups   groups that help people gain and maintain a sense of identity.

referent power   an ability for a practitioner to make the patient identify with the practitioner and want to be like him or her; great influence that the health care professional can have on the patient's health behavior to prevent noncooperation.

reinforcement   the process of rewarding a behavior by consequences so that it is more likely to occur in the future; operant conditioning.

relative risk   the risk of attaining a certain consequence for an action in comparison to the risk of the consequence without that action, such as the risk of mortality for smokers compared to the risk of mortality for nonsmokers.

relaxation response   a physiological result of successful meditation that can reduce an individual's blood pressure, respiration rate, and other physiological indicators of stressful arousal.

reliable assessment   to be able to repeat results each time the same thing is measured.

religiosity   the act of being religious or pious; a way of life that often has implications for good health because it involves beliefs of protecting and maintaining an individual's God-given body.

reward power   the ability to withdraw rewards for noncompliance; a limited power for a physician, since the physician controls few of the patient's needs.

role conflict   the dual identity that medical students feel when patients treat them like doctors but faculty and other students treat them like students; a common source of stress to medical students.

role training incongruities   a reality shock for newly hired health care professionals when it becomes apparent that there is a disparity between professional values and norms learned in school (such as the need to spend time talking with patients) and the bureaucratic norms set in hospitals (such as time limitations).

Roseto effect   a sense of community and social cohesiveness that may contribute to better health in a community overall.

salience   an important factor that influences the interpretation of symptoms as illness and produces the desire to seek medical care; the prominence of symptoms.

salutogenesis   a psychosocial equilibrium theory proposed by Antonovsky of how people stay healthy; points out that everyone is subject to environmental pressures, but some people thrive anyway.

secondary prevention   measures taken once a problem begins to develop, such as interventions designed to lower blood pressure to prevent stroke.

selection bias   bias that arises in a study when some people are more likely than others to be studied (thus deviating from a pure random sample).

self-actualization   the realization of personal growth and fulfillment.

self-efficacy   one's belief that he or she is in control of relevant actions.

self-healing personality   term coined by Howard Friedman to refer to the healing emotional style involving a match between the individual and the environment that maintains a physiological and psychosocial homeostasis and through which good mental health promotes good physical health.

self-healing subtypes   characteristic of individuals who differ but share an inherent resilience and an emotional equilibrium that comes from doing the right combination of activities appropriate for the individual.

self-identity   what a person thinks of himself or herself.

self-image   the way an individual perceives himself or herself with respect to his or her appearance and external characteristics; a self-concept that has direct relevance to the idea of a healthy body.

self-monitoring   a technique people use to lose weight, in which a written record of both the type and quantity of all food eaten each day as well daily weight is kept in order to promote awareness of the need for change and help prevent rationalization of poor eating habits.

self-presentation   a concept that involves the desire of an individual to appear normal or pleasurable to others.

sense of coherence   a person's confidence that the world is understandable, manageable, and meaningful; a belief that tends to be associated with healthy individuals.

SES gradient   a relation in public health that dictates that the higher a person's socioeconomic status, the lower is that person's risk of getting sick and of dying prematurely.

set point   the body's sense of its own ideal weight.

seven major tasks of adaptation   the seven major adaptive tasks researchers Rudolf Moos and Vivien Tsu suggested that the crisis of illness brings with it include, in order of occurrence, coping with the discomfort and physical incapacity, dealing with the medical technology, maintenance of adequate communication, preservation of emotional balance, preserving a satisfactory self-image, preserving relationships, and preparing for an uncertain future; a comprehensive framework for understanding reactions to illness.

sex roles   what is expected of people because of their sex, which may also contain a partial explanation of their illness behaviors.

sick role   a role in society adopted by people with symptoms and illness behaviors; a role that people can enter if a doctor, family, or influential friend confirms that the person is sick; a role in which the individual is exempt from normal activities and obligations, has a legitimate basis for seeking assistance from others, and is expected to feel uncomfortable and to try to cooperate with others to get well.

smoking prevention   any program designed to spread awareness about the dangers of smoking and that may incorporate activities that prevents individuals, specifically adolescents, from picking up the habit.

social comparison   a method of reducing patients' emotional uncertainty by looking to those around them—often medical personnel—for subtle clues to help them understand what they are feeling and how they should respond.

social death   a psychosocial state a patient experiences prior to biological death, during which others in the social environment may assume the patient's life is coming to a close and may act as if the patient has already passed.

social distance   one of Edward Hall's four spatial zones, in which usual social interaction occurs.

Social Readjustment Rating Scale (SRRS)   a scale to measure the general stressful impact of major events, constructed by having a large number of people rate various events as to how much readjustment was required.

social support   support of family and friends, which can be a significant aid to coping with stress; information, clarification, assistance, and reassurance that an individual receives from others in regard to his or her chronic illness.

socioeconomic and sociopolitical models   models of health promotion that focus on the economic and the legal pressures on people's health-relevant behavior.

socioemotional   one of the two aspects of the practitioner-patient relationship that involves the rapport between the health practitioner and patient.

socioemotional care   one of the two functions of the health care professional that involves the emotional and interpersonal dimension of care, such as the communication of caring to the patient and the understanding of the patient's feelings and problems.

somatic weakness   a component of grief during which a grieving individual may be exhausted or sometimes restless.

somatization   the presenting of symptoms that have no known medical explanation and that seem affected by psychological processes.

somatopsychology   the study of the influence of so-called physical states on so-called mental states.

stigma   some characteristic or attribute of a person that is deeply discrediting and takes priority over all other characteristics that the person has.

stress   state of an organism when reacting to challenging new circumstances.

stressors   challenging new environmental events that evoke reaction from an organism.

student culture   communication and shared understanding among students in a medical school class.

suicide   the act of purposely killing oneself.

sympathetic nervous system   part of the autonomic nervous system that mobilizes the body, such as by increasing heart rate, and that stimulates the adrenals to secrete catecholamines (epinephrine and norepinephrine) to enter the blood, travel throughout the body, and further increase the general arousal.

tend-and-befriend   a biobehavioral response to challenge that is normally found in females where there is more of a focus on tending to their young and creating associations with others to provide resources and protection.

thanatology   the study of death.

therapeutic touching   touching for therapeutic purposes; a relatively unresearched medical "art."

tone of voice   sounds, primarily pitch variations, that accompany the spoken word.

total institutions   institutions that manage every aspect of the patient's life, such as hospitals where people forfeit almost all control over their lives by relinquishing their clothes for hospital gowns, are rarely addressed in familiar terms, are highly restricted in where they can go, encounter a fixed schedule of eating and sleeping, and have little privacy.

touch   a sensation that occurs when two physical bodies come into contact; one of the oldest and most widespread forms of traditional medical treatment; a major category of nonverbal communication that incorporates any sort of contact to communicate a specific message.

traditional biomedical model of disease   mechanical model of health care; a way in which physicians and patients view illness; the model compares physicians to auto mechanics with the idea that physicians treat a patient's illness in a mechanical way, where each patient is treated with a routine procedure; an approach to disease that reached prominence in the 1950s and 1960s due to advanced medical technology.

transcutaneous nerve stimulation   a treatment in which a mild electrical current is applied to the skin to reduce pain; a treatment based on the belief that stimulation of one part of the nervous system can interfere with the sensation of pain produced by stimulation of another part of the nervous system; a treatment that has been shown to ease chronic pain in some people.

Type A behavior pattern   a characteristic that is displayed by people who are involved in a constant struggle to do more and more things in less and less time and are quite hostile or aggressive in their efforts to achieve them; a pattern associated with people who have coronary heart disease.

Type B behavior pattern   a characteristic that is displayed by people who are able to relax, do not worry about time, and are less concerned with accomplishment and more content with themselves compared to Type A people.

Type C behavior pattern   a characteristic that is displayed by people who are repressed, apathetic, and hopeless, in sharp contrast to Type A people; sometimes called the cancer-prone personality.

utilization   the usage of medical care in the field of health care.

validity   measuring or uncovering what is claimed to be measured and not something else in a study.

vector   an organism that transmits a pathogen, such as a disease-carrying mosquito.

visualization   a technique in which patients are taught to relax and form a mental picture, heavily employed in coping with cancer.

wellness   a term health practitioners have adopted to describe people not only free of disease but also who take positive action to improve their health; a sensible antidote to the narrow view that achieving health involves the "fixing" of a passive, diseased body by emphasizing that there are many aspects of a person's lifestyle that affect well-being.

white coat hypertension   the higher blood pressure that results from the patient's anxiety about the high-status physician in a white coat.

wisdom of the body   the amazing ability of the body to correct and internally regulate itself through the use of the nervous and endocrine systems.

work of worrying   the mental rehearsal of solutions to realistic problems, a moderate level of anticipatory fear, and a preparatory "working through" of difficulties.

years of life lost   the number of potential years an individual is no longer able to experience as a result of his or her early death.

zone of discontinuity   the realms in which inconsistency is experienced

REFERENCES

Aasland, O. G., Ekeberg, O. & Schweder, T. (2001). Suicide rates from 1960 to 1989 in Norwegian physicians compared with other educational groups. *Social Science & Medicine, 52,* 259–265.

Abel, E. L. (1998). *Fetal alcohol abuse syndrome.* New York: Plenum Press.

Abram, H. S. (1970). Survival by machine: The psychological stress of chronic hemodialysis. *Psychiatry in Medicine, 1,* 37–51.

ACS 1979 Survey. (1979). *Report on the social, economic and psychological needs of cancer patients in California.* San Francisco: American Cancer Society.

Adams, H. E., Feuerstein, M., & Fowler, J. (1980). Migraine headache: Review of parameters, etiology, and intervention. *Psychological Bulletin, 87,* 217–237.

Aday, L. (2001). *At risk in America: The health and health care needs of vulnerable populations in the United States,* 2nd ed. San Francisco: Jossey-Bass Publishers.

Ader, R. (Ed.). (1981). *Psychoneuroimmunology.* New York: Academic Press.

Ader, R., & Cohen, N. (1998). Psychoneuroimmunology. In H. S. Friedman (editor-in-chief), *Encyclopedia of Mental Health* (Vol. 3, pp. 315–323). San Diego: Academic Press.

Adler, A. (1943). Neuropsychiatric complications in victims of Boston's Coconut Grove diaster. *Journal of the American Medical Association, 123,* 1098–1101.

Adler, M. L. (1972). Kidney transplantation and coping mechanisms. *Psychosomatics, 13,* 337–341.

Adler, N. E., Boyce, T., Chesney, M. A., & Cohen, S. (1994). Socioeconomic status and health: The challenge of the gradient. *American Psychologist, 49,* 15–24.

Ajzen, I., & Fishbein, M. (1980). *Understanding attitudes and predicting social behavior.* Englewood Cliffs, NJ: Prentice-Hall.

Albee, G. W. (1982). Preventing psychopathology and promoting human potential. *American Psychologist, 37,* 1043–1050.

Albert, R. K., & Condie, F. (1981). Hand-washing patterns in medical intensive care units. *New England Journal of Medicine, 304,* 1465–1466.

Aldwin, C. M. (1994). *Stress, coping, and development: An integrative perspective.* New York: Guilford Press.

Alessandri, S. M., Sullivan, M. W., Bendersky, M. & Lewis, M. (1995). Temperament in cocaine-exposed infants. In M. Lewis & M. Bendersky (Eds.), *Mothers, babies, and cocaine: The role of toxins in development* (pp. 273–286). Hillsdale, NJ: Lawrence Erlbaum Associates.

Alexander, F. (1950). *Psychosomatic medicine, its principles and applications.* New York: W.W. Norton.

Allen, W. (1976). *Without feathers.* New York: Warner Books.

Allport, G. W. (1954). *The nature of prejudice.* Reading, MA: Addison-Wesley.

Allport, G. W. (1961). *Pattern and growth in personality.* New York: Holt, Rinehart, & Winston.

Aloise-Young, P. A., Hennigan, K. M., & Graham, J. W. (1996). Role of the self-image and smoker stereotype in smoking onset during early adolescence: A longitudinal study. *Health Psychology, 15*(6), 494–497.

Alpert, J. J. (1964). Broken appointments. *Pediatrics, 34,* 127–132.

Altman, D. G., & Cahn, J. (1987). Employment options for health psychologists. In G. Stone et. al. (Eds.), *Health psychology: A discipline and a profession* (pp. 231–244). Chicago: University of Chicago Press.

Altman, D. G., & Revenson, T. A. (1985). Children's understanding of health and illness concepts. *Journal of Primary Prevention, 6,* 53–67.

Amato, P. R. & Keith, B. (1991). Parental divorce and the well-being of children: A meta-analysis. *Psychological Bulletin, 110,* 26–46.

American Hospital Association. (2001). *Hospital statistics 2001 edition.* Chicago: Health Forum Publications.

Amirkhan, J. H. (1998). Attributions as predictors of coping and distress. *Personality and Social Psychology Bulletin, 24,* 1006–1018.

Anda, R., Williamson, D., Jones, D., Macera, C., Eaker, E., Glassman, A., Marks, J. (1993). Depressed affect, hopelessness, and the risk of ischemic heart disease in a cohort of U.S. Adults. *Epidemiology, 4,* 285–294.

Anderson, O. W., & Gevitz, N. (1983). The general hospital: A social and historical perspective. In D. Mechanic (Ed.). *Handbook of health, health care, and the health professions* (pp. 305–317). New York: Free Press.

Angell, M. (1985). Disease as a reflection of the psyche. *The New England Journal of Medicine, 312,* 1570–1572.

Anthony, S. (1972). *The discovery of death in childhood and after.* New York: Basic Books. (Revision of *The child's discovery of death.* New York: Harcourt, Brace, and World, 1940).

Antoni, M. H. (1987). Neuroendocrine influences in psychoimmunology and neoplasia: A review. *Psychology and Health, 1,* 3–24.

Antonovsky, A. (1979). *Health, stress, and coping.* San Francisco: Jossey-Bass.

Antonovsky, A. (1987). *Unraveling the mystery of health: How people manage stress and stay well.* San Franscisco: Jossey-Bass.

Archer, D., & Gartner, R. (1976). Violent acts and violent times: A comparative approach to postwar homicide rates. *American Sociological Review, 41,* 937–963.

Argyle, M. (1975). *Bodily communication.* New York: International Universities Press.

Artz, C. P., Moncrief, J. A., & Pruitt, B. A. Jr. (Eds.). (1979). *Burns: A team approach.* Philadelphia: Saunders.

Asch, S. E. (1951). Effects of group pressure upon the modification and distortion of judgements. In H. Gretzkow (Ed.), *Groups, leadership, and men* (pp. 177–190). Pittsburgh: Carnegie Press.

Aspinwall, L. G., & Taylor, S. E. (1992). Modeling cognitive adaptation: A longitudinal investigation of the impact of individual differences and coping on college adjustment and performance. *Journal of Personality & Social Psychology, 63*(6), 989–1003.

Aspinwall, L. G., & Taylor, S. E. (1997). A stitch in time: Self-regulation and proactive coping. *Psychological Bulletin. 121,* 417–436.

Astin, J. A. (1998). Why patients use alternative medicine: Results of a national study. *Journal of the American Medical Association, 279,* 1548–1553.

Auerbach, J. A., & Krimgold, B. K. (Eds.). (2001). *Income, socioeconomic status, and health: Exploring the relationships.* Washington, DC: National Policy Association Academy for Health Services Research and Health Policy.

Avorn, J., Chen, M., & Hartley, R. (1982). Scientific vs. commercial sources of influence on the prescribing behavior of physicians. *The American Journal of Medicine, 73,* 4–8.

Babbott, D., Baldwin, D. C., Killian, C. D., & Weaver, S. O. (1989). Racial-ethnic background and specialty choice: A study of U.S. medical school graduates in 1987. *Academic Medicine, 64,* 595–599.

Baekeland, F., & Lundwall, L. (1975). Dropping out of treatment: A critical review. *Psychological Bulletin, 82,* 738–783.

Baer, J. S., Marlatt, G. A., & McMahon, R. J. (Eds.). (1993). *Addictive behaviors across the life span: Prevention, treatment, and policy issues.* Newbury Park, CA: Sage Publications, Inc.

Bailer, A. J., Stayner, L. T., Stout, N. A., Reed, L. D., & Gilbert, S. J. (1998, July). Trends in rates of occupational fatal injuries in the United States. (1983–92). *Occupational and Environmental Medicine, 55*(7), 485–489.

Bakal, D. A. (1975). Headache: A biopsychological perspective. *Psychological Bulletin, 82,* 369–382.

Balint, M. (1957). *The doctor, his patient, and the illness.* New York: International Universities Press.

Barefoot, J., Dodge, K., Peterson, B., Dahlstrom, W., & Williams, R. (1989). The Cook-Medley hostility scale: Item content and ability to predict survival. *Psychosomatic Medicine, 51,* 46–57.

Barnard, P., Morland, I. & Nagy, J. (1999). *Children, bereavement, and trauma: Nurturing resilience.* Philadelphia: Jessica Kingsley Publishers.

Barnlund, D. C. (1976). The mystification of meaning: Doctor-patient encounters. *Journal of Medical Education, 51,* 716–725.

Barron-McBride, A. (1976). *Living with contradictions.* New York: Harper-Colophon.

Bartrop, R. W., Lazarus, L., Luckherst, E., Kiloh, L., & Penny, R. (1977). Depressed lymphocyte function after bereavement. *Lancet, 1,* 834–836.

Basbaum, A. I., & Fields, H. L. (1984). Endogenous pain control systems. *Annual Review of Neuroscience, 7,* 309–338.

Baum, A. (1990). Stress, intrusive imagery, and chronic distress. *Health Psychology, 9*(6), 653–675.

Baum, A., Cohen, L., & Hall, M. (1993). Control and intrusive memories as possible determinants of chronic stress. *Psychosomatic Medicine, 55,* 274–286.

Beck, A. T. (1976). *Cognitive therapy and the emotional disorders.* New York: International Universities Press.

Becker, E. (1973). *The denial of death.* New York: Free Press.

Becker, H. S., & Geer, B. (1958). The fate of idealism in medical school. *American Sociological Review, 23,* 50–56.

Becker, H. S., Geer, B., Hughes, E. C., & Strauss, A. M. (1961). *Boys in white: Student culture in medical school.* Chicago: University of Chicago Press.

Becker, M. H. (Ed.). (1974). *The health belief model and personal health behavior.* Thorofare, NJ: Charles B. Slack.

Becker, M. H., & Maiman, L. A. (1980). Strategies for enhancing patient compliance. *Journal of Community Health, 6*(2), 113–135.

Becker, M. H., Maiman, L. A., Kirscht, J. P., Haefner, D. P., Drachman, R. H., & Taylor, D. W. (1979). Patient perceptions and compliance: Recent studies of the Health Belief Model. In R. B. Haynes, D. W. Taylor, and D. L. Sackett (Eds.), *Compliance in health care* (pp. 78–109). Baltimore: Johns Hopkins University Press.

Beecher, H. K. (1959). *Measurement of subjective responses: Quantitative effects of drugs.* New York: Oxford University Press.

Belgrave, F. Z. (1998). *Psychosocial aspects of chronic illness and disability among African Americans.* Westport, CT: Auburn House.

Belisle, M., Roskies, E., & Levesque, J. M. (1987). Improving adherence to physical activity. *Health Psychology, 6,* 159–172.

Bem, D. J. (1965). An experimental analysis of self-persuasion. *Journal of Experimental Social Psychology, 1,* 199–218.

Benison, S., Barger, A. C., & Wolfe, E. (1987). *Walter B. Cannon: The life and times of a young scientist.* Cambridge, MA: Harvard University Press.

Bennett, M. E., & Miller, W. R. (1998). Alcohol problems. In H. S. Friedman (editor-in-chief) *Encyclopedia of Mental Health* (Vol. 1, pp. 53–63). San Diego: Academic Press.

Benoliel, J. Q. (1975). Childhood diabetes: The commonplace in living becomes uncommon. In A. L. Strauss (Ed.) *Chronic illness and the quality of life* (pp. 89–98). St. Louis: C. V. Mosby.

Ben-Sira, Z. (1976). The function of the professional's affective behavior in client satisfaction: A revised approach to social interaction theory. *Journal of Health and Social Behavior, 17,* 3–11.

Ben-Sira, Z. (1980). Affective and instrumental components in the physician-patient relationship: An additional dimension of interaction theory. *Journal of Health and Social Behavior, 21,* 170–180.

Benson, H. (1975). *The relaxation response.* New York: Wm. Morrow.

Berkanovic, E. (1972). Lay conceptions of the sick role. *Social Forces, 51,* 53–64.

Berkman, L. F., & Breslow, L. (1983). *Health and ways of living: The Alameda County study.* New York: Oxford University Press.

Berkman, L. F., & Syme, S. L. (1979). Social networks, host resistance, and mortality: A nine-year follow-up study of Alameda County residents. *American Journal of Epidemiology, 109,* 186–204.

Berkman, L. F., & Syme, S. L. (1994). Social networks, host resistance, and mortality: A nine year follow-up study of Alameda County residents. In A. Steptoe & J. Wardle (Eds.), *Psychosocial processes and health: A reader* (pp. 43–67). Cambridge, England: Cambridge University Press.

Bernard, V. W., Ottenberg, P., & Redl, F. (1971). Dehumanization. In N. Sanford, and C. Comstock (Eds.), *Sanctions for evil* (pp. 102–124). Boston: Beacon Press.

Bertakis, K. D., Azari, R., Helms, L. J., Callahan, E. J., & Robbins, J. A. (2000). Gender differences in the utilization of health care services. *Journal of Family Practice, 49,* 147–152.

Biegel, D. E., Sales, E., & Schulz, R. (1991). *Family caregiving in chronic illness: Alzheimer's disease, cancer, heart disease, mental illness, and stroke:* Newbury Park, CA: Sage Publications.

Biener, L., Aseltine, R. H., Cohen, B., & Anderka, M. (1998). Reactions of adult and teenaged smokers to the Massachusetts Tobacco Tax. *American Journal of Public Health, 88,* 1389–1391.

Bierman, S. M. (1983). A possible psychoneuroimmunologic basis for recurrent genital herpes simplex. *Western Journal of Medicine, 139,* 547–552.

Birbaumer, N., & Kimmel, H. (Eds.). (1979). *Biofeedback and self-regulation.* Hillsdale, NJ: L. Erlbaum.

Birch, L. L. & Fisher, J. A. (1996). The role of experience in the development of children's eating behavior. In E. D. Capaldi (ed.), *Why we eat what we eat: The psychology of eating* (pp. 113–141). Washington, DC: American Psychological Association.

Blackman, S. L. (1980). The effects of nonverbal expression and cognition on the perception of pain. [Ph.D. dissertation]. University of California, Riverside.

Blanck, P. D. (Ed.). (1993). *Interpersonal expectations: Theory, research, and applications.* New York: Cambridge University Press.

Blau, P. (1968). Social exchange. In D. Sills (Ed.), *International encyclopedia of the social sciences* (pp. 452–457). New York: Macmillan.

Bleeker, J. K., Lamers, L. M., Leenders, I. M., & Kruyssen, D. C. (1995). Psychological and knowledge factors related to delay of help-seeking by patients with acute myocardial infarction. *Psychotherapy & Psychosomatics, 63,* 151–158.

Bloch, M. (1973). *The royal touch.* Translated by J. E. Anderson. London: Routledge and K. Paul. (Originally published, 1961).

Block, J. H., Block, J., & Gjerde, P. F. (1986). The personality of children prior to divorce: A prospective study. *Child Development, 57,* 827–840.

Block, J., Block, J. H., & Keyes, S. (1988). Longitudinally foretelling drug usage in adolescence: Early childhood personality and environmental precursors. *Child Development, 59,* 336–355.

Blondis, M. N., & Jackson, B. E. (1977). *Nonverbal communication with patients: Back to the human touch.* New York: John Wiley.

Bloom, F. E., & Kupfer, D. J. (Eds.). (1995). *Psychopharmacology: The fourth generation of progress.* NewYork: Raven Press.

Bloom, S. W. (1963). *The doctor and his patient: A sociological interpretation.* New York: Russell Sage Foundation.

Blum, R. H. (1960). *The management of the doctor-patient relationship.* New York: McGraw-Hill.

Blumenthal, J. A., & McCubbin, J. A. (1987). Physical exercise as stress management. In A. Baum & J. E. Singer (Eds.), *Handbook of psychology and health* (Vol. 5: Stress). Hillsdale, NJ: Erlbaum.

Blumenthal, J. A., Shocken, D., Needels, T., & Hindle, P. (1982). Psychological and physiological effects of physical conditioning on the elderly. *Journal of Psychosomatic Research, 26,* 505–510.

Boerner, K., & Wortman, C. B. (1998). Grief and loss. In H. S. Friedman (editor-in-chief), *Encyclopedia of Mental Health* (Vol. 2, pp. 289–300). San Diego: Academic Press.

Bok, D. (1984). *The president's report, 1982–83.* Cambridge, MA: Harvard University Press.

Bolger, N., Foster, M., Vinokur, A. D., & Ng, R. (1996). Close relationships and adjustments to a life crisis: The case of breast cancer. *Journal of Personality & Social Psychology, 70,* 283–294.

Bolger, N., Zuckerman, A. & Kessler, R. C. (2000). Invisible support and adjustment to stress. *Journal of Personality & Social Psychology, 79,* 953–961.

Bolles, R. C., & Fanselow, M. S. (1980). A perceptual-defensive-recuperative model of fear and pain. *Behavioral & Brain Sciences, 3,* 291–323.

Booth-Kewley, S., & Friedman, H. S. (1987). Psychological predictors of heart disease: A quantitative review. *Psychological Bulletin, 101,* 343–362.

Boscarino, J. A. (1996). Posttraumatic stress disorder, exposure to combat, and lower plasma cortisol among Vietnam veterans: Findings and clinical implications. *Journal of Consulting & Clinical Psychology, 64,* 191–201.

Boscarino, J. A. (1997). Diseases among men 20 years after exposure to severe stress. *Psychosomatic Medicine, 59,* 605–614.

Bowling, A., & Grundy, E. (1998). The association between social networks and mortality in later life. *Reviews in Clinical Gerontology, 8,* 353–361.

Bowsher, D., Mumford, J., Lipton, S., & Miles, J. (1973). Treatment of intractable pain by acupuncture. *Lancet, 2,* 57–60.

Boyd, J. R., Covington, T. R., Stanaszek, W. F., & Coussons, R. T. (1974). Drug-defaulting. II. Analysis of noncompliance patterns. *American Journal of Hospital Pharmacy, 31,* 485–491.

Brehm, J. W. (1966). *A theory of psychological reactance.* New York: Academic Press.

Breslau, N., & Andreski, P. (1995). Migraine, personality, and psychiatric comorbidity. *Headache, 35,* 382–386.

Breslau, N., Chilcoat, H. D., & Andreski, P. (1996). Further evidence on the link between migraine and neuroticism. *Neurology, 47*(3), 663–667.

Brezinka, V. & Kittel, F. (1996). Psychosocial factors of coronary heart disease in women: A review. *Social Science & Medicine, 42,* 1351–1365.

Bride's Magazine. (1987, February/March).

Brown, F. (1961). Depression and childhood bereavement. *Journal of Mental Science, 107,* 754–777.

Brown, G. W. (1974). Meaning, measurement, and stress of life events. In B. S. Dohrenwend and B. P. Dohrenwend (Eds.), *Stressful life events: Their nature and effects* (pp. 217–244). New York: John Wiley.

Brown, R. T. (ed.) (1999). *Cognitive aspects of chronic illness in children.* New York: Guilford Press.

Brummett, B. H., Babyak, M. A., Barefoot, J. C., Bosworth, H. B., Clapp-Channing, N. E., Siegler, M. I. C., Williams, R. B., & Mark, D. B. (1998). Social support and hostility as predictors of depressive symptoms in cardiac patients one month after hospitalization: A prospective study. *Psychosomatic Medicine, 60,* 707–713.

Bryer, K. (1979). The Amish way of death. *American Psychologist, 34,* 255–261.

Buck, R. (1984). *The communication of emotion.* New York: Guilford Press.

Bukstein, O. G. (1995). *Adolescent substance abuse.* New York: Wiley.

Buller, D. B., & Street, R. L., Jr. (1992). Physician-patient relationships. In R. S. Feldman (Ed.), *Applications of nonverbal behavioral theories and research* (p. 119–141). Hillsdale, NJ: Lawrence Erlbaum Associates, Inc.

Burg, M., & Seeman, T. E. (1994). Families and health: The negative side of social ties. *Annals of Behavioral Medicine, 16*(2), 109–115.

Burish, T. G., & Bradley, L. A. (Eds.). (1983). Coping with chronic diseases: Research and applications. New York: Academic Press.

Burman, B., & Margolin, G. (1992). Analysis of the association between marital relationships and health problems: An interactional perspective. *Psychological Bulletin, 112,* 39–63.

Caine, E. D., Grossman, H. T., La Rue, A., Yang, J., Osato, S., Kemp, B. J., Mitchell, J. M., Newton, N. A., Lazarus, L. W. (1992). Assessment, treatment, and prevention. In J. E. Birren, et. al. (Eds.), *Handbook of mental health and aging* (2nd ed., pp. 603–890). San Diego: Academic Press.

Caine, L. (1975). *Widow.* New York: Bantam Books.

Caine, L. (1978). *Lifelines.* Garden City, NY: Doubleday.

Calle, E. E., Thun, M. J., Petrelli, J. M., Rodriguez, C., & Heath, C. W., Jr. (1999). Body-mass index and mortality in a prospective cohort of U.S. adults. *New England Journal of Medicine, 341*(15), 1097–1105.

Campbell, D. T., & Stanley, J. C. (1963). *Experimental and quasi-experimental designs for research.* New York: Houghton Mifflin.

Cannell, C. F., Oksenberg, L., & Converse, J. M. (Eds.). (1977) *Experiments in interviewing techniques: Field experiments in health reporting, 1971–1977.* Ann Arbor: Survey Research Center Institute for Social Research.

Cannon, W. B. (1932). *Wisdom of the body.* New York: W. W. Norton.

Cannon, W. B. (1942). Voodoo death. *American Anthropologist, 44,* 169–181.

Canter, A., Imboden, J. B., & Cluff, L. E. (1966). The frequency of physical illness as a function of prior psychological vulnerability and contemporary stress. *Psychosomatic Medicine, 28,* 344–350.

Cantor, R. C. (1978). *And a time to live: Toward emotional well-being during the crisis of cancer.* New York: Harper and Row.

Capaldi, Elizabeth D. (Ed.). (1996). *Why we eat what we eat: The psychology of eating.* Washington, D.C.: American Psychological Association.

Caplan, E. K., & Sussman, M. B. (1966). Rank-order of important variables for patient and staff satisfaction. *Journal of Health and Human Behavior, 7,* 133–138.

Caplan, R. D. (1979). Patient, provider, and organization: Hypothesized determinants of adherence. In S. J. Cohen (Ed.), *New directions in patient compliance* (pp. 75–100). Lexington, MA: Lexington Books.

Caplan, R. D., Robinson, E. A. R., French, J. R. P., Jr., Caldwell, J. R., & Shinn, M. (1976). *Adhering to medical regimens: Pilot experiments in patient education and social support.* Ann Arbor: Research Center for Group Dynamics, Institute for Social Research, University of Michigan.

Caporael, L. R. (1981). The paralanguage of caregiving. *Journal of Personality and Social Psychology, 40,* 876–884.

Cartwright, A. (1964). *Human relations and hospital care.* London: Routledge and Kegan Paul.

Cartwright, L. K. (1978). Career satisfaction and role harmony in a sample of young women physicians. *Journal of Vocational Behavior, 12,* 184–196.

Cartwright, L. K. (1979). Sources and effects of stress in health careers. In G. C. Stone, F. Cohen, and N. E. Adler (Eds.), *Health psychology* (p. 419). San Francisco: Jossey-Bass.

Cartwright, L. K. (1987). Occupational stress in women physicians. In Roy Payne, Jenny Firth-Cozens , et. al. (Eds.), *Stress in health professionals.* (pp. 71–87). New York: John Wiley & Sons.

Cassem, N. H., & Hackett, T. P. (1973). Psychological rehabilitation of myocardial infarction patients in the acute phase. *Heart and Lung, 2,* 382.

Cassileth, B. R. (Ed.). (1979). *The cancer patient: Social and medical aspects of care.* Philadelphia: Lea & Febiger.

Cassileth, B. R., & Donovan, J. A. (1983). Hospice: History and implications of the new legislation. *Journal of Psychosocial Oncology, 1,* 59–69.

Cassileth, B. R., & Steinfeld, A. D. (1987). Psychological preparation of the patient and family. *Cancer, 60,* 547–552.

CDC. (1996). Years of potential life lost from suicide and homicide. *Morbidity and Mortality Weekly Report, 35* (22), 357–365.

CDC. (1987, July 24). Traumatic occupational fatalities. *Morbidity and Mortality Weekly Report.*

Chaiken, S., & Pliner, P. (1987). Women but not men are what they eat. *Personality and Social Psychology Bulletin, 13,* 166–176.

Chang, R. S. (Ed.). (1981). *Preventative health care.* Boston: G. K. Hall.

Chapman, G. B. & Elstein, A. S. (2000). Cognitive processes and biases in medical decision making. In Chapman, G. B., & Sonnenberg, F. A. (Eds.), *Decision making in health care: Theory, psychology, and applications* (pp. 183–210). New York: Cambridge University Press.

Chapman, G. B., & Sonnenberg, F. A. (Eds.) (2000). *Decision making in health care: Theory, psychology, and applications.* New York: Cambridge University Press.

Charney, E. (1972). Patient-doctor communication: Implications for the clinician. *Pediatric Clinics of North America, 19,* 263–279.

Chassin, L., Presson, C. C., Sherman, S. J., Corty, E., & Olshavsky, R. W. (1984). Predicting the onset of cigarette smoking in adolescents: A longitudinal study. *Journal of Applied Social Psychology, 14,* 224–243.

Chaves, J., & Barber, T. X. (1975). Hypnotism and surgical pain. In M. Weisenberg, (Ed.), *Pain: Clinical and experimental perspectives* (pp. 225–239). St. Louis: C. V. Mosby.

Chesney, M. A., & Rosenman, R. H. (Eds.). (1985). *Anger and hostility in cardiovascular and behavioral disorders.* New York: Hemisphere.

Chiles, J., Lambert, M., & Hatch, A. (1999). The impact of psychological interventions on medical cost offset: A meta-analytic review. *Clinical Psychology: Science and Practice 6,* 204–219.

Chilman, C. S., Nunnally, E. W., & Cox, F. M. (Eds.). (1988). *Chronic illness and disability.* Newbury Park, CA: Sage Publications.

Cho, Z. H., Chung, S. C., Jones, J. P., Park, J. B., Park, H. J., Lee, H. J., Wong, E. K., & Min, B. I. (1998). New findings of the correlation between acupoints and corresponding brain cortices using functional MRI. *Proceedings of the National Academy of Sciences, USA, 95,* 2670–3.

Chochinov, H. M., & Breitbart, W. (Eds.). (2000). *Handbook of psychiatry in palliative medicine.* NY: Oxford University Press.

Choi, W. S., Pierce, J. P., Gilpin, E. A., Farkas, A. J., & Berry, C. C. (1997). Which adolescent experimenters progress to established smoking in the United States. *American Journal of Preventive Medicine, 13,* 385–391.

Chrisman, N. J., & Kleinman, A. (1983). Popular health care, social networks, and cultural meanings: The orientations of medical anthropology. In D. Mechanic (Ed.), *Handbook of health, health care, and the health professions* (pp. 569–590). New York: The Free Press.

Christensen, A. J., Moran, P. J., Wiebe, J. S. (1999). Assessment of irrational health beliefs: Relation to health practices and medical regimen adherence. *Health Psychology, 18,* 169–176.

Christie, R., & Merton, R. K. (1958). Procedures for the sociological study of the value climate in medical schools. *Journal of Medical Education, 33,* 125–133 (part 2).

Christy, N. P. (1979). English is our second language. *New England Journal of Medicine, 300*(17), 979–981.

Cioffi, D. (1991). Beyond attentional strategies: A cognitive-perceptual model of somatic interpretation. *Psychological Bulletin, 109,* 25–41.

Clark, K. M., Friedman, H. S., & Martin, L. R. (1999). A longitudinal study of religiosity and mortality risk. *Journal of Health Psychology, 4,* 381–391.

Clark, M. (1970). *Health in the Mexican-American culture: A community study* (2nd. ed.). Berkeley: University of California Press.

Clayson, D., & Mensh, I. N. (1987). Psychologists in medical schools. *American Psychologist, 42,* 859–862.

Clayton, P. J. (1974). Mortality and morbidity in the first year of widowhood. *Archives of General Psychiatry, 30,* 747–750.

Clayton, P. J., Desmarais, L., & Winokur, G. (1968). A study of normal bereavement. *American Journal of Psychiatry, 125,* 168–178.

Clendening, L. (Ed.). (1960). *Source book of medical history.* New York: Dover.

Coates, T. J., Temoshok, L., & Mandel, J. (1984). Psychosocial research is essential to understanding and treating AIDS. *American Psychologist, 39,* 1309–1314.

Cobb, B. (1954). Why do people detour to quacks? *The Psychiatric Bulletin, 3,* 66–69.

Cobb, S. (1976). Social support as a moderator of life stresses. *Psychosomatic Medicine, 38*(5), 300–314.

Cobb, S., & Kasl, S. (1977). *Termination: The Consequences of Job Loss.* Washington: DHEW, US Government Printing Office.

Cohen, F. (1979). Personality, stress, and the development of physical illness. In G. C. Stone, F. Cohen, & N. E. Adler, (Eds.), *Health psychology* (pp. 71–111). San Francisco: Jossey-Bass.

Cohen, F., & Lazarus, R. S. (1979). Coping with the stresses of illness. In G. C. Stone, F. Cohen, & N. E. Adler, (Eds.), *Health psychology* (p. 217). San Francisco: Jossey-Bass.

Cohen, F., & Lazarus, R. S. (1983). Coping and adaptation in health and illness. In D. Mechanic (Ed.), *Handbook of health, health care, and the health professions* (pp. 608–635). New York: Free Press.

Cohen, L. L., Blount, R. L., Cohen, R. J., Schaen, E. R., & Zaff, J. F. (1999, November). Comparative study of distraction versus topical anesthesia for pediatric pain management during immunizations. *Health Psychology, 18*(6), pp. 591–598.

Cohen, S., Evans, G., Krantz, D. S., & Stokols, D. (1980). Physiological, motivational, and cognitive effects of aircraft noise on children. *American Psychologist, 35,* 231–243.

Cohen, S., Frank, E., Doyle, W. J., Skoner, D. P., Rabin, B. S., & Gwaltney, J. M. (1998). Types of stressors that increase susceptibility to the common cold in healthy adults. *Health Psychology, 17,* 214–223.

Cohen, S., & Herbert, T. B. (1996). Health psychology: psychological factors and physical disease from the perspective of human psychoneuroimmunology. *Annual Review of Psychology, 47,* 113–42.

Cohen, S., Kessler, R. C., & Gordon, L. U. (Eds.). (1997). *Measuring stress: A guide for health and social scientists.* New York: Oxford University Press.

Cohen, S., & McKay, G. (1984). Social support, stress, and the buffering hypothesis. In A. Baum, S. E. Taylor, & J. E. Singer (Eds.), *Handbook of psychology and health* (Vol. 4: Social psychological aspects of health). Hillsdale, NJ: L. Erlbaum.

Cohen, S., & Wills, T. A. (1985). Stress, social support, and the buffering hypothesis. *Psychological Bulletin, 98,* 310–357.

Cohen, S., Underwood, L. G., & Gottlieb, B. H. (Eds.). (2000). *Social support measurement and intervention: A guide for health and social scientists.* New York: Oxford University Press.

Colligan, M. J., Pennebaker, J. W., & Murphy, L. R. (Eds.). (1982). *Mass psychogenic illness: A social psychological analysis.* Hillsdale, NJ: L. Erlbaum Associates.

Conley, F. K. (1998). Walking out on the boys. New York: Farrar, Straus, & Giroux.

Conrad, C. D., Galea, L. A., Kuroda, Y., & McEwen, B. S. (1996). Chronic stress impairs rat spatial memory on the Y maze, and this effect is blocked by tianeptine pretreatment. *Behavioral Neuroscience, 110,* 1321–1334.

Conrad, K. M., Flay, B. R., & Hill, D. (1992). Why children start smoking cigarettes: Predictors of onset. *British Journal of Addiction, 87,* 1711–1724.

Contrada, R. J., Ashmore, R. D., Gary, M. L., Coups, E., Egeth, J. D., Sewell, A., Ewell, K., Goyal, T., & Chasse, V. (2000). Ethnicity-related sources of stress and their effects on well-being. *Current Directions in Psychological Science, 9,* 136–139.

Cooley, C. H. (1922). *Human nature and the social order (Rev. ed.).* New York: Scribner's. (Originally published, 1902).

Cooper, I. S. (1981). *The vital probe: My life as a brain surgeon.* New York: W. W. Norton.

Cooperstock, R. (1971). Sex differences in the use of mood-modifying drugs: An explanatory model. *Journal of Health and Social Behavior, 12,* 238–244.

Coser, R. L. (1962). *Life in the ward.* East Lansing: Michigan State University Press.

Costa, P. T., & McCrae, R. R. (1985). Hypochondriasis, neuroticism, and aging: When are somatic complaints unfounded? *American Psychologist, 40,* 19–28.

Costa, P. T., & McCrae, R. R. (1987, June). Neuroticism, somatic complaints, and disease: Is the bark worse than the bite? *Journal of Personality, 55,* 299–316.

Costa, P. T., Jr., & VandenBos, G. R. (Eds.). (1990). *Psychological aspects of serious illness: chronic conditions, fatal diseases, and clinical care.* Washington, DC: American Psychological Association.

Council Report. (1987). Results and implications of the AMA-APA physician mortality project. *Journal of the American Medical Association, 257,* 2949–2954.

Cousins, N. (1979). *Anatomy of an illness as perceived by the patient: Reflections on healing and regeneration.* New York: W. W. Norton.

Cowan, G., Warren, L. W., & Young, J. L. (1985). Medical perceptions of menopausal symptoms. *Psychology of Women Quarterly, 9,* 3–14.

Cramond, W. A. (1967). Renal homotransplantation—some observations on recipients and donors. *British Journal of Psychology, 113,* 1223–1230.

Crary, B., Borysenko, M., Sutherland, D., Kutz, I., Borysenko, J., & Benson, H. (1983). Decrease in mitogen responsiveness of mononuclear cells from peripheral blood after epinephrine administration in humans. *Journal of Immunology, 130,* 606–697.

Creer, T. (1978). Asthma: Psychological aspects and management. In E. Middleton, C. Reed, & E. Ellis (Eds.), *Allergy: Principles and practice* (pp. 796–811). St. Louis: C. V. Mosby.

Criqui, M. H. (1996). Alcohol and coronary heart disease: consistent relationship and public health implications. *Clinica Chimica Acta, 246,* 51–57.

Croog, S. H., & Levine, S. (1982). *Life after a heart attack: Social and psychological factors eight years later.* New York: Human Sciences Press.

Crook, T., & Eliot, J. (1980). Parental death during childhood and adult depression: A critical review of the literature. *Psychological Bulletin, 87,* 252–259.

Culbertson, G. H., & Caporael, L. R. (1983). Baby talk speech to the elderly. *Personality and Social Psychology Bulletin, 9,* 305–312.

Cummings, N. A., & Follette, W. T. (1976). Brief psychotherapy and medical utilization. In H. Dorken (Ed.), *The professional psychologist today.* San Francisco: Jossey-Bass.

Cunningham, A. J. (1985). The influence of mind on cancer. *Canadian Psychology, 26,* 13–29.

Dahl, J. C. (1977). Rational management of hypertension. *Minnesota Medicine, 60,* 311–314.

Darwin, C. (1872). *The expression of the emotions in man and animals.* London: John Murray.

Daubenmire, M. J. (1976). Nurse-patient-physician communicative interaction process. In H. Werley, A. Zuzich, M. Zajkowski, & A. Zngornik, (Eds.), *Health research: The systems approach* (pp. 139–154). New York: Springer.

Davies, B. (1999). *Shadows in the sun: The experiences of sibling bereavement in childhood.* Philadelphia: Brunner/Mazel.

Davies, C. (1995). *Gender and the professional predicament in nursing.* Philadelphia: Open University Press.

Davis, F. (1960). Uncertainty in medical prognosis: Clinical and functional. *American Journal of Sociology, 66,* 41–47.

Davis, M. C., Matthews, K. A., & McGrath, C. E. (2000). Hostile attitudes predict elevated vascular resistance during interpersonal stress in men and women. *Psychosomatic Medicine, 62,* 17–25.

Davis, M. C., & Swan, P. D. (1999). Association of negative and positive social ties with fibrinogen levels in young women. *Health Psychology, 18,* 131–139.

Davitz, L. J., Sameshima, Y., & Davitz, J. (1976, August). Suffering as viewed in six different cultures. *American Journal of Nursing, 76*(8), 1296–1297.

DeLongis, A., Coyne, J. C., Dakof, S., Folkman, S., & Lazarus, R. S. (1982). Relationship of daily hassles, uplifts, and major life events to health status. *Health Psychology, 1,* 119–136.

DeLongis, A., & Newth, S. (1998). Coping with stress. In H. S. Friedman (editor-in-chief), *Encyclopedia of Mental Health* (Vol. 1, pp. 583–593). San Diego: Academic Press.

Dembroski, T. M., Weiss, S. M., Shields, J. L., Haynes, S. G., & Feinlieb, M. (Eds.). (1978). *Coronary-prone behavior.* New York: Springer-Verlag.

DePaulo, B. M., & Friedman, H. S. (1998). Nonverbal Communication. In D. Gilbert, S. Fiske, & G. Lindzey (Eds.) *Handbook of Social Psychology* (4th ed., Vol. II, pp. 3–40). Boston: McGraw Hill.

Depue, R. A., & Monroe, S. M. (1986). Conceptualization and measurement of human disorder in life stress research: The problem of chronic disturbance. *Psychological Bulletin, 99,* 36–51.

Derlega, V. J., Winstead, B. A., & Folk-Barron, L. (2000). Reasons for and against disclosing HIV-seropositive test results to an intimate partner: A functional perspective. In S. Petronio (Ed.), *Balancing the secrets of private disclosures* (pp. 53–69). Mahwah, NJ: Lawrence Erlbaum Associates,

Dershewitz, R. A. (1984). Childhood household safety. In J. D. Matarazzo, S. Weiss, J. A. Herd, N. E. Miller, & S. M. Weiss (Eds.), *Behavioral health*. New York: Wiley.

Descartes. (1955). *Selections*. Edited by R. Eaton. New York: Scribner's.

Deutsch, F., Jones, A., Stokuis, B., Fryberger, H., & Stunkard, A. (Eds.). (1964). *Advances in psychosomatic medicine*. New York: Hafner.

Deutsch, M. (1983). The prevention of world war III: A psychological perspective. *Journal of Political Psychology, 4*, 3–31.

Devins, G. M., & Seland, T. P. (1987). Emotional impact of multiple sclerosis: Recent findings and suggestions for future research. *Psychological Bulletin, 101*, 363–375.

Dew, M. A., & Bromet, E. J. (1993). Predictors of temporal patterns of psychiatric distress during 10 years following the nuclear accident at Three Mile Island. *Social Psychiatry & Psychiatric Epidemiology, 28*, 49–55.

Dew, M. A., Goycoolea, J. M., Stukas, A. A., Switzer, G. E., Simmons, R. G., Roth, L. H., & DiMartini, A. (1998). Temporal profiles of physical health in family members of heart transplant recipients: Predictors of health change during caregiving. *Health Psychology, 17*(2), 138–151.

Diamond, M., & Karlen, A. (1980). *Sexual decisions*. Boston: Little, Brown.

Dienstbier, R. A. (1991). Behavioral correlates of sympathoadrenal reactivity: The toughness model. *Medicine & Science in Sports & Exercise, 23*, 846–852.

Dijkstra, A., De Vries, H., Roijackers, J., & van Breukelen, G. (1998). Tailoring information to enhance quitting in smokers with low motivation to quit: Three basic efficacy questions. *Health Psychology, 17*, 513–519.

DiMatteo, M. R., & DiNicola, D. D. (1982). *Achieving patient compliance*. New York: Pergamon Press.

DiMatteo, M. R., Friedman, H. S., & Taranta, A. (1979). Sensitivity to bodily nonverbal communication as a factor in practitioner-patient rapport. *Journal of Nonverbal Behavior, 4*, 18–26.

DiMatteo, M. R., Hays, R., & Prince, L. M. (1986). Relationship of physicians' nonverbal communication skills to patient satisfaction, appointment compliance, and physician workload. *Health Psychology, 5*, 581–594.

DiMatteo, M. R., Taranta, A., Friedman, H. S., & Prince, L. M. (1980). Predicting patient satisfaction from physician's nonverbal communication skills. *Medical Care, 18*, 376–387.

Dishman, R. K. (1982). Compliance/adherence in health-related exercise. *Health Psychology, 1*, 237–267.

Dishman, R. K. (1998). Physical activity and mental health. In H. S. Friedman (editor-in-chief), *Encyclopedia of Mental Health* (Vol. 3, pp. 171–188). San Diego: Academic Press.

Distlehorst, L. H., Dunnington, G. L., & Folse, J. R. (eds.). (2000). *Teaching and learning in medical and surgical education: Lessons learned for the 21st century*. Mahwah, NJ: Erlbaum.

Ditto, P. H., Danks, J. H., Smucker, W. D., Bookwala, J., Coppola, K. M., Dresser, R., Fagerlin, A., Gready, R. M., Houts, R. M., Lockhart, L. K., & Zyzanski, S. (2001). Advance Directives as Acts of Communication: A Randomized Controlled Trial. *Archives of Internal Medicine, 161,* 421–430.

Doherty, K., Militello, F. S., Kinnunen, T., & Garvey, A. J. (1996). Nicotine gum dose and weight gain after smoking cessation. *Journal of Consulting & Clinical Psychology, 64,* 799–807.

Donald, C. A., Ware, J. E., Jr., Brook, R. H., & Davies-Avery, A. (1978). *Conceptualization and measurement of health for adults in the health insurance study.* Social Health (Vol. 4). Santa Monica: The Rand Corporation R-4-HEW.

Donavan, M., & Pierce, S. (1976). *Cancer care nursing.* New York: Appleton-Century-Crofts.

Dougall, A. L., & Baum, A. (1998). Stress. In H. S. Friedman (editor-in-chief), *Encyclopedia of Mental Health* (Vol. 3, pp. 599–606). San Diego: Academic Press.

Dracup, K., Moser, D. K., Eisenberg, M., & Meischke, H. (1995). Causes of delay in seeking treatment for heart attack symptoms. *Social Science & Medicine, 40,* 379–392.

Druley, J. A., Stephens, M. A. P., Coyne, J. C. (1997, November). Emotional and physical intimacy in coping with lupus: Women's dilemmas of disclosure and approach. *Health Psychology,16*(6), 506–514.

Dubbert, P. M. (1995). Behavioral (life-style) modification in the prevention and treatment of hypertension. *Clinical Psychology Review, 15,* 187–216.

Dubos, R. (1968). *Man, medicine, and environment.* New York: Praeger.

Dubos, R. (1978). Bolstering the body against disease. *Human Nature, 1*(8), 68–72.

Duff, R. S., & Hollingshead, A. B. (1968). *Sickness and society.* New York: Harper and Row.

Dunbar, F. H. (1943). *Psychosomatic diagnosis.* New York: Hoeber.

Duncan, D. S., Jr., & Rosenthal, R. (1968). Vocal emphasis in experimenters' introduction reading as unintended determinant of subjects' responses. *Language and Speech, 11,* 20–26.

Dunkel-Schetter, C. (1984). Social support and cancer: Findings based on patient interviews and their implications. *Journal of Social Issues, 40,* 77–98.

Dunkel-Schetter, C., & Wortman, C. (1982). The interpersonal dynamics of cancer. In H. S. Friedman, & M. R. DiMatteo (Eds.), *Interpersonal issues in health care* (pp. 69–100). New York: Academic Press.

Earthquake in Chicago. *Time,* April 9, 1951.

Eddy, D. M. (1994). A piece of my mind: A conversation with my mother. *Journal of the American Medical Association, 272,* 179–81.

Egbert, L. D., Battit, G. E., Turndorf, H., & Beecher, H. K. (1963). The value of the pre-operative visit by an anesthetist. *Journal of the American Medical Association, 185,* 553–555.

Egbert, L. D., Battit, G. E., Welch, C. E., & Bartlett, M. K. (1964). Reduction of post-operative pain by encouragement and instruction of patients: A study of doctor-patient rapport. *New England Journal of Medicine, 270,* 825–827.

Eitel, P., Hatchett, L., Friend, R., Griffin, K. W., & Wadhwa, N. K. (1995) Burden of self-care in seriously ill patients: Impact on adjustment. *Health Psychology, 14*(5), 457–463.

Ekman, P., & Friesen, W. (1969). Nonverbal leakage and clues to deception. *Psychiatry, 32,* 88–105.

Ekman, P., & Friesen, W. (1975). *Unmasking the face.* Englewood Cliffs, NJ: Prentice-Hall.

Ekman, P., Friesen, W., & Ellsworth, P. (1972). *Emotion in the human face: Guidelines for research and an integration of findings.* New York: Pergamon Press.

Elliott, T. R., Jackson, W. T., Layfield, M., & Kendall, D. (1996). Personality disorders and response to outpatient treatment of chronic pain. *Journal of Clinical Psychology in Medical Settings, 3,* 219–234.

Ellsworth, P. (1975). Direct gaze as a social stimulus: The example of aggression. In P. Pliner, L. Krames, & T. Alloway (Eds.), *Nonverbal communication of aggression* (pp. 53–75). New York: Plenum.

Ellsworth, P., Friedman, H., Perlick, D., & Hoyt, M. (1978). Some effects of gaze on subjects motivated to seek or to avoid social comparison. *Journal of Experimental Social Psychology, 14,* 69–87.

Elstein, A. S., & Bordage, G. (1979). Psychology of clinical reasoning. In G. C. Stone, F. Cohen, and N. E. Adler, (Eds.), *Health Psychology* (p. 333). San Francisco: Jossey-Bass.

Emery, C. F., Schein, R. L., Hauck, E. R., & MacIntyre, N. R. (1998, May). Psychological and cognitive outcomes of a randomized trial of exercise among patients with chronic obstructive pulmonary disease. *Health Psychology, 17*(3), 232–240.

Emmons, R. A. (1986). Personal strivings: An approach to personality and subjective well being. *Journal of Personality and Social Psychology, 51,* 1058–1068.

Emmons, R. A., & King, L. A. (1988). Conflict among personal strivings. *Journal of Personality and Social Psychology, 54,* 1040–1048.

Engel, G. L. (1968). A life setting conducive to illness: The giving up-given up complex. *Bulletin of the Menninger Clinic, 32,* 355–365.

Engel, G. L. (1971). Sudden and rapid death during psychological stress: Folklore or folk wisdom? *Annals of Internal Medicine, 74,* 771–782.

Engel, G. L. (1977a). The need for a new medical model: A challenge for biomedicine. *Science, 196,* 129–136.

Engel, G. L. (1977b). The care of the patient: Art of science? *The Johns Hopkins Medical Journal, 140,* 222–232.

Engel, G. L., & Schmale, A. H. (1967). Psychoanalytic theory of somatic disorder. *Journal of the American Psychoanalytic Association, 15,* 344–363.

Engolf, E., Lasker, J., Wolf, S., & Potvin, L. (1992). The Roseto effect: A 50-year comparison of mortality rates. *American Journal of Public Health, 82,* 1089–1092.

Environmental Protection Agency. (1990). *Health effects of passive smoking: Assessment of lung cancer in adults and respiratory disorders in children.* Washington, DC: U.S. Environmental Protection Agency.

Epstein, L. H., & Wing, R. R. (1987). Behavioral treatment of childhood obesity. *Psychological Bulletin, 101,* 331–342.

Eraker, S. A., Kirscht, J. P., & Becker, M. H. (1984). Understanding and improving patient compliance. *Annals of Internal Medicine, 100,* 258–268.

Erickson, R. C., & Hyerstay, B. J. (1979). The dying patient and the double-bind hypothesis. In C. A. Garfield (Ed.), *Stress and survival* (pp. 298–306). St. Louis: C. V. Mosby.

Erikson, E. H. (1950). *Childhood and society.* New York: Norton.

Erikson, K. (1976). *Everything in its path: Destruction of community in the Buffalo Creek flood.* New York: Simon and Schuster.

Escobar, J. I., & Gara, M. A. (1998). Somatization and hypochondriasis. In H. S. Friedman (editor-in-chief), *The Encyclopedia of Mental Health* (Vol. III, pp. 571–580). San Diego, CA: Academic Press.

Esterling, B. A., Kiecolt-Glaser, J. K., Bodnar, J. C., & Glaser, R. (1994, July). Chronic stress, social support, and persistent alterations in the natural killer cell response to cytokines in older adults. *Health Psychology, 13*(4), 291–298.

Esterling, B. A., L'Abate, L., Murray, E. J., & Pennebaker, J. W. (1999). Empirical foundations for writing in prevention and psychotherapy: Mental and physical health outcomes. *Clinical Psychology Review, 19,* 79–96.

Evans, D., Clark, N. M., Feldman, C. H., & Wasilewski, Y. (1990). School health education for children with asthma. In S. Shumaker & B. Schrom (Eds.), *The handbook of health behavior change* (pp. 144–152). New York: Springer.

Evans, G. W., Hygge, S., & Bullinger, M. (1995). Chronic noise and psychological stress. *Psychological Science, 6,* 333–338.

Evans, R. I., Rozelle, R. M., Maxwell, S. E., Raines, B. E., Dill, C. A., Guthrie, T. J., Henderson, A. H., & Hill, P. C. (1981). Social modeling films to deter smoking in adolescents. *Journal of Applied Psychology, 66,* 399–414.

Evans, R. I., Rozelle, R. M., Mittelmark, M. B., Hansen, W. B., Bane, A. L., & Havis, J. (1978). Deterring the onset of smoking in children. *Journal of Applied Social Psychology, 8,* 126–135.

Everson, R. B., & Fraumeni, J. F. (1975). Mortality among medical students and young physicians. *Journal of Medical Education, 50,* 809–811.

Exline, R. V. (1972). Visual interaction: The glance of power and preference. In J. Cole (Ed.), *Nebraska Symposium on Motivation 1971.* Lincoln: University of Nebraska Press.

Eysenck, H. J. (1967). *The biological basis of personality.* Springfield, IL: Charles C. Thomas.

Eysenck, H. J. (1984). Lung cancer and the stress personality inventory. In C. L. Cooper (Ed.), *Psychosocial stress and cancer.* Chichester, England: Wiley.

Falvo, D. R. (1999). *Medical and psychosocial aspects of chronic illness and disability* (2nd ed.). Gaithersburg, MD: Aspen Publishers.

Fanselow, M. S., & Sigmundi, R. A. (1986). Species-specific danger signals, endogenous opioid analgesia, and defensive behavior. *Journal of Experimental Psychology: Animal Behavior Processes, 12,* 301–309.

Farberow, N. L., & Shneidman, E. S. (Eds.). (1965). *The cry for help.* New York: McGraw-Hill.

Farquhar, J. W. et al. (1984). The Stanford five-city project: An overview. In J. D. Matarazzo, S. Weiss, J. A. Herd, N. E. Miller, & S. M. Weiss (Eds.), *Behavioral health.* New York: Wiley.

Feifel, H. (Ed.). (1959). *The meaning of death.* New York: McGraw-Hill.

Feifel, H. (1965). The function of attitudes toward death. In Group for the Advancement of Psychiatry (Eds.), *Death and dying: Attitudes of patient and doctor* (Vol. 5, Symposium 11, pp. 632–641). New York: Mental Health Materials Center.

Feldman, M. D., & Eisendrath, S. J. (Eds.). (1996). *The spectrum of factitious disorders.* Washington, DC: American Psychiatric Press.

Felton, B. J., Revenson, T. A., & Hinrichsen, G. A. (1984). Stress and coping in the explanation of psychological adjustment among chronically ill adults. *Social Science and Medicine, 18,* 889–898.

Fernandez, E., & Turk, D. C. (1995). The scope and significance of anger in the experience of chronic pain. *Pain, 61,* 165–175.

Ferraro, K. F. (1998). Firm believers? Religion, body weight, and well-being. *Review of Religious Research, 39,* 224–244.

Fidell, L. S. (1980). Sex role sterotypes and the American physician. *Psychology of Women Quarterly, 4,* 313–330.

Field, M. J., & Cassel, C. K. (Eds.). (1997). *Approaching death: Improving care at the end of life.* Committee on Care at the End of Life, Division of Health Care Services, Institute of Medicine. Washington, DC: National Academy Press.

Field, T. M. (1998). Massage therapy effects. *American Psychologist, 53,* 1270–1281.

Field, T. M. (1998). Touch therapies. In R. R. Hoffman, M. F. Sherrick, & J. S. Warm (Eds.), *Viewing psychology as a whole: The integrative science of William N. Dember* (pp. 603–624). Washington, DC: American Psychological Association.

Fields, H. L., & Liebeskind, J. C. (Eds.). (1994). *Pharmacological approaches to the treatment of chronic pain: New concepts and critical issues.* The Bristol-Myers Squibb Symposium on Pain Research (4th). Seattle: IASP Press.

Fishoff, J., & O'Brien, N. (1976). After a child dies. *Pediatrics, 88,* 140–146.

Fiske, S. T. (1987). People's reactions to nuclear war: Implications for psychologists. *American Psychologist, 42,* 207–217.

Flannery, R. B., & Flannery, G. J. (1990). Sense of coherence, life stress, and psychological distress: A prospective methodological inquiry. *Journal of Clinical Psychology, 46,* 415–420.

Flay, B. R., Miller, T. Q., Hedeker, D., Siddiqui, O., Britton, C. F., Brannon, B. R., Johnson, C. A., Hansen, W. B., Sussman, S., & Dent, C. (1995). The television, school, and family smoking prevention and cessation project: VIII. Student outcomes and mediating variables. *Preventive Medicine: An International Journal Devoted to Practice & Theory, 24,* 29–40.

Flay, B. R., Ryan, K. B., Best, J. A., Brown, K. S., Kersell, M. W., d'Avernas, J. R., & Zanna, M. P. (1985). Are social psychological smoking prevention programs effective? The Waterloo study. *Journal of Behavioral Medicine, 8,* 37–59.

Folkins, C. H., & Sime, W. E. (1981). Physical fitness training and mental health. *American Psychologist, 36,* 373–389.

Folkman, S., & Lazarus, R. S. (1980). An analysis of coping in a middle-aged community sample. *Journal of Health and Social Behavior, 21,* 219–239.

Fordyce, W. E. (1976). *Behavioral methods for chronic pain and illness.* St. Louis: C. V. Mosby.

Fox, B. H., & Newberry, B. (Eds.). (1984). *Impact of psychoendocrine systems in cancer and immunity.* New York: Hogrefe.

Fox, R. C. (1959). *Experiment perilous: Physicians and patients facing the unknown.* Glencoe, IL: Free Press.

Fox, R. C., & Swazey, J. P. (1974). *The courage to fail: A social view of organ transplants and dialysis.* Chicago: University of Chicago Press.

Francis, V., Korsch, B. M., & Morris, M. J. (1969). Gaps in doctor-patient communications: Patients' response to medical advice. *New England Journal of Medicine, 280,* 535–540.

Frank, J. D. (1946). Emotional reactions of American soldiers to an unfamiliar disease. *American Journal of Psychiatry, 101,* 631–640.

Frank, J. D. (1977). Mind-body relationships in illness and healing. *Journal of the International Academy of Preventive Medicine, 2*(3).

Frank, J. D. (1987). The drive for power and the nuclear arms race. *American Psychologist, 42,* 337–344.

Frankenhaeuser, M. (1972). Biochemical events, stress, and adjustment. Reports from the Psychological Laboratories, University of Stockholm. (368).

Frankenhaeuser, M. (1977). Quality of life: Criteria for behavorial adjustment. *International Journal of Psychology, 12,* 99–110.

Frankenhaeuser, M. (1980). Psychobiological aspects of life stress. In S. Levine, & H. Ursin (Eds.), *Coping and health* (pp. 203–223). New York: Plenum.

Frankl, V. E. (1962). *Man's search for meaning; an introduction to logotherapy. A newly rev. ed. of From death-camp to existentialism.* Tr. by Ilse Lasch. Boston: Beacon Press.

Freemon, B., Negrete, V. F., Davis, M., & Korsch, B. M. (1971). Gaps in doctor-patient communication: Doctor-patient interaction analysis. *Pediatric Research, 5,* 298–311.

French, J. R. P., Jr., & Raven, B. H. (1959). The bases of social power. In D. Cartwright (Ed.), *Studies in social power* (pp. 150–167). Ann Arbor: Institute for Social Research, University of Michigan.

French-Belgian Collaborative Group. (1982). Ischemic heart disease and psychological patterns: Prevalence and incidence studies in Belgium and France. *Advanced Cardiology, 29,* 25–31.

Freud, S. (1955). *Collected works.* (Vol. 2: Studies of hysteria). New York: Hogarth Press.

Friedman, H. S. (1979a). The interactive effects of facial expressions of emotion and verbal messages on perceptions of affective meaning. *Journal of Experimental Social Psychology, 15,* 453–469.

Friedman, H. S. (1979b). Nonverbal communication between patients and medical practitioners. *Journal of Social Issues, 35*(1), 82–99.

Friedman, H. S. (1982). Nonverbal communication in medical interaction. In H. S. Friedman, & M. R. DiMatteo (Eds.), *Interpersonal issues in health care* (pp. 51–66). New York: Academic Press.

Friedman, H. S. (1987a). Cassandra genes: Do we want to know our medical future? [Unpublished manuscript], University of California, Riverside.

Friedman, H. S. (1987b). A long-term apprenticeship model of medical training. [Manuscript]. University of California, Riverside.

Friedman, H. S. (1991). *Self-healing personality: Why some people achieve health and others succumb to illness.* New York: Henry Holt.

Friedman, H. S. (1994). Intelligence and health. In R. J. Sternberg (Ed.), *Encyclopedia of Intelligence* (pp. 521–525). New York: MacMillan.

Friedman, H. S. (1998). Self-healing personalities. In H. S. Friedman (editor-in-chief), *Encyclopedia of Mental Health* (pp. 453–459). San Diego: Academic Press.

Friedman, H. S. (2000a). *The Self-Healing Personality: Why some people achieve health and others succumb to illness.* iUniverse.com.

Friedman, H. S. (2000b). Long-term relations of personality and health: Dynamisms, mechanisms, tropisms. *Journal of Personality, 68,* 1089–1108.

Friedman, H. S., & Booth-Kewley, S. (1987a). Personality, Type A behavior, and coronary heart disease: The role of emotional expression. *Journal of Personality and Social Psychology, 53,* 783–792.

Friedman, H. S., & Booth-Kewley, S. (1987b). The "disease-prone personality": A meta-analytic view of the construct. *American Psychologist, 42,* 539–555.

Friedman, H. S., DiMatteo, M. R., & Taranta, A. (1980). A study of the relationship between individual differences in nonverbal expressiveness and factors of personality and social interaction. *Journal of Research in Personality, 14,* 351–364.

Friedman, H. S., Hall, J., & Harris, M. J. (1985). Type A behavior, nonverbal expressive style, and health. *Journal of Personality and Social Psychology, 48,* 1299–1315.

Friedman, H. S., Harris, M. J., & Hall, J. A. (1984). Nonverbal expression of emotion: Healthy charisma or coronary-prone behavior? In C. Van Dyke, L. Temoshok, & L. S. Zegans (Eds.), *Emotions in health and illness: Applications to clinical practice* (pp. 151–165). San Diego: Grune & Stratton.

Friedman, H. S., Tucker, J. S., & Reise, S. (1995). Personality dimensions and measures potentially relevant to health: A focus on hostility. *Annals of Behavioral Medicine, 17,* 245–253.

Friedman, H. S., Tucker, J., Schwartz, J. E., Martin, L. R., Tomlinson-Keasey, C., Wingard, D., & Criqui, M. (1995). Childhood conscientiousness and longevity: Health behaviors and cause of death. *Journal of Personality and Social Psychology, 68,* 696–703.

Friedman, H. S., Tucker, J. S., Schwartz, J. E., Tomlinson-Keasey, C., Martin, L. R., Wingard, D. L., & Criqui, M. H. (1995). Psychosocial and behavioral predictors of longevity: The aging and death of the "Termites." *American Psychologist, 50,* 69–78.

Friedman, H. S., Tucker, J. S., Tomlinson-Keasey, C., Schwartz, J., Wingard, D., & Criqui, M. H. (1993). Does childhood personality predict longevity? *Journal of Personality and Social Psychology, 65,* 176–185.

Friedman, M. A., & Brownell, K. D. (1998). Obesity. In H. S. Friedman (editor-in-chief), *Encyclopedia of Mental Health* (Vol. 3, pp. 1–14). San Diego: Academic Press.

Friedman, M., & Rosenman, R. H. (1974). *Type A behavior and your heart.* New York: Alfred A. Knopf.

Friedman, M., Thoresen, C. E., & Gill, J. J. (1986). Alteration of Type A behavior and its effect on cardiac recurrences in post myocardial infarction patients. *American Heart Journal, 112,* 653–665.

Friedman, M., Thoresen, C., Gill, J., Powell, L., Ulmer, D., Thompson, L., et al. (1984). Alteration of Type A behavior and reduction in cardiac occurances in post myocardial infarction patients. *American Heart Journal, 108,* 237–248.

Funk, S. C., & Houston, B. K. (1987). A critical analysis of the hardiness scale's validity and utility. *Journal of Personality and Social Psychology, 53,* 572–578.

Furman, E. F. (1974). *A child's parent dies: Studies in childhood bereavement.* New Haven: Yale University Press.

Futterman, E. H., Hoffman, I., & Sabshin, M. (1972). Parental anticipatory mourning. In B. Schoenberg, A. C. Carr, D. Peretz, and A. H. Kutscher (Eds.), *Psychosocial aspects of terminal care* (pp. 243–272). New York: Columbia University Press.

Gallant, S. J., Keita, G. P., & Royak-Schaler, R. (Eds.). (1997). *Health care for women: Psychological, social, and behavioral influences.* Washington, DC: American Psychological Association.

Gallup survey on food. (1987, October). *American Health,* 43–49.

Gallup, G. G., Jr. (1977). Self-recognition in primates: A comparative approach to the bidirectional properties of consciousness. *American Psychologist, 32,* 329–338.

Gamino, L. A., Elkins, G. R., & Hackney, K. U. (1989). Emergency management of mass psychogenic illness. *Psychosomatics, 30,* 446–449.

Garfield, C. A. (1979). (Ed.). *Stress and survival: The emotional realities of life threatening illness.* St. Louis: C. V. Mosby.

Garland, C., Barrett-Conner, E., Suaret, L., Criqui, M. H., & Wingard, D. L. (1985). Effects of passive smoking on ischemic heart disease mortality of nonsmokers. *American Journal of Epidemiology, 121,* 645–650.

Gatchel, R. J., Polatin, P. B., & Kinney, R. K. (1995). Predicting outcome of chronic back pain using clinical predictors of psychopathology: A prospective analysis. (Special Section: The interface of mental and physical health). *Health Psychology, 14,* 415–420.

Gatchel, R. J., & Turk, D. C. (Eds.). (1996). *Psychological approaches to pain management: A practitioner's handbook.* New York: Guilford Press.

Gentry, W. D. (1979). Preadmission behavior. In W. D. Gentry, & R. B. Williams (Eds.), *Psychological aspects of myocardial infarction and coronary care* (2nd ed., pp. 67–77). St. Louis: C. V. Mosby.

Gentry, W. D., & Haney, T. (1975). Emotional and behavioral reaction to acute myocardial infarction. *Heart and Lung, 4,* 738.

Gerrard, M., Gibbons, F. X., Reis-Bergan, M., & Russell, D. W. (2000). Self-esteem, self-serving cognitions, and health risk behavior. *Journal of Personality, 68,* 1177–1201.

Gersten, J. C., Langer, T. S., Eisenberg, J. G., & Orzeck, L. (1974). Child behavior and life events: Undesirable change or change per se? In B. S. Dohrenwend, & B. P. Dohrenwend (Eds.), *Stressful life events: Their nature and effects* (pp. 159–170). New York: John Wiley.

Gillum, R. F., & Barsky, A. J. (1974). Diagnosis and management of patient non-compliance. *Journal of the American Medical Association, 228,* 1563–1567.

Glantz, S. A., Slage, J., Bero, L. A., Hanauer, P., & Barnes, D. H. (1996). *The cigarette papers.* Berkeley: University of California Press.

Glass, D. C. (1977a). *Behavior patterns, stress, and coronary disease.* Hillsdale, NJ: L. Erlbaum.

Glass, D. C. (1977b). Stress, behavior patterns, and coronary disease. *American Scientist, 65,* 177.

Glass, D. C., & Singer, J. E. (1972). *Urban stress.* New York: Academic Press.

Glass, G. V., McGaw, B., & Smith, M. L. (1981). *Meta-analysis in social research.* Beverly Hills: Sage Publications.

Glick, I. O., Weiss, R. S., & Parkes, C. M. (1974). *The first year of bereavement.* New York: Wiley-Interscience.

Goffman, E. (1961). *Asylums: Essays on the social situation of mental patients and other inmates.* Garden City, NY: Doubleday.

Goffman, E. (1963). *Stigma: Notes on the management of spoiled identity.* Englewood Cliffs, NJ: Prentice-Hall.

Goldbaum, G. M., Remington, P. L., Powell, K. E., Hogelin, G. C., & Gentry, E. M. (1986). Failure to use seat belts in the United States. *Journal of the American Medical Association, 255,* 2459–2462.

Goldberg, L., Elliot, D., Clarke, G. N. , MacKinnon, D. P., Moe, E., Zoref, L., Green, C., Wolf, S. L., Greffrath, E., Miller, D. J., Lapin, A. (1996). Effects of a multidimensional anabolic steroid prevention intervention: The Adolescents Training and Learning to Avoid Steroids (ATLAS) Program. *Journal of the American Medical Association, 276,* 1555–1562.

Golden, J. S., & Johnston, G. D. (1970). Problems of distortion in doctor-patient communications. *Psychiatry in Medicine, 1,* 127–149.

Goldfarb, J., Lawry, K. W., Steffen, R., & Sabella, C. (1998). Infectious diseases presentations of Munchausen syndrome by proxy: Case report and review of the literature. *Clinical Pediatrics, 37,* 179–185.

Goldman, A. (Ed.). (1994). *Care of the dying child.* NY: Oxford University Press.

Goldstein, D. S., Eisenhofer, G., & McCarty, R. (Eds.). (1998). *Catecholamines: Bridging basic science with clinical medicine.* San Diego: Academic Press.

Goldston, D. B., Kovacs, M., Obrosky, D. S., & Iyengar, S. (1995, September). A longitudinal study of life events and metabolic control among youths with insulin-dependent diabetes mellitus. *Health Psychology, 14*(5), 409–414.

Goodkin, K., Antoni, M. H., & Blaney, P. H. (1986). Stress and hopelessness in the promotion of cervical intraepithelial neoplasis to invasive squamous cell carcinoma of the cervix. *Journal of Psychosomatic Research, 30,* 67–76.

Goodman, R., & Gorlin, R. (1970). *The face in genetic disorders.* St. Louis: C. V. Mosby.

Gordis, L. (1979). Conceptual and methodologic problems in measuring patient compliance. In R. B. Haynes, D. W. Taylor, & D. L. Sackett (Eds.), *Compliance in health care* (pp. 23–45). Baltimore: Johns Hopkins University Press.

Gordis, L., Markowitz, M., & Lilienfeld, A. M. (1969). Studies in the epidemiology and preventability of rheumatic fever. IV. A quantative determination of compliance in children on oral penicillin prophylaxis. *Pediatrics, 43,* 173–182.

Gordon, R. L. (1980). *Interviewing: Strategy, techniques, and tactics.* Homewood, IL: Dorsey Press.

Gordon, T., & Edwards, W. S. (1995). *Making the patient your partner: Communication skills for doctors and other caregivers.* Westport, CT: Auburn House/Greenwood Publishing Group, Inc.

Gore, S. (1978). The effect of social support in moderating the health consequences of unemployment. *Journal of Health and Social Behavior, 19*(2), 157–165.

Gorer, G. D. (1965). *Death, grief, and mourning.* Garden City, NY: Doubleday. (Reprinted by Arno Press, 1977).

Gorsuch, R., & Butler, M. (1976). Initial drug abuse: A review of predisposing social psychological factors. *Psychological Bulletin, 83,* 120–137.

Gosselin, C., & Cabanac, M. (1996). Ever higher: Constant rise of body weight set-point in growing Zucker rats. *Physiology & Behavior, 60,* 817–821.

Gottlieb, B. H. (1983). Social support as a focus for integrative research in psychology. *American Psychologist, 38,* 278–287.

Gough, H. G., & Hall, W. B. (1977). Physicians' retrospective evaluations of their medical education. *Research in Higher Education, 7,* 29–42.

Goyert, G., Bottoms, S., Treadwell, M., & Nehra, P. (1989). The physician factor in cesarean birth rates. *New England Journal of Medicine, 320,* 706–709.

Graham, K., & Vidal-Zeballos, D. (1998). Analyses of use of tranquilizers and sleeping pills across five surveys of the same population (1985–1991): The relationship with gender, age and use of other substances. *Social Science & Medicine, 46,* 381–395.

Graham, S. (1974). The sociological approach to epidemiology. *American Journal of Public Health, 64,* 1046–1049.

Grant, I. (1985). The social environment and neurological disease. *Advances in Psychosomatic Medicine, 13,* 26–48.

Gray, P. G., & Cartwright, A. (1953, December 19). Choosing and changing doctors. *The Lancet,* 1308.

Greenfield, N. S., Roessler, R., & Crosley, A. P. (1959). Ego strength and length of recovery from infectious mononucleosis. *Journal of Nervous and Mental Disease, 128,* 125–128.

Greer, D. S., & Mor, V. (1986). An overview of national hospice study findings. *Journal of Chronic Diseases, 39,* 5–7.

Greer, D. S., Mor, V., Morris, J. N., Sherwood, S., Kidder, D., & Birnbaum, H. (1986). An alternative in terminal care: Results of the national hospice study. *Journal of Chronic Diseases, 39,* 9–26.

Greer, S., & Morris, T. (1975). Psychological attributes of women who develop breast cancer. *Journal of Psychosomatic Research, 19,* 147–153.

Gregory, K. D., Hackmeyer, P., Gold, L., Johnson, A. I., & Platt, L. D. (1999, December). Using the continuous quality improvement process to safely lower the cesarean section rate. *Joint Commission Journal on Quality Improvement, 25*(12), 619–29.

Gross, C. P., Anderson, G. F., & Powe, N. R. (1999). The relation between funding by the National Institutes of Health and the burden of disease. *New England Journal of Medicine, 340,* 1881–7.

Guck, T. P., Skultety, F., Meilman, P., & Dowd, E. (1985). Multidisciplinary pain center follow-up study. *Pain, 21,* 295–306.

Gumbiner, J. (1981). Psychotherapeutic drug use: Personality, health, and demographic factors [Ph.D. dissertation]. University of California, Riverside.

Gunby, P. (1983). Gential herpes research. *Journal of the American Medical Association, 250,* 2417–2427.

Guyll, M., & Contrada, R. J. (1998). Trait hostility and ambulatory cardiovascular activity: Responses to social interaction. *Health Psychology, 17,* 30–39.

Haan, N. (1977). *Coping and defending: Processes of self-environment organization.* New York: Academic Press.

Haan, N. G. (1979). Psychosocial meanings of unfavorable medical forecasts. In G. C. Stone, F. Cohen, & N. E. Adler (Eds.), *Health psychology* (pp. 113–140). San Francisco: Jossey-Bass.

Hakim A. A., Curb, J. D., Petrovitch, H., Rodriguez, B. L., Yano, K., Ross, G. W., White, L. R., & Abbott, R. D. (1999). Effects of walking on coronary heart disease in elderly men: The Honolulu Heart Program. *Circulation, 100*(1), 9–13.

Hall, E. T. (1966). *The hidden dimension.* Garden City, NY: Doubleday.

Hall, J. A., Roter, D., & Rand, C. (1981). Communication of affect between patient and physician. *Journal of Health and Social Behavior, 22,* 18–30.

Haller, J. A., Talbert, J. L., & Dombro, R. H. (1967). *The hospitalized child and his family.* Baltimore: Johns Hopkins University Press.

Hanson, L. C., Danis, M., & Garrett, J. (1997). What is wrong with end-of-life care? Opinions of bereaved family members. *Journal of the American Geriatrics Society, 45,* 1339–1344.

Hanson, M. A., Spencer, J. A., & Rodeck, C. H. (Eds.). (1995). *Growth.* New York: Cambridge University Press.

Harlow, H. F., & Zimmermann, R. R. (1959). Affectional responses in the infant monkey. *Science, 130,* 421–432.

Harper, A. E. (1984). A healthful diet and its implications for disease prevention. In J. D. Matarazzo, S. Weiss, J. A. Herd, N. E. Miller, & S. M. Weiss (Eds.), *Behavioral health.* New York: Wiley.

Haruki, Y., Ishii, Y., & Suzuki, M. (Eds.). (1996). *Comparative and psychological study on meditation.* Delft, Netherlands: Eburon Publishers.

Harvey, J. H., & Miller, E. D. (1998). Toward a psychology of loss. *Psychological Science, 9,* 429–434.

Hawkins, J. D., Catalano, R. F., & Miller, J. Y. (1992). Risk and protective factors for alcohol and other drug problems in adolescence and early adulthood: Implications for substance abuse prevention. *Psychological Bulletin, 112,* 64–105.

Haynes, R. B. (1979). Introduction. In R. B. Haynes, D. W. Taylor, & D. L. Sackett (Eds.), *Compliance in health care* (pp. 1–7). Baltimore: Johns Hopkins University Press.

Haynes, R. B. (1980). Taking medication: Short- and long-term strategies. Paper delivered at conference, "Promoting Long-Term Health Behaviors." Institute for Advancement of Human Behavior. New York: Guilford Publications.

Haynes, R. B., Taylor, D. W., & Sackett, D. L. (1979). (Eds.), *Compliance in health care.* Baltimore: Johns Hopkins University Press.

Haynes, S. G., Feinleib, M., & Kannel, W. B. (1980). The relationship of psychosocial factors to coronary heart disease in the Framingham Study: III. Eight-year incidence of coronary heart disease. *American Journal of Epidemiology, 111,* 37–58.

Hegsted, D. M. (1984). What is a healthful diet? In J. D. Matarazzo, S. Weiss, J. A. Herd, N. E. Miller, & S. M. Weiss (Eds.), *Behavioral health.* New York: Wiley.

Helgeson, V. S., Cohen, S., Schulz, R., Yasko, J. (2000). Group support interventions for women with breast cancer: Who benefits from what? *Health Psychology, 19*(2), 107–114.

Henderson, J. B., & Enelow, A. J. (1976). The coronary risk factor program: A behavioral perspective. *Preventative Medicine, 5,* 128–148.

Henley, N. M. (1977). *Body politics: Power, sex, and nonverbal communication.* Englewood Cliffs, NJ: Prentice-Hall.

Herrick, J. W. (1976). Placebos, psychosomatic, and psychogenic illness and psychotherapy. *The Psychological Record, 26,* 327–342.

Herzberger, S. D., & Potts, D. A. (1982). Interpersonal relations during the childbearing years. In H. S. Friedman, & M. R. DiMatteo (Eds.), *Interpersonal issues in health care* (pp. 101–117). New York: Academic Press.

Hetherington, E. M. (1991). Presidential address: Families, lies, and videotapes. Presidential Address of the Society for Research in Adolescence. *Journal of Research on Adolescence, 1,* 323–348.

Hilfiker, D. (1984). Facing our mistakes. *New England Journal of Medicine, 310,* 118–122.

Hinrichsen, G. A., Revenson, T. A., & Shinn, M. (1985). Does self-help help? An empirical investigation of scoliosis peer support groups. *Journal of Social Issues, 41,* 65–87.

Hippocrates. (1923). *On decorum and the physician* (Vol. II). Translated by W. H. S. Jones. London: William Heinemann, Ltd.

Hippocrates. (1950). *The medical works of Hippocrates.* Translated by J. Chadwick and W. N. Mann. Oxford: Blackwell Scientific Publications.

Hobfoll, S. E., Spielberger, C. D., Breznitz, S., Figley, C., Folkman, S., Leooer-Green, B., Meichenbaum, D., & Milgram, N. A. (1991). War-related stress: Addressing the stress of war and other traumatic events. *American Psychologist, 46,* 848–855.

Hofling, C. K., Brotzman, S. D., Graves, N., & Pierce, C. M. (1966). An experimental study in nurse-physician relationships. *Journal of Nervous and Mental Disease, 143,* 171–180.

Holmes, T. H., & Masuda, M. (1974). Life change and illness susceptibility. In B. S. Dohrenwend, & B. P. Dohrenwend (Eds.), *Stressful life events: Their nature and effects* (pp. 45–72). New York: John Wiley.

Holmes, T. H., & Rahe, R. H. (1967). *Schedule of recent experiences.* Seattle: School of Medicine, University of Washington.

Holmes, T. H., & Rahe, R. H. (1967). The social readjustment rating scale. *Journal of Psychosomatic Research, 11,* 213–218.

Hoon, E. F., Hoon, P. W., Rand, K. H., & Johnson, J. (1991). A psycho-behavioral model of genital herpes recurrence. *Journal of Psychosomatic Research, 35,* 25–36.

House, J. S. (1981). *Work stress and social support.* Reading, MA: Addison-Wesley.

House, J. S., Robbins, C., & Metzner, H. L. (1982). The association of social relationships and activities with mortality. *American Journal of Epidemiology, 116,* 123–140.

Hughes, J. R. (1984). Psychological effects of habitual aerobic exercise. *Preventive Medicine, 13,* 66–78.

Hughes, P. H., Storr, C. L., Brandenburg, N. A., Baldwin, D. C., Anthony, J. C., & Sheehan, D.V. (1999). Physician substance use by medical specialty. *Journal of Addictive Diseases, 18,* 23–37.

Hulka, B., Cassel, J., Kupper, L., & Burdette, J. (1976). Communication, compliance, and concordance between physicians and patients with prescribed medications. *American Journal of Public Health, 66,* 847–853.

Hull, J. G., Van Treuren, R. R., & Virnelli, S. (1987). Hardiness and health: A critique and alternative approach. *Journal of Personality and Social Psychology, 53,* 518–530.

Hunt, M. (1974). *Sexual behavior in the 1970s.* Chicago: Playboy Press.

Hunt, W. A., & Matarazzo, J. D. (1982). Changing smoking behavior: A critique. In R. J. Gatchel, A. Baum, & J. E. Singer (Eds.), *Handbook of psychology and health* (Vol. 1, pp. 171–209). Hillsdale, NJ: Erlbaum.

Hurwitz, B. E., & Schneiderman, N. (1998). Cardiovascular reactivity and its relation to cardiovascular disease risk. In D. S. Krantz, & A. Baum (Eds.), *Technology and methods in behavioral medicine.* (pp. 245–273). Mahwah, NJ: Lawrence Erlbaum Associates, Inc.

Idler, E. L., & Kasl, S. V. (1997). Religion among disabled and nondisabled persons II: Attendance at religious services as a predictor of the course of disability. *Journals of Gerontology: Series B: Psychological Sciences & Social Sciences, 52,* S306–S316.

Iglehart, J. K. (1984). Smoking and public policy. *New England Journal of Medicine, 310,* 539–544.

Illich, I. (1976). *Medical nemesis: The expropriation of health.* New York: Random House.

Ironson, G., Field, T., Scafidi, F., Hashimoto, M., Kumar, M., Kumar, A., Price, A., Goncalves, A., Burman, I., Tetenman, C., Patarca, R., Fletcher, M. A. (1996). Massage therapy is associated with enhancement of the immune system's cytotoxic capacity. *International Journal of Neuroscience, 84,* 205–217.

Ironson, G., Wynings, C., Schneiderman, N., Baum, A., Rodriguez, M., Greenwood, D., Benight, C., Antoni, M., LaPerriere, A., Huang, H. S., Klimas, N., & Fletcher,

M. A. (1997). Posttraumatic stress symptoms, intrusive thoughts, loss, and immune function after Hurricane Andrew. *Psychosomatic Medicine, 59,* 128–141.

Irwin, M., Daniels, M., Bloom, E. T., Smith, T. L., & Weiner, H. (1987a). Life events, depressive symptoms, and immune function. *American Journal of Psychiatry, 144,* 437–441.

Irwin, M., Daniels, M., Smith, T. L., Bloom, E., & Weiner, H. (1987b). Impaired natural killer cell activity during bereavement. *Brain, Behavior, and Immunity,* 1, 98–104.

Istook, E. Jr. (1997). Research funding on major diseases is not proportionate to taxpayers' needs. *The Journal of NIH Research, 9,* 26–28.

Istvan, J. (1986). Stress, anxiety, and birth outcomes: A critical review of the evidence. *Psychological Bulletin, 100,* 331–348.

Jacobs, D. (Ed.). (1998). *Harvard Medical School Guide to Assessment and Intervention in Suicide.* San Francisco: Jossey-Bass.

Jacobs, M. K., & Goodman, G. (1989). Psychology and self-help groups. *American Psychologist, 44,* 536–545.

Jacobs, S., & Ostfeld, A. M. (1977). An epidemiological review of the mortality of bereavement. *Psychosomatic Medicine, 39,* 344–357.

Jaffe, D. (1980). *Healing from within.* New York: Knopf.

James, W. (1890). *The principles of psychology* (Vols. 1 and 2). New York: Henry Holt.

James, W. (1910). *The principles of psychology.* New York: Henry Holt.

Janis, I. L. (1958). *Psychological stress: Psychoanalytic and behavioral studies of surgical patients.* New York: John Wiley.

Janz, N. K., & Becker, M. H. (1984). The health belief model: A decade later. *Health Education Quarterly, 11,* 1–47.

Jarvinen, K. A. J. (1955). Can ward rounds be a danger to patients with myocardial infarction? *British Medical Journal, 1,* 318–320.

Jarvis, G. K., & Northcott, H. C. (1987). Religion and differences in morbidity and mortality. *Social Science Medicine, 25,* 813–824.

Jaycox, L. H., & Foa, E. B. (1998). Posttraumatic stress. In H. S. Friedman (editor-in-chief). *Encyclopedia of Mental Health* (Vol. 3, pp. 209–218). San Diego: Academic Press.

Jellinek, M. S., & Slovik, L. S. (1981). Current concepts in psychiatry: Divorce. Impact on children. *New England Journal of Medicine, 305,* 557–560.

Jemmott, J. B. (1987). Social motives and susceptibility to disease: Stalking individual differences in health risks. *Journal of Personality, 55*(2), 267–298.

Jemmott, J. B., Croyle, R. T., & Ditto, P. H. (1987). Commonsense epidemiology: Self-based judgements from laypersons and physicians. *Health Psychology, 7,* 55–73.

Jemmott, J. B., Ditto, P. H., & Croyle, R. T. (1986). Judging health status: Effects of perceived prevalence and personal relevance. *Journal of Personality and Social Psychology, 50,* 899–905.

Jemmott, J. B., & Locke, S. E. (1984). Psychosocial factors, immunological mediation, and human susceptibility to infectious diseases: How much do we know? *Psychological Bulletin, 95,* 78–108.

Jemmott III, J. B., Jemmott, L. S., & Fong, G. T. (1989). Abstinence and safer sex HIV risk-reduction interventions for African American adolescents. *Journal of the American Medical Association, 279*(19), 1529–1536.

Jenkins, C. D., Zyzanski, S. J., & Rosenman, R. H. (1978). *Manual for the Jenkins Activity Survey.* New York: Psychological Corporation.

Jensen, M. R. (1987). Psychobiological factors predicting the course of breast cancer. *Journal of Personality, 55,* 317–342.

Jessor, R., Van Den Bos, J., Vanderryn, J., Costa, F. M., & Turbin, M. S. (1995). Protective factors in adolescent problem behavior: Moderator effects and developmental change. *Developmental Psychology, 31,* 923–933.

Jiang, W., Babyak, M., Krantz, D. S., Waugh, R. A., Coleman, R. E., Hanson, M. M., Frid, D. J., McNulty, S., Morris, J. J., O'Connor, C. M., & Blumenthal, J. A. (1996). Mental stress-induced myocardial ischemia and cardiac events. *Journal of the American Medical Association, 275,* 1651–1656.

Johnson, B. S. (1965). The meaning of touch in nursing. *Nursing Outlook, 13,* 59–60.

Johnson, J. E. (1973). Effects of accurate expectations about sensations on the sensory and distress components of pain. *Journal of Personality and Social Psychology, 27,* 261–275.

Johnson, J. E., & Leventhal, H. (1974). Effects of accurate expectations and behavioral instructions on reactions during a noxious medical examination. *Journal of Personality and Social Psychology, 29,* 710–718.

Johnson, S. B., Tomer, A., Cunningham, W. R., & Henretta, J. C. (1990). Adherence in childhood diabetes: Results of a confirmatory factor analysis. *Health Psychology, 9*(4), 493–501.

Joiner, T. E., Jr. (1999, June). The clustering and contagion of suicide. *Current Directions in Psychological Science, 8*(3), 89–92.

Jonas, B. S., & Mussolino, M. E. (2000). Symptoms of depression as a prospective risk factor for stroke. *Psychosomatic Medicine, 62,* 463–471.

Jones, E. E., Kanouse, D. E., Kelley, H. H., Nisbett, R. E., Valins, S., & Weiner, B. (1972). *Attribution: Perceiving the causes of behavior.* Morristown, NJ: General Learning Press.

Jones, E. E., & Nisbett, R. E. (1972). The actor and the observer: Divergent perceptions of the causes of behavior. In E. E. Jones (Ed.), *Attribution: Perceiving the causes of behavior* (pp. 79–94). Morristown, NJ: General Learning Press.

Jones, K., & Vischi, J. (1979). Impact of alcohol, drug abuse, and mental health treatment on medical care utilization. *Medical Care, 17,* 1–82.

Jones, R. A. (1977). *Self-fulfilling prophecies: Social, psychological, and physiological effects of expectancies.* Hillsdale, NJ: Erlbaum.

Jones, R. A. (1982). Expectations and illness. In H. S. Friedman, & M. R. DiMatteo (Eds.), *Interpersonal issues in health care* (pp. 145–167). New York: Academic Press.

Jorgensen, H. S., Nakayama, H., Reith, J., Raaschou, H. O., & Olsen, T. S. (1996). Factors delaying hospital admission in acute stroke: The Copenhagen Stroke Study. *Neurology, 47,* 383–387.

Jospe, M. (1978). *The placebo effect in healing.* Lexington, MA: Lexington Books.

Jourard, S. M. (1966). An exploratory study of body-accessibility. *British Journal of Social and Clinical Psychology, 5,* 221–231.

Kabat, G. C., & Wynder, E. L. (1987). Determinants of quitting smoking. *American Journal of Public Health, 77,* 1301–1305.

Kahana, R. J., & Bibring, G. L. (1964). Personality types in medical management. In N. E. Zinberg (Ed.), *Psychiatry and medical practice in a general hospital* (pp. 108–123). New York: International Universities Press.

Kahn, H. S., Tatham, L. M., Patel, A. V., Thun, M. J., & Heath, C. W., Jr. (1998). Increased cancer mortality following a history of nonmelanoma skin cancer. *Journal of the American Medical Association, 280,* 910–912.

Kahn, J. P., Kornfeld, D. S., Frank, K. A., Heller, S. S., & Hoar, P. F. (1980). Type A behavior and blood pressure during coronary artery bypass surgery. *Psychosomatic Medicine, 42,* 407–414.

Kahn, R. L., Wolfe, D. M., Quinn, R. P., Snoek, J., & Rosenthal, R. A. (1964). *Organizational stress: Studies in role conflict and ambiguity.* New York: Wiley.

Kahneman, D., & Tversky, A. (1972). Subjective probability: A judgement of representativeness. *Cognitive Psychology, 3,* 430–454.

Kahneman, D., & Tversky, A. (1973). On the psychology of prediction. *Psychological Review, 80,* 237–251.

Kamarck, T. W., & Jennings, J. R. (1991). Biobehavioral factors in sudden cardiac death. *Psychological Bulletin, 109,* 42–75.

Kanfer, F. H. (1980). Self-management methods. In F. H. Kanfer, & A. P. Goldstein (Eds.), *Helping people change: A textbook of methods* (2nd ed., pp. 334–389). New York: Pergamon Press.

Kanner, A. D., Coyne, J. C., Schaeffer, C., & Lazarus, R. S. (1981). Comparison of two modes of stress measurement: Daily hassles and uplifts vs. major life events. *Journal of Behavioral Medicine, 4,* 1–39.

Kaplan, G. A., Seeman, T. E., Cohen, R. D., Knudsen, L. P., & Guralnik, J. (1987). Mortality among the elderly in the Alameda County study: Behavioral and demographic risk factors. *American Journal of Public Health, 77,* 307–312.

Kaplan, J. R., & Manuck, S. B. (1998). Monkeys, aggression and the pathobiology of atherosclerosis. *Aggressive Behavior, 24,* 323–334.

Kaplan, R. M. (1982). Coping with stressful medical examinations. In H. S. Friedman, & M. R. DiMatteo (Eds.), *Interpersonal issues in health care* (pp. 187–206). New York: Academic Press.

Kaplan, R. M. (1984). The connection between clinical health promotion and health status: A critical overview. *American Psychologist, 39,* 755–765.

Kaplan, R. M. (2000). Two pathways to prevention. *American Psychologist, 55*(4), 382–396.

Kaplan, R. M., Atkins, C., & Lenhard, L. (1982). Coping with a stressful sigmoidoscopy: Evaluation of cognitive and relaxation preparations. *Journal of Behavioral Medicine, 5,* 67–82.

Kaplan, R. M., & Criqui, M. H. (Eds.). (1985). *Behavioral epidemiology and disease prevention.* New York: Plenum.

Kaplan, R. M., Patterson, T. L., Kerner, D. N., Atkinson, J. H., Heaton, R. K., & Grant, I. (1997). The Quality of Well-being scale in asymptomatic HIV-infected patients. *Quality of Life Research: An International Journal of Quality of Life Aspects of Treatment, Care & Rehabilitation, 6,* 507–514.

Kaplan, R. M., Ries, A. L., Prewitt, L. M., & Eakin, E. (1994). Self-efficacy expectations predict survival for patients with chronic obstructive pulmonary disease. *Health Psychology, 13,* 366–368.

Kaplan, R. M., & Simon, H. J. (1990). Compliance in medical care: Reconsideration of self-predictions. *Annals of Behavioral Medicine, 12,* 66–71.

Kaprio, J., Koskenvuo, M., & Rita, H. (1987). Mortality after bereavement: A prospective study of 95,647 widowed persons. *American Journal of Public Health, 77,* 283–287.

Karasek, R. A., Theorell, T., Schwartz, J., Pieper, C., & Alfredsson, L. (1982). Job, psychological factors, and coronary heart disease. *Advances in Cardiology, 29,* 62–67.

Karasek, R. A., Theorell, T., Schwartz, J. E., Schnall, P. L., Pieper, C. F., & Michela, J. L. (1988). Job characteristics in relation to the prevalence of myocardial infarction in the U.S. HES and HANES. *American Journal of Public Health, 78,* 910–918.

Karoly, P. (1980). Operant methods. In F. H. Kanfer, & A. P. Goldstein (Eds.), *Helping people change: A textbook of methods* (2nd ed., pp. 210–247). New York: Pergamon Press.

Karoly, P. (Ed.). (1998). *Handbook of child health assessment: Biopsychosocial perspectives.* New York: John Wiley & Sons.

Kasl, S. V. (1975). Issues in patient adherence to health care regimens. *Journal of Human Stress, 1,* 5–17.

Kasl, S. V. (1983). Pursuing the link between stressful life experiences and disease. In C. L. Cooper (Ed.), *Stress research* (pp. 79–102). New York: Wiley.

Kasl, S. V., & Cobb, S. (1966). Health behavior, illness behavior, and sick role behavior. I., *Archives of Environmental Health, 12,* 246–266 (February 1966); II., 12, 534–541 (April 1966).

Kasteler, J., Kane, R. L., Olsen, D. M., & Thetford, C. (1976). Issues underlying prevalence of "doctor-shopping" behavior. *Journal of Health and Social Behavior, 17,* 328–339.

Kastenbaum, R. (1977). *Death, society, and human experience.* St. Louis: C. V. Mosby.

Kastenbaum, R. (1982). Dying is healthy and death a bureaucrat: Our fantasy machine is alive and well. In H. S. Friedman, & M. R. DiMatteo (Eds.), *Interpersonal issues in health care* (pp. 233–251). New York: Academic Press.

Kastenbaum, R. (1992). *The psychology of death* (2nd ed.). New York: Springer.

Kastenbaum, R., & Aisenberg, R. B. (1972). *The psychology of death.* New York: Springer.

Katcher, M. L. (1987). Prevention of tap water scald burns. *American Journal of Public Health, 77,* 1195–1197.

Kastenbaum, R. J. (1998). *Death, society, and human experience.* (6th ed.) Boston: Allyn and Bacon.

Kato, P. M., & Mann, T. (Eds.). (1996). *Handbook of diversity issues in health psychology: The Plenum series in culture and health.* New York: Plenum Press.

Katz, I. R. (1982). Is there a hypoxic affective syndrome? *Psychosomatics, 23,* 846–853.

Keane, T. M., Scott, W. O., Chavoya, G. A., Lamparski, D. M., & Fairbank, J. A. (1985). Social support in Vietnam veterans with posttraumatic stress disorder: A comparative analysis. *Journal of Consulting and Clinical Psychology, 53,* 95–102.

Kegeles, S. S., & Lund, A. K. (1984). Adolescents' acceptance of caries-preventive procedures. In J. D. Matarazzo, S. Weiss, J. A. Herd, N. E. Miller, & S. M. Weiss (Eds.), *Behavioral health.* New York: Wiley.

Kelleher, M. D., & Kelleher, C. L. (1998). *Murder most rare: The female serial killer.* Westport, CT: Praeger Publishers/Greenwood Publishing Group, Inc.

Kelley, H. H. (1967). Attribution theory in social psychology. In D. Levine (Ed.), *Nebraska Symposium on Motivation, 1967* (Vol. 15, pp. 192–238). Lincoln: University of Nebraska Press.

Kelley, J. E., Lumley, M. A., & Leisen, J. C. C. (1997). Health effects of emotional disclosure in rheumatoid arthritis patients. *Health Psychology, 16,* 331–340.

Kelly, J. A., Otto-Salaj, L. L., Sikkema, K. J., Pinkerton, S. D., & Bloom, F. R. (1998). Implications of HIV treatment advances for behavioral research on AIDS: Protease inhibitors and new challenges in HIV secondary prevention. *Health Psychology, 17,* 310–319.

Kelly, O. E. (1975). *Make today count.* New York: Delacorte Press.

Kemeny, M., Zegans, L., & Cohen, F. (1987). Stress, mood, immunity, and recurrence of genital herpes. *Annals of New York Academy of Sciences, 496,* 735–745.

Kemeny, M. E., Cohen, F., Zegans, L. S., & Conant, M. A. (1989). Psychological and immunological predictors of genital herpes recurrence. *Psychosomatic Medicine, 51*(2), 195–208.

Kennell, J. H., & Klaus, M. H. (1976). Caring for parents of an infant who dies. In M. H. Klaus, & J. H. Kennell (Eds.), *Maternal-infant bonding: The impact of early separation or loss on family development* (pp. 209–239). St. Louis: C. V. Mosby.

Kerchoff, A. C., & Back, K. W. (1968). *The june bug: A study of hysterical contagion.* New York: Appleton-Century-Crofts.

Kessler, R., & Whalen, T. (1999). Hypnotic preparation in anesthesia and surgery. In R. Temes (Ed.), *Medical hypnosis: An introduction and clinical guide* (pp. 43–57). New York: Churchill Livingstone Inc.

Kiecolt-Glaser, J. K., Page, G. G., Marucha, P. T., MacCallum, R. C., & Glaser, R. (1998). Psychological influences on surgical recovery. *American Psychologist, 53,* 1209–1218.

Kiev, A. (1968). *Curanderismo; Mexican-American folk psychiatry.* New York: Free Press.

Killed by a word (1994). *The Lancet, 344,* 695.

King, H. (1970). Health in the medical and other learned professions. *Journal of Chronic Diseases, 23,* 257–281.

King, S. H. (1962). *Perceptions of illness and medical practice.* New York: Russell Sage Foundation.

King, T. K., Borrelli, B., Black, C., Pinto, B. M., & Marcus, B. H. (1997). Minority women and tobacco: Implications for smoking cessation interventions. *Annals of Behavioral Medicine, 19,* 301–313.

Kinsey, A. C., Pomeroy, W. B., & Martin, C. E. (1948). *Sexual behavior in the human male.* Philadelphia: W. B. Saunders.

Kinsey, A. C., Pomeroy, W. B., Martin, C. E., & Gebhard, P. H. (1953). *Sexual behavior in the human female.* Philadelphia: W. B. Saunders.

Kirsch, I., Capafons, A., Cardena-Buelna, E., & Amigo, S. (Eds). (1999). *Clinical hypnosis and self-regulation: Cognitive-behavioral perspectives.* Washington, DC: American Psychological Association.

Kleck, R. (1968). Physical stigma and nonverbal cues emitted in face-to-face interaction. *Human Relations, 21,* 119–128.

Knapp, M. L., & Hall, J. A. (1997). *Nonverbal communication in human interaction.* (4th ed.) Fort Worth, TX: Harcourt Brace College Publishers.

Knapp, M. L., Hart, R. P., & Dennis, H. S. (1974). An exploration of deception as a communication construct. *Human Communication Research, 1,* 15–29.

Knapp, R. J. (1987, July). When a child dies. *Psychology Today.*

Knowles, J. H. (1977). The responsiblity of the individual. *Daedalus, 106,* 57–80.

Kobasa, S. C. (1982). Commitment and coping in stress resistance among lawyers. *Journal of Personality and Social Psychology, 42,* 707–717.

Kobasa, S. C., Maddi, S. R., & Kahn, S. (1982). Hardiness and health: A prospective study. *Journal of Personality and Social Psychology, 42,* 168–177.

Koenig, H. G., Kvale, J. N., & Ferrel, C. (1988). Religion and well-being in later life. *Gerontologist, 28,* 18–28.

Koh, K. B., & Lee, B. K. (1998). Reduced lymphocyte proliferation and interleukin-2 production in anxiety disorders. *Psychosomatic Medicine, 60,* 479–483.

Kohn, L. T., Corrigan, J. M., & Donaldson, M. S. (2000). *To err is human: Building a safer health system.* Washington, DC: National Academy Press.

Kohn, P. M., Lafreniere, K., & Gurevich, M. (1991). Hassles, health, and personality. *Journal of Personality & Social Psychology, 61,* 478–482.

Koocher, G. P. (1986). Coping with death from cancer. *Journal of Consulting in Clinical Psychology, 54,* 623–631.

Koop C. E. (1989). A parting shot at tobacco. *Journal of the American Medical Association, 262,* 2894–2895.

Koos, E. (1954). *The health of Regionville, what the people thought and did about it.* New York: Columbia University Press.

Korsch, B. M., Gozzi, E. K., & Francis, V. (1968). Gaps in doctor-patient communication. I. Doctor-patient interaction and patient satisfaction. *Pediatrics, 42,* 855–871.

Korsch, B. M., & Negrete, V. F. (1972). Doctor-patient communication. *Scientific American, 227,* 66–74.

Kostrubala, T. (1976). *The joy of running.* Philadelphia: Lippincott.

Krackow, A., & Blass, T. (1995). When nurses obey or defy inappropriate physician orders: Attributional differences. *Journal of Social Behavior & Personality, 10,* 585–594.

Kramer, M. (1974). *Reality shock: Why nurses leave nursing.* St. Louis: C. V. Mosby.

Krantz, D. S., Baum, A., & Singer, J. E. (1983). (Eds.), *Handbook of psychology and health* (Vol. 3: Cardiovascular disorders and behavior). Hillsdale, NJ: Erlbaum.

Krantz, D. S., & Durel, L. (1983). Psychobiological substrates of the Type A behavior pattern. *Health Psychology, 2,* 393–411.

Krantz, D. S., Lundberg, U., & Frankenhaeuser, M. (1987). Stress and Type A behavior. In A. Baum, & J. E. Singer (Eds.), *Handbook of psychology and health* (Vol. 5: Stress). Hillsdale, NJ: Erlbaum.

Krause, N. (1998). Stressors in highly valued roles, religious coping, and mortality. *Psychology & Aging, 13,* 242–255.

Krupnick, J. L. (1984). Bereavement during childhood and adolescence. In M. Osterweis, F. Salomon, & M. Green (Eds.), *Bereavement: Reactions, consequences, and care* (pp. 99–141). Washington, DC: National Academy Press.

Kübler-Ross, E. (1969). *On death and dying.* New York: Macmillan.

Kumanyika, S. K., Bowen, D., Rolls, B. J., Van Horn, L., Perri, M. G., Czajkowski, S. M., Schron, E. (2000). Maintenance of dietary behavior change. *Health Psychology, 19* (Suppl 1), 42–56.

Labbe, E. (1998). Biofeedback. In H. S. Friedman (editor-in-chief), *The Encyclopedia of Mental Health* (Vol. I, pp. 247–256). San Diego, CA: Academic Press.

Ladd, C. O., Owens, M. J., & Nemeroff C. B. (1996). Persistent changes in corticotropin-releasing factor neuronal systems induced by maternal deprivation. *Endocrinology, 137*(4):1212–8.

Lander, L. (1978). *Defective medicine: Risk, anger, and the malpractice crisis.* New York: Farrar, Straus, Giroux.

Lanzetta, J. T., Cartwright-Smith, J., & Kleck, R. (1976). Effects of nonverbal dissimulation on emotional experience and autonomic arousal. *Journal of Personality and Social Psychology, 33,* 354–370.

Largey, G. P., & Watson, D. R. (1972). The sociology of odors. *American Journal of Sociology, 77,* 1021–1033.

Larson, D. (1993). *The helper's journey: Working with people facing grief, loss, and life-threatening illness.* Champaign, IL: Research Press.

Lasagna, L. (1970). Physicians' behavior toward the dying patient. In O. Brim, H. Freeman, S. Levine, & N. Scotch (Eds.), *The dying patient* (pp. 83–101). New York: Russell Sage Foundation.

Lasegue, E. C. (1873). Essay on hysterical anorexia. *Medical Times, 2,* 265.

Lasser, T. (1974). *Reach to recovery.* New York: American Cancer Society.

Lazarus, R. S. (1966). *Psychological stress and the coping process.* New York: McGraw-Hill.

Lazarus, R. S., & Folkman, S. (1984). *Stress, appraisal, and coping.* New York: Springer.

Lazarus, R. S., & Launier, R. (1978). Stress related transactions between person and environment. In L. Pervin, & M. Lewis (Eds.), *Perspectives in interactional psychology.* New York: Plenum.

Leake, R., Friend, R., & Wadhwa, N. (1999). Improving adjustment to chronic illness through strategic self-presentation: An experimental study on a renal dialysis unit. *Health Psychology, 18*(1), 54–62.

Lederer, H. D. (1952). How the sick view their world. *Journal of Social Issues, 8,* 4–16.

Leedham, B., Meyerowitz, B. E., Muirhead, J., & Frist, W. H. (1995). Positive expectations predict health after heart transplantation. *Health Psychology, 14,* 74–79.

Lehrer, P. M., Isenberg, S., & Hochron, S. M. (1993) Asthma and emotion: A review. *Journal of Asthma, 30,* 5–21.

Leibowitz, J. O. (1970). *The history of coronary heart disease.* Berkeley: University of California Press.

Leigh, H., & Reiser, M. (1980). *The patient: Biological, psychological, and social dimensions of medical practice.* New York: Plenum Medical Book Co.

Leiter, M. P., & Maslach, C. (1998). Burnout. In H. S. Friedman (editor-in-chief), *Encyclopedia of Mental Health.* (Vol. I, pp. 347–358). San Diego: Academic Press.

Lepore, S. J. (1995). Cynicism, social support, and cardiovascular reactivity. *Health Psychology, 14,* 210–216.

Lepore, S. J., Silver, R. C., Wortman, C. B., & Wayment, H. A. (1996). Social constraints, intrusive thoughts, and depressive symptoms among bereaved mothers. *Journal of Personality & Social Psychology, 70,* 271–282.

Lerman, C., Caporaso, N. E., Audrain, J., Main, D., Bowman, E. D., Lockshin, B., Boyd, N. R., Shields, P. G. (1999). Evidence suggesting the role of specific genetic factors in cigarette smoking. *Health Psychology, 18*(1), 14–20.

Lerner, M. (1970). The desire for justice and reactions to victims. In J. Macaulay, & L. Berkowitz (Eds.), *Altruism and helping behavior; social psychological studies of some antecedents and consequences* (pp. 205–229). New York: Academic Press.

Letter (1988). It may seem obvious to you. Giving medication instructions to patients. *Journal of the American Medical Association, 260*(9), 1243–1244.

Levav, I., Friedlander, Y., Kark, J. D., & Peritz, E. (1988). An epidemiologic study of mortality among bereaved parents. *New England Journal of Medicine, 319,* 457–61.

Levenstein, S. (2000). The very model of a modern etiology: A biopsychosocial view of peptic ulcer. *Psychosomatic Medicine, 62,* 176–185.

Leventhal, H., & Cleary, P. D. (1980). The smoking problem: A review of the research and theory in behavioral risk modification. *Psychological Bulletin, 88,* 370–405.

Leventhal, H., & Everhart, D. (1979). Emotion, pain, and physical illness. In C. E. Izard (Ed.), *Emotions and psychopathology* (pp. 263–299). New York: Plenum.

Leventhal, H., & Sharp, E. (1965). Facial expressions as indicators of distress. In S. S. Tomkins, & C. E. Izard (Eds.), *Affect, cognition, and personality: Empirical studies* (pp. 296–318). New York: Springer.

Levin, J. S., & Schiller, P. L. (1987). Is there a religious factor in health? *Journal of Religion and Health, 26,* 9–36.

Levine, J. D., Gordon, N., & Fields, H. (1978). The mechanism of placebo analgesia. *Lancet, 2,* 654–657.

Levy, B. S., & Sidel, V. W. (1997). *War and Public Health.* New York: Oxford University Press.

Levy, L. H. (1984). Issues in research and evaluation. In A. Gartner, & F. Riessman (Eds.), *The self-help revolution* (pp. 155–172). New York: Human Sciences Press.

Levy, L., & Herzog, A. (1974). Effects of population density and crowding on health and social adaptation in the Netherlands. *Journal of Health and Social Behavior, 15,* 228–240.

Levy, S. M. (1985). *Behavior and cancer: Life-style and psychosocial factors in the initiation and progression of cancer.* San Francisco: Jossey-Bass.

Lewis, C. E., Freeman, H. E., & Corey, C. R. (1987). AIDS-related competence of California's primary care physicians. *American Journal of Public Health, 77,* 795–799.

Lewis, S., & Armstrong, S. H. (1977). Children with terminal illness: A selected review. *International Journal of Psychiatry in Medicine, 8*(1), 73–82.

Ley, P., & Spelman, M. S. (1965). Communication in an outpatient setting. *British Journal of Social and Clinical Psychology, 4,* 114–116.

Ley, P., & Spelman, M. S. (1967). *Communicating with the patient.* London: Staples Press.

Lichtman, R. R., Wood, J. V., & Taylor, S. E. (1982). Close relationships after breast surgery. Paper presented at American Psychological Association convention, Washington, DC.

Lieberman, M. A. (1979). *Self-help groups for coping with crisis: Origins, members, processes, and impact.* San Francisco: Jossey-Bass.

Lief, H. I., & Fox, R. C. (1963). Training for "detached concern" in medical students. In H. I. Lief, V. F. Leif, and N. R. Leif (Eds.), *The psychological basis of medical practice* (pp. 12–35). New York: Harper and Row, Hoeber Medical Books.

Lief, H. I., & Karlen, A. (Eds.). (1976). *Sex education in medicine.* New York: Spectrum.

Liem, J. H., & Liem, R. (1976). Life events, social supports and physical and psychological well-being. Paper presented at annual meetings of the American Psychological association, Washington, DC.

Liggett, J. (1974). *The human face.* New York: Stein and Day.

Light, R. J., & Pillner, D. B. (1984). *Summing up: The science of reviewing research.* Cambridge, MA: Harvard University Press.

Lin, E. H., & Peterson, C. (1990). Pessimistic explanatory style and response to illness. *Behaviour Research & Therapy, 28,* 243–248.

Lin, N., Simeone, R. S., Ensel, W. M., & Kuo, W. (1979). Social support, stressful life events, and illness: A model and an empirical test. *Journal of Health and Social Behavior, 20*(2), 108–119.

Lindemann, E. (1944). The symptomatology and management of acute grief. *American Journal of Psychiatry, 101,* 141–148.

Llewelyn, S. P., & Fielding, R. G. (1987). Nurses: Training for new job demands. *Work & Stress, 1,* 221–233.

Lobel, M., Dunkel-Schetter, C., & Scrimshaw, S. C. (1992). Prenatal maternal stress and prematurity: A prospective study of socioeconomically disadvantaged women. *Health Psychology, 11*(1), 32–40.

Lobel, M. (1998). Pregnancy and mental health. In H. S. Friedman (editor-in-chief), *The Encyclopedia of Mental Health* (Vol. III, pp. 229–238). San Diego, CA: Academic Press.

Locke, S. E., Kraus, L., Leserman, J., et al. (1984). Life change stress, psychiatric symptoms, and natural killer cell activity. *Psychosomatic Medicine, 46,* 441–453.

Loesser, J. D. (1980). Low back pain. In J. Bonica (Ed.), *Pain* (pp. 363–377). New York: Raven Press.

LoPiccolo, J., & LoPiccolo, L. (Eds.). (1978). *Handbook of sex therapy.* New York: Plenum.

Lorber, J. (1975). Good patients and problem patients: Conformity and deviance in a general hospital. *Journal of Health and Social Behavior, 16,* 213–225.

Lorig, K. R., Sobel, D. S., Stewart, A. L., Brown, B. W., Jr., Bandura, A., Ritter, P., Gonzalez, V. M., Laurent, D. D., & Holman, H. R. (1999). Evidence suggesting that a chronic disease self-management program can improve health status while reducing hospitalization. *Medical Care, 37*(1), 5–14.

Lowman, C., Hunt, W. A., Litten, R. Z., & Drummond, D. C. (2000). Research perspectives on alcohol craving: An overview. *Addiction, 95* (Suppl2), S45–S54.

Lown, B. (1979). Sudden cardiac death. *American Journal of Cardiology, 43,* 313–328.

Lown, B. (1996). *The lost art of healing.* Boston: Houghton Mifflin.

Lurie, H. J., & Lawrence, G. L. (1972). Communication problems between rural Mexican-American patients and their physicians: Description of a solution. *American Journal of Orthopsychiatry, 49*(5), 777–783.

Lurie, P., & Reingold, A. L. (Eds.). (1993). Public health impact of needle exchange programs in the United States and abroad: Summary, conclusions, and recommendations. Berkeley: School of Public Health, University of California, Berkeley, Institute for Health Policy Studies, University of California, San Francisco.

Lustman, P. J., Freedland, K. E., Griffith, L. S., & Clouse, R. E. (1998). Predicting response to cognitive behavior therapy of depression in type 2 diabetes. *General Hospital Psychiatry, 20,* 302–306.

Lustman, P., Griffith, L., Freedland, K., Kissel, S., & Clouse, R. (1998). Cognitive behavior therapy for depression in type 2 diabetes: A randomized controlled trial. *Annals of Internal Medicine, 129,* 613–621.

Lutgendorf, S. K., Vitaliano, P. P., Tripp-Reimer, T., Harvey, J., & Lubaroff, D. M. (1999). Sense of coherence moderates the relationship between life stress and natural killer cell activity in healthy older adults. *Psychology & Aging, 14,* 552–563.

Lynch, J. J. (1977). *The broken heart: The medical consequences of loneliness.* New York: Basic Books.

Lynch, J. J., Thomas, S. A., Mills, M. E., Malinow, K., & Katcher, A. H. (1974). The effects of human contact on cardiac arrhythmia in coronary care patients. *The Journal of Nervous and Mental Disease, 158,* 88–99.

Maccoby, N., Farquhar, J. W., Wood, P. D., & Alexander, J. (1977). Reducing the risk of cardiovascular disease: Effects of a community-based campaign on knowledge and behavior. *Journal of Community Health, 3,* 100–114.

MacCoun, R. J. (1998). Toward a psychology of harm reduction. *American Psychologist, 53,* 1199–1208.

MacDonald, M. E., Hagberg, K. L., & Grossman, B. J. (1963). Social factors in relation to participation in follow-up care of rheumatic fever. *Journal of Pediatrics, 62,* 503–513.

Maddi, S. R., & and Kobasa, S. C. (1984). *The Hardy Executive.* Homewood, IL: Dow Jones-Irwin.

Mahoney, M. J., & Mahoney, K. (1976). *Permanent weight control.* New York: W. W. Norton.

Maier, S. F., & Watkins, L. R. (2000). The immune system as a sensory system: Implications for psychology. *Current Directions in Psychological Science, 9,* 98–102.

Mandell, H., & Spiro, H. (Eds.). (1987). *When Doctors Get Sick.* New York: Plenum Press.

Manuck, S. B., Kaplan, J. R., & Matthews, K. A. (1986). Behavioral antecedents of coronary heart disease atherosclerosis. *Arteriosclerosis, 6,* 2–14.

Maris, R. W. (1998). Suicide. In H. S. Friedman (editor-in-chief), *Encyclopedia of Mental Health* (Vol. 3, pp. 621–634). San Diego: Academic Press.

Marlatt, G. A., & Gordon, J. R. (Eds.). (1985). *Relapse prevention.* New York: Guilford.

Marlatt, G. A., & VandenBos, G. R. (Eds.). (1997). *Addictive behaviors: Readings on etiology, prevention, and treatment.* Washington, DC: American Psychological Association.

Marmot, M. G., & Syme, S. L. (1976). Acculturation and coronary heart disease in Japanese-Americans. *American Journal of Epidemiology, 104,* 225–246.

Marquis, K. H. (1970). Effects of social reinforcement on health reporting in the household interview. *Sociometry, 33*(2), 203–215.

Marsland, D. W., Wood, M. B., & Mayo, F. (1976). The databank for patient care, curriculum, and research in family practice: 526,196 patient problems. *Journal of Family Practice, 3,* 25–28.

Martin, L. R., Friedman, H. S., Tucker, J. S., Schwartz, J. E., Criqui, M. H., Wingard, D. L., & Tomlinson-Keasey, C. (1995). An archival prospective study of mental health and longevity. *Health Psychology, 14,* 381–387.

Martin, L. R., & Friedman, H. S. (2000). Comparing personality scales across time: An illustrative study of validity and consistency in life-span archival data. *Journal of Personality, 68,* 85–110.

Martin, R. A., Kuiper, N. A., Olinger, L. J., & Dobbin, J. (1987). Is stress always bad? Telic versus paratelic dominance as a stress-moderating variable. *Journal of Personality & Social Psychology, 53*(5), 970–982.

Maslow, A. H. (1971). *The farther reaches of human nature.* New York: Viking Press.

Mason, J. W. (1974). Specificity in the organization of neuroendocrine response profiles. In P. Seeman, & G. M. Brown (Eds.), *Frontiers in neurology and neuroscience research: First international symposium of the neuroscience institute, University of Toronto* (pp. 68–80). Toronto: University of Toronto.

Mason, J. W. (1975). A historical view of the stress field: Part I. *Journal of Human Stress, 1*(1), 6–12.

Masters, W. H., & Johnson, V. E. (1966). *Human sexual response.* Boston: Little, Brown.

Matarazzo, J. D. (1982). Behavioral health's challenge to academic, scientific, and professional psychology. *American Psychologist, 37,* 1–14.

Mathis, J. L. (1964). A sophisticated version of voodoo death. *Psychosomatic Medicine, 26*(2), 104–107.

Matthews, K. A. (1982). Psychological perspectives on the Type A behavior pattern. *Psychological Bulletin, 81,* 293–323.

Matthews, K. A., & Haynes, S. G. (1986). Type A behavior pattern and coronary disease risk: Update and critical evaluation. *American Journal of Epidemiology, 123,* 923–960.

Matthews, K. A., & Siegel, J. M. (1987). Training health psychologists in schools of public health. In G. Stone et al. (Eds.), *Health Psychology.* Chicago: University of Chicago Press.

Matthews, K. A., Siegel, J. M., Kuller, L. H., Thompson, M., & Varat, M. (1983). Determinants of decisions to seek medical treatment by patients with acute myocardial infarction symptoms. *Journal of Personality and Social Psychology, 44,* 1144–1156.

Mattson, M. E., Pollack, E. S., & Cullen, J. W. (1987). What are the odds that smoking will kill you? *American Journal of Public Health, 77,* 425–431.

Mattsson, A. (1972). The crisis of illness: Chronic conditions. *Pediatrics, 50,* 801–811.

Mauss, M. (1967). *Essai sur le don, forme archaique de l'exchange* (1925). Translated by I. Cunnison. New York: W. W. Norton.

Mayhall, C. G. (Ed.). (1999). *Hospital epidemiology and infection control* (2nd ed.). Philadelphia: Lippincott Williams & Wilkins.

Mazullo, J. M., Lasagna, L., & Griner, P. F. (1974). Variations in interpretation of prescription instructions. *Journal of the American Medical Association, 227*(8), 929–930.

McCabe, P. M., Schneiderman, N., Field, T., & Wellens, A. R. (Eds.). (2000). *Stress, coping, and cardiovascular disease.* Mahwah, NJ: Lawrence Erlbaum Associates.

McCann, S. M., Lipton, J. M., Sternberg, E. M., & Chrousos, G. P. (Eds.). (1998). *Annals of the New York Academy of Sciences: Neuroimmunomodulation: Molecular aspects, integrative systems, and clinical advances.* (Vol. 840). New York: New York Academy of Sciences.

McCorkle, R., Robinson, L., Nuamah, I., & Lev, E. (1998). The effects of home nursing care for patients during terminal illness on the bereaved's psychological distress. *Nursing Research, 47,* 2–10.

McCullough, M. E., Hoyt, W. T., Larson, D. B., Koenig, H. G., & Thoresen, C. E. (2000). Religious involvement and mortality: A meta-analytic review. *Health Psychology, 19,* 211–222.

McEwen, B. S. (1998). Stress, adaptation, and disease: Allostasis and allostatic load. *Annals of the New York Academy of Sciences, 840,* 33–44.

McEwen, B. S., Biron, C. A., Brunson, K. W., Bulloch K., Chambers, W. H., Dhabhar, F. S., Goldfarb, R. H., Kitson R. P., Miller, A. H., & Spencer, R. L. (1997). The role of adrenocorticoids as modulators of immune function in health and disease: Neural, endocrine and immune interactions. *Brain Research Reviews, 23,* 79–133.

McFadden, S. H., & Levin, J. S. (1996). Religion, emotions, and health. In Magai, C., & McFadden, S. H. (Eds.), *Handbook of emotion, adult development, and aging.* (pp. 349–368). San Diego: Academic Press.

McFarlane, T., Polivy, J., & Herman, C. P. (1998). Dieting. In H. S. Friedman (editor-in-chief), *Encyclopedia of Mental Health* (Vol. I, pp. 743–754). San Diego: Academic Press,

McGinnis, J. M., & Foege, W. H. (1993). Actual causes of death in the United States. *Journal of the American Medical Association, 270,* 2207–2212.

McIntosh, J. (1974). Processes of communication, information seeking, and control associated with cancer: A selective review of the literature. *Social Science and Medicine, 8,* 167–187.

McIntyre, J. G., & Dusek, J. B. (1995). Perceived parental rearing practices and styles of coping. *Journal of Youth & Adolescence, 24,* 499–509.

McKeown, T. (1979). *The role of medicine.* Princeton: University of Princeton Press.

McKinlay, J. (1973). Social networks, lay consultation, and help-seeking behavior. *Social Forces, 51,* 275–292.

McKinlay, J. (1975). Who is really ignorant? *Journal of Health and Social Behavior, 16,* 3–12.

McKinney, C. H., Antoni, M. H., Kumar, M., Tims, F. C., & McCabe, P. M. (1997, July). Effects of guided imagery and music (GIM) therapy on mood and cortisol in healthy adults. *Health Psychology, 16*(4), 390–400.

McNulty, E. G., & Holderby, R. A. (1983). *Hospice: A caring challenge.* Springfield, IL: C. C. Thomas.

Mead, G. H. (1934). *Mind, self, and society from the standpoint of a social behaviorist.* Chicago: University of Chicago Press.

Meaney, M. J., Tannenbaum, B., & Francis, D. (1994). Early environmental programming: Hypothalamic-pituitary-adrenal responses to stress. *Seminar in Neuroscience, 6,* 247–59.

Mechanic, D. (1959). Illness and social disability: Some problems and analysis. *Pacific Sociological Review, 2,* 37–41.

Mechanic, D. (1962). The concept of illness behavior. *Journal of Chronic Disease, 15,* 189–194.

Mechanic, D. (1966). Response factors in illness: The study of illness behavior. *Social Psychiatry, 1,* 11–20.

Mechanic, D. (1968). *Medical sociology: A selective view.* New York: Free Press.

Mechanic, D. (1972). Social psychological factors affecting the presentation of bodily complaints. *New England Journal of Medicine, 286,* 1132–1139.

Mechanic, D. (1978). *Medical sociology* (2nd ed.). New York: Free Press.

Mechanic, D. (Ed.). (1982). *Symptoms, illness behavior, and help-seeking.* New York: Prodist.

Mechanic, D. (Ed.). (1983). *Handbook of health, health care, and the health professions.* New York: Free Press.

Mechanic, D., & Volkart, E. H. (1960). Illness behavior and medical diagnoses. *Journal of Health and Human Behavior, 1,* 86–94.

Mechanic, D., & Volkart, E. H. (1961). Stress, illness behavior, and the sick role. *American Sociological Review, 26,* 51–58.

Meerloo, J. A. M. (1964). *Unobtrusive communication: Essays in psycholinguistics.* Assen, Netherlands: Koninklijke Van Gorcum.

Melamed, B. G., & Fogel, J. (2000). The psychologist's role in the treatment of dental problems. In D. I. Mostofsky & D. H. Barlow (Eds.), *The management of stress and anxiety in medical disorders.* (pp. 268–281). Needham Heights, MA: Allyn & Bacon.

Melzack, R. (1973). *The puzzle of pain.* New York: Basic Books.

Melzack, R. (1983). *Pain measurement and assessment.* New York: Raven Press.

Melzack, R., & Wall, P. D. (1965). Pain mechanisms: A new theory. *Science, 150,* 971.

Melzack, R., & Wall, P. D. (1982). *The challenge of pain.* New York: Basic Books.

Mendelson, M. A. (1975). *Tender loving greed.* New York: Vintage Books.

Menninger, K. A., & Menninger, W. C. (1936). Psychoanalytic observations in cardiac disorders. *American Heart Journal, 11*(10).

Menza, M. A., & Liberatore, B. L. (1998). Psychiatry in the geriatric neurology practice. *Neurologic Clinics, 16,* 611–633.

Mesters, I., Meertens, R., Crebolder, H., & Parcel, G. (1993, March). Development of a health education program for parents of preschool children with asthma. *Health Education Research, 8*(1), 53–68.

Metry, J-M, & Meyer, U. A. (Eds.). (1999). *Drug regimen compliance: Issues in clinical trials and patient management.* NY: Wiley.

Meyer, A. (1948). Cited in A. Lief (Ed.), *The commonsense psychiatry of Dr. Adolf Meyer.* New York: McGraw-Hill.

Meyer, R., & Haggerty, R. (1962). Streptococcal infections in families. *Pediatrics, 29,* 539–549.

Meyers, T. M., Eichhorn, D. J., Guzzetta, C. E., Clark, A. P., Klein, J. D., Taliaferro, E., & Calvin, A. (2000). Family presence during invasive procedures and resuscitation. *American Journal of Nursing , 100.*

Michela, J. L., & Contendo, I. R. (1986). Cognitive, motivational, social, and environmental influences on children's food choices. *Health Psychology, 5,* 209–230.

Michela, J. L., & Wood, J. V. (1986). Causal attributes in health and illness. In P. C. Kendell (Ed.), *Advances in cognitive-behavioral reserch and therapy* (Vol. 5, pp. 79–236). New York: Academic Press.

Michela, J. M. (1987). Interpersonal and individual impacts of a husband's heart attack. In A. Baum, & J. Singer (Eds.), *Handbook of psychology and health* (Vol. 5 Stress, pp. 255–301). Hillsdale, NJ: Erlbaum.

Milgram, S. (1974). *Obedience to authority: An experimental view.* New York: Harper and Row.

Miller, G. E, Cohen, S., & Herbert, T. B. (1999). Pathways linking major depression and immunity in ambulatory female patients. *Psychosomatic Medicine, 61,* 850–860.

Miller, G. E., & Cohen, S. (2001). Psychological interventions and the immune system: A meta-analytic review and critique. *Health Psychology, 20,* 47–63.

Miller, S. M., & Diefenbach, M. A. (1998). The Cognitive-Social Health Information-Processing (C-SHIP) model: A theoretical framework for research in behavioral oncology. In D. S. Krantz, & A. Baum (Eds.), *Technology and methods in behavioral medicine* (pp. 219–244). Mahwah, NJ: Lawrence Erlbaum Associates, Inc.

Miller, S. M., Rodoletz, M., Schroeder, C. M., Mangan, C. E., & Sedlacek, T. V. (1996). Applications of the monitoring process model to coping with severe long-term medical threats. *Health Psychology, 15,* 216–225.

Miller, T. Q., Smith, T. W., Turner, C. W., Guijarro, M. L., & Hallet, A. J. (1996). Meta-analytic review of research on hostility and physical health. *Psychological Bulletin, 119,* 322–348.

Miller, T. Q., Turner, C. W., Tindale, R. S., Posavac, E. J., & Dugoni, B. L. (1991). Reasons for the trend toward null findings in research on Type A behavior. *Psychological Bulletin, 110,* 469–485.

Miller, W. R., & Heather, N. (Eds.) (1998). *Treating addictive behaviors* (2nd ed.). New York: Plenum Press.

Millman, M. (1976). *The unkindest cut: Life in the backrooms of medicine.* New York: William Morrow.

Milmoe, S., Rosenthal, R., Blane, H. T., Chafetz, M. E., & Wolf, I. (1967). The doctor's voice: Postdictor of successful referral of alcoholic patients. *Journal of Abnormal Psychology, 72,* 78–84.

Minuchin, S., Lee, W., & Simon, G. M. (1996). *Mastering family therapy: Journeys of growth and transformation.* New York: John Wiley & Sons.

Minuchin, S., Montalvo, B., Guerney, B. Jr., Rosman, B., & Schumer, K. (1967). *Families of the slums: an exploration of their structure and treatment.* New York: Basic Books.

Minuchin, S., Rosman, B. L., & Baker, L. (1978). *Psychosomatic families: Anorexia nervosa in context.* Cambridge, MA: Harvard University Press.

Montague, A. (1978). *Touching: The human significance of the skin.* New York: Harper and Row.

Moos, R. (Ed.). (1977). *Coping with physical illness.* New York: Plenum.

Moos, R. H. (1979). Social-ecological perspectives on health. In G. C. Stone, F. Cohen, & N. E. Adler (Eds.), *Health psychology* (p. 523). San Francisco: Jossey-Bass.

Moos, R. H., & Tsu, V. D. (1977). The crisis of physical illness: An overview and perspective. In R. H. Moos (Ed.), *Coping with physical illness* (pp. 3–21). New York: Plenum.

Morera, O. F., Johnson, T. P., Freels, S., Parsons, J., Crittenden, K. S., Flay, B. R., & Warnecke, R. B. (1998). The measure of stage of readiness to change: Some psychometric considerations. *Psychological Assessment, 10,* 182–186.

Morgan, W. P. (1997). *Physical activity and mental health.* Washington, DC: Taylor & Francis Publishers.

Moriarty, D. M. (Ed.). (1967). *The loss of loved ones: The effects of a death in the family on personality development.* Springfield, IL: Charles C. Thomas.

Moss, A. J., & Goldstein, S. (1970). The pre-hospital phase of acute myocardial infarction. *Circulation, 41,* 737.

Moss, G. E. (1973). *Illness, immunity and social interaction: The dynamics of biosocial resonation.* New York: John Wiley.

Muehrer, P. (2000). Research on adherence, behavior change, and mental health: A workshop overview. *Health Psychology, 19,* 304–307.

Mumford, E., Schlesinger, H. J., & Glass, G. V. (1982). The effects of psychological intervention on recovery from surgery and heart attacks: An analysis of the literature. *American Journal of Public Health, 72,* 141–151.

Mumford, E., Schlesinger, H. J., Glass, G. V., Patrick, C., & Cuerdon, B. A. (1984). A new look at evidence about reduced cost of medical utilization following mental health treatment. *American Journal of Psychiatry, 141,* 1145–1158.

Murdock, G. P. (1980). *Theories of illness: A world survey.* Pittsburgh: University of Pittsburgh Press.

Mussell, M. P., & Mitchell, J. E. (1998). Anorexia nervosa and bulimia nervosa. In H. S. Friedman (editor-in-chief), *Encyclopedia of Mental Health.* (Vol. I, pp. 111–118). San Diego: Academic Press.

Myers, R. E. (1977). Production of fetal asphyxia by maternal psychological stress. *Pavlovian Journal of Biological Sciences, 12,* 51–62.

Nagy, M. (1948). The child's theories concerning death. *Journal of Genetic Psychology, 73,* 3–27.

Nall, F., & Speilberg, J. (1967). Social and cultural factors in responses of Mexican-Americans to medical treatment. *Journal of Health and Social Behavior, 8,* 299–308.

Name withheld to protect the guilty. (1986). Why would a girl go into surgery? *Journal of the American Women's Medical Association, 41,* 58–60.

Nathan, P. E. (1984). Johnson & Johnson's live for life. In J. D. Matarazzo, S. Weiss, J. A. Herd, N. E. Miller, & S. M. Weiss (Eds.), *Behavioral health.* New York: Wiley.

Nathanson, C. (1975). Illness and the feminine role. *Social Science and Medicine, 9,* 57–62.

National Center for Injury Prevention and Control. (2000). *Fact book for the year 2000: Working to prevent and control injury in the United States.* Atlanta, GA: Center for Disease Control and Prevention.

National Institutes of Health. (1996). *Alcoholism, getting the facts* (NIH Publication No. 96–4153). Rockville, MD: National Institute on Alcohol Abuse and Alcoholism, National Institutes of Health.

Newsweek. March 14, 1977.

Newsweek. Medicine. December 8, 1952.

Newsweek. Medicine. June 27, 1977.

New York Times. (1994, Aug 20). Obituary of John Bonica.

NIH. (1982). *Consensus development conference on cesarean childbirth.* Bethesda, MD: NIH Publication 82–2067.

Norman, J. C. (Ed.). (1969). *Medicine in the ghetto.* New York: Appleton-Century-Crofts.

Ockene, J. K. (1987). Physician-delivered interventions for smoking cessation. *Preventive Medicine, 16,* 723–737.

Olin, H. S., & Hackett, T. P. (1964). The denial of chest pain in 32 patients with acute myocardial infarction. *Journal of the American Medical Association, 190,* 977.

Orleans, C. T., Boyd, N. R., Bingler, R., & Sutton, C. (1998). A self-help intervention for African American smokers: Tailoring Cancer Information Service counseling for a special population. *Preventive Medicine: An International Journal Devoted to Practice & Theory, 27,* S61–S70.

Orth-Gomer, K., & Wamala, S. P. (2001). Marital stress and coronary heart disease: Reply. *Journal of the American Medical Association, 285,* 10.

Orwell, G. (1949). *1984.* New York: Harcourt, Brace.

Osler, W. (1904). *The master-word in medicine.* Aequanimitas with other addresses to medical students, nurses, and practitioners of medicine (pp. 369–371). London: H. K. Lewis.

Ostrow, David G. (1997). Disease, disease course, and psychiatric manifestations of HIV. In M. F. O'Connor, & I. D. Yalom, (Eds.), *Treating the psychological consequences of HIV* (pp. 33–71). San Francisco: Jossey-Bass.

Overmier, J. B., & Murison, R. (2000). Anxiety and helplessness in the face of stress predisposes, precipitates, and sustains gastric ulceration. *Behavioural Brain Research, 110,* 161–174.

Padilla, A., & Ruiz, R. A. (1973). *Latino mental health: A review of the literature.* Rockville, MD: National Institute of Mental Health.

Paffenberger, R. S., Hyde, R. T., Wing, A. L., & Steinmetz, E. H. (1984). A natural history of athleticism and cardiovascular health. *Journal of the American Medical Association, 252,* 491–495.

Paige, K. (1973). Women learn to sing the menstrual blues. *Psychology Today, 7,* 41–46.

Pakenham, Kenneth I. (1999, July). Adjustment to multiple sclerosis: Application of a stress and coping model. *Health Psychology, 18*(4), 383–392.

Panksepp, J. (1998). *Affective neuroscience: The foundations of human and animal emotions.* New York: Oxford University Press.

Parkes, C. M. (1972). *Bereavement: Studies of grief in adult life.* New York: International Universities Press.

Parkes, C. M., & Weiss, R. (1983). *Recovery from bereavement.* New York: Basic Books.

Parsons, T. (1951). *The social system.* New York: Free Press.

Parsons, T. (1958). Definitions of health and illness in the light of American values and social structure. In E. G. Jaco (Ed.), *Physicans, patients, and illness: Sourcebook in behavioral science and medicine* (pp. 165–187). Glencoe, IL: Free Press.

Parsons, T. (1975). The sick role and the role of the physician reconsidered. *Millbank Memorial Fund Quarterly, 53,* 257–278.

Pate, R. R., Trost, S. G., Mullis, R., Sallis, J. F., Wechsler, H., & Brown, D. R. (2000, August). Community interventions to promote proper nutrition and physical activity among youth. *Preventive Medicine: An International Journal Devoted to Practice & Theory, 31*(2, Pt.2), S138–S149.

Pavlov, I. P. (1927). *Conditioned reflexes: An investigation of the physiological activity of the cerebral cortex.* Oxford, England: Oxford University Press.

Payne, B. C., Harrison, R. V., & Harel, Y. (1986). *Medical malpractice claims.* Institute for Social Research, University of Michigan.

Peabody, F. W. (1927). The care of the patient. *Journal of the American Medical Association, 88,* 877–882.

Pearlin, L. I., Aneshensel, C. S., & LeBlanc, A. J. (1997). The forms and mechanisms of stress proliferation: The case of AIDS caregivers. *Journal of Health & Social Behavior, 38,* 223–236.

Pearlin, L. I., & Schooler, C. (1978). The structure of coping. *Journal of Health and Social Behavior, 19*(1), 2–21.

Pelletier, K. (1977). *Mind as healer, mind as slayer: A holistic approach to preventing stress disorders.* New York: Dell.

Pelletier, K. R. (1979). *Holistic medicine: From stress to optimum health.* New York: Delacorte Press.

Penn, N. E., Kar, S., Kramer, J., Skinner, J., & Zambrana, R. E. (1995). Ethnic minorities, health care systems, and behavior. *Health Psychology, 14*(7), 641–646.

Pennebaker, J., & Skelton, J. (1978). Psychological parameters of physical symptoms. *Personality and Social Psychology Bulletin, 4,* 524–530.

Pennebaker, J. W. (1980). Perceptual and environmental determinants of coughing. *Basic and Applied Social Psychology, 1,* 83–91.

Pennebaker, J. W. (1982). *The psychology of physical symptoms.* New York: Springer-Verlag.

Pennebaker, J. W. (1985). Traumatic experience and psychosomatic disease. *Canadian Psychology, 26,* 82–95.

Pennebaker, J. W., & Beall, S. K. (1986). Confronting a traumatic event: Toward an understanding of inhibition and disease. *Journal of Abnormal Psychology, 95,* 274–281.

Pennebaker, J. W., Burnan, M. A., Schaeffer, M. A., & Harper, D. C. (1977). Lack of control as a determinant of perceived physical symptoms. *Journal of Personality and Social Psychology, 35,* 167–174.

Pennebaker, J. W., & Traue, H. C. (1993). Inhibition and psychosomatic processes. In Traue, H. C., & Pennebaker, J. W. (Eds.), *Emotion inhibition and health* (pp. 146–163). Goettingen, Germany: Hogrefe & Huber Publishers.

Pennebaker, J. W. (Ed.). (1995). *Emotion, disclosure & health.* Washington, DC: American Psychological Association.

Penninx, B. W. J. H., van Tilburg, T., Boeke, A. J. P., Deeg, D. J. H., Kriegsman, D. M. W., & van Eijk, J. T. M. (1998). Effects of social support and personal coping resources on depressive symptoms: Different for various chronic diseases? *Health Psychology, 17*(6), 551–558.

Perry, C. L., Sellers, D. E., Johnson, C., Pedersen, S., Bachman, K. J., Parcel, G. S., Stone, E. J., Luepker, R. V., Wu, M., Nader, P. R., & Cook, K. (1997). The Child and Adolescent Trial for Cardiovascular Health (CATCH): Intervention, implementation, and feasibility for elementary schools in the United States. *Health Education & Behavior, 24*(6), 716–735.

Peters, A. S., Greenberger-Rosovsky, R., Crowder, C., Block, S. D., & Moore, G. T. (2000 May). Long-term outcomes of the new pathway program at Harvard medical school: A randomized controlled trial. *Academic Medicine, 75*(5), 470–479.

Peterson, C., & Bossio, L. M. (1991). *Health and optimism.* New York, NY: Free Press.

Peterson, C., & Seligman, M. E. (1984). Causal explanations as a risk factor for depression: Theory and evidence. *Psychological Review, 91,* 347–374.

Peterson, C., Seligman, M. E. P., Yurko, K. H., Martin, L. R., & Friedman, H. S. (1998). Catastrophizing and untimely death. *Psychological Science, 9,* 127–130.

Peterson, L., Crowson, J., Saldana, L., & Holdridge, S. (1999 March). Of needles and skinned knees: Children's coping with medical procedures and minor injuries for self and other. *Health Psychology, 18*(2), 197–200.

Petraitis, J., Flay, B. R., & Miller, T. Q. (1995). Reviewing theories of adolescent substance use: Organizing pieces in the puzzle. *Psychological Bulletin, 117,* 67–86.

Petrie, K. J., Booth, R. J., Pennebaker, J. W., & Davison, K. P. (1995). Disclosure of trauma and immune response to a hepatitis B vaccination program. *Journal of Consulting & Clinical Psychology, 63,* 787–792.

Petrie, K. J., & Weinman, J. A. (1997). Illness representations and recovery from myocardial infarction. In K. J. Petrie, & J. A. Weinman (Eds.), *Perceptions of health and illness: Current research and applications* (pp. 441–461). Singapore: Harwood Academic Publishers.

Pettingale, K. W. (1984). Coping and cancer prognosis. *Journal of Psychosomatic Research, 28,* 363–364.

Pfungst, O. (1965). *Clever Hans: The horse of Mr. Von Osten.* New York: Holt, Rinehart, and Winston.

Phillips, D. L. (1963). Rejection: A possible consequence of seeking help for mental disorders. *American Sociological Review, 28,* 963–972.

Phillips, D. L. (1965). Self-reliance and the inclination to adopt the sick role. *Social Forces, 43,* 555–563.

Piaget, J. (1960). *The child's conception of the world.* Totowa, NJ: Littlefield, Adams.

Pilowsky, I., & Spence, N. D. (1977). Ethnicity and illness behaviors. *Psychological Medicine, 7,* 447–452.

Placek, P. J. (1986). Cesarean rate still rising. *Statistical Bulletin, 67*(3), 9–10.

Polivy, J., & Herman, C. P. (1999, September). Distress and eating: Why do dieters overeat? *International Journal of Eating Disorders, 26*(2), 153–164.

Pomeroy, W. B. (1972). *Dr. Kinsey and the institute for sex research.* New York: Harper & Row.

Pope, M. K., & Smith, T. W. (1991). Cortisol excretion in high and low cynically hostile men. *Psychosomatic Medicine, 53,* 386–392.

Porter, A. (1969). Drug defaulting in a general practice. *British Medical Journal, 1,* 218–222.

Powell, L. H., & Thoresen, C. E. (1988). Effects of Type behavioral counseling and severity of prior acute myocardial infarction on survival. *Journal of Cardiology, 62,* 1159–1163.

Power, M., Bullinger, M., & Harper, A. (1999, September). The World Health Organization Quality of Life Group, Switzerland. The World Health Organization WHO-QOL-100: Tests of the universality of quality of life in 15 different cultural groups worldwide. *Health Psychology, 18*(5), 495–505.

Pratt, L., Seligmann, A., & Reader, G. (1957). Physicians' views on the level of medical information among patients. *American Journal of Public Health, 47,* 1277–1283.

Pyszczynski, T., Wicklund, R. A., Floresku, S., Koch, H., Gauch, G., Solomon, S., & Greenberg, J. (1996). Whistling in the dark: Exaggerated consensus estimates in response to incidental reminders of mortality. *Psychological Science, 7,* 332–336.

Quesada, G. M. (1976). Language and communication barriers for health delivery to a minority group. *Social Science and Medicine, 10,* 323–327.

Quittner, A. L., Espelage, D. L., Opipari, L. C., Carter, B., Eid, N., Eigen, H. (1998). Role strain in couples with and without a child with a chronic illness: Associations with marital satisfaction, intimacy, and daily mood. *Health Psychology, 17*(2), 112–124.

Rabinowitz, H. K. (1988, August). Evaluation of a selective medical school admissions policy to increase the number of family physicians in rural and underserved areas. *New England Journal of Medicine, 319*(8), 480–6.

Rabkin, J. G., & Struening, E. L. (1976). Life events, stress, and illness. *Science, 194,* 1013–1020.

Radest, H. B. (2000). *From clinic to classroom: Medical ethics and moral education.* Westport, CT: Praeger.

Rahe, R. H. (1972). Subjects' recent changes and their near-future illness susceptibility. *Advances in Psychosomatic Medicine, 8,* 2–19.

Rahe, R. H. (1974). The pathway between subjects' recent life changes and their near-future illness reports: Representative results and methodological issues. In B. S. Dohrenwend, & B. P. Dohrenwend (Eds.), *Stressful life events: Their nature and effects* (pp. 73–86). New York: John Wiley.

Rahe, R. H. (1987). Recent life changes, emotions and behaviors in coronary heart disease. In A. Baum, & J. Singer (Eds.), *Handbook of psychology and health* (Vol. 5: Stress). Hillsdale, NJ: Erlbaum.

Rahe, R. H., & Arthur, R. H. (1978). Life change and illness studies. *Journal of Human Stress, 4*(1), 3–15.

Rando, T. A. (1993). *Treatment of complicated mourning.* Champaign, IL: Research Press.

Rando, T. A. (Ed.). (2000). *Clinical dimensions of anticipatory mourning: Theory and practice in working with the dying, their loved ones, and their caregivers.* Champaign, IL: Research Press.

Rank, S. G., & Jacobson, C. K. (1977). Hospital nurses' compliance with medication overdose orders: A failure to replicate. *Journal of Health and Social Behavior, 18,* 188–193.

Rapoport, A. M., & Sheftell, F. D. (1996). *Headache disorders: A management guide for practitioners.* Philadelphia: Saunders.

Ratti, L. A., Humphrey, L. L., & Lyons, J. S. (1996). Structural analysis of families with a polydrug-dependent, bulimic, or normal adolescent daughter. *Journal of Consulting & Clinical Psychology, 64,* 1255–1262.

Ravaja, N., Keltikangas-Jaervinen, L., & Keskivaara, P. (1996). Type A factors as predictors of changes in the metabolic syndrome precursors in adolescents and young adults: A 3-year follow-up study. *Health Psychology, 15,* 18–29.

Raven, B. H., & Haley, R. W. (1980). Social influence in a medical context: Hospital acquired infections as a problem in medical social psychology. In L. Bickman (Ed.), *Applied social psychology annual* (Vol. 1). Beverly Hills: Sage Publications.

Rebuffe-Scrive, M., Walsh, U., McEwen, B., & Rodin, J. (1992). Effect of chronic stress and exogenous glucocorticoids on regional fat distribution and metabolism. *Physiology and Behavior, 52,* 583–590.

Reed, G. M., Kemeny, M. E., Taylor, S., Wang, H. J., & Visscher, B. R. (1994). Realistic acceptance as a predictor of decreased survival time in gay men with AIDS. *Health Psychology, 13,* 299–307.

Reichsman, F., & Levy, N. B. (1972). Problems in adaptation to maintenance. *Archives of Internal Medicine, 130,* 859–865.

Revenson, T. A. (1986). Debunking the myth of loneliness in late life. In E. Seidman, & J. Rappaport (Eds.), *Redefining social problems* (pp. 115–135). New York: Plenum.

Revenson, T. A., & McFarlane, T. A. (1998). Women's health. In H. S. Friedman (editor-in-chief), *Encyclopedia of Mental Health* (Vol. III, pp. 707–719). San Diego: Academic Press.

Revenson, T. A., Schiaffino, K. M., Majerovitz, D. S., & Gibofsky, A. (1991). Social support as a double-edged sword: The relation of positive and problematic support to depression among rheumatoid arthritis patients. *Social Science & Medicine, 33,* 807–813.

Revenson, T. A., Wollman, C. A., & Felton, B. J. (1983). Social supports as stress buffers for adult cancer patients. *Psychosomatic Medicine, 45,* 321–331.

Richards, J. M., & Gross, J. J. (1999). Composure at any cost? The cognitive consequences of emotion suppression. *Personality & Social Psychology Bulletin, 25,* 1033–1044.

Richardson, J. L., Marks, G., Johnson, C. A., Graham, J. W., Chan, K. K., Selser, J. N., Kishbaugh, C., & Barranday, Y. (1987). Path model of multidimensional compliance with cancer therapy. *Health Psychology, 6,* 183–207.

Richman, J., & Goldthorp, W. O. (1978). Fatherhood: The social construction of pregnancy and birth. In S. Kitzinger, & J. A. Davis (Eds.), *The place of birth: A study of the environment in which birth takes place with special refernce to home confinements* (pp. 157–173). Oxford: Oxford University Press.

Richter, C. P. (1957). On the phenomenon of sudden death in animals and man. *Psychosomatic Medicine, 19,* 191–198.

Rimal, R. N. (2000). Closing the knowledge-behavior gap in health promotion: The mediating role of self-efficacy. *Health Communication, 12,* 219–237.

Riscalla, L. (1975). Healing by laying on of hands: Myth or fact. *Ethics in Science and Medicine, 2,* 167–171.

Roberts, A. H., Kewman, D. G., Mercier, L., & Hovell, M. F. (1993). The power of nonspecific effects in healing: Implications for psychosocial and biological treatments. *Clinical Psychology Review, 13,* 375–391.

Robinson, V. M. (1977). *Humor and the health professions.* Thorofare, NJ: Charles B. Slack.

Rochlin, G. (1967). How younger children view death and themselves. In E. A. Grollman (Ed.), *Explaining death to children* (pp. 51–88). Boston: Beacon Press.

Rodin, J. (1986). Health, control, and aging. In M. Baltes, & P. Baltes (Eds.), *The Psychology of Control and Aging.* Hillsdale, NJ: Erlbaum.

Rodin, J., & Janis, I. L. (1979). The social power of health-care practitioners as agents of change. *Journal of Social Issues, 35*(1), 60–81.

Rodin, J., & Janis, I. L. (1982). The social influence of physicians and other health care practitioners as agents of change. In H. S. Friedman, & M. R. DiMatteo (Eds.), *Interpersonal issues in health care* (pp. 33–49). New York: Academic Press.

Rodin, J., & Langer, E. (1977). Long-term effects of a control-relevant intervention with institutionalized aged. *Journal of Personality and Social Psychology, 35,* 897–902.

Rodin, J., Silberstein, L. R., & Striegel-Moore, R. H. (1985). Women and weight: A normative discontent. *Nebraska symposium on motivation* (Vol. 32). Lincoln: University of Nebraska Press.

Rodriguez, M. S., & Cohen, S. (1998). Social support. In H. S. Friedman (editor-in-chief), *Encyclopedia of Mental Health* (Vol. 3, pp. 535–544). San Diego: Academic Press.

Roethlisberger, F. J., & Dickson, W. (1939). *Management and the worker; an account of a research program conducted by the Western electric company.* Cambridge, MA: Harvard University Press.

Rogers, C. R. (1961). *On becoming a person; a therapist's view of psychotherapy.* Boston: Houghton Mifflin.

Rogoff, N. (1957). The decision to study medicine. In R. K. Merton, G. G. Reader, & P. L. Kendall (Eds.), *The student physician; introductory studies in the sociology of medical education* (pp. 109–129). Cambridge, MA: Harvard University Press.

Rook, K. S., & Schuster, T. L. (1996). Compensatory processes in the social networks of older adults. In G. R. Pierce, & B. R. Sarason (Eds.), *Handbook of social support and the family* (pp. 219–248). New York: Plenum Press.

Rose, K. D., & Rosow, I. (1973). Physicians who kill themselves. *Archives of General Psychiatry, 29,* 800–805.

Rosenberg, E. L., Ekman, P., & Blumenthal, J. A. (1998). Facial expression and the affective component of cynical hostility in male coronary heart disease patients. *Health Psychology, 17,* 376–380.

Rosenberg, P. P. (1979). Catch 22—the medical model. In E. C. Shapiro, & L. M. Lowenstein (Eds.), *Becoming a physician: Development of values and attitudes in medicine* (pp. 81–92). Cambridge, MA: Ballinger.

Rosenman, R. H., Brand, R. J., Jenkins, C. D., Friedman, M., Straus, R., & Wurm, M. (1975). Coronary heart disease in the western collaborative group study: Final follow-up experience of 8 1/2 years. *Journal of the American Medical Association, 233,* 872–877.

Rosenman, R. H., Friedman, M., Straus, R., Jenkins, D., Zyzanski, S., & Wurm, M. (1970). Coronary heart disease in the western collaborative group study: A follow-up experience of 4 1/2 years. *Journal of Chronic Disease, 23,* 173.

Rosenstock, I. M. (1974). The health belief model and preventative health behavior. In M. H. Becker (Ed.), *The health belief model and personal health behavior* (pp. 27–59). Thorofare, NJ: Charles B. Slack.

Rosenthal, R. (1966). *Experimenter effects in behavioral research.* New York: Appleton-Century-Crofts.

Rosenthal, R. (1984). *Meta-analytic procedures for social research.* Beverly Hills: Sage Publications.

Rosenthal, R., Hall, J. H., DiMatteo, M. R., Rogers, P. L., & Archer, D. (1979). *Sensitivity to nonverbal communication: The PONS test.* Baltimore: Johns Hopkins University Press.

Rosenthal, R., & Rubin, D. B. (1982). A simple, general purpose display of magnitude of experimental effect. *Journal of Educational Psychology, 74,* 166–169.

Roter, D. L. (1984). Patient question asking in physician-patient interaction. *Health Psychology, 3,* 395–409.

Roter, D. L. (2000). The enduring and evolving nature of the patient-physician relationship. *Patient Education and Counseling, 39,* 5–15.

Roter, D. L., & Hall, J. A. (1992). *Doctors talking with patients/patients talking with doctors: Improving communication in medical visits.* Westport, CT: Auburn House.

Roth, J. A. (1972). Some contingencies of the moral evaluation and control of clientele: The case of the hospital emergency service. *American Journal of Sociology, 77,* 839–856.

Rothenberg, M. (1967). Reactions of those who treat children with cancer. *Pediatrics, 40,* 507.

Rotter, J. B. (1954). *Social learning and clinical psychology.* New York: Prentice-Hall.

Rotter, J. B. (1966). Generalized expectancies for internal versus external control of reinforcement. *Psychological Monographs, 80*(1), No. 609.

Rouse, B. A. (Ed.). (1998). *Substance abuse and mental health statistics sourcebook* (2nd ed.). Rockville, MD: Dept. of Health and Human Services, Substance Abuse and Mental Health Services Administration, Office of Applied Studies.

Rowland, K. R. (1977). Environmental events predicting death for the elderly. *Psychological Bulletin, 84,* 349–372.

Rozin, P. (1984). The acquisition of food habits and preferences. In J. D. Matarazzo, S. Weiss, J. A. Herd, N. E. Miller, & S. M. Weiss (Eds.), *Behavioral health.* New York: Wiley.

Ryan, W. (1971). *Blaming the victim.* New York: Pantheon Books.

Ryle, G. (1949). *The concept of mind.* New York: Barnes & Noble.

Sackett, D. L. (1979). A compliance practicum for the busy practitioner. In R. B. Haynes, D. W. Taylor, & D. L. Sackett (Eds.), *Compliance in health care* (pp. 286–294). Baltimore: Johns Hopkins University Press.

Sackett, D. L., & Snow, J. C. (1979). The magnitude of compliance and noncompliance. In R. B. Haynes, D. W. Taylor, & D. L. Sackett (Eds.), *Compliance in health care* (pp. 11–22). Baltimore: Johns Hopkins University Press.

Saito, K., Kim, J. I., Maekawa, K., Ikeda, Y., & Yokoyama, M. (1997). The great Hanshin-Awaji earthquake aggravates blood pressure control in treated hypertensive patients. *American Journal of Hypertension, 10,* 217–21.

Sallis, J. F. (1986). Exercise adherence and motivation. *Focal Points (U. S. Public Health Service), 2,* 1–3.

Sallis, J. F., Prochaska, J. J., Taylor, W. C., Hill, J. O., & Geraci, J. C. (1999). Correlates of physical activity in a national sample of girls and boys in Grades 4 through 12. *Health Psychology, 18,* 410–415.

Saltman, P., Gurin, J., and Mothner, I. (Eds.). (1993). *The University of California San Diego nutrition book.* Boston: Little, Brown.

Samarel, N. (1991). *Caring for life and death.* Washington, DC: Hemisphere Publishing Corp.

Samora, J., Saunders, L., & Larson, R. F. (1961). Medical vocabulary knowledge among hospital patients. *Journal of Health and Human Behavior, 2,* 83–89.

Sanford, N., & Comstock, C. (Eds.). (1971). *Sanctions for evil; sources of social destructiveness.* Boston: Beacon Press.

Sapolsky, R. M. (1994). *Why zebras don't get ulcers: A guide to stress, stress related diseases, and coping.* New York: W.H. Freeman.

Sarason, I. G., Johnson, J. H., & Siegel, J. M. (1978). Assessing the impact of life changes: Development of the life experiences survey. *Journal of Consulting and Clinical Psychology, 46,* 932–946.

Sarason, I. G., & Sarason, B. R. (1984). Life changes, moderators of stress, and health. In A. Baum, S. E. Taylor, & J. E. Singer (Eds.), *Handbook of psychology and health* (Vol. 4: Social psychological aspects of health). Hillsdale, NJ: L. Erlbaum.

Saunders, L. (1954). *Cultural differences and medical care; the case of the Spanish-speaking people of the southwest.* New York: Russell Sage Foundation.

Savidge, C. J., & Slade, P. (1997). Psychological aspects of chronic pelvic pain. *Journal of Psychosomatic Research, 42,* 433–444.

Schab, F. R., & Crowder, R. G. (Eds.). (1995). *Memory for odors.* Hillsdale, NJ: Lawrence Erlbaum Associates.

Schachter, S. (1959). *The psychology of affiliation; experimental studies of the sources of gregariousness.* Palo Alto, CA: Stanford University Press.

Schachter, S. (1982). Recidivism and self-cure of smoking. *American Psychologist, 37,* 436–444.

Schachter, S., & Singer, J. E. (1962). Cognitive, social and physiological determinants of emotional state. *Psychological Review, 69,* 379–399.

Scheier, M. F., & Carver, C. S. (1987). Dispositional optimism and physical well-being: The influence of generalized outcome expectancies on health. *Journal of Personality, 55,* 169–210.

Schermerhorn, G. R., Colliver, J. A., Verhulst, S. J., & Schmidt, E. L. (1986). Factors that influence career patterns of women physicians. *Journal of the American Women's Medical Association, 41,* 74–78.

Schiffman, S. S., Graham, B. G., Sattely-Miller, E. A., & Warwick, Z. S. (1998). Orosensory perception of dietary fat. *Current Directions in Psychological Science, 7,* 137–143.

Schinke, S., Cole, K., Diaz, T., & Botvin, G. J. (1997). Developing and implementing interventions in community settings. *Journal of Child & Adolescent Substance Abuse, 6,* 49–67.

Schmale, A. H., Jr. (1972). Giving up as a final common pathway to changes in health. *Advances in Psychosomatic Medicine, 8,* 20–40.

Schmale, A. H., Jr., & Engel, G. L. (1967). The giving up-given up complex illustrated on film. *Archives of General Psychiatry, 17,* 135–145.

Schmale, A. H., Jr., & Iker, H. P. (1966). The affect of hopelessness and the development of cancer. I. Identification of uterine cancer in women with atypical cytology. *Psychosomatic Medicine, 28,* 714–721.

Schmale, A. H., Jr., & Iker, H. P. (1971). Hopelessness as a predictor of cervical cancer. *Social Science and Medicine, 5,* 95–100.

Schooler, C., Chaffee, S. H., Flora, J. A., Roser, C. (1998). Health campaign channels: Tradeoffs among reach, specificity and impact. *Human Communication Research, 24,* 410–432.

Schowalter, J. E. (1970). Multiple organ transplantation and the creation of surgical siblings. *Pediatrics, 46*(4), 576–580.

Schultz, D. (1977). *Growth psychology: Models of the healthy personality.* New York: Van Nostrand, Reinhold Co.

Schwalbe F. C. (1990). Relationship between Type A personality and coronary heart disease. Analysis of five cohort studies. *Journal of the Florida Medical Association, 77,* 803–5.

Schwartz, C. E., Kaplan, R. M., Anderson, J. P., Holbrook, T., & Genderson, M. W. (1999). Covariation of physical and mental symptoms across illnesses. *Annals of Behavioral Medicine, 21,* 122–127.

Schwartz, H. (1986). *Never satisfied: A cultural history of diets, fantasies, and fat.* New York: Free Press.

Schwartz, J. E., Friedman, H. S., Tucker, J. S., Tomlinson-Keasey, C., Wingard, D. L., & Criqui, M. H. (1995). Sociodemographic and psychosocial factors in childhood as predictors of longevity across the life-span. *American Journal of Public Health, 85,* 1237–1245.

Sebregts, E. H. W. J., Falger, P. R. J., & Baer, F. W. H. M. (2000). Risk factor modification through nonpharmacological interventions in patients with coronary heart disease. *Journal of Psychosomatic Research, 48,* 425–441.

Seeman, M., & Evans, J. W. (1962). Alienation and learning in a hospital setting. *American Sociological Review, 27,* 772–783.

Seeman, T. E., Kaplan, G. A., Knudsen, L., Cohen, R., & Guralnik, J. (1987). Social network ties and mortality among the elderly in the Alameda County study. *American Journal of Epidemiology, 126,* 714–723.

Seeman, T. E., McEwen, B. S., Singer, B. H., Albert, M. S., & Rowe, J. W. (1997). Increase in urinary cortisol excretion and memory declines: MacArthur studies of successful aging. *Journal of Clinical Endocrinology and Metabolism, 93,* 2458–65.

Seeman, T. E., Singer, B. H., Rowe, J. W., Horwitz, R. I., & McEwen, B. S. (1997). Price of adaptation-allostatic load and its health consequences: MacArthur studies of successful aging. *Archives of Internal Medicine, 157,* 2259–68.

Segall, A. (1972, June). The sick role concept: Understanding illness behavior. *Journal of Health and Social Behavior, 17,* 163–170.

Segall, A. (1976). Sociocultural variation in sick role behavioral expectations. *Social Science and Medicine, 10,* 47–51.

Segall, A., & Roberts, L. W. (1980). A comparative analysis of physician estimates and levels of medical knowledge among patients. *Sociology of Health and Illness, 2*(3), 317–334.

Seligman, M. E. P. (1975). *Helplessness: On depression, development, and death.* San Francisco: W. H. Freeman.

Seligman, M. E. P., Reivich, K., Jaycox, L., & Gillham, J. (1995). *The optimistic child.* Boston: Houghton Mifflin.

Selye, H. (1956). *The stress of life.* New York: McGraw-Hill.

Selye, H. (1978). *The stress of life.* (Rev. ed.). New York: McGraw-Hill.

Shaper, A. G., Wannamethee, G., & Walker, M. (1998). Alcohol and mortality in British men: Explaining the U-shaped curve. *Lancet, 2,* 1267–1273.

Shapiro, A. K. (1960). A contribution to a history of the placebo effect. *Behavioral Science, 5,* 109–135.

Shapiro, A. K. (1971). Placebo effects in medicine, psychotherapy, and psychoanalysis. In A. E. Bergin, & S. L. Garfield (Eds.), *Handbook of psychotherapy and behavior change: An empirical analysis* (pp. 439–473). New York: JohnWiley.

Shapiro, A. K., & Shapiro, E. (1984). Patient-provider relationships and the placebo effect. In J. Matarazzo, et al. (Eds.), *Behavioral Health.* New York: Wiley.

Shapiro, D. E., Boggs, S. R., Melamed, B. G., & Graham-Pole, J. (1992). The effect of varied physician affect on recall, anxiety, and perceptions in women at risk for breast cancer: An analogue study. *Health Psychology, 11*(1), 61–66.

Shattuck, F. C. (1907). The science and art of medicine in some of their aspects. *Boston Medical and Surgical Journal, 157,* 63–67.

Shaw, D. S., Emery, R. E., & Tuer, M. D. (1993). Parental functioning and children's adjustment in families of divorce: A prospective study. *Journal of Abnormal Child Psychology, 21,* 119—134.

Sheehan, G. (1975). *Dr. Sheehan: On running.* Mt. View, CA: World Publications.

Shem, S. (1978). *The house of God.* New York: Dell.

Shephard, M. (1975). *Someone you love is dying: A guide for helping and coping.* New York: Charter.

Sherman, R. A. (Ed.). (1997). *Phantom pain.* New York: Plenum Press.

Shiffman, S., Gnys, M., Richards, T. J., Paty, J. A., Hickcox, M., & Kassel, J. D. (1996). Temptations to smoke after quitting: A comparison of lapsers and maintainers. *Health Psychology, 15,* 455–461.

Shipley, R. H., Butt, J. H., & Horowitz, E. (1979). Preparation to reexperience a stressful medical examination. *Journal of Consulting and Clinical Psychology, 47,* 485–492.

Shively, C. A. (1998). Social subordination stress, behavior, and central monoaminergic function in female cynomolgus monkeys. *Biological Psychiatry, 44,* 882–891.

Shively, C. A., Watson, S. L., Williams, J. K., & Adams, M. R. (1998). Social stress, reproductive hormones, and coronary heart disease risk in primates. In K. Orth-Gomer, & M. Chesney, (Eds.), *Women, stress, and heart disease* (pp. 205–217). Mahwah, NJ: Lawrence Erlbaum Associates, Inc.

Shore, J. H. (1987). The Oregon experience with impaired physicians on probation. *Journal of the American Medical Association, 257,* 2931–2934.

Shumaker, S. A., Schron, E. B., Ockene, J. K., & McBee, W. L. (Eds.). (1998). *The handbook of health behavior change* (2nd ed.). New York: Springer Publishing Co., Inc.

Siegel, J. M. (1984). Type A behavior: Epidemiologic foundations and public health implications. *Annual Review of Public Health, 5,* 343–367.

Siegel, J. M. (1993). Companion animals: In sickness and in health. *Journal of Social Issues, 49,* 157–167.

Sifneos, P. E. (1973). The prevalence of alexithymic characteristics in psychosomatic patients. *Psychotherapy and Psychosomatics, 22,* 255–262.

Sime, W. E. (1984). Psychological benefits of exercise training in the healthy individual. In J. D. Matarazzo et al. (Eds.), *Behavioral Health.* New York: Wiley.

Simon, A. B., Feinleib, M., Thompson, H. (1972). Components of delay in the prehospital phase of acute myocardial infarction. *American Journal of Cardiology, 30,* 476–482.

Simon, T. R., Richardson, J. L., Dent, C. W., Chou, C. P., & Flay, B. R. (1998, June). Prospective psychosocial, interpersonal, and behavior predictors of handgun carrying among adolescents. *American Journal of Public Health, 88*(6), 960–963.

Simon, W. (1986). Suicide among physicians: Prevention and postvention. *Crisis, 7,* 1–13.

Simmonds, M. J., Kumar S., & Lechelt, E. (1996). Psychosocial factors in disabling low back pain: Causes or consequences? *Disability & Rehabilitation: An International Multidisciplinary Journal, 18*(4), 161–168.

Simonton, C., Matthews-Simonton, S., & Creighton, J. (1978). *Getting well again: A step-by-step self-help guide to overcoming cancer for patients and their families.* New York: St. Martin's Press.

Skinner, J., & Wennberg, J. E. (1998). *How much is enough? Efficiency and medicare spending in the last six months of life.* Cambridge, MA: National Bureau of Economic Research.

Skipper, J. K., & Leonard, R. C. (Eds.). (1965). *Social interaction and patient care.* Philadelphia and Toronto: J. B. Lippincott.

Skipper, J. K., Tagliacozzo, D., & Mauksch, H. (1964). Some possible consequences of limited communication between patients and hospital functionaries. *Journal of Health and Human Behavior, 5,* 34–39.

Smelser, N. J. (1963). *Theory of collective behavior.* New York: Free Press.

Smith, T. W., McGonigle, M. A., & Benjamin, L. S. (1998). Sibling interactions, self-regulation, and cynical hostility in adult male twins. *Journal of Behavioral Medicine, 21,* 337–349.

Snow, C. E., & Ferguson, C. A. (Eds.). (1977). *Talking to children: Language input and acquisition.* New York: Cambridge University Press.

Snow, L. (1974). Folk-medical beliefs and their implications for care of patients. *Annals of Internal Medicine, 81,* 82–96.

Snyder, S. H. (1977). Opiate receptors in the brain. *New England Journal of Medicine, 296,* 266–271.

Sobel, D. S. (1995, May-June). Rethinking medicine: Improving health outcomes with cost-effective psychosocial interventions. *Psychosomatic Medicine, 57*(3), 234–244.

Soll, I. A., & Isenberg, J. I. (1983). Duodenal ulcer diseases. In M. H. Sleisenger, & J. S. Fortran (Eds.), Gastrointestinal diseases: Pathophysiology, diagnosis, and management (3rd edition, pp. 625–672). Philadelphia: W. B. Saunders.

Solomon, G. F., & Amkraut, A. A. (1983). Emotions, immunity, and disease. In L. Temoshok, C. Van Dyke, & L. Zegans (Eds.), *Emotions in health and illness: Theoretical and research foundations* (pp. 167–186). San Diego: Grune & Stratton.

Sontag, S. (1978). *Illness as a metaphor.* New York: Farrar, Straus, and Giroux.

Sourkes, B. M. (1982). *The deepening shade: Psychological aspects of life-threatening illness.* Pittsburgh: University of Pittsburgh Press.

Spiegel, D., Sephton, S. E., & Stites, D. P. (1998). Effects of psychosocial treatment in prolonging cancer survival may be mediated by neuroimmune pathways. In S. M. McCann, & J. M. Lipton (Eds.), *Neuroimmunomodulation: Molecular aspects, integrative systems, and clinical advances* (pp. 674–683). New York: Academy of Sciences.

Spoont, M. R. (1992). Modulatory role of serotonin in neural information processing: Implications for human psychopathology. *Psychological Bulletin, 112,* 330–350.

Stallone, D. D., & Stunkard, A. J. (1991). The regulation of body weight: Evidence and clinical implications. *Annals of Behavioral Medicine, 13*(4), 220–230.

Stanberry, L. R. (1996). Genital and neonatal herpes. New York: John Wiley.

Stanwyck, D., & Anson, C. (1986). Is personality related to illness?: Cluster profiles of aggregated data. *Advances, Institute for the Advancement of Health, 3,* 4–15.

Starr, P. (1982). *The social transformation of American medicine.* New York: Basic Books.

Stephenson, J. S. (1985). *Death, grief, and mourning.* New York: Free Press.

Sterling, P., & Eyer, J. (1988). Allostasis: A new paradigm to explain arousal pathology. In S. Fisher & J. Reason (Eds.), *Handbook of Life Stress: Cognition and Health* (pp. 629–649). NY: John Wiley & Sons.

Sternbach, R. A. (1974). *Pain patients: Traits and treatments.* New York: Academic Press.

Sternbach, R. A., & Tursky, B. (1965). Ethnic differences among housewives in psychological and skin potential responses to electric shock. *Psychophysiology, 1,* 241–246.

Stewart, G. M., & Gregory, B. C. (1996). Themes of a long-term AIDS support group for gay men. *Counseling Psychologist, 24,* 285–303.

Stiles, W. B., Putnam, S. M., & Jacob, M. C. (1982). Verbal exchange structure of initial medical interviews. *Health Psychology, 1,* 315–336.

Stiles, W. B., Putnam, S. M., Wolf, M. H., & James, S. A. (1979). Interaction exchange structure and patient satisfaction with medical interviews. *Medical Care, 17,* 667–679.

Stoddard, S. (1978). *The hospice movement: A better way of caring for the dying.* New York: Vintage Books.

Stolzenberg, L., & D'Alessio, S. J. (2000). Gun availability and violent crime: New evidence from the National Incident-Based Reporting System. *Social Forces, 78,* 1461–1482.

Stone, A. A., Cox, D. S., Valdimarsdottie, H., Jandorf, L., & Neale, J. M. (1987). Evidence that secretory IgA antibody is associated with daily mood. *Journal of Personality and Social Psychology, 52,* 988–993.

Stone, G. C. (1979). Patient compliance and the role of the expert. *Journal of Social Issues, 35*(1), 34–59.

Stone, G. C., Weiss, S. M., Matarazzo, J. D., Miller, N. E., Rodin, J., Belar, C. D., Follick, M. J., & Singer, J. E. (Eds.). (1987). *Health psychology: A discipline and a profession.* Chicago: University of Chicago Press.

Stoney, C. M., Bausserman, L., Niaura, R., Marcus, B., & Flynn, M. (1999). Lipid reactivity to stress: II. Biological and behavioral influences. *Health Psychology, 18*(3), 251–261.

Stoney, C. M., & West, S. (1997). Lipids, personality, and stress: Mechanisms and modulators. In M. Hillbrand, & R. T. Spitz (Eds.), *Lipids, health, and behavior* (pp. 47–66). Washington, DC: American Psychological Association.

Storms, M. D., & Nisbett, R. E. (1970). Insomnia and the attribution process. *Journal of Personality and Social Psychology, 16,* 319–328.

Stoudemire, A. (Ed.). (1995). *Psychological factors affecting medical conditions.* Washington, DC: American Psychiatric Press, Inc.

Stout, C., Morrow, J., Brandt, E., & Wolf, S. (1964). Unusually low incidence of death from myocardial infarction in an Italian-American community in Pennsylvania. *Journal of the American Medical Association, 188,* 845–849.

Strauss, A. L., & Glaser, B. G. (1975). *Chronic illness and the quality of life.* St. Louis: C. V. Mosby.

Strawbridge, W. J., Cohen, R. D., Shema, S. J., & Kaplan, G. A. (1997). Frequent attendance at religious services and mortality over 28 years. *American Journal of Public Health, 87,* 957–961.

Striegel-Moore, R. H., Silberstein, L. R., & Rodin, J. (1986). Toward an understanding of risk factors for bulimia. *American Psychologist, 41,* 246–263.

Stroebe, M. S., & Stroebe, W. (1987). *Bereavement and health: The psychological and physical consequences of partner loss.* New York: Cambridge University Press.

Stroebe, M. S., Stroebe, W., & Hansson, R. O. (Eds.). (1993). *Handbook of bereavement: Theory, research, and intervention.* New York: Cambridge University Press.

Stroebe, M. S., Stroebe, W., Schut, H., & van den Bout, J. (1998). Bereavement. In H. S. Friedman (editor-in-chief), *Encyclopedia of Mental Health* (Vol. 1, pp. 235–246). San Diego: Academic Press.

Stroebe, W., Stroebe, M., Gergen, K., & Gergen, M. (1982). The effects of bereavement on mortality. In J. R. Eiser (Ed.), *Social psychology and behavioral medicine* (pp. 527–560). New York: John Wiley.

Sugisawa, H., Liang, J., & Liu, X. (1994). Social networks, social support, and mortality among older people in Japan. *Journals of Gerontology, 49,* S3–S13.

Suitor, J. (1981). Husband's participation in childbirth. *Journal of Family History, 6,* 278–293.

Suls, J., Green, P., & Hillis, S. (1998). Emotional reactivity to everyday problems, affective inertia, and neuroticism. *Personality & Social Psychology Bulletin, 24,* 127–136.

Suls, J., Wan, C. K., & Costa, P. T. (1995). Relationship of trait anger to resting blood pressure: A meta-analysis. *Health Psychology, 14,* 444–456.

Sunday Telegraph (1997). Strange But True: Africa's manhood snatched by sorcery witchcraft. March 9, 1997, p. 19.

SUPPORT Principal Investigators. (1995). A controlled trial to improve care for seriously ill hospitalized patients: The study to understand prognoses and preferences for outcomes and risks of treatments. *Journal of the American Medical Association, 274,* 1591–1598.

Surgeon General of the United States. (1979). *Healthy people: The surgeon general's report on health promotion and disease prevention.* Washington, DC: USDHEW Pub. 79-55071. Public Health Service.

Surwit, R., & Williams, P. (1996). Animal models provide insight into psychosomatic factors in diabetes. *Psychosomatic Medicine, 58,* 582–589.

Suzuki, M. (1996). A study of posture: Relationships between self-evaluations of each part of the body, depressive mood, sense of health, and self-esteem. *Japanese Journal of Health Psychology, 9,* 1–8.

Svarstad, B. (1976). Physician-patient communication and patient conformity with medical advice. In D. Mechanic (Ed.), *The growth of bureaucratic medicine: An inquiry into the dynamics of patient behavior and the organization of medical care* (pp. 220–238). New York: John Wiley.

Swain, A., & Suls, J. (1996). Reproducibility of blood pressure and heart rate reactivity: A meta-analysis. *Psychophysiology, 33,* 162–174.

Swan, G. E., Ward, M. M., Jack, L. M., & Javitz, H. S. (1993 Nov.). Cardiovascular reactivity as a predictor of relapse in male and female smokers. *Health Psychology, 12*(6), 451–458.

Syme, S. L. (1987). Social determinants of disease. *Annals of Clinical Research, 19*(2), 44–52.

Szasz, T. S. (1957). *Pain and pleasure: A study of bodily feelings.* New York: Basic Books.

Szasz, T. S., & Hollender, M. H. (1956). A contribution to the philosophy of medicine: The basic models of the doctor-patient relationship. *Archives of Internal Medicine, 97,* 585–592.

Taffel, S. M., Placek, P. J., & Liss, T. (1987). Trends in the United States cesarean section rate and reasons for the 1980–1985 rise. *American Journal of Public Health, 77,* 955–959.

Takeshige, C., Oka, K., Mizuno, T., & Hisamitsu, T. (1993). The acupuncture point and its connecting central pathway for producing acupuncture analgesia. *Brain Research Bulletin, 30,* 53–67.

Talbott, G. D., Gallegos, K. V., Wilson, P. O., & Porter, T. L. (1987). The medical association of Georgia's impaired physicians program. *Journal of the American Medical Association, 257,* 2927–2930.

Tarrier, N. (1995, February). Psychological morbidity in adult burn patients: Prevalence and treatment. *Journal of Mental Health (UK), 4*(1), 51–62.

Taylor, P. (1984). *Smoke ring: Tobacco, money, and multinational politics.* New York: Pantheon.

Taylor, S. E. (1982). Hospital patient behavior: Reactance, helplessness, or control? In H. S. Friedman, & M. R. DiMatteo (Eds.), *Interpersonal issues in health care* (pp. 209–232). New York: Academic Press.

Taylor, S. E. (1989). *Positive illusions: Creative self-deception and the healthy mind.* New York: Basic Books.

Taylor, S. E. (1998). Positive illusions. In H. S. Friedman (editor-in-chief), *Encyclopedia of Mental Health* (Vol. 3, pp. 199–208). San Diego: Academic Press.

Taylor, S. E., & Brown, J. D. (1994). Positive illusions and well-being revisited: Separating fact from fiction. *Psychological Bulletin, 116,* 21–27.

Taylor, S. E., Kemeny, M. E., Aspinwall, L. G., Schneider, S. G., Rodriguez, R., & Herbert, M. (1992). Optimism, coping, psychological distress, and high-risk sexual behavior among men at risk for acquired immunodeficiency syndrome (AIDS). *Journal of Personality & Social Psychology, 63,* 460–473.

Taylor, S. E., Kemeny, M. E., Reed, G. M., Bower, J. E., & Gruenewald, T. L. (2000). Psychological resources, positive illusions, and health. *American Psychologist, 55,* 99–109.

Taylor, S. E., Klein, L. C., Lewis, B. P., Gruenewald, T. L., Gurung, R. A. R., & Updegraff, J. A. (2000). Biobehavioral responses to stress in females: Tend-and-befriend, not fight-or-flight. *Psychological Review, 107,* 411–429.

Taylor, W. C., & Moore, G. T. (1994). Health promotion and disease prevention: Integration into a medical school curriculum. *Medical Education, 28*(6), 481–487.

Temoshok, L. (1990). On attempting to articulate the biopsychosocial model: Psychological-psychophysiological homeostasis. In H. S. Friedman (Ed.), *Personality and disease* (pp. 203–225). New York: John Wiley.

Temoshok, L. (1998). HIV/AIDS. In H. S. Friedman (editor-in-chief), *Encyclopedia of Mental Health* (Vol. 2, pp. 375–392). San Diego: Academic Press.

Temoshok, L., & Fox, B. H. (1984). Coping styles and other psychosocial factors related to medical status and to prognosis in patients with cutaneous malignant melanoma. In B. H. Fox, & B. Newberry (Eds.), *Impact of psychoendocrine systems in cancer and immunity* (pp. 258–287). New York: Hogrefe.

Temoshok, L., Heller, B. W., Sagebiel, R., Blois, M., Sweet, D. M., DiClemente, R. J., & Gold, M. L. (1985). The relationship of psychosocial factors to prognostic indicators in cutaneous malignant melanoma. *Journal of Psychosomatic Research, 29,* 139–154.

Tennant, C. (1988). Parental loss in childhood: Its effect in adult life. *Archives of General Psychiatry, 45,* 1045–1050.

Tennen, H., & Affleck, G. (1987). The costs and benefits of optimistic explanations and dispositional optimism. *Journal of Personality, 55,* 377–393.

Terman, G. W., Shavit, Y., Lewis, J., Cannon, J., & Liebeskind, J. (1984). Intrinsic mechanisms of pain inhibition. *Science, 226,* 1270–1277.

Terman, L. M., & Oden, M. H. (1947). *The gifted child grows up; twenty-five years' follow-up of a superior group.* Stanford: Stanford University Press.

Tesser, A., & Rosen, S. (1975). The reluctance to transmit bad news. In L. Berkowitz (Ed.), *Advances in experimental social psychology* (pp. 193–232). New York: Academic Press.

Thoits, P. A. (1994). Stressors and problem-solving: The individual as psychological activist. *Journal of Health & Social Behavior, 35,* 143–160.

Thompson, J. Kevin, & Smolak, Linda (Eds.). (2001). *Body image, eating disorders, and obesity in youth: Assessment, prevention, and treatment.* Washington, D.C.: American Psychological Association.

Thompson, R. F. (1985). *The brain.* New York: W. H. Freeman.

Thompson, T. (1971). *Hearts; of surgeons and transplants, miracles and diasters along the cardiac frontier.* New York: Academic Press.

Time. Medicine. July 26, 1963.

Time. Medicine. June 20, 1977.

Tinsley, B. J. (1997). Maternal influences on children's health behavior. In D. S. Gochman (Ed.), *Handbook of health behavior research 1: Personal and social determinants* (pp. 223–240). New York: Plenum Press.

Tinsley, B. J., Holtgrave, D. R., Reise, S. P., & Erdley, C. (1995). Developmental status, gender, age, and self-reported decision-making influences on students' risky and preventive health behaviors. *Health Education Quarterly, 22,* 244–259.

Tjoe, S. L., & Luria, M. H. (1972). Delays in reaching the cardiac care unit: An analysis. *Chest, 61,* 617.

Toffler, A. (1971). *Future shock.* New York: Bantam Books.

Tomaka, J., Blascovich, J., Kibler, J., & Ernst, J. M. (1997). Cognitive and physiological antecedents of threat and challenge appraisal. *Journal of Personality & Social Psychology, 73,* 63–72.

Tomar, S. L., & Giovino, G. A. (1998). Incidence and predictors of smokeless tobacco use among U.S. youth. *American Journal of Public Health, 88,* 20–26.

Toombs, S. K., Barnard, D., & Carson, R. A. (Eds.). (1995). *Chronic illness: From experience to policy.* Bloomington: Indiana University Press.

Totman, R. (1979). *Social causes of illness.* London: Souvenir Press.

Train, J. (1989, Jan./Feb.). *Harvard Magazine, 91,* 6.

Tuchfeld, B. S., & Marcus, S. H. (1984). Social models of prevention in alcoholism. In J. D. Matarazzo, S. Weiss, J. A. Herd, N. E. Miller, & S. M. Weiss (Eds.), *Behavioral health.* New York: John Wiley.

Tucker, J. S., Friedman, H. S., Schwartz J. E., Criqui, M. H., Tomlinson-Keasey, C., Wingard, D. L., & Martin, L. R. (1997). Parental divorce: Effects on individual behavior and longevity. *Journal of Personality & Social Psychology, 73,* 381–391.

Tucker, J. S, Friedman, H. S., Tsai, C. M., & Martin, L. R. (1995). Playing with pets and longevity among the elderly. *Psychology and Aging, 10,* 3–7.

Tucker, J. S., Friedman, H. S., Wingard, D. L., & Schwartz, J. E. (1996). Marital history at mid-life as a predictor of longevity: Alternative explanations to the protective effect of marriage. *Health Psychology, 15,* 94–101.

Turk, D. C., Meichenbaum, D. H., & Genest, M. (1983). *Pain and behavioral medicine.* New York: Guilford.

Turk, D. C., & Okifuji, A. (1998). Pain. In H. S. Friedman (editor-in-chief), *The Encyclopedia of Mental Health* (Vol. III, pp. 61–72). Sand Diego, CA: Academic Press.

Tversky, A., & Kahneman, D. (1974). Judgement under uncertainty: Heuristics and biases. *Science, 185,* 1124–1131.

U.S. Department of Agriculture. (1995). *Report of the dietary guidelines advisory committee on the dietary guidelines for Americans, 1995.* Springfield, VA: National Technical Information Services.

U.S. Department of Health and Human Services (1996). *Physical Activity and Health: A Report of the Surgeon General.* Atlanta, GA: U.S. Dept. of Health and Human Services, Centers for Disease Control and Prevention.

U.S. Department of Health and Human Services (2000). *Healthy People 2010: Tracking healthy people 2010.* Washington, DC: U.S. Dept. of Health and Human Services.

United States General Accounting Office. (1987). *Cancer patient survival: What progress has been made?* Washington DC: GAO/PEMD-87-13.

U.S. National Center for Health Statistics. (1999). *Vital Statistics of the United States 1997.* Hyattsville, MD: National Center for Health Statistics.

U.S. Public Health Service. (1979). *Healthy people: The surgeon general's report on health promotion and disease prevention.* Washington, DC: U.S. Government Printing Office.

U.S. Public Health Service. (1987). *Health, United States, 1986.* DHHS Publication: No. 87-1232. Washington, DC.

U.S. Public Health Service. (1999). Achievements in public health, 1900–1999: Tobacco use, United States, 1900–1999. *Morbidity and Mortality Weekly Report, 48*(43), 986–993.

Vaccarino, J. M. (1977). Malpractice: The problem in perspective. *Journal of the American Medical Association, 238,* 861–863.

Vaillant, G. E. (1983). *The natural history of alcoholism.* Cambridge, MA: Harvard University Press.

Vaillant, G. E., Sobowale, N. C., & McArthur, C. (1972). Some psychologic vulnerabilities of physicians. *New England Journal of Medicine, 287,* 372–375.

VanderPlate, C., & Aral, A. (1987). Psychosocial aspects of genital herpes virus infection. *Health Psychology, 6,* 57–72.

van Doornen, L. J. P. (1997). Lipids and the coronary-prone personality. In M. Hillbrand, & R. T. Spitz (Eds.), *Lipids, health, and behavior* (pp. 81–98). Washington, DC: American Psychological Association.

van Dyke, C., & Kaufman, I. C. (1983). Psychobiology of bereavement. In L. Temoshok, C. van Dyke, & L. S. Zegans (Eds.), *Emotions in health and illness: Theoretical and research foundations* (pp. 37–49). New York: Grune & Stratton.

Vega, W. A., & Miranda, M. R. (Eds.). (1985). *Stress & Hispanic mental health: Relating research to service delivery.* Rockville, MD: National Institute of Mental Health.

Vernon, D., Foley, J., Sipowicz, R., & Schulman, J. (1965). *The psychological responses of children to hospitalization and illness: A review of the literature.* Springfield: IL: Charles C. Thomas.

Verrier, R., DeSilva, R., & Lown, B. (1983). Psychological factors in cardiac arrhythmias and sudden death. In D. Krantz, A. Baum, & J. Singer (Eds.), *Handbook of psychology and health* (Vol. 3, pp. 125–154). Hillsdale, NJ: Erlbaum.

Vine, I. (1970). Communication by facial-visual signals. In J. H. Crook (Ed.), *Social behavior in birds and mammals* (pp. 279–354). London and New York: Academic Press.

Vitaliano, P. P., Schulz, R., Kiecolt-Glaser, J., & Grant, I. (1997). Research on physiological and physical concomitants of caregiving: Where do we go from here? *Annals of Behavioral Medicine, 19,* 117–123.

Vitaliano, P. P., Scanlan, J. M., Siegler, I. C., McCormick, W. C., & Knopp, R. H. (1998). Coronary heart disease moderates the relationship of chronic stress with the metabolic syndrome. *Health Psychology, 17*(6), 520–529.

Volkow, N. D., Fowler, J. S., & Wang, G. (1999). Imaging studies on the role of dopamine in cocaine reinforcement and addiction in humans. *Journal of Psychopharmacology, 13,* 337–345.

Von Dras, D. D., & Siegler, I. C. (1997). Stability in extraversion and aspects of social support at midlife. *Journal of Personality & Social Psychology, 72,* 233–241.

Wadden, T. A., & Brownell, K. D. (1984). The development and modification of dietary practices in individuals, groups, and large populations. In J. D. Matarazzo, S. Weiss, J. A. Herd, N. E. Miller, & S. M. Weiss (Eds.), *Behavioral health.* New York: John Wiley.

Wadhwa, P. D. (1998). Prenatal stress and life-span development. In H. S. Friedman (editor-in-chief), *The Encyclopedia of Mental Health* (Vol. III, pp. 265–280). San Diego, CA: Academic Press.

Wagner, B. M. (1997). Family risk factors for child and adolescent suicidal behavior. *Psychological Bulletin, 121,* 246–298.

Wagner, R. V. (1985). Psychology and the threat of nuclear war. *American Psychologist, 40,* 531–535.

Waitzkin, H., & Stoeckle, J. D. (1972). The communication of information about illness: Clinical, sociological and methodological considerations. *Advances in Psychosomatic Medicine, 8,* 180–215.

Waitzkin, H., & Waterman, B. (1974). The exploitation of illness in capitalist society. Indianapolis: Bobbs-Merrill.

Wallston, K. A. (1992). Hocus-pocus, the focus isn't strictly on locus: Rotter's social learning theory modified for health. *Cognitive Therapy & Research, 16,* 183–199.

Wallston, K. A., Malcarne, V. L., Flores, L., Hansdottir, I., Smith, C. A., Stein, M. J., Weisman, M. H., Clements, P. J. (1999). Does God determine your health? The God Locus of Health Control Scale. *Cognitive Therapy & Research, 23,* 131–142.

Wallston, K. A., & Wallston, B. S. (Eds.). (1978). Health locus of control. *Health Education Monographs, 6*(2) (whole issue).

Walsh, D. M., Lowe, A. S., McCormack, K., Willer, J. C., Baxter, G. D., & Allen, J. M. (1998). Transcutaneous electrical nerve stimulation: Effect on peripheral nerve conduction, mechanical pain threshold, and tactile threshold in humans. *Archives of Physical Medicine and Rehabilitation, 79,* 1051–1058.

Wannamethee, S. G., Shaper, A. G., & Walker, M. (1998, May). Changes in physical activity, mortality, and incidence of coronary heart disease in older men. *Lancet, 351*(9116), 1603–8.

Ward, A., & Mann, T. (2000, April). Don't mind if I do: Disinhibited eating under cognitive load. *Journal of Personality & Social Psychology, 78*(4), 753–763.

Warner, K. E. (1986). *Selling smoke: Cigarette advertising and public health.* Washington, DC: American Public Health Association.

Warner, L. A., Kessler, R. C., Hughes, M., Anthony, J. C., & Nelson, C. B. (1995). Prevalence and correlates of drug use and dependence in the United States: Results from the National Comorbidity Survey. *Archives of General Psychiatry, 52,* 219–229.

Wazana, A. (2000). Physicians and the pharmaceutical industry: Is a gift ever just a gift? JAMA*: Journal of the American Medical Association, 283,* 373–380.

Wear, D., & Bickel, J. (Eds.). (2000). *Educating for professionalism: Creating a culture of humanism in medical education.* Iowa City, IA: University of Iowa Press.

Weinberger, M., Hines, S. L., & Tierney, W. M. (1987). In support of hassles as a measure of stress in predicting health outcomes. *Journal of Behavioral Medicine, 10,* 19–31.

Weiner, H. (1977). *Psychobiology and human disease.* New York: Elsevier.

Weiner, H., Thaler, M., Reiser, M. F., & Mirsky, I. A. (1957). Etiology of duodenal ulcer. *Psychosomatic Medicine, 19,* 1–10.

Weinstein, N. D. (1988). The precaution adoption process. *Health Psychology, 7*(4), 355–386.

Weisenberg, M. (1977). Pain and pain control. *Psychological Bulletin, 84,* 1008–1044.

Weisman, A. D., & Worden, J. W. (1975). Psychosocial analysis of cancer deaths. *Omega, 6,* 61–65.

Weisman, C. S., Levine, D. M., & Steinwachs, D. M. (1980). Male and female physician career patterns. *Journal of Medical Education, 55,* 813–825.

Weiss, J. M. (1968). Effects of coping response on stress. *Journal of Comparative and Physiological Psychology, 65,* 251–260.

Weiss, J. M. (1971). Effects of coping behavior in different warning signal conditions of stress pathology in rats. *Journal of Comparative and Physiological Psychology, 77,* 1–13.

Weiss, J. M. (1972, June). Psychological factors in stress and disease. *Scientific American*, 105–113.

Weiss, S. M. (1982). Health psychology: The time is now. *Health Psychology, 1*, 81–91.

Whitcher, S., & Fisher, J. (1979). Multidimensional reaction to therapeutic touch in a hospital setting. *Journal of Personality and Social Psychology, 37*, 87–96.

White, K. L., & Henderson, M. M. (1976). *Epidemiology as a fundamental science, its uses in health services, planning, administration, and evaluation.* New York: Oxford University Press.

White, K. L., Williams, T. F., & Greenberg, B. G. (1961). The ecology of medical care. *New England Journal of Medicine, 265*, 885–892.

White, L., & Tursky, B. (1982). *Clinical biofeedback: Efficacy and mechanisms.* New York: Guilford.

White, R. W. (1959). Motivation reconsidered: The concept of competence. *Psychological Review, 66*, 297–333.

Whorf, B. L. (1956). *Language, thought, and reality: Selected writings of Benjamin Lee Whorf.* Edited by J. Carroll. Cambridge, MA: MIT Press.

Wiebe, D. J., & Smith, T. W. (1997). Personality and health: Progress and problems in psychosomatics. In R. Hogan, J. A. Johnson, & S. R. Briggs (Eds.), *Handbook of personality psychology* (pp. 891–918). San Diego: Academic Press.

Wiener, J. M. (1970). Response of medical personnel to the fatal illness of a child. In B. Schoenberg, G. C. Carr, S. Peretz, & A. H. Kutscher (Eds.), *Loss and grief: Psychological management in medical practice* (pp. 102–115). New York: Columbia University Press.

Williams, G. C., Rodin, G. C., Ryan, R. M., Grolnick, W. S., & Deci, E. L. (1998). Autonomous regulation and long-term medication adherence in adult outpatients. *Health Psychology, 17*, 269–276.

Williams, M. V., Parker, R. M., Baker, D. W., Parikh, N. S., Pitkin, K., Coates, W. C., & Nurss, J. R. (1995). Inadequate functional health literacy among patients at two public hospitals. *Journal of the American Medical Association, 274*, 1677–82.

Williams, R. B. (1988). Biological mechanisms mediating the relationship between behavior and coronary heart disease. In A. W. Siegman, & T. M. Dembroski (Eds.), *In search of coronary behavior.* Hillsdale, NJ: Erlbaum.

Williams, R. B., Lane, J. D., Kuhn, C. M., Melosh, W., White, A. D., & Schanberg, S. M. (1982). Type A behavior and elevated physiological and neuroendocrine response to cognitive tasks. *Science, 218*, 483–485.

Wills, T. A. (1986). Stress and coping in early adolescence: Relationships to substance use in urban school samples. *Health Psychology, 5*, 503–529.

Wills, T. A. (1998). Substance abuse. In H. S. Friedman (editor-in-chief), *Encyclopedia of Mental Health.* (Vol. 3, pp. 607–619). San Diego: Academic Press..

Wills, T. A., Gibbons, F. X., Gerrard, M., & Brody, G. H. (2000). Protection and vulnerability processes relevant for early onset of substance use: A test among African American children. *Health Psychology, 19*, 253–263.

Wilmore, J. H., & Costill, D. L. (1999). *Physiology of sport and exercise* (2nd ed.). Champaign, IL: Human Kinetics Press.

Wilson, C. C. (1991). The pet as an anxiolytic intervention. *Journal of Nervous and Mental Diseases, 179,* 482–489.

Wilson, R. (1963). The social structure of a general hospital. *Annals of the American Academy of Political and Social Science, 346,* 67–76.

Winkleby, M. A., Flora, J. A., Kraemer, H. C. (1994). A community-based heart disease intervention: Predictors of change. *American Journal of Public Health, 84,* 767–772.

Winkler, A., Fairnie, H., Gericevich, F., & Long, M. (1989). The impact of a resident dog on an institution for the elderly: Effect on perceptions and social interactions. *Gerontologist, 29,* 216–223.

Wisely, D. W., Masur, F. T., & Morgan, S. B. (1983). Psychological aspects of severe burn injuries in children. *Health Psychology, 2*(1), 45–72.

Wolf, S. (1959). The pharmacology of placebos. *Pharmacology Review, 11,* 698.

Wolf, S., & Wolff, H. G. (1947). *Human gastric function.* New York: Oxford.

Wolff, H., & Goodell, H. (1968). *Stress and disease* (2nd ed.). Springfield, IL: Charles C. Thomas.

Worden, J. W. (1991). *Grief counseling and grief therapy: A handbook for the mental health practitioner* (2nd ed.). New York: Springer Pub. Co.

Wortman, C. B., & Dunkel-Schetter, C. (1979). Interpersonal relationships and cancer: A theoretical analysis. *Journal of Social Issues, 35*(1), 120–155.

Wortman, C. B., & Dunkel-Schetter, C. (1987). Conceptual and methodological issues in the study of social support. In A. Baum, & J. Singer (Eds.), *Handbook of psychology and health* (Vol. 5: Stress, pp. 63–108). Hillsdale, NJ: Erlbaum.

Wortman, C. B., & Silver, R. C. (1989). The myths of coping with loss. *Journal of Consulting & Clinical Psychology, 57,* 349–357.

Wortman, C. B., & Silver, R. C. (1992). Reconsidering assumptions about coping with loss: An overview of current research. In L. Montada, S-H. Filipp, & M. J. Lerner (Eds.), *Life crises and experiences of loss in adulthood* (pp. 341–365). Hillsdale, NJ: Lawrence Erlbaum Associates.

Wyatt, N. (1991). Physician-patient relationships: What do doctors say? *Health Communication, 3,* 157–174.

Yehuda, R. (Ed.). (1998). *Psychological trauma.* Washington, DC: American Psychiatric Press.

Yehuda, R., Resnick, H., Hahana, B., & Giller, E. (1993). Long-lasting hormonal alterations to extreme stress in humans: Normative or maladaptive. *Psychosomatic Medicine, 55,* 287–297.

Zautra, A. J., Burleson, M. H., Matt, K. S., Roth, S., & Burrows, L. (1994). Interpersonal stress, depression, and disease activity in rheumatoid arthritis and osteoarthritis patients. *Health Psychology, 13,* 139–148.

Zborowski, M. (1952). Cultural components in responses to pain. *Journal of Social Issues, 8,* 16–30.

Zborowski, M. (1969). *People in pain.* San Francisco: Jossey-Bass.

Zill, N., Morrison, D. R., & Coiro, M. J. (1993). Long-term effects of parental divorce on parent-child relationships, adjustment, and achievement in young adulthood. *Journal of Family Psychology, 7,* 91–103.

Zola, I. (1963). Problems of communication, diagnosis and patient care. *Journal of Medical Education, 10,* 829–838.

Zola, I. K. (1964). Illness behavior of the working class. In A. Shostak, & W. Gomberg (Eds.), *Blue-collar world: Studies of the American worker* (pp. 350–361). Englewood Cliffs, NJ: Prentice-Hall.

Zola, I. K. (1966). Culture and symptoms: An analysis of patients presenting complaints. *American Sociological Review, 31,* 615.

Zola, I. K. (1972). Studying the decisions to see a doctor. *Advances in Psychosomatic Medicine, 8,* 226–227.

Zorrilla, E. P., Redei, E., & DeRubeis, R. J. (1994). Reduced cytokine levels and T-cell function in healthy males: Relation to individual differences in subclinical anxiety. *Brain, Behavior, and Immunity, 8,* 293–312.

INDEX

NAME INDEX

SUBJECT INDEX